IN THE KITCHEN

....

IN THE KITCHEN

The new BIBLE OF HOME COOKING

MICHELE CURTIS & ALLAN CAMPION

hardie grant books

IN THE KITCHEN

Introduction

It's back! This book almost feels like an autobiography – the dishes I've cooked, the meals I've shared, the special occasions spent with friends and family. It's all in here.

In the Kitchen is a special book. It contains recipes that date back to my training as a chef in the 1980s, and spans so many parts of my life: working in London, my relationship with Allan, having children, jobs in Melbourne, writing *The Foodies' Diary* and the original Campion and Curtis *In the Kitchen* (circa 2002), the friends who have shared their recipes with me, and the businesses I have set up, worked in and owned. Still, whenever I get the chance, I love cooking in my kitchen at home and creating new dishes.

When my publisher, Jane Willson from Hardie Grant, said she was interested in reprinting *In the Kitchen*, I was ecstatic – then I realised it would need an update, as a lot has happened in 15 years. I've changed and the food I cook has changed – just a quick flick through the original book confirmed this, as there are no kale or quinoa recipes! This revision has been my project but, as Allan and I initially wrote the book together, there's still plenty of the original good stuff in here, too.

It has been a cathartic process, culling old recipes and adding new favourites, revisiting old friends and tweaking them (it's incredible how much sugar was in some of the cake recipes), and introducing new techniques and ingredients.

Not only have the recipes changed, my life has changed. When Allan and I wrote the original book we had a young family and worked from home, allowing us the freedom to cook yummy meals. Today Allan and I have a great friendship, our children have grown up and I now live with my son, Luke (who's studying to become a chef), and our crazy pug, George. Throughout the years I've set up numerous food shops and time at home has been tight. I recall saying in one of the earlier books, 'Make sure you take the time out to create a good wholesome dinner that satisfies your soul and replenishes your energy after a day's work'. Ha! How hard is that reality? Some days when I got home at 8 pm, the only thing that satisfied my soul was a packet of chips and a bottle of red wine.

However, I still believe that making time to cook a tasty dinner is so important (it would help enormously if there was food in the kitchen, though). Cook for your friends and, if you're lucky, they will repay your hospitality when you need it most. When you cook, make double and freeze the extra. Find the energy to put effort into what you eat and you will function better.

To quote every contestant on a TV cooking show, this book is 'me on a plate'. As I finish writing this, I feel so proud of the book and the recipes in it and all the people who have come into my life and influenced my food and me. As one door closes another opens, but some dishes remain firm favourites, such as spaghetti with breadcrumbs, tuna, parsley and lemon; braised lamb shanks with mint and harissa; and one-pot chocolate cake. They are now joined by zingy beef and ramen noodle salad bowl, spice-perfumed slow-roasted lamb shoulder and gluten-free chocolate brownies.

Simplicity, seasonality and freshness are still the key to each and every one of the recipes, and serving friends and family dinner – whether it's a quick bowl of pasta or something more elaborate – is what makes me tick. A big thank you to everyone who came and ate – especially Mia and Luke, who are still always hungry at 6 pm, but can wait till 8 pm.

Michele Curtis

Everyday ingredients

It's often the basic ingredients that raise the most queries in a recipe. Chefs and food writers take huge leaps of faith, assuming that everybody else knows as much about the ingredients as they do. To prevent any confusion, here's my take on the basic stuff to get you started.

Black pepper All pepper used in these recipes is freshly ground black pepper, unless otherwise stated. It brings freshness and spice to any dish. As these properties will dissipate with cooking, add a little more before you serve a dish.

Chicken I use only free-range chickens. Given the amount of chicken I eat, this is my compromise on flavour and cost, though I do upgrade to corn-fed or organic poultry for special occasions. It's worth it for the flavour.

Eggs Eggs used in these recipes are medium-sized and free-range (59 g/ 2 oz each).

Egg wash Egg wash is lightly beaten egg yolk with a little milk, usually brushed onto raw pastry to add a shiny finish when cooked (see page 419).

Herbs All herbs used in these recipes are fresh unless otherwise stated.

Oil for cooking Well, this is interesting. This is all going to come down to personal preference. Recent research (and this is probably already out of date by now) shows that saturated fats, such as coconut oil and butter, are better oils for deep-frying as they produce less aldehydes (chemicals that can cause heart disease and cancer). Olive oil is the best all-rounder, but extra-virgin olive oil has a low smoke point, which makes it unsuitable for heavy frying. However, regular olive oil is considered okay for general light frying.

Vegetable and sunflower oils should be avoided, as they produce high levels of aldehydes when heated. I tend to use extra-virgin olive oil for light cooking, often with the addition of butter for flavour, except in a few cases where peanut or sesame oil is called for to give a different flavour. I use coconut oil for stir-frying.

Olive oil Extra-virgin olive oil has the best flavour, as well as healthy qualities, so use one that suits your tastebuds and budget. Prices will vary, but aim to buy a locally produced oil to reduce food miles. I also try to buy recently pressed oil. Consider buying a large tin, then decant the oil into a clean, dry, wine bottle and seal it with an olive oil pourer. This is more economical if you use a lot of oil.

Parmigiano Reggiano Be sure to buy Parmigiano Reggiano or Grana Padano, rather than imitation parmesan, as true Parmigiano comes only from Italy. To ensure freshness, it's best to buy a block and grate it as needed.

Pulses and beans I have become healthier as I have grown older, and I now eat pulses, chickpeas and beans much more often. So often, in fact, that due to time constraints I often use tinned varieties. If using tinned, I recommend you soak them in lots of cold water for 15 minutes to get rid of the metallic taste. Some recipes, however, require long, slow cooking, for which only dried pulses will do. If you are using dried beans, they are best soaked overnight in plenty of cold water, drained, then cooked in boiling water until tender.

Red chilli Unless otherwise stated, small red chillies (not bird's eye) are used. Take care when removing the seeds and membrane as these contain the capsaicin (the source of the heat).

Salt I prefer to use sea salt, as it has a finer mineral flavour than common table salt. Living in Australia, Murray River pink salt is my favourite for cooking with, and I also use Sicilian Iblea fine crystals as they dissolve easily in dressings and are ideal for last-minute seasoning. However, you can use any good-quality, locally produced salt.

Seasonal produce I am a big fan of seasonal produce – mostly because it tastes the best and requires little work to enhance its flavour, but also because quality is highest and price is lowest when produce is in season.

Stock Stocks provide the essential base for all good sauces, casseroles and stews. The variety and quality of ready-made stocks are now better than ever, but it's very easy to make your own. (See pages 450–2 for stock recipes.)

Tomato passata Passata, also called tomato purée or sugo, is simply a ready-to-use tomato sauce. The best passatas come from Italy and are an essential pantry item for pasta sauces and casseroles. I have stopped using tinned tomatoes in some dishes as I prefer the smoothness of passata. Choose one with no added flavours like garlic or herbs, as it's always best to add your own to ensure freshness.

Vanilla extract As the name suggests, this is a pure extract from crushed vanilla beans, producing a thick, aromatic liquid. Use it wherever vanilla is called for. Vanilla essence is a poor substitute.

Measurements

This book uses metric cup measurements, i.e. 250 ml (8½ fl oz) for 1 cup; in the US a cup is 237 ml (8 fl oz), so American cooks should be generous with their cup measurements; in the UK, a cup is 284 ml (9½ fl oz), so British cooks should be scant with their cup measurements.

As well, 20 ml (¾ fl oz) tablespoons are used; cooks with 15 ml (½ fl oz) tablespoons should be generous with their tablespoon measurements.

TIP

Breakfast & brunch

Far from being a chore, the first meal of the day should be something to savour and enjoy. Breakfast is fast disappearing as something to be enjoyed at home so, if you are one of those people who eat in the car on the way to work, try getting up a few minutes earlier. It doesn't take long to pour some muesli into a bowl or make a few slices of toast, and it will give you enough energy to at least get through to mid-morning.

Fuel for the day

In this chapter I've included the basics: how to poach an egg, make an omelette, prepare a pot of porridge and put together a simple bowl of muesli. I've also given you plenty of creative ideas for weekends, when breakfast can easily be turned into brunch with friends by preparing a selection of dishes and adding coffee and perhaps a glass of sparkling wine. Don't forget that muffins and savoury tarts are also a great addition to brunch, and see the Preserves chapter (page 431) for ideas on making your own jams and marmalades.

Quick ideas

- Serve Cauliflower polpetti (page 45) with sautéed spinach, poached eggs and Kale pesto (page 476).
- A Sunday breakfast can be as simple as warmed croissants served with jam and a cup of properly brewed coffee.

If you have a good-quality loaf of bread, the options are endless:

- Top the toasted bread with Roasted roma tomatoes (page 264) and some good-quality feta or goat's cheese.
- Turn bread into Bruschetta (page 23) and top with Tomato and basil salsa (page 479). Add sautéed English spinach and Pan-fried mushrooms (page 254) and maybe even a poached egg.
- Add slices of avocado on wholegrain toast.
- Mash half an avocado with 1 teaspoon wasabi paste, then serve on toast with crispy bacon and poached eggs.
- Combine Pan-fried haloumi, Roasted roma tomatoes (page 264) and pesto (pages 476–7) on toast or fritters.
- Take slices of Banana bread (page 374), toast them lightly, top with fresh banana slices and serve with honey and fresh ricotta.
- Toast some slices of coconut bread and top with Marmalade cream (page 488), mascarpone cream and fresh blueberries.

JUICE INSPIRATION

Whether you like to use a cold-press, a nutribullet or a juicer, here are some combos to try:

- Fruit cocktail – whatever is at hand: apple, orange, pineapple, watermelon, berries or kiwi fruit
- For getting caught in the rain, a piña colada–inspired orange, pineapple and lime juice
- Strawberry, watermelon and orange
- Pineapple, apple, mint and English spinach (or even wheatgrass)
- Peach and raspberry
- Blood orange, pink grapefruit and mandarin
- Carrot, apple and ginger
- Beetroot (beet), orange, ginger and apple
- Kale, cucumber, apple, English spinach and celery

SMOOTHIES

- Strawberry, banana and coconut milk – or swap the strawberries for blueberries and the coconut milk for almond milk
- Pineapple, passionfruit, mint and apple
- Banana, cinnamon, milk of your choice, ice and maybe a shot of raw cacao powder
- Mango, yoghurt, cinnamon and coconut milk
- English spinach, coconut water, banana, mango and ice
- Pineapple, apple, English spinach, kiwi fruit and matcha

Things to remember
about breakfast & brunch

- You will need a large heavy-based pan for frying eggs and bacon, making scrambled eggs, hotcakes, fritters and French toast.

- Try making your own freshly squeezed juices every now and then (see the ideas on the opposite page).

- Eggs need to be free-range, and organic free-range eggs are even better. You don't need to buy barn-laid or omega-3 enhanced eggs.

- Eggs usually benefit from a little salt, so buy some top-quality sea salt flakes from a specialist food store – it'll be well worth the extra expense.

- Breakfast doesn't have to mean a fry-up, but that style of food is okay every now and then. It's been proven that a big fry-up is the most effective way of sorting out a hangover – what more excuse do you need?

- Liven up toast for breakfast by making your own jams and marmalades (see the Preserves chapter, page 431).

- There is no reason why you can't have a 'second' breakfast each day, as well as lunch and dinner.

Breakfast & brunch recipes

Breakfast muesli

This is easy to make and much more delicious than bought mueslis. I vary the flavours every time I make this, often adding additional ingredients, such as desiccated coconut, cranberries, wheatgerm, pepitas (pumpkin seeds) or sunflower seeds. Make a huge batch, divide it into smaller bags and give them to your friends as gifts. Makes just over 1.5 kg (3 lb 5 oz)

1 kg (2 lb 3 oz/10 cups) rolled (porridge) oats
120 g (4½ oz/¾ cup) dried apricots, chopped
90 g (3 oz/¾ cup) toasted slivered almonds
150 g (5½ oz/1 cup) oat bran
200 g (7 oz) sultanas (golden raisins) or cranberries

Combine all the ingredients. Divide the muesli into plastic containers with tight-fitting lids and store in a cool dark place. It will keep for 2–3 months.

Apple and hazelnut muesli
Substitute hazelnuts for the almonds and dried apple rings for the apricots.

Date and walnut muesli
Substitute walnuts (or pecans) for the almonds and dried dates for the apricots.

Gluten-free muesli
Make sure you buy gluten-free oats. Substitute 120 g (4½ oz) puffed quinoa and 120 g (4½ oz/2 cups) shredded coconut for 500 g (1 lb 2 oz/5 cups) of the oats, and substitute Buckinis (caramelised buckwheat) for the oat bran.

Granola

The beauty of this recipe is you can add whatever seeds, nuts and fruits you like, so no batch ever has to be the same. If using a measuring cup for the wet ingredients, measure the oil first, add it to the bowl, then use the oil-coated cup for the sweetener – this means the sweetener won't stick to the cup. Genius! This is delicious with yoghurt and fresh or poached fruits.
Makes 400 g (14 oz/3 cups)

200 g (7 oz/2 cups) rolled (porridge) oats
70 g (2½ oz) raw nuts, such as almonds, hazelnuts or pecans
70 g (2½ oz/½ cup) pepitas (pumpkin seeds) or sunflower seeds, or half/half
½ teaspoon ground cinnamon
½ teaspoon fine salt
60 ml (2 fl oz/¼ cup) melted coconut oil
60 ml (2 fl oz/¼ cup) sweetener, such as honey, agave syrup or rice syrup
100 g (3½ oz) dried fruit, such as cranberries, sliced apricots or figs
30 g (1 oz/½ cup) shredded coconut

Preheat the oven to 180°C (350°F).

In a large bowl mix together the oats, nuts, seeds, cinnamon and salt. Pour in the coconut oil and sweetener of your choice. Toss well to ensure all the dry ingredients are coated with the wet ingredients.

Spread the granola out in a deep, lined baking dish and bake until golden, about 18–20 minutes – make sure you stir every 5 minutes to ensure the granola toasts evenly.

Remove the granola from the oven and allow to cool. Stir through the dried fruits and coconut and store in an airtight container.

Gluten-free granola
Substitute gluten-free oats.

Bircher muesli

Traditionally bircher muesli is soaked overnight. I often don't know that I want bircher muesli for breakfast until 5 minutes before, so I've started mixing it as I need to and I kinda like the crunchy approach, particularly when I make it with granola. Add as much or as little fruit as you desire – apple and berries is my favourite combination. Serves 6–8

150 g (5½ oz) muesli or granola
30 g (1 oz/⅓ cup) flaked almonds
250 ml (8½ fl oz/1 cup) milk of your choice
250 g (9 oz/1 cup) natural yoghurt
1 apple, grated
150 g (5½ oz) berries
Honey (optional)

Mix the muesli with the almonds, milk and yoghurt. Refrigerate for as long as you desire. In the morning, add the apple and berries and toss together lightly.

Add honey to taste and more milk or yoghurt if needed to adjust the consistency – it should be moist, but not runny.

Traditional porridge

Porridge is perfect for cold winter mornings when you need a warming start to the day. I like to top my porridge with a sprinkling of coconut sugar, as it adds such a lovely caramel flavour, and some poached fruit – whatever is to hand – or slices of fresh banana. Serves 4

150 g (5½ oz/1½ cups) rolled (porridge) oats
375 ml (12½ fl oz/1½ cups) milk, plus extra to serve
Poached fruit (optional)
Honey or coconut sugar to serve

Place the oats, 500 ml (17 fl oz/2 cups) water and the milk in a heavy-based saucepan. Add a pinch of salt, if desired, and bring to the boil. Reduce to a gentle simmer and cook for 10–15 minutes, stirring occasionally. Top with fruit, if desired, and serve with the extra milk and honey or coconut sugar.

Porridge with stewed apple, raisins and honey
Place two peeled, cored and thinly sliced apples in a small saucepan with 85 g (3 oz/⅔ cup) raisins, 60 ml (2 fl oz/¼ cup) water, 2 tablespoons caster (superfine) sugar and a pinch of ground cinnamon. Cover and cook over medium heat for 10-12 minutes, stirring often, until the apples are tender but not cooked to a purée. Serve the cooked porridge with a dollop of the stewed apple and raisins on top. Add milk and a drizzle of honey if desired.

Berry porridge
Add 100 g (3½ oz) frozen berries to the cooking porridge - blueberries or raspberries are ideal.

Chai porridge
Infuse milk with chai tea, strain and then use this to cook the porridge in. Add chopped dates and fresh banana at the end for a complementary taste.

Protein porridge

There are a couple of different ways to make this porridge. You can soak the quinoa, millet and buckwheat overnight in water, which will reduce the cooking time by 5 minutes. You can cook the grains in soaked water, keeping all the nutrients intact, adding more water as you need, or you can cook the grains in the milk of your choice for a bit more of a protein punch. Serves 2

50 g (1¾ oz) quinoa flakes

50 g (1¾ oz) millet

50 g (1¾ oz) buckwheat

25 g (1 oz/¼ cup) ground almonds

2 tablespoons LSA (optional)

½ teaspoon ground cinnamon (optional)

Milk of your choice

Agave syrup to sweeten (optional)

200 g (7 oz) blueberries

2 tablespoons chopped pistachio nuts

Place the grains (soaked if you like), ground almonds, LSA and cinnamon (if using), in a medium saucepan. Add more water or milk as needed to get a good consistency. Cook over medium heat for 20–25 minutes, stirring often until all the grains are cooked through. Check the taste – add 1–2 teaspoons of agave syrup if you like. Divide between two bowls, top with the fruit and nuts and serve.

Coconut quinoa porridge

If you can, soak the quinoa in the coconut milk overnight, or even for 30 minutes before, as it will help to reduce the cooking time. Serves 3–4

100 g (3½ oz/½ cup) quinoa

750 ml (25½ fl oz/3 cups) coconut milk, plus extra to serve if desired

2 bananas, sliced

90 g (3 oz/¾ cup) chopped walnuts

Agave nectar or honey to taste

Place the quinoa and coconut milk in a medium saucepan. Bring to the boil over medium–high heat. Reduce to a simmer, cover and cook for 18–20 minutes, stirring occasionally. Check that the quinoa is cooked. If not, cook for a further 2–3 minutes, adding more coconut milk if needed.

When cooked, divide between serving bowls and top with banana slices and chopped walnuts. Serve with agave nectar or honey and extra coconut milk if required.

Chia bowl with fresh berries and pistachio nuts

You can serve whatever type of fruit and nuts you like on top of this chia – you are limited only by your imagination. In spring I would add fresh mango slices and fresh grated coconut; roasted apricot halves in early summer; berries at any time of the year; and poached quince or rhubarb in winter. I also eat this for dessert – it's protein-packed, gluten-free and low in sugar. Winner! Serves 3–4

500 ml (17 fl oz/2 cups) orange juice

60 g (2 oz/½ cup) chia seeds

1–2 tablespoons sweetener, such as agave or rice syrup (optional)

330 g (11½ oz) fresh berries

100 g (3½ oz) pistachio nut slivers

Place the orange juice and chia seeds in a bowl. Add the sweetener to taste (if using), and stir to combine the ingredients. Refrigerate for at least 4 hours or overnight to soak the chia.

Divide the chia between three to four bowls. Divide the berries between the bowls and scatter the slivered pistachio nuts over the top.

Coconut chia bowl
Substitute coconut water for the orange juice, or use half coconut water and half coconut milk.

Moroccan spiced breakfast couscous

A very sophisticated and exotic way to start the day. This is also delicious served with poached or stewed fruit on top. Serves 4–6

250 ml (8½ fl oz/1 cup) orange juice

½ teaspoon ground cinnamon

¼ teaspoon freshly grated nutmeg

2 teaspoons caster (superfine) sugar

250 g (9 oz/1⅓ cups) instant couscous

100 g (3½ oz) natural yoghurt

2 tablespoons honey

60 g (2 oz/⅔ cup) flaked almonds

Place the orange juice, cinnamon, nutmeg and sugar in a small saucepan. Heat to almost boiling. Remove from the heat, stir in the couscous, cover and allow to rest for 2 minutes.

Place the saucepan over low heat and stir with a fork to break up the grains.

Mix the yoghurt and honey together in a bowl and refrigerate until required.

To serve, heap the couscous into bowls, spoon the sweet yoghurt on top and scatter over the almonds.

Breakfast quinoa
Place 100 g (3½ oz/½ cup) quinoa in a small saucepan along with the orange juice and spices. Bring to the boil, reduce the heat and cover with a lid. Cook until the quinoa is tender, approximately 10-12 minutes.

Fruit compote

Make this with the season's best available ingredients: nectarines, apricots and berries in summer; plums and quince in autumn; rhubarb and apples in winter; and cherries in spring. This compote is great with muesli or porridge, or simply with a dollop of yoghurt. It's also good for dessert. Serves 4–6

3 nectarines, cut into thick wedges

6 plums, quartered

6 apricots, quartered

Pulp from 4 passionfruit

Pinch of saffron threads or 1 cinnamon stick

55 g (2 oz/¼ cup) caster (superfine) sugar

Place the prepared fruit, saffron, 80 ml (2½ fl oz/⅓ cup) water and the caster sugar in a heavy-based saucepan and cook over medium heat until the liquid comes to the boil. Reduce the heat and simmer for 20 minutes, stirring occasionally. Discard the cinnamon. Allow to cool slightly before serving.

Ricotta hotcakes with poached raspberries

These ricotta hotcakes make a perfect brunch dish. They can be served with a range of different fruit, from banana and maple syrup to oven-roasted apricots or poached berries. Serves 4–6

115 g (4 oz/½ cup) caster (superfine) sugar, plus 2 tablespoons extra

300 g (10½ oz) raspberries

2 eggs

250 g (9 oz/1 cup) ricotta

60 ml (2 fl oz/¼ cup) milk

125 g (4½ oz/½ cup) natural yoghurt

150 g (5½ oz/1 cup) self-raising flour

½ teaspoon baking powder

Oil for cooking

Preheat the oven to 180°C (350°F).

Place the caster sugar and 180 ml (6 fl oz) water in a medium saucepan over low heat to allow the sugar to dissolve. Increase the heat and bring to the boil. Place the berries in the hot syrup and heat them through. Strain the berries immediately, reserving the cooking liquid. Return the cooking liquid to the saucepan and boil to reduce by half. Allow the syrup to cool a little, then add the berries. Set aside.

Beat the eggs and ricotta together. Add the milk, yoghurt and the extra 2 tablespoons caster sugar, and beat until smooth. Sift the flour with the baking powder and ½ teaspoon salt, and add to the ricotta base. Stir until combined – it should be quite thick.

Heat a heavy-based frying pan over medium–low heat. Add a splash of oil, then add ladlefuls of the ricotta mixture to form 7.5 cm (3 in) hotcakes. Cook until the bases are golden brown. Turn the hotcakes over and cook for a further 2–3 minutes. Repeat until the mixture is used up, adding more oil as needed and keeping the cooked hotcakes warm in the oven. This mixture makes at least 12 hotcakes. Serve the hotcakes with the poached raspberries on top.

Ricotta hotcakes with banana and maple syrup
Once the hotcakes are cooked, turn the heat up slightly and add a splash more oil. Add two sliced bananas and cook for 1-2 minutes on each side. Serve the hotcakes with the bananas on top and drizzle with maple syrup.

Gingerbread waffle cakes with honeycomb butter and banana

If you love waffles you'll be smitten by this dish, which is inspired by an American recipe. If, like me, you don't have a waffle maker, just cook small circles of the batter in a warm frying pan. I have dreams about these waffle cakes and, on waking, I proceed to the kitchen instantly to make a batch. Serves 6

200 g (7 oz/1⅓ cups) self-raising flour

1 teaspoon ground cinnamon

1 teaspoon ground ginger

¼ teaspoon ground cloves

4 eggs, separated

250 ml (8½ fl oz/1 cup) milk

50 g (1¾ oz/¼ cup firmly packed) brown sugar

60 ml (2 fl oz/¼ cup) golden syrup

Oil for cooking

4 bananas

Honeycomb butter (page 487), chilled

Preheat the oven to 180°C (350°F). Sift together the flour, cinnamon, ginger and cloves.

Beat the egg whites until stiff peaks form. Beat together the egg yolks, milk, brown sugar and golden syrup until thoroughly blended. Add the egg yolk mixture to the sifted ingredients and stir until combined. Fold through the egg whites.

Place a large frying pan over medium heat and add a splash of oil. Make sure the frying pan isn't too hot or the waffle cakes will burn. Spoon in some waffle mixture to form 6 cm (2½ in) circles. Cook until bubbles form on top and the bases are golden brown. Turn the waffle cakes over and cook for a further 2–3 minutes. Repeat until the mixture is used up, adding more oil as needed and keeping the cooked waffle cakes warm in the oven.

Slice the bananas and honeycomb butter. Top the waffle cakes with slices of both and serve.

Green goddess bowl

You can literally add anything you like to this bowl of goodness. For an extra protein punch, add a poached egg on top. Simply multiply the ingredients for extra people. Serves 1

Oil for cooking

50 g (1¾ oz) kale, cavolo nero or English spinach, chopped into 5 cm (2 in) pieces

50 g (1¾ oz) broccoli or broccolini florets, blanched

50 g (1¾ oz) cooked quinoa

1 tablespoon Tamari seed mix (page 471)

Extra-virgin olive oil

2 tablespoons kimchi or sauerkraut

½ avocado

Raw nuts (optional)

Chopped herbs (optional)

Poached egg (optional)

Heat a heavy-based frying pan over medium–high heat. Add a splash of oil and the greens and cook for 1–2 minutes, stirring occasionally. Season well with salt and freshly ground black pepper and add a splash of water to steam the greens, allowing them to cook completely. Transfer the greens to a serving bowl.

Toss the quinoa with the seed mix, some salt and pepper and a splash of extra-virgin olive oil, and arrange in a bowl next to the greens. (If you like, you can add raw nuts — activated, if that does anything for you — and chopped herbs.) Add a mound of broccoli and kimchi and lastly slice the avocado and add it to the bowl. Top with a poached egg, if desired, and serve.

Sweetcorn and ricotta hotcakes with smoked salmon

These hotcakes work well as breakfast, a light lunch or an appetiser. Make smaller versions and you have a pre-dinner nibble. Serves 6

2 eggs

250 g (9 oz/1 cup) ricotta

125 ml (4 fl oz/½ cup) milk

125 g (4½ oz/½ cup) natural yoghurt

150 g (5½ oz/1 cup) self-raising flour (gluten-free if preferred)

½ teaspoon baking powder

2 corn cobs, kernels removed with a sharp knife

2 tablespoons chopped flat-leaf (Italian) parsley

Oil for cooking

Rocket (arugula) to serve

12 slices smoked salmon to serve

Preheat the oven to 180°C (350°F). Beat the eggs and ricotta together. Add the milk and yoghurt and beat until smooth.

Sift the flour with the baking powder and ½ teaspoon salt and add to the ricotta base. Stir until combined. Stir the corn kernels and parsley through the pancake mixture.

Heat a heavy-based frying pan over medium heat. Add a splash of oil, then add spoonfuls of the ricotta mixture to form 7.5 cm (3 in) hotcakes. Cook until bubbles form on top and the bases are golden brown. Turn the hotcakes over and cook for a further 2–3 minutes. Repeat until the mixture is used up, adding more oil as needed and keeping the cooked hotcakes warm in the oven. You will need at least 12 hotcakes.

Place one hotcake on each plate. Top each with a handful of rocket leaves, followed by another hotcake. Add more rocket leaves and arrange two slices of smoked salmon on top. Serve immediately.

Zucchini and feta fritters

These zucchini fritters make a great brunch dish and are terrific served alongside bacon and tomatoes. If you've ever wondered what to do with zucchini, wonder no more! Makes 20–24

2 zucchini (courgettes), coarsely grated

2 eggs, separated

125 ml (4 fl oz/½ cup) milk

125 g (4½ oz/½ cup) natural yoghurt

100 g (3½ oz) soft feta, chopped

30 g (1 oz/⅔ cup) firmly packed chopped basil leaves

150 g (5½ oz/1 cup) self-raising flour

½ teaspoon baking powder

Oil for cooking

Put the grated zucchini in a clean tea towel (dish towel). Tightly squeeze the tea towel to force out as much liquid from the zucchini as you can.

Mix the egg yolks, milk, yoghurt, feta and basil leaves together. Sift the flour with the baking powder and ¼ teaspoon salt, and add to the wet mixture. Stir until combined. Stir in the grated zucchini and plenty of freshly ground black pepper. Whisk the egg whites until thick, then fold them gently into the fritter mixture. It should be a nice dropping consistency.

Heat a heavy-based frying pan over medium–high heat. Add a splash of oil. Fry spoonfuls of the fritter mixture until golden brown on both sides and allow to drain on paper towel. Serve hot.

Haloumi and potato cakes with smoked salmon

Use waxy potatoes for this recipe. Serves 6

4 potatoes, peeled
125 g (4½ oz) haloumi
Chopped fresh herbs
Oil for cooking
100 g (3½ oz) rocket (arugula)
12 slices smoked salmon to serve
Sour cream to serve

Preheat the oven to 180°C (350°F).

Coarsely grate the potatoes and squeeze away any excess moisture.

Grate the haloumi and place it in a bowl along with the potato and chopped herbs. Season with salt and freshly ground black pepper. Mix well.

Heat a heavy-based frying pan over medium–high heat. Add a generous amount of oil. Spoon in the potato mixture, aiming for rough circles 6 cm (2½ in) wide. Allow to cook for a couple of minutes, without stirring. The mixture will begin to brown and hold itself together. Using a palette knife, loosen the base of each potato cake. Turn the cakes over and cook for a further 5 minutes. Transfer the cakes from the pan to a baking tray and cook in the oven for 10–12 minutes.

To serve, top each cake with a handful of rocket, two slices of smoked salmon and a spoonful of sour cream.

French toast

Good-quality bread or brioche is the key to good French toast. Ideally, it should be a day old – the slight staleness will ensure the bread soaks up more egg mixture. Take care not to oversoak the bread, though, or it will take longer to cook. Serves 4

3 eggs
60 ml (2 fl oz/¼ cup) milk
4 pieces of brioche or thick, day-old bread
Oil for cooking
Maple syrup to serve

Whisk the eggs, milk and some salt and freshly ground pepper together until combined.

Take the brioche and soak one side and then the other in the egg mixture until well coated on both sides.

Heat a large heavy-based frying pan over medium–high heat. Add a generous splash of oil and one to two pieces of bread (you may need to cook it in two batches, depending on the size of the bread). Cook for 3–4 minutes on each side until well browned. Cut in half diagonally and serve immediately with maple syrup.

Chipotle French toast with guacamole
Add two diced chipotles en adobo to the egg mixture along with 2 tablespoons chopped coriander (cilantro). Use cornbread in place of brioche and cook as directed. Serve with Guacamole (page 474).

French toast sandwiches filled with chocolate
Take eight thin slices of brioche or bread, spread chocolate and hazelnut spread thickly on half of them, then top with the remaining bread slices to make sandwiches. Take each sandwich and soak one side and then the other in the egg mixture until well coated on both sides. Cook as directed, cut in half diagonally and serve immediately. These are delicious with Raspberry sauce (page 487) and fresh raspberries or strawberries.

Smashed avocado on toast

The ultimate Melbourne breakfast dish. Depending on the avocados and how large they are, you may need to allow a whole avocado per person – or less depending on how much you love avocado and how hungry you are. Serves 1

½ large avocado

1 tablespoon Tamari seed mix (page 471)

1 piece goat's cheese feta

1 tablespoon lemon juice

1 tablespoon extra-virgin olive oil

1 tablespoon chopped herbs: flat-leaf (Italian) parsley, basil or mint (a mixture of all three or just one)

1–2 slices wholegrain bread, toasted, to serve

Poached egg (optional)

Cut the avocado in half and remove the stone. Criss-cross the flesh with a small knife and, using a spoon, scoop the avocado into a bowl.

Add the remaining ingredients and season well with salt and freshly ground black pepper. Mash together roughly and serve on top of the warm toast. Top with a poached egg if desired.

Smashed avocado with bacon and smoked paprika
Take two rashers (slices) of bacon and pan-fry them until crispy. Drain well on paper towel and place the bacon in a bowl along with a diced avocado, 1 tablespoon each lemon juice and olive oil, 1 teaspoon smoked sweet paprika and 1 tablespoon chopped flat-leaf (Italian) parsley. Season well and mix together. Serve on top of warm toast – again, this is delicious with a poached egg on top.

Bruschetta

You can go all out with this recipe and use slices of sourdough bread and add chopped coriander (cilantro) to the tomato mixture, or even diced fresh chilli. Makes 6

4 ripe tomatoes

6 basil leaves, thinly sliced

7 g (¼ oz/¼ cup) roughly chopped flat-leaf (Italian) parsley

½ small red onion, finely diced

6 slices day-old bread

Oil for cooking

1–2 garlic cloves, peeled and cut in half (optional)

Dice the tomatoes finely. Mix the tomato, basil, parsley and onion together and season to taste with salt and freshly ground black pepper.

Heat a chargrill pan, or a heavy-based frying pan, over medium heat. Brush the bread with oil and cook until quite toasty. Remove the bread from the pan and rub with peeled garlic, if desired. While the bread is still warm, top with the tomato mixture and serve straight away.

Bruschetta with goat's cheese
Spread the toasted bread with soft goat's cheese, then top with the tomatoes.

Bruschetta with tapenade
Spread the toasted bread with tapenade, then top with the tomatoes.

Bacon and fried eggs

This is a classic in its own right.

Oil for cooking

2 or 3 rashers (slices) bacon per person

1 or 2 medium eggs per person

Toast and Irish breakfast tea to serve

Heat a large heavy-based frying pan over medium–high heat. Add a splash of oil and cook the bacon until crispy on each side. (If you are cooking for a few people, place the bacon in a warm oven to keep it hot while you cook the eggs.)

Everyone has their own view on how much oil to use when frying eggs: some say lots, others keep it to a minimum. Practice and experience will teach you how much oil to add, but start with enough to coat the base of the pan.

Crack the eggs into the pan and cook for 2–3 minutes. If the eggs are spluttering a lot, turn the heat down. Serve the eggs sunny side up or turn them over and cook for 1–2 minutes on the other side.

Season with salt and freshly ground black pepper and serve on hot buttered toast with a big pot (or two) of Irish breakfast tea.

The big brekkie

A big brekkie doesn't always have to include bacon (crazy I know). Instead, think about fried or poached eggs with grilled tomatoes and mushrooms, sautéed English spinach and maybe a dollop of pesto (see pages 476-7), all served on sourdough toast. This big brekkie is also great with Thai corn fritters (page 46) or Zucchini and feta fritters (page 21).

Poached eggs

Cooking poached eggs is like riding a bike. Learning is often painful and messy but, once mastered, it's a skill to relish for life. You will need a deep-sided frying pan and a slotted spoon. An egg poacher will make things much easier, but patience and the freshest eggs are the real essentials. Some people say that adding a teaspoon of acid, such as vinegar or lemon juice, will help keep the eggs in shape. To my way of thinking, this just adds an unnecessary sour flavour.

Eggs, 2 per person

Toast to serve

Fill your deep-sided frying pan with 2–3 cm (¾–1¼ in) water. Place the pan over medium heat and bring to a slow simmer, with bubbles gently popping on the surface. Some people like to swirl the water as they add the eggs to get the whites to stay together. This works for the first egg but is very tricky for the second. (If you are using fresh eggs you won't have this problem anyway; and if a bit of white floats away it's hardly the end of the world, is it?)

Crack the eggs gently into the simmering water. Add as many eggs as you are comfortable dealing with (four is good). Leave them to cook for 3 minutes, making sure

the water doesn't boil. Gently spoon the cooking water over the top of the eggs, as this helps them to cook.

Okay, nearly there. Have a gentle poke at the eggs; the whites should be firm, but the yolks still soft. Have a paper towel nearby. Lift out the eggs, one by one, using the slotted spoon. Rest the spoon briefly on the paper towel to absorb water, then carefully slide each egg onto a slice of hot buttered toast and serve. Bear in mind that the yolk is about to be broken in 5 seconds, so if you do it at this stage, just think of it as an extra service to your breakfast companions. Season with salt and freshly ground black pepper and serve.

Eggs benedict

Now that we are poached eggs experts (see opposite page), let's make eggs benedict. If you are still struggling with poached eggs, treat yourself to a morning off and go out for breakfast. Then try them again next weekend. Serves 4

16 rashers (slices) bacon
4 English muffins, split in half
8 eggs
Hollandaise sauce (page 454)
Chives to garnish

Set up the frying pan as directed for poached eggs (see opposite). Start cooking the bacon by pan-frying it until brown and crispy. Place it in the oven to keep warm.

Toast the muffins and also keep them warm. Then, last but not least, begin poaching the eggs.

When the eggs are ready, place two toasted muffin halves on each plate. Add a piece of cooked bacon to each muffin. Place the eggs on top of the bacon, then add a spoonful of hollandaise sauce. Garnish with chives.

Eggs florentine
Omit the bacon and spoon hot blanched English spinach onto the toasted muffins just before the eggs. Then top with a spoonful of hollandaise sauce and garnish with chives.

Eggs royale
Swap the bacon for smoked salmon if you are feeling really fancy. You can also add the grated zest of one lemon and/or some chopped dill to the hollandaise sauce.

Eggs mexicano
Swap the bacon for Mexican pulled pork (page 177) and add one or two chopped chipotles en adobo to the hollandaise sauce.

Scrambled eggs

The trick with scrambled eggs is to take the mixture from the heat when just under-cooked, as it will continue to cook a while longer. When just done, serve immediately. If you overcook your eggs, simply add another raw egg to the pan and stir gently. It will bring them back to moist, fluffy gorgeousness. Serves 2

40 g (1½ oz) ghee
6 eggs
60 ml (2 fl oz/¼ cup) pouring (single/light) cream
Chopped chives
Toast to serve

Heat a heavy-based saucepan or frying pan over medium heat and add the ghee.

Beat together the eggs and cream and season with salt and freshly ground black pepper. Pour the mixture into the pan. Cook for 3–4 minutes, stirring frequently. Serve with chopped chives and slices of hot buttered toast.

Herb scrambled eggs
In place of the chives add 2 tablespoons chopped fresh herbs of your choice to the cooked eggs. Basil and flat-leaf (Italian) parsley are particularly good.

Saffron scrambled eggs
Cook 10 saffron threads in the butter for 2-3 minutes, or until fragrant, before adding the egg mixture.

Chilli scrambled eggs
Cook two seeded and diced small red chillies in the butter for 2-3 minutes, or until fragrant, before adding the egg mixture.

Parmesan scrambled eggs
Add 50g (1¾ oz/½ cup) finely grated parmesan to the cooked eggs.

Omelettes

Knowing how to make a great omelette is an essential life skill. It's also a handy little thing to have up your sleeve for those times when there's nothing in the refrigerator except, hopefully, a couple of eggs. Finishing the omelette under a grill (broiler) or in the oven helps to puff it up, so it's worth doing. Makes 1 omelette

3 eggs
20 g (¾ oz) ghee
Handful of grated parmesan or your favourite cheese
Chopped fresh herbs

Whisk the eggs together with a pinch of salt and some freshly ground black pepper.

Heat a heavy-based, ovenproof frying pan over medium heat. Give the pan plenty of time to heat properly. Add the ghee and allow it to melt. Pour the egg mixture into the pan, spread it evenly and cook for 1–2 minutes, or until the base has set.

Place the cheese and fresh herbs on half of the omelette and fold the remaining half over. Finish under a grill (broiler) or in a hot oven and serve straight away.

Ham and tomato omelette
Add a handful of chopped ham and two or three tomato slices along with the cheese.

Mushroom omelette
Allow two button mushrooms per person. Cook the sliced mushrooms in a little butter with fresh herbs and salt and freshly ground black pepper until soft. Add to the omelette with the cheese and herbs.

Spinach and feta omelette
Substitute feta for the parmesan and add a handful of chopped blanched English spinach.

Breakfast frittata

This is a really light frittata packed with sweet cherry tomatoes and full-flavoured parmesan. Serves 4–6

2 tablespoons oil
2 onions, finely diced
½ red capsicum (bell pepper), diced
100 g (3½ oz) cherry tomatoes, halved
150 g (5½ oz) baby English spinach leaves
6 eggs
100 g (3½ oz/1 cup) grated parmesan
3 tablespoons chopped fresh herbs, such as flat-leaf (Italian) parsley, thyme and chives

Preheat the oven to 190°C (375°F).

Heat a small ovenproof frying pan over medium heat. Add the oil and cook the onion and capsicum until slightly softened. Add the tomato halves and cook together for 5 minutes. Add the spinach at the last moment and cook until it just starts to wilt.

Beat the eggs, cheese and herbs in a large bowl. Pour over the mixture in the pan. Cook for 4–5 minutes until the egg forms a cooked base. Place the pan in the oven to finish cooking, about 10–15 minutes. Serve warm.

Broccoli frittata
Use the onion as a base, add blanched broccoli florets, parmesan and cook in the same way. For a little extra, serve with smoked salmon slices and fresh rocket (arugula) leaves.

Roast vegetable frittata
Add a selection of roasted vegetables, such as zucchini (courgette) or eggplant (aubergine), and cook in the same way.

Prosciutto and olive frittata
Cook three or four slices of prosciutto with the onions. Add the egg mixture, grated parmesan, 90 g (3 oz) pitted kalamata olives and cook in the same way.

Potato tortilla

This classic Spanish dish is very similar to a frittata, combining a simple trio of eggs and vegetables. The secret is in the free-range eggs, the slow-cooked onions and the addition of flavour-filled potatoes, such as nicola, desiree, kipfler (fingerling), or any other waxy potato.
Serves 6

6 potatoes (800 g/1 lb 12 oz), peeled
80 ml (2½ fl oz/⅓ cup) olive oil for cooking
4 onions, sliced
2–3 thyme sprigs (optional)
6 eggs

Place the peeled potatoes in a saucepan and cover with water. Cook until just tender. Drain and set aside.

Heat a large heavy-based frying pan over medium–low heat. Add the oil, onion and thyme (if using), and season with salt and freshly ground black pepper. Cook for 15–20 minutes, stirring often, until the onion softens and caramelises.

Beat the eggs together with some more salt and pepper. Cut the potatoes into 1 cm (½ in) slices and add them to the caramelised onion, tossing gently to combine and taking care not to break up the potatoes. Pour the egg mixture over the onion and potatoes; it should just cover the potatoes. Cook for 8–10 minutes over low heat until well set.

Slide the tortilla onto a plate and turn it over gently, then slide it back into the frying pan. Cook for a further 5–6 minutes on a low heat, or until the egg is set and cooked. If you prefer, you can finish cooking the tortilla in a preheated 180°C (350°F) oven – if so, you would need to use an ovenproof pan.

Mediterranean eggs with tomato and chorizo

This tomato, onion and chorizo sauce is cooked in a large pan with eggs and served on toasted sourdough bread. It makes a full-flavoured brunch dish to share. Serves 4

1 red capsicum (bell pepper)
Oil for cooking
1 onion, diced
1 hot chorizo sausage, cut into 5 mm (¼ in) slices
1 garlic clove, crushed
1 teaspoon Harissa (page 467)
4 tomatoes, diced
125 ml (4 fl oz/½ cup) chicken stock or water
1 tablespoon chopped basil or flat-leaf (Italian) parsley
4 eggs
Toasted sourdough to serve

Preheat the oven to 180°C (350°F).
Rub the capsicum with oil, salt and freshly ground black pepper. Place on a baking tray and roast for

20 minutes, or until the skin blisters. Set aside to cool. Peel the skin, remove the seeds and slice the capsicum flesh into 1 cm (½ in) slices.

Heat a large frying pan over medium–high heat. Add a generous splash of oil and the onion and chorizo. Cook for 7–8 minutes, until the onion is softened and golden brown. Add the garlic and harissa and cook for 1–2 minutes, until fragrant. Add the tomatoes, stock, herbs and capsicum, season with salt and pepper, then simmer for 10–15 minutes, until the tomatoes are cooked to a rich sauce. Check the seasoning.

Crack the eggs on top of the sauce and cook until the whites are cooked but the yolks are still runny. Don't stir the sauce after adding the eggs.

Divide the eggs, tomato and chorizo mixture between slices of toasted sourdough and serve.

Deep-fried eggs with sweet chilli, coriander and lime sauce

A very decadent dish guaranteed to get rid of all hangovers – or at least make you forget about them for a short time. Serve with fresh crusty bread. Serves 6

220 g (8 oz) caster (superfine) sugar

20 g (¾ oz/⅔ cup) coriander (cilantro) roots and stems, finely chopped, plus 7 g (¼ oz/¼ cup) coriander leaves, sliced

1 small red chilli, cut in half

2 cm (¾ in) piece fresh ginger, thinly sliced

80 ml (2½ fl oz/⅓ cup) lime juice

Finely grated zest of 2 limes

1 tablespoon fish sauce

12 eggs

100 g (3½ oz) bean sprouts

½ red capsicum (bell pepper), thinly sliced

500 ml (17 fl oz/2 cups) oil for deep-frying

Put the sugar and 250 ml (8½ fl oz/1 cup) water in a small saucepan and cook over medium heat until the sugar has dissolved. Continue cooking until the liquid has reduced by half, approximately 5 minutes.

Add the chopped coriander roots and stems, chilli and ginger and simmer for a further 5 minutes. Remove from the heat, add the lime juice, zest and fish sauce and allow to cool. Strain the sauce into a small saucepan.

Fill a deep frying pan with 2–3 cm (¾–1¼ in) water. Place it over medium heat and bring to a gentle simmer, with bubbles gently popping on the surface (you don't want large bubbles to break the surface). If necessary, turn the heat down a little.

Crack the eggs, two or three at a time, into the simmering water, and cook for 1½ minutes, or until the whites are just set and the yolks still runny. Spoon the eggs gently onto a tray lined with paper towel, pat dry and allow to cool. Continue until all the eggs are poached.

Mix together the bean sprouts, sliced coriander leaves and capsicum strips. Toss with 3 tablespoons of the sweet chilli, coriander and lime sauce.

Pour the oil into a wok or deep saucepan over medium–high heat to a depth of 4 cm (1½ in). If the oil begins to smoke, it is too hot.

Reheat the remaining lime sauce, season to taste with salt and freshly ground black pepper and keep warm.

Deep-fry the eggs, three at a time, until golden. Keep the eggs warm until all are cooked.

To serve, place two deep-fried eggs in the centre of each plate and a mound of dressed salad on top. Drizzle some lime sauce over to finish.

Baked beans with smoky ham hock

Give store-bought baked beans the flick and make your own. It takes a little effort to prepare the beans and the ham hock but the end result is well worth it. If your tastebuds prefer a hit of spice, add 1–2 chopped chillies. Serves 6

1 ham hock

250 g (9 oz/1¼ cups) white beans, soaked in cold water overnight, drained

Oil for cooking

2 onions, diced

2 garlic cloves, crushed

1 teaspoon smoked sweet paprika

250 ml (8½ fl oz/1 cup) tomato passata (puréed tomatoes)

2 tablespoons chopped flat-leaf (Italian) parsley

Toasted fresh crusty bread to serve

Place the ham hock in a large saucepan. Cover with water and bring to the boil. Reduce to a simmer and cook for 1 hour, or until the meat is cooked and beginning to fall off the bone. Remove any scum that comes to the surface during cooking. Set the meat aside to cool in the cooking liquid.

Place the beans in a saucepan, cover with plenty of water and bring to the boil. Reduce the heat to a simmer and cook for 30–40 minutes, until the beans are tender. Remove any scum that comes to the surface during cooking.

Remove the ham hock from the cooking liquid. Remove the skin, bone and tendons, and discard. Chop the ham meat into chunks. Strain the cooking liquid and set aside.

Preheat the oven to 180°C (350°F).

Heat a large, heavy-based ovenproof saucepan over medium–high heat. Add a splash of oil and the onion. Cook for 3–4 minutes, until the onion has softened. Add the garlic and paprika and cook for 1–2 minutes, until fragrant. Add 250 ml (8½ fl oz/1 cup) of the reserved ham cooking liquid and the tomato passata. Bring to the boil and add the cooked beans and chopped ham. Cover and cook in the oven for 15–20 minutes, stirring occasionally. Add more cooking liquid if needed.

Season with salt and freshly ground black pepper, add the parsley and serve with the toast.

Smoked salmon and prawn kedgeree

Traditionally a kedgeree is made with smoked haddock, but this can be hard to find, so I tend to make it with salmon and prawns. It's a great rice dish that's good for brunch or even supper. Serves 4

Oil for cooking

2 onions, diced

2 teaspoons mild curry paste

400 g (14 oz/2 cups) long-grain rice

200 g (7 oz) green (raw) prawns (shrimp), shells removed

2 hardboiled eggs, peeled and cut into wedges

60 g (2 oz) butter, diced

150 g (5½ oz) smoked salmon, cut into wide strips

2 tablespoons chopped flat-leaf (Italian) parsley

Preheat the oven to 180°C (350°F). Heat a medium saucepan over medium–high heat. Add the oil and onion and cook until tender. Add the curry paste and stir together for 1 minute. Add the rice and 750 ml (25½ fl oz/3 cups) water and bring to the boil. Reduce the heat to low, cover and cook until all the water has been absorbed.

Place the rice in a buttered casserole dish and add the prawns and egg wedges on top. Dot the rice with butter and cover the casserole with foil. Place in the oven and cook for 15 minutes. Remove the foil and gently stir in the smoked salmon. Scatter the parsley on top and serve.

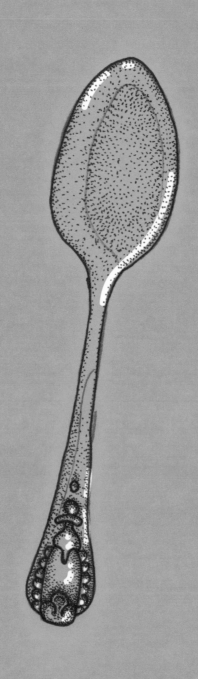

Bite-sized

There's only one thing better than a few tasty bite-sized nibbles to start a meal off on the right foot, and that's a glass of bubbles – or two. Choose your nibbles well, as it sets the tone for the rest of the meal. They can be as simple as a bowl of spiced nuts, or something more exotic, such as betel leaves stuffed with crabmeat and flavoured with kaffir lime and chilli.

Preparing the palate

At a typical dinner party I serve two or three nibbles followed by a more formal appetiser, which we sit at the table to enjoy. Most of the appetisers tend to be vegetarian or seafood-based, mainly because I am saving the meat for the main course, but there are many options. Light salads, steamed mussels, smoked salmon and cheese-based dishes largely make up my repertoire, though pasta sneaks in from time to time – and soups, of course.

Along with the recipes in this chapter, there are many other dishes you can try. The Moroccan chicken rolls (page 306) and Spiced eggplant parcels (page 308) from the Pastry chapter make great finger food. For more formal appetisers, try the recipes at the end of this chapter – and don't forget soups and light pasta dishes.

Balance the first course with what you will be serving next. Consider the style of food; keep to one type of cuisine to avoid confusing the palate. If serving shellfish, check with your guests that no one has an allergy; there's nothing worse than everyone tucking into a delicious crab salad while one guest nibbles miserably on a piece of bread.

Quick ideas

- Warm garlic and fennel olives
- Roasted chestnuts with jamon
- Spiced nuts (page 470)
- Cherry tomatoes with buffalo mozzarella sticks
- Grissini with prosciutto and truffle oil
- Dates with blue cheese

- Raw vegetable crudités with a selection of dips
- Grilled haloumi in vine leaves (page 38)
- Chicken larb (page 132) in lettuce leaf cups
- Soups, pasta and salads are also great for appetisers – think small, appetite inducing–sized bowls, not filling portions.

Things to remember
when serving bite-sized food

- If you plan to serve cocktail food, make sure it can be eaten with one hand.

- Remember to offer serviettes.

- Keep it simple and seasonal: light dishes for spring and summer and hearty dishes for winter.

- Don't serve too much alcohol, too early.

- If you expect your guests to be drinking a lot of alcohol, increase the amount of food you'll be serving to help soak up the liquor.

- Never attempt something outside your capabilities.

- Don't serve the same food group for appetiser and main course.

- Allow 250 g (9 oz) shellfish, 75 g (2¾ oz) fish, 75–100 g (2¾–3½ oz) raw meat or 250 ml (8½ fl oz/1 cup) soup per person.

- Keep the dishes small – they're only supposed to be a beginning to your meal.

- Serve two to three pieces per person before dinner, or eight to ten pieces per person to substitute for a meal.

- For a full-on cocktail party experience, allow at least seven items per person for the first hour and add two more for each hour after that.

- If you're game enough to serve a soufflé, make sure all your guests are sitting down before you bring it to the table – there's nothing quite like the 'wow' reaction.

- Another idea is to buy antipasto ingredients from your favourite deli, then serve up a platter. Antipasto can range from marinated artichokes, olives and sun-dried tomatoes to baby bocconcini, thinly sliced prosciutto or salami and strips of roasted red capsicum (bell pepper). Antipasto can also be supplemented with crispy grissini breadsticks or sliced ciabatta bread, plus a few fresh ingredients, such as sliced fresh capsicum (bell pepper), cherry tomatoes, asparagus, green beans and radishes.

- A Middle Eastern platter might include some Dolmades (page 50), Sweet potato and cashew falafels (page 152), black or green olives, thinly sliced bastourma (a spice-coated air-dried beef) and thinly sliced salami, along with Hummus (page 473), Baba ghanoush (page 472) and Tzatziki (page 475). A bowl of Dukkah (page 469) and olive oil is also an excellent match with these foods. Serve with toasted crispbreads or pitta bread.

- A typical crudité platter might include carrots, red capsicum (bell pepper), fennel and celery stalks, all cut into long sticks; mushrooms, washed and quartered; cucumber cut into thin slices; tomatoes cut into wedges; and cherry tomatoes. Provide a few dips, such as Guacamole (page 474), Beetroot dip (page 474) or Hummus (page 473). Serve with grissini sticks, corn (taco) chips and crispbreads.

Bite-sized recipes

Toppings

A few topping suggestions for any of the following recipes: Blini (opposite page), Crostini (page 36), Potato rösti (page 36) and Parmesan wafers (page 37).

TIP

- Tapenade (page 477) and goat's cheese
- Pesto (see pages 476–7) and goat's cheese
- Pesto (see pages 476–7) with roasted capsicum (bell pepper) and a dollop of ricotta
- Marinated artichoke with roasted capsicum (bell pepper)
- Rocket (arugula) leaves with pesto (see pages 476–7) and goat's cheese
- Thinly sliced ham with dijon mustard
- Salami with Tapenade (page 477)
- Smoked salmon, sour cream, freshly ground black pepper and dill
- Smoked salmon with sour cream and horseradish
- Salmon caviar, crème fraîche and chives
- Green olive salsa (page 478)
- Thin slices of roast pumpkin (squash) and feta
- Pumpkin mole (page 262)

Pitta crisps

Using pitta bread to make your own crispbreads may sound like a lot of work, but they are so good it's well worth the effort. Use them with dips. Makes 80

450 g (1 lb) packet pitta bread

Oil as required

Salt flakes

Poppy or sesame seeds or toasted cumin seeds

Preheat the oven to 180°C (350°F).

Using scissors, cut around the edge of the pitta bread to split it and produce two large circles. Brush the brown side of each pitta bread circle with oil, then sprinkle on the salt and poppy seeds. Lay the circles on top of each other.

Cut into crisps by cutting each circle in half, then quarters, then into three triangles. Lay them flat on baking trays and cook in the oven for 5–10 minutes or until crisp.

Lemon and pepper pitta crisps
The lemon and pepper mix you can buy from the supermarket is perfect on pitta crisps.

Cheese and sesame seed pitta crisps
Brush the pitta bread with oil, then sprinkle on grated parmesan and sesame seeds. Cut and cook.

Blini

Blini are small buckwheat pancakes from Russia, traditionally served with caviar. Even if you're not serving caviar, blini make a great base for many other toppings. See the topping ideas on the opposite page. Serves 20–25

1 sachet (7 g/¼ oz) dried yeast

200 ml (7 fl oz) milk, plus 2 tablespoons warm milk

125 g (4½ oz/¾ cup) buckwheat flour

2 eggs, separated

40 g (1½ oz) melted butter

Whisk the yeast and the 2 tablespoons warm milk together in a large bowl. Leave in a warm place until bubbles form on the surface. Whisk in the remaining milk, flour, egg yolks and a pinch of salt. Cover and leave until bubbles again form on the surface.

Beat the egg whites until stiff. Fold the whites into the blini mixture.

Heat a heavy-based frying pan over medium heat. Brush the melted butter over the base of the pan, then spoon in level tablespoons of the blini mixture. Allow to cook until bubbles appear on the surface, then turn them over and cook on the other side for 1–2 minutes, until just golden brown.

Place the cooked blini on a flat tray to cool. Continue cooking until all the mixture is used. When all the blini are cooked, cover them with plastic wrap until you are ready to add the toppings.

Crostini

Crostini are slices of baguette that have been baked until they are crisp. They can be topped with an endless array of ingredients or served with dips. See the topping ideas on page 34.
Makes 20–30

1 baguette
Olive oil as required

Preheat the oven to 160°C (320°F).

Slice the bread into 1 cm (½ in) slices. Brush each slice with oil. Place on flat baking trays and cook in the oven for 10–15 minutes, or until crisp on top. Turn the crostini slices over and continue cooking for a further 10 minutes, or until golden.

Prawn and chorizo pinchos
Take 125 g (½ oz) cherry tomatoes, drizzle with olive oil and sprinkle with salt. Roast in a 160°C (320°F) oven for 10-12 minutes, or until slightly soft. Take one chorizo sausage, slice it thinly and either grill (broil) or barbecue it until crispy on each side. Drain on paper towel to remove any excess fat. Take 12 cooked prawns (shrimp) and peel and devein them, then cut them in half lengthways. To assemble, lay the crostini out and spread with Smoked paprika mayonnaise (page 463), top with a slice of chorizo, half a prawn and a cherry tomato, and sprinkle with chopped flat-leaf (Italian) parsley. Makes 18-24.

Potato rösti

These are very tasty potato fritters, which will disappear as quickly as you can make them. You can also make these rösti the size of a small saucer and eat them for breakfast, or even for dinner – they are great with steak. See the topping ideas on page 34. Makes 20 cocktail-sized rösti

500 g (1 lb 2 oz) waxy potatoes
4 spring onions (scallions), thinly sliced (optional)
Oil for cooking

Peel and grate the potatoes. Place in a clean tea towel (dish towel) and squeeze out all the moisture. Place the potato in a small bowl and mix with the spring onion (if using), and some salt and freshly ground black pepper.

Place a little of the mixture (about 2 tablespoons) in the palm of your hand, roll up tightly then flatten. Repeat with all the potato mixture.

Pour a layer of oil into a heavy-based frying pan over medium heat. Add the potato rösti to the hot pan. Cook until golden brown on each side. Continue until all the rösti are cooked. Drain on paper towel.

Ocean trout tartare on potato rösti with wasabi
Finely dice 250 g (9 oz) skinless ocean trout and mix with 2 tablespoons lime juice, some freshly ground black pepper and a pinch of salt. Lay the rösti out and spread each with a thin layer of wasabi. Top with a heaped teaspoon of ocean trout. Sprinkle the trout with diced Pickled ginger (page 439) and chopped chives. Serve immediately. Makes 20.

Parmesan wafers

These wafers are great for nibbles as they are gluten-free as well as tasty. Take care as they can be quite fragile – assemble them just before serving. See the topping ideas on page 34. Makes 15–20

250 g (9 oz) packet shredded parmesan

Preheat the oven to 180°C (350°F). Line two baking trays with baking paper.

Place 1 tablespoon amounts of grated parmesan on the trays, leaving approximately 5 cm (2 in) between each to allow room for spreading.

Bake in the oven for 8–10 minutes or until golden brown. Remove and allow to cool. When cool, top with your desired ingredients.

Parmesan wafers with celeriac roulade and rare roast beef
Make celeriac roulade by peeling, then coarsely grating one celeriac into a bowl. Add 2 teaspoons dijon mustard, 2 tablespoons lemon juice and enough thickened (whipping) cream (approximately 3-4 tablespoons) to bring the mixture together. Check the seasoning – it should have a similar flavour to coleslaw. To serve, arrange the parmesan wafers on a serving platter. Top with a spoonful of the roulade, half a slice of roast beef and a sprinkling of chopped chives.

Baby caramelised onion tarte tatin

You can eat these as they are – and they are delicious enough in their own right – or top them with just about anything, such as roast beef and horseradish. Makes 20

250 g (9 oz/1⅔ cups) self-raising flour
100 ml (3½ fl oz) milk
40 g (1½ oz) melted butter, plus extra for greasing
1 teaspoon dijon mustard
1 egg
½ quantity Caramelised onions (page 251)
60 g (2 oz/½ cup) grated cheddar or gruyère

Preheat the oven to 180°C (350°F). Sift the flour and 1 teaspoon salt into a bowl. Beat together the milk, melted butter, mustard and egg. Pour the wet mixture into the flour mixture and stir with a fork to combine.

Tip the mixture onto a floured work surface and knead briefly until smooth. Roll the dough out to a 1 cm (½ in) thickness and cut into 2.5 cm (1 in) circles.

Grease 20 holes in mini muffin tins with butter and add a spoonful of caramelised onion in the bottom of each hole. Top with a pinch of grated cheese, then top each one with a disc of dough. Cook in the oven for about 10–15 minutes, or until golden on top.

Remove from the oven and allow to stand for about 3–4 minutes. To turn them out of the tin, cover the tin with a large plate and turn upside down. Place on a flat surface and remove the muffin tin.

Pan-fried haloumi with pomegranate and za'atar

Need a pre-dinner nibble in a hurry? This is the one for you. If pomegranates aren't in season, scatter coriander (cilantro) leaves over instead. You can buy za'atar from Middle Eastern food shops and good delis if you don't want to make your own. Makes 12

400 g (14 oz) haloumi

Oil for cooking

Za'atar (page 470) to sprinkle

Pomegranate molasses

Juice of 1 lemon

Fresh pomegranate seeds

Cut the haloumi into 12 equal slices.

Heat a heavy-based frying pan over medium–high heat. Add a splash of oil and cook the haloumi for 2–3 minutes on each side until golden brown. (You may need to do this in batches.)

Arrange on a serving platter and sprinkle the za'atar over. Drizzle with pomegranate molasses, squeeze over the lemon juice, sprinkle over the pomegranate seeds and serve.

Grilled haloumi in vine leaves

This is a simple dish but, to make it even simpler, you can just grill the haloumi cheese and squeeze some lemon juice over to serve. Makes 12

400 g (14 oz) haloumi

12 preserved vine leaves, soaked in cold water for 30 minutes

Oil for cooking

Cut the haloumi into 12 equal pieces.

Dry the vine leaves and lay them out flat. Place a piece of haloumi in the centre of each leaf. Roll each leaf up to cover the haloumi. Brush with oil then barbecue until golden brown on each side. Serve immediately.

Eggplant and feta rolls

A simple yet stylish nibble. If you don't want to cook the eggplant slices you could buy grilled eggplant from the deli, or substitute grilled capsicum (bell pepper). Makes 12

2 eggplants (aubergines)

Oil for cooking

2 tablespoons shredded basil leaves

100 g (3½ oz) feta, crumbled

Cut the eggplants lengthways into thin slices and sprinkle with salt. Leave to drain in a colander for 30 minutes. Rinse the eggplant slices and dry them well with paper towel.

Pan-fry the slices in oil over medium heat until golden brown on both sides. Drain and allow to cool.

Top the eggplant slices with the chopped basil and crumbled feta, then roll up. Place the rolls on a platter and serve immediately.

Sushi rice

This is the rice that is used to make the ever-popular California rolls (see below) and sushi.
Makes 1 kg (2 lb 3 oz/6 cups)

400 g (14 oz/2 cups) medium-grain (sushi) rice
60 ml (2 fl oz/¼ cup) rice wine vinegar
1 teaspoon sugar

Place the rice and 625 ml (21 fl oz/2½ cups) water in a saucepan. Cover with a lid, bring to the boil, then reduce to a low simmer. It's important to keep the pan covered with a lid, so as not to allow the steam to escape. This helps the rice to cook correctly. It will take about 8–10 minutes for all the water to be absorbed.

Remove the pan from the heat and allow the rice to stand, covered, for 5 minutes before using.

Warm the rice wine vinegar in a small saucepan over low heat for 2–3 minutes. Add the sugar and 1 teaspoon salt and stir until dissolved. Stir this into the rice while still hot. Allow the rice to cool slightly before using to make sushi or California rolls (see below).

California rolls

California rolls make perfect party food. However, they take a bit of practice to get just right. You'll need a bamboo mat to make the rolling easier, plus a few other Japanese ingredients, including wasabi and pickled ginger. You can vary the flavour of these rolls by using whatever you have on hand – fried chicken, tofu, Peking duck, egg omelette, raw or tinned tuna, seaweed or raw salmon. Makes 4–5 rolls (40–48 pieces)

1 quantity Sushi rice (see above)
1 packet nori sheets
Wasabi
1 cucumber, cut into thin julienne
1 carrot, cut into thin julienne
1 avocado, peeled and thinly sliced
Pickled ginger (page 439)
Seafood, such as smoked salmon, cooked peeled prawns (shrimp), or crabmeat (optional)
Soy sauce to serve

Prepare the sushi rice as directed. Lay out one nori sheet on your bamboo mat. Cover most of the nori with cooked rice, leaving the top 1 cm (½ in) free of rice.

Near the bottom, spread a small layer of wasabi across the rice. Add a row of cucumber, carrot, avocado and pickled ginger. Add a layer of seafood, if desired. Wet the top 1 cm (½ in) of nori with a little pickled ginger juice. Roll the nori around the fillings, compressing it tightly with the bamboo mat. Continue rolling until all the rice and nori is used.

Chill the rolls for 20 minutes before slicing each one into 10 pieces. Serve with pickled ginger, wasabi and soy sauce.

Peking duck and hoisin rice-paper rolls

Rice-paper rolls are perfect for a light pre-dinner nibble, particularly in warmer weather. You can add any filling you like, from roast chicken through to prawns (shrimp) or vegetables – or even crayfish if you're feeling flash. The Vietnamese dipping sauce can be served with Southeast Asian food of any description. Makes 12

50 g (1¾ oz) cellophane noodles

½ Chinese roast duck, flesh removed and thinly sliced

80 g (2¾ oz/½ cup) chopped roasted peanuts

2 tablespoons chopped coriander (cilantro)

1 small carrot, finely grated or julienned

1 tablespoon hoisin sauce

12 Vietnamese mint leaves, shredded

12 rice-paper wrappers

Vietnamese dipping sauce

1 tablespoon shaved palm sugar (jaggery)

2 tablespoons lime juice

3 tablespoons fish sauce

1 small red chilli, sliced

To make the dipping sauce, put the palm sugar and lime juice in a bowl and stir to dissolve the sugar. Stir in the fish sauce, chilli and 1 tablespoon water. Set aside for 30 minutes before using, to let the flavours infuse.

Place the noodles in a large bowl and cover completely with boiling water. Stand for 5 minutes to soften, then drain well.

Place the noodles, duck meat, peanuts, coriander, carrot, hoisin sauce and Vietnamese mint in a large bowl and mix well. Season to taste with salt and freshly ground black pepper.

Fill a large bowl with hot water, then soak the rice-paper wrappers, one at a time, until softened. Remove the wrappers carefully and drain them on paper towel or a tea towel (dish towel).

Lay the wrappers out flat, then place the filling on the bottom centre of each softened wrapper. Roll the end up over the filling, fold in the sides and continue rolling up to the top. Serve with the dipping sauce.

Vegetable and egg rice-paper rolls
Beat two eggs lightly. Heat a small frying pan or wok over medium heat. Add a splash of oil then enough beaten egg to form a thin layer, as you would with an omelette. Cook briefly on both sides, then remove from the heat and allow to cool. Slice thinly and toss with noodles, as directed, but add more vegetables, such as bean sprouts, shredded cucumber and chopped capsicum (bell pepper).

Prawn rice-paper rolls
Instead of duck, use six cooked prawns (shrimp) cut in half. Swap the hoisin sauce for Sweet chilli sauce (page 437).

Spring rolls

I like to make tiny finger-sized spring rolls to serve before a meal, particularly if it's to be one with Asian flavours. Makes 36

50 g (1¾ oz) cellophane noodles

250 g (9 oz) minced (ground) pork

1 garlic clove, crushed

1 teaspoon grated fresh ginger

4 spring onions (scallions), green tops only, thinly sliced

1 tablespoon kecap manis

1 tablespoon Sweet chilli sauce (page 437)

1½ teaspoons fish sauce

200 g (7 oz) packet small spring roll wrappers

1 egg, lightly beaten

Oil for deep-frying

80 ml (2½ fl oz/⅓ cup) soy sauce

2 small red chillies, chopped

Place the noodles in a large bowl and cover them completely with boiling water. Stand for 5 minutes to soften, then drain well.

Place the noodles, minced pork, garlic, ginger, spring onion, kecap manis, sweet chilli sauce and fish sauce together in a large bowl and mix well.

Peel a spring roll pastry wrapper off the stack and place it in front of you with one corner facing downwards (like a diamond). Brush liberally with the beaten egg. Place a teaspoon of the mixture near the bottom of the pastry, fold the bottom corner up over the filling, then fold the sides in. Roll up to the top and ensure the wrapper seals well. Repeat with the remaining ingredients.

Pour the oil into a wok or a deep saucepan to a depth of 4 cm (1½ in) and heat until 180°C (350°F). Deep-fry four spring rolls at a time until golden brown, then allow to drain on a wok rack or some paper towel.

Mix the soy sauce and chopped chilli together in a small bowl and serve as a dipping sauce with the spring rolls.

Chicken and water chestnut spring rolls
Substitute minced (ground) chicken for the pork and add 80 g (2¾ oz) chopped water chestnuts.

Chicken liver pâté

This pâté recipe is from my good friend Ruth Wirtz and is one of the smoothest, most delicious pâtés I've ever tasted. It is cooked at a fairly low temperature to retain its smooth texture, and has a great flavour combination of bacon, onion, garlic and chicken livers. Make it just once and you too will be hooked. Serves 8–10

250 g (9 oz) butter

2 onions, diced

2 garlic cloves, crushed

4 bacon rashers (slices), diced

500 g (1 lb 2 oz) chicken livers, trimmed of any white sinew

1 tablespoon brandy (optional)

Preheat the oven to 160°C (320°F).

Heat a heavy-based frying pan over medium heat. Melt 40 g (1½ oz) of the butter then add the onion and garlic. Cook gently until the onion begins to soften, about 6–7 minutes. Season well with salt and freshly ground black pepper. Add the bacon and livers to the pan and continue to cook over low heat for 5–6 minutes.

Transfer the ingredients to an ovenproof dish, cover and cook in the oven for 20 minutes.

Melt the remaining butter in a frying pan over medium heat, or in a microwave on Medium (50%).

Allow the livers to cool for 5 minutes, then transfer to a food processor. Purée until smooth, then add the melted butter. Purée again until very smooth. Add the brandy (if using), then season to taste as required. Pour the mixture into a sieve and strain any remaining lumps.

Spoon the pâté into a terrine dish or a few small ramekins. Cover with plastic wrap and chill overnight. Serve with hot toast triangles or crackers.

Duck liver pâté
For a richer pâté, replace the chicken livers with duck livers, or any combination of pheasant, duck or goose livers.

Other pâté flavours
This pâté can easily be varied by the addition of green peppercorns, port, Madeira, grated orange zest or cooked mushrooms.

Smoked trout pâté

I often use this recipe with smoked fish other than trout. Smoked mackerel is also excellent, but it will need a little more lemon juice to cope with the oiliness of the fish. Serves 8–10

200 g (7 oz) smoked trout

90 g (3 oz/⅓ cup) cream cheese

2 teaspoons Horseradish cream (page 456)

2–3 tablespoons lemon juice

Remove the skin and all the bones from the trout. Flake the fish pieces and place them in a food processor. Add the cream cheese and process until smooth. Add the horseradish cream and enough lemon juice to get a good consistency, then season with salt and freshly ground black pepper.

Refrigerate until ready to serve. Will keep for 3–4 days.

Country pork, veal and pistachio terrine

You'll need thin rashers of bacon for this terrine. Ideally, go for thin, fatty rashers from a butcher. Make the terrine the day before you want to serve it, to allow the flavours to develop overnight. This also firms up the terrine, making it easier to slice. Serves 8

Oil for cooking

1 onion, finely diced

16–20 thin rashers (slices) bacon

2 garlic cloves, crushed

3–4 juniper berries

300 g (10½ oz) minced (ground) pork

300 g (10½ oz) minced (ground) veal

50 g (1¾ oz/⅓ cup) pistachio nuts

55 g (2 oz/1 cup) fresh breadcrumbs

1 tablespoon thyme leaves

Pinch of freshly ground nutmeg

2 tablespoons brandy

1 egg

1 bay leaf

Cornichons to serve

Toast or crusty baguette to serve

Heat a small frying pan over medium heat. Add a splash of oil and cook the onion for 3–4 minutes, until soft but not coloured. Dice four rashers of bacon and add them to the onion, along with the garlic. Cook for 2–3 minutes until fragrant. Place the ingredients in a large bowl and allow to cool.

Preheat the oven to 180°C (350°F).

Crush the juniper berries lightly using either a mortar and pestle or a knife handle. Add it to the onion and bacon, along with the pork and veal, the pistachio nuts, breadcrumbs, thyme, nutmeg, 1 teaspoon salt, a decent grinding of black pepper and the brandy. Add the egg to the mixture and mix well to combine.

Line a medium terrine dish (21 × 9 × 6 cm/8¼ × 3½ × 2½ in) with the remaining bacon rashers, allowing the rashers to hang over the sides of the dish – you want to be able to fold the bacon over to encase the mixture.

Place the terrine mixture in the dish, pushing it down into the corners. Place the bay leaf on top and fold the bacon rashers over the terrine. Cover with foil or a lid.

Half-fill a deep baking tray with boiling water to make a water bath. Place the terrine in the water and cover the tray with foil. Cook in the oven for 1–1½ hours, or until firm to the touch. Remove from the water bath and allow to cool at room temperature. Refrigerate overnight.

Slice the terrine into 1 cm (½ in) slices. Arrange on plates with five to six cornichons and slices of hot toast or crusty baguette.

Summer vegetable terrine

Layers of my favourite summer vegetables sandwiched together with basil and goat's cheese equals total yumminess. Although it takes a little bit of time to put together, come dinnertime it's just a matter of slicing and serving. Serves 6–8

2 eggplants (aubergines)

3 small zucchini (courgettes)

Olive oil

2 red capsicums (bell peppers)

3 roma (plum) tomatoes

150 g (5½ oz) firm goat's cheese

2 tablespoons red-wine vinegar

125 ml (4 fl oz/½ cup) extra-virgin olive oil

100 g (3½ oz) rocket (arugula)

20 g (¾ oz/⅓ cup) basil leaves

Preheat the oven to 200°C (400°F).

Slice the eggplants lengthways into 5 mm (¼ in) slices and sprinkle with salt. Leave to drain in a colander for 30 minutes. Rinse under cold running water, then dry well.

Slice the zucchini lengthways into 5 mm (¼ in) slices.

Heat a heavy-based frying pan over medium–high heat. Add a splash of olive oil and cook the eggplant, then the zucchini slices, until tender and golden brown. Set aside.

Rub the red capsicums all over with olive oil and roast them in the oven on a baking tray for 20–25 minutes until the skins blister. Place the capsicums in a plastic bag and seal. Set aside to allow the steam to lift the skins. When cool, remove and discard the skins and seeds. Cut the capsicum into thick strips.

Slice the tomatoes and goat's cheese.

Line a 23.5 × 13.5 × 7 cm (9¼ × 5¼ × 2¾ in) baking tin with plastic wrap lengthways and across, leaving plenty of overhang.

Begin layering the vegetables, starting with one-third of the eggplant slices across the bottom. Sprinkle with a few drops of vinegar, olive oil, salt and freshly ground black pepper. Continue to sprinkle with vinegar, oil, salt and pepper between each layer. Add a layer of zucchini slices, then half the rocket, half the capsicum, all the basil, tomato and goat's cheese, then another third of the eggplant slices. Add the remaining rocket and capsicum and finish with eggplant slices. Push down firmly when adding the rocket leaves.

Fold the overhanging plastic wrap over the vegetables. Place the filled baking tin on a baking tray to catch any overflowing juices. Cut a piece of thick cardboard to fit snugly in the top of the terrine. Weigh down with a heavy weight such as two 2 litre (68 fl oz) juice or milk cartons (around 4 kg/8 lb 13 oz in total is required to compress the ingredients together). Refrigerate overnight with the weights on top of the terrine.

To serve, remove the weights and cardboard from the terrine. Peel back the top layer of wrap and place a chopping board on top. Turn the board and the tin over carefully. Remove the tin and plastic wrap from the pressed terrine. Wipe away any excess juices. Evenly slice the terrine, carefully place onto plates and serve.

Cauliflower polpetti

My friend Rosa Mitchell showed me the knack of making polpetti (Italian fritters) when I helped out at a big Slow Food dinner in Mildura, Victoria. As with all batters, you need to adjust the amount of milk you add to get the right consistency. Makes 20–25

½ cauliflower, thick stalk removed and cut into florets

75 g (2¾ oz/½ cup) self-raising flour

2 eggs

25 g (1 oz/¼ cup) grated parmesan

2 tablespoons chopped flat-leaf (Italian) parsley

2–3 tablespoons milk

Oil for cooking

Bring a large saucepan of water to the boil. Add a sprinkling of salt and cook the cauliflower florets for 3–4 minutes. Drain and set aside to cool.

In a large bowl, mix the flour with the eggs, parmesan and parsley until smooth. Add the cauliflower and mix until combined. Add the milk, as needed, and season with salt and freshly ground black pepper.

Heat a large heavy-based frying pan over medium heat and add a generous splash of oil. Drop large spoonfuls of the polpetti mixture into the pan – you want them around 8 cm (3¼ in) wide and 1 cm (½ in) thick. Pan-fry the polpetti until golden brown on each side. Serve immediately.

Zucchini polpetti
Substitute grated zucchini (courgette) for the cauliflower, and add chopped mint if desired.

Spinach and ricotta fritters

You can make these fritters extra special by searching out wild greens, such as purslane, warrigal greens, dandelion leaves, nettles and wild cress in laneways or your own backyard. If not, your local farmers' market might have some – or you can try sorrel. Ensure that any wild greens are chemical-free and safe to eat. Makes 12–15

200 g (7 oz) baby English spinach leaves

2 eggs

100 g (3½ oz/⅔ cup) self-raising flour

50 g (1¾ oz/⅓ cup) polenta

250 g (9 oz/1 cup) ricotta

Oil for cooking

Blanch the spinach in boiling water for 1–2 minutes. Refresh under cold running water, then squeeze out any excess water and chop roughly.

Beat together the eggs, flour, polenta, ricotta and spinach and mix until smooth. Season with salt and freshly ground black pepper.

Heat a heavy-based frying pan over medium–high heat, add a splash of oil and 3–4 tablespoonfuls batter to the pan. Cook for 2–3 minutes on each side or until golden brown. Turn over and cook for a further 1–2 minutes.

Keep the fritters warm in a preheated oven until all the batter mixture is cooked.

Thai corn fritters

This is a variation of my favourite corn fritters, which I often serve with crispy bacon. Light and easy to eat, they can be enjoyed on their own or dressed up with rocket (arugula), smoked salmon and cucumber. Makes 30

75 g (2¾ oz/½ cup) self-raising flour
185 g (6½ oz/1¼ cups) polenta
½ teaspoon baking powder
1 egg
250 ml (8½ fl oz/1 cup) milk
2 corn cobs, kernels removed with a sharp knife
25 g (1 oz/½ cup) chopped coriander (cilantro) leaves
4 spring onions (scallions), thinly sliced
1 small red chilli, seeded and diced
Oil for frying
Sweet chilli sauce (page 437) to serve

Preheat the oven to 180°C (350°F).

In a bowl, combine the flour, polenta, baking powder and ½ teaspoon salt. Add the egg and milk and mix until the batter is smooth.

Add the corn kernels to the mixture, along with the coriander leaves, spring onion and chilli. If the mixture seems too thin, add 1–2 tablespoons extra flour; if it's too thick, add 1–2 tablespoons extra milk.

Heat a heavy-based frying pan over medium heat. Add 1–2 tablespoons oil and tablespoonfuls of batter. Cook on one side until golden brown, with bubbles forming on top. Turn the fritters over and cook until golden brown on the other side.

Repeat until the mixture is used up, keeping the cooked fritters warm in the oven. Serve with the sweet chilli sauce.

Mexican corn fritters
Omit the spring onions and red chilli. Add two diced chipotles en adobo, 1 teaspoon smoked sweet paprika and 1 teaspoon ground cumin. Serve with Yoghurt tahini sauce (page 455).

Onion bahjis

Onion bahjis are deep-fried fritters of crisp onion and spices but, to many English people, they also mean a late-night Indian snack on the way home from the pub. Makes 20–24

3 onions
140 g (5 oz/1⅓ cups) besan (chickpea flour)
150 g (5½ oz/1 cup) plain (all-purpose) flour
2 teaspoons baking powder
1 egg
3 teaspoons ground cumin
3 teaspoons ground coriander
Oil for deep-frying

Finely dice the onions and blanch them in a saucepan of boiling water for 2–3 minutes. Drain the onion well and reserve 250 ml (8½ fl oz/1 cup) of the cooking liquid for the batter mixture.

Combine the besan, plain flour, baking powder, egg, 1 teaspoon salt, the cumin, coriander and reserved cooking liquid. Whisk until smooth. Add the onion and mix well.

Pour the oil into a wok or a deep saucepan to a depth of 4 cm (1½ in) and heat until it reaches 180°C (350°F). Deep-fry tablespoonfuls of the onion bahji mixture until golden brown, then allow to drain on a wok rack or some paper towel.

Cauliflower pakoras

Cauliflower has to be one of my favourite vegetables and deep-frying it in Indian spices creates a perfect combination. These are delicious with Tzatziki (page 475). Serves 4–6

1 small cauliflower

140 g (5 oz/1⅓ cups) besan (chickpea flour)

½ teaspoon baking powder

2 teaspoons ground cumin

2 teaspoons ground coriander

½ teaspoon ground turmeric

Pinch of chilli or cayenne pepper

Oil for deep-frying

Bring a saucepan of water to the boil. Cut the cauliflower into small florets. Blanch the cauliflower in the boiling water for 2–3 minutes – you want it to keep a good bite. Drain and refresh. I like to keep the cooking water to make the batter. If you want to do this, set it aside to cool.

Mix together the besan, baking powder, spices and a pinch of salt. Add enough water (cooled cooking water if you want) to form a thick batter. Add the cauliflower and mix together well until the cauliflower is coated.

Pour the oil into a wok or a deep saucepan to a depth of 4 cm (1½ in) and heat until approximately 180°C (350°F). Deep-fry the cauliflower (you will need to do this in batches) until golden brown, then allow to drain on a wok rack or some paper towel. Serve hot.

Fried cheesy piquillo peppers

Most piquillo peppers come in a jar, but look out for these chillies in late summer when the local crop comes into season. Makes 12

12 whole piquillo peppers

125 g (4½ oz) grated gruyère, or other hard cheese

160 g (5½ oz/⅔ cup) ricotta

1 tablespoon chopped flat-leaf (Italian) parsley

1 tablespoon Za'atar (page 470)

1 small red chilli, seeded and diced

100 g (3½ oz) cornflour (cornstarch)

150 g (5½ oz/1 cup) plain (all-purpose) flour

2 teaspoons baking powder

Sparkling mineral or soda water (club soda)

Oil for deep-frying

Rinse the peppers well and set them aside to dry. Mix together the gruyère, ricotta, parsley, za'atar and chilli and season with salt and freshly ground black pepper.

Stuff the filling into the peppers and place in the refrigerator for at least 20 minutes to firm up.

Make the batter by mixing together the two flours with the baking powder. Add enough sparkling mineral water to produce a smooth batter.

Pour the oil into a wok or a deep saucepan to a depth of 4 cm (1½ in) and heat until approximately 180°C (350°F).

Dip the peppers into the batter, shake off any excess then lower them into the oil. Deep-fry the peppers (you will need to do this in batches) for 2 minutes on each side until golden brown, then allow to drain on a wok rack or some paper towel. Serve immediately.

Pea arancini balls

Arancini balls are always a hit. You can change the flavour of these by adding other vegetables, such as mushrooms, roast pumpkin (squash) and feta, or English spinach and blue cheese.
Makes 25

Oil for cooking
1 onion, diced
1 garlic clove, crushed
1 leek, white part only, thinly sliced (optional)
1 carrot, finely diced (optional)
300 g (10½ oz/1⅓ cups) arborio rice
125 ml (4 fl oz/½ cup) white wine
1 litre (34 fl oz/4 cups) hot vegetable or chicken stock
155 g (5½ oz/1 cup) frozen peas
40 g (1½ oz/½ cup) grated parmesan
15 g (½ oz/¼ cup) chopped flat-leaf (Italian) parsley
Seasoned flour
1 egg
125 ml (4 fl oz/½ cup) milk
200 g (7 oz/2⅓ cups) panko breadcrumbs
Oil for deep-frying
Herb aïoli (page 463) to serve

Heat a large heavy-based saucepan over medium heat. Add the oil, onion, garlic, leek and carrot (if using), and cook for 3–4 minutes, until fragrant and soft. Add the rice and stir to coat with oil, then cook briefly. Add the wine and stir until it is absorbed.

Begin adding the hot stock – just enough to cover the rice at first, then a ladleful at a time as the stock is absorbed. Stir well with each addition of stock. Continue cooking for 15–20 minutes, until the rice is just done but each grain is still slightly firm in the centre. Add the peas for the last 2–3 minutes of cooking.

Remove from the heat. Add the parmesan and half the parsley and stir until the risotto is creamy and the cheese has melted. Check the seasoning. Pour into a large, reasonably flat container, such as a baking tray or plastic tray to cool the mixture quickly. Set aside to cool.

Put the seasoned flour in a shallow bowl. Beat the egg and milk together in another bowl. Place the breadcrumbs and remaining parsley in a third bowl.

Roll the cooled risotto mixture into golf ball–sized balls. Roll each ball first in the flour, then the egg and finally the breadcrumbs, ensuring they are completely coated.

Pour the oil into a wok or a deep saucepan to a depth of 4 cm (1½ in) and heat until approximately 180°C (350°F). Cook the balls in batches for 3–4 minutes, until golden brown. Drain on paper towel, season with salt and serve with herb aïoli.

Coconut laksa fried chicken

Who doesn't love fried chicken? I love the combo of laksa paste and coconut in this recipe.
Serves 4–6

3 tablespoons laksa paste
125 ml (4 fl oz/½ cup) coconut milk
500 g (1 lb 2 oz) chicken tenderloins, cut in half
Oil for deep-frying
75 g (2¾ oz/½ cup) plain (all-purpose) flour
75 g (2¾ oz) cornflour (cornstarch)
90 g (3 oz/1 cup) desiccated coconut

Mix together the laksa paste and coconut milk. Pour over the chicken and set aside to marinate for up to 4 hours.

Pour the oil into a wok or a deep saucepan to a depth of 4 cm (1½ in) and heat until approximately 180°C (350°F).

Mix together the flours and coconut and ½ teaspoon salt. Dip the chicken in the flour mixture then cook in the hot oil for 5–6 minutes, until golden brown and cooked through. Drain on paper towel, season with salt and serve.

Spicy lip-smacking drumettes

The flavours in this garlic and spice mix are perfect on chicken – you can use chicken wings or ribs if you like. Cooking the meat on the bone makes the chicken beautifully moist. Serves 4–6

1 garlic clove, crushed

1 teaspoon chilli powder

1 teaspoon sweet paprika

1 teaspoon mustard powder

½ teaspoon ground coriander

½ teaspoon ground cumin

½ teaspoon freshly ground black pepper

½ teaspoon salt

2 tablespoons olive oil

1 kg (2 lb 3 oz) chicken drumettes

Mix all the ingredients, except the chicken, together in a bowl. Rub the mixture over the chicken drumettes and allow to marinate for at least 2 hours.

Preheat the oven to 180°C (350°F).

Place the chicken in a lined baking tin and cook in the oven for 1 hour, turning often, until golden brown and cooked through. (Or place the drumettes on a medium–hot barbecue plate and cook for 30 minutes, turning often until cooked.)

Tequila and lime chicken wings
Mix together 80 ml (2½ fl oz/⅓ cup) tequila, the grated zest and juice of two limes, 1 teaspoon dried chilli flakes, 80 ml (2½ fl oz/⅓ cup) olive oil and 2 tablespoons chopped coriander (cilantro), and season well with salt. Pour over the chicken wings and mix well to ensure all the chicken is coated. Allow to marinate for 40 minutes. Cook as normal.

Barbecued lime and chilli chicken wings

This one is finger lickin' good. Children wolf these wings down without even realising the chilli is in there. Serves 4–6

125 ml (4 fl oz/½ cup) lime juice

1 small red chilli, seeded and finely diced

1 teaspoon caster (superfine) sugar

2 tablespoons olive oil

1 kg (2 lb 3 oz) chicken wings

Coriander (cilantro) leaves to serve

Lime wedges to serve

Mix the lime juice, chilli, sugar, oil and ½ teaspoon salt together. Add the chicken wings, turning well to coat, and marinate for 1 hour. Drain off the excess marinade and use it for basting during cooking.

Preheat a barbecue to medium–high.

Place the chicken on the oiled barbecue grill. Cook for 20 minutes, turning often.

If you prefer, place the chicken in a lined baking tin and cook in a preheated 200°C (400°F) oven for 40–50 minutes, turning often, until the chicken is golden brown and cooked through.

To serve, arrange the chicken wings on a platter, scatter with coriander leaves and add some lime wedges.

Dolmades

There's no doubt that the very best dolmades are those made at home. Commercially produced dolmades are typically laden with oil and lack texture and flavour. Makes 25–30

25–30 preserved vine leaves

Oil for cooking

1 onion, finely diced

2 garlic cloves, crushed

100 g (3½ oz/½ cup) long-grain rice

50 g (1¾ oz/⅓ cup) toasted pine nuts

50 g (1¾ oz/⅓ cup) currants

1 tablespoon chopped mint

1 tablespoon chopped flat-leaf (Italian) parsley

Pinch of allspice

Pinch of ground cinnamon

375 ml (12½ fl oz/1½ cups) water or chicken stock

1 tablespoon lemon juice

Olive oil for drizzling

Carefully unfold the vine leaves and discard any brine. Separate the leaves and place them in a large bowl. Pour boiling water over to completely cover them and leave them to soak for 20 minutes. Drain well, then cover with cold water and leave to soak for another 20 minutes. Drain the leaves well once again and pat them dry with paper towel. They are now ready to use.

Heat a small frying pan over medium–high heat. Add 2 tablespoons oil and the onion and cook for 4–5 minutes, until soft. Add the garlic and rice and cook for 1–2 minutes, until fragrant. Remove from the heat and transfer to a bowl.

To the onion mixture, add the pine nuts, currants, herbs, spices and season with salt and freshly ground black pepper. Mix well.

Spread out the vine leaves, shiny side down, and place 1 heaped tablespoon of the filling at one end of each leaf. Fold over the two sides and roll it up. Continue with the remaining leaves until all the filling is used.

Line a saucepan that's big enough to hold all the dolmades snugly in one layer, with three to four parcels in each row. Pack the vine leaves as closely together as possible. Cover with water or chicken stock, lemon juice and a drizzle of olive oil. Put a plate on top to stop the parcels moving around.

Place the saucepan over medium–high heat and bring to the boil. Reduce the heat and simmer for about 40–45 minutes, or until the dolmades are soft and shiny. You may like to remove one of the dolmades to check that the rice is completely cooked. If necessary, add some more water or stock and cook for a further 5 minutes.

Allow to cool in the saucepan. Serve warm or at room temperature.

Chicken and pistachio dolmades
Add 500 g (1 lb 2 oz) minced (ground) chicken to the onion while cooking. Substitute chopped pistachio nuts for the pine nuts. Makes an extra 12-15 dolmades. (You will need extra vine leaves.)

Lamb and mint dolmades
Add 500 g (1 lb 2 oz) minced (ground) lamb to the onion while cooking. Add an additional 1 tablespoon chopped mint. Makes an extra 12-15 dolmades. (You will need extra vine leaves.)

Cheese and za'atar kataifi parcels

These great little parcels look and taste fantastic, but beware when eating them as the pastry tends to fall everywhere. Provide serviettes! If you don't want to make your own za'atar, you can buy it from Middle Eastern food shops and good delis. If you can't find kataifi pastry, use filo instead. Makes 20

100 g (3½ oz) haloumi, grated

100 g (3½ oz) feta, crumbled

80 g (2¾ oz/½ cup) toasted pine nuts

1 tablespoon chopped flat-leaf (Italian) parsley

180 g (6½ oz) kataifi pastry

125 g (4½ oz/½ cup) melted butter

Za'atar (page 470) as required

Preheat the oven to 180°C (350°F). Line a baking tray with baking paper.

Mix the cheeses, pine nuts and parsley together. Form the mixture into twenty 2 cm (¾ in) balls.

Separate the pastry into strands of 10–12 lengths. Place one ball of cheese on each pastry section and roll up, enclosing the filling entirely. Place on the prepared baking tray. Brush the pastries with melted butter and bake for 10–12 minutes, or until crisp.

Pile the kataifi parcels on a platter, sprinkle with za'atar and serve.

Oyster shooters

These oysters look fantastic served in shot glasses but, if you don't have any to hand, you can simply spoon the oysters back into their shells. Liven them up by adding a splash of vodka or tequila, if you like. Makes 24

250 ml (8½ fl oz/1 cup) tomato juice

1 Lebanese (short) cucumber, finely diced

1 tomato, finely diced

½ red onion, finely diced

2–3 tablespoons lemon juice

Tabasco to taste

2 dozen oysters, freshly opened and with juices intact, if possible

Mix the tomato juice, cucumber, tomato and onion together. Season to taste with lemon juice, Tabasco, salt and freshly ground black pepper. Tip the oysters into the tomato mixture, along with any juices. Allow the oysters to absorb the flavours for at least 10 minutes, but no longer than 30 minutes.

Either spoon the oysters back into their shells, adding some of the liquid, or put them in shot glasses, covering with the liquid. Serve immediately.

Oysters with jamon and harissa

Here's a twist on oysters kilpatrick – and it's much more grown up. If you can't find jamon, use prosciutto or pancetta. For a sophisticated appetiser, you could serve six oysters nestled around a mound of bitter lettuce leaves, such as frisée, radicchio, rocket (arugula) or mizuna, with a light dressing. Makes 24

6–8 slices jamon

125 g (4½ oz/½ cup) Harissa mayonnaise (page 463)

2 dozen oysters, freshly opened

Preheat the oven to 180°C (350°F).

Place the jamon slices on a baking tray and cook for 4–5 minutes, until crispy. You can also pan-fry them if you prefer.

Arrange the oysters on a platter and top each one with ½ teaspoon harissa mayonnaise.

Break the jamon into small pieces and place one segment on top of the mayonnaise. Serve immediately.

Oysters with Vietnamese flavours

You should be able to make an Asian-inspired dressing with the ingredients you have to hand in the cupboard. I love the zingy combination of Vietnamese mint with fish sauce and chilli – perfect on a hot night with a glass of riesling. Makes 24

2 teaspoons grated palm sugar (jaggery)

2 teaspoons fish sauce

2 teaspoons lime juice

1 spring onion (scallion), shredded

7 g (¼ oz/¼ cup) coriander (cilantro) leaves

7 g (¼ oz/¼ cup) Vietnamese mint leaves

1 green chilli, seeded and sliced

2 dozen oysters, freshly opened and with juices intact, if possible

Place the palm sugar in a small bowl. Add the fish sauce, lime juice and some freshly ground black pepper. Stir until the sugar dissolves. Add the spring onion, coriander, mint and chilli. Toss to combine.

Tip the oysters into the Vietnamese mixture, along with any juices. Allow the oysters to absorb the flavours for at least 10 minutes, but no longer than 30 minutes.

Spoon the oysters back into their shells, adding some of the liquid. Serve immediately.

Betel leaves with crab, kaffir lime and chilli

These make a beautiful nibble. You will have to go looking for betel leaves, but that will probably be the hardest part of the recipe. You can find crispy fried shallots at Asian food stores. Makes 20

150 g (5½ oz) crabmeat

1 long red chilli, seeded and sliced

2 kaffir lime leaves, thinly sliced

30 g (1 oz/1 cup) coriander (cilantro) leaves

1 French shallot, peeled and diced

4 mint leaves, thinly sliced

1 tablespoon crispy fried shallots

1 tablespoon lime juice

1 tablespoon fish sauce

20 betel leaves

50 g (1¾ oz) salmon caviar (optional)

Combine all the ingredients, except the betel leaves and caviar, in a large bowl. Spoon the mixture onto the betel leaves and top with the caviar (if using).

Pandan chicken parcels

Pandan chicken parcels are pieces of black bean–marinated chicken wrapped in an aromatic pandan leaf. They are easily cooked in the oven. Makes 20

1 tablespoon black beans, soaked and drained

1 teaspoon chilli paste

1 tablespoon kecap manis

1 kg (2 lb 3 oz) boneless skinless chicken thighs

20 pandan leaves

Toothpicks or skewers

Finely chop the black beans, then mix them with the chilli paste and kecap manis.

Cut each chicken thigh into four even-sized pieces. Marinate the chicken in the black bean mixture for 1 hour.

Preheat the oven to 180°C (350°F).

Place one piece of chicken at one end of each pandan leaf, then roll the pandan leaf around the chicken. Secure the pandan leaf by putting a toothpick through it and the chicken.

Place the parcels on a baking tray and cook in the oven for 10–15 minutes, turning once. Serve the parcels and advise the guests to remove the toothpick and pandan leaf before eating.

Pork gyoza

Gyoza dumplings make an excellent start to a Japanese meal and are really very easy to prepare. Round dumpling wrappers for making gyoza can be easily sourced at Asian food stores, as can chilli jam if you don't want to make your own. Makes 20–25

500 g (1 lb 2 oz) minced (ground) pork

2 spring onions (scallions), sliced

1 tablespoon grated fresh ginger

2 tablespoons Chilli jam (page 437)

1 packet gyoza wrappers

1 tablespoon caster (superfine) sugar

125 ml (4 fl oz/½ cup) red-wine vinegar

1 tablespoon lime juice

60 ml (2 fl oz/¼ cup) soy sauce

Combine the pork with the spring onion, ginger and chilli jam. Place a teaspoon of the mixture in the centre of a gyoza wrapper. Brush the edges of the wrapper with water, then pull them together so that they meet. Crimp to seal. Keep making the gyoza until all of the filling is used.

For the sauce, combine the sugar, vinegar, lime juice, 2 tablespoons water and the soy sauce, stirring to dissolve the sugar.

Poach the dumplings in a pan of simmering water for 5–6 minutes. Toss the cooked gyoza with the sauce and serve immediately.

Wontons with Thai curry sauce

These are very spectacular, but simple to make. You can buy crispy fried shallots from Asian food stores. Makes 40

250 g (9 oz) minced (ground) pork or chicken

2 spring onions (scallions), sliced

2 teaspoons grated fresh ginger

1 tablespoon soy sauce

1 tablespoon chopped coriander (cilantro)

180 g (6½ oz) wonton wrappers

250 ml (8½ fl oz/1 cup) coconut cream

1 tablespoon Red Thai curry paste (page 465)

Fish sauce to taste

Lime juice (optional)

Crispy fried shallots to serve

Mix together the minced pork or chicken, spring onion, ginger, soy sauce and chopped coriander.

Arrange four to five wonton wrappers on a plate and place 1 teaspoon of the meat mixture in the centre of each one. Brush the edges with water and fold over diagonally to form a small triangular parcel. Press the edges together and hold firmly to seal. Repeat until all the meat mixture is used.

Place the coconut cream and Thai curry paste in a small saucepan and bring to the boil. Stir and allow to simmer over low heat for 5 minutes. Season to taste with fish sauce and, if desired, add a squeeze of lime juice. Keep the sauce warm until required.

Bring a large saucepan of water to the boil. Cook the wontons in batches of 8–10 for 5 minutes. Remove and drain well. Place the wontons on serving spoons, drizzle with hot sauce and garnish with crispy fried shallots.

Twice-cooked goat's cheese soufflés

Don't be put off by the scary 'soufflé' tag, as they're not as tricky to make as most people think. It's just a basic cheese sauce, with whipped egg whites folded through. This one is particularly easy as you do the majority of the cooking well beforehand, then reheat them before you serve. This avoids those anxious moments of worrying about whether the soufflés will rise or not. Go get 'em! Serves 6

60 g (2 oz) butter

2 tablespoons plain (all-purpose) flour

350 ml (12 fl oz) milk, warmed

150 g (5½ oz) fresh goat's cheese

1 tablespoon grated parmesan

3 eggs, separated

500 ml (17 fl oz/2 cups) pouring (single/light) cream

Preheat the oven to 180°C (350°F).

Melt 20 g (¾ oz) of the butter and grease six 150 ml (5 fl oz) ramekins. Line a deep baking dish with a tea towel (dish towel) and place the buttered ramekins in the dish.

Melt the remaining butter in a small saucepan over low heat. Add the flour and stir together. Cook for 2 minutes, stirring occasionally. Gradually add the milk, stirring well with each addition to ensure it makes a smooth sauce. Allow the sauce to come to the boil, then reduce the heat and simmer for 2 minutes.

Remove from the heat and crumble in the goat's cheese and parmesan. Allow to cool for a few minutes, then add the egg yolks and season with salt and freshly ground black pepper (if you add the egg yolks while the sauce is really hot, you run the risk of curdling the yolks).

Whip the egg whites until stiff. Stir a spoonful of the beaten egg whites through the sauce first – this helps the remaining whites to fold through easily. Add the remaining egg whites and fold through carefully using a flat spoon or spatula.

Divide the mixture between the buttered ramekins. Pour enough boiling water into the prepared baking dish to come two-thirds of the way up the sides of the ramekins. Bake in the oven for 20 minutes, until well risen and firm to touch.

Set aside for 5 minutes, allowing the soufflés to deflate. Ease them out of their ramekins and place them in a greased ovenproof dish. Cover with plastic wrap and refrigerate – you can leave them for several hours, if not cooking immediately.

When you are ready to serve, preheat the oven to 180°C (350°F).

Pour the cream over the top of the soufflés. Bake in the oven for 15 minutes. Place the soufflés on individual plates, spoon the cooking cream around the soufflés and serve.

Crab cakes with Thai cucumber salad

These crab cakes make a great start to a memorable meal. One large crab weighing about 1.5 kg (3 lb 5 oz) will be perfect for this recipe, otherwise 200 g (7 oz) of smaller crabs is fine. Or even easier, buy fresh crabmeat from your local fishmonger. This recipe is just as delicious with lobster or crayfish meat. Serves 4

200 g (7 oz) fresh crabmeat

1 egg

2 tablespoons chopped coriander (cilantro)

1 tablespoon lime juice

200 g (7 oz/2½ cups) fresh breadcrumbs

4 spring onions (scallions), very finely chopped

Tabasco to taste

2 cucumbers

15 g (½ oz/½ cup) coriander (cilantro) leaves

6 French shallots, thinly sliced

1 small red chilli, seeded and finely diced

½ tablespoon palm sugar (jaggery)

1 tablespoon lime juice

1 tablespoon fish sauce

2 teaspoons rice vinegar

2 tablespoons peanut oil

Ghee or olive oil for cooking

2 limes, cut into wedges, to serve

Place the crabmeat, egg, coriander, lime juice, breadcrumbs and spring onion in a bowl and mix lightly. Add a pinch of salt and a few drops of Tabasco to season and combine. Divide the mixture into eight and pat into burger shapes. Refrigerate until needed.

Peel the cucumbers. Using a vegetable peeler, slice strips of cucumber from one end to the other, discarding the centre seeds. Place the cucumber strips in a colander and leave to drain for 30 minutes. Toss the cucumber with the coriander leaves, shallot and chilli and set aside until ready to serve.

Prepare the dressing by dissolving the palm sugar in the lime juice and fish sauce. Add freshly ground black pepper to season and whisk in the vinegar. Finally, add the peanut oil.

Heat a heavy-based frying pan over medium heat. Add 1–2 tablespoons ghee, add the crab cakes and cook for 5–8 minutes on each side until golden brown on the outside and hot in the middle. It is essential to cook the crab cakes slowly over medium heat to ensure they cook right through to the centre without browning too much. You can pan-fry them until crispy on the outside and put them in a 180°C (350°F) preheated oven for 10 minutes if you prefer.

Meanwhile, toss the cucumber with the dressing and divide between four plates. Place two crab cakes on each plate and serve with the lime wedges.

Coriander-cured salmon

This recipe takes the theory behind gravlax salmon and cures it in a similar manner using coriander in place of dill, making it more Middle Eastern than Scandinavian. Add a splash of soy sauce to make it more Asian. Serves 8–10

1 Atlantic salmon fillet, approximately 1 kg (2 lb 3 oz)

2 tablespoons coriander seeds

1 tablespoon juniper berries

200 g (7 oz/1½ cups) salt flakes

145 g (5 oz/⅔ cup) caster (superfine) sugar

Grated zest of 1 lemon

1 bunch coriander (cilantro) with roots

2 garlic cloves, crushed

1½–2½ tablespoons lemon juice

80–125 ml (2½–4 fl oz/⅓–½ cup) olive oil

Rocket (arugula) leaves to serve

Ask your fishmonger to remove the fine bones that run down the centre of the salmon – you can do it yourself if you have tweezers.

Place the salmon, skin side down, in a deep baking dish.

Crush the coriander seeds and juniper berries coarsely in a mortar and pestle. Mix with the salt flakes, sugar and lemon zest. Chop the roots of the coriander and mix through the salt mixture.

Pack the salt mixture down on the salmon flesh, cover with plastic wrap and weigh it down with something heavy, such as a bag of rice. Refrigerate for 12 hours. Turn the salmon over and refrigerate for a further 6 hours.

Remove the plastic wrap and salt mixture. Rinse the salmon under cold water and pat dry.

You can slice the salmon whenever you are ready. Take a sharp knife and, starting at the tail, on an angle (as you would smoked salmon), cut into paper-thin slices. Don't worry if the first few are a bit uneven – you'll get better. Place the slices on a large tray or platter with plastic wrap between the layers. Refrigerate until needed.

Make the dressing by placing the coriander leaves and stems in a food processor along with the garlic. Process until chopped. Add 2 tablespoons of the lemon juice, blend and then drizzle in the oil to form a smooth sauce. Check the seasoning, adding salt and freshly ground black pepper as needed. Add more lemon juice if needed and refrigerate.

Toss the rocket leaves with around 1–2 tablespoons of the dressing.

Arrange four to five slices of salmon in the centre of each plate. Arrange a handful of dressed rocket leaves in the centre and drizzle a spoonful of dressing over the salmon. Grind a little more black pepper over the top if desired and serve.

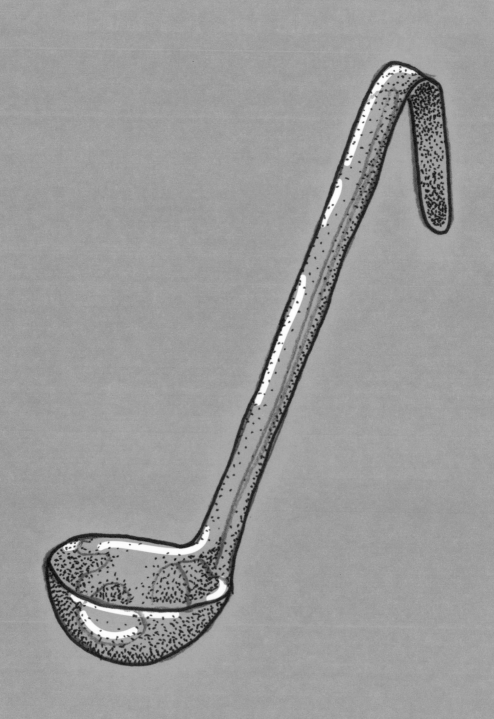

Soup

As a general rule of cooking, the higher the quality of the raw ingredients, the better the dish will be. This is particularly the case with soup. It's well worth the effort to ensure you have good-quality stock, fresh vegetables, and quality meats and noodles.

A nourishing meal or starter

Whether it's a simple pot of creamy pumpkin or a more robust hearty dish, I'm a big soup fan, especially for lunch in cooler weather and to provide an energy boost to keep me going. Everyone should learn how to make a few soups – they're very easy to prepare and it only takes 10 minutes or so to get a pot of soup onto the stove. Then it just simmers away gently and virtually cooks itself. Growing up in England, I remember there was an advertisement on TV for a cereal that put a warm glow around you – it almost looked like you were radioactive. That's how I feel when I have a bowl of soup – nourished, comforted and protected against Melbourne weather.

Good stock is essential for most soups (see Stocks, page 450). The best stock is home-made, but of course we don't all have the time to make our own stock and there are plenty of good alternatives available. Quality food stores and butchers sell home-made or high-quality stock, but you can get cartons of stock at the supermarket and, if you're really stuck, a stock cube can do the job. I have to confess that I am a big user of packaged liquid stock, but mostly the low-salt ones.

Soup with fresh crusty bread, and maybe a nice chunk of farmhouse cheddar, is a perfect meal, and very healthy. Slow-cooker owners can get it going in the morning and come home to a substantial dinner. I like to make a big pot of soup and enjoy it over the course of the week; it's great for mid-week lunches as well as dinner. I often freeze half for a rainy day and those manic weeks when time is short.

Things you should know
about soup

- Virtually all soups freeze well, so you can usually make enough for more than one meal.

- Soup will keep well for 2–3 days in the refrigerator and up to 3 months in the freezer.

- I prefer to thicken my soups with potato where possible, rather than using flour and butter in a roux. Simply add a peeled and diced potato to a soup that will be puréed to ensure a good consistency, or add a grated potato to broth soups that are to be served as they are.

- Take care when puréeing soups: hot soup will cause nasty burns if it splashes onto your skin.

- Deep bowls are perfect for serving soup, keeping the liquid hot to the very last spoonful.

- Don't forget to try barley, rice, pasta, noodles, lentils, borlotti (cranberry) beans, split peas, chickpeas and haricot beans in your soup.

- I cook dried beans in a separate saucepan until they are tender, then add them to the soup in the later stages. This ensures that they are completely tender and it also stops the soup going cloudy.

- It's best to add cream to soup after it has been taken off the heat. Boiling liquid can curdle the cream.

- Soup recipes sometimes call for a bouquet garni. This is a bundle of fresh herbs that includes bay leaves, thyme, flat-leaf (Italian) parsley and celery leaves, tied with string or wrapped in muslin (cheesecloth). You add the bouquet garni while the stock is simmering and remove it during straining. I always have the basics of a bouquet garni growing in the backyard.

- Use chicken stock (page 450) or vegetable stock (page 452) at your discretion in vegetable soups. I prefer chicken for its fuller flavour, but vegetable stock is just as good.

Soup recipes

Classic tomato soup

You can't go too far wrong with this old favourite. A good tip is to add a pinch of sugar after puréeing the tomatoes, as it increases the soup's sweetness. Serves 4

Oil for cooking

1 onion, peeled and quartered

2 garlic cloves, peeled

8 ripe tomatoes, chopped

250–500 ml (8½–17 fl oz/1–2 cups) vegetable or chicken stock

125 ml (4 fl oz/½ cup) pouring (single/light) cream

30 g (1 oz/½ cup) chopped basil leaves

Heat a large heavy-based saucepan over medium heat. Add a splash of oil and the onion and cook for 5–6 minutes, stirring well. Add the garlic and tomatoes, then reduce the heat to low and cook for 10 minutes, stirring often.

Add enough stock to cover the tomatoes. Raise the heat and bring to the boil. Reduce to a simmer, cover the saucepan and cook for 20 minutes, or until the tomatoes are tender. Purée the soup and strain into a clean saucepan.

Return the soup to the boil and add more stock if it is too thick. Remove from the heat, whisk in the cream and season to taste with salt and freshly ground black pepper. Stir in the chopped basil and serve immediately.

Tomato and fennel soup
Add one chopped fennel bulb along with the tomatoes.

Moroccan carrot and coriander soup

Fresh carrots are wonderfully highlighted by coriander, which adds a lovely zing. Serves 4

Oil for cooking

1 onion, diced

2 celery stalks, diced

1 leek, white part only, sliced

4 carrots, peeled and diced

1 garlic clove, crushed

½ bunch coriander (cilantro)

60 ml (2 fl oz/¼ cup) orange juice

1 litre (34 fl oz/4 cups) chicken or vegetable stock

Pouring (single/light) cream to taste (optional)

Heat a heavy-based saucepan over medium–high heat. Add a generous splash of oil, then add the onion, celery and leek. Cook for 5–6 minutes, stirring often. Add the carrot and garlic and cook for a further 3–4 minutes.

Wash the coriander well and chop the roots and stems, reserving the leaves for garnish.

Add the chopped coriander to the saucepan and cook for 2–3 minutes. Add the orange juice, enough stock to just cover the vegetables, and salt and freshly ground black pepper to taste. Bring to the boil. Reduce the heat and simmer for 15 minutes, or until the carrots are tender.

Remove from the heat. Purée the soup using a food processor or blender, then pass through a sieve into a clean saucepan.

To serve, bring the soup back to the boil, check the seasoning, and add cream, if desired. Garnish with the coriander leaves.

Carrot, coriander and lentil soup
Add 200 g (7 oz/1 cup) cooked red lentils after the soup has been puréed.

Creamy potato and leek soup

Potato and leek soup is nutritious, tasty and easy to make. Every young person should learn how to make this soup before leaving home. You can see from all the variations below how easy it is to change this soup to suit your tastes, or whatever vegetables you have in the refrigerator at the time. Serves 4

Oil for cooking

1 onion, diced

2 celery stalks, diced

2 leeks, white part only, sliced

4 potatoes, peeled and diced

1 garlic clove, crushed

1 litre (34 fl oz/4 cups) chicken or vegetable stock

Pouring (single/light) cream to taste (optional)

Fresh chopped herbs to garnish

Heat a heavy-based saucepan over medium–high heat. Add a generous splash of oil, the onion, celery and leek. Cook for 5–6 minutes, stirring often. Add the potatoes and garlic and cook for a further 3–4 minutes. Add enough stock to just cover and a little salt and freshly ground black pepper, then bring to the boil. Reduce the heat and simmer for 15 minutes, or until the potatoes are tender.

Remove from the heat. Purée the soup using a food processor or blender and pass through a sieve into a clean saucepan.

To serve, bring the soup back to the boil, check the seasoning, and add cream, if desired. Garnish with the chopped herbs.

Potato and watercress soup
Use only one leek and cook as directed. Adding a few handfuls of freshly picked watercress to the soup when it is about to be puréed will give it a fresh green colour and a gutsy watercress flavour.

Asparagus soup
Use only one leek and one potato and then add 300 g (10½ oz) asparagus tips to the soup just before you purée it.

Creamy corn soup
Use only one leek and two potatoe. Add the kernels from four corn cobs along with the potatoes and cook as directed.

Curried parsnip soup
Use only one leek and one potato and add 1 tablespoon curry paste along with the potatoes and garlic. Add 750 g (1 lb 11 oz) peeled parsnip pieces and cook as directed.

Mushroom soup
Add 300 g (10½ oz) mushrooms along with the potatoes and garlic.

Mushroom and freekeh soup
Add 300 g (10½ oz) mushrooms with the potatoes and garlic. Cook 85 g (3 oz/½ cup) cracked freekeh in boiling water for 12-15 minutes, or until tender. Drain and rinse well and add to the puréed soup.

Asian-inspired pumpkin soup

This soup came about when I got totally fed up with regular pumpkin soup. All I've done is add some Thai curry paste for flavour and coconut milk for creaminess, and now it's anything but boring. I was delighted when this recipe was included in Stephanie Alexander's updated version of *The Cook's Companion*. Serves 6–8

Oil for cooking

2 tablespoons Red Thai curry paste (page 465)

1 onion, diced

1 celery stalk, diced

1 tomato, chopped (optional)

1 kg (2 lb 3 oz) pumpkin (squash), peeled and diced

1 litre (34 fl oz/4 cups) vegetable or chicken stock

400 ml (13½ fl oz) coconut milk

Coriander (cilantro) leaves to serve

Heat a large heavy-based saucepan over medium heat. Add a splash of oil and the Thai curry paste and cook for 5 minutes, stirring often, until fragrant. Add the onion, celery, tomato (if using) and pumpkin, and season with salt and freshly ground black pepper. Reduce the heat and cook for 15 minutes, stirring often.

Add the stock to the saucepan, increase the heat and bring to the boil. Reduce to a simmer, cover the saucepan and cook for 20 minutes, or until the pumpkin is tender.

Purée the soup and strain it into a clean saucepan. Return the soup to the boil, whisk in the coconut milk and adjust the seasoning. Garnish with the coriander leaves and serve.

Asian-inspired sweet potato soup
Substitute two peeled and diced sweet potatoes for the pumpkin.

Sweet potato and ginger soup
Substitute two peeled and diced sweet potatoes for the pumpkin. Omit the Thai curry paste and add a 3 cm (1¼ in) piece of peeled and sliced fresh ginger along with the onion and other ingredients.

Roast tomato and capsicum soup

Despite the roasting and puréeing involved, this soup is very quick to make. The flavour is so good it can also be served chilled on a hot summer night. Serves 4–6

4 red capsicums (bell peppers)

Oil for cooking

6 tomatoes, halved

1 onion, peeled and quartered

2 garlic cloves, peeled

1 red chilli

250–500 ml (8½–17 fl oz/1–2 cups) vegetable or chicken stock

Preheat the oven to 180°C (350°F).

Rub the capsicums with oil. Place them on a baking tray and roast them for 30 minutes, or until their skins blister.

Put the tomatoes, onion, garlic and chilli on another baking tray, toss with oil, salt and freshly ground black pepper and roast at the same temperature for 30 minutes, or until soft.

Remove and discard the seeds and skins from the tomatoes and capsicums. Purée the tomato, capsicum, onion, garlic and chilli with the cooking juices. Pass through a sieve.

Place the purée in a saucepan and add enough stock to bring the soup to a good consistency. Bring to the boil. Check the seasoning and serve.

Roast tomato and coriander pesto soup
Serve with a spoonful of Coriander pesto (page 477) and garnish with the coriander (cilantro) leaves.

French onion soup

Serve huge bowls of this intensely flavoured soup with a loaf of good bread, a wedge of full-flavoured cheese (such as English farmhouse cheddar) and a green salad. It will prove once and for all the theory of how satisfying the holy trinity of soup, bread and cheese can be. Serves 4–6

40 g (1½ oz) butter

1 tablespoon olive oil

6 onions, diced

2 garlic cloves, crushed

2 tablespoons plain (all-purpose) flour

1.5 litres (51 fl oz/6 cups) beef stock

12–18 slices baguette

125 g (4½ oz/1 cup) grated cheddar

Heat a heavy-based saucepan over medium heat. Add the butter and oil, allow them to melt, then add the onion and garlic. Cook and stir occasionally for 30 minutes, by which time the onion should develop a pale golden colour. Sprinkle in the flour and cook for 3–4 minutes, stirring often.

Add the stock and bring to the boil, whisking occasionally to ensure that the flour is incorporated. Reduce to a simmer, cover the pan and cook for 45 minutes. By this stage it should have achieved a good gutsy flavour. Season to taste with salt and freshly ground black pepper.

Top the bread slices with the grated cheese and cook under a hot grill (broiler) until the cheese melts.

Pour the soup into bowls and place the cheese croutons on top.

Creamy onion soup
Add one diced potato to the cooked onions, use chicken instead of beef stock and purée the soup when cooked. Stir in a few tablespoons of pouring (single/light) cream just before serving. Sprinkle with chopped flat-leaf (Italian) parsley and freshly grated black pepper.

Beetroot soup

This soup is rich, warming and restorative, and is a great use of beetroot – a vegetable that I happen to adore. The soup is easy to prepare as it's a simple matter of cooking diced beetroot in an aromatic broth until tender. Serves 4

2 tablespoons olive oil

1 onion, diced

1 celery stalk, diced

1 garlic clove, crushed

3 large beetroot (beets), peeled and cut into 1 cm (½ in) dice

80 ml (2½ fl oz/⅓ cup) orange juice

750 ml (25½ fl oz/3 cups) chicken or beef stock

1 tablespoon balsamic vinegar

Natural yoghurt or sour cream to serve

Heat a heavy-based saucepan over medium heat. Add the oil, onion and celery and cook for 4–5 minutes, stirring often. Add the garlic and beetroot and cook for a further 5 minutes, stirring often. Add the orange juice, stock and vinegar and bring to the boil.

Lower the heat and cook for 15–20 minutes, or until the beetroot is tender.

Add lots of freshly ground black pepper, check the salt and serve each bowl with a spoonful of yoghurt or sour cream on top.

Classic chicken noodle soup

Here is the ultimate chicken noodle soup; the dish that's said to be able to cure anything.

Serves 6

1 whole chicken

A few whole black peppercorns

2 bay leaves

2 onions

2 carrots

1 leek

2 celery stalks

Olive oil

100 g (3½ oz) thin spaghetti, broken into 5 cm (2 in) pieces, or egg noodles

2 tablespoons chopped flat-leaf (Italian) parsley to serve

Place the chicken in a large saucepan and cover with water. Add the peppercorns and bay leaves.

Roughly chop 1 onion and 1 carrot and add to the pan along with the green tops of the leek and celery and bring to the boil.

Remove any scum from the surface, reduce to a simmer and cook for 1–2 hours. Remove the chicken and set aside to cool.

Strain the liquid and press down hard on the ingredients to extract all the flavour. When the cooking liquid has cooled slightly, refrigerate to allow the fat to set on the surface. Skim the fat off the surface and the stock is ready to use.

Remove the skin and bone from the chicken and thinly slice the chicken meat. Finely dice the remaining onion and carrot along with the white parts of the leek and celery stalks.

In a clean saucepan, add the oil and cook the finely diced vegetables gently, without colouring, for 4–5 minutes, stirring often. Add the reserved stock and bring to the boil. Add the spaghetti or noodles and simmer for 10 minutes, until the pasta is cooked. Add the chicken and return to the boil. Remove from the heat, season with salt and freshly ground black pepper, garnish with parsley and serve.

Chinese chicken noodle soup
Instead of spaghetti, use thin Chinese noodles, either fresh or dried, and season with soy sauce. Serve with sliced spring onions (scallions) instead of parsley.

Asian noodle soup
Flavour the broth with grated fresh ginger, sliced chilli, thinly sliced lemongrass and a few drops of fish sauce. Replace the spaghetti with rice noodles and serve topped with coriander (cilantro) leaves, a handful of bean sprouts and some crispy fried shallots (available in Asian food stores).

Chicken and corn soup
Add the kernels from two corn cobs (or a small tin of kernels, rinsed) to the broth after cooking the chicken. Instead of spaghetti, use thin Chinese noodles, either fresh or dried, and season with a little soy sauce. Just before serving, lightly whisk an egg and stir it into the soup. Serve with sliced spring onions (scallions) instead of parsley.

Carrot, red lentil and coriander soup

This is a great winter warmer. I like to dice the carrots small so there's no need to purée the soup – anything to keep things simpler. The roast pumpkin variation is a slight twist – roasting the pumpkin adds an extra dimension and, if you're feeling lazy, you can just mash it roughly, add it to the cooked soup and not worry about puréeing. Serves 4

Oil for cooking

1 onion, finely diced

1 leek, white part only, thinly sliced

2 celery stalks, finely diced

4 carrots, finely diced

2 garlic cloves, crushed

Pinch of saffron stems

1 teaspoon ground coriander

1 teaspoon ground cumin

2 teaspoons Harissa (page 467)

1 litre (34 fl oz/4 cups) vegetable stock

185 g (6½ oz/¾ cup) red lentils

2 tablespoons chopped coriander (cilantro)

Heat a medium saucepan over medium heat and add the oil. Add the onion, leek, celery and carrot and cook, stirring often, for 5 minutes or until the vegetables are beginning to soften. Add the garlic, saffron, spices and harissa and cook for 2–3 minutes until fragrant. Add the stock and bring to the boil. Reduce the heat and cook for 15–20 minutes.

Rinse the lentils under cold running water and cook in a small saucepan with plenty of water until tender. Drain and rinse well and then add to the soup. Season with salt and freshly ground black pepper, add the coriander and serve.

Roast pumpkin and Moroccan lentil soup
Substitute 500 g (1 lb 2 oz) peeled pumpkin (squash) pieces for the carrot. Toss the pumpkin with oil, salt and freshly ground black pepper and roast in a preheated 180°C (350°F) oven for 15-20 minutes or until tender. Add the pumpkin to the soup and purée it roughly – I like to keep the soup chunky. Add the cooked lentils after this and then check the seasoning,

Tomato, pancetta and chickpea soup

This is the first recipe in the book to use pancetta – but there are quite a few others! If you can't get hold of it easily, bacon can be substituted. Serve with crusty bread. Serves 4

Oil for cooking

1 onion, diced

1 carrot, finely diced

1 leek, white part only, thinly sliced

2 × 5 mm (¼ in) thick slices of pancetta, diced

2 garlic cloves, crushed

1 teaspoon smoky paprika

400 g (14 oz) tinned chopped tomatoes

750 ml (25½ fl oz/3 cups) chicken stock

400 g (14 oz) tinned chickpeas, drained and rinsed

2 tablespoons chopped flat-leaf (Italian) parsley or basil

Basil pesto (page 476) to serve (optional)

Heat a large heavy-based saucepan over medium–high heat. Add a splash of oil and the onion, carrot and leek and cook for 3–4 minutes, stirring often, until softened. Add the pancetta and cook for 4–5 minutes until golden brown. Add the garlic and paprika and cook for 1–2 minutes until fragrant. Add the chopped tomatoes and stock and bring to the boil.

Season with salt and freshly ground black pepper, reduce to a simmer and cook for 15–20 minutes. Add the chickpeas, check the seasoning and finish with the chopped herbs. Dollop with pesto (if using) and serve.

Minestrone

The ingredients list might look somewhat daunting, but don't be alarmed. You can swap any of the vegetables listed here with whatever you have on hand. Corn kernels, peas, green beans, English spinach leaves, chopped cabbage and cooked chickpeas are some of my other favourite ingredients to add. Be warned: minestrone seems to grow and grow. Serves 4

Oil for cooking
1 onion, diced
1 celery stalk, diced
1 leek, white part only, thinly sliced
1 carrot, diced
½ red capsicum (bell pepper), diced
1 potato, diced
2 garlic cloves, crushed
250 ml (8½ fl oz/1 cup) tomato passata (puréed tomatoes)
750 ml (25½ fl oz/3 cups) chicken or vegetable stock
75 g (2¾ oz (⅓ cup) risoni
20 g (¾ oz/⅓ cup) chopped flat-leaf (Italian) parsley and basil or a dollop of Basil pesto (page 476)

Heat a large heavy-based saucepan over medium–high heat. Add a generous splash of oil and add the onion, celery, leek, carrot, capsicum and potato. Cook for 8–10 minutes, stirring often. Add the garlic and cook for 1–2 minutes more. Add the tomato passata, stock, salt and freshly ground black pepper and bring to the boil. Add the risoni and reduce the heat to a simmer. Cook for 10 minutes, check the seasoning, add the herbs and serve.

Chickpea harira

A filling and hearty soup – all it needs is a loaf of crusty bread. I love chickpeas, whether in soups, curries, casseroles, made into hummus or spice-coated and roasted. I just love 'em. Serves 4

Oil for cooking
1 onion, diced
2 celery stalks, diced
1 carrot, diced
Pinch of saffron (optional)
1 teaspoon ground cumin
1 teaspoon ground coriander
1 teaspoon smoky paprika
1 teaspoon Harissa (page 467)
750 ml (25½ fl oz/3 cups) vegetable or chicken stock
125 ml (4 fl oz/½ cup) tomato passata (puréed tomatoes)
400 g (14 oz) tinned chickpeas, drained and rinsed
420 g (15 oz) tinned red lentils, drained and rinsed
7 g (¼ oz/¼ cup) chopped coriander (cilantro)

Heat a large heavy-based saucepan over medium–high heat. Add a splash of oil and the onion, celery and carrot and cook for 5–6 minutes, stirring often, until softened. Add the saffron (if using), the spices and harissa and cook for 2–3 minutes until fragrant. Add the stock and tomato passata and bring to the boil.

Season with salt and freshly ground black pepper, reduce to a simmer and cook for 15–20 minutes, stirring often. Add the chickpeas, lentils and coriander and heat through. Check the seasoning and serve.

Harira with chorizo
Add one diced chorizo sausage with the onions.

Pasta e fagioli

This classic Italian dish is part soup, part stew. Some people reckon it's a hangover cure and, without a doubt, it's a lifesaver that cures most ailments – hunger being the main one. Serves half the neighbourhood, and then some

500 g (1 lb 2 oz) borlotti (cranberry) beans, soaked in cold water overnight

6 potatoes, peeled and diced

2 carrots, chopped

2 onions, diced

2 celery stalks, diced

2 garlic cloves, crushed

1 small red chilli, seeded and diced

2 tablespoons tomato paste (concentrated purée)

200 g (7 oz) pasta, such as spaghetti or fettuccine

Grated parmesan to serve

Olive oil to serve

2 tablespoons chopped flat-leaf (Italian) parsley to garnish

Place the drained borlotti beans, potatoes, carrots, onion, celery, garlic, chilli, tomato paste and 1 teaspoon salt in a large saucepan. Add enough cold water to cover everything completely. Bring to the boil, reduce the heat and simmer gently for 1–2 hours. Take care to stir often and well to prevent the beans and vegetables sticking to the bottom of the saucepan. Cook until the vegetables and beans are well cooked.

Cool slightly, then purée half the soup. Return the puréed soup to the saucepan. Bring back to the boil, adding more water if necessary. Add the pasta and cook for 10 minutes. Season with salt and freshly ground black pepper.

To serve, ladle the soup into bowls, add a generous sprinkling of grated parmesan, a swirl of olive oil and some chopped parsley.

Pea and ham soup

A classic soup and a perfect winter warmer. This recipe makes lots so there's enough for lunch the next day. Serves 4–6

1 ham hock

Oil for cooking

2 onions, diced

2 carrots, diced

1 leek, white part only, sliced

2 celery stalks, diced

2 garlic cloves, crushed

220 g (8 oz/1 cup) split peas

Chopped flat-leaf (Italian) parsley to serve

Place the ham hock in a large saucepan. Cover with at least 1 litre (34 fl oz/4 cups) water, and bring to the boil. Reduce the heat and cook for 1 hour, or until the ham is cooked and beginning to fall off the bone. (I often do this the day before, allowing the stock to be refrigerated and the fat to set overnight.) Set the ham hock aside to cool and reserve the strained cooking stock.

Heat a large saucepan over medium heat. Add a splash of oil and the onion, carrot, leek and celery. Cook for 5–6 minutes, stirring often, until the vegetables soften. Add the garlic and cook for a further 1–2 minutes. Pour in the strained cooking stock and bring to the boil. Add the split peas and cook for 30–45 minutes, or until the peas are tender.

Remove the skin from the cooled ham hock and dice the meat, discarding any sinew and gristle. Add the ham meat to the soup. Check the seasoning – you may not need to add salt as ham hocks are sometimes very salty, but add some freshly ground black pepper. Garnish with a good pinch of chopped parsley and serve.

Lamb shank, vegetable and barley broth

A great Aussie classic that's so substantial it can easily be served as dinner on a chilly winter's night. Serves 6

2 lamb shanks

220 g (8 oz/1 cup) pearl barley

2 onions, diced

1 leek, white part only, thinly sliced

2 celery stalks, diced

2 carrots, cut into 1 cm (½ in) dice

1 swede (rutabaga), cut into 1 cm (½ in) dice

2 small turnips, cut into 1 cm (½ in) dice

¼ green or savoy cabbage, sliced

2 tablespoons chopped flat-leaf (Italian) parsley
  to serve

Place the lamb shanks in a large saucepan. Cover with 2–3 litres (68–101 fl oz/8–12 cups) water and bring to the boil. Remove any scum that comes to the surface and discard. Reduce the heat and simmer for 1 hour, or until the lamb is tender.

Remove the lamb shanks and strain the broth. If you refrigerate the broth when it has cooled, the fat will rise to the top and set, allowing it to be easily removed.

Place the barley in a small saucepan. Cover with water and bring to the boil. Reduce to a simmer and cook for 20–30 minutes, or until the barley is tender. Drain and set aside.

Pour the broth into a clean saucepan and bring to the boil. Add the onion, leek, celery, carrot, swede and turnip and cook over low heat for 30 minutes, or until the vegetables are tender. Add the cabbage, season with salt and freshly ground black pepper and cook for a further 10 minutes.

Cut the meat off the lamb shank bones, discarding any skin, sinew and the bones. Add the meat to the broth along with the pearl barley. Cook for a further 10 minutes and check the seasoning again. Garnish with the chopped parsley and serve.

Tofu, broccolini and noodle miso soup

I'm addicted to tofu and this is a great light dinner. Many people don't like tofu because they have been served the hard rubbery stuff. Most tofu now is softer and very easy to cook with. Take care with silken tofu – delicious as it is, it breaks up if handled too roughly. Serves 4

1 litre (34 fl oz/4 cups) vegetable stock

2 tablespoons miso paste

2 tablespoons tamari

1 bunch of broccolini

200 g (7 oz) udon noodles

300 g (10½ oz) tofu, cut into 1 cm (½ in) dice

2 spring onions (scallions), sliced

15 g (½ oz/½ cup) coriander (cilantro) leaves

Bring the stock to the boil. Mix the miso paste and tamari together and add to the boiling stock. Add the broccolini and noodles and cook for 1–2 minutes. Add the tofu and spring onion and allow to heat through. Add the coriander leaves and serve.

Chicken, bok choy and udon miso
Cut one boneless skinless chicken breast thinly and add it to the simmering miso. Cook for 5 minutes. Add the washed leaves of one bunch of baby bok choy (pak choy) instead of broccolini and cook for 1-2 minutes.

Udon soup with shiitake mushrooms and roast duck
To the boiling miso, add 150 g (5½ oz) sliced shiitake mushrooms and 60 g (2 oz) sliced broccoli in place of the tofu. Cook for 2 minutes. Add half a Chinese roast duck (flesh removed from the bone and sliced) and two thinly sliced spring onions (scallions). Return to the boil, then remove from the heat. Add the coriander leaves and check the seasoning.

Beijing dumpling soup

I love this style of soup, where the simplicity of the broth is combined with the silky softness of delicate wontons. Serves 6

250 g (9 oz) minced (ground) pork or chicken

4 spring onions (scallions), sliced, plus 2 extra sliced spring onions for garnish

3 teaspoons grated fresh ginger

2 tablespoons soy sauce, plus extra to taste

2 tablespoons chopped coriander (cilantro) leaves, plus whole coriander leaves to garnish

1 packet wonton wrappers

1.25 litres (42 fl oz/5 cups) chicken stock

Mix together the minced meat, spring onion, ginger, soy sauce and chopped coriander.

Lay four to five wonton wrappers out flat in front of you. Place a teaspoon of the prepared mixture in the centre of each. Brush the edges with water and fold over, diagonally, to form a small triangular parcel. Press the edges together and hold firmly to seal. Repeat until all the meat mixture is used.

Bring the chicken stock to the boil, then reduce to a simmer. Carefully add the wontons to the simmering stock and cook for 3–4 minutes. Season to taste with soy sauce.

To serve, spoon four to five wontons into each bowl, ladle the hot broth over and garnish with the sliced spring onion and coriander leaves.

Prawn and coconut tom yum

Tom yum is a classic Asian soup and one of the most popular dishes on Thai restaurant menus. For many people, it is their first introduction to ingredients such as kaffir lime leaves, lemongrass, coriander, chillies, palm sugar and fish sauce. Here, prawns and coconut milk are added to the base ingredients to make a creamy version of this soup. Serves 4

500 g (1 lb 2 oz) green (raw) peeled prawns (shrimp)

2 tablespoons tom yum paste

750 ml (25½ fl oz/3 cups) chicken stock

2 kaffir lime leaves, shredded

3 spring onions (scallions), chopped

1 lemongrass stem, thinly sliced

4 Asian shallots, sliced

½ bunch coriander (cilantro) stems and roots, chopped, plus whole coriander leaves to garnish

1 tablespoon grated palm sugar (jaggery)

2 tablespoons fish sauce

2 tablespoons lime juice

125 ml (4 fl oz/½ cup) coconut milk

Sliced red chillies (optional)

Brush the prawns with the tom yum paste and marinate for 30 minutes.

Place the stock and 750 ml (25½ fl oz/3 cups) water in a large saucepan. Add the kaffir lime leaves, spring onion, lemongrass, shallot, coriander, palm sugar and fish sauce. Bring to the boil, then reduce to a simmer and cook for 20 minutes.

Strain into a clean saucepan. Add the prawns, lime juice and coconut milk and simmer for 5–6 minutes. Check the seasoning, adding salt and freshly ground black pepper to taste and more fish sauce if necessary. Serve with the coriander leaves and chillies (if using).

Duck and macadamia wonton soup

Chinese roast duck is widely available from all Asian roast-house restaurants. They will often supply a little tub of cooking juices if requested. If they do, this makes a great addition to the cooking stock. Serves 4

¼ Chinese roast duck

60 ml (2 fl oz/¼ cup) light soy sauce

5 cm (2 in) piece fresh ginger, sliced

1 small red chilli, split

6 Asian shallots, sliced

2 tablespoons chopped coriander (cilantro)

60 g (2 oz) macadamia nuts, chopped

1 packet wonton wrappers

4 spring onions (scallions), chopped, to serve

Remove the meat from the duck. Thinly slice the meat and set aside.

Place the duck bones, cooking juices (if available), 750 ml (25½ fl oz/3 cups) water, the soy sauce, ginger and chilli in a saucepan and bring to the boil. Reduce to a simmer and cook for 25 minutes, removing any scum as it comes to the surface. Strain into a clean saucepan. You should have 1 litre (34 fl oz/4 cups). Add more water if necessary.

Combine the duck meat with the shallots, coriander and macadamia nuts. Season to taste with salt and freshly ground black pepper.

Lay six to eight wonton wrappers out flat in front of you. Brush two edges of each wonton with water. Place 1 teaspoon of the duck mixture in the centre of each wrapper. Fold each wonton in half, press the edges together and hold firmly to seal. Repeat until all the mixture is used.

To serve, bring the reserved stock to the boil. Add the wontons and poach for 3–4 minutes. Divide the wontons between the bowls, ladle the broth over and garnish with the spring onion.

Traditional laksa

I was tossing up which chapter this dish should be in – is it a noodle dish, a curry or a soup? As you can see, the soup chapter won. But boy, oh boy, what a soup! Serves 4

200 g (7 oz) dried vermicelli noodles

Oil for cooking

2 tablespoons laksa paste

500 ml (17 fl oz/2 cups) chicken stock

400 ml (13½ fl oz) coconut milk

2 tablespoons fish sauce

2 tomatoes, diced (optional)

½ red capsicum (bell pepper), thinly sliced

12 green (raw) prawns (shrimp), heads and shells removed

Handful of bean sprouts

100 g (3½ oz) fried tofu, sliced

Handful of mixed herbs, including Vietnamese mint, coriander (cilantro) and Thai basil

Crispy fried shallots to serve

2 limes, cut into wedges, to serve

Place the vermicelli noodles in a large bowl and cover with boiling water. Soak for 8–10 minutes, or until the noodles soften. Drain and set aside.

Heat a large saucepan or wok over medium heat and add a splash of oil. Add the laksa paste and stir for 2–3 minutes, or until aromatic. Add the chicken stock, 250 ml (8½ fl oz/1 cup) water and the coconut milk and bring to the boil. Add the fish sauce, tomato (if using), capsicum and prawns. Simmer until the prawns are cooked, about 3–4 minutes.

To serve, divide the noodles between four bowls. Add the bean sprouts and slices of tofu. Ladle the broth into the bowls and top with a large handful of fresh herbs and some crispy shallots. Serve with lime wedges.

Chicken laksa
Substitute one sliced boneless skinless chicken breast for the prawns.

Moroccan-style fish soup

This soup is simple but a great way to enjoy seafood. You can use chicken, fish or vegetable stock. I prefer chicken myself, as I find fish stock makes it too fishy. Serves 4

Oil for cooking
1 onion, sliced
1 small fennel bulb, sliced
2 garlic cloves, crushed
2 teaspoons Ras el hanout (page 468)
Pinch of saffron threads
500 ml (17 fl oz/2 cups) chicken, fish or vegetable
  stock
250 ml (8½ fl oz/1 cup) tomato passata (puréed
  tomatoes)
500 g (1 lb 2 oz) diced firm white fish
8 peeled green (raw) prawns (shrimp)
500 g (1 lb 2 oz) baby clams (vongole) or mussels
15 g (½ oz/½ cup) coriander (cilantro) leaves
Crusty bread to serve

Heat a large, heavy-based saucepan over medium–high heat. Add a splash of oil, the onion and fennel and cook for 3–4 minutes until soft. Add the garlic, ras el hanout and saffron and cook for 1–2 minutes until fragrant. Add the stock and tomato passata and bring to the boil. Season with salt and freshly ground black pepper, reduce the heat to a simmer and cook for 10 minutes.

Add the fish and seafood, cover and simmer until the seafood is cooked, 3–4 minutes.

Check the seasoning, add the coriander leaves and serve with crusty bread.

Ribollita

A classic Italian soup and just the thing to give you a warm lining for a cold winter's day. Cavolo nero is an Italian cabbage with long black leaves. Its popularity has increased in recent years and I have seen it for sale in greengrocers and even the supermarket. Kale also makes a good substitute, or even English spinach or silverbeet (Swiss chard). Serves 4–6

Oil for cooking
1 onion, diced
2 celery stalks, diced
2 carrots, diced
3 garlic cloves, crushed
Pinch of dried chilli flakes
400 g (14 oz) tinned tomatoes
500 ml (17 fl oz/2 cups) chicken or vegetable stock
1–2 bay leaves
400 g (14 oz) tinned cannellini (lima) beans, drained
  and rinsed
1 bunch cavolo nero (approximately 250 g/9 oz),
  leaves and stalks finely sliced
2 large handfuls of stale sourdough bread, torn into
  chunks
60 ml (2 fl oz/¼ cup) extra-virgin olive oil to serve

Heat a heavy-based saucepan over medium–high heat and add a splash of oil, the onion, celery and carrot. Cook for 4–5 minutes until softened, stirring occasionally. Add the garlic and chilli and cook for 1–2 minutes, stirring, until fragrant, taking care not to burn them. Add the tomatoes, stock and bay leaves and bring to the boil.

Season with salt and freshly ground black pepper and allow to simmer for 5 minutes. Add the beans and cavolo nero and allow it to cook down.

Moisten the bread with water and add it to the soup. Allow to cook for 30 minutes, stirring often, adding more stock if necessary – the soup should become soft and silky.

To serve, check the seasoning, then add the olive oil to give a glossy texture.

Sweetcorn chowder

I have been making and enjoying this creamy, chunky sweetcorn soup forever. Make it once and it's sure to become a favourite of yours, too. Remember to keep all the vegetables finely diced, as this soup is not puréed. I have tweaked this recipe slightly from my original version – the flour has gone, making the recipe gluten-free, and I've added kale, which is not a traditional chowder ingredient, but the soup cries out for some greenery. Serves 4

2–3 tablespoons olive oil

1 onion, finely diced

2 garlic cloves, crushed

1 leek, white part only, finely diced

2 celery stalks, finely diced

1 zucchini (courgette), finely diced

2 carrots, finely diced

2 potatoes, finely diced

1 litre (34 fl oz/4 cups) vegetable or chicken stock

2 corn cobs, kernels removed with a sharp knife

100 g (3½ oz) kale, thinly shredded

250 g (9 oz/1 cup) creamed cottage cheese

2 tablespoons sour cream

1 tablespoon chopped flat-leaf (Italian) parsley

1 tablespoon chopped basil

Heat a heavy-based saucepan over medium heat. Add the oil, onion, garlic, leek, celery, zucchini and carrot. Cook for 4–5 minutes, stirring often. Add the diced potato and cook for a further 3–4 minutes.

Pour in the stock and return to the boil, whisking occasionally. When boiling, add the corn kernels and kale and then simmer for 10 minutes.

Remove from the heat and whisk in the cottage cheese and sour cream. Add the chopped parsley and basil, then check the seasoning before serving.

Bowl food

Bowl food is the ultimate easy dinner –
quick and easy to make, comforting and
there's not too much washing up! Whether
it's a bowl of pasta, rice or stir-fried noodles,
or a one-pot wonder, bowl food is always
an excellent dinner choice.

One-bowl wonders

The Italians were onto a good thing when they invented pasta. It's the ultimate quick dinner. By the time a pot of water has boiled, you can easily have made a quick sauce. My kitchen is relatively close to the garden and I'm always popping outside for a handful of parsley or thyme to finish off a sauce. Furthermore, I have proof that you can make pasta for dinner in less time than it takes to fetch takeaway.

It's said that more people throughout the world sit down to a meal that uses rice than to any other food. It's not really surprising when you consider that virtually every country has its favourite rice dishes. What would Italian food be without risotto, North African food without pilaf, or Spanish food without paella?

These dishes that originate from Italy, the Middle East, India and Spain all use a particular grain of rice significant to that dish. There's arborio rice for risotto, scented long-grain jasmine or basmati for pilafs and calasparra for paella. Each type of rice has its own characteristics but, at a pinch, you can use any type of long-grain rice in pilaf and any type of short-grain rice in risotto and paella, though it won't have the same authenticity.

All of these recipes require a short frying time for ingredients before the rice is added along with stock, then cooked. In the case of pilafs you can place the entire pot (as long as it's ovenproof) in the oven to finish cooking. I find this gives a better finish as it cooks more evenly than with a direct heat underneath.

For simple steamed rice I can't encourage you enough to buy a rice cooker. These are the greatest kitchen invention. You can pop the rice and water in there, switch it on and leave it to do its own thing, and it will keep the rice hot once it's finished cooking.

A stir-fry is possibly my favourite quick meal. Just 10 minutes of chopping, followed by 5 minutes of cooking will result in a healthy, tasty meal.

There are several tricks to successful stir-frying. The first one is to ensure all your ingredients are cut and ready to go before you start – you can't interrupt stir-frying to chop up extra ingredients. The second trick is to not overload the wok. Ideally, you would cook for two to three people at a go. Any more than this and the wok struggles to retain its heat and you start stewing rather than stir-frying. Trick number three is to remember that stir-frying is actually two cooking methods. You have the original frying part and then you cover the wok with a lid to steam. This ensures the ingredients cook through. Finally, keep your stir-fry simple – add garlic, fresh ginger and chilli for flavour and keep the salty soy, black bean and oyster sauces for seasoning at the end. If you add them to the stir-fry while it's cooking, the high salt content of these ingredients will draw the liquid from your leafy vegetables, making the stir-fry swampy.

A stir-fry can be served with steamed rice or noodles, or both can be added. The variety of noodles you can get is outstanding, and they are a great resource to have on hand in the kitchen cupboard. I typically have dried vermicelli, udon and buckwheat noodles, and buy fresh hokkien and chow mein noodles to refrigerate or freeze for longer storage. I also source fresh rice noodles from Asian grocery stores as the need arises.

Things you need to know
about pasta

- Unless you are making a slow-cooked dish like ragu, remember to put a saucepan of water on to boil for the pasta before starting to prepare your sauce.

- Allow 100 g (3½ oz) dried pasta per person.

- Allow 150 g (5½ oz) fresh pasta per person.

- Cook pasta in plenty of gently boiling salted water.

- Always drain your pasta well.

- Toss pasta with the sauce before serving.

- Always serve pasta piping hot.

- Never overcook your pasta.

Things you need to know
about rice

- The best way to cook rice is by the absorption (steaming) method. I strongly recommend buying a rice cooker.

- Don't stir rice during cooking as this allows steam and heat to escape.

- Generally speaking, rice doesn't have to be washed before cooking. You only need to wash rice if you want to get rid of the starch, but this isn't necessary if you use the absorption method.

- 1 cup of raw rice equals 3 cups of cooked rice.

- The addition of salt depends on personal taste.

- Make sure you use the right type of rice to suit the dish: arborio for risotto, calasparra for paella and long-grain white for stir-fries and steaming.

- Pilaf often needs a little more water or stock than steamed rice as the extra ingredients also soak up the liquid.

Things you need to know
about noodles

- Fresh egg and rice noodles need to be heated before adding to the wok. The simplest way of doing this is to place them in a bowl, pour boiling water over them and let them sit for 2–3 minutes before draining and adding to the wok.

- You can also add fresh noodles to a pot of boiling water – allow the water to return to the boil and then drain the noodles before using.

- Dried noodles need to be cooked in boiling water before using, unless you're making soups and broths – you can then add dried noodles as there is no need for precooking.

- Dried soba noodles and udon noodles are great to have on hand for use in Japanese salads and soups. They need to be cooked in boiling water for 4 minutes until tender.

Pasta essentials

A BIG PASTA POT

I'm talking a 10 litre (338 fl oz) pot here, one that's especially made for cooking pasta. Inside the pasta pot is a large colander so you lift your cooked pasta from the boiling water, rather than pouring the boiling water over the cooked pasta in a colander. The drained pot is then perfect for tossing the pasta with its sauce.

FRESH OR DRIED?

Fresh pasta produces a soft eating experience and is perfect for filled pastas, such as ravioli, lasagne and cannelloni. Dried pasta, which is an essential modern pantry item, is firmer to the bite than fresh pasta. Choose one that suits your taste and budget.

WHAT SHAPE?

It all comes down to personal taste. I always cook spaghetti for pasta bolognese; it just doesn't seem right with anything else. Likewise, it has to be macaroni in macaroni cheese though, at a pinch, penne will do. However, if you want farfalle with bolognese sauce, be my guest. Younger members of the family love the different shapes of pasta, so it's well worth experimenting.

CHEESE

Parmigiano Reggiano (often labelled as parmesan) is the classic Italian pasta cheese. It's quite expensive, but the flavour is so good that only a little is needed. For the best flavour, buy it in large chunks or blocks, rather than pre-grated, and grate as required. Serve a bowl of grated or shaved parmesan with most pasta dishes, although seafood and cream sauces rarely need cheese. The slightly cheaper Grana Pandano is also parmesan, but from a different region. Some prefer its sweeter flavour. Pecorino can also be used with pasta dishes. This hard cheese is made from sheep's milk. Fresh ricotta is also delicious with pasta in place of parmesan. It's lighter and has an interesting texture.

TOMATO PASSATA (PURÉED TOMATOES)

Simply heat this ready-to-use Italian tomato sauce while your pasta is cooking – you can add chilli and olives, a few chunks of tuna, a spoonful of pesto, or nothing at all! I tend to use tomato passata, or sugo as it's also called, as a base for most of my sauces. I like the consistency it brings to the sauce, though tinned tomatoes are making a comeback in my kitchen. Please avoid buying passata or tinned tomatoes with added flavours, such as herbs, wine or garlic. You should add your own flavouring, preferably fresh, in the quantity you want. Depending on the acidity of the tomatoes, you may need to add a pinch of sugar to tomato-based recipes.

OLIVE OIL

Good olive oil is essential when cooking pasta. You'll need it for making sauces, to toss with pasta so that the strands don't stick to each other, and for pan-cooking or oven-roasting vegetables to go with your dish. The better the quality, the deeper the flavour that olive oil will bring to your pasta dishes. Research has shown that extra-virgin olive oil is much better for you as it's a monounsaturated fat and contains antioxidants. Use it as your preferred oil as it's a healthier substitute for saturated fats, such as butter and palm oil.

Extra-virgin olive oil is the first extraction from the olives. It has the most flavour and, depending on the variety of olives, can be fruity, spicy, grassy or peppery in flavour. High-quality oils are cold pressed, as the heat affects the flavour of the oil and no chemicals are used.

Virgin olive oil is the second pressing. It doesn't have the same complexity of flavours and has less of the nutrients. Pure, light and extra-light oils are produced from the last pressing of the olives; they are the lowest quality and have usually been heat extracted.

Olive oil should be used when fresh. Heat and light will damage the oil so keep it in a cool, dark place. Imported oil won't be as fresh as local stuff because it's probably been travelling on a ship around the globe for several months.

Bowl food recipes

Pasta

Pasta Napoletana

This recipe is dead simple, though pretty basic when it comes to taste. I would serve this with a filled tortellini or ravioli to add more flavour, or over penne for an uncomplicated meal.
Serves 4

Oil for cooking

1 onion, diced

1 garlic clove, crushed

1 tablespoon tomato paste (concentrated purée)

6 tomatoes, diced, or 400 g (14 oz) tinned chopped tomatoes

Chopped fresh herbs (basil and flat-leaf/Italian parsley are both good)

400 g (14 oz) pasta of your choice

Bring a large saucepan of water to the boil over high heat. Add a good pinch of salt.

Heat a medium saucepan over medium heat. Add a splash of oil and cook the onion for 3–4 minutes, stirring often, until it softens slightly. Add the garlic and cook for 1–2 minutes, or until fragrant. Add the tomato paste and cook briefly before adding the tomatoes. Bring to the boil, reduce the heat and cook for 5–8 minutes, stirring often. When the sauce has thickened to the desired consistency, season with salt and freshly ground black pepper and add the fresh herbs to taste.

Add the pasta to the boiling water and stir until the water has returned to the boil. Reduce the heat, cover and cook the pasta at a fast simmer for 8 minutes, or following the packet instructions. Check that the pasta is cooked, drain and toss with the sauce.

Napoletana sauce with basil
Add chopped basil to the sauce for a fresh taste.

Napoletana sauce with chilli
Add two seeded and finely diced red chillies with the cooking onions.

Napoletana sauce with roasted eggplant
Add one diced roasted eggplant (aubergine) with the tomatoes.

Napoletana sauce with roasted capsicum
Add one diced roasted red capsicum (bell pepper) with the tomatoes.

Napoletana sauce with olives
Add 85 g (3 oz/⅔ cup) pitted olives to the sauce.

Napoletana sauce with tuna
Add 300 g (10½ oz) tinned tuna chunks to the sauce.

Napoletana sauce with pesto
Finish the sauce with a spoonful of pesto (see pages 476-7) per person.

Napoletana sauce with mushrooms
Add 100 g (3½ oz) sliced mushrooms after cooking the onion for 3-4 minutes.

Napoletana sauce with spinach
Add 100 g (3½ oz) washed English spinach leaves for the last 3-4 minutes of cooking.

Napoletana sauce with bacon, spicy salami (or chorizo)
Add 150 g (5½ oz) diced bacon, spicy salami or chorizo after cooking the onion for 3-4 minutes and continue cooking for another 4-5 minutes.

Quick-and-easy bolognese

As the name suggests, this is a quick and easy dish. Make double or even triple this recipe and keep it on hand in the freezer for emergency dinners. Add it to pasta bakes, to chilli with kidney beans or to shepherd's pie with a potato mash topping. Serves 4–6

Oil for cooking

2 onions, diced

2 garlic cloves, crushed

1 kg (2 lb 3 oz) lean minced (ground) beef

3 tablespoons tomato paste (concentrated purée)

250 ml (8½ fl oz/1 cup) tomato passata (puréed tomatoes)

375 ml (12½ fl oz/1½ cups) beef stock

2 tablespoons chopped fresh herbs, such as basil, thyme or flat-leaf (Italian) parsley

Heat a medium saucepan over medium heat. Add a splash of oil and the onion and cook for 3–4 minutes, stirring often, until the onion softens slightly. Add the garlic and cook for a further 1–2 minutes, or until the garlic is fragrant. Add the beef and cook until well browned, stirring well. Add the tomato paste and cook for 1–2 minutes, stirring often. Add the passata, beef stock and herbs and bring to the boil.

Reduce the heat and cook for 10–15 minutes, stirring often. When the sauce has thickened to the desired consistency, season with salt and freshly ground black pepper and serve.

Spicy bolognese
Add two finely diced and seeded chillies along with the onions.

Beef and mushroom bolognese
Add 150 g (5½ oz) sliced mushrooms.

Veal ragu

This is it, the king of pasta sauces – rich, decadent and well worth the effort. This is delicious used in lasagne. Serves 4–6

Oil for cooking

1 onion, diced

2 celery stalks, diced

1 carrot, diced

1 garlic clove, crushed

125 g (4½ oz) pancetta, diced

1 kg (2 lb 3 oz) coarsely ground veal (silverside is excellent)

2 tablespoons tomato paste (concentrated purée)

125 ml (4 fl oz/½ cup) white wine

375 ml (12½ fl oz/1½ cups) beef stock

250 ml (8½ fl oz/1 cup) tomato passata (puréed tomatoes)

1 rosemary sprig

2–3 thyme sprigs

2 tablespoons chopped flat-leaf (Italian) parsley

Heat a heavy-based saucepan over medium heat. Add a splash of oil and the onion, celery and carrot. Cook for 5–6 minutes, stirring often. Add the garlic and cook for a further 1–2 minutes, or until the garlic is fragrant. Add the pancetta and veal and cook until well browned, stirring well. Add the tomato paste, then lower the heat and cook for 2–3 minutes.

Raise the heat, then add the wine, stock, passata, rosemary and thyme. Bring to the boil, then reduce the heat and simmer for 1 hour, stirring often. Sesason with salt and freshly ground black pepper, add the parsley and serve.

Pasta with pancetta, roast pumpkin and rosemary

There's something going on here with the saltiness of the pancetta and the sweetness of the roasted pumpkin – a perfect combination. Serves 4

200 g (7 oz) pumpkin (squash), peeled and cut into 2 cm (¾ in) dice

1 tablespoon rosemary leaves

Oil for cooking

400 g (14 oz) pasta of your choice

1 onion, diced

2 thick slices pancetta (approximately 125 g/4½ oz), diced

2 tablespoons chicken stock

80 g (2¾ oz/1⅔ cups) baby English spinach leaves

100 g (3½ oz) goat's cheese, crumbled (optional)

Preheat the oven to 180°C (350°F).

Toss the pumpkin with the rosemary, drizzle with oil and season with salt and freshly ground black pepper. Roast in the oven for 15–20 minutes, or until the pumpkin is tender and golden. Set aside.

Bring a large saucepan of water to the boil over high heat. Add a good pinch of salt. Add the pasta and stir until the water has returned to the boil. Reduce the heat, cover and cook the pasta at a fast simmer for 8 minutes.

Heat a medium frying pan over medium–high heat. Add a splash of oil and the onion and cook for 3–4 minutes. Add the pancetta and cook for 3–4 minutes, until it starts to turn golden brown. Add the stock and spinach and cook for 1–2 minutes until the spinach wilts. Add the roasted pumpkin to the pan and toss to combine. Drain your pasta and toss with the sauce to serve. Crumble the goat's cheese over (if using) and serve.

Orecchiette with rich mushroom sauce

If wild mushrooms, such as pine mushrooms or slippery jacks, are in season, they will add extra oomph to this sauce. If not, a combination of readily available Swiss browns, field and shiitake is good. Serves 4

Oil for cooking

1 onion, diced

500 g (1 lb 2 oz) mushrooms, sliced

2 garlic cloves, crushed

125 ml (4 fl oz/½ cup) white wine

125 ml (4 fl oz/½ cup) chicken stock

125 ml (4 fl oz/½ cup) tomato passata (puréed tomatoes)

400 g (14 oz) dried orecchiette

2 tablespoons chopped flat-leaf (Italian) parsley or basil to serve

Heat a medium saucepan over medium–high heat. Add a generous splash of oil and the onion and cook for 3–4 minutes. Add the mushrooms and cook for 4–5 minutes, stirring often. Add the garlic and cook for 1–2 minutes, until fragrant. Pour in the wine and cook until reduced by half. Add the stock and tomato passata and bring to the boil. Reduce to a simmer and cook for 10–15 minutes.

Bring a large saucepan of water to the boil over high heat. Add a good pinch of salt. Add the orecchiette and stir until the water has returned to the boil. Reduce the heat, cover and cook the pasta at a fast simmer for 8 minutes.

Once the sauce is cooked, season with salt and freshly ground black pepper. Drain the pasta and toss with the sauce and herbs to serve.

Penne with prosciutto, peas and mint

With this type of dish it's easy to serve the sauce on the side for fussy eaters, then toss the rest of the sauce together for those with grown-up tastes. In spring I like to swap the peas for double-podded broad beans – their season is short so make the most of them. Serves 4

400 g (14 oz) dried penne

Oil for cooking

1 onion, chopped

1 garlic clove, crushed

250 ml (8½ fl oz/1 cup) chicken stock

90 g (3 oz) prosciutto (about 8 thin slices), chopped

255 g (9 oz/1⅔ cups) peas

40 g (1½ oz) butter

1 tablespoon chopped fresh mint

Preheat the oven to 180°C (350°F).

Heat a large shallow pan over medium heat. Add a splash of oil and the onion and cook for 3–4 minutes, stirring often, until the onion softens slightly. Add the garlic and cook for a further 1–2 minutes or until fragrant. Add the stock, bring to the boil, and then reduce the heat. Simmer for 5 minutes, allowing the stock to reduce slightly.

Bring a large saucepan of water to the boil over high heat. Add a good pinch of salt. Add the pasta to the boiling water and stir until the water has returned to the boil. Reduce the heat, cover and cook the pasta at a fast simmer for 8 minutes.

Lay the prosciutto slices flat on a baking tray and cook in the oven for 6–7 minutes, or until crisp.

Add the peas to the pan and cook for 3–4 minutes, turning the heat up if necessary. Remove from the heat, whisk in the butter and add salt and loads of freshly ground black pepper. Add the mint.

Drain the pasta, toss with the sauce, crumble the crispy prosciutto over the top of each bowl and serve.

Pasta with prawns and rocket

I'm not a big fan of seafood with pasta, but every now and again the fancy takes hold of me. That's when I cook this dish. Serves 4

400 g (14 oz) pasta of your choice

Olive oil for cooking

2 garlic cloves, crushed

½ teaspoon dried chilli flakes

500 g (1 lb 2 oz) peeled green (raw) prawns (shrimp), deveined

125 ml (4 fl oz/½ cup) white wine

Grated zest and juice of 1 lemon

2 handfuls of rocket (arugula), roughly chopped

Bring a large saucepan of water to the boil over high heat. Add a good pinch of salt. Add the pasta and stir until the water has returned to the boil. Reduce the heat, cover and cook the pasta at a fast simmer for 8 minutes.

Heat a heavy-based frying pan over medium–high heat and add a generous slug of olive oil. Add the garlic and chilli and cook for 2–3 minutes until the garlic just starts to colour. Add the prawns and cook for 1–2 minutes, tossing them to coat with the garlic–chilli mixture. Add the white wine and bring to the boil, then reduce to a simmer and cook for 2–3 minutes.

Drain the pasta and add it to the pan along with the lemon zest and juice and rocket. Toss to combine, and serve.

Spaghetti with silverbeet, raisins and pine nuts

My good friend Daniele blew me away with this simple pasta recipe. I felt I just had to share it with you. You can substitute the silverbeet for cavolo nero or kale if you prefer. Serves 4

85 g (3 oz/⅔ cup) raisins
60 ml (2 fl oz/¼ cup) brandy
400 g (14 oz) dried spaghetti
3–4 silverbeet (Swiss chard) stems
Oil for cooking
1 onion, diced
50 g (1¾ oz/⅓ cup) pine nuts
1 garlic clove, crushed
1 small red chilli, seeded and diced
Grated zest of 1 orange
125 ml (4 fl oz/½ cup) chicken stock

Soak the raisins in the brandy and set aside.

Bring a large saucepan of water to the boil over high heat. Add a good pinch of salt. Add the pasta and stir until the water has returned to the boil. Reduce the heat, cover and cook the pasta at a fast simmer for 8 minutes.

Wash the silverbeet well. Discard the stalks and roughly chop the leaves.

Heat a frying pan over medium–high heat and add a splash of oil, the onion and pine nuts. Cook for 4–5 minutes, stirring often, until the pine nuts turn golden brown. Add the garlic, chilli, orange zest and silverbeet, and cook for 2–3 minutes. Add the stock, cover with a lid and cook for 1–2 minutes, until the silverbeet collapses. Season with salt and freshly ground black pepper.

Add the brandy-soaked raisins and toss everything together well. Drain the pasta and toss with the sauce.

Spaghetti with breadcrumbs, tuna, parsley and lemon

This is a great meal for when all you have is a tin of tuna and some day-old bread. The success of the recipe really lies in the quality of the ingredients – good bread and olive oil make all the difference. Serves 4

400 g (14 oz) dried spaghetti
Olive oil for cooking
175 g (6 oz) sourdough bread, chopped into coarse breadcrumbs
350 g (12½ oz) tinned tuna, drained
Grated zest and juice of 1 lemon
15 g (½ oz/½ cup) roughly chopped flat-leaf (Italian) parsley

Bring a large saucepan of water to the boil over high heat. Add a good pinch of salt. Add the pasta and stir until the water has returned to the boil. Reduce the heat, cover and cook the pasta at a fast simmer for 8 minutes.

Heat a large heavy-based frying pan over medium–high heat. Add a very generous splash of oil and the breadcrumbs and cook for 4–5 minutes, stirring often, until the breadcrumbs are golden and crunchy. Remove and drain on paper towel.

Drain the pasta and add the breadcrumbs, tuna, lemon zest and juice and parsley. Season with salt and freshly ground black pepper and serve.

Spaghetti with braised chicken meatballs

I've fallen in love with the simplicity of this dish. It can easily be made in advance and be cooking away in the oven when your guests arrive. Serves 4

Oil for cooking

2 onions, diced

2 small red chillies, seeded and diced (optional)

2 garlic cloves, crushed

125 ml (4 fl oz/½ cup) dry white wine

500 ml (17 fl oz/2 cups) chicken stock

250 ml (8½ fl oz/1 cup) tomato passata (puréed tomatoes)

500 g (1 lb 2 oz) minced (ground) chicken

7 g (¼ oz/¼ cup) chopped flat-leaf (Italian) parsley

1 tablespoon chopped basil

1 egg

50 g (1¾ oz) dry breadcrumbs or quinoa flakes

400 g (14 oz) dried spaghetti

Preheat the oven to 180°C (350°F).

Heat a large saucepan over medium heat. Add 80 ml (2½ fl oz/⅓ cup) oil and the onions. Cook for 5–6 minutes, stirring often, ensuring that the onions don't colour. Add the chillies (if using) and the garlic and cook for a further 1–2 minutes, until fragrant. Pour in the white wine, bring to the boil and cook until reduced by half, about 10–15 minutes. Add the stock and passata and bring to the boil. Season with salt and freshly ground black pepper.

Mix the minced chicken, 2 tablespoons of the chopped parsley, basil, egg, breadcrumbs and some salt and pepper together. Roll into 3 cm (1¼ in) balls.

Heat a heavy-based frying pan over medium–high heat. Add a generous splash of oil and cook the meatballs until golden brown. Transfer to an ovenproof casserole dish. Pour the hot sauce over the meatballs. Cover the dish with foil and bake in the oven for 1 hour.

After 1 hour, bring a large saucepan of water to the boil over high heat. Add a good pinch of salt. Add the spaghetti and stir until the water comes back to the boil. Cook the pasta at a fast simmer for 8 minutes.

Drain the pasta and serve with the meatballs and sauce, sprinkled with the remaining chopped parsley.

Moroccan chicken meatballs
Swap the chilli for 2 teaspoons Harissa (page 467) and serve the cooked meatballs with couscous.

Mexican meatballs
Swap the chilli for two diced chipotles en adobo, or add both if you like it spicy. Serve with Basic pilaf (page 481).

Spaghetti with smoked chicken and asparagus

Smoked chicken and asparagus is a gorgeous combination, especially in spring when the new season's asparagus arrives. Serves 4

400 g (14 oz) dried spaghetti

Oil for cooking

1 onion, chopped

1 garlic clove, crushed

2 smoked boneless skinless chicken breasts, sliced

250 ml (8½ fl oz/1 cup) chicken stock

1 bunch asparagus, woody ends removed, cut into 2 cm (¾ in) lengths

40 g (1½ oz) butter

2 tablespoons chopped flat-leaf (Italian) parsley

Bring a large saucepan of water to the boil over high heat. Add a good pinch of salt. Add the pasta to the boiling water and stir until the water has returned to the boil. Reduce the heat, cover and cook the pasta at a fast simmer for 8 minutes.

Heat a large frying pan over medium–high heat. Add a generous splash of oil and the onion and cook for 3–4 minutes, stirring often, until the onion softens slightly. Add the garlic and cook for a further 1–2 minutes, or until the garlic is fragrant. Add the smoked chicken and stock and bring to the boil. Add the asparagus and cook for 2–3 minutes.

Remove the pan from the heat, whisk in the butter and season with salt and loads of freshly ground black pepper. Add the parsley.

Drain the pasta, toss with the sauce and serve.

Smoked trout and asparagus cream sauce
Swap the smoked chicken for smoked trout, being sure to remove all the bones.

Spiced pipis with risoni

Risoni is pasta shaped like a grain of rice and pipis are small, silvery coloured shellfish. Together they make a delicious combination. Serve with crusty bread. Serves 4

500 g (1 lb 2 oz) pipis or clams (vongole)

Oil for cooking

1 onion, finely diced

1 carrot, finely diced

1 leek, white part only, thinly sliced

1 garlic clove, crushed

2 small red chillies, seeded and finely diced

1 tablespoon tomato paste (concentrated purée)

1 litre (34 fl oz/4 cups) chicken stock

220 g (8 oz) risoni

1 tablespoon chopped flat-leaf (Italian) parsley

Rinse the pipis under cold water and discard any opened shells. Keep refrigerated until needed.

Heat a large saucepan over medium heat. Add a splash of oil and the onion, carrot and leek. Cook for 5 minutes, stirring often. Add the garlic, chilli and tomato paste and cook for a further 2 minutes. Add the stock and bring to the boil. Once boiling, add a pinch of salt and the risoni. Return to the boil, then lower the heat, cover with a lid and cook for 6 minutes.

Check the risoni is al dente, add the pipis, cover again and cook for 2 minutes. Uncover and watch for the pipis beginning to open. Remove the pipis as they open and place them in a warm bowl. Continue cooking until most of the pipis have opened – discard any that don't open. Add the parsley to the risoni and season with salt and freshly ground black pepper.

Divide the pipis and risoni evenly between four warmed soup bowls.

Spaghetti with seafood and tomato

Serve this seafood pasta for dinner or in smaller portions for an appetiser. Serves 4

400 g (14 oz) spaghetti

Olive oil for cooking

2 onions, finely diced

2 small red chillies, seeded and finely diced

2 garlic cloves, crushed

125 ml (4 fl oz/½ cup) white wine

500 ml (17 fl oz/2 cups) tomato passata (puréed tomatoes)

300 g (10½ oz) firm white fish fillets, cut into 5 mm (¼ in) slices

500 g (1 lb 2 oz) green (raw) prawns (shrimp), peeled and deveined

500 g (1 lb 2 oz) pipis or small clams (vongole)

2 tablespoons chopped flat-leaf (Italian) parsley

Bring a large saucepan of water to the boil over high heat. Add a good pinch of salt. Add the pasta and stir until the water has returned to the boil. Reduce the heat, cover and cook the pasta at a fast simmer for 8 minutes.

Heat a large shallow pan over medium heat. Add 60 ml (2 fl oz/¼ cup) olive oil, onion and chilli and cook for 3–4 minutes, stirring often, until the onion softens slightly. Add the garlic and cook for a further 1–2 minutes or until the garlic is fragrant. Turn up the heat, add the white wine and boil until reduced by half. Add the passata, allow to come to the boil, then reduce the heat and cook for 5–10 minutes.

Heat another pan over medium heat. Add a splash of oil and first cook the fish, then the prawns, for 2–3 minutes, or until just cooked through. Remove and set aside.

Add the pipis to the cooking sauce, cover with a lid and simmer for 3–4 minutes, until most of the shells have opened (if space is tight, take the cooked pipis and set them aside in a warmed bowl in a warm place). Add the cooked fish and prawns, season with salt and freshly ground black pepper and add the parsley.

Drain the pasta and toss together well with the sauce. Tip into a large warm bowl and serve.

Macaroni cheese

This is a classic you just can't pass up. Littlies love it, especially when it's all crispy on top. Be sure to remove the white sauce from the heat before adding the cheese, as otherwise the sauce may curdle. Serves 4

400 g (14 oz) dried macaroni

40 g (1½ oz) butter

2 tablespoons plain (all-purpose) flour

750 ml (25½ fl oz/3 cups) hot milk

1 teaspoon dijon mustard

200 g (7 oz) grated cheese (mix of parmesan and cheddar)

Bring a large saucepan of water to the boil over high heat. Add a good pinch of salt. Add the pasta and stir until the water has returned to the boil. Reduce the heat, cover and cook the pasta at a fast simmer for 8 minutes.

Place a medium saucepan over medium heat and melt the butter, without browning. Add the flour and stir well to incorporate and form a roux. Reduce the heat and 'cook' the flour for 2–3 minutes, stirring often.

Raise the heat under the roux and add 1 ladleful of hot milk. Whisk in well, then continue to add the milk, 1 ladleful at a time, until it's all incorporated. Add the mustard, reduce the heat and cook for 3–4 minutes, stirring often.

Remove from the heat, add three-quarters of the grated cheese and stir well until melted. Season well with salt and freshly ground black pepper.

Drain the pasta and stir through the cheese sauce. Pour into an ovenproof dish. Sprinkle the remaining cheese on top and place under a hot grill (broiler) until golden brown.

Macaroni cheese with ham
Dice two 1 cm (½ in) thick slices of leg ham and add the ham to the sauce with the cheese.

Macaroni cheese with corn
Add 200 g (7 oz) corn kernels to the sauce with the cheese.

Spaghettini carbonara

Spaghettini is a thin spaghetti, and it's perfect for a creamy sauce such as this. Serves 4

400 g (14 oz) dried spaghettini

Oil for cooking

125 g (4½ oz) bacon, thinly sliced

4 egg yolks

2 tablespoons pouring (single/light) cream

2 tablespoons grated parmesan

2 tablespoons chopped flat-leaf (Italian) parsley

Bring a large saucepan of water to the boil over high heat. Add a good pinch of salt. Add the pasta and stir until the water has returned to the boil. Reduce the heat, cover and cook the pasta at a fast simmer for 8 minutes.

Heat a frying pan over medium heat. Add a splash of oil, cook the bacon until crispy, then chop it into small pieces.

Beat the egg yolks, cream, cheese, some salt and plenty of freshly ground black pepper together – the pepper needs to be plentiful, so it dominates in the finished dish.

Drain the pasta and toss with the egg mixture, bacon and parsley and serve.

Bolognese pasta bake

If you have been smart enough to make extra bolognese, this dish is a quick and easy mid-week option. I often call it cheat's lasagne because it's your sauce, cheese and pasta all in one dish. I like to cook the pasta and heat the sauce and, while it's all still hot, pop it under the grill (broiler) to get golden brown and toasty. You can make it in advance and cook it in the oven to heat through, but make sure your bolognese is very wet – add more stock and tomato passata (puréed tomatoes), as the pasta absorbs the liquid and you could end up with a dry dish. Serves 4

250 g (9 oz) dried penne
300 g (10½ oz) Quick-and-easy bolognese (page 84)
125 g (4½ oz/1 cup) grated cheddar
150 g (5½ oz/1 cup) grated mozzarella

Bring a large saucepan of water to the boil over high heat. Add a good pinch of salt. Add the pasta to the boiling water and stir until the water has returned to the boil. Reduce the heat, cover and cook the pasta at a fast simmer for 8 minutes.

Preheat a grill (broiler).

Heat the bolognese and mix the cheeses together. Drain the pasta and mix together with the bolognese and two-thirds of the cheese. Spoon into a 1 litre (34 fl oz/4 cup) capacity baking dish and scatter the remaining cheese over the top. Cook under the grill until golden brown, about 8–10 minutes, and serve.

If making this in advance, drain and refresh the pasta under cold running water. Toss the cold pasta with the bolognese and two-thirds of the cheese. Spoon into a 1 litre (34 fl oz/4 cup) baking dish and scatter the remaining cheese over the top.

When ready to serve, preheat the oven to 180°C (350°F). Place the pasta bake in the oven and cook for 30–40 minutes until golden brown on top and heated through. (You could always microwave the dish and pop it in the hot oven for 10–15 minutes to finish off.)

As-good-as-it-gets lasagne

The name says it all, really. For those moments when life doesn't get any better, here's the recipe that's the icing on the cake, so to speak. Serves 4

40 g (1½ oz) butter
2 tablespoons plain (all-purpose) flour
750 ml (25½ fl oz/3 cups) hot milk
1 teaspoon dijon mustard
200 g (7 oz) grated cheese (mix of parmesan and cheddar)
1 quantity Veal ragu (page 84)
300 g (10½ oz) fresh or instant lasagne sheets

Preheat the oven to 180°C (350°F).

Place a medium saucepan over medium heat and melt the butter, without browning. Add the flour and stir well to incorporate and form a roux. Reduce the heat and 'cook' the flour for 2–3 minutes, stirring often.

Raise the heat under the roux and add 1 ladleful of hot milk. Whisk in well, then continue to add the milk, 1 ladleful at a time, until it's all incorporated. Add the mustard, reduce the heat and cook for 3–4 minutes, stirring often.

Remove from the heat, add three-quarters of the grated cheese and stir well until melted. Season well with salt and freshly ground black pepper.

Place half of the ragu in a rectangular baking dish. Top with a single layer of lasagne sheets, then a layer of cheese sauce, another layer of lasagne sheets, the remainder of the ragu, more lasagne sheets and a final layer of cheese sauce. Sprinkle with grated cheese and bake in the oven for 30–40 minutes until golden brown and the pasta is cooked.

Beef lasagne
Replace the veal ragu with Quick-and-easy bolognese (page 84).

Cheesy bean and tomato pasta bake

Pasta bake is the new black in my house and my family eats many variations of this dish. This is my favourite, but not the kids' – they prefer the meatier option. Serves 4

250 g (9 oz) dried penne

Oil for cooking

1 onion, diced

1 garlic clove, crushed

1 small red chilli, seeded and diced

375 ml (12½ fl oz/1½ cups) chicken or vegetable stock

375 ml (12½ fl oz/1½ cups) tomato passata (puréed tomatoes)

400 g (14 oz) tinned cannellini (lima) beans, drained and rinsed

125 g (4½ oz/1 cup) grated cheddar

150 g (5½ oz/1 cup) grated mozzarella

Preheat the oven to 180°C (350°F).

Bring a large saucepan of water to the boil over high heat. Add a good pinch of salt. Add the pasta to the boiling water and stir until the water has returned to the boil. Reduce the heat, cover and cook the pasta at a fast simmer for 8 minutes. If making in advance, drain and refresh the pasta under cold running water. Toss the cold pasta with 1 tablespoon oil to prevent it sticking together and set aside until needed. If baking straight away, add the hot pasta to the finished sauce.

Heat a large frying pan over medium–high heat. Add a splash of oil and the onion and cook for 3–4 minutes, stirring often, until the onion softens slightly. Add the garlic and chilli and cook for a further 1–2 minutes, or until the garlic is fragrant. Add the stock and tomato passata and bring to the boil. Add the beans, then reduce to a simmer and cook for 8–10 minutes, stirring often. Season with salt and freshly ground black pepper. Add the pasta to the sauce and stir well to combine.

Pour the pasta mixture into a 3 litre (101 fl oz/12 cup) capacity ovenproof dish. Mix the cheddar and mozzarella together. Scatter the cheeses over the pasta and bake in the oven for 30–40 minutes, until golden brown on top and heated through.

Baked ricotta and spinach cannelloni

Surprisingly quick and easy, and a worthwhile addition to any home cook's repertoire. Serves 4

200 g (7 oz/4 cups) baby English spinach leaves

300 g (10½ oz) ricotta

50 g (1¾ oz) feta, crumbled (optional)

2 tablespoons chopped basil

1 packet dried cannelloni or fresh cannelloni sheets

500 ml (17 fl oz/2 cups) tomato passata (puréed tomatoes)

150 g (5½ oz/1 cup) grated mozzarella

2 tablespoons chopped flat-leaf (Italian) parsley

Bring a large saucepan of water to the boil. Blanch the spinach for 1–2 minutes, then refresh under cold water. Squeeze out the excess water. Chop roughly. (Or put the spinach in a microwave-proof container with a splash of water and zap for 1–2 minutes.)

Place the cool spinach, ricotta, feta (if using) and basil in a large bowl, season well with salt and freshly ground black pepper and mix to combine.

Take the cannelloni tubes and fill them with the ricotta mixture. If using dried tubes, a piping bag is the easiest way to do this. If using fresh sheets, lay them out flat, spoon a strip of the ricotta mixture along one edge of the sheet and roll up, enclosing the filling.

Preheat the oven to 200°C (400°F).

Take a 2 litre (68 fl oz/8 cup) capacity ovenproof baking dish and pour half of the tomato passata into the base. Arrange the cannelloni rolls side by side in the dish, nice and snug. Spoon over the remaining tomato passata. Sprinkle with the mozzarella and parsley and bake for 25 minutes or until golden.

Potato gnocchi

Floury potatoes are best for making gnocchi. A pasta pot fitted with a large metal colander inside will enable you to lift your cooked gnocchi from the boiling water, rather than pouring the boiling water over it into a colander (cooked gnocchi is quite fragile). Serve with some Napoletana sauce (page 83) or Quick-and-easy bolognese (page 84). Serves 4

1 kg (2 lb 3 oz) potatoes, such as Toolangi Delight, desiree, bintje, or any other waxy or all-purpose potato, peeled
75 g (2¾ oz) butter
3 eggs, plus 3 egg yolks
Pinch of freshly grated nutmeg
300 g (10½ oz/2 cups) plain (all-purpose) flour, plus extra for dusting

Boil or steam the potatoes until tender. Drain well. Mash the potatoes while they're still hot, then add the butter, eggs, egg yolks, nutmeg and flour, and season with salt and freshly ground black pepper. Stir until incorporated.

Divide the potato mixture into four portions on a floured work surface. Roll each portion into 2 cm (¾ in) thick sausages. Cut into 2 cm (¾ in) lengths.

Bring a large saucepan of water to the boil. Add a good pinch of salt. Plunge the gnocchi into the boiling salted water.

Allow the gnocchi to rise to the surface, then cook for a further 2 minutes. Remove and serve straight away with a piping hot sauce.

If desired, the gnocchi can be pre-cooked, set aside to cool and tossed gently with olive oil. Reheat by gently placing the gnocchi back into boiling water for 1 minute, or by reheating in a microwave.

Spinach and ricotta gnocchi

You will feel like an Italian nonna with this recipe – it's so easy and quick, too. This is delicious tossed with Napoletana sauce with chilli (page 83) and parmesan. Serves 2

250 g (9 oz/1 cup) ricotta
1 egg
50 g (1¾ oz) blanched, chopped English spinach
2 tablespoons grated parmesan, plus extra to serve
75 g (2¾ oz/½ cup) plain (all-purpose) flour
Semolina as needed

Mix the ricotta with the egg, blanched spinach, parmesan and flour until combined. Season well with salt and freshly ground black pepper.

Divide the mixture into easily workable amounts and place on a chopping board sprinkled with semolina. Roll into 2 cm (¾ in) thick sausages, then cut into 2 cm (¾ in) lengths. Repeat until all the mixture is used.

Bring a large saucepan of water to the boil. Add a good pinch of salt. Cook the gnocchi in the boiling salted water for 3–4 minutes, or until the gnocchi float to the surface.

Gnocchi with blue cheese sauce

This is a rich dining experience that demands the very best blue cheese to be enjoyed at its smooth-textured best. Serves 4

125 ml (4 fl oz/½ cup) pouring (single/light) cream

150 g (5½ oz) blue cheese, such as gorgonzola

100 g (3½ oz/1 cup) grated parmesan

800 g (1 lb 12 oz) Potato gnocchi (see opposite) or 1 packet gnocchi

60 g (2 oz/½ cup) chopped walnuts (optional) to serve

Place the cream and cheeses in a saucepan and bring to the boil. Reduce the heat and allow to simmer for 3–4 minutes. Season with freshly ground black pepper.

Bring a large saucepan of water to the boil over high heat. Add a good pinch of salt. Add the gnocchi and stir until the water has returned to the boil. Reduce the heat, cover and cook the gnocchi at a fast simmer for 3–4 minutes, until the gnocchi is cooked through.

Drain the pasta and toss gently with the blue cheese sauce. Serve with the chopped walnuts sprinkled over the top, if desired.

Roast tomato, pancetta and sweet onions with gnocchi

You don't have to serve this chunky, rich sauce with gnocchi. But take it from me – it's a magic combination. Serves 2

4 tomatoes

Olive oil for cooking

Pinch of caster (superfine) sugar

2 onions, diced

2–3 thyme sprigs

150 g (5½ oz) pancetta, diced

2 tablespoons chopped flat-leaf (Italian) parsley

2–3 tablespoons shaved parmesan

300 g (10½ oz) Potato gnocchi (see opposite)

Preheat the oven to 180°C (350°F).

Cut the tomatoes into quarters. Lay them on a baking tray, skin side down, and drizzle with olive oil. Season them with salt and freshly ground black pepper and sprinkle with the sugar. Roast in the oven for 30 minutes.

Heat 60 ml (2 fl oz/¼ cup) olive oil in a heavy-based frying pan over medium–high heat. Add the onions, thyme and some salt and pepper. Cook over low heat for 20–30 minutes or until the onions are soft and slightly coloured. Turn the heat up, add the pancetta and cook for 3–4 minutes, until the pancetta is crispy. Add the roasted tomatoes, parsley and parmesan. Check the seasoning.

Bring a large saucepan of water to the boil over high heat. Add a good pinch of salt.

Plunge the gnocchi into the boiling salted water, allow them to rise to the surface and cook for a further 2–3 minutes. Toss the cooked gnocchi in the sauce and serve.

Roast pumpkin, pancetta and sweet onions with gnocchi
Substitute 200 g (7 oz) diced pumpkin (squash) for the tomatoes.

Broccoli with chilli, ricotta, lemon and pasta

I love the simplicity of this dish. You can add a dollop of pesto (see pages 476–7) if you like or even some crispy pancetta. Make sure you search out the best-quality ricotta you can find – none of that low-fat stuff, please. Serves 4

1 head of broccoli (approximately 250 g/9 oz)

400 g (14 oz) dried pasta

Oil for cooking

175 g (6 oz) sourdough bread, chopped into coarse breadcrumbs

2 small red chillies, seeded and diced

2 garlic cloves, crushed

Juice of 1 lemon

2 tablespoons chopped flat-leaf (Italian) parsley

250 g (9 oz/1 cup) ricotta, crumbled

Cut the broccoli into bite-sized florets and blanch in boiling water for 1–2 minutes. Drain and refresh under cold water. Set aside.

Bring a large saucepan of water to the boil over high heat. Add a good pinch of salt. Add the pasta and stir until the water has returned to the boil. Reduce the heat, cover and cook the pasta at a fast simmer for 8 minutes.

Heat a large heavy-based frying pan over medium–high heat. Add a very generous splash of oil and the breadcrumbs and cook for 4–5 minutes, stirring often, until the breadcrumbs are golden and crunchy. Remove from the heat and set aside.

Return the pan to the heat and add a splash of oil. Add the chillies and garlic and cook for 30 seconds, stirring often, until fragrant. Add the broccoli and lemon juice. Allow to simmer for 2–3 minutes, stirring often, until the broccoli is heated through.

Drain the pasta and toss with the crunchy breadcrumbs, broccoli mixture, chopped parsley and ricotta. Season to taste with salt and freshly ground black pepper and serve immediately.

Seafood

Steamed mussels with garlic

A bowl of garlicky mussels makes a great start to any meal; it's also a dish that takes only a few minutes to prepare. Remember to buy mussels with their shells closed and discard any that fail to open during cooking. You can serve the mussels in individual portions, but it's more fun to throw them into a big bowl and invite everyone to dive in and share. Serves 4

2 tablespoons olive oil

4 garlic cloves, crushed

125 ml (4 fl oz/½ cup) dry white wine

Pinch of saffron threads

1 kg (2 lb 3 oz) mussels, shells scrubbed and beards removed

2 tablespoons chopped flat-leaf (Italian) parsley

Knob of butter

Heat a wok or large frying pan over high heat. Add the oil, then the garlic. Stir for 1 minute, or until fragrant.

Add the white wine and saffron. Allow the liquid to come to the boil, then toss in the mussels. Cover with a lid and leave to steam for 3−4 minutes.

Have a serving bowl ready. Remove the lid of the pan, shake the pan well and remove the cooked mussels as they open, placing them into the bowl.

Remove the pan from the heat and discard any mussels that didn't open during cooking. Add the chopped parsley and butter to the cooking liquid and whisk it through. Check the seasoning and add salt and freshly ground black pepper if needed. Pour the cooking juices over the mussels and serve immediately.

How to clean mussels

TIP

Rinse the mussels under cold running water and pull sharply at the beards to remove them, discarding any open shells. Scrub the shells if necessary. Place the clean mussels under a damp cloth in the refrigerator until needed.

Mussels with Thai chilli broth

This dish is great for lunch, or as a smart appetiser for a dinner party. You have to believe me when I say mussels are easy to cook; they just look difficult. Serves 6 as an appetiser or 4 as a main course

3 tomatoes, quartered

2 small red chillies, halved

3 garlic cloves, bruised

5 cm (2 in) piece fresh ginger, sliced

2 lemongrass stems, white part only, sliced

400 ml (13½ fl oz) coconut cream

2 tablespoons fish sauce

250 ml (8½ fl oz/1 cup) fish or chicken stock

1 bunch coriander (cilantro)

6 Asian shallots, sliced

½ red capsicum (bell pepper), sliced

250 g (9 oz) chow mein noodles

2 kg (4 lb 6 oz) fresh mussels, cleaned

Place the tomatoes, chillies, garlic, ginger and lemongrass in a heavy-based saucepan. Add the coconut cream, fish sauce and stock.

Wash the coriander well, roughly chop the roots and stems, reserving the leaves for later, and add it to the saucepan. Bring to a gentle boil and allow to simmer for 20 minutes.

Remove from the heat and strain the infused coconut cream into a clean saucepan. Using a ladle, force any remaining liquid through the sieve.

Bring the infused coconut cream to the boil. Add the shallots and capsicum and allow to simmer until needed.

Put a kettle of water on to boil. Pour the boiling water over the noodles and set aside.

Heat a wok, add 2 cm (¾ in) of boiling water and toss the mussels in. Cover with a lid and allow to steam for 2 minutes. Remove the mussels as they open and keep them warm until the remainder are opened.

Drain the noodles.

To serve, divide the noodles into bowls, add eight mussels per person for an appetiser, or 12 for a main course, discarding any that are not open. Add a handful of the reserved coriander leaves to the infused coconut cream, pour over the noodles and serve.

Rice

Chicken pilaf

Making a chicken pilaf is an easy introduction to this Middle Eastern style of cooking Once mastered, you can move on to more complex versions by adding vermicelli noodles, nuts, pumpkin (squash) or chickpeas. Pilaf can easily be cooked over low heat on the stove top or in your oven, as in this recipe. Serves 4–6

2 tablespoons oil

2 onions, diced

1 garlic clove, crushed

Pinch of saffron threads

500 g (1 lb 2 oz) boneless skinless chicken thighs, diced

400 g (14 oz/2 cups) long-grain rice

750 ml (25½ fl oz/3 cups) chicken stock

2 tablespoons chopped flat-leaf (Italian) parsley

Preheat the oven to 180°C (350°F).

Heat a large heavy-based ovenproof saucepan over medium heat. Add the oil, onion, garlic and saffron and cook for 4–5 minutes, until fragrant and soft. Add the chicken and cook until it starts to colour. Add the rice and cook for 2–3 minutes, stirring often, then add the stock.

Bring to the boil, stirring often. Reduce the heat, cover and cook in the oven for 30 minutes, or until the rice is tender and the stock has been absorbed. Allow to stand for 5 minutes before serving. Season with salt and freshly ground black pepper, add the parsley and serve.

Chicken, almond and harissa pilaf
Add 80 g (2¾ oz/½ cup) blanched almonds and 1 teaspoon Harissa (page 467) to the pilaf along with the onions.

Chicken, sultana and sweet spice pilaf
Add 1 teaspoon each of ground cinnamon, allspice and ground cardamom with the onions and saffron. Cook until fragrant. Continue as directed, adding 75 g (2¾ oz) sultanas (golden raisins) and a handful of toasted flaked almonds along with the chicken.

Chicken and broad bean pilaf
Add 150 g (5½ oz) double-podded broad beans once the rice is cooked. Allow to stand for 5 minutes, then stir the beans through.

Lamb and saffron pilaf
Brown 500 g (1 lb 2 oz) lean diced lamb in oil, remove and set aside. Return the lamb to the pan with the stock and cook as directed.

Quinoa, beetroot and almond pilaf

Every now and again my inner hippy has to come out and eat dishes like this. This is real comfort food, but ultra healthy. I feel so much better after eating this than I would a burger with the lot. Serves 4

3 beetroot (beets)

Oil for cooking

1 red onion, diced

1 carrot, diced

40 g (1½ oz/¼ cup) blanched almonds

200 g (7 oz/1 cup) quinoa

375 ml (12½ fl oz/1½ cups) vegetable stock

1 tablespoon pomegranate molasses

60 ml (2 fl oz/¼ cup) orange juice

2 tablespoons chopped coriander (cilantro)

1 tablespoon chopped mint

Place the beetroot in a saucepan, cover with water and bring to the boil. Reduce the heat, cover with a lid and cook for 30–40 minutes, depending on the size of the beetroot, until tender. Drain, allow to cool and then peel and cut into 1 cm (½ in) chunks.

Heat a heavy-based saucepan over medium–high heat. Add a splash of oil and the onion and cook for 2–3 minutes until the onion is softened. Add the carrot and almonds and cook for a further 4–5 minutes or until the almonds start to turn golden brown.

Rinse the quinoa well under cold running water and add it to the saucepan along with the stock and some salt and freshly ground black pepper. Bring to the boil, reduce the heat to a simmer and cook for about 20–25 minutes or until the quinoa is cooked and the stock has been absorbed.

Stir through the diced beetroot, pomegranate molasses, orange juice, coriander and mint, and serve immediately.

Hainanese chicken

Traditionally a Chinese dish that has spread across Southeast Asia, this is an intriguing combination of delicate poached chicken with flavoured rice and a spicy chilli sauce to tantalise the taste buds. Serves 4

1 × 1.6 kg (3½ lb) free-range chicken

2 tablespoons Chinese rice wine

2 tablespoons light soy sauce

6 slices fresh ginger, plus 2 tablespoons grated fresh ginger

1 garlic clove, slightly bruised, plus 3–4 garlic cloves, chopped

1 teaspoon sesame oil

400 g (14 oz/2 cups) long-grain rice

4 spring onions (scallions), thinly sliced, to serve

Chilli sauce to serve (optional)

Place the chicken in a large saucepan so that it fits snugly, then cover with water. Add the rice wine, soy sauce, sliced ginger, whole garlic clove and sesame oil. Cover with a lid, bring to the boil and then remove from the heat and allow to stand for 1 hour.

Strain the stock and reserve. Remove the chicken and, when cool enough to handle, remove the skin – reserving some of the skin for later – and discard the bones. Cut the chicken into small pieces.

For the chicken rice, fry the reserved chicken skin until the oil is released. Add the grated ginger and chopped garlic and cook for 1–2 minutes, until just fragrant, taking care not to burn the garlic. Remove the chicken skin, add the rice and cook for 2–3 minutes until all the flavours are mixed together. Add 500 ml (17 fl oz/ 2 cups) of the reserved stock (still reserve the remaining stock), season with salt, cover with a lid and bring to the boil. Once boiling, reduce the heat so the rice is just cooking. Keep covered with the lid and cook until all the stock has been absorbed and the rice is cooked. Remove from the heat and keep warm until ready to serve.

Heat the remaining stock to use as a broth. Season with salt and freshly ground black pepper and add more soy sauce if needed. Spoon the rice into bowls, add a ladleful of hot stock, some pieces of the cooked chicken, sprinkle with the spring onion and serve with chilli sauce, if desired.

Chicken risotto

Risotto is the iconic one-pot meal. You can add any flavours you like to this dish, depending on the season: asparagus, English spinach, mushrooms, broad beans or roast pumpkin (squash).
Serves 4–6

2 tablespoons olive oil

1 onion, diced

1 garlic clove, crushed

1 leek, white part only, thinly sliced (optional)

1 carrot, finely diced (optional)

2 boneless skinless chicken thighs, diced

300 g (10½ oz) arborio rice

125 ml (4 fl oz/½ cup) white wine

750 ml–1 litre (25½–34 ml/3–4 cups) hot vegetable or chicken stock

35 g (1½ oz/⅓ cup) grated parmesan

50 g (1¾ oz) butter, diced

2 tablespoons chopped flat-leaf (Italian) parsley

Heat a large heavy-based saucepan over medium heat. Add the oil, onion, garlic, and leek and carrot (if using), and cook for 3–4 minutes, until fragrant and soft. Add the chicken and cook for 3–4 minutes, or until beginning to brown. Add the rice and stir to coat with oil, then cook briefly. Add the wine and stir until it is absorbed.

Begin adding the hot stock – just enough to cover the rice at first, then a ladleful at a time as the stock is absorbed. Stir well with each addition of stock. Continue cooking for 15–20 minutes, until the rice is just done but each grain is still slightly firm in the centre.

Remove from the heat. Add the parmesan, butter and parsley and stir until the risotto is creamy and the cheese has melted. Season with salt and freshly ground black pepper and serve.

Chicken and asparagus risotto
Prepare 300 g (10½ oz) asparagus by snapping off the woody ends and cutting the spears into 3 cm (1¼ in) pieces. Blanch in boiling water for 2–3 minutes, then refresh under cold running water. Add for the last 2–3 minutes of cooking.

Chicken and mushroom risotto
Add 150 g (5½ oz) sliced mushrooms along with the chicken.

Pea risotto

A simple basic risotto that I eat with roast chicken, grilled lamb or pan-fried fish. You can swap the peas for asparagus or double-podded broad beans, or even use all three together. Serves 4–6

2 tablespoons olive oil

1 onion, diced

1 garlic clove, crushed

1 leek, white part only, thinly sliced (optional)

1 carrot, finely diced (optional)

300 g (10½ oz) arborio rice

125 ml (4 fl oz/½ cup) white wine

750 ml–1 litre (25½–34 fl oz/3–4 cups) hot vegetable or chicken stock

155 g (5½ oz/1 cup) frozen peas

40 g (1½ oz/½ cup) grated parmesan

50 g (1¾ oz) butter, diced

2 tablespoons chopped flat-leaf (Italian) parsley

Heat a large heavy-based saucepan over medium heat. Add the oil, onion, garlic, and leek and carrot (if using), and cook for 3–4 minutes, until fragrant and soft. Add the rice and stir to coat with oil, then cook briefly. Add the wine and stir until it is absorbed.

Begin adding the hot stock – just enough to cover the rice at first, then a ladleful at a time as the stock is absorbed. Stir well with each addition of stock. Continue cooking for 15–20 minutes, until the rice is just done but each grain is still slightly firm in the centre. Add the peas for the last 2–3 minutes of cooking.

Remove from the heat. Add the parmesan, butter and parsley and stir until the risotto is creamy and the cheese has melted. Season with salt and freshly ground black pepper and serve.

Roast pumpkin, pine nut and feta risotto

Roast pumpkin and feta is a classic combination. Pine nuts add a touch of luxury, but you could also add toasted almonds and even swap feta for blue cheese if you're a fan. Serves 4–6

200 g (7 oz) pumpkin (squash), cut into 2 cm (¾ in) dice

Oil for cooking

1 onion, diced

1 garlic clove, crushed

1 leek, white part only, thinly sliced (optional)

1 carrot, finely diced (optional)

300 g (10½ oz) arborio rice

125 ml (4 fl oz/½ cup) white wine

750 ml–1 litre (25½–34 fl oz/3–4 cups) hot vegetable or chicken stock

50 g (1¾ oz/⅓ cup) toasted pine nuts

90 g (3 oz) baby English spinach or sliced English spinach leaves (optional)

25 g (1 oz/¼ cup) grated parmesan

60 g (2 oz) feta, crumbled

40 g (1½ oz) butter

2 tablespoons chopped flat-leaf (Italian) parsley

Preheat the oven to 180°C (350°F).

In a baking tin, drizzle the pumpkin with oil and season with salt and freshly ground black pepper. Roast the pumpkin in the oven for 15–20 minutes, or until tender and golden. Set aside.

Heat a large heavy-based saucepan over medium heat. Add 2 tablespoons oil, the onion, garlic, and leek and carrot (if using), and cook for 3–4 minutes until fragrant and soft. Add the rice and stir to coat with the oil, then cook briefly. Add the wine and stir until it is absorbed.

Begin adding the hot stock – just enough to cover the rice at first, then a ladleful at a time as the stock is absorbed. Stir well with each addition of stock. Continue cooking for 15–20 minutes, until the rice is just done. Add the pumpkin, pine nuts and spinach (if using) and stir through, then cook for 2–3 minutes.

Remove from the heat. Add the cheeses, butter and parsley and stir until the risotto is creamy and the cheese has melted. Check the seasoning and serve.

Mushroom risotto

Being fairly rich, this risotto lends itself to small portions. I typically have it alongside things like roast chicken, pot-roasted veal or pan-fried steaks. It is delicious with Chicken saltimbocca (page 128). Served on its own it would make a beautiful appetiser. Serves 4–6

2 tablespoons olive oil

1 onion, diced

1 garlic clove, crushed

1 leek, white part only, thinly sliced (optional)

1 carrot, finely diced (optional)

250 g (9 oz) Swiss brown mushrooms, sliced

500 g (1 lb 2 oz) arborio rice

250 ml (8½ fl oz/1 cup) white wine

1–1.25 litres (34–42 fl oz/4–5 cups) hot vegetable stock

75 g (2¾ oz/¾ cup) grated parmesan

90 g (3 oz) butter, diced

2 tablespoons chopped flat-leaf (Italian) parsley

2–3 teaspoons truffle oil (optional)

Heat a large heavy-based saucepan over medium heat. Add the oil, onion, garlic, and leek and carrot (if using), and cook for 3–4 minutes until fragrant and soft. Add the mushrooms and cook for 3–4 minutes, or until soft. Add the rice and stir to coat with oil, then cook briefly. Add the wine and stir until it is absorbed.

Begin adding the hot stock — at first just enough to cover the rice, then a ladleful at a time as the stock is absorbed. Stir well with each addition. Continue cooking until the rice is just done, about 15–20 minutes.

Remove from the heat. Add the parmesan, butter, parsley and truffle oil (if using), and stir until the risotto is creamy and the cheese has melted. Season with salt and freshly ground black pepper and serve.

Porcini and truffle oil risotto
Use only half of the mushrooms. Soak 10 g (¼ oz) dried porcini mushrooms in 90 ml (3 fl oz) boiling water. Add this soaking liquid to the risotto, reducing the stock by the same amount, and combine the porcini mushrooms with the other mushrooms.

Sweet potato, pancetta and pea risotto

Sweet vegetables and salty pancetta is another of my favourite flavour combinations. Ask your local deli to cut you a thick slice of pancetta, or substitute bacon or prosciutto. Serves 4–6

1 large sweet potato, peeled, halved and cut into
   5 mm (¼ in) slices
Oil for cooking
100 g (3½ oz) pancetta, diced
1 onion, diced
1 garlic clove, crushed
1 leek, white part only, thinly sliced (optional)
1 carrot, finely diced (optional)
495 g (1 lb 2 oz/2¼ cups) arborio rice
250 ml (8½ fl oz/1 cup) white wine
1–1.25 litres (34–42 fl oz/4–5 cups) hot vegetable or
   chicken stock
155 g (5½ oz/1 cup) peas
100 g (3½ oz/1 cup) grated parmesan
90 g (3 oz) butter, diced
2 tablespoons chopped flat-leaf (Italian) parsley

Preheat the oven to 180°C (350°F).

Drizzle the sweet potato with oil and season with salt and freshly ground black pepper. Roast in the oven for 15–20 minutes, or until the sweet potato is tender and golden. Set aside.

Heat a large heavy-based saucepan over medium heat. Add a splash of oil and the pancetta and cook for 5–6 minutes until crispy. Remove the pancetta from the heat and set aside.

Wipe the pan clean of any fat and return to the heat. Add 2 tablespoons oil, the onion, garlic, and leek and carrot (if using), and cook for 3–4 minutes until fragrant and soft. Add the rice and stir to coat with the oil, then cook briefly. Add the wine and stir until it is absorbed.

Begin adding the hot stock – just enough to cover the rice at first, then a ladleful at a time as the stock is absorbed. Stir well with each addition. Continue cooking for 15–20 minutes, until the rice is just done but each grain is still slightly firm in the centre. Add the pancetta, sweet potato and peas for the last 5 minutes of cooking.

Remove from the heat. Add the parmesan, butter and parsley and stir until the risotto is creamy and the cheese has melted. Check the seasoning and serve.

Prawn and lemon risotto

I'm not a big fan of seafood with risotto. I would much rather eat a simple risotto, such as the pea one on page 103, and place some pan-fried fish on top. Every now and again, though, I succumb to a prawn risotto, but one in which the prawn is a back-up ingredient and not the main star. Serves 4-6

2 tablespoons olive oil

1 onion, diced

1 garlic clove, crushed

1 leek, white part only, thinly sliced (optional)

1 carrot, finely diced (optional)

300 g (10½ oz) arborio rice

125 ml (4 fl oz/½ cup) white wine

750 ml–1 litre (25½–34 fl oz/3–4 cups) hot vegetable or chicken stock

155 g (5½ oz/1 cup) peas (optional)

500 g (1 lb 2 oz) green (raw) prawns (shrimp), peeled and deveined

50 g (1¾ oz) baby English spinach leaves (optional)

Grated zest and juice of 1 lemon

35 g (1¼ oz/⅓ cup) grated parmesan

50 g (1¾ oz) butter, diced

2 tablespoons chopped flat-leaf (Italian) parsley

Heat a large heavy-based saucepan over medium heat. Add the oil, onion, garlic, and leek and carrot (if using), and cook for 3-4 minutes until fragrant and soft. Add the rice and stir to coat with oil, then cook briefly. Add the wine and stir until it is absorbed.

Begin adding the hot stock – just enough to cover the rice at first, then a ladleful at a time as the stock is absorbed. Stir well with each addition. Continue cooking for 15-20 minutes, until the rice is just done but each grain is still slightly firm in the centre. Add the peas (if using) for the last 5 minutes of cooking.

When the risotto is almost ready, add the prawns and cook for 2 minutes. Add the spinach and cook for a further 2 minutes. Stir through the lemon zest and juice.

Remove from the heat. Add the parmesan, butter and parsley and stir until the risotto is creamy and the cheese has melted. Season with salt and freshly ground black pepper and serve.

Risotto of roast duck, oyster mushrooms and star anise

This risotto sounds like a weird mix of Chinese flavours with Italian techniques, but believe me, if you like roast duck you'll love this dish. It was created when our book *Chilli Jam* came out in 1997 and I think it's a great example of what can be achieved by carefully combining ingredients and cooking methods. Serves 4–6

½ Chinese roast duck, including bones and juices

2 star anise

3 cm (1¼ in) piece fresh ginger, thinly sliced

12 Asian shallots, peeled and quartered

2 tablespoons olive oil

150 g (5½ oz) oyster mushrooms, halved (or quartered if large)

295 g (10½ oz/1⅓ cups) arborio rice

Remove the meat from the duck and slice it thinly, discarding the fat as you go. Set the duck meat aside.

Place the duck bones, duck juices, 1 litre (34 fl oz/ 4 cups) water, star anise and ginger in a large saucepan and bring to the boil. Reduce the heat and simmer for 20 minutes, removing any scum that comes to the surface. Strain the stock into a saucepan and discard the bones. You will need 1.2 litres (41 fl oz) of stock. Add water or chicken stock to make up this amount if required. Reheat the stock to a simmer.

Heat a heavy-based pan over medium heat and add the shallots and 125 ml (4 fl oz/½ cup) of the stock. Cover and cook for 10 minutes. Set aside the shallots and any cooking juices.

Wipe the pan dry and reheat over medium–high heat. Add the oil, then the mushrooms and stir for 3–4 minutes or until the mushrooms begin to wilt. Add the rice and cook for 1 minute, stirring occasionally. Begin adding the hot stock — at first just enough to cover the rice, then a ladleful at a time as the stock is absorbed. Stir well with each addition. Continue cooking until the rice is just done, about 15–20 minutes. Stir in the duck and shallots. Season with salt and freshly ground black pepper and serve.

One-pot curried chicken and rice

This has to be one of my greatest inventions. Chicken curry in a pot and no need to cook the rice separately. Serves 4

Oil for cooking

1 onion, diced

½ tablespoon grated fresh ginger

1 small red chilli, seeded and diced

500 g (1 lb 2 oz) boneless skinless chicken thighs, diced

1 tablespoon curry paste – Indian korma paste (page 464) or Tikka paste (page 466)

155 g (5½ oz/½ cup) cashew nuts

250 g (9 oz/1¼ cups) jasmine rice

375 ml (12½ fl oz/1½ cups) chicken stock

100 g (3½ oz/2 cups) baby English spinach leaves

Heat a large heavy-based saucepan over medium–high heat. Add a splash of oil, the onion, ginger and chilli and cook for 3–4 minutes, stirring often until fragrant. Add the chicken and cook until golden brown all over. Add the curry paste and cashew nuts and cook for 1–2 minutes until fragrant. Add the rice and cook, stirring for 1–2 minutes. Add the stock, season with salt and freshly ground black pepper and bring to the boil. Reduce to a simmer, cover with a lid and cook for 25 minutes – do not stir.

Remove from the heat and stand for 5 minutes. Stir through the spinach leaves, and serve.

Paella

Paella is made with short-grain rice, or you can buy special paella (calasparra) rice at most top-quality food stores. A special paella pan makes light work of keeping all the ingredients together. Serves 4

2 tablespoons olive oil

2 onions, diced

6–8 small garlic cloves

Pinch of saffron threads

1 teaspoon smoked paprika

400 g (14 oz) paella (calasparra) rice

1 litre (34 fl oz/4 cups) chicken stock

90 g (3 oz/¾ cup) pitted olives

500 g (1 lb 2 oz) chicken drumettes or winglets, roasted until golden

1 red capsicum (bell pepper), roasted, peeled, seeded and cut into long strips

500 g (1 lb 2 oz) green (raw) prawns (shrimp), peeled and deveined

500 g (1 lb 2 oz) mussels, debearded

2 tablespoons chopped flat-leaf (Italian) parsley to serve

Place a large heavy-based frying pan over medium heat. Heat the oil, add the onion, garlic and saffron and cook for 4–5 minutes, stirring often. Add the paprika, cook for 1–2 minutes, then add the rice and cook briefly for 2–3 minutes, stirring often. Add most of the stock and allow to come to the boil, stirring often.

Add the olives, roasted chicken and capsicum. Reduce the heat and allow to cook for 15 minutes. The trick now is not to stir the paella so a crispy base will form on the bottom. Make sure all the ingredients are tucked down in the rice so everything cooks evenly – if necessary you can cover the top with foil to keep the steam in and cook everything on top. You may need to add more stock.

Check that the rice is nearly cooked, then add the prawns and mussels and cook until the mussels open (discard any that do not) and the prawns turn pink. Serve immediately with the chopped parsley.

Sticky chicken with cucumber–ginger pickle

The addition of sugar makes this dish delightfully sticky, but also sweet. The contrast of the cucumber–ginger pickle contrasts beautifully and adds a great crunch. Serves 4

2 boneless skinless chicken breasts

60 ml (2 fl oz/¼ cup) soy sauce

60 ml (2 fl oz/¼ cup) Chinese cooking wine

2 teaspoons sesame oil

2 teaspoons caster (superfine) sugar

2 tablespoons grated fresh ginger

1 cucumber, peeled, seeded and sliced

2 tablespoons Pickled ginger (page 439), thinly sliced

2 tablespoons rice vinegar

1 teaspoon black sesame seeds

Oil for cooking

125 ml (4 fl oz/½ cup) chicken stock

Steamed rice (page 480) to serve

Cut the chicken into thin strips. Mix together the soy sauce, wine, sesame oil, sugar and ginger. Pour over the chicken and marinate for 10 minutes.

While the chicken is marinating, make the cucumber–ginger pickle by mixing together the sliced cucumber, pickled ginger, rice vinegar and sesame seeds. Toss to combine and set aside until ready to serve.

Drain the chicken, but reserve the marinade.

Heat a wok until hot, add a splash of oil and the chicken and stir-fry for 2–3 minutes, until browned. Add the stock and 1–2 tablespoons of the reserved marinade. Cook for a further 3–4 minutes, stirring often.

Serve the chicken on top of the steamed rice with the cucumber–ginger pickle.

Spring Spanish rice with chicken, peas and lemon

This dish is inspired by the wonderful tapas restaurant MoVida in Melbourne. It is basically a paella using chicken, and is livened up with fiery harissa, the crunch of new-season peas and the zest of lemons. A one-pot meal, all it needs is a green salad. Serves 4–6

2 red capsicums (bell peppers)

Olive oil

600 g (1 lb 5 oz) boneless skinless chicken thighs, cut into 2 cm (¾ in) dice

2 garlic cloves, chopped

Grated zest of 1 lemon

2 teaspoons Harissa (page 467)

2 teaspoons smoky paprika

2 red onions, chopped

Pinch of saffron threads

500 g (1 lb 2 oz) paella (calasparra) rice

125 ml (4 fl oz/½ cup) white wine

750 ml (25½ fl oz/3 cups) chicken stock

155 g (5½ oz/1 cup) peas

7 g (¼ oz/¼ cup) chopped flat-leaf (Italian) parsley

2 tablespoons lemon-infused olive oil

Preheat the oven to 180°C (350°F).

Rub the capsicums with oil. Place them on a baking tray and roast for 30 minutes, or until their skins blister. Allow to cool, then remove the skin and seeds. Cut the flesh into 1 cm (½ in) strips.

Meanwhile, place the chicken in a bowl with the garlic, lemon zest, harissa, smoky paprika and 60 ml (2 fl oz/¼ cup) olive oil. Season with salt and freshly ground black pepper. Marinate for at least 20 minutes.

Heat a paella pan or large frying pan over medium heat. Add the chicken and fry for 6–8 minutes, stirring often, until golden brown. Remove the chicken from the pan and set aside.

Return the pan to the heat, add a splash more oil if needed and fry the onion for 4–5 minutes. Add the saffron and cook for 1–2 minutes until fragrant. Add the rice and cook for 2–3 minutes, stirring often, until lightly toasted. Add the wine, stirring well, and cook until it has reduced slightly, then add the stock.

Bring to the boil, return the chicken to the pan, reduce the heat to a simmer and cook for 15–20 minutes, stirring often, until almost all the stock has been absorbed by the rice. Add the peas and capsicum and cook for another 3–4 minutes.

Stir well for the last 2–3 minutes, ensuring the peas cook through and the remaining stock is absorbed. Add more stock or water if necessary. Taste for seasoning and add the parsley and lemon-infused olive oil. Stir through and serve.

Hoisin chicken, broccolini and egg fried rice

You can use left-over rice in this dish. I like to reheat it in the microwave before adding it to the stir-fry to ensure it's hot or, better still, cook fresh rice and tip it in while it's still hot. Serves 3–4

Oil for cooking

2 eggs, lightly beaten

2 garlic cloves, crushed

1 small red chilli, seeded and finely diced

1 teaspoon grated fresh ginger

2 boneless skinless chicken breasts, thinly sliced

4 spring onions (scallions), thinly sliced

200 g (7 oz) snow peas (mangetout)

1 bunch broccolini, trimmed and sliced

Chicken stock or water as needed

3 tablespoons soy sauce

100 g (3½ oz/⅔ cup) frozen peas

200 g (7 oz) hot cooked long-grain rice

90 g (3 oz/1 cup) bean sprouts

2 tablespoons hoisin sauce

Heat a wok over high heat. Add a splash of oil, then the lightly beaten eggs. Swirl well to coat the side of the wok with the egg mix. Cook briefly, then lift one edge away from the wok and roll up the omelette. Tip onto a chopping board and allow to cool.

Return the wok to the heat and add another splash of oil and the garlic, chilli and ginger. Cook for 1–2 minutes, stirring often to avoid burning, until fragrant. Add the sliced chicken and cook for a further 2–3 minutes, until browned. Remove, cover to keep hot and set aside.

Return the wok to the heat, add more oil if necessary and add the spring onion. Cook for 2–3 minutes, stirring often. Add the snow peas and broccolini. Add a splash of stock or water, cover with a lid and cook for 2 minutes. Add 1 tablespoon of the soy sauce, the peas and then the rice, breaking it up if necessary. Continue cooking and stirring constantly, until the rice is coloured by the sauce and heated through.

Slice the omelette and add it to the rice along with the chicken and bean sprouts, and cook until heated through. Add the hoisin sauce and the remaining soy sauce to taste, and serve.

Stir-fried rice with tofu, egg and broccolini

I cook this as my dinner treat when it's just me at home. I usually cook the rice first and add it while it's still hot. However, if I have left-over rice, I zap it in the microwave before adding it to the wok. This makes enough for me for dinner and leftovers for lunch the next day. Serves 1–2

Oil for cooking

2 eggs, lightly beaten

4 spring onions (scallions), thinly sliced

1 tablespoon grated fresh ginger

2 small carrots, peeled and finely diced

1 bunch broccolini, cut into 2 cm (¾ in) lengths

60 ml (2 fl oz/¼ cup) chicken or vegetable stock or Chinese cooking wine

200 g (7 oz) hot cooked long-grain rice

220 g (8 oz) tofu, cut into 2 cm (¾ in) dice

155 g (5½ oz/1 cup) frozen peas

2 tablespoons soy sauce

Heat a wok over high heat. Add a splash of oil, then the lightly beaten eggs. Swirl well to coat the side of the wok with the egg mixture. Cook briefly, then lift one edge away from the wok and roll up the omelette. Tip onto a chopping board and allow to cool.

Return the wok to the heat and add another splash of the oil, along with the spring onion and ginger. Cook for 2–3 minutes, stirring often. Add the carrot and broccolini and cook for 1–2 minutes until softened. Add the stock, cover with a lid and cook for 2–3 minutes. Add the hot rice, tofu and peas and cook for 2–3 minutes, stirring often. Check everything is hot, add the soy sauce and sliced egg omelette and serve.

Sushi bowl

This is great for using left-over rice. You can more or less add any vegetables you like or add some chicken, beef or omelette instead of tofu. I like to use the Chinese-flavoured tofu you can buy in the supermarket. It has loads of flavour. Just chop it up and away you go. Serves 2

Grated zest of ½ orange

1 tablespoon orange juice

1 tablespoon brown rice vinegar

1 tablespoon tamari or shoyu

185 g (6½ oz/1 cup) hot cooked brown rice

300 g (10½ oz) tofu

1 carrot, julienned or grated

Handful of bean sprouts

1 small cucumber, julienned

½ avocado, sliced

Pickled ginger (page 439)

½ sheet toasted nori, shredded

1 teaspoon toasted sesame seeds

Coriander (cilantro) leaves to garnish

Mix together the orange zest, juice, vinegar and tamari. Season with freshly ground black pepper.

Divide the rice between two bowls. Arrange the tofu, vegetables and pickled ginger on top in individual mounds. Place the shredded nori in the middle of the bowl, sprinkle sesame seeds over the top and scatter with the coriander leaves.

Beef and green bean donburi

Although donburi is good with brown rice, too, not everyone in my family likes brown rice. I often cook both so everyone's happy. Best mother in the world! The poached eggs are an optional extra – some say that donburi is not complete without an egg. Serves 4

Oil for cooking

400 g (14 oz) scotch fillet (rib eye), thinly sliced

1 onion, sliced

250 ml (8½ fl oz/1 cup) dashi

60 ml (2 fl oz/¼ cup) soy sauce

90 ml (3 fl oz) mirin

200 g (7 oz) green beans or asparagus, cut into
  5 cm (2 in) lengths

740 g (1 lb 10 oz) hot cooked rice, white or brown

Pickled ginger (page 439) or pickles to serve

1 toasted nori sheet, shredded

Togarashi (page 469) (optional)

Eggs, poached (optional)

Preheat the oven to 180°C (350°F).

Heat a heavy-based ovenproof frying pan over high heat. Add a splash of oil and cook the scotch fillet until browned all over. Place the beef in the preheated oven for 15–20 minutes, or until cooked medium–rare. Allow to cool and reserve the pan juices. Slice the meat into thick strips, discarding the fat and gristle.

Make your broth by combining the onion, dashi, soy and mirin in a small saucepan. Bring to the boil over medium heat, reduce to a simmer and cook for 10 minutes.

When the beef is resting, add the beans to the simmering dashi and allow to cook for 2 minutes.

Divide the hot rice, the sliced steak and the broth with onions and beans between the bowls. You can add pickled ginger, nori and togarashi to each bowl, or serve them on the side and allow everyone to help themselves. Serve with poached eggs, if desired.

Noodles

Pad Thai (Thai rice noodles)

What I really like about this dish is that I generally have most of these ingredients on hand, so it's become a cupboard-dinner stand-by. Serves 2–3

100 g (3½ oz) thin rice-stick noodles

Oil for cooking

3 spring onions (scallions), thinly sliced

1 garlic clove, crushed

2 small red chillies, seeded and finely diced, or 2 teaspoons chilli sauce

2 eggs, lightly beaten

2 tablespoons fish sauce

1 tablespoon shaved palm sugar (jaggery)

120 g (4 oz/1⅓ cups) bean sprouts

60 g (2 oz) roasted peanuts

Fresh coriander (cilantro) leaves to serve

Lime wedges to serve

Put a kettle on to boil. Pour boiling water over the noodles and set aside.

Place a wok over high heat. Add a splash of oil, the spring onion, garlic and chilli and cook for 1–2 minutes, stirring often to avoid burning, until fragrant. Push the vegetables to one side and add the eggs to the wok. Allow the eggs to just set, then scramble them by stirring well.

Drain the noodles and add them to the wok along with the fish sauce, palm sugar, bean sprouts and peanuts. Stir constantly until heated through, about 3–4 minutes. Serve with the coriander leaves and lime wedges.

Sesame and ginger beef fillet with coriander noodles

If you can marinate the beef fillet for 30 minutes it will increase the flavour, but don't worry about it if you don't have time. Serves 4

60 ml (2 fl oz/¼ cup) soy sauce

2 tablespoons honey

1 tablespoon sesame oil

1 tablespoon grated fresh ginger

Oil for cooking

400 g (14 oz) beef eye fillet (tenderloin)

375 g (13 oz) fresh egg noodles

2 spring onions (scallions), thinly sliced

7 g (¼ oz/¼ cup) coriander (cilantro) leaves

1 teaspoon toasted sesame seeds

Whisk together the soy sauce, honey, sesame oil, ginger and oil. Pour half over the beef fillet. Set the remaining half aside.

Preheat the oven to 180°C (350°F). Heat a heavy-based ovenproof frying pan over medium–high heat. Add a splash of oil and the beef and cook for 2–3 minutes on each side until browned. Transfer the beef to the oven and cook until medium–rare. Remove and rest for 10 minutes.

Cook the noodles in boiling water for 3–4 minutes, or until al dente. Drain. Mix the noodles with the reserved marinade, spring onion, coriander and sesame seeds. Slice the beef and serve it on top of the noodles.

Stir-fried sesame chicken with noodles

I love sesame and you can make this dish with any type of noodles that takes your fancy.
Serves 2–3

180 g (6½ oz) soba noodles

Oil for cooking

1 teaspoon grated fresh ginger

1 small red chilli, seeded and diced

1 teaspoon sesame oil

1 boneless skinless chicken breast, cut into thin strips

1 bunch broccolini, cut into 2 cm (¾ in) lengths

4 mushrooms, sliced

100 g (3½ oz) snow peas (mangetout)

½ red capsicum (bell pepper), thinly sliced

60 ml (2 fl oz/¼ cup) chicken stock or Chinese cooking wine

2 tablespoons soy sauce

1 teaspoon sesame seeds, toasted

Bring a saucepan of water to the boil. Add the noodles and cook for 3–4 minutes or until tender. Drain and keep warm until needed.

Heat a wok over high heat. Add a splash of oil, then the ginger and chilli. Cook for 1–2 minutes, stirring often to avoid burning, until fragrant. Add the sesame oil and sliced chicken and cook for a further 2–3 minutes, until browned.

Add the broccolini and mushrooms and cook for 2–3 minutes, stirring often. Add the snow peas and capsicum, then add the stock. Cover with a lid and cook for 2–3 minutes.

Add the noodles to the wok together with the soy sauce and sesame seeds and toss until combined. Serve immediately.

Chilli beef stir-fry

This is one of the quickest stir-fries around, and one of the tastiest. I like it because it's easy, spicy and great for an iron hit – not to mention the decadence of using eye fillet. All you'll need is a bowl of steamed rice or some noodles to serve with it. Add a handful of toasted cashew nuts if you like. Serves 4

400 g (14 oz) beef eye fillet (tenderloin)

1 tablespoon peanut oil

1 bunch baby bok choy (pak choy), leaves separated and washed

80 ml (2½ fl oz/⅓ cup) Sweet chilli sauce (page 437)

80 ml (2½ fl oz/⅓ cup) soy sauce

3 spring onions (scallions), thinly chopped

110 g (4 oz/⅔ cup) roasted peanuts (optional)

Steamed rice (page 480) or hot noodles to serve

Cut the beef into 1 cm (½ in) slices, and then cut each slice into 1 cm (½ in) strips.

Heat a wok over high heat. Add the oil, swirl it around the wok and add the beef. Toss and cook for 2–3 minutes, or until the beef is well browned. Add the bok choy, stir well, then add the chilli sauce, soy sauce, spring onion and peanuts (if using). Allow to heat through and serve immediately with steamed rice or hot noodles.

Chilli beef and lime stir-fry
Add two shredded kaffir lime leaves along with the bok choy.

Chilli beef and mushroom stir-fry
Add 125 g (4½ oz) quartered mushrooms at the same time as the beef.

Chilli kangaroo stir-fry
Substitute sliced kangaroo sirloin for the beef.

Zingy beef and ramen noodle salad bowl

Feel free to swap the cabbage and carrots for other vegetables, depending on your tastes and what's in the refrigerator. As with all recipes, you can vary or omit the garlic, ginger and chilli to suit your tastes. You can also add more, too! Serves 2

Oil for cooking

2 garlic cloves, crushed

2 tablespoons grated fresh ginger

2 diced small red chillies, seeded if you like

300 g (10½ oz) minced (ground) beef

150 g (5½ oz) ramen noodles

1 carrot, julienned

75 g (2¾ oz/1 cup) shredded red cabbage

2 spring onions (scallions), thinly sliced

1 tablespoon soy sauce

1 tablespoon fish sauce

2 tablespoons lime juice

1 tablespoon sesame oil

110 g (4 oz/⅔ cup) roasted peanuts

Bring a saucepan of water to the boil for the noodles.

Heat a wok over high heat and add a splash of oil and the garlic, ginger and chilli. Cook for 1 minute, stirring until fragrant. Add the beef and cook for 4–5 minutes, using a wooden spoon to break it up, allowing it to be coated with the aromatics. Cook until brown and crispy.

Cook the noodles in the boiling water for 3–4 minutes. Drain and divide between two bowls. Divide the vegetables between the bowls.

Season the beef with the soy and fish sauce, lime juice and sesame oil. Add the peanuts. Divide the beef over the noodles and vegetables, and serve.

Barbecue pork and bok choy stir-fry

Chinese barbecued pork, or char siu as it is also called, can be bought at any Asian roast house.
Serves 3–4

200 g (7 oz) cellophane noodles

1 tablespoon peanut oil

4 spring onions (scallions), thinly sliced

½ red capsicum (bell pepper), thinly sliced

250 g (9 oz) Chinese barbecued pork (char siu), thinly sliced

2 bunches bok choy (pak choy), washed and sliced

Splash of chicken stock or water

90 g (3 oz/1 cup) bean sprouts

2 tablespoons soy sauce

Crispy shallots to garnish

Put a kettle on to boil, then pour boiling water over the noodles and set aside.

Place a wok over high heat. Add the peanut oil, then the spring onion and capsicum. Cook for 1–2 minutes, stirring often. Add the barbecued pork, bok choy and a splash of stock. Cover with a lid and cook for 3–4 minutes.

Drain the noodles and add them to the wok with the bean sprouts and soy sauce. Stir until hot, top with the crispy shallots and serve.

Honey roast pork with stir-fried noodles

Whether served at a dinner-party or as an everyday meal, this pork dish is an absolute winner.
Serves 3–4

2 tablespoons soy sauce, plus extra to serve

2 tablespoons honey

½ teaspoon sesame oil

500 g (1 lb 2 oz) pork fillet

375 g (13 oz) dried rice noodles

1 bunch Chinese broccoli (gai larn)

2 tablespoons peanut oil

1 garlic clove, crushed

1 small red chilli, seeded and diced

2–3 teaspoons grated fresh ginger

4 spring onions (scallions), sliced

100 g (3½ oz/⅔ cup) roasted cashew nuts

Chicken stock or water as needed

Preheat the oven to 180°C (350°F).

Place the 2 tablespoons soy sauce, the honey and the sesame oil in a small saucepan. Cook over medium heat until reduced to a thick syrup.

Place the pork in a baking dish. Brush the honey mixture over it and cook in the oven for 15–20 minutes, by which stage it should be cooked to medium.

Put the kettle on to boil. Pour boiling water over the noodles and set them aside.

Wash the Chinese broccoli well. Remove the tough outer leaves and slice the stems and leaves on an angle into 2 cm (¾ in) slices.

Place a wok over high heat. Add the peanut oil, garlic, chilli, ginger and spring onion. Cook for 1–2 minutes, stirring often to avoid burning, until fragrant. Add the sliced Chinese broccoli and cashew nuts. Cook briefly, then add a splash of stock or water. Cover with a lid and cook for 2 minutes.

Drain the noodles and add them to the wok, along with more stock or water if the stir-fry is looking a little dry. Cook, tossing constantly, for 2–3 minutes, until well combined. Season with extra soy sauce to taste.

Slice the roast pork. Place the stir-fried noodles on a serving platter and arrange the pork over the top. Serve immediately.

Soy ginger salmon with green vegetables and noodles

The nori sprinkle in this recipe will keep in an airtight container for a while, so feel free to add it to other dishes as the fancy takes you. Serves 2

2 teaspoons grated fresh ginger

1 small red chilli, seeded and diced

60 ml (2 fl oz/¼ cup) soy sauce

4 × 200 g (7 oz) salmon fillets

1 teaspoon sesame seeds, toasted

½ teaspoon dried chilli flakes

1 nori sheet, toasted and torn into pieces

Oil for cooking

1 head of broccoli, cut into florets

100 g (3½ oz) sugar snap or snow peas (mangetout)

200 g (7 oz) asparagus or green beans, cut into 3 cm (1¼ in) lengths

200 g (7 oz) brown rice noodles

Combine the ginger, chilli and soy sauce and pour the mixture over the salmon fillets. Marinate for up to 30 minutes, if time permits. Set aside.

Place the sesame seeds, chilli flakes and nori in the food processor and blitz to form a crumb or sprinkle. Set aside.

Preheat the oven to 180°C (350°F).

Bring a saucepan of water to the boil.

Heat a heavy-based frying pan over high heat. Drain the excess marinade from the salmon fillets. Add a generous splash of oil and cook the salmon fillets for 3–4 minutes on each side, until golden brown and medium–rare. Cook for 1–2 minutes longer if you prefer your salmon cooked to medium. When ready, place the salmon fillets in the hot oven to keep warm while you cook the greens.

While the salmon is cooking, blanch all the green vegetables for 2–3 minutes until just cooked. Remove and keep warm. Add the noodles to the water and cook for 1–2 minutes. Drain and keep warm.

Divide the noodles between two bowls and then add the vegetables. Top with a piece of salmon and sprinkle over the nori mix.

Tofu and ginger stir-fry

Cleansing and refreshing, this dish always makes me feel better, especially if I've been over-indulging. It must be something to do with that ginger, so add as much as you like or need.
Serves 2

Oil for cooking

3 spring onions (scallions), sliced

1 small red chilli, seeded and finely diced

2–3 teaspoons grated fresh ginger

1 bunch Chinese broccoli (gai larn), chopped

Stock or water as needed

100 g (3½ oz) snow peas (mangetout)

300 g (10½ oz) tofu, cut into 1 cm (½ in) dice

60 g (2 oz/⅔ cup) bean sprouts

Soy sauce to season

Steamed rice (page 480) or noodles to serve

Heat a wok over high heat. Add a splash of oil and the spring onion, chilli and ginger and cook for 1–2 minutes, stirring, until fragrant. Add the broccoli, stir briefly, then add a splash of stock or water. Cover with a lid and steam for 2–3 minutes.

Remove the lid, add the snow peas, plus more stock or water if required. Cover and steam for 1 minute. Add the tofu and bean sprouts, cover and steam for a further 2 minutes. Toss to combine the ingredients, but do so carefully so as not to break up the tofu. Season with soy sauce. Serve immediately with steamed rice or noodles.

Stir-fried rice noodles with prawns and snow peas

In this recipe, a classic combination of rice noodles, garlic, ginger and chilli is tossed with fresh prawns and tender snow peas to make a special meal. Serves 2–3

100 g (3½ oz) dried rice-stick noodles

2–3 tablespoons peanut oil

3 spring onions (scallions), sliced

1 garlic clove, crushed

2 teaspoons grated fresh ginger

2 small red chillies, seeded and diced

250 g (9 oz) green (raw) prawns (shrimp), peeled and deveined

100 g (3½ oz) snow peas (mangetout)

1 tablespoon fish sauce

2 tablespoons soy sauce

500 g (1 lb 2 oz/5½ cups) bean sprouts

1 lime, cut into wedges, to serve

Put a kettle on to boil. Pour boiling water over the noodles and set them aside.

Place a wok over high heat. Add the oil, spring onion, garlic, ginger and chillies. Cook for 1 minute, stirring often to avoid burning. Add the prawns and cook for 1 minute, then add the snow peas plus a small ladleful of water. Cover and cook for 2 minutes.

Drain the noodles and add them to the wok with the fish sauce and soy sauce. Stir for 3–4 minutes, until heated through. Add the bean sprouts and serve immediately with the lime wedges.

Chinese stir-fried vegetables with noodles

There are times when it's vegetables and noodles that you crave, and meat or seafood doesn't enter into the picture. This is just the thing to satisfy that need. Serves 3–4

375 g (13 oz) hokkien noodles

Oil for cooking

1 garlic clove, crushed

1 teaspoon grated fresh ginger

1 small red chilli, seeded and finely diced

4 spring onions (scallions), thinly sliced

½ capsicum (bell pepper), finely diced

1 carrot, peeled and thinly sliced

4 broccoli florets, chopped

90 g (3 oz) sugar snap peas

Stock or water as needed

1 bunch Chinese broccoli, (gai larn) cut into 5 cm (2 in) chunks

2–3 tablespoons soy sauce

Coriander (cilantro) leaves to garnish

Put a kettle on to boil. Pour boiling water over the noodles and set aside.

Place a wok over high heat, add a splash of oil and the garlic, ginger, chilli and spring onion. Cook briefly, stirring frequently, until fragrant. Add the capsicum, carrot, broccoli and sugar snap peas and add a splash of stock or water. Cover the wok with a lid and cook for 2–3 minutes, stirring once or twice. Add the Chinese broccoli and more stock or water if necessary. Cover and cook for a further 1–2 minutes.

Drain the noodles and add them to the wok. Stir, adding soy sauce to taste. Serve immediately with the coriander leaves scattered on top.

Stir-fried vegetables and egg with noodles
Make an omelette using two eggs, as in Hoisin chicken, broccolini and egg fried rice (page 110). Add with the Chinese broccoli.

Stir-fried vegetables with tofu and noodles
Add 300 g (10½ oz) firm, diced tofu with the Chinese broccoli.

Chilli stir-fried vegetables with noodles
Add an extra finely diced chilli and a dash of Sweet chilli sauce (page 437) to taste.

Light soy sauce

Light soy sauce is not some dietary special, but the first pressing of soy beans. It has a superior flavour, much like extra-virgin olive oil does, and is mostly used as a seasoning because it is saltier, a lighter colour and adds a distinct flavour.

Dark soy sauce is aged longer and is slightly thicker and darker. It is usually used in longer, slower methods of cooking because its flavour develops.

TIP

Teriyaki chicken

A classic, but also a quick and easy stir-fry. Serves 3–4

2 boneless skinless chicken breasts, sliced into strips

80 ml (2½ fl oz/⅓ cup) soy sauce

2 tablespoons mirin

2 teaspoons grated fresh ginger

1 teaspoon sesame oil

1 teaspoon caster (superfine) sugar

1 garlic clove, crushed

375 g (13 oz) udon noodles

Oil for cooking

1 onion, sliced

1 carrot, sliced

1 small bunch baby bok choy (pak choy), washed

2 spring onions (scallions), green tops only, thinly sliced

Place the chicken in a bowl, then add the soy sauce, mirin, ginger, sesame oil, caster sugar and garlic. Leave to marinate in the refrigerator for 1 hour. Drain the chicken well and reserve the marinade.

Put a saucepan of water on to boil for the noodles.

Place a wok over high heat, add a splash of oil and seal the chicken until golden brown – you will need to do this in two batches.

Wipe the wok clean and return it to the heat. Add a splash of oil and cook the onion for 1–2 minutes until soft. Add the carrot and the sealed chicken and cook for 2–3 minutes, stirring often. Add the marinade and bok choy, cover the wok and allow to simmer for 5 minutes.

Cook the udon noodles in boiling water for 2–3 minutes, until tender. Drain well, then add them to the wok, tossing them briefly with the chicken. Scatter with the spring onion and serve immediately.

Teriyaki beef
Substitute 500 g (1 lb 2 oz) beef fillet for the chicken.

Spicy sichuan noodles

This is a traditional Asian dish that is often called 'Chinese spaghetti bolognese'. It does, in fact, look like bolognese and it's served on noodles, but it cooks in a fraction of the time and has the flavours of ginger, chilli and soy sauce. Serves 3–4

375 g (13 oz) hokkien noodles

1–2 tablespoons peanut oil

2 cloves garlic, crushed

2 teaspoons grated fresh ginger

2 small red chillies, seeded and finely diced

4 red Asian or French shallots, peeled and diced

500 g (1 lb 2 oz) minced (ground) meat – traditionally pork but could be chicken or beef

2 tablespoons Chinese rice wine

2 tablespoons soy sauce

125 ml (4 fl oz/½ cup) chicken stock

1 teaspoon sichuan peppercorns, roasted and ground

Put a kettle on to boil. Pour boiling water over the noodles and set aside.

Heat a wok until hot. Add the oil, garlic, ginger, chillies and shallots and cook until fragrant. Add the pork and cook, stirring often, until the colour changes. Add the Chinese rice wine, soy sauce and enough chicken stock to just cover. Stir until well combined, then simmer for 5–6 minutes, lowering the heat if necessary.

Check the seasoning of the pork and add salt and freshly ground black pepper if needed. Drain the noodles and serve immediately with the sauce on top. Sprinkle with the sichuan pepper and serve.

30-minute dinners

Whether cooking for one or for ten, the hardest question you face every day is: what's for dinner? What's ideal is something that's quick and easy, that can be made from ingredients to hand and that everybody is going to enjoy – not to mention something that results in minimal washing up.

Weeknight saviours

Some families follow a strict order of meals for dinner each week. Monday is tuna mornay, Tuesday spaghetti bolognese, and so on. I find this hard to imagine as I generally decide what I'm going to eat for dinner based on the contents of the refrigerator at 5.30 pm each day. But if you can get organised, preparing a menu at the beginning of each week is a lifesaver come 5.30 pm when the cry goes up.

Hopefully this chapter will give you some new ideas. Most recipes can be prepared in under 30 minutes and the dishes are fairly straightforward, though I have included a bit of variety for the more adventurous palate. Stir-fries, pasta and noodles are all ideal quick dinners, too, so don't forget to look at the Bowl food chapter (see page 77) when dinnertime comes around.

Most of the meals cooked in our house start on the stove. The frying pan is everyone's answer to a quick and easy meal; whether it's a simple pan-fried chicken breast or a more involved burger recipe, steak and sauce or a classic vegetarian meal.

You can pan-fry with any type of oil you have handy. I prefer extra-virgin olive oil as it's a pure oil that hasn't been processed. It has a reasonably high burn temperature so the oil won't break down, and it will add some colour to meat but won't let it burn.

The secret to cooking on the stove is a good-quality heavy-based frying pan, such as a Le Creuset – this is what I use all the time. You need to use one of these pans to retain the heat when you start adding your meat. (I also have a smaller pan, which is great for two chicken breasts or two steaks.) Never overcrowd a frying pan or it will lose its heat and you run the risk of stewing the meat instead of achieving the nice caramelisation of the natural sugars in the meat that you want.

One of the tricks to pan-frying is getting the heat just right. Put the pan on a gas burner (or electric pad) that suits the size of the pan – you don't want flames or heat coming up the side of the pan. You shouldn't have to have the power going full bore – three-quarters strength should be enough. Allow the pan to heat up properly before adding any food.

Sometimes if I'm cooking larger items, I get them going in the pan by increasing the heat a bit. I get the meat or fish in there and get some colour on both sides and then transfer them to a hot tray in a hot oven to continue cooking while I get the next lot going in the pan.

Things you need to know
about 30-minute dinners

- A chargrill pan is also fantastic for cooking meats, as the flesh cooks on the hot metal ridges, while most of the oil drains away.

- Just how much oil you fry with depends largely on what you are cooking. Crumbed food will soak up a lot of oil, as does some meat, though generally 1–2 tablespoons will do it.

- When I am feeling indulgent, I cook with a splash of oil and a knob of butter. This adds the richness of butter to the high cooking temperature of oil. Butter also turns food a lovely golden brown.

- The ideal amount of time for marinating meat is 40 minutes, but less is acceptable when you need to get dinner on the table fast.

- Try to serve a bowl of salad with every evening meal. Not only is this a good standard to set for the younger generation, but it's also a fantastic way to cleanse your palate after dinner. It also makes you less likely to stray towards the treat box later on.

- It's a great idea to get your children used to sitting at a dinner table with adults from the earliest age possible. This means no television, no digital devices, good table manners and joining in conversations. It's the perfect way to find out exactly what your children have been up to. Encourage your children's friends to join you for dinner, too.

- Rather than serving up food on individual plates for everyone, place it on platters and ask them to help themselves. There's less waste and it encourages children to come back for seconds or, heaven forbid, thirds.

Deglazing and reducing

Deglazing and reducing are the two basic principles of making a sauce.

Deglazing is the process of adding liquid (usually alcohol, such as wine, but when I'm cooking for the family I simply use stock) to a hot pan after meat has been browned and transferred to the oven to finish cooking. Tip any oil from the pan away and return the pan to the heat. Always take care when adding alcohol as it may ignite. This is fine – good, actually – but you don't want to have your hand in the way. Let the alcohol evaporate, but make sure some liquid stays in the base of the pan. Once you have added the alcohol, use a wooden spoon to scrape the nice caramelised bits of meat from the bottom of the pan to add more flavour. Then add your stock and continue reducing.

Reducing is adding stock to the remaining juices in the pan and boiling rapidly to evaporate the liquid. Usually the liquid is reduced by half; any more and the flavour can become too concentrated. Once the stock is reduced, any finishing ingredients such as herbs or cream are added. Don't add the cream any earlier as it will curdle, but you want it to reduce a little to thicken the sauce. A knob of butter whisked in at the end will also thicken slightly, as well as adding sheen and richness.

TIP

30-minute dinner recipes

Chicken

Pan-fried herb chicken breasts

A boneless skinless chicken breast coated lightly with fresh herbs is a great-tasting combo.
If anyone partaking of this meal has a problem with herbs, leave a breast or two plain.
This dish is good with Soft polenta (page 483) or Mashed potatoes (page 257). Serves 4

Handful of chopped herbs (flat-leaf/Italian parsley,
   thyme, rosemary, oregano)
Grated zest of 1 lemon
Oil for cooking
4 small boneless skinless chicken breasts

Mix together the herbs, lemon zest, enough oil to coat
the chicken and some salt and freshly ground black
pepper. Rub the mixture over the chicken breasts
and leave to marinate for at least 10 minutes or up to
3 hours if time permits.

Preheat the oven to 180°C (350°F).

Heat a heavy-based frying pan over medium–high heat.
Add a generous splash of oil and the chicken breasts
and cook for 2–3 minutes on each side until well
browned. Place in the oven and continue to cook for
10 minutes. Remove and rest, covered, in a warm place
for 5 minutes before serving.

Spiced chicken breasts
Add 1 teaspoon each of ground cumin, ground
coriander and sweet smoky paprika along with
the herbs and lemon zest.

Thai-marinated chicken

If the weather permits, this dish benefits from cooking on the barbecue grill. Fire up the
barbie, get it nice and hot, and cook the chicken breasts for 4–5 minutes on each side or until
cooked through. This is delicious with Asian coleslaw (page 275) or sautéed greens. Serves 4

2–3 tablespoons Thai curry paste, red or green
   (page 465)
Oil for cooking
4 small boneless skinless chicken breasts
Steamed rice (page 480) to serve

Mix the Thai curry paste and enough oil to coat the
chicken together and rub the mixture all over the bird.

Preheat the oven to 180°C (350°F).

Heat a heavy-based frying pan over medium–high heat.
Add a generous splash of oil and the chicken breasts
and cook for 2–3 minutes on each side until well
browned. Place in the oven and continue to cook for
10 minutes. Remove and rest, covered, in a warm place
for 5 minutes before serving. Slice the breasts thickly
and serve.

Chilli, lime and coconut chicken

Kaffir lime leaves can be hard to find on a regular basis. I usually buy a packet at the market and then freeze the remaining leaves in small bags in the freezer so I always have some on hand. More recently I have planted a kaffir lime tree. Serves 4

2 boneless skinless chicken breasts

2 small red chillies, seeded and diced

2 garlic cloves, chopped

3 kaffir lime leaves, finely shredded (optional)

Grated zest and juice of 1 lime

Oil for cooking

125 ml (4 fl oz/½ cup) coconut milk

Fish sauce to season

1 bunch baby bok choy (pak choy), washed and trimmed

15 g (½ oz/½ cup) coriander (cilantro) leaves

Steamed rice (page 480) to serve

Preheat the oven to 180°C (350°F).

Take each chicken breast and cut it into thin slices, starting at the thin end of the breast, to make two escalopes. If necessary, flatten the thick top pieces using a meat mallet.

Mix the chilli, garlic, kaffir lime, lime zest and 1 tablespoon oil. Pour the mixture over the chicken and marinate for 10 minutes.

Heat a heavy-based frying pan over medium–high heat. Remove the chicken from the marinade (but reserve the remaining marinade). Add a generous splash of oil and cook the chicken pieces, in batches, for 2–3 minutes on each side until well browned. As they cook, remove and place them on a baking tray in the oven. Once all the chicken is cooked, tip out any excess fat from the pan. Add any of the remaining marinade and the coconut milk and bring to the boil. Season with the fish sauce and some freshly ground black pepper.

Add the bok choy and cook for 2–3 minutes until soft. Finish with a squeeze of lime juice and the coriander leaves. Serve the chicken and bok choy with the sauce on top of steamed rice.

Chicken with cherry tomatoes and olives

If you can get them, chicken tenderloins are perfect for this recipe. Allow three to four per person. Alternatively, I cut chicken breasts into escalopes. Serves 4

2 boneless skinless chicken breasts or 16 chicken tenderloins

Oil for cooking

2 garlic cloves, crushed

1 small red chilli, seeded and diced

125 ml (4 fl oz/½ cup) verjuice or white wine

2 tablespoons chopped oregano or basil

40 g (1½ oz/¼ cup) pitted black olives

125 g (4½ oz) cherry tomatoes, halved

2 tablespoons chopped flat-leaf (Italian) parsley

If using tenderloins, check to see if you need to trim any sinew or fat from them. Otherwise, take each chicken breast and cut it into thin slices, starting at the thin end of the breast, to make two escalopes. If necessary, flatten the thick top pieces using a meat mallet.

Heat a heavy-based frying pan over medium–high heat. Add a splash of oil and cook the chicken in a single layer (you may need to cook the chicken in batches) until golden brown on each side. Add the garlic and chilli, then the verjuice and oregano, and season with salt and freshly ground black pepper. Reduce the heat, cover with a lid and cook for 10 minutes. Add the olives and tomatoes and cook for a further 4–5 minutes. Check the seasoning, sprinkle over the chopped parsley and serve.

Tandoori chicken wraps

I enjoy this dish with alarming regularity. Sometimes I make my own naan bread, but I usually just buy it from the supermarket or Indian takeaway for convenience. This dish is also known as Pambula chicken, as it was a must on family camping trips to that destination. Serves 4

250 g (9 oz/1 cup) natural yoghurt

2 tablespoons Tandoori paste (page 464)

2 tablespoons lemon juice

4 boneless skinless chicken thighs, cut into 3 cm (1¼ in) dice

12 skewers

2 tomatoes, finely diced

1 Lebanese (short) cucumber, finely diced

2 spring onions (scallions), thinly sliced

1 tablespoon chopped mint

2 tablespoons olive oil

12 naan or roti wraps

Mix together the yoghurt, tandoori paste and half the lemon juice. Rub the mixture over the chicken and leave to marinate for 1 hour.

Preheat a barbecue or grill (broiler) to medium–high.

Thread four or five pieces of chicken onto 12 skewers. Cook the skewers for 12 minutes in total, turning three or four times.

To make a salad, mix together the tomato, cucumber, spring onion, mint, remaining lemon juice and oil.

Heat the bread for 1–2 minutes before serving, either on the barbecue or in the oven.

Remove the chicken from the skewers and serve wrapped in the hot bread with the salad over the top.

Chicken yakitori skewers with sesame dipping sauce

Yakitori is generally a sweet marinade but, because I try to eliminate sugar wherever possible, I usually omit it from this recipe. Makes 12

60 ml (2 fl oz/¼ cup) light soy sauce

2 tablespoons mirin

1 teaspoon sesame oil

1 teaspoon sesame seeds

½ teaspoon caster (superfine) sugar (optional)

12 chicken tenderloins or 2–3 boneless skinless chicken breasts, cut into 3 cm (1¼ in) dice

12 skewers

Mix together the soy sauce, mirin, sesame oil, sesame seeds and sugar (if using). Pour half the mixture over the chicken and marinate for at least 20 minutes.

Thread the chicken pieces onto the skewers. Preheat a barbecue or heavy-based frying pan to medium–high (you will need oil if using a frying pan). Cook the skewers for 4–5 minutes on each side until cooked through. Serve with the remaining sauce for dipping.

Satay chicken skewers
Prepare the chicken as directed but substitute satay marinade (see Beef satay kebabs, page 139) for the yakitori marinade. Serve with additional satay sauce on the side.

Chicken saltimbocca

This is a chicken version of veal saltimbocca. You end up with thin slices of chicken, each wrapped in prosciutto and filled with sage leaves. They are beautiful served with Mushroom risotto (page 104) or polenta. Serves 4

4 boneless skinless chicken breasts

Sage leaves

8 slices prosciutto

Oil for cooking

250 ml (8½ fl oz/1 cup) white wine

250 ml (8½ fl oz/1 cup) chicken stock

90 g (3 oz) butter

2 tablespoons chopped flat-leaf (Italian) parsley

Cut each chicken breast in half through the middle, so you end up with two thin escalopes. Lay a large square of plastic wrap on a chopping board, put one or two pieces of chicken inside, fold half of the plastic wrap over the top (this will prevent the meat from sticking to the mallet) and then pat the chicken breasts gently two or three times on each side, until they are flat and have an even thickness.

Lay three to four sage leaves on each piece of chicken. Season lightly with salt and freshly ground black pepper and wrap one piece of prosciutto around each piece of chicken. Pat with the meat mallet to bond the prosciutto to the chicken.

Heat a heavy-based frying pan over medium–high heat. Add a splash of oil and fry the chicken pieces, in batches if necessary, until golden brown on each side. Place the cooked chicken in a warm oven while you prepare the sauce.

Tip out any excess oil from the pan and raise the heat to high. Add the wine and reduce by half. Add the stock and again reduce by half. Remove from the heat and whisk in the butter in small amounts. Check the seasoning and add the parsley.

Serve two chicken pieces per person, drizzle with the sauce and serve.

Breadcrumbs

TIP

I'm going to get a bit technical here for a moment. There are many ways you can bind a meatball, burger or pattie together. My preference is to soak day-old bread (the slight staleness means the bread absorbs better) in milk; this produces a nice soft binding mass. Dry breadcrumbs are not only processed and have lots of nasty additives, they often make the finished product a bit sawdust-like. Another option – and I think you're going to love this – is to use quinoa flakes. Not only are they the perfect binder, they are gluten-free. Just chuck them in – the amount will always vary depending on the wetness of your base mix, but start with 100 g (3½ oz/ ½ cup) and see how you go.

Chicken schnitzel

Schnitzel is an ever-popular dish, and the variations are endless – you can change not only the meat but also the breadcrumbs. Schnitzel is great with Mashed potatoes (page 257) and peas.
Serves 4–6

2–3 boneless skinless chicken breasts

Seasoned flour

1 egg

125 ml (4 fl oz/½ cup) milk

90 g (3 oz/1½ cups) panko breadcrumbs

Grated zest of 1 lemon

1 tablespoon sesame seeds

2 tablespoons grated parmesan

1 tablespoon chopped flat-leaf (Italian) parsley

Oil for cooking

Lemon wedges to serve

Remove the small chicken breast from underneath each larger breast, and then cut the remaining piece into three or four pieces lengthways, depending on the original size.

Cut each chicken breast in half through the middle, so you end up with two thin escalopes. Lay a large square of plastic wrap on a chopping board, put one or two pieces of chicken inside, fold half of the plastic wrap over the top (this will prevent the meat from sticking to the mallet) and then pat the chicken breasts gently two or three times on each side, until they are flat and have an even thickness.

Put the flour in a shallow bowl. Beat the egg and milk together in another bowl. Place the breadcrumbs into a third bowl and add as many or as few of the flavourings (lemon zest, sesame seeds, parmesan and parsley) as you like – personally, I like all of them in together.

Dip the chicken pieces in the flour, shaking off the excess, then dip them into the egg and finally into the breadcrumbs, making sure each piece of chicken is well coated at each stage. If desired, the chicken can now be placed in the refrigerator until you are ready to cook it.

Preheat the oven to 160°C (320°F).

Heat a large heavy-based frying pan over medium–high heat. Add a generous splash of oil and the chicken pieces to the pan. Make sure that the chicken doesn't overlap or it won't cook properly. Cook for 2–3 minutes, until golden brown on one side. If the pan becomes dry, add more oil as needed. Turn each piece of chicken over and cook for 2 minutes on the other side, or until golden brown. Remove and place on a tray in the warm oven. It's a good idea to line the tray with plain brown paper or paper towel to absorb the excess oil and keep the food crisp.

Repeat this process until all the chicken is cooked. Serve with the lemon wedges.

Chicken parmigiano
While the schnitzels are hot, place them on a tray, spread them with Napoletana sauce (page 83) and then sprinkle with grated mozzarella. Grill (broil) until golden brown, or bake in the oven until the cheese melts.

Veal schnitzel
Use thin veal escalopes instead of chicken.

Chicken nuggets
Chop the chicken into three 3 cm (1¼ in) chunks, then crumb as directed.

Fish fingers
Swap the chicken for flathead tails or other firm white fish fillets.

Lemon chicken polpettini

These meatballs are one of my son, Luke's, favourite meals – alongside chicken wraps, that is. I often double this recipe in the hope that there'll be leftovers for lunch boxes the next day. The polpettini can be served with Polenta wedges (page 484), or as a great pre-dinner nibble with Almond skordalia (page 475). Serves 4

100 g (3½ oz) day-old bread
250 ml (8½ fl oz/1 cup) milk
1 egg yolk
500 g (1 lb 2 oz) minced (ground) chicken
7 g (¼ oz/¼ cup) chopped flat-leaf (Italian) parsley
2 garlic cloves, crushed
Grated zest of 1 lemon
65 g (2¼ oz/⅔ cup) grated parmesan
Plain (all-purpose) flour for dusting
Oil for cooking
2 lemons, cut into wedges, to serve

Tear the bread into small pieces and soak it in the milk for 10–15 minutes.

Squeeze the bread well to remove the excess liquid and place in a bowl with the egg yolk, chicken, parsley, garlic, lemon zest and parmesan and season with salt and freshly ground black pepper. Mix well. Roll the mixture into small 3 cm (1¼ in) balls. Roll each ball lightly in the flour.

Preheat the oven to 180°C (350°F).

Heat a heavy-based pan over medium–high heat. Add a splash of oil and cook the polpettini in batches for 5–6 minutes, shaking the pan often, until they are golden brown. Remove from the pan and keep warm in the preheated oven until all the polpettini are cooked. Serve with the lemon wedges.

Chicken and veal polpettini
Swap half the minced chicken for veal.

Thai chicken balls
To 500 g (1 lb 2 oz) minced chicken, add three thinly sliced spring onions (scallions), one grated carrot, 1 tablespoon Sweet chilli sauce (page 437), 1 tablespoon chopped coriander (cilantro), one egg yolk, 40 g (1½ oz) quinoa flakes and an optional 100 g (3½ oz) cooked vermicelli noodles. Omit the flour. Shape into balls or small burgers and cook as for polpettini.

Japanese chicken meatballs
To 500 g (1 lb 2 oz) minced chicken, add three thinly sliced spring onions (scallions), 2 teaspoons grated fresh ginger, the grated zest of one lemon, 1 tablespoon barbecue sauce, 2 tablespoons white or black sesame seeds along with one egg yolk and 40 g (1½ oz/⅓ cup) quinoa flakes. Omit the flour. Shape into balls or small burgers and cook as for polpettini.

Chicken, sweet potato and feta burgers

I eat these a lot, and I mean a lot. Most days it's just my son, Luke, and I at home and this makes enough for us for dinner and then some extra for the next day's lunch or snack. I've even made the mixture into meatballs and taken them away hiking. They make the perfect protein-packed lunch and are yummy with Hummus (page 473). They're also delicious with Potato wedges (page 258). Serves 3–4

100 g (3½ oz) day-old bread or 40 g (1½ oz) quinoa flakes

250 ml (8½ fl oz/1 cup) milk

Oil for cooking

1 onion, diced

2 garlic cloves, crushed

500 g (1 lb 2 oz) minced (ground) chicken

1 egg yolk

2 tablespoons chopped flat-leaf (Italian) parsley

125 g (4½ oz/1 cup) grated sweet potato

100 g (3½ oz) feta, crumbed

Lemon wedges to serve

Tear the bread into small pieces and soak in the milk for 10–15 minutes. (Omit this step if using quinoa flakes.)

Heat a small saucepan over medium–high heat. Add a splash of oil and the onion and cook for 3–4 minutes, stirring often, until softened. Add the garlic, cook for a further 1–2 minutes, then place the mixture in a large bowl.

Squeeze the bread well to remove any excess liquid and place it in the bowl with the onion, garlic, chicken, egg yolk, parsley, sweet potato and feta. Season well with salt and freshly ground black pepper. Divide the mixture into eight and shape into burgers.

Preheat the oven to 180°C (350°F).

Heat a heavy-based pan over medium–high heat. Add a splash of oil and cook the burgers until golden brown on each side. You may need to do this in batches. When the burgers brown, transfer them to the oven for a further 8–10 minutes or until cooked through. Serve with lemon wedges.

Chicken and haloumi sausages

Delicious parcels of chicken flavoured with haloumi cheese and topped off with crispy prosciutto. Makes 8

500 g (1 lb 2 oz) minced (ground) chicken

100 g (3½ oz) grated haloumi

Grated zest of 1 lemon

2 tablespoons chopped flat-leaf (Italian) parsley or sage

1 egg yolk

40 g (1½ oz) quinoa flakes

8 slices prosciutto

Place the chicken in a bowl with the haloumi, lemon zest, chopped herbs, egg yolk and quinoa flakes. Season with salt and freshly ground black pepper and mix everything together well.

Form the mixture into eight sausage shapes. Wrap each sausage in a slice of prosciutto.

Either heat a heavy-based frying pan over medium–high heat, or heat a barbecue grill until hot. Cook the sausages for 4–5 minutes on each side.

Chicken larb

A dish that really packs a punch in the flavour department. You can serve it in lettuce leaf cups or serve it with steamed rice. You can also use minced (ground) pork in this recipe if you prefer. Serves 2–3

2 tablespoons jasmine rice

Oil for cooking

500 g (1 lb 2 oz) minced (ground) chicken

1 lemongrass stem, white part only, finely chopped

2 green chillies, finely chopped

½ small red onion, thinly sliced

1 kaffir lime leaf, finely shredded, or the finely grated zest of 1 lime

2 tablespoons lime juice

1 tablespoon fish sauce

1 teaspoon grated palm sugar (jaggery)

15 g (½ oz/½ cup) coriander (cilantro) leaves

50 g (1¾ oz/⅓ cup) roasted peanuts, chopped finely

Iceberg lettuce leaves to serve

Heat a wok over high heat, add the rice and cook for 1–2 minutes, stirring until lightly toasted. Remove and crush the rice until fine, either using a mortar and pestle or a food processor.

Heat the wok again until hot, add a splash of oil and add the minced chicken. Cook for 3–4 minutes, stirring often, until browned. Add the lemongrass, chillies, red onion and kaffir lime. Cook for a further 2–3 minutes, stirring often, until the chicken is cooked and the onion has softened.

Add the lime juice, fish sauce and palm sugar. Cook briefly, then add the coriander leaves and peanuts. Toss to combine and remove from the heat. Spoon the chicken larb into the lettuce leaves and serve.

Southern fried chicken

You can use whichever cut of chicken you like for this recipe, though the cooking time will vary slightly. Great served with Slaw (page 274). Serves 4

8 chicken drumsticks, skin removed

250 ml (8½ fl oz/1 cup) buttermilk

Oil for deep-frying (approximately 2 litres/68 fl oz/ 8 cups)

90 g (3 oz/¾ cup) cornflour (cornstarch)

2 teaspoons sweet paprika

1 teaspoon ground coriander

½ teaspoon cayenne pepper

1 teaspoon ground oregano

1 teaspoon ground cumin

½ teaspoon ground cardamom

Lemon wedges to serve

The next day, place the chicken in a colander to allow the excess buttermilk to drain away.

In a deep-fryer or deep frying-pan, heat the oil to 180°C (350°F). Preheat the oven to 180°C (350°F).

Mix the cornflour with 1 teaspoon salt and the spices in a bowl and toss the chicken pieces in the mixture.

Deep-fry the chicken in the oil until each piece is golden brown.

Place the chicken pieces on a baking tray and cook in the oven for 20 minutes or until cooked through. Serve with the lemon wedges.

Place the chicken in a bowl and add the buttermilk. Refrigerate overnight.

Steamed ginger chicken

Steaming may not be the first thing that springs to mind when deciding how to cook chicken, but this is a dish that everyone should try. The result is an incredibly tender and amazingly flavoured meal. Go on, try it. Serves 4

4 skinless chicken breasts on the bone, or off the bone if it's easier for you

125 ml (4 fl oz/½ cup) light soy sauce

2 garlic cloves, peeled and sliced

2 small red chillies, sliced

1 tablespoon fish sauce

60 ml (2 fl oz/¼ cup) rice wine vinegar

2 teaspoons sesame oil

4 cm (1½ in) piece fresh ginger, peeled and shredded

Steamed rice (page 480) to serve

Place the chicken in a deep bowl. Mix together the soy sauce, garlic, chilli, fish sauce, 80 ml (2½ fl oz/⅓ cup) water, rice wine vinegar and sesame oil.

Pour the mixture over the chicken and leave to marinate in the refrigerator for 4 hours, turning the chicken once.

Place a wok over high heat, add 6 cm (2½ in) water and bring to the boil. Rest a plate in the bottom of a bamboo steamer and place this in the wok. Arrange the chicken breasts on the plate and pour the marinade over. Spread the ginger over the chicken, cover and steam for 20 minutes, or until the chicken is just cooked. Remove and allow the chicken to rest for 5 minutes in a warm place.

Cut each piece of chicken into four and serve immediately with the cooking juices and steamed rice.

Duck

Chinese five-spiced duck

Child number one loves duck. If we are celebrating an achievement of one of our children, they get to choose their favourite dinner, and this is Mia's favourite. Serve with Soy mushrooms (page 254), Steamed rice (page 480) or soba noodles. Serves 4

3 duck breasts (approximately 250 g/9 oz) each)

1 teaspoon Chinese five-spice

½ teaspoon chilli flakes

Oil for cooking

Score the fat of the duck breast using a small sharp knife. Cut the breast into 2 cm (¾ in) fingers.

In a bowl mix together 1 teaspoon salt, the five-spice and chilli and sprinkle this mixture over the duck.

Heat a large heavy-based frying pan over medium–high heat. Add a splash of oil and cook the duck breasts for 3–4 minutes on each side, until just cooked. Cover and rest for 5 minutes before serving.

Quail

Crispy-skin quail with sichuan pepper and salt

This dish can easily be served as a main course by adding an extra half quail per person. If you have a wok burner on your barbecue, I suggest you cook the birds outside. Serves 6

Master stock (page 451)

6 quail, spatchcocked (see page 160)

Oil for cooking

Sichuan salt and pepper spice (page 467)

Lime wedges

Bring the master stock to a gentle boil in a medium saucepan. Add the quail and cook for 10 minutes, making sure the liquid doesn't boil, but just trembles.

Remove the quail and allow them to cool. Once cool, lay them, skin side down, on paper towel and refrigerate.

When you're ready to fry the quail, make sure that their skin is completely dry. In a wok, heat 4 cm (1½ in) oil, or enough oil to deep-fry the birds two to three at a time. Cook the quail until crispy. Drain on paper towel.

Arrange the quail pieces on a platter and sprinkle with the sichuan salt and pepper spice. Serve with the lime wedges and an additional bowl of the sichuan mix on the side.

Kashmiri quail

I love quail on the barbecue. They are quite easy to spatchcock and deliciously sweet to eat. Beautiful served with Freekeh and chickpea salad (page 283). Serves 4

125 g (4½ oz/½ cup) natural yoghurt

1 teaspoon grated fresh ginger

1 garlic clove, crushed

1 teaspoon ground cumin

¼ teaspoon ground white pepper

½ teaspoon ground turmeric

½ teaspoon chilli powder

¼ teaspoon ground cinnamon

1 tablespoon lemon juice

2 tablespoons olive oil

6 quail, spatchcocked (see page 160)

Mix the yoghurt with the ginger, ½ teaspoon salt, the spices, lemon juice and oil. Pour the mixture over the quail – if time permits you can marinate it for up to 2 hours.

Preheat a barbecue to hot and oil the barbecue plate.

Place the quail on the barbecue grill. Cook for 5 minutes, rotating once. Turn over and cook for a further 5 minutes, rotating once. Cut each quail in half along the breastbone. Serve 1½ quails per person.

Beef

Steak with oven chips

The oven chips included here are wicked. Seeing that they are so easy to make, I can't understand why anyone buys those frozen ones. It's these or nothing as far as I am concerned. Serve with a green salad and some fried mushrooms, if you like. Serves 4

500 g (1 lb 2 oz) desiree or other waxy potatoes

Olive oil

2 tablespoons rosemary leaves

1 tablespoon chopped flat-leaf (Italian) parsley

4 × 200 g (7 oz) fillet or porterhouse steaks

Preheat the oven to 200°C (400°F).

Cut the potatoes into thick wedges. Combine 2–3 tablespoons oil and the herbs in a large bowl and season with salt and freshly ground black pepper. Add the potato wedges and toss well. Place the wedges on a large baking tray, skin side down, and cook in the oven for 45–55 minutes, turning the tray occasionally. The potatoes will be golden brown when ready.

Heat a heavy-based frying pan over medium–high heat and add a splash of oil. Add the steaks and cook for 4–5 minutes on both sides. Rest briefly in a warm place, then serve with lots of potato wedges.

Steak with chimichurri

You can use whatever type of steak you prefer for this recipe; it's up to your personal preference. Be aware that the cooking time may vary depending on the thickness of your steak and, of course, how you like it cooked. Take four steaks and pour half the Chimichurri (page 459) over the steaks. At this stage they can be marinated for up to 4 hours. Heat a barbecue grill and cook the steaks for 3–4 minutes on each side. Remove and rest, covered, in a warm place for 5 minutes. Slice thickly and pour the remaining chimichurri over to serve.

Teriyaki steak

Cook the steaks as directed and brush both sides of the steaks with Teriyaki glaze (page 457) as they are cooking. Serve with Stir-fried Chinese greens (page 248) and Steamed rice (page 480). I love this dish – don't be surprised at how much you're gonna love it too!

Cooking steaks

TIP

You could write a whole book on how to cook the perfect steak and, regardless of whether you cook it in a frying pan, a chargrill pan or on the barbecue, the principle is the same.

The most important thing to remember is not to move the steak too much – get the heat at a nice medium-high strength, make sure the pan/grill is nice and hot, then add the steaks. You may rotate them, but don't flip them. Cook for 3–4 minutes, depending on the thickness of the steak. You will see blood start to bead on top of the steak. This is your cue to turn the steak over.

You then repeat this process, again looking for the blood. This indicates that the steak is cooked medium-rare. If you prefer your steak cooked a bit more, allow another minute or two. Transfer the steaks to a plate, cover with foil and a tea towel (dish towel) to keep them warm, and rest in a warm place for 5 minutes. This allows the meat to relax, making it more tender and juicy.

Fillet steak with red wine mushroom sauce

If you didn't want to run to the expense of beef fillet you could use scotch fillet (rib eye) or porterhouse in its place. Delicious served with Catalan potatoes (page 259). Serves 4

Oil for cooking

1 kg (2 lb 3 oz) beef eye fillet (tenderloin)

40 g (1½ oz) butter

250 g (9 oz) Swiss brown mushrooms, sliced

2 onions, diced

2 garlic cloves, crushed

250 ml (8½ fl oz/1 cup) red wine

375 ml (12½ fl oz/1½ cups) beef stock

Preheat the oven to 200°C (400°F).

Heat a heavy-based frying pan over medium heat. Add a splash of oil and cook the beef on all sides until golden brown, about 3–4 minutes for each side.

Transfer the beef to a baking tray, place the beef in the oven and cook for 20 minutes. Check if the steaks are cooked to your liking. If so, remove, cover with foil and allow to rest for 5 minutes. If not, cook for a further 2–3 minutes and check again.

Return the frying pan to the heat, add the butter, then the mushrooms and cook for 10 minutes, stirring occasionally until softened and golden brown. Season with salt and freshly ground black pepper and then remove the mushrooms from the frying pan.

Heat a saucepan over medium–high heat. Add more oil if necessary and cook the onion for 5 minutes until softened but not coloured. Add the garlic and cook for 2–3 minutes. Add the red wine and bring to the boil. Reduce the heat slightly and cook for 2–3 minutes, allowing the wine to reduce. Add the stock and return to the boil, whisking until well combined. Simmer for 30 minutes. Return the mushrooms to the sauce and correct the seasoning. Slice the beef thickly and serve.

Beef tataki

Traditionally, this dish is served very rare and eaten with textural vegetables, such as daikon (white radish) and spring onions. You can, of course, cook it longer to suit your palate and serve it with some crunchy Asian coleslaw (page 275) or even soba noodles. Serves 2

300 g (10½ oz) beef eye fillet (tenderloin)

Oil for cooking

2 tablespoons soy sauce

60 ml (2 fl oz/¼ cup) rice vinegar

2 spring onions (scallions), thinly sliced

1 tablespoon finely chopped chives

Radish shoots or shiso shoots (optional)

1 daikon (white radish), shredded (optional)

1 teaspoon toasted sesame seeds (optional)

Ponzu sauce (page 453)

Heat a heavy-based frying pan over medium–high heat. Brush the beef fillet with oil and season with salt and freshly ground black pepper. Add the beef to the hot pan and cook on each side for about 2–3 minutes until golden brown and well sealed. It's ideal is to serve the beef very rare, but you may prefer to cook it longer, either by cooking on each side for 4–5 minutes, or by finishing it in a preheated 180°C (350°F) oven for 10 minutes. Set aside to cool.

To make the tataki dressing, mix the soy sauce and rice vinegar together in a bowl.

Slice the beef thinly and arrange it neatly on a plate. Garnish with the spring onion and chives, and the shoots, daikon and sesame seeds (if using). Pour over the ponzu sauce just before serving. Serve with the tataki dressing on the side.

Mexican spiced beef with chilli beans and tortillas

I love Mexican tortillas. I do them with chicken and fish too, but this spiced beef is my favourite, with a real explosion of spice, contrasted with cold sour cream and crispy lettuce.
Serves 3–4

1 garlic clove, crushed

½ teaspoon chilli powder

1 teaspoon sweet smoked paprika

½ teaspoon ground coriander

½ teaspoon ground cumin

1 teaspoon mustard seeds, crushed, or mustard powder

½ teaspoon freshly ground black pepper

Olive oil

2 × 250 g (9 oz) porterhouse steaks

400 g (14 oz) tinned red kidney beans

1 small red chilli, seeded and diced

15 g (½ oz/½ cup) coriander (cilantro) or flat-leaf (Italian) parsley leaves

½ red onion, finely diced

1 tomato, finely diced

1 tablespoon lime or lemon juice

8 Tortillas (page 424), hot

½ iceberg lettuce, shredded

Sour cream

Mix the garlic, ½ teaspoon salt and the spices together with 1 tablespoon olive oil. Pour over the beef and marinate for at least 40 minutes.

Rinse the beans well and mix them with the fresh chilli, herbs, onion, tomato and citrus juice.

Heat a heavy-based frying pan over medium–high heat. Brush the steaks with oil and cook for 4–5 minutes on each side, until well browned. Remove and allow to rest for 3–4 minutes, covered, in a warm place.

Slice the beef thinly and serve with the hot tortillas, chilli beans, lettuce and sour cream.

Cevapcici

This cevapcici recipe is the base mix from which a multitude of different types of sausages can be made. You can swap the minced (ground) beef for lamb or veal, or vary the flavours to suit your tastes by adding more chilli, spices or fresh herbs. Makes 20

500 g (1 lb 2 oz) minced (ground) beef

500 g (1 lb 2 oz) minced (ground) pork

¼ teaspoon ground white pepper

1 garlic clove, crushed

Large pinch of chilli powder

Oil for barbecue

Rustic bread to serve

Chilli salsa (page 479) to serve

Preheat a barbecue to medium–high.

Mix together the minced meats, white pepper, garlic, chilli, 1 teaspoon salt and ½ teaspoon freshly ground black pepper, then divide the mixture into twenty portions. Pat them into thin sausage shapes, then flatten them slightly.

Oil the barbecue plate and cook the cevapcici for 10 minutes, turning three to four times. Serve with rustic bread and the chilli salsa.

Classic beef and mushroom kebabs

I call these my 'classic' kebabs because everyone loves them, children and grown-ups alike. I've been making them since I was 16, when I was training to be a chef. It was one of the first dishes I cooked for my parents. Makes 14 kebabs

2 teaspoons dijon mustard
2 teaspoons chopped rosemary
2 tablespoons olive oil
60 ml (2 fl oz/¼ cup) red wine
1 kg (2 lb 3 oz) tender beef (fillet, porterhouse or rump), cut into 2 cm (¾ in) dice
1 red capsicum (bell pepper)
16 button mushrooms (approximately 200 g/7 oz)
14 skewers
Oil

Mix the mustard, rosemary, oil and red wine together and season with salt and freshly ground black pepper. Pour over the beef and marinate for 1 hour.

Cut the capsicum in half, remove the seeds and cut into 2 cm (¾ in) dice. Wipe the mushrooms clean and cut them in half.

Drain the excess marinade from the beef and set aside for basting during cooking. Thread the ingredients onto 14 skewers.

Heat a heavy-based frying pan over medium–high heat. Add a generous splash of oil and cook the kebabs for 8–10 minutes, turning often.

Pinchito beef kebabs
Follow the method described but swap the marinade for Pinchito marinade (page 459).

Spanish veal and pork rissoles

This recipe takes burgers to a whole new level. I use a heavy-based casserole dish to cook these in, as I can fry the rissoles and then put the whole lot in the oven to finish cooking. These are perfect with Mashed potatoes (page 257). Who can eat rissoles without thinking about the Australian movie *The Castle*, darl? Serves 4

100 g (3½ oz) day-old bread
160 ml (5½ fl oz) milk
500 g (1 lb 2 oz) minced (ground) veal and pork
2 tablespoons chopped flat-leaf (Italian) parsley
½ teaspoon freshly grated nutmeg
1 egg yolk
Plain (all-purpose) flour for coating
Oil for cooking
1 onion, diced
1 teaspoon smoky paprika
80 ml (2½ fl oz/⅓ cup) white wine or sherry
125 ml (4 fl oz/½ cup) chicken stock

Soak the bread in the milk for 10 minutes and then squeeze out the excess milk.

Place the bread in a bowl along with the minced meat, parsley, nutmeg and egg yolk and season with salt and

freshly ground black pepper. Mix well to combine and shape into eight rissoles. Coat lightly with flour.

Preheat the oven to 180°C (350°F).

Heat a heavy-based ovenproof saucepan or casserole dish over medium–high heat. Add a splash of oil and cook the rissoles – you may need to do this in batches – until golden brown on each side. Remove from the pan and set aside.

Add the onion to the pan, add more oil if needed and cook for 3–4 minutes until softened. Add the smoky paprika and cook for 1–2 minutes until fragrant. Add the wine and bring to the boil. Add the stock, check the seasoning and return the rissoles to the pan. Cover with a lid and place in the oven for 20 minutes. Serve the rissoles with the sauce.

Beef satay kebabs

These satay kebabs are ideal as a starter or as part of a larger spread of food. Serves 10

1 small onion, diced
1 tablespoon soy sauce
60 ml (2 fl oz/¼ cup) peanut oil
2 teaspoons ground coriander
1 teaspoon ground cumin
1 teaspoon ground turmeric
¼ teaspoon ground cinnamon
1 teaspoon salt
1 teaspoon sugar
50 g (1¾ oz/⅓ cup) roasted peanuts
500 g (1 lb 2 oz) beef fillet, cut into 3 cm (1¼ in) dice
20 skewers

Preheat a barbecue to high and oil the barbecue grill.

Make the satay sauce by placing all the ingredients, except the beef, in a food processor and blending until smooth. Marinate the beef in the satay sauce for 1 hour.

Thread four to five pieces of beef onto each skewer. Place the beef skewers on the barbecue grill. Cook for 10 minutes, turning two or three times.

Chicken satay kebabs
Substitute chicken for the beef.

Lamb

Greekish lamb kebabs

Who doesn't love a lamb kebab on the barbecue? Serve with a simple Greek salad or Cherry tomato and pomegranate salad (page 271). Makes 8

Grated zest of 1 lemon
60 ml (2 fl oz/¼ cup) olive oil
2 garlic cloves, crushed
1 tablespoon Za'atar (page 470)
2 tablespoons chopped coriander (cilantro)
500 g (1 lb 2 oz) lean lamb, cut into 2 cm (¾ in) dice
8 skewers

Mix the lemon zest, oil, garlic, za'atar and coriander together and season with salt and freshly ground black pepper. Pour over the diced lamb and toss to coat the lamb well. Marinate for at least 20 minutes.

Thread four to five pieces of lamb onto each skewer. Either heat a heavy-based frying pan over medium–high heat or place the lamb on a hot barbecue grill and cook for 6–7 minutes, turning once or twice.

Lamb and haloumi kebabs
Replace the marinade with the grated zest of one lemon, 2 tablespoons oil, 1 tablespoon chopped oregano and season with salt and freshly ground black pepper. When threading the lamb onto the skewers, alternate with diced haloumi. Continue as directed.

Soy, chilli and lime lamb cutlets

Lamb and Asian flavours go together really well. You could swap the cutlets for chops or fillets if you prefer. You can use this marinade over any cut of lamb, such as chops, fillets or rumps; just adjust the cooking time to suit the cut. Serves 4

Grated zest and juice of 1 lime
60 ml (2 fl oz/¼ cup) light soy sauce
2 small red chillies, seeded and finely diced
1 tablespoon oil
12–16 trim lamb cutlets

Mix together the lime zest and juice with the soy sauce, chilli and oil. Season with freshly ground black pepper. Pour over the lamb and toss to combine. You can set the lamb aside to marinate for up to 4 hours if time permits. Drain the excess marinade.

Heat a heavy-based frying pan or barbecue until hot. Cook the cutlets for 3–4 minutes on each side until golden brown, but still pink in the centre. Rest briefly in a warm place and then serve.

Lamb cutlets with cumin and yoghurt
Mix together 125 g (4 oz/½ cup) natural yoghurt, 1 tablespoon cumin, 2 crushed garlic cloves, the leaves from 1-2 thyme sprigs and the grated zest of one lemon, and season well with salt and freshly ground black pepper. Pour over the lamb cutlets and marinate, time permitting, for 20 minutes. Continue as directed.

Tikka–yoghurt lamb chops
Mix together 90 g (3 oz/⅓ cup) natural yoghurt, 3 tablespoons Tikka paste (page 466), 1 teaspoon ground coriander, 1 teaspoon ground cumin, ½ teaspoon ground cardamom and 2 tablespoons lemon juice . Brush over the lamb cutlets and marinate for up to 30 minutes, time permitting. Continue as directed.

Pomegranate mojo lamb cutlets
Toast 2 teaspoons cumin seeds, either in a small frying pan over medium-high heat or in a preheated 180°C (350°F) oven, until fragrant. Allow to cool, then grind using a mortar and pestle. Mix together 1 tablespoon sesame seeds, 1 teaspoon ground cumin seeds, 60 ml (2 fl oz/¼ cup) pomegranate molasses, the zest and juice of one lemon, and season well with salt and freshly ground black pepper. Pour over 12 lamb cutlets and allow to marinate for up to 4 hours, time permitting. Heat a barbecue grill or chargrill pan and cook the lamb for 4-5 minutes on each side or until medium-rare. Rest briefly and then serve.

Greek lamb and feta meatballs

Supermarkets have an array of minced meats available, which is great because it makes it easier to make quick dishes like this. Serve the meatballs with a Greek salad. Serves 4

500 g (1 lb 2 oz) minced (ground) lamb
1 onion, finely diced
½ tablespoon chopped mint leaves
½ tablespoon chopped oregano leaves
2 teaspoons ground cumin
1 teaspoon ground coriander
2 eggs
100 g (3½ oz) feta, crumbled
Oil for cooking
Tzatziki (page 475) to serve

In a large bowl, combine the lamb, onion, herbs, spices, eggs and feta and season with salt and freshly ground black pepper. Divide the mixture and roll into small golf ball–sized pieces.

Preheat the oven to 180°C (350°F).

Heat a heavy-based frying pan over medium–high heat. Add a splash of oil and cook the balls, in batches, for 3–4 minutes on each side until brown. Transfer to a baking tray and place in the hot oven for 10–12 minutes to finish cooking. Serve with the tzatziki.

Moorish lamb and sour cherry patties
Omit the feta and add 100 g (3½ oz) dried cherries instead. Shape into small patties.

Lamb and pistachio burgers
Omit the feta and add 100 g (3½ oz) chopped pistachio nuts and 2 teaspoons ground sumac. Shape into small patties.

Moorish lamb with quince glaze

Quince, smoky paprika, garlic and fresh thyme combine to flavour the lamb and create a great tasting sauce to serve over it. This sauce would be equally good with boneless skinless chicken breasts. The lamb goes well with Polenta wedges (page 484) and Rocket, pear, parmesan and pomegranate salad (page 271). Serves 4

2 garlic cloves, crushed
1 teaspoon smoky paprika
1 tablespoon vinegar or lemon juice
1 tablespoon thyme leaves
1 tablespoon olive oil
4 lamb backstraps or steaks
Oil for cooking
2 tablespoons quince paste
125 ml (4 fl oz/½ cup) white wine

Mix together the garlic, paprika, vinegar, thyme, oil and salt and freshly ground black pepper to taste. Brush over the lamb and marinate for up to 1 hour.

Heat a heavy-based frying pan over medium–high heat. Add a splash of oil and cook the lamb for 3–4 minutes on each side until golden brown. Remove the lamb from the pan and set aside in a warm place to rest.

Tip away the excess oil from the pan. Add the quince paste and white wine and bring to the boil. Whisk well and cook until the sauce reduces to a syrupy consistency. Check the seasoning. To serve, slice the lamb thickly and pour the quince glaze over.

Pork

Plum and ginger pork steaks

A very simple and quick dinner, perfect for those nights when time is short. Serves 4

2 teaspoons grated fresh ginger

2 tablespoons plum sauce

4 pork butterfly steaks

Oil for cooking

Steamed rice (page 480) to serve

Mix the ginger and plum sauce together and brush over the pork steaks. Season with salt and freshly ground black pepper.

Heat a heavy-based frying pan over medium–high heat. Add a splash of oil and cook the pork steaks for 3–4 minutes on each side. Serve with the steamed rice.

Korean barbecued pork

You can use any cut of pork in this recipe, such as pork chops, cutlets or belly pork. Adjust the cooking time as needed. Serves 4

80 ml (2½ fl oz/⅓ cup) soy sauce

1 tablespoon sesame oil

2–3 garlic cloves, crushed

2–3 spring onions (scallions), thinly sliced

2 teaspoons grated fresh ginger

1 tablespoon brown sugar

1 teaspoon toasted sesame seeds

1 tablespoon Korean chilli paste (optional)

Freshly ground black pepper

500 g (1 lb 2 oz) pork fillet, sliced into 2 cm (¾ in) dice

Kimchi fried rice (page 480) to serve

Mix together all the ingredients, except the pork, and pour the mixture over the pork. Set aside to marinate for up to 4 hours.

Either heat the barbecue or a heavy-based frying pan until hot. Tip off the excess marinade. Cook the pork for 2–3 minutes on each side until golden brown and cooked through. Serve with the kimchi fried rice.

Korean barbecued beef
Use beef fillet instead of pork.

Spanish pork cutlets

After eating this, my son, Luke, smacked his lips and claimed it was the best-ever dinner. Both my children love meat with bones as they don't have to use their cutlery. Serves 4

2 tablespoons olive oil

Grated zest of 1 orange

2 teaspoons smoky sweet paprika

1 teaspoon ground cumin

½ teaspoon ground coriander

1 tablespoon chopped flat-leaf (Italian) parsley

4 pork cutlets

Mix together the oil, orange zest, spices and parsley and season with salt and freshly ground black pepper. Brush over the pork cutlets.

Heat a heavy-based frying pan over medium–high heat and add the pork cutlets. Cook for 5–6 minutes, turn over and cook for a further 5–6 minutes or until the pork is cooked through.

Sticky lemongrass pork patties

I love this recipe and have cooked it numerous times in a relatively short time. It's one of my favourites. Lovely served with Stir-fried Chinese greens (page 248). Serves 4

500 g (1 lb 2 oz) minced (ground) pork

1 tablespoon grated fresh ginger

2 spring onions (scallions), thinly sliced

1 lemongrass stem, white part only, finely chopped

1 egg

Oil for cooking

1 tablespoon palm sugar (jaggery)

2 tablespoons soy sauce

60 ml (2 fl oz/¼ cup) chicken stock

Coriander (cilantro) leaves (optional)

Steamed rice (page 480) to serve

In a bowl, combine the pork, ginger, spring onion, lemongrass and egg, season with salt and freshly ground black pepper and mix well. Shape into eight patties.

Preheat the oven to 180°C (350°F).

Heat a heavy-based frying pan over medium–high heat, add a splash of oil and fry the patties for 3–4 minutes on each side until golden brown – you may need to do this in batches depending on the size of your pan. As the patties cook, place them on a tray in the oven to continue cooking.

Once all the patties have been browned, return the pan to the heat and add the palm sugar, soy sauce and stock. Allow to come to the boil, stir to scrape up all the cooking flavours from the bottom of the pan and cook for 3–4 minutes until the sauce thickens slightly.

Return the patties to the pan, cook for a further 1–2 minutes, garnish with the coriander and serve with the steamed rice.

San choy bau

San choy bau is a classic Asian dish, often made with minced quail, though minced pork is easier to come by. You can add mushrooms, water chestnuts, bean sprouts, bamboo shoots or anything else that takes your fancy. Serves 4

1 iceberg lettuce

1–2 tablespoons peanut oil

2 garlic cloves, crushed

2 teaspoons grated fresh ginger

2 small red chillies, seeded and finely diced

750 g (1 lb 11 oz) minced (ground) pork

2 tablespoons Chinese rice wine

Soy sauce to taste

4 spring onions (scallions), chopped

Fresh coriander (cilantro) leaves to serve

Chilli sauce to serve

Peel whole leaves away from the lettuce, wash them well and chill until needed.

Heat a wok until hot. Add the peanut oil, garlic, ginger and chillies and cook until fragrant. Add the pork and cook, stirring often, until the meat changes colour. Add the Chinese rice wine and soy sauce to taste, along with the spring onions. Toss until combined.

Spoon the minced pork into the lettuce leaf cups, add the coriander and chilli sauce to taste, roll up and away you go.

Katsudon (Japanese crumbed pork)

I love Japanese food and dishes like this one creep into my cooking repertoire more and more often. Serves 4

1 pork fillet (approximately 500 g/1 lb 2 oz)

Seasoned flour

4 eggs

125 ml (4 fl oz/½ cup) milk

100 g (3½ oz/1⅔ cups) panko breadcrumbs

1 onion, sliced

250 ml (8½ fl oz/1 cup) dashi

60 ml (2 fl oz/¼ cup) soy sauce

80 ml (2½ fl oz/⅓ cup) mirin

Oil for cooking

Steamed rice (page 480) to serve

Cut the pork into slices. Using a meat mallet, pat each piece of pork gently two or three times on each side until flat and of an even thickness. (Cover the pork with plastic wrap to prevent the pork from sticking to the mallet.)

Put the flour in a shallow bowl. Beat 1 egg and the milk together in another bowl and put the breadcrumbs in a third bowl. Coat the pork in the flour and shake off the excess. Then coat with the egg and finally the breadcrumbs, making sure each piece of pork is well coated at each stage. If you want, you can now place the pork in the refrigerator until you are ready to cook it.

Make your broth by combining the onion, dashi, soy and mirin in a small saucepan. Bring to the boil over medium heat, reduce to a simmer and cook for 10 minutes.

Heat a large heavy-based frying pan over medium–high heat. Add a generous splash of oil and enough pork pieces to fit into the pan, making sure the pork doesn't overlap or else it will not cook properly. Cook for 2–3 minutes until golden brown on one side. If the pan becomes dry, add more oil as needed. When golden brown on one side, turn the pork over and cook for 2 minutes on the other side, or until golden brown.

Beat the remaining eggs together and pour them into the pan around the pork pieces. (If cooking in batches, pour half the egg in and keep the remaining beaten eggs for the second batch.) Cook for 1–2 minutes until the egg sets. Serve the pork over steamed rice with a spoonful of the hot broth.

Barbecued pork sausage with spiced lentils

If it's raining and I can't get to the barbecue, I cook the sausage slices for this dish in a pan before serving them on top of the spiced lentils. This means I can eat the dish all year round. Serves 4–6

185 g (6½ oz/1 cup) puy lentils or tiny blue-green lentils

1 tablespoon olive oil

1 onion, diced

1 garlic clove, crushed

2 carrots, peeled and finely diced

1 celery stalk, finely diced

2 tablespoons curry paste

500 ml (17 fl oz/2 cups) vegetable or chicken stock

2 tablespoons chopped flat-leaf (Italian) parsley

500 g (1 lb 2 oz) Polish pork sausage

Oil for cooking

Sort through the lentils, discarding any brown ones and pieces of grit, then rinse well.

Heat a heavy-based pan over medium–high heat. Add the oil, onion, garlic, carrot and celery and cook for 5–6 minutes until soft. Add the curry paste and cook until fragrant. Add the lentils and cook for a few moments. Add enough stock to just cover and bring to the boil. Lower the heat, season with salt and cook for 30–40 minutes, or until the lentils are soft. Add more stock as necessary and stir frequently. Stir through the parsley and season with salt and freshly ground black pepper.

Slice the pork sausage into 5 mm (¼ in) slices. Brush with olive oil and barbecue or grill for 3–4 minutes on each side, or until brown and crispy.

Spoon the lentils into a bowl, arrange slices of grilled sausage on top and serve.

Seafood

Lime salmon skewers

Salmon is great on the barbecue as the natural oils stop it from drying out and it holds its shape well. Makes 12

1 tablespoon shoyu

Grated zest of 1 lime

2 tablespoons chopped coriander (cilantro)

2 tablespoons chopped fresh mint

4 salmon fillets

12 skewers

Oil for cooking

Mix together the shoyu, lime zest and herbs and season with freshly ground black pepper. Remove the skin from the salmon and cut the fish into 2 cm (¾ in) chunks. Pour the marinade over the fish and marinate for 20 minutes, if time permits.

Heat a barbecue until hot. Thread four chunks of fish onto each skewer. Cook on the barbecue for 3–4 minutes on each side, drizzling with oil as needed.

Pan-fried fish fillets

Once a week I will have this for dinner and my children eat just as much of it as I do, sometimes more. Usually I choose flathead or rockling for flavour and firmness. I eat fish with everything: rice; boiled, baked, mashed or fried potatoes; and sometimes noodles.
Serves 4

500 g (1 lb 2 oz) firm white fish fillets
Seasoned flour
Oil and butter for cooking
Lemon wedges to serve

Cut the fish into 10 cm (4 in) pieces. Coat with the flour, shaking off any excess.

Heat a heavy-based frying pan over medium–high heat. Add a splash of oil and a knob of butter (for both flavour and browning). Cook the fish for 3–4 minutes, or until golden brown. Turn over, add more oil and butter if needed and continue cooking for a further 2–3 minutes.

Remove and serve immediately with the lemon wedges. (I usually have to cook mine in two batches to fit in the pan, which means the children get a head start on dinner.)

Pan-fried fish with coconut curry sauce
Pan-fry the fish as directed and keep warm in a preheated oven. Tip the excess oil out of the frying pan and return the pan to the heat. Add 300 ml (10 fl oz) coconut milk and 2 tablespoons Red Thai curry paste (page 465) and bring to the boil, stirring occasionally. Once boiling, reduce the heat and cook for 2-3 minutes. Serve the sauce on top of the fish. This is great over a bowl of noodles.

Pan-fried fish with lime butter and bok choy
Cook the fish as directed. Allow one to two baby bok choy (pak choy) per person and cut in half lengthways. Blanch in a pan of boiling water for 2-3 minutes until just cooked, drain and dress with a drizzle of soy sauce and a squeeze of lime. Place the bok choy on the plate, add the fish and top with a generous knob of Lime butter sauce (page 454).

Miso-blackened fish

Marinating the fish in miso adds a lovely flavour. But it's called miso-blackened for a reason – it does burn. It's part of the process and adds a lovely flavour, but you don't want it cremated.
Serves 6

100 g (3½ oz) white miso paste
60 ml (2 fl oz/¼ cup) mirin
1 tablespoon caster (superfine) sugar
6 firm fish fillets, such as blue-eye, trevally or salmon
Oil for cooking
7 g (¼ oz/¼ cup) coriander (cilantro) leaves
1–2 teaspoons black sesame seeds
Slaw (page 274) to serve

Mix the miso paste with the mirin and sugar in a bowl and add the fish fillets, tossing to coat. Marinate in the refrigerator overnight or for at least 8 hours.

Heat a heavy-based frying pan over medium–high heat. Add a generous splash of oil and place the fish fillets,

flesh side down, in the pan. Cook for 4–5 minutes, then turn over and cook for a further 4 minutes or until just cooked though. Place some slaw on a plate, put a piece of fish on top and sprinkle with coriander leaves and sesame seeds.

Steamed fish with miso dressing
Place a wok over high heat. Add 6 cm (2½ in) water and bring to the boil. Rest a plate in the bottom of a bamboo steamer and place this in the wok. Arrange the marinated fish fillets on the plate. Steam for 5-6 minutes, or until the fish is cooked through. The timing will depend on the thickness of the fish fillets. Top with salad and serve with cooking juices and Steamed rice (page 480).

Lemon and chilli fish tortillas

I'm always trying to get the children to eat more fish. They love Mexican food and this is so easy, it's a winner all round. Serves 4

500 g (1 lb 2 oz) flathead or other firm white fish fillets

1 teaspoon chilli flakes

Grated zest of 1 lemon

60 ml (2 fl oz/¼ cup) lemon juice

2 garlic cloves, crushed

Olive oil

200 g (7 oz) cherry tomatoes, halved

1 baby cos (romaine) lettuce

1 avocado

8 Tortillas (page 424)

Cut the flathead fillets into 7 cm (2¾ in) fingers. Mix together the chilli, lemon zest and juice, garlic and 2 tablespoons olive oil and season with salt and freshly ground black pepper. Pour half of the lemon–chilli mixture over the fish and marinate briefly. Don't leave the fish too long in the marinade before cooking as the acid in the lemon juice will start to 'cook' the fish – 5 minutes is perfect. Pour the remaining lemon–chilli mixture over the tomatoes and toss to combine.

Wash the lettuce and slice the avocado. Arrange on a platter and top with the tomatoes.

Heat a heavy-based frying pan over medium–high heat. Add a splash of oil and cook the drained fish for 3–4 minutes on each side until golden brown and cooked through.

Heat the tortillas. Serve each tortilla with the salad and fish.

Deep-fried fish fillets in beer batter

This batter is guaranteed to be light and fluffy because of the yeast in the beer. If you live in Australia, small fish fillets like flathead and strips of rockling are perfect for this dish. Use this recipe as a stepping stone to get to crispy fish tacos. These are delicious served with Lemon mayonnaise and a salad. Serves 4

250 ml (8½ fl oz/1 cup) beer

Olive oil

1 egg

170 g (6 oz/1⅓ cups) plain (all-purpose) flour, plus seasoned flour for coating

500 g (1 lb 2 oz) firm white fish fillets

Oil for deep-frying

Lemon wedges to serve

Lemon mayonnaise (page 463) to serve

Whisk together the beer, 2 tablespoons olive oil and the egg. Sift the flour and a pinch of salt, add to the beer mixture and whisk until smooth. Set aside for 30 minutes.

Coat the fish in the seasoned flour, then the batter, allowing any excess to drip off.

Pour the oil into a wok or a deep saucepan to a depth of 4 cm (1½ in) and heat to 180°C (350°F).

Ease the fish gently into the hot oil and cook until golden, turning the fish over once. Drain on paper towel, sprinkle with salt and serve with the lemon wedges and lemon mayonnaise.

Crispy fish tacos
Serve the battered fish with Tortillas (page 424), Slaw (page 274), Guacamole (page 474) and Harissa mayonnaise (page 463).

Moroccan-crumbed snapper

You can swap the snapper for other firm white fish fillets, such as flathead or rockling (if you live in Australia), or even for boneless skinless chicken breasts. It's basically glammed up fish fingers. Serve with Harissa mayonnaise (page 463) and a simple salad. Serves 6

200 g (7 oz) day-old soft white bread

50 g (1¾ oz/⅓ cup) pine nuts

2 tablespoons chopped flat-leaf (Italian) parsley

2 teaspoons smoky paprika

1 egg

125 ml (4 fl oz/½ cup) milk

6 × 180 g (6½ oz) snapper fillets or other firm white fish

Oil for cooking

Lemon wedges to serve

Place the bread in a food processor and process until coarse breadcrumbs form. Add the pine nuts, parsley and smoky paprika and season with salt and freshly ground black pepper. Process until well combined and the mixture resembles fine breadcrumbs. Tip into a large bowl.

Beat the egg and milk together in a separate bowl.

Coat each fish fillet in the egg mixture and then the breadcrumbs until the fish is well coated. Repeat with the remaining fish and refrigerate until needed.

Heat a heavy-based frying pan over medium–high heat, add a generous splash of oil and cook the fish, in batches if necessary, until golden brown on each side. Keep the cooked fish warm in a hot oven while you finish cooking the rest of the fish. Serve with the lemon wedges.

Tuna patties

This is another favourite dinner, and a great one because there's usually a tin of tuna in the cupboard and potatoes on hand, so I can avoid a trip to the shops. Serves 4

750 g (1 lb 11 oz) potatoes

20 g (¾ oz) butter

Grated zest of 2 lemons

2 tablespoons chopped flat-leaf (Italian) parsley

1 tablespoon mayonnaise

1 teaspoon dijon mustard

475 g (1 lb 1 oz) tinned tuna, drained

1 egg, lightly beaten with 80 ml (2½ fl oz/⅓ cup) milk

60–120 g (2–4½ oz/1–2 cups) panko breadcrumbs

Oil for cooking

Peel, boil and mash the potatoes. Add the butter, lemon zest, parsley, mayonnaise and mustard and season with salt and freshly ground black pepper.

Break up the tuna and add it to the mashed potatoes. Mix to combine and shape into fish cakes – you should get 8–10. Allow to cool.

Put the egg and milk mixture in a bowl and the breadcrumbs in another.

Take the fish patties and coat them with the egg mixture and then dip them in the breadcrumbs to coat completely. Repeat with all the patties.

Preheat the oven to 180°C (350°F).

Place a heavy-based frying pan over high heat. Add a generous splash of oil and cook the fish cakes for 3–4 minutes on each side until golden brown. You may have to do this in batches. Transfer the fish cakes to a baking tray and cook in the oven for a further 10 minutes.

Salmon fish cakes
Swap the tuna for 400 g (14 oz) pan-fried salmon.

Blue-eye with tomato and chilli broth

This easy-to-prepare and absolutely gorgeous dish will knock your dining companions sideways. The richness of the fish is perfectly matched with the tangy lemongrass, while the tomatoes – the star of the dish – add an extra vibrancy. Serve with crusty bread and a green salad. Serves 6

15 g (½ oz) chopped coriander (cilantro) roots and stems, plus 30 g (1 oz/1 cup) coriander leaves

1 lemongrass stem, white part only, roughly chopped

3 spring onions (scallions), roughly chopped

4 roughly chopped ripe tomatoes plus 3 whole tomatoes

3–4 slices fresh ginger

2 garlic cloves, peeled

3 small red chillies, cut in half, plus 2–3 thinly sliced small red chillies

2 kaffir lime leaves (optional)

Fish sauce

40–60 ml (1¼–2 fl oz) fresh lime juice

Oil for cooking

6 × 180–200 g (6½–7 oz) blue-eye or other white fish fillets

4 spring onions (scallions), thinly sliced

For the broth, place the coriander roots and stems in a large saucepan. Add the lemongrass, spring onion, the chopped tomatoes, the ginger, garlic, halved chillies and the kaffir lime leaves (if using). Add 1.5 litres (51 fl oz/6 cups) water and bring to the boil over medium heat. Reduce to a simmer and cook for 45 minutes. Strain the liquid through a sieve, pushing down well to extract all the flavour from the vegetables.

Take the whole tomatoes, remove the eyes and cut a cross on the base with a sharp knife. Plunge into boiling water and blanch for 10 seconds. Remove and refresh under cold water. Peel, cut into quarters, remove the seeds and finely dice the flesh. Set aside.

When ready to serve, bring the broth to the boil, season with fish sauce and lime juice to taste and simmer until ready to serve.

Place a large frying pan over medium heat and add a splash of oil. Place the fish, flesh side down, in the pan and cook for 3–4 minutes. You may need to cook them in two batches, or use two pans. Turn the fish over and cook for a further 3 minutes or until just cooked.

Place each fish fillet in a shallow bowl. Scatter the spring onion, diced tomato, coriander leaves and sliced chilli over the top. Ladle over the broth, and serve.

Tuna teriyaki skewers

As with all oily fish, you should cook these tuna teriyaki skewers only to medium-rare to enjoy them at their best. Makes 12 skewers

750 g (1 lb 11 oz) tuna
80 ml (2½ fl oz/⅓ cup) shoyu
2 tablespoons mirin
2 teaspoons grated fresh ginger
1 teaspoon sesame oil
12 skewers

Cut the tuna into 2 cm (¾ in) chunks. Mix the remaining ingredients together, pour over the tuna and marinate for 30 minutes.

Preheat a barbecue to high and oil the barbecue plate.

Thread four chunks of tuna onto each skewer. Set aside the remaining marinade for basting during cooking.

Place the tuna on the barbecue plate and cook for 2 minutes. Turn over and cook for a further 2 minutes.

Skewers

I find it best to use metal skewers for two reasons. One, you don't have to worry about soaking them. The soaking theory is good - soak the bamboo skewers in water for 20 minutes so that when you put them on the barbecue they don't catch fire - but if you ever want to make skewers in advance and store them in the refrigerator, they will dry out, and they often still catch fire even when they have been soaked. The other reason is purely environmental; it's always better to reuse!

TIP

Steamed Thai fish

Steaming is a simple way to cook delicate food like fish, yet it's a method that's rarely used by most home cooks. Well, this could just be the recipe to inspire you to give it a try. Serves 4

½ bunch coriander (cilantro)

2 garlic cloves, crushed

2 fresh green chillies, finely diced

60 ml (2 fl oz/¼ cup) lime juice

2–3 teaspoons caster (superfine) sugar

2 tablespoons fish sauce

1 teaspoon sesame oil

4 firm white fish fillets or 1 whole fish

2 tablespoons julienned fresh ginger

2 spring onions (scallions), thinly sliced

Steamed rice (page 480) to serve

Trim the roots from the coriander and chop them finely. Mix together the coriander roots, ½ teaspoon salt, the garlic, chilli, lime juice, caster sugar, fish sauce and sesame oil. Pound briefly with a mortar and pestle or whizz briefly in a food processor.

Pick the coriander leaves from the stems and set aside for garnish.

Place a wok over high heat. Add 6 cm (2½ in) of water and bring to the boil. Rest a plate in the bottom of a bamboo steamer and place the steamer in the wok. Arrange the fish on the plate, then pour the marinade over and top with the ginger. Cover and steam for 6–8 minutes, depending on the thickness of the fish. A whole fish may take up to 12–15 minutes.

Serve the fish with the cooking juices, spring onion, coriander leaves and steamed rice.

Baked fish parcels with coconut milk and kaffir lime

I can't express how simple fish parcels are to make and how dramatic they look as you serve them. Serves 4

1 carrot

8 choy sum (Chinese flowering cabbage) stems

4 kaffir lime leaves

2 spring onions (scallions), sliced

Coriander (cilantro) sprigs

1 lemongrass stem, white part only, sliced

2 tablespoons fish sauce

4 firm white fish fillets

60 ml (2 fl oz/¼ cup) coconut milk

Jasmine rice to serve

Preheat the oven to 180°C (350°F).

Peel the carrot, then cut long strips from the carrot using a vegetable peeler. Cut the choy sum into 6 cm (2½ in) lengths.

Lay four 25 cm (10 in) baking paper squares out flat. Divide the carrot and choy sum between the paper squares and lay one kaffir lime leaf on top of each pile. Divide the spring onion, coriander sprigs and lemongrass between the piles. Sprinkle with fish sauce. Place the fish on top and pour coconut milk over.

Fold the paper ends in and pull the remaining two edges up together. Roll over tightly to finish on top of the fish. Cook the fish in the oven for 15 minutes. Serve with jasmine rice.

Vegetarian

Moroccan lentil burgers

Ras el hanout is a Middle Eastern spice mix. You can use any Moroccan-inspired spice mix you have handy, or simply add 1 teaspoon each of ground cumin, coriander and smoky paprika, plus 1 teaspoon of Harissa (page 467). You can serve the lentil burgers with Beetroot fattouche (page 281) and Tzatziki (page 475). Serves 4

Olive oil

1 onion, diced

1 tablespoon Ras el hanout (page 468)

200 g (7 oz) red lentils, washed

500 ml (17 fl oz/2 cups) vegetable stock

2 tablespoons chopped coriander (cilantro)

125 g (4½ oz/½ cup) ricotta

100 g (3½ oz/1 cup) dry breadcrumbs

Oil for cooking

Heat a medium saucepan over medium heat. Add 1–2 tablespoons olive oil and the onion and cook for 3–4 minutes, until the onion is soft. Add the spice and cook for 3–4 minutes, until aromatic. Add the lentils, stir well, and add enough stock to cover. Bring to the boil, then reduce the heat and cook for 15 minutes, adding more stock as necessary. Cook until the lentils are tender and all the liquid is absorbed.

Put the cooked lentils in a bowl and add the coriander, ricotta and breadcrumbs. Mix well and season to taste with salt and freshly ground black pepper. Divide into 12 portions and form into burger shapes.

Preheat the oven to 180°C (350°F).

Heat a heavy-based frying pan over medium heat, add a splash of oil and cook for 5–6 minutes on each side, until golden brown. Place in the oven and cook for a further 3–4 minutes before serving.

Sweet potato and cashew falafels

Traditionally, falafels are deep-fried but, in the interests of being a bit healthier, I have opted for pan-frying. Serve with Green tahini sauce (page 455), Hummus (page 473) and Cabbage, pea, mint and chilli salad (page 272). For a more substantial meal, serve with Black quinoa and baby carrot salad (page 282). Serves 4

1 small sweet potato, peeled and grated

40 g (1½ oz) quinoa flakes

2 tablespoons chopped coriander (cilantro)

2 spring onions (scallions), thinly sliced

80 g (2¾ oz/½ cup) chopped cashew nuts, optional

2 teaspoons Ras el hanout (page 468)

1 egg yolk

1 tablespoon cashew or peanut butter

Oil for cooking

Place all the ingredients, except the oil, in a food processor and pulse until just combined.

Roll the mixture into large golf ball–sized balls and flatten them slightly.

Heat a heavy-based frying pan over medium–high heat, add a splash of oil and cook the falafels for 3–4 minutes on each side until golden brown. You may need to cook them in batches – if so, heat the oven to 180°C (350°F) and keep the cooked falafels hot while you cook the remaining falafels.

Caramelised onion, spinach and chickpea patties

I have been making this recipe for as long as I can remember and I love it. Remember, you can always substitute the breadcrumbs for quinoa flakes if you like. Makes 12

60 ml (2 fl oz/¼ cup) olive oil

4 onions, sliced

2 teaspoons ground cumin

2 teaspoons ground coriander

1 teaspoon sweet paprika

150 g (5½ oz/3 cups) baby English spinach leaves, chopped

3 tablespoons chopped coriander (cilantro)

1 egg

100–150 g (3½–5½ oz/1–1½ cups) dry breadcrumbs

400 g (14 oz) tinned chickpeas, drained, rinsed and roughly mashed

Oil for cooking

Heat the oil in a medium saucepan, add the onion and cook over low heat, stirring often, for 15–20 minutes until the onion softens but doesn't colour. Add the spices and cook for 1–2 minutes. Add the spinach, remove from the heat and stir until the spinach wilts. Season well with salt and freshly ground black pepper and add the coriander.

Allow to cool slightly, then mix in the egg, breadcrumbs and mashed chickpeas. Divide into 12 and form into burger pattie shapes.

Preheat the oven to 180°C (350°F).

Heat a heavy-based frying pan over medium heat, add a splash of oil and cook for 5–6 minutes on each side, until golden brown. Place in the oven and cook for a further 3–4 minutes.

Mexican bean cakes with chilli salsa

These bean cakes are well suited to both vegetarians and vegans. They can also be made smaller and served as an appetiser. Makes 12

300 g (10½ oz) dried pinto beans, soaked in cold water, soaked overnight, then drained

Oil for cooking and brushing

1 onion, diced

1 red capsicum (bell pepper), diced

4 small red chillies, seeded and diced, or 1 tablespoon chilli paste

2 garlic cloves, crushed

2–3 tablespoons chopped coriander (cilantro)

1 tablespoon ground cumin

1 tablespoon ground coriander

100 g (3½ oz/⅔ cup) polenta

Chilli salsa (page 479) to serve

Place the soaked beans in a large saucepan, cover with cold water and bring to the boil. Cook for about 30–40 minutes, until tender, topping up the water if needed. Drain and mash roughly.

Heat a small frying pan over medium heat. Add a splash of oil, the onion and capsicum and cook for 4–5 minutes, until soft. Add the chilli and garlic and cook for a further 1–2 minutes, until fragrant. Add to the mashed beans, along with the fresh coriander and spices. Season with salt and freshly ground black pepper and shape into 12 cakes. Coat lightly with the polenta.

Preheat a barbecue to hot and brush with oil.

Place the bean cakes on the barbecue plate and cook for 5–6 minutes, rotating as needed. Turn them over and cook for a further 5 minutes, again rotating as needed. Serve with the chilli salsa.

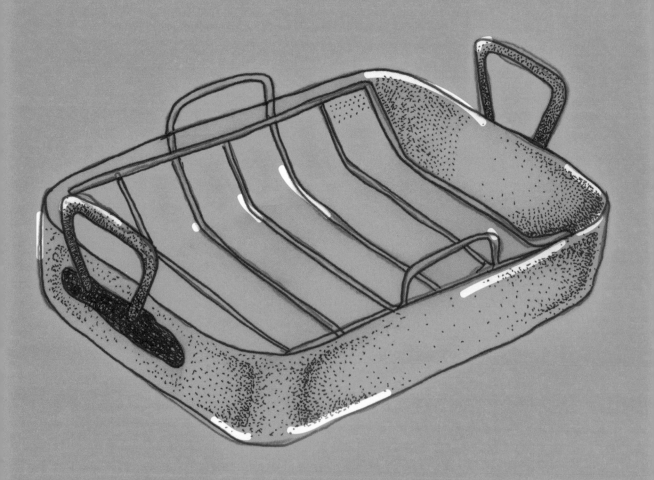

Roasts

A roast dinner is one of the most satisfying meals you can prepare. Anticipation builds from the moment the first aromas start to waft from the oven, culminating in the presentation of the cooked meat with all the trimmings. I grew up with the tradition of the weekly Sunday roast and, while I no longer regularly indulge, having a roast dinner on a Sunday is a treat I still savour.

Traditional family dinners

A roast is such a family dinner. It's a convivial celebration of important times spent together. Even children get excited … 'There *is* going to be gravy, isn't there?'. Whether you're a roast chook, lamb, pork or beef kind of person, a traditional roast deserves roast potatoes, a variety of seasonal vegetables and proper gravy. Try one of the time-honoured recipes, or go for something more modern and exotic.

A good roast means top-quality meat and it needs fat to keep it moist. Meat cooked on the bone, such as racks, ribs, shoulders and leg, will have much more juice and a meatier flavour than a boned roast. Always ensure the oven is preheated before adding the meat. Prime cuts of meat, such as beef fillet, need to be sealed before being put in the oven. Not only does this cut the cooking time, it ensures all the juices are kept in the meat. You can also start the roast off at a higher temperature for the initial cooking, which has the same effect.

There are two ways to cook a red meat roast (lamb and beef). You either go medium–rare – nice and juicy with a pink centre – which usually takes about 1 hour. Or you can go the other extreme and do it long and slow until the meat is almost falling part. If you end up somewhere in between (chef's purgatory), the meat will be dry and tough.

Don't forget to rest your roast once it's cooked. Allow at least 10 minutes. Remove the meat from the roasting tin, wrap it in foil, place it on a plate and cover with a dry tea towel (dish towel). Add any juices to the gravy and always carve across the grain of the meat.

Things you need to know
about roasts

- Meat can be browned before roasting to create a crust. This can be done by placing the joint in a very hot 220°C (430°F) oven for 10 minutes, then lowering the oven to 180°C (350°F) and cooking as required. You can also brown the meat in a hot frying pan before placing the roast in the oven. The only exception to this rule is poultry, as the high temperatures can cause the flesh to dry out.

- Poultry comes with its own rules. Stuff the bird and it will take up to an extra 30 minutes to cook. Start the bird off upside down, as this keeps the juices in the breast and prevents the flesh from drying out. Finish cooking by turning the bird the right way up for the last 30 minutes to crisp the skin.

- A free-range chicken has loads more flavour than an ordinary chook.

- If you want pork crackling, be sure to score the skin on your cut of pork with a sharp knife, then rub lots of salt into it.

- Roast your veggies! They're delish cooked that way. Potatoes, obviously, but also carrots, parsnips and just about every root vegetable, as well as cauliflower and zucchini (courgettes). Just don't roast green vegetables, such as beans and broccoli.

- Good gravy can make or break a roast.

- Add trimmings, such as mint sauce, bread sauce, mustards, horseradish, Yorkshire puddings and stuffing to suit your own tastes. These are all optional extras.

- A good heavy-based roasting tin is a fantastic asset – one that doesn't wobble or warp during cooking, that's large enough to fit the meat and the potatoes together, and that sits neatly soaking in the sink while you enjoy the fruits of your labour.

Roasting times and temperatures

BEEF AND VEAL ROASTING TIMES

NO BONE

15 minutes per 500 g (1 lb 2 oz), plus 15 minutes (medium–rare)

Add 5 minutes per 500 g (1 lb 2 oz) (medium)

Add another 5 minutes per 500 g (1 lb 2 oz) (well done)

BONE IN

20 minutes per 500 g (1 lb 2 oz), plus 15 minutes (medium–rare)

Add 5 minutes per 500 g (1 lb 2 oz) (medium)

Add another 5 minutes per 500 g (1 lb 2 oz) (well done)

LAMB ROASTING TIMES

NO BONE

20 minutes per 500 g (1 lb 2 oz), plus 15 minutes (medium–rare)

Add 5 minutes per 500 g (1 lb 2 oz) (medium)

Add another 5 minutes per 500 g (1 lb 2 oz) (well done)

BONE IN

25 minutes per 500 g/1 lb 2 oz, plus 20 minutes (medium–rare)

Add 5 minutes per 500 g/1 lb 2 oz (medium)

Add another 5 minutes per 500 g (1 lb 2 oz) (well done)

PORK ROASTING TIMES

NO BONE 25 minutes per 500 g (1 lb 2 oz), plus 25 minutes (cooked through)

BONE IN 30 minutes per 500 g (1 lb 2 oz), plus 25 minutes (cooked through)

POULTRY ROASTING TIMES

WHOLE CHICKEN 20 minutes per 500 g (1 lb 2 oz), plus 20 minutes (cooked through)

TURKEY 20 minutes per 500 g (1 lb 2 oz) plus 20 minutes (cooked through)

NOTE If the roast is stuffed, allow at least an additional 20–30 minutes overall

HOW TO TELL IF A ROAST IS COOKED

Insert a small knife into the meat as described below and count to five. Then test the temperature of the knife blade by placing it, cautiously, on the fleshy part of your thumb. (You may prefer to use a meat thermometer.)

BEEF AND LAMB Insert a small kitchen knife into the centre of the roast. Count to five. If the knife feels warm (tepid), the meat is rare. If it feels bearably hot, the meat is medium – it will have some pink left but no rare bits. This is ideal.

The colour of the juices that come to the surface can also indicate how well the meat is cooked. It takes a bit of getting used to, as well as some trial and error, but it works.

POULTRY Insert the knife in between the leg and the body. If the juices that come to the surface are pink, return the roast to the oven for a further 5–10 minutes. If the juices run clear (no sign of blood), the poultry is ready and there's no need to test for temperature.

PORK AND TURKEY Insert the knife into the thickest part of the joint. Unless the knife feels unbearably hot, indicating a high internal temperature, return the roast to the oven. These meats need to be thoroughly cooked through.

ROASTING TEMPERATURES

If using a meat thermometer, use these temperatures as a guide:

RARE	55°C (130°F)
MEDIUM–RARE	60°C (140°F)
MEDIUM	65°C (150°F)
MEDIUM–WELL DONE	70°C (160°F)
WELL DONE	70–75°C (160–170°F)

Roast recipes

Chicken

Roast chicken

A proper roast chook is one of life's simple pleasures. Buy a free-range corn-fed bird if you can, and serve it with all the trimmings. Serves 4

1.6 kg (3½ lb) chicken
Oil for cooking

Preheat the oven to 180°C (350°F).

Rub the chicken with oil and sprinkle salt and freshly ground black pepper all over, including in the cavity. Place the chicken upside down in a roasting tin or, better still, sit it on a wire rack in the roasting tin.

Cook in the oven for 45 minutes, until the skin is crisp. Turn over and cook for a further 30 minutes, until the skin is golden brown and crisp. Check whether the chicken is cooked by inspecting the juices for any sign of blood (pinkness). Allow to rest for 10 minutes before carving.

Lemon and oregano roast chicken
Mix together the grated zest and juice of 1 lemon, 1 tablespoon chopped oregano, 2-3 tablespoons olive oil, two crushed garlic cloves and season with salt and freshly ground black pepper. Rub the mixture all over the chicken.

Honey roast chicken
Mix 2 tablespoons oil and 2 tablespoons warm honey together and brush all over the chicken.

Herb roast chicken
Roughly chop herbs, such as thyme, rosemary or sage, and mix with a little melted butter. Brush all over the chicken and put some in the cavity.

Chermoula chicken
Mix 1 tablespoon Chermoula (page 468) with 2 tablespoons lemon juice and 60 ml (2 fl oz/¼ cup) olive oil and rub all over the chicken.

Sticky Asian chicken
In a saucepan, mix together 125 ml (4 fl oz/½ cup) soy sauce, 60 ml (2 fl oz/¼ cup) hoisin sauce, 60 ml (2 fl oz/¼ cup) Sweet chilli sauce (page 437), 2 teaspoons grated fresh ginger, two crushed garlic cloves and 1 tablespoon mirin. Place over medium heat and bring to the boil. Reduce to a simmer and cook until reduced by half. Allow the sauce to cool slightly, then brush it all over the chicken.

Spatchcocking a chicken

TIP

The beauty of spatchcocking a chicken is that it allows the bird to cook quickly. Allow 20 minutes, skin side down, then turn over and cook for another 20 minutes. Use any of the above marinades to mix it up.

You can ask your friendly butcher to spatchcock your chicken for you, or you can do it yourself.

Insert a sharp knife into the cavity and out through the neck. Hold the point of the knife and cut through, pressing down firmly. Trim the backbone away and remove any excess skin. Press the bird flat and trim the rib bones, if desired.

Chinese crispy-skin chicken

Crispy-skin chicken is a bit of an addiction with me – I can't go to a Chinese restaurant without ordering it. To recreate it at home I rub the chicken with a sichuan salt and pepper spice mix, fry it to give it a crispy skin, then roast it to finish cooking. Serves 4

1.6 kg (3½ lb) chicken
Sichuan salt and pepper spice (page 467)
1–2 tablespoons grated fresh ginger
1½ tablespoons rice wine vinegar
1½ tablespoons soy sauce
1½ tablespoons Chinese rice wine (shaoxing)
Oil for cooking
Steamed rice (page 480) to serve
1 lemon, cut into wedges, to serve

Cut the chicken in half through the backbone and trim away the rib bones. Cut off any excess fat and skin.

Place 1 teaspoon of the spice mix in a deep bowl, along with the ginger, vinegar, soy sauce and Chinese rice wine. Mix well, then add the chicken and rub the marinade all over it. Marinate the chicken, skin side down, for 1–2 hours, if time permits.

Preheat the oven to 200°C (400°F).

Heat a wok over high heat and add 3–4 cm (1¼–1½ in) oil. Remove the chicken from the marinade and pat it dry on paper towel.

Carefully place the chicken in the hot oil and cook it, skin side down, for 3–4 minutes, until golden. Turn the chicken over and cook for a further 4–5 minutes. Place the chicken, skin side up, in a roasting tin and cook in the oven for 15 minutes.

To serve, chop the chicken into thick slices and sprinkle with extra spice mix. Serve with the steamed rice and lemon wedges.

Peri-peri chicken

Forget fast food chains. Make your own peri-peri chicken. It's healthier, cheaper and generally more rewarding. Serves 4

1 tablespoon dried hot chilli flakes
15 g (½ oz/½ cup) chopped flat-leaf (Italian) parsley
1.6 kg (3½ lb) chicken, spatchcocked (see opposite), or 8 chicken drumsticks
Lemon wedges to serve
Potato wedges (page 257) to serve

Peri-peri marinade
4 garlic cloves, coarsely chopped
4 cm (1½ in) piece fresh ginger, peeled and coarsely chopped
160 ml (5½ fl oz) olive oil
160 ml (5½ fl oz) fresh lemon juice

To make the peri-peri marinade, place the garlic, ginger, oil and lemon juice in a food processor and blitz until puréed. Add the chilli flakes and parsley. Stir until combined.

Place the chicken in a large sealable plastic bag. Add the peri-peri marinade to the bag and seal. Rub the bag to coat the chicken in the marinade. Refrigerate for 4 hours, or preferably overnight, to develop the flavours.

Preheat the oven to 200°C (400°F).

Line a roasting tin with baking paper. Remove the chicken from the bag. Discard the bag and the excess marinade. Place the chicken, skin side up, in the prepared roasting tin. Season with salt and freshly ground black pepper. Roast in the oven, brushing occasionally with the pan juices, for 1 hour or until the chicken is golden and the juices run clear when the thickest part is pierced with a skewer. Set aside for 10 minutes to rest before cutting into eight pieces. Serve immediately with the lemon and the potato wedges.

Middle Eastern twice-cooked chicken with coriander relish

This recipe has a number of small stages in its preparation, but is quite simple at the serving up stage. One important step here is to get the chicken as dry as possible after cooking it in the stock. Otherwise, when you cook it the second time, it will splash and splutter a lot. Serves 4

1 onion, chopped

2 garlic cloves, peeled

1 cinnamon stick

Pinch of saffron threads

2 small red chillies, halved

3 cardamom pods, cracked

1 bunch coriander (cilantro)

1.6 kg (3½ lb) chicken

Oil for cooking

1½ tablespoons ground cumin

1 tablespoon salt

Coriander relish (page 477) to serve

Persian rice (page 481) to serve

Place the onion, garlic, cinnamon, saffron, chillies and cardamom in a saucepan large enough to hold the chicken snugly.

Chop the coriander roots and stems, reserving the leaves for garnish. Add the roots and stems to the pan, along with 2 litres (68 fl oz/8 cups) water. Add the chicken, ensuring there is enough water to cover it. Cover with a lid. Place the saucepan over medium–high heat and bring to the boil. Once boiling, remove it from the heat, keeping the saucepan covered, and allow the chicken to cool in the liquid. Once cool, remove the chicken from the liquid. Dry it well, wrap it in a tea towel (dish towel) and refrigerate, overnight if possible.

Preheat the oven to 180°C (350°F).

Cut the chicken into portions (see below). Heat a large frying pan over medium heat, add a splash of oil and cook the chicken portions for 3–4 minutes on each side until golden brown. Place in a roasting tin and cook in the oven for 10 minutes. Remove, cover and rest for 5 minutes before slicing.

Mix the cumin and salt together to make cumin salt.

Arrange the chicken on a platter, sprinkle with the cumin salt, garnish with the coriander relish and serve with the Persian rice.

Cutting a chicken into portions

TIP

To cut a chicken into portions, place the chicken on a chopping board. I put a tea towel (dish towel) underneath first to stop the board moving, but also to soak up any cooking juices.

Using a sharp knife, cut down one side of the breastbone (if you run your fingers along the top of the chicken you can feel it). Follow the bone cavity with your knife, cutting the breast away down to where it joins the wing. Using the heel of the knife, press down firmly on the wing knuckle and cut through it. Remove the breast and set aside. Repeat on the other side of the breastbone to remove that breast. Cut these breasts in half to get four portions. Place on a serving plate.

Using your hand, pull the thigh meat away from the carcass of the chicken. As you pull the thigh part away, use your knife to cut through the skin down to the thigh joint. Again using the heel of the knife, cut through the knuckle of the joint. Remove the leg quarter. Cut through the thigh and drumstick by pressing the heel of the knife through the joint. Repeat on the other side. You now have eight chicken pieces.

Sticky lemon roast chicken with sweet tomatoes

Roasting chicken pieces takes less time than roasting a whole chicken and enables the chicken pieces to get well coated in all the flavours and become deliciously rich and caramelised. Serves 4–6

1 chicken (1.6 kg/3½ lb), cut into 8 joints, or 1.5 kg (3 lb 5 oz) chicken pieces

Oil for coating the chicken

1 kg (2 lb 3 oz) new potatoes, cut in half if large

1 Preserved lemon (page 434), thinly sliced

Handful of garlic cloves

250 g (9 oz) cherry tomatoes

Juice of 1 lemon

Handful of roughly chopped flat-leaf (Italian) parsley

Preheat the oven to 180°C (350°F).

Place the chicken in a deep roasting tin and add enough oil to coat the chicken. Add the potatoes, preserved lemon and garlic cloves. Season well with salt and freshly ground black pepper.

Bake in the oven for 60 minutes, turning occasionally until the chicken is golden brown and cooked through. Add the cherry tomatoes and cook for 10–15 minutes or until soft. Finish with the lemon juice and chopped parsley, and serve.

Roast chicken drumsticks with chorizo and tomatoes

You can use your favourite cut of chicken in this dish, but thigh chops or drumsticks are best. You can even take a whole chicken and cut it into eight portions if you like (see opposite). Serves 4

2 tablespoons extra-virgin olive oil

1 garlic clove, crushed

2 teaspoons smoky paprika

2 tablespoons chopped coriander (cilantro)

8 chicken drumsticks

2 chorizo sausages, thickly sliced

500 g (1 lb 2 oz) small potatoes

1 red onion, sliced

Oil for cooking

125 ml (4 fl oz/½ cup) chicken stock

125 g (4½ oz) cherry tomatoes

2 tablespoons sherry vinegar

Mix together the extra-virgin olive oil, garlic, paprika and coriander, and season with salt and freshly ground black pepper. Pour the mixture over the chicken and marinate for up to 4 hours, time permitting.

Preheat the oven to 180°C (350°F).

Heat a heavy-based frying pan over medium–high heat. Add the chorizo slices and cook for 6–8 minutes, stirring often until the fat renders out. Drain the chorizo well on paper towel.

Place the marinated chicken drumsticks in a large roasting tin. Add the potatoes, cut in half if necessary. Add the chorizo and red onion, toss in oil and season with salt and pepper. Pour the chicken stock over and cook in the oven for 30 minutes.

Remove the pan from the oven, stir well, add the cherry tomatoes and replace in the oven to continue cooking for a further 30–45 minutes, or until the chicken is golden brown and most of the stock has been absorbed. Sprinkle with sherry vinegar and serve.

Roast chicken drumsticks with lime, ginger and honey

Chicken drumsticks generally take less time to cook, but I love cooking them at a lower temperature for a bit longer so they are really crispy and falling apart. Serves 4

8 chicken drumsticks

Grated zest and juice of 2 limes

2 small red chillies, seeded and diced

1 tablespoon grated fresh ginger

4 spring onions (scallions), thinly sliced

2 garlic cloves, crushed

2 tablespoons honey

Preheat the oven to 200°C (400°F).

Take the chicken drumsticks and slash the flesh to the bone two or three times.

Mix together the lime zest and juice, chilli, ginger, spring onion and garlic. Season well with salt and freshly ground black pepper. Pour the mixture over the drumsticks and massage well into the chicken flesh. Place in a roasting tin and cook in the oven for 30 minutes.

Remove the chicken from the oven, add the honey and toss to combine. Return the chicken to the oven and roast for a further 20 minutes or so, until golden brown all over.

Turkey

Stuffed turkey breast

Ask your butcher to even out the thickness of the breast if necessary. Better still, if you ask nicely and bring your stuffing with you, your poultry person will stuff and roll the breast for you. Just don't forget to say please. Serves 4–6

1 boneless skinless turkey breast (approximately
  1 kg/2 lb 3 oz)

Stuffing of your choice (see pages 485–6)

Oil for cooking

Preheat the oven to 180°C (350°F).

Lay the turkey on a chopping board, skin side down. Push the under-fillet (the small fillet under the main part of the breast) to one side, keeping it attached. Lay the stuffing down the centre and wrap the turkey around the stuffing.

Roll the breast up carefully so the skin is at the top. Take a piece of string, about 30 cm (12 in) long, and tie the thick part of the breast tightly. Continue to wrap the string around the turkey, 2 cm (¾ oz) from the previous tie. Thread the end of the string under the string to form a knot. Repeat this action until the turkey is evenly rolled.

Rub the turkey with oil and sprinkle with salt and freshly ground black pepper. Place the turkey in a roasting tin and cook in the oven for 1 hour and 20 minutes, or until the turkey is cooked through. Remove the turkey from the tin, wrap it in foil and rest in a warm place for 10–15 minutes. Carve and serve.

Moroccan roast turkey

A turkey buffe is a turkey with the legs and wings removed. It takes a shorter time to cook than a whole turkey and has white meat only. I often prepare this dish for Christmas Day and cook it in my kettle barbecue. It comes out moist, tender and full of flavour. You can, of course, cook the turkey without the spice mix if you prefer. This is excellent with Roast pumpkin, chickpea, feta and coriander salad (page 277). Serves 10–12

1 × 3.5–4 kg (7 lb 12 oz–8 lb 13 oz) turkey buffe

4 teaspoons ground cumin

4 teaspoons ground coriander

2 teaspoons ground ginger

2 pinches saffron threads (about 20)

½ teaspoon ground cinnamon

Pinch of ground cloves

60 ml (2 fl oz/¼ cup) olive oil

Preheat the oven to 180°C (350°F). Pat the turkey dry.

Mix together the spices, ½ teaspoon salt and ¼ teaspoon freshly ground black pepper with the olive oil and brush the mixture over the turkey skin. Place the turkey in a large roasting tin and roast in the oven for 1¼ hours. Turn over, baste well and cook for a further 45 minutes.

Remove the turkey from the oven, cover with foil and rest for 20 minutes before carving and serving.

Christmas roast turkey with all the trimmings

I'm still a traditionalist when it comes to the festive season. To me, it's just not Christmas without turkey and, as this is a special purchase, I always take care to search out the very best organic, free-range bird I can find. The quality and flavour make the extra effort and expense well worthwhile. Serves 10–12

1 × 3.5–4 kg (7 lb 12 oz–8 lb 13 oz) turkey

75 g (2¾ oz) butter

1 tablespoon chopped flat-leaf (Italian) parsley

2–3 thyme sprigs, chopped

Grated zest of 1 lemon

10–12 rashers (slices) streaky bacon

10–12 chipolata sausages

Cranberry sauce to serve

Classic gravy (page 456) to serve

Preheat the oven to 180°C (350°F). Pat the turkey dry.

Place the butter in a small saucepan and cook over low heat until it just melts. Combine the melted butter with the chopped herbs and lemon zest and brush the mixture over the turkey skin. Season well with salt and freshly ground black pepper.

Place the turkey upside down in a large roasting tin and roast in the oven for 1¼ hours. Remove the turkey from the oven and turn it over. Cook for a further 45 minutes.

Wrap a piece of bacon around each chipolata sausage. Add the bacon-wrapped sausages to the roasting tin with the turkey. Return to the oven and cook for a further 20–30 minutes.

Check to see if the turkey is cooked by inspecting the juices for any sign of blood (pinkness). Remove the turkey from the oven and rest for 20 minutes before carving. Serve with the bacon-wrapped chipolatas, cranberry sauce and gravy.

Duck

Roast duck

Most people put roasting a duck into the 'too hard basket' but, essentially, it's no different from roasting a chicken. Quite a bit of fat will come from the duck as it cooks, but all you need to do is pour this away from time to time. Serves 6

1 × 2–2.5 kg (4 lb 6 oz–5½ lb) duck
Olive oil
1 orange

Preheat the oven to 200°C (400°F).

Remove any giblets, neck and loose fat from the duck. Wipe the duck inside and out to remove any moisture. Make a few small cuts in the duck skin to allow some of the fat to come out during cooking. Rub the duck all over with olive oil and season the inside and out with salt and freshly ground black pepper.

Cut the orange into quarters and stuff it into the cavity.

Place the duck upside down in a roasting tin. Roast for 20 minutes, then remove the tin from the oven and tip any excess fat away. Return to the oven for a further 20 minutes. Again, tip any excess fat away and then turn the duck breast side up. Return to the oven for a further 30 minutes, checking once to see if more fat needs to be drained.

Check to see if the duck is cooked by inserting a knife between the thigh and the body – clear juices should run out. Rest the duck in a warm place for 15 minutes before carving.

Chinese roast duck
Use Sweet sticky marinade (page 459) on the duck. Roast as directed.

Sumac and pomegranate roast duck
Mix together 60 ml (2 fl oz/¼ cup) pomegranate molasses, 80 ml (2½ fl oz/⅓ cup) olive oil and 3 teaspoons sumac. Rub over the duck and marinate for 1 hour. Drain any excess marinade away. Roast as directed.

Roast duck with orange and cardamom caramel sauce

This is a jazzier version of the classic duck a l'orange. The cardamom adds a taste of the Middle East, so why not go all out and prepare Spiced couscous (page 483) to accompany the dish!
Serves 6

1 × 2–2.5 kg (4 lb 6 oz–5½ lb) duck

3 oranges

1–2 bay leaves

1–2 thyme sprigs

1 teaspoon ground sichuan pepper

1 teaspoon ground cardamom

115 g (4 oz/½ cup) caster (superfine) sugar

250 ml (8½ fl oz/1 cup) orange juice

3–4 cardamom pods, smashed

250 ml (8½ fl oz/1 cup) chicken stock

80–125 ml (2½–4½ oz/⅓–½ cup) lemon juice

Preheat the oven to 200°C (400°F).

Remove any giblets, neck and loose fat from the duck. Wipe the duck inside and out to remove any moisture. Make a few small cuts in the duck skin to allow some of the fat to come out during cooking.

Cut 1 orange into six segments and stuff them into the cavity along with the bay leaves and thyme. Place the duck upside down in a roasting tin and sprinkle with half the sichuan pepper and cardamom, then season with salt and freshly ground black pepper.

Roast the duck for 30 minutes. Remove the tin from the oven and tip any excess fat away, if necessary. Turn the duck over and sprinkle with the remaining sichuan pepper and cardamom and season with salt and pepper. Return the duck to the oven and continue cooking for a further 40 minutes.

Check to see if the duck is cooked by inserting a knife between the thigh and the body – clear juices should run out. Rest the duck in a warm place for 15 minutes before carving.

Remove the zest from the remaining oranges and set aside. Using a small sharp knife, remove the orange segments from the pith and set aside.

To make the sauce, place the caster sugar and 80 ml (2½ fl oz/⅓ cup) water in a small saucepan. Cook over low heat until the sugar dissolves. Increase the heat and bring to the boil. Continue boiling until the sugar turns to a dark caramel. Remove from the heat and carefully add the orange juice – be careful as it will splutter as it hits the hot sugar. Bring back to the boil and add the orange zest, cardamom pods and stock. Continue to boil until reduced by half. Strain and return to a clean saucepan. Check the seasoning. Add the lemon juice to counteract the sweetness of the caramel sauce.

Just before serving, add the reserved orange segments to the sauce and allow to heat through. Serve the duck with the sauce.

Crispy duck with spiced plum sauce

Everyone seems to love this combination of crispy-skin duck with spiced plum sauce. It's great with Stir-fried Chinese greens (page 248). Serves 4–6

Master stock (page 451)

4 boneless skinless duck breasts

115 g (4 oz/½ cup) caster (superfine) sugar

2 star anise

2–3 cinnamon sticks

4–6 plums, halved and stoned

Oil

80 ml (2½ fl oz/⅓ cup) fish sauce

80–125 ml (2½–4½ fl oz/⅓–½ cup) lemon or lime juice

Steamed rice (page 480) to serve

Bring the master stock to the boil in a large saucepan. Add the duck breasts, cover and cook for 10 minutes at a gentle simmer. Remove from the heat and allow the duck to cool in the stock. Once cool, remove the duck from the stock and refrigerate. Reserve the stock.

Preheat the oven to 180°C (350°F).

To make the sauce, place 500 ml (17 fl oz/2 cups) of the master stock in a saucepan over medium heat. Bring to the boil, add the caster sugar and stir to dissolve. Add the star anise and cinnamon and cook for 10 minutes to infuse the flavours. Add the plums and cook for 2–3 minutes. Remove the saucepan from the heat. Discard the cinnamon.

Heat a large frying pan over medium heat. Add a splash of oil and cook the duck breasts for 3–4 minutes on each side, until golden brown. Place the duck in a roasting tin and cook in the oven for 10 minutes. Remove from the oven, cover and rest for 5 minutes.

Reheat the plum sauce and add the fish sauce and lemon or lime juice to taste. The sauce should be tart, sweet and sour.

Carve each duck breast into six to seven slices. Arrange the duck pieces on a platter, pour over the hot sauce and serve with the steamed rice.

Duck confit

To make duck confit you are basically drawing out moisture with salt, then cooking the meat slowly in fat. Traditionally, this is done with duck fat or lard, but my mate Macka goes for the low-fat option (if you can call it that) with olive oil. The resulting meat can then be served in all manner of ways, from roasting or pan-frying, as a salad ingredient or to make the classic Duck cassoulet (page 221). Serves 6

100 g (3½ oz) coarse salt

6 duck legs

1 kg (2 lb 3 oz) duck fat or lard, or 1 litre (34 fl oz/ 4 cups) olive oil

Rub the salt over the duck legs, then cover and refrigerate overnight.

Preheat the oven to 180°C (350°F).

Rinse the duck legs well and dry the meat. Place a large ovenproof casserole dish over medium heat and melt the fat or lard. Submerge the duck legs in the fat,

cover with a lid and cook in the oven for 2–2½ hours, or until the duck meat is tender and the legs are almost falling apart. Allow to cool slightly before removing the legs and setting them aside to drain well.

Once the fat is tepid, strain it into a clean saucepan and bring to the boil, skimming if necessary. Strain once again and cool.

Keep the fat for the next time you want to make confit. Refrigerate the duck legs until needed.

Duck confit with cherry and verjuice sauce

Confit duck legs can be prepared at home or bought at a specialist food store. Either way, once you have the confit duck, the rest of the recipe is easy to prepare. Serves 6

6 Confit duck legs (see Duck confit, opposite page)

Oil for cooking

1 onion, diced

1 carrot, finely diced

1 garlic clove, crushed

250 ml (8½ fl oz/1 cup) verjuice

2 bay leaves

250 ml (8½ fl oz/1 cup) beef stock

300 g (10½ oz) cherries, halved and pitted

2 tablespoons chopped flat-leaf (Italian) parsley

Preheat the oven to 180°C (350°F).

Place the confit duck legs in a roasting tin and roast in the oven for 20–30 minutes.

To make the sauce, heat a medium saucepan over medium–high heat. Add a splash of oil and the onion and carrot and cook for 4–5 minutes, stirring often. Add the garlic and cook for 1 minute until fragrant. Add the verjuice and bay leaves and reduce the liquid by half. Add the stock and also reduce by half. Season with salt and freshly ground black pepper.

Just before serving, add the cherries and parsley and serve the duck confit with the sauce.

Beef

Roast beef rib

This is classic dinner-party fare and minimal work once it's in the oven. You might like to serve it with some steamed vegetables or a simple green salad. Serves 4–6

Oil for cooking

2 × 3 ribs of beef (1 rib per person)

250 ml (8½ fl oz/1 cup) red wine

250 ml (8½ fl oz/1 cup) beef stock

Preheat the oven to 180°C (350°F).

Heat a heavy-based frying pan over medium heat. Add a splash of oil and brown the ribs all over. Season well with salt and freshly ground black pepper and transfer the meat to a baking tin.

Place the beef in the oven. Cook for 40 minutes, then check the beef – it should be medium–rare. Once cooked, remove from the oven, cover with foil and rest for 10 minutes.

Return the frying pan to a high heat and tip away any excess fat. Add the red wine and allow to reduce by half. Add the stock and bring to the boil. Set aside.

To serve, reheat the red wine sauce. Carve the beef, arranging a rib on each plate. Serve immediately with the red wine sauce.

Roast beef with Yorkshire pudding

I always had trouble finding a small cut of beef for roasting – until I tried scotch fillet. Scotch is usually considered to be a steak cut, rather than a roast, but it's actually very good for roasting, particularly with Yorkshire pudding. Just make sure any excess fat is trimmed from the top, leaving a nice thin layer to baste the meat while it's in the oven. Serves 6

1.5 kg (3 lb 5 oz) scotch fillet (rib eye), trimmed of excess fat

Oil for cooking

300 ml (10½ fl oz) milk

150 g (5½ oz/1 cup) plain (all-purpose) flour

2 tablespoons olive oil

1 teaspoon salt

2 eggs

Roast potatoes (page 257) to serve

Classic gravy (page 456) to serve

Preheat the oven to 220°C (430°F).

Rub the beef all over with oil and salt and freshly ground black pepper.

Place the beef on a baking rack set in a roasting tin and cook in the oven for 20 minutes. Lower the temperature to 180°C (350°F) and cook for a further hour, for medium–rare. Remove the beef, wrap in foil and rest in a warm place.

While the beef is cooking, prepare the Yorkshire puddings. Whisk the milk, flour, olive oil, salt and eggs together until smooth. Allow to stand for 30 minutes.

When the beef is cooked and resting, raise the oven temperature to 220°C (430°F). Brush 12 large muffin tin holes with oil and heat them in the oven for 5 minutes. Pour the batter into the hot tins and return to the oven for 15–20 minutes or until risen and golden brown.

Slice the beef and serve with the Yorkshire puddings, the roast potatoes and the gravy in a warmed jug alongside.

Mustard roast beef
Rub the beef with wholegrain mustard.

Horseradish Yorkshire pudding
Add 2 teaspoons Horseradish cream (page 456) to the batter.

Pomegranate-glazed beef

I just love the combination of the sweet-and-sour pomegranate and the meatiness of the roast beef. Serve with Roasted summer vegetable and quinoa salad (page 279). Serves 4

2 tablespoons pomegranate molasses

60 ml (2 fl oz/¼ cup) olive oil

2 tablespoons lemon juice

2 teaspoons sumac

½ teaspoon ground coriander

½ teaspoon ground cumin

Pinch of ground allspice

2 garlic cloves, crushed

1 kg (2 lb 3 oz) rolled beef porterhouse

Mix the pomegranate molasses, olive oil, lemon juice, spices, garlic and some salt and freshly ground black pepper together. Rub over the beef and marinate in the refrigerator for 4 hours.

Preheat the oven to 180°C (350°F).

Drain any excess marinade from the beef and place the meat in a roasting tin. Roast for 1 hour, or until medium–rare. Set aside to rest for 20 minutes. Carve into thick slices and serve.

Slow-roasted pulled beef

How did we ever survive before slow-cooked pulled meats became so popular? I cook this style of food more and more. It takes very little work to get it going and then you can put it in the oven and forget about it. Leftovers make for great sandwiches the next day, too. Great served with tacos, Slaw (page 274) and Guacamole (page 474). Serves 4–6

2 kg (4 lb 6 oz) beef brisket
Barbecue baste (page 457)
500 ml (17 fl oz/2 cups) beef stock
2 bay leaves
3–4 red chillies, cut in half (optional)

Marinate the beef in the barbecue baste, ideally overnight. If time doesn't permit, just move straight on to the cooking stage.

Preheat the oven to 160°C (320°F).

Place the beef and marinade in a large casserole dish. Add the stock, bay leaves and chilli (if using), and season well with salt and freshly ground black pepper.

Cover and cook in the oven for 4–5 hours, turning the beef over every hour or so, and adding water if needed. The beef will be cooked when it starts to fall apart and you can 'pull' or shred it with two forks.

Pull the beef apart while still warm and return it to the cooking juices. Serve hot.

Roast sirloin with mustard and balsamic crust

The crust on this roast beef adds extra texture and flavour. You may like to use wholegrain mustard instead of dijon, or different herbs to suit your tastes. Serves 6

Oil for cooking
1.5 kg (3 lb 5 oz) beef sirloin
2 teaspoons dijon mustard
2 teaspoons balsamic vinegar
2 teaspoons olive oil
2 tablespoons chopped herbs (thyme, rosemary and flat-leaf/Italian parsley)
25 g (1 oz/⅓ cup) fresh breadcrumbs

Heat a large frying pan over medium–high heat. Add a splash of oil and the beef and cook until golden brown on all surfaces. Remove from the heat and allow to cool.

Preheat the oven to 180°C (350°F).

Mix the mustard, vinegar, the 2 teaspoons olive oil, the herbs and some salt and freshly ground black pepper to form a smooth paste. Add enough breadcrumbs to hold the paste together. Spread the paste on top of the sirloin and press firmly to ensure that it sticks to the meat's surface.

Place the beef in a roasting tin and cook in the oven for 45 minutes. To check if it is done, insert a small kitchen knife into the centre of the roast. Count to five, then pull the knife out. If the knife feels warm (tepid), the meat is rare. If it feels bearably hot, the meat is medium. You're aiming for medium to medium–rare. If necessary, cook for a further 5 minutes and test again.

Remove the beef from the oven, wrap in foil and rest in a warm place for 10 minutes. Carve into thin slices and serve immediately.

Beef pot-roast

This recipe is an absolute must to cook several times in the cooler months. The first sign of a cool night and I'm into it. The simple method and ingredients combined with a long, slow cooking time mean that you are still in good shape to enjoy it when it finally appears as a magnificent roast complete with its own gravy. Serves 4–6

1.5 kg (3 lb 5 oz) beef (fresh silverside or bolar blade)
2 tablespoons olive oil
125 ml (4 fl oz/½ cup) beef stock
125 ml (4 fl oz/½ cup) red wine
2 tablespoons tomato paste (concentrated tomato purée)
1 onion, diced
2 carrots, diced
1 garlic clove, crushed
1 bay leaf
2–3 thyme sprigs

Preheat the oven to 180°C (350°F).

Heat a large heavy-based casserole dish or roasting tin over medium heat. Rub the beef with the olive oil and add it to the casserole dish. Cook the meat on all sides until well browned all over, about 10 minutes.

Add the stock, wine and tomato paste. Scatter the vegetables around the meat. Add the fresh herbs along with a sprinkling of salt and freshly ground black pepper. Cover with a tightly fitting lid or with foil and place in the oven. Cook for 2½ hours, then check the meat for tenderness and adjust the seasoning of the sauce if required. Cut into thick slices and serve with vegetables and the sauce.

Mustard-crusted rack of veal

This is a beautiful dish and, while I don't eat a lot of veal, this dish reminds me that I should eat more of it. Cook the veal until it's medium–rare (still pink) for the best results. Best served with Pan-fried kale or cavolo nero (page 253). Serves 8

20 g (¾ oz/1 cup) flat-leaf (Italian) parsley leaves, plus 7 g (¼ oz/¼ cup) chopped flat-leaf parsley
2 tablespoons coarsely chopped chives
3 garlic cloves, finely chopped
2 tablespoons dijon mustard
60 ml (2 fl oz/¼ cup) extra-virgin olive oil
160 g (5½ oz/2 cups) fresh breadcrumbs
1.8 kg (4 lb) veal rack (approximately 8 points)
100 g (3½ oz) butter
Finely grated zest and juice of 1 lemon

For the crust, place the 20 g (¾ oz/1 cup) parsley leaves, the chives, garlic, mustard, oil and breadcrumbs in a food processor and pulse until a paste forms. Season with salt and freshly ground black pepper.

Preheat the oven to 160°C (320°F).

Season the veal with salt and pepper, then place it in a roasting tin. Using your hands, press the breadcrumb mixture evenly over the flesh side of the veal rack to cover. Roast for 1–1½ hours or until the veal is cooked through, but still pink. Remove, cover with foil and allow to rest for 20 minutes in a warm place.

To finish the dish, melt the butter in a small saucepan over medium heat. Add the chopped parsley, lemon zest and juice and cook for 2 minutes or until foamy.

Cut the veal into cutlets, drizzle with the herb butter and serve.

Lamb

Garlic and rosemary roast lamb

Garlic and rosemary is the classic combination to enhance the flavour of roast lamb.

Serves 4–6

1 × 1.5 kg (3 lb 5 oz) easy-carve leg of lamb

10–12 garlic cloves, peeled

2–3 rosemary sprigs

Oil for cooking

Preheat the oven to 180°C (350°F).

Using a small knife, make 10–12 cuts, 2 cm (¾ in) deep, evenly over the lamb. Push one garlic clove and a piece of rosemary into each cut. Rub the lamb with oil and season well with salt and freshly ground black pepper. Cook in the oven for 1–1½ hours.

To check if the lamb is done, insert a small kitchen knife into the centre of the roast. Count to five, then pull the knife out. If the knife feels warm (tepid), the meat is rare. If it feels bearably hot, the meat is medium. You're aiming for medium to medium-rare. If necessary, cook for a further 5 minutes and test again.

Remove the lamb from the oven. Cover and rest for 10 minutes in a warm place before carving.

Pesto roast lamb
Smear 60 g (2 oz/¼ cup) Basil pesto (page 476) all over the lamb and roast as directed.

Mustard roast lamb
Rub 2–3 tablespoons wholegrain mustard all over the lamb and roast as directed.

Stuffed leg of lamb with za'atar, preserved lemon and herbs
Soak one Preserved lemon (page 434) in cold water for 10-15 minutes. Drain, discard the pulpy centre and dice the zest finely. Mix with 3 tablespoons each of chopped coriander (cilantro) and flat-leaf (Italian) parsley, and 1 tablespoon Za'atar (page 470). Take the leg of lamb, remove the string if necessary and spread the meat out flat. Sprinkle the lemon, herbs and za'atar mix in the centre. Roll the lamb back up, enclosing the mixture. Tie with string to keep the lamb rolled in shape. Rub the lamb all over with oil, sprinkle with salt and freshly ground black pepper and place in a roasting tin and cook as directed.

Slow-roasted lamb shoulder

Slow-roasted lamb is a sensation. The shoulder has more flavour, but a leg of lamb will work just as well. Keep the oven temperature low and roast for hours – the aromas will tantalise your tastebuds. Cooking on the bone will add extra flavour, but you can use a boneless piece of shoulder if you like – it will take less time to cook, though. Serves 6

1 lamb shoulder (approximately 2 kg/4 lb 6 oz)

60 ml (2 fl oz/¼ cup) olive oil

2 tablespoons lemon juice

2 garlic cloves, crushed

2–3 thyme sprigs

Preheat the oven to 160°C (320°F). Cut slashes all over the lamb, going right down to the bone.

Combine the olive oil, lemon juice, garlic and thyme and add some salt and freshly ground black pepper. Rub the mixture all over the lamb, getting into the slashes. Place the lamb in a roasting tin, add 2 cm (¾ oz) water to the dish, cover with foil and roast for 5 hours, turning occasionally.

When the lamb has cooked for 5 hours, remove the foil. Return to the oven for a further hour, turning the lamb two or three times. Ensure the lamb is cooked until it is literally falling apart. Remove the lamb from the tray and keep warm.

To serve, place the lamb on a serving platter. Use two forks to roughly pull the meat off the bone, breaking it into large chunks.

Slow-roasted lamb with pomegranate and sumac glaze
Prepare the glaze by mixing together 2 tablespoons pomegranate molasses, 2 tablespoons olive oil, 125 ml (4 fl oz/½ cup) water, two crushed garlic cloves, 2 teaspoons sumac and some salt and freshly ground black pepper. Take a leg or shoulder of lamb, score the lamb flesh and rub the mixture over the lamb, getting right into the slashes. Continue as directed.

Spice-perfumed lamb shoulder
Taking inspiration from Sabrina Ghayour's book Persiana, *this beautiful spice mix adds a lovely perfumed flavour to the lamb shoulder. Grind 2 tablespoons (organic, unsprayed) rose petals. Add 2 tablespoons sumac, 1 tablespoon ground cumin, ½ tablespoon ground cardamom and season well with salt and freshly ground black pepper. Rub olive oil over the lamb, place the meat in a roasting tin, sprinkle the spice mixture all over and continue as directed.*

Lamb with broad beans, cherry tomatoes and anchovies

This recipe takes roast lamb to a whole new dimension. The tartness of the cherry tomatoes and the saltiness of the anchovies are the perfect accompaniments to this dish. Serves 6

1 × 1.5 kg (3 lb 5 oz) easy-carve leg of lamb

Oil for cooking

1 red onion, finely diced

Pinch of dried chilli flakes

4–6 anchovy fillets, chopped

250 g (9 oz) cherry tomatoes, halved

125 ml (4 fl oz/½ cup) chicken stock

150 g (5½ oz) broad beans, blanched and double-podded

2 tablespoons chopped flat-leaf (Italian) parsley

Preheat the oven to 180°C (350°F).

Rub the lamb with oil and season well with salt and freshly ground black pepper. Place the lamb in a roasting tin and cook in the oven for 1–1½ hours.

To check if the lamb is done, insert a small kitchen knife into the centre of the roast. Count to five, then pull the knife out. If the knife feels warm (tepid), the meat is rare. If it feels bearably hot, the meat is medium. You're aiming for medium to medium–rare. If necessary, cook for a further 5 minutes and test again.

Remove the lamb from the oven. Cover and rest for 20 minutes in a warm place before carving.

Heat a heavy-based frying pan over medium–high heat. Add a splash of oil, the onion and chilli and cook for 3–4 minutes until softened. Add the anchovies and cook for a further 1–2 minutes, then add the tomatoes. Cook for 4–5 minutes, stirring often, until the tomatoes start to break down and caramelise. Add the stock, season with pepper and bring to the boil. Reduce to a simmer and cook until the sauce reduces. If required, set aside until almost ready to serve. To serve, bring the sauce back to the boil and add the broad beans to heat through.

Carve the lamb, adding any juices to the sauce, and check the seasoning. Stir the parsley through the sauce and pour into a deep platter. Arrange the sliced lamb on top and serve.

Pork

Roast rack of pork

I often cook a roast rack of pork for a mid-year 'Christmas' dinner. The tender slices of crackling-topped meat with creamy potatoes really hit the spot on a cold winter's night.
Serves 6

2 kg (4 lb 6 oz) rack of pork, trimmed and scored

2 tablespoons olive oil

500 ml (17 fl oz/2 cups) chicken stock

2 kg (4 lb 6 oz) potatoes, peeled and sliced

40–60 g (1½–2 oz) butter

Preheat the oven to 220°C (430°F).

Rub the pork with the oil, 2 tablespoons salt (yes, really) and some freshly ground black pepper. Pour the stock into a deep roasting tin, place a wire baking rack in the tin and place the pork on top of it.

Cook the pork in the oven for 20–30 minutes. The crackling should rise and become puffy; if it doesn't start to crackle at this stage, then it probably isn't going to.

Lower the oven temperature to 180°C (350°F) and cook for 40 minutes. Add the sliced potatoes to the stock in the roasting tin, top with dobs of butter and sprinkle with salt and pepper. Return the dish to the oven, with the pork still sitting on top of the baking rack. Cook for a further hour.

Check that the pork is cooked by inserting a knife into the thickest part of the joint. Unless the knife is unbearably hot, indicating a high internal temperature, return the roast to the oven.

When the pork is ready, remove it from the oven, wrap it in foil and rest it in a warm place for 20 minutes.

Return the potatoes to the oven and cook for a further 20 minutes, until tender and the stock is absorbed. Carve the pork and serve with the potatoes.

Sweet sticky pork

This incomparable roast has a flavoured crust from the marinade. It's incredibly moist and tender and is also free of bones. You can buy pork neck from Asian butchers. Serves 6

250 ml (8½ fl oz/1 cup) dark soy sauce

125 ml (4 fl oz/½ cup) rice vinegar

2 tablespoons honey

1 teaspoon sesame oil

2 garlic cloves, crushed

2 teaspoons grated fresh ginger

2 tablespoons hot bean paste

½ teaspoon Chinese five-spice

1–1.5 kg (2 lb 3 oz–3 lb 5 oz) pork neck or
   scotch fillet

Mix the soy sauce, rice vinegar, honey, sesame oil, garlic, ginger, hot bean paste and five-spice together. Rub the mixture onto the pork and set aside to marinate for 2 hours, turning occasionally.

Preheat the oven to 190°C (375°F).

Drain the excess marinade off the pork. Place the pork in a deep roasting tin and cook in the oven for 45–50 minutes, turning occasionally. Check that the pork is cooked by inserting a knife into the thickest part of the joint. Unless the knife is unbearably hot, indicating a high internal temperature, return the roast to the oven. When ready, rest for 10 minutes before carving.

Slow-roasted pork belly with fennel and garlic

The longer you cook this fabulous pork roast, the more the fat will break down and the more the meat will melt in your mouth. For a twist on apple sauce, serve the pork with Quince aïoli (page 475), which will bring a beautiful sweetness to the meat. Serves 4–6

4 garlic cloves, crushed

1 tablespoon fennel seeds

2 tablespoons olive oil

1.5 kg (3 lb 5 oz) pork belly, skin scored

Preheat the oven to 220°C (430°F).

Mix the garlic, fennel seeds, oil and 1–2 tablespoons salt together. Rub over the skin of the pork, massaging it well into the flesh. Set aside for 2–3 hours to allow the flavours to penetrate the pork.

Place the pork in a large roasting tin, skin side up, and add enough water to half-cover the meat. Cook for 30 minutes, until the skin crackles. Lower the heat to 180°C (350°F) and cook for a further 2–2½ hours. Check the water level during cooking and top up as necessary, as the liquid will evaporate.

Remove the pork from the oven. If the skin needs to be crisper, remove it in one piece using a sharp knife, place it on a wire baking rack in a shallow roasting tin and return it to the oven, or place it under a hot grill (broiler) to crisp up. Once crisp, chop it into pieces.

Cut the pork into 2 cm (¾ oz) thick slices and serve with the crackling.

Mexican pulled pork

Pork shoulder is the best cut to use for 'pulling'. It can cope with the long, slow cooking and the forequarter cut has a good amount of fat through it to keep it moist. You can use belly pork if you like – just make sure when you pull it you get all the bones and cartilage out as you go. Some people like to add Barbecue sauce (page 440) to the pork as it warms, but I prefer it sauceless. I like to serve it with Tortillas (page 424), Guacamole (page 474) and Mexican black barley with corn, tomato and avocado (page 280). Serves 6–8

2 kg (4 lb 6 oz) pork shoulder, skin removed

Double quantity of Spicy Mexican marinade (page 458)

Pour three-quarters of the marinade over the pork. Set aside to marinate, ideally overnight, or for at least 4 hours. If you've failed to pre-read this part of the recipe and are planning on eating the pork shortly, you can still cook it now, but it just will not have the same depth of flavour.

Preheat the oven to 150°C (300°F).

Place the pork in a roasting tin along with the remaining marinade. Add 250–500 ml (8½–17 fl oz/1–2 cups) water, to come almost halfway up the pork. Cover with foil and cook in the oven for 3–4 hours, depending on the thickness of the pork, until it is cooked through and starting to fall apart. As the pork is cooking, add more water as needed to keep it moist.

Pull the pork meat apart with two forks, removing any gristle as you go. Warm gently as necessary to serve.

Roast pork loin with grapes and verjuice

If you happen to find the tiny purple currant grapes, they are ideal for this recipe, but other purple grapes such as muscat or Waltham Cross are also good. There are plenty of verjuices on the market, too. Maggie Beer's Sangiovese Verjuice is ideal for this recipe as it's made from purple grapes. Serves 6

1 × 1.5 kg (3 lb 5 oz) boned pork loin, skin scored
Olive oil for cooking
½ teaspoon fennel seeds
3–4 whole garlic cloves, peeled
2 bay leaves
250 ml (8½ fl oz/1 cup) verjuice
250 ml (8½ fl oz/1 cup) chicken stock
300 g (10½ oz) currant or other purple grapes

Preheat the oven to 220°C (430°F).

Rub the pork all over with olive oil and the fennel seeds. Season well with salt and freshly ground black pepper, rubbing it well into the scored skin.

Place the pork in a deep roasting tin and add the garlic cloves, bay leaves, verjuice and stock. Remove the grapes from the stalks and add them to the tin. Transfer to the oven and roast for 15–20 minutes. Lower the temperature to 180°C (350°F) and continue to roast for 1 hour.

Check if the pork is cooked by inserting a small sharp knife into the thickest part of the loin. Unless the knife feels unbearably hot, indicating a high internal temperature, return the roast to the oven and cook for a further 10 minutes and then try again.

When the pork is cooked, remove it from the tin and carefully slice off the crackling. Cover the pork with foil and rest in a warm place for 15–20 minutes.

Place the roasting tin over low heat on the stove top and crush the grapes and garlic with a wooden spoon. Allow the sauce to reduce to a syrupy consistency. Check the seasoning.

Slice the pork thinly and serve with the crackling and sauce.

Seafood

Baked salmon with herbs and lemon

Ask your fishmonger to pin-bone the salmon – that is, to remove the fine line of bones that runs down the middle of the fillet. I usually serve this classic dish around Christmas time when we are catching up with other families. It feeds a crowd, doesn't cost too much and has that wow factor. Lovely served with boiled minted potatoes, a green salad and a bowl of Lemon mayonnaise (page 463). Serves 4

1 side of salmon, pin-boned
2 tablespoons olive oil
1 tablespoon chopped flat-leaf (Italian) parsley
1 tablespoon chopped dill
1½ teaspoons chopped mint
Grated zest and juice of 2 lemons

Preheat the oven to 200°C (400°F).

Line a baking tray with baking paper and place the salmon on top. Rub the olive oil all over the fish and scatter the herbs and lemon zest over. Season with salt and freshly ground black pepper. Transfer to the oven and bake for 15–20 minutes, depending on the thickness of the salmon, until the fish is just cooked, but still a little pink in the centre.

Remove the salmon from the oven, squeeze the lemon juice over and serve.

Vegetarian

Nine-spiced roasted vegetables with chickpeas

This is a truly memorable dish – lots of chunky vegetables covered in an aromatic spice paste and roasted to perfection. The long list of ingredients makes this recipe look much harder than it really is, so don't be put off by it. Serves 4

165 g (6 oz/¾ cup) chickpeas, soaked overnight

1 teaspoon sweet paprika

½ teaspoon ground ginger

½ teaspoon chilli powder

½ teaspoon ground coriander

½ teaspoon ground white pepper

¼ teaspoon ground cardamom

¼ teaspoon ground cinnamon

¼ teaspoon allspice

Juice of 1 lemon

Olive oil

4 potatoes, peeled

1 eggplant (aubergine)

2 zucchini (courgettes)

2 large carrots

2 parsnips

½ pumpkin (squash)

375 ml (12½ fl oz/1½ cups) vegetable stock

Quick couscous (page 483) to serve

Tzatziki (page 475) to serve

Preheat the oven to 180°C (350°F).

Drain the chickpeas and place them in a medium saucepan. Cover with water and bring to the boil over medium heat. Reduce the heat and cook until soft, about 30–40 minutes. Drain and set aside.

Mix all the spices together with 1 teaspoon salt, the lemon juice and 2 tablespoons olive oil to form a smooth paste.

Cut the potatoes and eggplant into thick wedges. Salt the eggplant and let it stand for 30 minutes in a colander, until the juices bead. Rinse well and dry.

Cut the zucchini in half lengthways and then into quarters.

Heat a frying pan over medium heat and cook the eggplant and zucchini in a small amount of oil until golden brown. Peel the carrots and parsnips. Cut them the same way as the zucchini. Cut the pumpkin into thick fingers. Rub the spice mix over all the vegetables.

Arrange the potatoes, parsnips and carrots in a deep roasting tin. Pour half the stock over and bake in the oven for 30 minutes, turning occasionally.

Place the eggplant, zucchini, pumpkin and chickpeas in another dish and pour the remaining stock over. Cook for a further 20 minutes alongside the potatoes.

Check the seasoning, then serve the vegetables on top of the couscous accompanied by the tzatziki.

Moroccan stuffed eggplants

You can stuff these eggplants with just about anything, like Mexican black barley with corn, tomato and avocado (page 280), Red salad with berries and spiced nuts (page 281), Mexican spiced beef with chilli beans and tortillas (page 137) or even the harissa lentils from the Pan-fried blue eye with harissa lentils recipe (page 207). Serves 4

2 medium eggplants (aubergines)

Oil for cooking

1 onion, diced

2 garlic cloves, crushed

1 teaspoon Harissa (page 467)

1 teaspoon ground cumin

1 teaspoon ground coriander

100 g (3½ oz/1 cup) cooked quinoa or red rice or lentils

2 tablespoons chopped coriander (cilantro) or flat-leaf (Italian) parsley

2 tablespoons toasted slivered almonds or pine nuts (optional)

2 tablespoons currants or barberries

Seeds of ½ fresh pomegranate (optional)

Yoghurt tahini sauce (page 455) to serve

Preheat the oven to 180°C (350°F).

Cut the eggplants in half and, using a small knife, criss-cross the flesh taking care not to cut into the skin. Rub generously with oil and place on a baking tray. Cook in the oven for 25–30 minutes or until cooked through. Remove and allow to cool.

Heat a heavy-based saucepan over medium–high heat and add a splash of oil. Add the onion and cook for 3–4 minutes, stirring often. Add the garlic, harissa and spices, season with salt and freshly ground black pepper and cook for a further 2–3 minutes, until fragrant. Remove and place in a large bowl.

Scoop the cooked flesh out of the eggplant shells (reserving the shells). Dice the flesh roughly and add it to the onion mixture, along with the cooked grains, herbs, nuts and currants.

Divide the mixture between the four eggplants shells and return them to the oven and cook for an additional 15 minutes.

Serve while still hot – scatter the pomegranate seeds over the top (if using), and serve with the yoghurt tahini sauce.

Spice

I have always had a fascination with spices – how they can be subtle and perfumed, or spicy and heady, depending on the combination and how you cook them. Spices have long been a part of everyday cooking in many parts of the world, and flavours from Thailand, India, Malaysia and the Middle East influence other cuisines. Dishes such as tagines and curries often feature at the dinner table.

Spice up your dinner table

Many people find spice addictive. Once you have discovered the amazing array available, expect to find yourself adding more chilli and other spices to your food as your tastebuds are gradually won over and become more sophisticated.

Curry is a generic term applied to spicy food, usually from Asia, most commonly India. They are not called curries there, nor do traditional Indian chefs use pre-made curry pastes, sauces or spice mixes. Each dish is made up of selected spices, blended as they go into the saucepan. This is fine if you have plenty of time to spare, but most of us don't. My curries are a mixture of simple spice combinations, my own curry pastes and (more often) quick curries using store-bought curry pastes. I tend to eat one of these curries at least once a week.

Tagines use spices in a different way from curries, and they produce quite different results. The name 'tagine' comes from the traditional glazed earthenware dish that the meal is cooked in across North Africa. In a modern sense, tagines are slow-cooked stews, where meat and vegetables are combined with spices for flavour, fruit for sweetness and nuts for crunch. I'm big on tagines, both for everyday dinners and for entertaining, as they can be left to cook on their own and don't take much looking after.

Things you need to know
when cooking with spice

- The best accompaniments to cool down fiery curries include Tzatziki (page 475), Basic pilaf (page 481), Quick couscous (page 483) and lots of pitta bread.

- Curries don't require special cooking pots or equipment. A heavy-based saucepan with a tight lid will handle just about every curry we know.

- An everyday earthenware casserole dish with a tightly fitting lid is great if the long, slow cooking is to be done in the oven.

- Curries make inexpensive and flavoursome meals.

- When making a traditional curry you must have fresh spices, or it's not even worth starting.

- I often use two pastes in the same dish, such as Madras and hot, to get a more complex flavour.

- Start with mildly spiced curries and build up to spicier blends over time.

- You can choose to make quick curries using prime, tender cuts of meat, or there are slower curries using cheaper cuts, which are cooked long and slow to impart wonderful flavours and aromas.

- Tagines usually use tough, cheaper cuts of meat, which become extremely tender during the slow cooking process.

- Tagines often use special ingredients, such as pomegranate molasses, preserved lemons and harissa, which bring unique flavours and textures to the finished dish.

- Check the seasoning before serving, adding fish sauce for salt or freshly ground black pepper if needed – although the chillies should make the dish spicy enough.

- Virtually all recipes can have their meat component replaced with chunks of vegetables, although the cooking times will be shorter.

Spice recipes

Chicken

Thai green chicken and cashew curry

The basic method for all Thai curries is much the same. In a pan, you heat coconut cream until the natural oils appear on the surface, then you add the curry paste and cook the spices in the coconut oil. It sounds unusual, but it produces a curry that's much more pungent and has fuller flavours than those produced in the conventional way of cooking the spices in oil, then adding the coconut milk and meat. Serves 4

Oil for cooking

500 g (1 lb 2 oz) boneless skinless chicken thighs, diced

150 ml (5 fl oz) coconut cream

3 teaspoons Green Thai curry paste (page 465)

2 tablespoons grated palm sugar (jaggery)

2 tablespoons fish sauce

400 ml (13½ fl oz) coconut milk

400 g (14 oz) diced potato

100 g (3½ oz/⅔ cup) toasted cashew nuts

15 g (½ oz/½ cup) coriander (cilantro) leaves

Steamed rice (page 480) to serve

Heat a large heavy-based saucepan over medium heat. Add a splash of oil and the chicken thighs and cook until browned.

Remove the chicken from the saucepan and set aside. Spoon the coconut cream into the same saucepan and cook over medium–high heat for 5 minutes, until it separates and the oil floats on the surface.

Add the curry paste and cook for 5 minutes, stirring constantly, until fragrant. Add the palm sugar and cook briefly before adding the fish sauce and coconut milk. Bring the liquid to the boil, then return the chicken to the saucepan, along with the diced potato. Reduce the heat and simmer for 15–20 minutes, or until the potatoes are cooked. Add the cashew nuts and coriander leaves, check the seasoning and serve with the steamed rice.

Thai green chicken and spinach curry
In the last few minutes of cooking, add 90 g (3 oz) washed English spinach leaves – or other vegetables, such as peas, green beans or capsicum (bell pepper).

Thai red chicken curry
Substitute Red Thai curry paste (page 465) for the Green Thai curry paste.

Indian chicken curry

I've called this dish an 'Indian' chicken curry to differentiate it from the other curries. But it's just a basic curry I cook all the time, varying the ingredients according to what I feel like and what's in the refrigerator. I use a combination of medium and hot curry pastes to alter the flavour. However, you can make your own, or make it hotter or milder to suit yourself. Serves 4

Oil for cooking

1 onion, diced

3 tablespoons curry paste

500 g (1 lb 2 oz) boneless skinless chicken thighs, diced

4 potatoes, peeled and cut into 2 cm (¾ in) chunks

250 ml (8½ fl oz/1 cup) tomato passata (puréed tomatoes)

250 ml (8½ fl oz/1 cup) chicken stock

Steamed rice (page 480) to serve

Heat a large heavy-based saucepan over medium–high heat. Add a splash of oil and the onion and cook until the onion just begins to soften. Add the curry paste and cook for 5–10 minutes, until fragrant – but don't allow the spices to burn. Add the chicken and potatoes and cook for 2–3 minutes, just browning the meat. Add the passata and stock and bring to the boil. Reduce the heat and simmer for 15–20 minutes, uncovered. Serve with the steamed rice.

Indian chicken and spinach curry
Add a large handful of English spinach leaves for the last 2-3 minutes of cooking.

Indian chickpea and spinach curry
Omit the chicken and potatoes and add 200 g (7 oz/ 1 cup) cooked chickpeas. Add English spinach and coriander (cilantro) leaves for the last 2-3 minutes of cooking time.

Indian vegetable curry
Omit the chicken and add a selection of vegetables, such as sliced zucchini (courgette), cauliflower, green beans, peas, sliced red cabbage or bok choy (pak choy), to vary the textures.

Malaysian chicken curry

Malaysian curries are great when you want a really flavoursome, satisfying meal. Serve this with lots of steamed rice, natural yoghurt and roti bread for a real feast. Serves 4–6

6 Asian shallots, peeled

2 garlic cloves, peeled

1 lemongrass stem, pale part only, chopped

3 small red chillies, chopped

3 cm (1¼ in) piece of fresh galangal, peeled and chopped

Oil for cooking

1 teaspoon ground turmeric

4 boneless skinless chicken breasts, diced

1 tablespoon tomato paste (concentrated purée)

400 ml (13½ fl oz) coconut milk

2–3 kaffir lime leaves

200 g (7 oz) green beans

Steamed rice (page 480) to serve

Place the shallots, garlic, lemongrass, chilli, galangal, turmeric, 1–2 tablespoons water and 1 tablespoon oil in a food processor and blend until smooth.

Heat a medium saucepan over medium–high heat. Add a splash of oil and cook the chicken for 2–3 minutes, until golden brown. Remove from the heat and set aside. Return the saucepan to the heat and add the blended curry paste, along with more oil if necessary, and cook for 3–4 minutes until fragrant. Add the tomato paste, coconut milk and kaffir lime leaves. Return the chicken to the pan and bring to the boil. Reduce the heat, cover and simmer for 6–8 minutes.

Trim the ends off the beans and cut them in half. Add them to the saucepan and cook for a further 1–2 minutes. Season with salt and freshly ground black pepper and serve with the steamed rice.

Butter chicken

I never used to make butter chicken at home, instead preferring my local Indian restaurant to do all the hard work. Sorry guys, I will be staying in more now I have succeeded in creating this perfect butter chicken recipe. Serves 4

125 g (4½ oz/½ cup) natural yoghurt

1 tablespoon lemon juice

1 teaspoon turmeric

2 teaspoons garam masala

1 teaspoon chilli powder

1 teaspoon ground cumin

1 teaspoon ground cardamom

1 cinnamon stick

2 garlic cloves, crushed

2 teaspoons grated fresh ginger

1 kg (2 lb 3 oz) boneless skinless chicken thighs, diced

125 g (4½ oz) cashew nuts, roasted

Oil for cooking

1 onion, diced

1 bay leaf

2 teaspoons sweet paprika

250 ml (8½ fl oz/1 cup) tomato passata (puréed tomatoes)

250 ml (8½ fl oz/1 cup) chicken stock

125 ml (4 fl oz/½ cup) thickened (whipping) cream

Steamed rice (page 480) to serve

Place the yoghurt, lemon juice, spices, garlic and ginger in a bowl and mix together. Add the chicken and marinate for up to 4 hours, time permitting.

Place the cashew nuts in a food processor and blitz until finely ground.

Heat a heavy-based saucepan over medium–high heat. Add a splash of oil and the onion and cook for 3–4 minutes until softened. Add the chicken and the marinade, the bay leaf, paprika, tomato passata, stock and ground cashew nuts. Bring to the boil, reduce to a simmer and cook for 20–30 minutes, stirring often. Add the cream and cook for a further 10 minutes. Season with salt and freshly ground black pepper and serve with the steamed rice.

Chicken tagine with mushrooms, chorizo and sherry

This warming chicken dish will take the edge off chilly evenings as the weather starts to cool. The chorizo and mushrooms boost the flavour, making it very hearty. Use wild pine mushrooms, if available, and serve with Quick couscous (page 483) or Mashed potatoes (page 257). Serves 6

Oil for cooking

1 chorizo sausage (approximately 250 g/9 oz), diced

1.5 kg (3 lb 5 oz) chicken pieces (thigh and drumsticks) or diced boneless skinless chicken thighs

1 onion, sliced

300 g (10½ oz) mushrooms, sliced

2 garlic cloves, crushed

1 teaspoon Harissa (page 467)

2 teaspoons ground cumin

2 teaspoons ground coriander

1 teaspoon sweet paprika

½ teaspoon allspice

60 ml (2 fl oz/¼ cup) dry sherry

250–500 ml (8½–17 fl oz/1–2 cups) tomato passata (puréed tomatoes)

500 ml (17 fl oz/2 cups) chicken stock

Handful each of flat-leaf (Italian) parsley and coriander (cilantro) leaves

Heat a heavy-based frying pan over medium heat. Add a splash of oil and the chorizo and cook until the fat renders out. Remove from the frying pan and drain on paper towel.

Return the pan to the heat. Add a generous splash of oil and cook the chicken pieces until golden brown all over. Remove the chicken from the pan and set aside.

Return the frying pan to the heat and add more oil, if necessary. Add the onion and cook for 3–4 minutes, until it softens. Add the mushrooms, along with more oil if necessary, and cook until they soften. Add the garlic, harissa and spices and cook for 1–2 minutes, until fragrant. Add the sherry and stir well. Bring to the boil and cook until reduced by half. Add the passata and stock and bring to the boil.

Return the chorizo and chicken to the pan, and add more passata if necessary to just cover. Cover with a lid and cook over low heat for 1½ hours. Season with salt and freshly ground black pepper, add the fresh parsley and coriander, and serve.

Moroccan chicken with tomato saffron jam

This is a beauty of a recipe: one I'd serve up every week if time allowed. If you're as keen on this style of cooking as I am, this dish may become one of your favourites, too. Serves 6

Oil for cooking

1.5 kg (3 lb 5 oz) chicken pieces (thigh and drumsticks) or diced boneless skinless chicken thighs

1 onion, diced

2 garlic cloves, crushed

1 teaspoon ground cinnamon

1 teaspoon ground ginger

1 teaspoon ground cumin

¼ teaspoon ground cardamom

Pinch of saffron threads

6 tomatoes (500 g/1 lb 2 oz), diced

250 ml (8½ fl oz/1 cup) chicken stock

2 tablespoons honey

1 tablespoon orange blossom water

2 tablespoons flaked toasted almonds

7 g (¼ oz/¼ cup) coriander (cilantro) leaves

Quick couscous (page 483) to serve

Heat a heavy-based saucepan over medium–high heat. Add a generous splash of oil and cook the chicken pieces until golden brown all over. This may need to be done in batches. Remove the chicken and set aside.

Return the pan to the heat. Add more oil, if necessary, and cook the onion for 3–4 minutes, stirring often, until soft. Add the garlic, cinnamon, ginger, cumin, cardamom and saffron. Cook for 1–2 minutes, then add the diced tomatoes. Lower the heat and cook for 5 minutes, stirring occasionally. Raise the heat, add the stock and chicken and bring to the boil. Season with salt and freshly ground black pepper to taste. Reduce the heat and simmer for 30–40 minutes, or until the chicken is cooked.

Remove the chicken pieces and set them aside to keep warm. Raise the heat under the saucepan and reduce the cooking liquid until it's the consistency of thick cream. Add the honey and continue to cook for 5–6 minutes, stirring often, until it's reduced and like jam. Check the seasoning, add the orange blossom water and return the chicken to the pan to heat through.

Scatter the chicken with almonds and coriander and serve with the couscous.

Duck

Red curry of duck

This is another variation on the basic Thai curry theme, but the different herbs produce a slightly more complex result. The dish is smart enough for a dinner party, assuming you are serving several side dishes with it. Add vegetables such as Asian greens or bamboo shoots to balance the dish. You can buy Chinese roast duck from an Asian roast house. Barbecued quail is also a good substitute. Serves 4

1 Chinese roast duck
500 ml (17 fl oz/2 cups) coconut milk
4 teaspoons Red Thai curry paste (page 465)
2 tablespoons grated palm sugar (jaggery)
2 tablespoons fish sauce
125 ml (4 fl oz/½ cup) chicken stock
4 kaffir lime leaves (optional)
25 g (1 oz/½ cup) Thai basil leaves
Steamed rice (page 480) to serve

Using a sharp knife, remove all the flesh from the duck's carcass, taking care to leave the meat in reasonably large pieces, with the skin intact.

Discard the bones and chop the duck meat into 2 cm (¾ in) chunks, if necessary.

Place the coconut milk, curry paste, palm sugar and fish sauce in a large heavy-based saucepan over medium–high heat. Bring to the boil, reduce the heat and simmer for 5–10 minutes. Add the stock, duck meat and kaffir lime leaves (if using). Continue to simmer for 5–10 minutes, taking care not to let it boil or overcook as the duck pieces will start to break up. Add the basil leaves and serve immediately with the steamed rice.

Beef

Thai red beef and bok choy curry

This is the same base recipe used in Thai green chicken and cashew curry (page 187), but it uses red curry paste instead of green. The beef is cooked separately to ensure it remains tender, and it's added to the sauce just before serving. I have made it this way hundreds of times and it has always been a success. Serves 4

Oil for cooking

400 g (14 oz) scotch fillet (rib eye)

150 ml (5 fl oz) coconut cream

2 tablespoons Red Thai curry paste (page 465)

2 tablespoons grated palm sugar (jaggery)

2 tablespoons fish sauce

400 ml (13½ fl oz) coconut milk

1 bunch baby bok choy (pak choy), sliced

½ red capsicum (bell pepper), thinly sliced

100 g (3½ oz/⅔ cup) roasted cashew nuts

15 g (½ oz/½ cup) coriander (cilantro) leaves

Steamed rice (page 480) to serve

Preheat the oven to 180°C (350°F).

Heat a heavy-based ovenproof frying pan over high heat. Add a splash of oil and cook the beef until browned all over.

Transfer the beef to a roasting tin and cook it in the oven for 15–20 minutes, or until medium–rare. Allow to cool. Reserve the pan juices. Slice the meat into thick strips, discarding any fat and gristle.

Place the coconut cream in a heavy-based saucepan and cook over medium–high heat for 5 minutes, until the coconut cream separates and the oil floats on the surface. Add the curry paste and cook for 5 minutes, stirring constantly, until fragrant. Add the palm sugar and cook briefly before adding the fish sauce and coconut milk. Bring the liquid to the boil, then reduce the heat and simmer for 8–10 minutes. Add the bok choy and capsicum and cook until slightly softened. Add the beef and cashew nuts and cook until heated through. Add the coriander leaves to taste, season with salt and freshly ground black pepper and serve with the steamed rice.

Thai red fish curry
Swap the beef for firm white fish chunks and add them with the bok choy and capsicum. Vary the vegetables to suit your own tastes and finish with a squeeze of fresh lime juice to add zest.

Bloody good beef curry

It is indeed bloody good when you realise this dish needs few ingredients yet produces an aromatic curry that's perfect for Friday nights with a beer or two. Use any type of curry paste that takes your fancy. I like to use a mixture of two to add extra depth. Serves 6

Oil for cooking

2 onions, diced

2 teaspoons grated fresh ginger

2 garlic cloves, crushed

4 tablespoons curry paste

1.5 kg (3 lb 5 oz) blade steak, diced

2–3 cardamom pods

1 cinnamon stick

500 ml (17 fl oz/2 cups) beef stock

250 ml (8½ fl oz/1 cup) tomato passata (puréed tomatoes)

Steamed rice (page 480) to serve

Heat a large heavy-based saucepan over medium heat. Add the oil, onion and ginger and cook until the onion just begins to soften. Add the garlic and curry paste and cook for 5–10 minutes, until fragrant – but don't allow the spices to burn. Add the beef and cook briefly for 2–3 minutes, just browning the meat. Add the spices, stock and passata and bring to the boil.

Reduce the heat, cover and cook for 1½–2 hours, or until the beef is tender. Serve the beef with the steamed rice.

Massaman beef curry

This is a great curry. I prefer curries when they are cooked long and slow so all the flavours develop and the beef forms tender chunks. Serves 4–6

Oil for cooking

1 kg (2 lb 3 oz) beef (chuck or blade), diced

140 ml (4½ fl oz) coconut cream

2 tablespoons massaman curry paste

1 tablespoon grated palm sugar (jaggery)

2 tablespoons fish sauce

400 ml (13½ fl oz) coconut milk

3–4 cardamom pods, bruised

2 star anise

1 cinnamon stick

500 ml (17 fl oz/2 cups) beef stock

2 tablespoons tamarind

1 sweet potato, peeled and cut into 2 cm (¾ in) dice

40 g (1½ oz/¼ cup) roasted unsalted peanuts

4 spring onions (scallions), sliced

Steamed rice (page 480) to serve

Heat a large heavy-based saucepan over medium heat. Add a splash of oil and the beef and cook until browned. Remove the beef from the saucepan and set aside.

Spoon the coconut cream into the same saucepan and cook over medium–high heat for 5 minutes, until it separates and the oil floats on the surface. Add the curry paste and cook for 5 minutes, stirring constantly, until fragrant. Add the palm sugar and cook briefly before adding the fish sauce and coconut milk. Return the beef to the pan, along with the spices, beef stock, coconut milk and tamarind.

Bring to the boil, reduce to a simmer and cook over low heat for 1 hour. Add the diced sweet potato and cook for a further hour. Check the beef is tender – if not, cook for a further 10 minutes and test again.

When the beef is tender, add the peanuts and spring onions and serve with the steamed rice.

Beef rendang

Rendang is perfect with the usual accompaniments of steamed rice and hot roti bread. Together with my friends, Max and Sophie Allen, I've discovered that a magnum of Chimay stout with this dish will get us through a winter's night with considerable comfort. Serves 4

1 tablespoon tamarind pulp

125 ml (4 fl oz/½ cup) boiling water

Oil for cooking

200 g (7 oz) Rendang curry paste (page 466)

1 kg (2 lb 3 oz) blade steak, diced

250 ml (8½ fl oz/1 cup) coconut cream

1 star anise

1 cinnamon stick

Handful of coriander (cilantro) leaves for garnish

2 tablespoons toasted coconut (optional)

Steamed rice (page 480) to serve

Crisp roti bread to serve

Soak the tamarind in boiling water for 5–10 minutes. Use your fingers to work the pulp free from the tamarind seeds. Strain the tamarind, reserving the liquid.

Heat a heavy-based casserole dish over medium–high heat. Add a splash of oil and the rendang paste and fry for 5–6 minutes, stirring often, until fragrant. Add the beef and cook for 5–10 minutes, or until the beef starts to colour but before the spices begin to burn. Add the tamarind liquid, coconut cream, star anise and cinnamon to the casserole dish. Allow to come to the boil, reduce to a simmer, cover with a lid and cook for 1 hour, stirring occasionally.

Remove the lid and continue cooking the rendang for a further 30–45 minutes, until the beef is tender and most of the liquid has evaporated. Stir often to prevent the sauce from catching.

Sprinkle the coriander leaves and toasted coconut (if using) on top and serve with the steamed rice and crisp roti bread.

Beef and prune tagine

The casseroles and stews of the Middle East and North Africa typically include dried fruit, and the sweetness complements meats, vegetables and spices. This is a classic example of this style of cooking. Serves 4–6

1½ teaspoons sweet paprika

1½ teaspoons chilli powder

2 teaspoons ground cumin

2 teaspoons ground coriander

1 teaspoon ground white pepper

2 tablespoons lemon juice

60 ml (2 fl oz/¼ cup) olive oil

1 kg (2 lb 3 oz) beef (blade or skirt), diced

750 ml (25½ fl oz/3 cups) beef stock

250 g (9 oz) pitted prunes

Coriander (cilantro) leaves to serve

Combine the spices, 1 teaspoon salt, the lemon juice and oil to form a smooth paste. Coat the beef with the spice mixture and leave to marinate for at least 4 hours or preferably overnight.

Preheat the oven to 180°C (350°F).

Place the marinated beef in an ovenproof casserole dish with a tight-fitting lid. Add the stock, cover and cook in the oven for 1 hour. Add the prunes, replace the lid and return to the oven for a further 45 minutes.

Check to see if the beef is nearly cooked. If so, cook for a final 30 minutes with the lid removed to reduce the liquid. Sprinkle with coriander leaves and serve.

Indian beef curry

This is based on a vindaloo recipe and it's quite fiery, so make sure there's plenty of thirst-quenching beer and a big bowl of natural yoghurt nearby. Serves 4

2 tablespoons vinegar

3–4 curry leaves

1 tablespoon ground coriander

1 tablespoon ground cumin

1 teaspoon chilli powder

½ teaspoon turmeric

250 g (9 oz/1 cup) natural yoghurt

1 kg (2 lb 3 oz) blade steak, diced

2 tablespoons oil

2 onions, diced

2 teaspoons grated fresh ginger

2 garlic cloves, crushed

3 tomatoes, diced

1 teaspoon cumin seeds

2–3 cloves

2–3 cardamom pods

1 cinnamon stick

250 ml (8½ fl oz/1 cup) beef stock

Coriander (cilantro) leaves to serve

Steamed rice (page 480) to serve

Mix the vinegar, curry leaves, coriander, ground cumin, chilli powder, turmeric, yoghurt and a pinch of salt together. Pour over the beef and set aside to marinate for at least 2–3 hours, or overnight. Stir once or twice if possible.

Heat a heavy-based saucepan over medium heat. Add the oil and onion and cook for 5–6 minutes or until the onion is soft. Add the ginger and garlic and cook for a further 1–2 minutes. Add the marinated beef, tomatoes, cumin seeds, cloves, cardamom, cinnamon stick and stock and bring to the boil, stirring often. Cover with a lid, reduce the heat and cook for 1–1½ hours. Check to see if the beef is tender; if not, continue cooking. Discard the cinnamon stick.

Serve the curry with the coriander leaves and the steamed rice.

Chilli con carne

For a quick, easy, satisfying mid-week dinner it's hard to pass up a bowl of chilli con carne. I serve it with Steamed rice (page 480), sour cream, Tortillas (page 424) or tacos and Guacamole (page 474) and let everyone create their own masterpiece. Make extra and freeze it, as it's perfect for when time is short. Serves 4–6

Oil for cooking

2 onions, diced

2 garlic cloves, crushed

2 teaspoons Chipotle chilli powder or dried chilli flakes

3 chipotles en adobo, chopped

1 kg (2 lb 3 oz) lean minced (ground) beef

250 ml (8½ fl oz/1 cup) tomato passata (puréed tomatoes)

375 ml (12½ fl oz/1½ cups) beef stock

400 g (14 oz) tinned red kidney beans, rinsed

2 tablespoons chopped coriander (cilantro)

Heat a medium saucepan over medium heat. Add a splash of oil and the onion and cook for 3–4 minutes, stirring often, until the onion softens slightly. Add the garlic, chilli powder and chipotles en adobo and cook for a further 1–2 minutes, or until the garlic is fragrant.

Add the beef and cook until well browned, stirring well. Add the passata and beef stock, season well with salt and freshly ground black pepper and bring to the boil. Reduce the heat and cook for 30–40 minutes, stirring often. When the sauce has thickened to the desired consistency, check the seasoning, add the kidney beans and coriander, and serve.

Braised chipotle beef ribs

A perfect winter dish – long, slow braising, fall-apart beef, but with a kick of chilli to keep things interesting. Delicious served with Pumpkin mole (page 262) and Tomato pilaf (page 482). Serves 4–6

Oil for cooking

2 kg (4 lb 6 oz) beef short ribs

½ teaspoon chipotle chilli powder or dried chilli flakes

½ teaspoon ground coriander

½ teaspoon ground cumin

1 teaspoon mustard seeds, crushed

1 onion, diced

3–4 garlic cloves, chopped

2 cinnamon sticks

1 teaspoon ground cloves

1 teaspoon allspice

1 tablespoon tamarind

125 ml (4 fl oz/½ cup) boiling water

50 g (1¾ oz) tinned chipotles en adobo, chopped

½ bunch coriander (cilantro), chopped, plus extra coriander leaves to serve

2 tablespoons soy sauce

2 tablespoons balsamic vinegar

3 tablespoons brown sugar

375 ml (12½ fl oz/1½ cups) tomato passata (puréed tomatoes)

250 ml (8½ fl oz/1 cup) chicken or beef stock

Heat a large heavy-based frying pan over medium–high heat. Add a splash of oil and cook the beef ribs until golden brown and sealed on all sides. Remove and place in a large ovenproof baking dish.

Mix together the chilli powder, coriander, cumin and mustard seeds. Add some salt and freshly ground black pepper and sprinkle the mixture over the beef.

Preheat the oven to 180°C (350°F).

Soak the tamarind in the boiling water, then drain.

Heat a large heavy-based casserole dish over medium–high heat. Add a splash of oil and the onion and cook for 3–4 minutes until the onion is softened. Add the garlic and cook until fragrant. Add the spices and cook for 1–2 minutes, stirring often. Add the tamarind water and remaining ingredients and bring to the boil. Season well with salt and pepper. Allow to simmer for 30 minutes, then pour this mixture over the beef ribs.

Cover the baking dish with foil and cook in the oven for 2–3 hours, turning the beef ribs every hour or so. When the beef is cooked, check the seasoning, scatter the coriander leaves over and serve.

Lamb

Moroccan spiced rack of lamb

You can use this spice mix on any cut of lamb – leg, topside (round steak), chops or fillet (tenderloin). It's a bit more of a dinner party dish, mostly because lamb racks are so expensive. If I see them on special I usually grab them and make the most of them in a recipe like this. Great with Freekeh and chickpea salad (page 283) and Tzatziki (page 475). Serves 4

1 teaspoon ground cumin

1 teaspoon ground coriander

1 teaspoon smoky paprika

1 teaspoon Harissa (page 467)

Grated zest of 1 lemon

2 tablespoons olive oil

1–2 tablespoons pomegranate molasses

2 × 1.8 kg (4 lb/8 point) lamb racks

Preheat the oven to 180°C (350°F).

Mix together the spices, harissa, lemon zest, oil and pomegranate molasses. Rub all over the lamb. Cook in the oven for 20–30 minutes.

To check if the lamb is done, insert a small kitchen knife into the centre of the roast. Count to five, then pull the knife out. If the knife feels warm (tepid), the meat is rare. If it feels bearably hot, the meat is medium. You're aiming for medium to medium–rare. If necessary, cook for a further 5 minutes and test again.

Remove the lamb from the oven. Cover and rest for 10 minutes in a warm place before carving and serving.

Tikka roasted lamb

We eat a lot of slow-cooked lamb in our house; it's so easy and always popular. This is my favourite, as I love the slow-cooked richness of the lamb with the tang of tikka paste. I recommend serving with Basic pilaf (page 481), Tzatziki (page 475) and Cherry tomato and pomegranate salad (page 271). Serves 6

2 kg (4 lb 6 oz) shoulder of lamb, bone-in

4 heaped tablespoons Tikka paste (page 466)

2 long red chillies, sliced

4 garlic cloves, sliced

2–3 mint sprigs, leaves picked

Oil for cooking

500 ml (17 fl oz/2 cups) chicken stock

Lightly score the fat side of the lamb all over with a sharp knife, then stab it a few times and use your fingers to make little holes. Spread the tikka paste over the lamb and into the holes and then stuff the holes with slices of chilli, garlic and mint leaves. Cover and marinate in the refrigerator overnight.

When ready to cook, take your lamb out of the refrigerator to come up to room temperature.

Preheat the oven to 170°C (340°F).

Place the lamb in a deep baking tin, drizzle with oil and add the stock to the tin. Cover with a double layer of baking paper and foil.

Roast, basting occasionally, for 3½ hours or until the coating is dark and gnarly and the meat beautifully tender. Remove the lamb from the tin and pull apart the lamb with two forks to serve.

Kashmiri lamb

Diced leg of lamb will work nicely with this recipe. However, diced mutton, if you can find it, is even better. Because mutton is a tougher meat, it takes longer to cook, so the flavours of the dish have even longer to develop. Ask your local butcher if they can get some in for you; it will be well worth the effort. Serves 6–8

2 tablespoons garam masala

2 tablespoons Madras curry powder

1 teaspoon mixed spice

1 tablespoon sweet paprika

1 tablespoon ground ginger

125 g (4½ oz/½ cup) natural yoghurt

2 kg (4 lb 6 oz) lamb or mutton, diced

40 g (1½ oz) ghee

4 onions, diced

500–750 ml (17–25½ fl oz/2–3 cups) chicken stock

120 g (4½ oz/⅔ cup) dried apricots, sliced

125 g (4½ oz/1 cup) sultanas (golden raisins)

Steamed rice (page 480) to serve

Mix all the spices and yoghurt together and season with salt and freshly ground black pepper. Mix with the lamb and marinate overnight or for at least 2–3 hours.

Heat a large casserole dish over medium–high heat. Add the ghee and onion and cook until golden in colour, about 5–6 minutes, stirring often. Add the marinated lamb and enough chicken stock to just cover.

Simmer, uncovered, for 1–1½ hours, until almost tender. If using mutton, this could easily take an extra hour. Add the apricots and sultanas and cook for a further 30–45 minutes, or until the meat is tender. Serve with the steamed rice.

Sweet and sticky lamb ribs

Lamb ribs can cope with some good strong flavours. This meat is particularly gelatinous but with long, slow cooking will become tender and tasty. You could add some chilli to this recipe if you want a kick. Serve with Kimchi fried rice (page 480) and Asian coleslaw (page 275). Serves 6

2 kg (4 lb 6 oz) lamb ribs

80 ml (2½ fl oz/⅓ cup) oil

1 tablespoon ground cumin

1 tablespoon ground coriander

1 tablespoon smoky paprika

2 garlic cloves, crushed

1 teaspoon chilli paste (optional)

2 tablespoons brown sugar

2 tablespoons fish sauce

1 tablespoon tamarind paste

You may need to cut the lamb ribs into individual ribs, or ask your butcher to do this if you prefer. Simply slice down between each bone to separate.

Place the lamb in a large bowl. Mix together the oil, cumin, coriander, paprika, garlic and chilli (if using) and add salt and freshly ground black pepper to taste. Pour over the lamb ribs. Using your fingers, make sure the ribs are well coated. Set aside to marinate for up to 4 hours or overnight.

Preheat the oven to 170°C (340°F).

Spread the lamb ribs out flat in a large roasting tin (line it with baking paper to make cleaning easier). Cover the tin with foil and cook the lamb in the oven for 1 hour, turning occasionally.

Mix together the remaining ingredients and pour them over the lamb, making sure each rib is well coated. Increase the oven temperature to 180°C (350°F) and cook the ribs, uncovered, for a further hour, basting and turning occasionally until golden brown and crispy. Serve hot.

Braised lamb shanks with mint and harissa

I love slow-cooked lamb with a bit of spice – it helps to cut through the richness of the meat. If you like, add some vegetables to the lamb as it cooks. Serve with a green salad. Serves 6

Oil for cooking

6 lamb shanks

1½ teaspoons Harissa (page 467)

2 teaspoons ground cumin

1 teaspoon smoky sweet paprika

½ teaspoon allspice

⅓ bunch coriander (cilantro) with roots, chopped

2 mint sprigs, chopped

625 ml (21 fl oz/2½ cups) chicken stock

375 ml (12½ fl oz/1½ cups) tomato passata (puréed tomatoes)

Spiced couscous (page 483) to serve

Preheat the oven to 180°C (350°F).

Heat a large heavy-based saucepan over medium heat. Add a splash of oil and the shanks and cook until well browned on all sides. Add the harissa, spices, herbs, stock and passata and bring to the boil.

Transfer the lamb and sauce to a casserole dish, cover with a lid or foil and cook for 2 hours, or until the lamb is tender and almost falling off the bone. Season to taste with salt and freshly ground black pepper.

Arrange the shanks on top of the spiced couscous, pour the sauce over and serve.

Syrian lamb shanks

Shanks! I do love a lamb shank in winter. It's great food for sharing with friends – the hardest problem is finding a pot large enough to fit the shanks in. Serves 6

2 teaspoons ground cumin

2 teaspoons ground cinnamon

6 lamb shanks

Oil for cooking

1 onion, thinly sliced

10 cm (4 in) piece of fresh ginger, peeled and julienned

2 garlic cloves, crushed

2 small red chillies, diced

Pinch of saffron threads

2 tomatoes, coarsely chopped

2 tablespoons honey

100 g (3½ oz) dried apricots, sliced

500 ml (17 fl oz/2 cups) chicken stock

100 g (3½ oz) chickpeas, cooked

30 g (1 oz/1 cup) coriander (cilantro) leaves

Quick couscous (page 483) to serve

Preheat the oven to 180°C (350°F).

Combine the cumin, cinnamon, 2 teaspoons salt and 1 teaspoon freshly ground black pepper in a large bowl. Lightly coat the lamb shanks with the spice mix.

Heat a large ovenproof dish over medium–high heat and add a generous splash of oil. Add the lamb and cook, in batches if needed, until golden brown on all sides. Remove from the pan and set aside.

Add the onion and ginger and cook for 4–5 minutes, stirring often, until softened. Add the garlic, chilli and saffron and cook for a further 3 minutes or until fragrant. Add the tomatoes and cook for 2–3 minutes. Add the honey, apricots and lamb shanks and enough stock to cover. Season with salt and bring to the boil.

Reduce to a simmer, add the cooked chickpeas, cover with a lid and cook in the oven for 2 hours.

Stir in the coriander, check the seasoning and serve with the couscous.

Lamb tagine

This is one of my favourite lamb dishes. Extremely simple and impressive, this recipe can be doubled or even tripled if you are feeding lots of people. Serves 4

2 teaspoons sweet paprika

1 teaspoon ground ginger

1 teaspoon chilli powder

1 teaspoon ground cumin

1 teaspoon ground coriander

1 teaspoon ground white pepper

½ teaspoon ground cardamom

½ teaspoon ground cinnamon

½ teaspoon allspice

2 tablespoons lemon juice

60 ml (2 fl oz/¼ cup) olive oil

1 kg (2 lb 3 oz) diced lamb

Juice of 1 orange

500 ml (17 fl oz/2 cups) chicken stock

90 g (3 oz/½ cup) dried apricots, diced

90 g (3 oz/¾ cup) sultanas (golden raisins)

Handful of coriander (cilantro) leaves to serve

Mix the spices, 1 teaspoon salt, the lemon juice and oil to form a smooth paste. Coat the diced lamb with the spice mixture and leave to marinate for 4 hours or preferably overnight.

Preheat the oven to 180°C (350°F).

Place the lamb in a heavy-based casserole dish that has a well-fitting lid. Add the orange juice and stock and cook for 1 hour in the oven, covered, stirring occasionally.

Remove the lid, add the apricots and sultanas and return to the oven for a further 30–60 minutes, or until the lamb is tender. Serve the tagine garnished with the coriander leaves.

Pork

Chinese five-spiced pork loin

I love the simplicity of this dish. The five-spice adds a subtle flavour and lifts the dish from an ordinary roast to something quite special. Steamed rice and loads of Asian greens are compulsory. Serves 4

60 ml (2 fl oz/¼ cup) olive oil

1 kg (2 lb 3 oz) pork loin, skin scored

2 teaspoons Chinese five-spice (page 468)

1 teaspoon dried chilli flakes

60 ml (2 fl oz/¼ cup) plum sauce

60 ml (2 fl oz/¼ cup) hoisin sauce

Steamed rice (page 480) to serve

Preheat the oven to 220°C (430°F)

Rub the oil into the scored pork skin. Sprinkle liberally with the spices and 2 teaspoons salt. Rub in well to push the salt right into the skin. Place the pork in a baking tin or dish in which it fits snugly. Cook in the oven for 20 minutes

Reduce the oven to 180°C (350°F) and cook for a further hour. Check that the pork is cooked by inserting a knife into the thickest part of the joint. Unless the knife is unbearably hot, indicating a high internal temperature, return the roast to the oven.

When cooked through, remove the pork from the roasting tin, cut off the crackling and set it aside to serve. Wrap the pork loin in foil and rest in a warm place for 15–20 minutes.

Mix together the plum and hoisin sauces.

Slice the pork thinly and serve it with the crackling, sauce and steamed rice.

Seafood

Malaysian fish curry

Curry pastes sound harder to make than they actually are but, after the first couple of attempts, they become easy. A food processor cuts the work in half. Try doubling the paste and freezing half for next time. The fish can be left whole or diced, depending on how you like it. Serves 4

50 g (1¾ oz) tamarind

125 ml (4 fl oz/½ cup) boiling water

1 lemongrass stem, pale part only, chopped

2 dried red chillies, soaked in boiling water and drained

2 garlic cloves, peeled

1 tablespoon grated fresh ginger

1 onion, chopped

2 teaspoons ground coriander

2 teaspoons ground cumin

1 teaspoon ground fennel (optional)

1 teaspoon turmeric

125 ml (4 fl oz/½ cup) oil

250 ml (8½ fl oz/1 cup) coconut milk

4 firm white fish steaks or 750 g (1 lb 11 oz) diced fish, such as ling, cod, flathead or trevally, or other white-fleshed fish

Steamed rice (page 480) to serve

Soak the tamarind in boiling water for 15–20 minutes. Use your fingers to work the pulp free from the tamarind seeds. Strain the tamarind, reserving the liquid.

Place the lemongrass, chillies, garlic, ginger and onion in a food processor and blend until smooth (this can be done using a mortar and pestle if you want to give your biceps a workout). Add the spices, 1 teaspoon salt and half the oil and blend briefly until smooth.

Heat a large heavy-based saucepan over medium–high heat. Add the remaining oil and the paste and fry until fragrant. Add the tamarind liquid and coconut milk and bring to the boil. Reduce to a simmer and cook for 10–15 minutes.

Remove the skin from the fish if needed and add the fish to the pan. Simmer for a further 5–6 minutes, or until the fish is just cooked. Serve with the steamed rice.

Thai prawn and asparagus curry

This impressive seafood curry is actually very easy to make. It follows my basic Thai curry method, then the remaining ingredients are added and it's ready to serve. Who said cooking was hard, eh? Serves 4

140 ml (4½ fl oz) coconut cream

3 teaspoons Red Thai curry paste (page 465)

2 tablespoons grated palm sugar (jaggery)

2 tablespoons fish sauce

400 ml (13½ fl oz) coconut milk

500 g (1 lb 2 oz) green (raw) prawns (shrimp), peeled and deveined

150 g (5½ oz) asparagus, woody ends removed, cut into 5 cm (2 in) lengths

½ red capsicum (bell pepper), thinly sliced

15 g (½ oz/½ cup) coriander (cilantro) leaves

Steamed rice (page 480) to serve

Place the coconut cream in a heavy-based saucepan and cook over medium–high heat for 5 minutes, until it separates and the oil floats on the surface. Add the curry paste and cook for 5 minutes, stirring constantly, until fragrant. Add the palm sugar and cook briefly before adding the fish sauce and coconut milk.

Bring the liquid to the boil, then reduce the heat and simmer for 8–10 minutes. Add the prawns, asparagus and red capsicum. Return the curry to the boil, then reduce the heat and simmer for 2–3 minutes, or until the prawns are cooked.

Add the coriander leaves, check the seasoning and serve with the steamed rice.

Chermoula prawns with tzatziki

This is one of my favourite nibbles. You can also serve this as an appetiser with a simple rocket (arugula) salad. You can also make them with chicken or beef instead of prawns if you prefer. Makes 30 skewers

1 kg (2 lb 3 oz) green (raw) prawns (shrimp), peeled and deveined

2 tablespoons Chermoula (page 468)

30 skewers

Tzatziki (page 475)

Coat the prawns with the chermoula paste and marinate for 30 minutes.

Preheat the barbecue to hot and oil the barbecue plate.

Thread one prawn onto each skewer, through the centre lengthways.

Grill on the barbecue plate for 2 minutes on each side, or bake in a preheated 180°C (350°F) oven for 5–6 minutes. Serve with the tzatziki.

Sweet chipotle barbecued prawns
Make a paste by mixing together three finely diced chipotles en adobo, two crushed garlic cloves, 1 tablespoon coconut sugar or brown sugar, the zest and juice of one lime, 2 teaspoons fish sauce and some freshly ground black pepper. Pour this mixture over as many peeled and deveined prawns as you want to cook (ideally no more than 1 kg/2 lb 3 oz or you will have to double the recipe). Mix well to ensure the prawns are covered and set aside to marinate for 20 minutes. Cook on a hot, oiled barbecue plate for 2-3 minutes on each side and serve with lime wedges.

Sichuan salt and pepper calamari

I often eat this for dinner on a Friday night. It's my answer to fish and chips. I simply serve the calamari with lemon wedges, a green salad and crusty bread. If you want, you can buy a sichuan salt and pepper mix all ready to go, instead of making your own. Serves 4

75 g (2¾ oz/½ cup) plain (all-purpose) flour

Oil for cooking

3 calamari tubes

2 teaspoons Sichuan salt and pepper spice (page 467)

Lemon wedges to serve

Depending on your fishmonger, the calamari may already be scored. If not, ask them to do it. This helps to tenderise the flesh. Cut the calamari into 2 × 5 cm (¾ × 2 in) pieces.

Sift the flour with the sichuan salt and pepper spice, then season with salt and freshly ground black pepper to taste.

Heat a deep heavy-based frying pan over medium–high heat. Add a generous layer of oil – you want to really coat the base of the pan with about 2.5 mm (⅛ in) of oil. When hot, dip the calamari in the flour mix, shake the excess off and add them straight to the pan. Be careful not to overcrowd the pan.

As the calamari cook – they will take about 2–3 minutes on each side – remove them and drain on paper towel. Start serving as soon as the calamari is ready. Continue cooking until all the calamari is cooked. Serve with the lemon wedges.

Moroccan fish tagine

In this dish, firm white fish fillets are perfectly paired with sweet aromatic Moroccan spices. The fish only needs a brief cooking time right at the end – too much heat and you run the risk of overcooking the fish and it falling apart. Serves 4

Oil for cooking

1 onion, sliced

1 fennel bulb, sliced

1 small red chilli, seeded and diced

2 garlic cloves, crushed

½ teaspoon sweet paprika

Pinch of saffron threads

4 tomatoes, diced

2 bay leaves

250 ml (8½ fl oz/1 cup) fish stock or water

300 g (10½ oz) small potatoes

500 g (1 lb 2 oz) mussels, debearded

500 g (1 lb 2 oz) firm white fish, diced into 2 cm (¾ in) chunks

2 tablespoons chopped coriander (cilantro)

Quick couscous (page 483) to serve

Heat a large heavy-based saucepan over medium–high heat. Add a splash of oil, the onion and fennel. Cook for 4–5 minutes, stirring often, until softened. Add the chilli, garlic, paprika and saffron and cook for a further 1–2 minutes, stirring well. Add the tomatoes and cook briefly to soften, then add the bay leaves and stock and bring to the boil. Add the potatoes, season with salt and cook for 10–15 minutes or until the potatoes are cooked through.

Add the mussels and cook until they all open (discard any that remain closed). Add the fish pieces and allow to cook through.

Check the seasoning and spoon into a large serving bowl. Top the tagine with the coriander and serve with the couscous.

Mexican-style baked snapper with barbecued corn and coriander salsa

This dish makes a great centrepiece for a Mexican-inspired dinner party. It really doesn't need too much to serve with it. Serves 4–6

½ teaspoon salt

½ teaspoon chipotle chilli powder

1 teaspoon sweet paprika

½ teaspoon ground coriander

½ teaspoon ground cumin

1 teaspoon mustard seeds, crushed

½ teaspoon freshly ground black pepper

2 tablespoons olive oil

1 whole snapper, gutted and scaled (approximately 2 kg/4 lb 6 oz)

Barbecued corn and coriander salsa

3 corn cobs

Olive oil for cooking

1 green chilli, seeded and diced

30 g (1 oz/1 cup) coriander (cilantro) leaves

10 g (¼ oz/½ cup) flat-leaf (Italian) parsley leaves

2 tablespoons lime juice

½ red onion, thinly sliced

To make the barbecued corn and coriander salsa, preheat a barbecue to high and oil the plate.

To prepare the corn, roll the husks back and remove them, then pull off the silky tassels. Wash the cobs briefly to ensure that all the tassels have been removed. Brush the cobs all over with oil and then sprinkle with salt and freshly ground black pepper. Place the corn cobs on the barbecue and cook for 10 minutes, turning often. Set aside to cool.

Using a sharp knife, slice the kernels away from the corn cob by standing the cob on its end, holding the top and cutting downwards as close to the cob as possible.

Place the corn in a bowl along with the chilli, coriander, parsley, lime juice, 3 tablespoons olive oil and the red onion. Season with salt and freshly ground black pepper and mix to combine. Set aside.

To cook the fish, preheat the oven to 180°C (350°F).

Mix all the spices together with the oil. Trim the fins off the fish and slash the thick part of the fish, near the head, three to four times. This will help the fish to cook evenly. Rub the spice mix over the fish and place it on a baking tray lined with baking paper.

Cook the fish in the oven for 40 minutes. Check the fish is cooked, either by pressing down on the thick part of the fish, or peeking inside the gut to check the flesh is cooked. If the fish isn't cooked, return it to the oven and cook for a further 5 minutes and test again.

Place the cooked fish on a serving platter, spoon the corn salsa over the top and serve.

Pan-fried blue-eye with harissa lentils

Lentils provide the perfect background for this stunning fish dish. I prefer to use puy or tiny blue-green lentils, as they keep their shape better. Serves 6

Oil for cooking

6 × 150 g (5½ oz) blue-eye or other white fish fillets

15 g (½ oz/¼ cup) chopped coriander (cilantro) leaves

Harissa lentils

Oil for cooking

1 onion, diced

1 garlic clove, crushed

2 teaspoons Harissa (page 467)

1 teaspoon ground coriander

1 teaspoon ground cumin

125 g (4½ oz) puy or tiny blue–green lentils

500 ml (17 fl oz/2 cups) chicken or vegetable stock

125 ml (4 fl oz/½ cup) tomato passata (puréed tomatoes)

For the harissa lentils, heat a medium saucepan over medium–high heat. Add a splash of oil and cook the onion for 3–4 minutes. Add the garlic, harissa, coriander and cumin. Cook for a further 1–2 minutes, stirring often. Add the lentils, stock and tomato passata, and bring to the boil. Reduce the heat and cook for 45 minutes, stirring occasionally, until the lentils are cooked and the sauce is reduced. Season to taste with salt and freshly ground black pepper.

Heat a heavy-based frying pan over medium–high heat. Add a generous splash of oil and cook the blue-eye fillets for 4–5 minutes on each side, or until cooked through and golden brown.

Check the seasoning of the lentils and stir through the coriander leaves.

Spoon the lentils into six serving bowls, or one large platter. Top with the fish and serve immediately.

Vegetarian

Thai red roasted pumpkin, spinach and chickpea curry

This curry follows my method of cooking the curry paste in coconut cream, then adding the other ingredients. Here, these happen to be chickpeas, roasted chunks of pumpkin and tender English spinach leaves. All in all, it's a real beauty, and vegetarian to boot. Serves 4

110 g (4 oz/½ cup) dried chickpeas, soaked in cold water

350 g (12½ oz) pumpkin (squash), peeled, seeded and chopped into 3 cm (1¼ in) chunks

Oil for cooking

140 ml (4½ fl oz) coconut cream

3 teaspoons Red Thai curry paste (page 465)

2 tablespoons grated palm sugar (jaggery)

2 tablespoons soy sauce

400 ml (13½ fl oz) coconut milk

100 g (3½ oz/2 cups) baby English spinach leaves

15 g (½ oz/½ cup) coriander (cilantro) leaves

Steamed rice (page 480) to serve

Preheat the oven to 180°C (350°F).

Drain the chickpeas and place them in a medium saucepan over medium–high heat. Cover with plenty of water and cook for 30–40 minutes, until tender. Drain and set aside until needed.

Toss the pumpkin with a little oil and salt and freshly ground black pepper to taste. Roast in the oven for 20–30 minutes, until tender.

Place the coconut cream in a heavy-based saucepan and cook over medium–high heat for 5 minutes, until it separates and the oil floats on the surface. Add the curry paste and cook for 5 minutes, stirring constantly, until fragrant. Add the palm sugar and cook briefly before adding the soy sauce and coconut milk. Bring the liquid to the boil, then reduce the heat and simmer for 8–10 minutes. Add the roasted pumpkin and heat through. Add the cooked chickpeas and spinach and cook until the spinach leaves are wilted.

Add the coriander leaves, check the seasoning and serve with the steamed rice.

Sweet potato and cashew nut curry

In this simple curry, the sweetness of the potato is a perfect match for the spices, while the cashew nuts add crunch. You may, of course, add other vegetables if so desired. Serves 4

Oil for cooking

1 teaspoon brown mustard seeds

1 teaspoon ground coriander

1 teaspoon ground turmeric

2 garlic cloves, crushed

2 teaspoons grated fresh ginger

2 sweet potatoes, peeled and cut into 2 cm (¾ in) dice

1 tablespoon shaved palm sugar (jaggery)

250 ml (8½ fl oz/1 cup) coconut milk

250 ml (8½ fl oz/1 cup) vegetable stock or water

100 g (3½ oz/⅔ cup) toasted cashew nuts

Handful of basil leaves, torn

1 tablespoon soy sauce

Squeeze of lime juice

Steamed rice (page 480) to serve

Heat a heavy-based saucepan over medium–high heat. Add a splash of oil and the mustard seeds. Cook for 2–3 minutes, or until the seeds start to pop. Add the coriander and turmeric and cook for a further 2–3 minutes. Add the garlic and ginger and cook for another 2–3 minutes, stirring often. Add the sweet potato, sugar, coconut milk and stock. Stir well and bring to the boil. Reduce to a simmer and cook for 20 minutes, stirring often until the potato is cooked. Add the nuts, basil, soy sauce and a generous squeeze of lime juice. Check the seasoning and serve with the steamed rice.

Tunisian vegetable and lentil tagine

Use puy lentils or tiny blue-green lentils for this, as they hold their shape and don't break down into a mush. Serves 4–6

185 g (6½ oz) puy or tiny blue-green lentils

Oil for cooking

1 onion, diced

1½ teaspoons sweet paprika

1½ teaspoons chilli powder

2 teaspoons ground cumin

2 teaspoons ground coriander

1 teaspoon ground white pepper

2 carrots, cut into 3 cm (1¼ in) chunks

4 small potatoes, peeled and halved

1 sweet potato, cut into 3 cm (1¼ in) chunks

2 tablespoons lemon juice

500 ml (17 fl oz/2 cups) vegetable stock

250 ml (8½ fl oz/1 cup) tomato passata (puréed tomatoes)

¼ cauliflower

2 zucchini (courgettes), cut into quarters

100 g (3½ oz/2 cups) baby English spinach leaves

15 g (½ oz/½ cup) coriander (cilantro) leaves

Place the lentils in a saucepan, cover with plenty of water and bring to the boil. Reduce the heat and cook for 15–20 minutes or until the lentils are tender. Drain and set aside until needed.

Preheat the oven to 180°C (350°F).

Heat a large ovenproof casserole dish or saucepan over medium–high heat. Add a splash of oil, the onion and spices and cook for 3–4 minutes, stirring often, until softened. Add the carrot, potato and sweet potato. Cook for a further 3–4 minutes, stirring often. Add the lemon juice, stock and tomato passata and season with salt. Bring to the boil.

Cover with a lid and cook in the oven for 45 minutes. Check to see if the vegetables are tender. If so, add the cauliflower, zucchini and lentils and cook for a further 10 minutes. Add the spinach leaves and stir through until they wilt. Check the seasoning, sprinkle with the coriander leaves and serve.

Fragrant vegetable curry

The choice of vegetables here can be changed to suit personal tastes or to use what's best in season. During winter I use the mix listed below; during the warmer months I use mostly capsicum (bell pepper), eggplant (aubergine) and zucchini (courgette). Serves 4

Oil for cooking
1 teaspoon brown mustard seeds
½ teaspoon ground cumin
½ teaspoon ground coriander
½ teaspoon chilli powder
½ teaspoon ground turmeric
1 teaspoon curry powder
¼ teaspoon ground cardamom
¼ teaspoon ground cinnamon
1 onion, diced
1 potato, diced
1 parsnip, diced
1 carrot, diced
1 small swede (rutabaga), diced
1 small sweet potato, diced
Small wedge of pumpkin (squash), peeled and diced

250 ml (8½ fl oz/1 cup) vegetable stock
¼ cauliflower, cut into florets (optional)
Steamed rice (page 480) to serve

Heat a heavy-based saucepan over medium–high heat. Add a generous splash of oil and all the spices and cook for 2–3 minutes until distinctly fragrant but not burning. Add the diced vegetables and cook in the aromatic spice mix for 1–2 minutes.

Add enough stock to just cover, season with salt and freshly ground black pepper and bring to the boil. Reduce to a simmer and cook for 15–20 minutes, or until the vegetables are just tender. Add the cauliflower for the last 3–4 minutes of cooking.

Check the seasoning and add more stock or water if necessary to adjust the consistency. Serve with the steamed rice.

Lentil dal

Dal is one of the classic dishes of Indian cooking. I have adapted it by adding finely diced onion and carrot, as well as a little curry paste. I generally use whole green lentils, as they keep their shape and texture. Red lentils will cook much faster and turn into a fine purée. Serves 4

310 g (11 oz/1⅔ cups) whole green lentils
Oil for cooking
1 onion, finely diced
1 carrot, finely diced
2 tablespoons curry paste
250–500 ml (8½–17 fl oz/1–2 cups) vegetable stock
2 tablespoons chopped flat-leaf (Italian) parsley or coriander (cilantro)
Steamed rice (page 480) to serve
Natural yoghurt to serve

Sort through the lentils, discarding any brown ones and pieces of grit, then rinse well.

Heat a heavy-based saucepan over medium heat. Add a splash of oil, then cook the onion and carrot for 3–4 minutes, stirring occasionally, until softened. Add the curry paste and cook for 3–4 minutes, until aromatic. Add the lentils, stirring to coat them well with the curry mixture. Pour in enough stock to cover the lentils and bring to the boil. Reduce the heat and cook at a simmer for 30–40 minutes, or until the lentils are soft.

Pour in more stock as needed, but take care not to add too much near the end. Add the herbs and serve with the steamed rice and a dollop of natural yoghurt.

Aromatic vegetable tagine

You can add just about any vegetable you like to this dish – capsicum (bell pepper), eggplant (aubergine), pumpkin (squash), okra, cauliflower or even mushrooms, just to name a few.
Serves 4–6

Oil for cooking

1 onion, diced

1½ teaspoons sweet paprika

1½ teaspoons chilli powder

2 teaspoons ground cumin

2 teaspoons ground coriander

1 teaspoon ground white pepper

2 carrots, cut into 3 cm (1¼ in) chunks

8 small potatoes, peeled and cut in half

2 parsnips, cut into quarters

1 sweet potato, cut into 3 cm (1¼ in) chunks

2 tablespoons lemon juice

750 ml (25½ fl oz/3 cups) vegetable stock

2 zucchini (courgettes), cut into quarters

Coriander (cilantro) leaves to serve

Preheat the oven to 180°C (350°F).

Heat a large heavy-based ovenproof saucepan or casserole dish over medium–high heat. Add the oil, onion and spices and cook for 5–6 minutes, stirring often, until the onion has softened. Add the carrot, potato, parsnip and sweet potato. Cook for a further 3–4 minutes, stirring often. Add the lemon juice and stock and season with salt. Bring to the boil. Cover with a lid, reduce the heat and cook for 45 minutes – or cook in a preheated 180°C (350°F) oven.

Check whether the vegetables are tender. Add the zucchini and cook for a further 5 minutes. Check the seasoning and serve garnished with the coriander.

Potato, spinach and chickpea curry

This is one of my absolute favourite stand-bys for a mid-week meal. To make it even faster, use a tin of chickpeas, drained. Serves 4

110 g (4 oz/½ cup) dried chickpeas, soaked in cold water overnight

Oil for cooking

1 onion, diced

2 garlic cloves, crushed

2 tablespoons curry paste

6 potatoes, peeled and diced

250 ml (8½ fl oz/1 cup) tomato passata (puréed tomatoes)

250 ml (8½ fl oz/1 cup) chicken stock

100 g (3½ oz/2 cups) baby English spinach leaves

Handful of coriander (cilantro) leaves

Steamed rice (page 480) to serve

Place the drained chickpeas in a saucepan over medium–high heat. Cover with plenty of water and cook for 30–40 minutes, or until tender. Drain and set aside until needed.

Heat a large saucepan over medium–high heat. Add a splash of oil and the onion and cook for 5–6 minutes, or until the onion is soft. Add the garlic and curry paste and cook for 1–2 minutes. Add the potatoes, lower the heat and cook for a further 3–4 minutes, stirring often, until the curry is fragrant. Take care not to burn the curry paste. Add the passata and stock and bring to the boil. Season with salt.

Reduce the heat and simmer for 20 minutes, or until the potatoes are tender. Add the chickpeas and spinach and cook for 1–2 minutes. Check the seasoning. Add the coriander leaves and serve with the steamed rice.

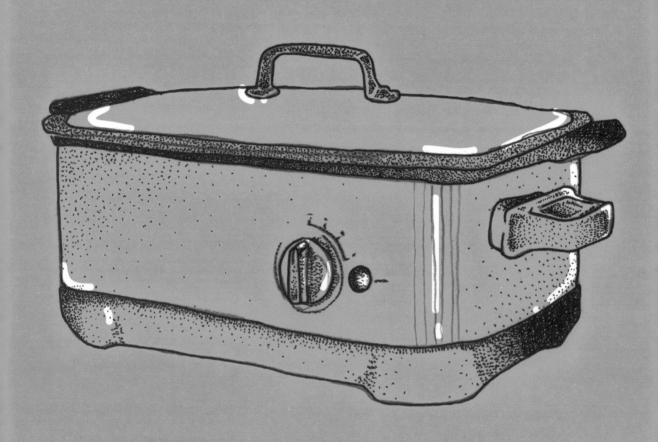

Slow cooking

This is cold-weather food, for those days when the winds are blowing and it's raining or snowing and you need some rib-sticking food to protect you against the worst Mother Nature has to offer. Casseroles and other slow-cooked dishes fit the bill perfectly.

Cold-weather comfort food

For a slow-cooked dish, you'll only spend 30 minutes or so dicing, chopping and frying, before you put the whole thing in the oven and leave it alone for 1½–2 hours. That will give you enough time to run down to footy practice, put the washing away, tidy up the bedroom or put your feet up and have a well-deserved drink before dinner. It's also very easy to transform a casserole into a pie. Simply cook as described until the meat is just tender. Transfer to a pie dish, cover with puff pastry, brush with Egg wash (page 419) and put it in a preheated oven for 30–40 minutes, or until the pastry is crisp and golden brown.

I have modified most of my casserole recipes to omit the flour traditionally used in thickening the sauce, for people suffering from gluten intolerance. Tomato paste (concentrated purée), tomato passata (puréed tomatoes) and ground nuts can be successfully used in most recipes as a natural thickener.

Many of these recipes can be cooked in a slow cooker. Personally, I'm not a fan of the slow cooker, as the liquid doesn't evaporate as much as when you slow cook traditionally – cooking in the oven creates an amazing depth of flavour. If you like the slow cooker, then you will know how much to reduce the cooking liquid.

Things you need to know
about slow cooking

- The beauty of casseroles is that they only work if you use the cheaper cuts. You are never going to get a tender beef stew from topside or sirloin; chuck or blade steak will melt in the mouth, though. Likewise, with lamb, go for diced leg. With chicken, choose boneless skinless chicken thighs – you get the picture.

- A casserole only works with long, slow cooking – you can't cheat and turn the oven up and hope it does its thing in 45 minutes – but it's well worth the wait.

- An important stage in most dishes of this type is cooking the meat first until it is lightly browned. This provides depth of flavour as the dish cooks, as well as good colour. The vegetables are often lightly cooked first, though there are some recipes that skip this step altogether. Be sure to deglaze the base of the pan with wine or stock to make sure all the flavour goes into the finished dish.

- I use a variety of cookware for my casseroles. The one that I use most often is a large Le Creuset saucepan made from enamelled cast iron. The thick metal base is perfect for the initial cooking of the ingredients, and the casserole can then be covered and popped straight into the oven for 1–2 hours. I know these pots are expensive – that's why I only have one – but one is usually enough and they tend to last a lifetime.

- Sometimes I cook the meat and vegetables in a frying pan, then transfer them to a casserole dish as they are ready. Terracotta or earthenware dishes are perfect for casseroles, stews and braises, as they are excellent conductors of heat in the oven, while also presenting well at the table. They seem to be on sale everywhere these days and are much cheaper than other dishes. Terracotta dishes must be soaked in water for 24 hours, then dried in the oven, before their first use.

- Try to buy skinless chicken pieces. The fat in the skin breaks down during the cooking process and floats to the top of a casserole, producing a layer of chicken fat.

- As well as the European-style dishes in this chapter, I've included a range of Asian braises. These are cooked without the addition of flour and are served with a light broth rather than a thick sauce.

- Casseroles can either be cooked over low heat on the stove top (a simmer pad makes sure the heat is spread over the base of the saucepan) or in the oven. It doesn't make any difference to the finished dish, though I fancy that cooking a casserole in the oven lessens the chances of the food catching or burning. If you have a slow cooker lurking in the back of the cupboard, take advantage of it: these are great for cooking all casseroles, stews and braised dishes (although I still prefer the oven).

- Cooking meat with the bone in adds to the finished flavour of the dish. You can easily substitute skinless casserole pieces for diced chicken thighs in any of these recipes. Just remember that thighs will take less time to cook.

Slow cooking recipes

Chicken

French chicken casserole

This traditional French approach to making a chicken casserole uses French shallots along with carrot and bacon to create the flavour base, while red wine produces a heartier result than many dishes cooked in this style. It's an absolute beauty of a meal to enjoy in cooler weather. If you like you can substitute a diced onion for the French shallots and omit the bacon. Serve with Mashed potatoes (page 257) and Cauliflower cheese (page 247). Serves 4

Oil for cooking

1 kg (2 lb 3 oz) chicken casserole pieces

10–12 French shallots, peeled

1 carrot, finely diced

6 rashers (slices) bacon, diced

1 garlic clove, crushed

125 ml (4 fl oz/½ cup) red wine

250 ml (8½ fl oz/1 cup) tomato passata (puréed tomatoes)

500 ml (17 fl oz/2 cups) chicken stock

1–2 tablespoons chopped flat-leaf (Italian) parsley to serve

Heat a heavy-based saucepan over medium heat. Add a generous splash of oil and cook the chicken pieces until golden brown all over. Remove the chicken from the saucepan and set aside.

Return the saucepan to the heat and add more oil, if necessary. Cook the shallots, carrot, bacon and garlic until soft. Add the wine, passata and stock and bring to the boil. Reduce the heat to a simmer, return the chicken to the saucepan, cover with a lid and cook for 1 hour, or until the chicken is tender. Season with salt and freshly ground black pepper, sprinkle the parsley on top and serve.

Chicken casserole with mushrooms
Add 100 g (3½ oz) sliced mushrooms with the onion and carrot.

Chicken, pancetta and mushroom casserole

Chicken is the quickest casserole to make, with chicken thighs only taking 30 minutes or so to turn deliciously tender. This is yummy with Soft polenta (page 483) or Mashed potatoes (page 257). Serves 4–6

Oil for cooking

1 onion, diced

2 × 5 mm (¼ in) thick slices pancetta (approximately 125 g/4½ oz), diced

600 g (1 lb 5 oz) boneless skinless chicken thighs, diced

250 g (9 oz) field mushrooms, sliced

2–3 bay leaves

2 carrots, cut into chunks

125 ml (4 fl oz/½ cup) white wine

250 ml (8½ fl oz/1 cup) tomato passata (puréed tomatoes)

500–750 ml (17–25½ fl oz/2–3 cups) chicken stock

2–3 thyme sprigs

2 tablespoons chopped flat-leaf (Italian) parsley

Heat a large heavy-based saucepan over medium–high heat. Add a splash of oil and the onion and cook for 3–4 minutes until soft. Add the pancetta and cook for 3–4 minutes, stirring often, until just starting to turn golden brown. Add the diced chicken and cook for 4–5 minutes until golden brown. Add the mushrooms, bay leaves, carrot, wine, passata and enough stock to just cover. Season with salt and freshly ground black pepper, bring to the boil, then reduce to a simmer, cover and cook for 30–35 minutes, stirring occasionally.

Check the chicken is cooked and adjust the seasoning if necessary. Add the herbs and serve.

Chicken, pancetta and mushroom pie
Cook the casserole as described above, then transfer it to an ovenproof pie dish. Place a sheet of butter puff pastry over the top, brush with egg wash, sprinkle with sesame or poppy seeds, if you like, and bake in a preheated 180°C (350°F) for 20-30 minutes or until the pastry is golden brown and cooked through.

Soy-braised chicken

You're going to love this: only a handful of ingredients, no chopping – and it tastes fantastic. I feel like chicken tonight, at its best. Serves 4–6

1.6 kg (3½ lb) chicken

250 ml (8½ fl oz/1 cup) soy sauce

250 ml (8½ fl oz/1 cup) Chinese rice wine

250 ml (8½ fl oz/1 cup) chicken stock

250 ml (8½ fl oz/1 cup) water

3 whole star anise

220 g (8 oz/1 cup) caster (superfine) sugar

Steamed rice (page 480) to serve

Stir-fried Chinese greens (page 248) to serve

Place the chicken, breast side up, in a saucepan that will fit it snugly and that comes with a lid. Add all the other ingredients and place over medium heat. Bring to the boil, then reduce the heat, cover with a lid and cook for 30 minutes.

Remove the lid, turn the chicken over, cover and cook for a further 15 minutes. Remove from the heat and allow to stand, covered, for 15–20 minutes before serving.

Chop the chicken into 10–12 pieces and serve with the steamed rice and greens.

Spring poached chicken

I love light dishes like this, where the meat is cooked in a broth, making it easier to digest and everything is wonderful and fresh. Serves 4

1.6 kg (3½ lb) chicken

Handful of flat-leaf (Italian) parsley

3–4 bay leaves

500 g (1 lb 2 oz) new potatoes

1 fennel bulb

1 bunch of baby (Dutch) carrots

100 g (3½ oz/⅔ cup) peas

100 g (3½ oz) broad beans, blanched and double podded

100 g (3½ oz) baby English spinach

Horseradish cream (page 456) to serve

Fill the cavity of the chicken with the parsley and bay leaves. Place the chicken, breast side down, in a large saucepan big enough to fit the chicken snugly, then add enough water to almost cover the chicken. Add a good pinch of salt and the potatoes. Place over medium–high heat and bring to the boil. Cover with a lid and simmer for 30 minutes.

Remove the lid and turn the chicken over so the breast side is facing up.

Take the fennel bulb, remove the feathery top leaves and set them aside. Cut the fennel into quarters, remove the core and chop it roughly. Add it to the pan along with the baby carrots, cover the pan with the lid and cook for a further 30 minutes.

Remove the chicken from the pan and cut it into portions.

Add the peas, broad beans and spinach to the simmering stock and cook for 2–3 minutes. Check the seasoning of the broth and add salt and freshly ground pepper as needed. Divide the vegetables between four bowls, add the chicken and ladle over the broth. Serve with the horseradish cream.

Spanish chicken and chorizo braise

Spanish flavours have such warmth; the combination of chicken and chorizo is such a classic, too. Serve with couscous. Serves 4–6

Oil for cooking

1.5 kg (3 lb 5 oz) skinless chicken casserole pieces

1 chorizo sausage, sliced

1 onion, diced

2 teaspoons ground cumin

2 teaspoons ground coriander

1 teaspoon sweet paprika

½ teaspoon allspice

Pinch of saffron threads

250 ml (8½ fl oz/1 cup) tomato passata (puréed tomatoes)

500 ml (17 fl oz/2 cups) chicken stock

3 tablespoons each of flat-leaf (Italian) parsley and coriander (cilantro) leaves to serve

Heat a heavy-based saucepan over medium heat. Add a generous splash of oil and cook the chicken pieces, until golden brown all over. Remove the chicken from the pan and set aside.

Return the saucepan to the heat and add more oil if necessary. Add the chorizo and cook for 5–6 minutes, stirring often, until golden brown. Remove and set aside with the chicken. If the chorizo has released a lot of fat, drain it away, then return the pan to the heat and cook the onion and spices until fragrant. Add the passata and stock and bring to the boil.

Return the chicken to the pan and season with salt and freshly ground black pepper. Cover and cook over low heat for 1½ hours. Check the seasoning and add the fresh herbs to serve.

Pot-roast chicken with Italian flavours

You will need a good casserole dish with a lid for this. It's an absolute beauty – just pop everything in the pot and let it do its magic. Serve with a green salad and Mashed potatoes (page 257). Serves 4

1.6 kg (3½ lb) chicken

1 onion, diced

1 carrot, diced

4 field or Swiss brown mushrooms, sliced

125 ml (4 fl oz/½ cup) wine (red or white)

250 ml (8½ fl oz/1 cup) chicken stock

250 ml (8½ fl oz/1 cup) tomato passata (puréed tomatoes)

1–2 bay leaves

2–3 fresh thyme stalks

Oil

Preheat the oven to 180°C (350°F).

Place the chicken upside down in a casserole dish that has a lid. Add the remaining ingredients, except for the oil, and season with salt and freshly ground black pepper. Cover with the lid and cook for 45 minutes.

Remove the casserole dish from the oven, turn the chicken breast side up, brush it with oil and return to the oven, without the lid. Cook for a further 45 minutes.

Cut the chicken into portions and either return it to the sauce, or arrange it on a plate and serve the sauce separately.

Miso chicken with walnuts and grapes

Grapes bring a lovely sweetness and texture to any dish. Take care to only add them during the last few minutes as they may overcook and soften too much. Serves 4

2 tablespoons white miso paste

80 ml (2½ fl oz/⅓ cup) mirin

1 tablespoon grated fresh ginger

1 tablespoon cider vinegar

8 boneless chicken thighs, skin left on

Oil for cooking

8 French shallots, diced

125 ml (4 fl oz/½ cup) chicken stock

125 g (4½ oz) walnuts, roughly chopped

250 g (9 oz) small seedless red grapes

Generous knob of butter

1 tablespoon chopped tarragon

2 tablespoons chopped flat-leaf (Italian) parsley

Mix together the miso, mirin, ginger and vinegar. Pour over the chicken thighs and set aside to marinate, ideally for 4 hours.

Preheat the oven to 180°C (350°F).

Place the chicken in a large roasting dish, strain off the excess marinade and set aside.

Heat a heavy-based frying pan over medium–high heat. Add a splash of oil and cook the French shallots for 4–5 minutes, stirring often, until softened. Add the excess marinade to the pan and cook until it is reduced by half. Add the chicken stock and bring to the boil. Season with salt and freshly ground black pepper.

Pour the cooking liquid and shallots over the chicken and bake in the oven for 40–50 minutes, turning often until the chicken is cooked through and golden brown.

Remove the chicken from the dish, cover and set aside. Return the dish to the heat and add the walnuts and grapes. Allow to cook for a few minutes, until the sauce reduces and the grapes soften. Add the butter, check the seasoning, add the herbs and pour the sauce over the chicken to serve.

Duck

Duck cassoulet

You'll be waiting for winter to kick in just so you can enjoy this confit duck casserole. It's become a regular 'celebrate the start of winter' meal for my good friend Steve, who reckons he can't get through winter without this extra layer of fat. Serve the cassoulet with a green salad.
Serves 6

Oil for cooking

75 g (2¾ oz/10½ oz) pork belly, skin removed and cut into 2 cm (¾ in) dice

2 onions, diced

1 celery stalk, chopped

½ leek, white part only, chopped

2 carrots, diced

2 garlic cloves, crushed

125 ml (4 fl oz/½ cup) white wine

250 g (9 oz/1¼ cups) haricot beans, soaked in cold water overnight

1–2 thyme sprigs

2 bay leaves

250 g (9 oz) saucisson lyonnaise or Polish sausage, sliced into 1 cm (½ in) rounds

6 confit duck legs (see Duck confit, page 168, or buy in a specialist food store)

250 ml (8½ fl oz/1 cup) tomato passata (puréed tomatoes)

Chicken stock as required

100 g (3½ oz/2 cups) fresh breadcrumbs

2 tablespoons chopped flat-leaf (Italian) parsley

Heat a large saucepan over medium heat. Add a generous splash of oil and cook the pork belly for 15 minutes, until browned. Remove the pork from the pan and set aside.

Return the saucepan to the heat and add more oil, if necessary. Cook the onion, celery, leek and carrot for 5–6 minutes, stirring often, until soft. Add the garlic and cook for 1–2 minutes, until fragrant. Pour in the wine and add the pork belly, beans, thyme and bay leaves. Cover with water, bring to the boil and simmer for 1 hour, until the beans are tender. Drain, reserving the stock, and set both aside.

Heat a large frying pan over medium heat. Add a splash of oil and lightly brown the sausage slices.

Place half the amount of cooked pork and beans in the bottom of a large ovenproof casserole dish. Arrange the duck legs on top and cover with the remaining pork and beans. Arrange the pork sausage on top of the beans, pushing the slices down into the bean mixture.

Bring the reserved stock to the boil, season with salt and add the passata. Pour the liquid over the beans, duck and sausage to almost cover. If you don't have enough liquid, top up with chicken stock. Sprinkle the breadcrumbs over the top.

Cover the dish with foil and cook in the oven for 40 minutes. Remove the foil and cook for a further 30–40 minutes, until golden brown. Sprinkle with parsley and serve.

Beef

Beef bourguignon

This is a traditional dish with classic flavours that will fill your home with hearty, appetite-inducing aromas. Master it, then adapt it with other flavours and ingredients that you love. Serve with steamed vegetables and Mashed potatoes (page 257). Serves 4

Oil for cooking

6 rashers (slices) bacon, cut into strips

16 French shallots, peeled, or 2 onions, sliced

1 kg (2 lb 3 oz) diced chuck or blade steak

250 ml (8½ fl oz/1 cup) red wine

250 ml (8½ fl oz/1 cup) tomato passata (puréed tomatoes)

250 ml (8½ fl oz/1 cup) beef stock

Bouquet garni (see page 61)

Preheat the oven to 180°C (350°F).

Heat a large heavy-based ovenproof saucepan or casserole dish over medium–high heat. Add a splash of oil, add the bacon and cook for 2–3 minutes, until it begins to brown. Remove with a slotted spoon and set aside. Add the shallots and more oil if needed, and cook until beginning to brown. Remove with a slotted spoon and set aside with the bacon.

Brown the beef in batches, using more oil as needed. Remove the beef from the pan, tip out any excess fat, then return the beef, bacon and shallots to the pan with the red wine, passata and stock. Bring to the boil, stirring often, then reduce the heat, add the bouquet garni and a pinch of salt. Cover with the lid and cook for 2 hours on minimum heat or in a 180°C (350°F) preheated oven.

Check to ensure the beef is tender. If not, continue cooking for a further 15–20 minutes before checking again. When ready, season with salt and freshly ground black pepper to taste, then serve.

Beef stew with dumplings
Add dumplings (see the recipe opposite) for the last 45 minutes to 1 hour of cooking.

Beef stew with mushrooms
Add 100 g (3½ oz) sliced mushrooms with the shallots/onions and cook for another 2-3 minutes.

Beef and Guinness casserole with dumplings

The heart-warming power of this luscious casserole will be most appreciated on a cold winter's night. Dumplings may seem like a very old-fashioned thing to add, but these are beautifully light and really take the dish to a new level. Serves 4–6

Seasoned flour for coating

1.5 kg (3 lb 5 oz) skirt or blade steak, diced

Oil for cooking

500 ml (17 fl oz/2 cups) Guinness

500 ml (17 fl oz/2 cups) beef stock

2 garlic cloves, crushed

250 g (9 oz) French shallots, peeled and cut into quarters

Dumplings

100 g (3½ oz/1 cup) dry breadcrumbs

150 g (5½ oz/1 cup) self-raising flour

75 g (2¾ oz) soft butter, diced

1 tablespoon chopped flat-leaf (Italian) parsley

1 egg

50 ml (1¾ fl oz/¼ cup) milk

Coat the beef with the seasoned flour and shake off any excess. Heat a large heavy-based saucepan over medium heat. Add a splash of oil and cook the beef in small batches until golden brown, adding more oil if needed. Add the Guinness, stock, garlic and shallots and bring to the boil. Season lightly with salt and freshly ground black pepper, cover and reduce the heat to low. Skim any impurities from the surface as needed. Cook for 1 hour.

While the beef is cooking, prepare the dumplings by combining the breadcrumbs and flour in a bowl. Rub the butter through to form a sandy texture. Add salt, pepper and the parsley and stir to combine. Add the egg and enough milk to bring the mixture together. Knead to form a smooth dough and roll into 3 cm (1¼ in) balls.

Add the dumplings to the casserole dish after the first hour of cooking and cook for an additional hour.

After the beef has been cooking for 2 hours, test to see if the meat is tender. If so, check the seasoning and serve. If not, cook for a further 20–30 minutes.

Beef and Guinness pie
Make the casserole as described above, but omit the dumplings. Prepare the pastry as follows. Combine 150 ml (5 fl oz) cold water, 100 g (3½ oz) butter and 1 teaspoon salt in a saucepan and place over medium heat until the butter melts. Remove from the heat, add 75 g (2¾ oz) self-raising flour and stir to combine quickly. Tip the dough onto a floured work surface and knead quickly until smooth. Divide the dough in two. Roll out a piece to fit a 2 litre (68 fl oz/8 cup) pie dish. Grease the pie dish and line it with the pastry. Spoon the hot pie filling into the dish. Roll out the remaining pastry and cover the pie. Trim the edges and brush with the egg wash. Bake in a preheated 180°C (350°F) oven until golden brown, about 15-20 minutes.

Braised steak and onions

Braised steak and onions is a dish that everyone should learn how to make. It's perfect during the cooler months, when you need some gutsy, rib-sticking food. Serve with Mashed potatoes (page 257) and lots of vegetables. Serves 4–6

Oil for cooking

4 onions, sliced

4 × 150 g (5½ oz) pieces blade steak

250 ml (8½ fl oz/1 cup) red wine

250 ml (8½ fl oz/1 cup) beef stock

1–2 tablespoons chopped fresh herbs, such as flat-leaf (Italian) parsley, rosemary or thyme

250 ml (8½ fl oz/1 cup) tomato passata (puréed tomatoes)

Preheat the oven to 180°C (350°F).

Heat a heavy-based ovenproof saucepan or casserole dish over medium heat. Add the oil and onions and cook until soft. Add the steak, red wine, stock, herbs, tomato passata and some salt and freshly ground black pepper. Cover with a lid and cook in the oven for 1½–2 hours, or until tender. Serve hot.

Slow-cooked beef with lemongrass and coconut

Serve with Steamed rice (page 480) and steamed bok choy (pak choy). Serves 4

2 lemongrass stems, white part only

2 garlic cloves, crushed

6 Asian shallots, peeled

Oil for cooking

1 kg (2 lb 3 oz) beef blade, cut into 6 cm (2½ in) pieces

400 ml (13½ fl oz) coconut milk

2 tablespoons fish sauce

1–2 kaffir lime leaves (optional)

125 ml (4 fl oz/½ cup) water or chicken stock, as needed

500 g (1 lb 2 oz) potatoes, peeled, halved and cut into 1 cm (½ in) slices

250 g (9 oz) green beans

Place the lemongrass, garlic and shallots in a food processor and blitz to form a paste. Add 1–2 tablespoons of oil as needed.

Heat a casserole dish over medium heat. Add a splash of oil and brown the beef pieces — you may need to do this in batches. Remove the beef and set aside.

Add the lemongrass paste to the pan, adding more oil if necessary, and cook for 2–3 minutes or until fragrant, stirring. Return the beef to the pan, along with the coconut milk, fish sauce and kaffir lime leaves (if using). Add water or chicken stock to just cover, bring to the boil, reduce the heat and cover with a lid.

Either cook on low on the stove top or in a preheated 180°C (350°F) oven for 1 hour. Add the potatoes and cook for another 1–1½ hours or until the beef is tender.

Add the green beans and cook for 3–4 minutes. Check the seasoning, adding more fish sauce if needed and freshly ground black pepper to taste. Serve hot.

Spezzatino

Only the Italians can make a humble beef stew sound so exotic. This version is inspired by the Australian godfather of Italian cooking, Stefano de Pieri. Spezzatino is great with Soft polenta (page 483) and Pear, candied walnut, goat's cheese and rocket salad (page 271). Serves 6

Oil for cooking

2 carrots, diced

2 onions, diced

2 celery stalks, diced

1.5 kg (3 lb 5 oz) diced blade steak

2 garlic cloves, peeled

250 ml (8½ fl oz/1 cup) red wine

4 potatoes, peeled and diced

400 g (14 oz) tinned chopped tomatoes

250 ml (8½ fl oz/1 cup) tomato passata (puréed tomatoes)

1 bay leaf

250–375 ml (1–1½ cups) beef stock

Heat a large heavy-based ovenproof saucepan or casserole dish over medium heat. Add a generous splash of oil and the diced carrot, onion and celery. Cook for 5–6 minutes, until soft but not coloured. Remove the vegetables from the pan and set aside.

Return the saucepan to the heat and add more oil, if needed. Cook the beef, in batches if necessary, until browned. Return the vegetables to the saucepan, along with the garlic, red wine, potatoes, tomatoes, passata and bay leaf, and season well with salt and freshly ground black pepper. Bring to a gentle simmer and add stock as needed to ensure that the meat is covered. Cook for 2½–3 hours over low heat, partially covered, until the meat is tender. Check the seasoning and serve.

Osso bucco with gremolata

A classic veal casserole that is delicious served with mounds of Mashed potatoes (page 257) or Soft polenta (page 483) to soak up all the lovely tasty juices. Serves 4

Oil for cooking

1 kg (2 lb 3 oz) veal osso bucco

1 onion, diced

2 celery stalks, diced

2 carrots, finely diced

3 garlic cloves, crushed

250 ml (8½ fl oz/1 cup) white wine

250 ml (8½ fl oz/1 cup) tomato passata (puréed tomatoes)

350–500 ml (12–17 fl oz/1½–2 cups) chicken stock

Finely grated zest of 1 lemon

3 tablespoons chopped flat-leaf (Italian) parsley

2 anchovy fillets, chopped

Place a large ovenproof casserole dish over medium heat. Add a splash of oil and brown the osso bucco well

on both sides, in batches if necessary. Remove the veal and set aside.

Add more oil to the pan if required, then cook the onion, celery and carrot for 6–8 minutes, stirring often, until soft. Add one-third of the crushed garlic and cook for a further minute.

Return the veal to the pan, add the white wine, bring to the boil and cook until the liquid is reduced by half. Add the passata and enough stock to cover the veal. Season with salt and freshly ground black pepper. Bring to the boil, reduce to a simmer, cover with the lid and cook for 1 hour. Check to see whether the veal is tender. If not, cook for a further 10 minutes and try again.

Mix the additional garlic, lemon zest, parsley and anchovy together. Sprinkle over the veal to serve.

Lamb

Slow-cooked leg of lamb with lemon and oregano

Cooking lamb with potatoes and garlic over a long period of time adds intensity to this dish. The potatoes will soak up all the fat from the lamb, making them irresistible. This is yummy with Potato gratin (page 259) and Sicilian brussels sprouts (page 245). Serves 4–6

Oil for cooking

1 leg of lamb on the bone

80 ml (2½ fl oz/⅓ cup) lemon juice

1 tablespoon chopped oregano

250–375 ml (8½–12½ fl oz/1–1½ cups) chicken stock

4–6 garlic cloves, peeled

Preheat the oven to 160°C (320°F).

Heat a heavy-based saucepan over medium–high heat. Add a splash of oil and cook the lamb until brown all over.

Transfer the meat to a casserole dish. Rub the lemon juice all over the lamb and season with oregano, salt and freshly ground black pepper. Pour stock around the meat and add the garlic. Cover with foil. Cook in the oven for 3–4 hours. Check every 45 minutes or so, turning the lamb to ensure it cooks evenly. Add more stock or water, as needed, to keep the dish moist. Remove the foil and cook for a further 30 minutes. The lamb should now be tender and falling apart.

To serve, simply break the meat into chunks and place on a large platter.

Braised lamb shanks with red wine and thyme

A very classic dish. If the amount of wine bothers you, substitute a tin of chopped tomatoes. Served with Mashed potatoes (page 257). Serves 4

Oil for cooking

1 onion, diced

2 carrots, diced

2 tablespoons tomato paste (concentrated purée)

4 lamb shanks

500 ml (17 fl oz/2 cups) red wine

500 ml (17 fl oz/2 cups) beef stock

3–4 fresh thyme stalks

1–2 bay leaves

2 tablespoons chopped flat-leaf (Italian) parsley to serve

Heat a heavy-based saucepan over medium–high heat. Add a splash of oil and the onion and carrot, and cook for 3–4 minutes until softened. Add the tomato paste, cook for 1–2 minutes and then add the shanks, red wine, stock, thyme and bay leaves. Bring to the boil and season with salt and freshly ground black pepper. Reduce to a simmer and cook for 2 hours or until the lamb is tender and falling off the bone. Sprinkle over the parsley and serve.

Lamb hot pot

Served piping hot, this is the perfect meal on a cold night. It's an all-in-one meal with a delicious mix of diced lamb and vegetables in a light sauce, all under a crust of golden potato slices. The traditional version uses lamb chops. If you prefer, you can use them in this recipe, but I choose to use diced lamb. Serves 4

Olive oil for cooking
1 kg (2 lb 3 oz) lamb, preferably shoulder, diced
1 onion, diced
1 garlic clove, crushed
1 carrot, diced
2 celery stalks, diced
1 tablespoon plain (all-purpose) flour
750 ml (25½ fl oz/3 cups) chicken or beef stock
400 g (14 oz) tinned chopped tomatoes
1 tablespoon tomato paste (concentrated purée)
1 tablespoon thyme leaves
1 kg (2 lb 3 oz) potatoes
40 g (1½ oz) melted butter

Preheat the oven to 180°C (350°F).

Heat a large heavy-based frying pan over medium–high heat. Add a splash of oil and cook the lamb in small batches until golden brown, adding more oil if needed. Set the lamb aside in a casserole dish.

Add extra oil to the pan if needed. Reduce the heat to medium, add the onion, garlic, carrot and celery and cook for 5–6 minutes, stirring often, until the vegetables soften. Sprinkle the flour over the vegetables and stir it in, then cook for another 3–4 minutes. Add the stock, tomatoes, tomato paste and thyme. Bring to the boil, reduce the heat and simmer for 10 minutes. Season with salt and freshly ground black pepper. Pour the sauce over the lamb.

Peel the potatoes and slice them into 5 mm (¼ in) rounds. Arrange the potatoes on top of the lamb. Brush the melted butter over the layer of potato. Place the hot pot in the oven, uncovered, and cook for 2½ hours. Brush the potato slices with some of the casserole juices every half hour. Serve hot.

Sicilian lamb stew with pecorino

The rustic flavours of this Italian-influenced slow-cooked stew include pancetta, garlic and red wine. Serves 4–6

Oil for cooking

2 onions, sliced

60 g (2 oz) pancetta, diced

1 kg (2 lb 3 oz) lamb, diced

2 garlic cloves, crushed

250 ml (8½ fl oz/1 cup) red wine

250 g (9 oz) small potatoes

250 ml (8½ fl oz/1 cup) chicken stock

125 ml (4 fl oz/½ cup) tomato passata (puréed tomatoes)

100 g (3½ oz) pecorino cheese, cut into 1 cm (½ in) dice

2 tablespoons red-wine vinegar

2 tablespoons chopped flat-leaf (Italian) parsley

Soft polenta (page 483) to serve

Preheat the oven to 180°C (350°F).

Heat a casserole dish over medium–high heat. Add a splash of oil and the onion and cook for 3–4 minutes, stirring often, until softened. Add the diced pancetta and cook for a further 3–4 minutes. Add the diced lamb and cook for 3–4 minutes, until golden brown on all sides. Add the garlic and cook briefly, then add the red wine. Allow to boil until reduced by half. Add the potatoes, stock and passata and bring to the boil. Season with salt and freshly ground black pepper.

Reduce the heat, cover with a lid and cook in the oven for 1–1½ hours or until the lamb is tender. Add the diced pecorino and red-wine vinegar and return to the oven for 5 minutes.

Check the seasoning, add the parsley and stir well to combine. Serve with the polenta.

Shepherd's pie

Okay, I have been known to take some beef bolognese and throw a bit of mashed potato on top and try to pass it off as the real deal, but nothing quite comes close to a genuine shepherd's pie. Serves 4

Oil for cooking

1 onion, diced

1 carrot, diced

2 celery stalks, diced (optional)

500 g (1 lb 2 oz) minced (ground) lamb

Pinch of ground cumin

A few shakes of worcestershire sauce

400 g (14 oz) tinned chopped tomatoes

250–500 ml (8½–17 fl oz/1–2 cups) beef stock

155 g (5½ oz/1 cup) frozen peas

Mashed potatoes (page 257) to serve

Heat a large heavy-based saucepan over medium–high heat. Add a splash of oil and the onion, carrot and celery (if using), and cook for 5–6 minutes, stirring often. Add the lamb and cook for a further 5–6 minutes, stirring often until brown. Add the cumin, worcestershire sauce, tomatoes and enough stock to cover. Bring to the boil and season with salt and freshly ground black pepper. Cook for 30 minutes, stirring often.

Preheat the oven to 180°C (350°F).

Check the seasoning and spoon the lamb mixture into a deep casserole dish. Cover with mashed potato. Bake in the oven for 20–30 minutes until golden brown and crispy.

Shepherd's pie with potato crust
Instead of mashed potato I sometimes cook peeled whole potatoes until just tender, slice them thinly and then arrange them in a layer over the top of the lamb. Brush with melted butter and cook as above.

Shepherd's pie with sweet potato topping
Top with Sweet potato mash (page 261) instead of regular potato mash.

Spanish lamb stew

I've cooked many variations of this dish over the years, the original hailing from my good friend Phillippa Grogan. I've added some almonds to increase the richness and I love including fresh broad beans if they are in season. Serves 6

2 red capsicums (bell peppers)

Olive oil for cooking

80 g (2¾ oz/½ cup) blanched almonds

1 kg (2 lb 3 oz) broad beans, podded (optional)

1.5 kg (3 lb 5 oz) lamb, diced

2 onions, diced

2 garlic cloves, crushed

2 teaspoons smoky paprika

Pinch of saffron threads

2–3 bay leaves

160 ml (5½ fl oz/⅔ cup) white wine

500 ml (17 fl oz/2 cups) chicken stock

375 ml (12½ fl oz/1½ cups) tomato passata (puréed tomatoes)

2 tablespoons chopped flat-leaf (Italian) parsley

Preheat the oven to 180°C (350°F).

Rub the capsicums with olive oil and roast them in the oven until the skins blister, about 20–30 minutes. Put them in a plastic bag and seal to allow the steam to lift the skins. When cool enough to handle, peel and discard the seeds and cut the capsicum into 1 cm (½ in) slices. Set aside.

Roast the almonds in the oven until golden brown, about 6–7 minutes. Allow to cool, then grind in a food processor. Set aside.

Bring a saucepan of water to the boil, blanch the broad beans for 1–2 minutes, then immediately refresh them under cold water. Remove the outer pale green skins and set the beans aside.

Heat a large casserole dish over medium–high heat. Add a splash of olive oil and cook the lamb until brown all over, in batches if necessary. Remove the lamb from the dish and return the dish to the heat. Add more oil if needed and cook the onion for 6–8 minutes until soft. Add the garlic, paprika, saffron and bay leaves and cook for 1–2 minutes until fragrant. Add the wine, bring to the boil and allow to reduce by half. Add the stock and passata and bring to the boil. Reduce the heat and simmer for 20–30 minutes.

Return the lamb to the dish and season with salt and freshly ground black pepper. Cover the casserole dish and cook in the oven for 1½–2 hours, or until the lamb is tender. Add the cooked capsicum and enough roasted ground almonds to thicken the sauce. Add the broad beans and parsley, season to taste and serve.

Pork

Braised pork with star anise (The pork dish)

Here, pork belly is braised with simple Asian ingredients to create a meal you will absolutely adore. Serve with Steamed rice (page 480) and Stir-fried Chinese greens (page 248) to complete the experience. Serves 4–6

1.5 kg (3 lb 5 oz) pork belly

3 spring onions (scallions), sliced

4 cm (1½ in) piece of fresh ginger, sliced

2 tablespoons soy sauce

2 tablespoons Chinese rice wine

2 tablespoons fish sauce

2 star anise

1 teaspoon crushed sichuan peppercorns

1 teaspoon crushed black peppercorns

2 small red chillies, halved

Preheat the oven to 180°C (350°F).

Cut the pork into 1 cm (½ in) thick slices. Place the meat in a casserole dish with a tight-fitting lid. Add the remaining ingredients and enough water to come halfway up the pork. Put the lid on and cook in the oven for 3 hours.

Carefully lift the slices of pork onto a deep serving platter, spoon over the cooking liquid and serve.

Baked sausages with potatoes and rosemary

This simple dish relies on the quality of the sausages. I prefer a good-quality pork sausage, Italian in style, with a bit of fennel and chilli to give it a kick. But you can use whatever you have at hand. It won't work with cheap supermarket barbecue sausages. Serve with a green salad. Serves 4

6 good-quality pork sausages

1 kg (2 lb 3 oz) waxy potatoes, such as kipfler (fingerling) or desiree

1½ teaspoons smoky paprika

1 tablespoon chopped rosemary

Handful of unpeeled garlic cloves

2 slices of white sourdough bread

60 ml (2 fl oz/¼ cup) extra-virgin olive oil

2 tablespoons chopped flat-leaf (Italian) parsley

Preheat the oven to 200°C (400°F).

Cut the sausages into 4 cm (1½ in) pieces and place them in a large roasting tin.

Scrub the potatoes well and slice them into chunks. Add the potatoes to the baking dish along with the smoky paprika, chopped rosemary and garlic cloves, and season with salt and freshly ground black pepper.

Tear the sourdough bread into chunks and add it to the pan along with the olive oil. Toss to combine. Cook in the oven for 40–50 minutes, turning the sausages and potatoes once or twice, until the potatoes are tender and the sausages are golden brown. Finish with the chopped parsley.

Rodriguez pork

Being a movie fan, I was intrigued by the cooking lesson included by director Robert Rodriguez in *Once Upon a Time in Mexico*. In the film the character Sands, played by Johnny Depp, chows down in restaurants across Mexico in search of the best Puerco Pibil, a classic dish of slow-cooked pork – only to shoot the chef at the end because it was so good. Serves 6

2 tablespoons annatto seeds

2 tablespoons cumin seeds

1 tablespoon black peppercorns

8 whole allspice

1 teaspoon whole cloves

125 ml (4 fl oz/½ cup) orange juice

170 ml (5½ fl oz/⅔ cup) lemon juice

125 ml (4 fl oz/½ cup) white-wine vinegar

2 tablespoons tequila

2 habanero chillies, seeded and diced

8 garlic cloves, peeled

2 tablespoons salt

2.5 kg (5½ lb) pork butt or leg

Banana leaves (optional)

Steamed rice (page 480) to serve

Grind the spices in a mortar and pestle until fine.

Place the ground spices, orange juice, lemon juice, vinegar, tequila, chillies, garlic and salt in a blender and purée until smooth.

Dice the pork into 2 cm (¾ in) chunks. Pour the marinade over the pork and refrigerate for at least 40 minutes or up to 4 hours.

Preheat the oven to 180°C (350°F).

Line a casserole dish with the banana leaves (if using), add the pork and cover with more leaves. If not using banana leaves, place the pork in a casserole dish and cover with foil.

Bake in the oven for 3–4 hours. Test after 3 hours – the pork should have a fall-apart character. If you cook the meat for too long it will become dry and stringy. Serve with the steamed rice.

Slow-cooked pork belly with Catalan potatoes and quince aïoli

This dish is basically a fabulous pork roast. The quince aïoli adds a beautiful sweetness to the meat, not dissimilar to apple sauce. The longer you cook the pork, the more the fat breaks down and the more it will melt in your mouth. Serve with a green salad. Serves 6

4 garlic cloves, crushed

1 tablespoon fennel seeds

1–2 tablespoons salt flakes

Oil for cooking

2 kg (4 lb 6 oz) pork belly, skin scored

Catalan potatoes (page 259)

Quince aïoli (page 475)

Preheat the oven to 220°C (430°F).

Mix the garlic, fennel seeds and salt flakes with 2 tablespoons oil. Rub over the skin of the pork, massaging it well down into the flesh. Set aside to allow the flavour to penetrate the pork – ideally overnight, or between 20 minutes and 4 hours. Place the pork in a deep baking tin, skin side up. Add enough water to come halfway up the pork, then cook for 30 minutes until the skin crackles.

Lower the heat to 180°C (350°F) and cook for a further hour. The water will evaporate during cooking.

Remove the pork from the oven. If the skin needs to be crisper, remove the crackling using a sharp knife, place it on a wire rack over a shallow baking tin and return to the oven, or place it under a hot grill (broiler), to crisp up. Once crisp, chop the crackling into pieces.

Cut the pork into 2 cm (¾ in) thick slices. Arrange on a platter with the potatoes and crackling. Serve with the quince aïoli.

Bean stew with chorizo

This is a really quick dish – the sort of thing I might have for dinner if I have had a big lunch. It's glammed-up baked beans, really. Serve with crusty bread. Serves 4

Oil for cooking

2 chorizo sausages, sliced

1 onion, diced

2 garlic cloves, crushed

250 ml (8½ fl oz/1 cup) tomato passata (puréed tomatoes)

250 ml (8½ fl oz/1 cup) chicken stock

400 g (14 oz) tinned cannellini (lima) beans, drained and rinsed

2 tablespoons chopped flat-leaf (Italian) parsley

Heat a large heavy-based saucepan over medium–high heat. Add the chorizo and cook for 5–6 minutes, stirring often until the fat renders out.

Remove the chorizo from the pan, drain the excess fat and add the onion to the pan. Cook for 3–4 minutes until the onion is softened. Add the garlic and cook for 1–2 minutes, until fragrant. Return the chorizo to the pan, add the passata, stock and beans and bring to the boil. Season with salt, reduce to a simmer and cook for 15–20 minutes, stirring often.

Check the seasoning, add the parsley and serve.

Seafood

Mediterranean fish stew

Cooking fish with tomatoes, herbs and potatoes is one of the easiest ways to enjoy seafood for dinner. It's a true one-pot wonder. Serve with crusty bread with some good-quality butter.
Serves 4–6

4 potatoes, peeled and diced

1 onion, sliced

2–3 garlic cloves, peeled

4 tomatoes, diced

2–3 thyme sprigs

1 tablespoon oregano leaves

1 kg (2 lb 3 oz) firm white fish fillets

Olive oil

2 tablespoons lemon juice

375 ml (12½ fl oz/1½ cups) fish or chicken stock

2 tablespoons chopped flat-leaf (Italian) parsley

Preheat the oven to 180°C (350°F).

Put the potato, onion, garlic, tomatoes and herbs in a casserole dish. Cut the fish into 3 cm (1¼ in) chunks and place it on top. Drizzle with olive oil and lemon juice.

Place the stock in a small saucepan and bring it to the boil. Pour this over the other ingredients. Season lightly with salt and freshly ground black pepper and cover with foil. Bake in the oven for 45 minutes.

Check to see if the potatoes are cooked. If not, cook for an additional 5 minutes and check again. Check the seasoning, scatter the parsley over and serve.

Vegetarian

Chickpea and vegetable casserole

This simple but satisfying casserole is for lovers of chickpeas and vegetables. Serves 4

1 eggplant (aubergine), diced

Oil for cooking

2 onions, diced

2 carrots, diced

1 red capsicum (bell pepper), diced

2 garlic cloves, crushed

2 small red chillies, seeded and finely diced

2 teaspoons ground turmeric

2 teaspoons sweet paprika

1 teaspoon Harissa (page 467)

2 tablespoons tomato paste (concentrated purée)

250 ml (8½ fl oz/1 cup) vegetable stock

400 g (14 oz) tinned chickpeas, drained and rinsed

Steamed rice (page 480) to serve

Sprinkle the diced eggplant with salt and set aside for 20 minutes to allow the juices to bead. Rinse the eggplant well and pat dry.

Heat a medium saucepan over medium–high heat. Add a splash of oil and cook the onion, carrot, capsicum and eggplant for 6–8 minutes, or until softened. Add the garlic, chilli, turmeric, paprika and harissa and cook for a further 3–4 minutes, stirring occasionally, until aromatic. Add the tomato paste and cook for 1 minute.

Add the stock and bring to the boil. Season with salt and freshly ground black pepper and add the chickpeas. Reduce to a simmer and cook for 10–12 minutes, until the liquid thickens. Check the seasoning and serve with the steamed rice.

Moroccan lentil and sweet potato shepherd's pie

A great option for vegetarians or meat-free Mondays. Serves 4

Oil for cooking

1 onion, diced

1 garlic clove, crushed

2 teaspoons Harissa (page 467)

1 teaspoon ground coriander

1 teaspoon ground cumin

200 g (7 oz/1 cup) puy lentils or tiny blue-green lentils

750 ml (125½ fl oz/3 cups) vegetable stock

125 ml (4 fl oz/½ cup) tomato passata (puréed tomatoes)

15 g (½ oz/¼ cup) chopped coriander (cilantro) leaves

500 g (1 lb 2 oz) sweet potatoes

Heat a medium saucepan over medium–high heat. Add a splash of oil and cook the onion for 3–4 minutes. Add the garlic, harissa, ground coriander and cumin. Cook for a further 1–2 minutes, stirring often. Add the lentils, stock and tomato passata and bring to the boil. Reduce the heat and cook for 45 minutes, stirring occasionally, until the lentils are cooked and the sauce is reduced. Season to taste with salt and freshly ground black pepper and stir through the coriander leaves.

Preheat the oven to 180°C (350°F).

Peel and dice the sweet potatoes, place in a saucepan, cover with water and cook until tender, about 10 minutes. Drain and mash the potatoes, then season with salt and pepper.

Pour the lentil mixture into a 2 litre (68 fl oz/8 cup) deep casserole dish. Cover with the mashed sweet potato and bake in the oven for 20 minutes or until crispy and golden brown.

Vegetables

Most people master how to pan-fry chicken or barbecue a steak, but few take the time to learn to prepare vegetables correctly. Or, if they do, it's just the basics – peas, carrots and green beans. Well-prepared vegetables should be part of every meal; in fact, they can even be the highlight. Think of baby carrots drizzled with honey, new-season peas with mint and butter, or something as simple as beautifully smooth mashed potatoes.

Season's best

This chapter gives instructions on how to prepare a wide selection of vegetables correctly, plus ways to jazz them up and add complementary flavours. Always use the season as your guide to ensure what you're buying is ripe and full of flavour. To help you choose, I've included an easy-to-follow seasonal vegetable chart on page 240. Don't forget that Mother Nature can act at will and may bring on plums early with a spell of hot weather, or delay winter greens with a lack of rain. So, always use your senses – sight, touch and smell – when choosing the season's best.

Things you need to know
about vegetables

- Asparagus really signifies spring. Choose asparagus spears of an even thickness so they will cook at the same time. Most commonly you will see green asparagus, though white and purple can be found at the height of the season. See page 242 for a tip on how to trim the woody ends.

- Asian greens are more widely available than ever, so they can easily become a part of your weekly menu. When preparing them, ensure you wash them well to remove any dirt.

- One of my favourite Asian greens is Chinese flowering cabbage (choy sum), with tender fleshy stems, bright green leaves and yellow flowers. Another is Chinese broccoli (gai larn) – it's almost identical, except the flowers are white.

- Leafy greens, such as brussels sprouts, cabbage and broccoli, aren't everyone's cup of tea, but usually it's because they've been overcooked. If leafy greens are cooked for longer than necessary, sulphur compounds are released giving the veggies an unpleasant aroma. The exception is slow-braised red cabbage. However, leafy greens are fabulous when carefully cooked, which in their case means cooked only briefly.

- When buying corn, look for even-coloured cobs with the green husks free from decay. Fine, silky white tassels extending out of the top are another sign of freshness. Corn's natural sweetness means it is a vegetable that appeals to children and adults alike, so make full use of it throughout the warmer months.

- The pungent aniseed flavour of fennel can be overpowering for some people. However, cooking transforms fennel from an intense taste to a mild one. When buying fennel bulbs, choose those with their feather-like tops still attached – this is a sign of freshness.

- Green beans are without doubt the most popular of all the bean family. There are lots of other varieties to try at various times of the year, including yellow butter beans, broad beans, borlotti (cranberry) beans and large, flat runner beans.

- The array of mushrooms now on offer is fantastic, from the everyday cultivated button and field mushrooms to the more full-flavoured Swiss brown, shiitake, enoki and oyster mushrooms.

- Wild mushrooms appear in the damp autumn (fall) months when the weather conditions are just right. The most widely available are pine mushrooms (saffron milk cap) and slippery jacks. These are usually picked in secret spots dotted around the countryside, often near pine trees.

- Fresh garden peas seem to have been replaced in our kitchens by packets of frozen peas. I use frozen peas myself sometimes, but please make the effort every now and then to pod fresh peas, even if it's just to let our kids know that peas don't grow in supermarket freezers.

- It's best to buy potatoes with the dirt still attached. This way they will last longer and be protected against some bruising. Unwashed potatoes will keep in a cool dark place for up to 1 month.

- Pumpkin (squash) has a delightfully sweet flesh and is a great staple in my winter cooking. There are many different varieties to choose from, but there is little discernible difference in flavour between them. Take care when cutting pumpkins due to their uneven shape and tough skin. It is best to chop the top or bottom off, and then stand the pumpkin upright. When balanced like this it is safe to cut it into wedges. Peel the tough skin away using a sharp knife. Cut the wedges in half and discard the seeds.

- Root vegetables are one of the largest groups of vegetables and perhaps one of the least utilised. They include parsnip, swede (rutabaga), turnip, celeriac, Jerusalem artichoke, kohlrabi and, of course, carrot. Good root vegetables should have a deep, earthy aroma and be firm and appealing to the eye. Their harvesting is perfectly timed to coincide with the hearty comfort foods of winter, such as roasts and casseroles.

- English spinach is a quick and easy vegetable to prepare, especially now that pre-washed spinach leaves are so readily available. It has a delicate flavour and appeals to those who find cabbage and brussels sprouts too strong.

- There is nothing quite like a tomato in its prime, sun-kissed, fragrant and oozing with flavour. The arrival of heirloom varieties, such as green zebras, black Russians and tigerella, means there is now a range of new varieties to include in our cooking.

- Zucchini (courgette) is one of the classic summer vegetables. Pan-fry a few slices briefly in butter or olive oil to taste just how good they can be. The flowers that are attached to the ends of baby zucchini are also highly sought after. They are best stuffed and then deep-fried.

Seasonal vegetable chart

I am a big fan of seasonal produce and encourage everyone to use veggies at their peak for the best quality and flavour. Use the following list, which shows when each vegetable is in season, as a general guide. However, there may be variations depending on your local climate.

SPRING

artichoke
asparagus
avocado
broad bean
broccoli
cabbage
carrot
cauliflower
cucumber
green bean
leek
lettuce
pea
potato
salad (white) onion
silverbeet (Swiss chard)
snow pea (mangetout)
spinach, English
sugar snap pea
sweetcorn
tomato
zucchini (courgette) flower

SUMMER

asparagus
avocado
borlotti (cranberry) bean
butter bean
capsicum (bell pepper)
celery
cucumber
eggplant (aubergine)
green bean
leek
lettuce
pea
radish
snow pea (mangetout)
squash
sugar snap pea
sweetcorn
tomato
zucchini (courgette)
zucchini (courgette) flower

AUTUMN

Asian greens
avocado
beetroot (beet)
borlotti (cranberry) bean
broccoli
brussels sprout
butter bean
cabbage
capsicum (bell pepper)
carrot
cauliflower
celery
cucumber
eggplant (aubergine)
fennel
green bean
leek
lettuce
onion
parsnip
pea
potato
pumpkin (squash)
silverbeet (Swiss chard)
spinach, English
squash
swede (rutabaga)
sweetcorn
sweet potato
tomato
turnip
wild mushrooms

WINTER

Asian greens
avocado
beetroot (beet)
broccoli
brussels sprout
cabbage
carrot
cauliflower
celeriac
celery
fennel
horseradish
Jerusalem artichoke
kale
kohlrabi
leek
okra
olive
onion
parsnip
pea
potato
pumpkin (squash)
silverbeet (Swiss chard)
spinach, English
swede (rutabaga)
sweet potato
turnip

Vegetable recipes

Asparagus with feta

Asparagus goes well with a great variety of sauces and other ingredients. In this recipe, marinated feta is melted slightly on the warm asparagus – delicious! Serves 4

500 g (1 lb 2 oz) asparagus
Oil for cooking
100 g (3½ oz) marinated feta
1 tablespoon red-wine vinegar

Trim the woody ends from the asparagus. You can do this by holding the end of the stalk in one hand and the remainder in the other and then bending the asparagus. The stalk will break at the appropriate point. If preferred, trim off the bottom 5 cm (2 in) or so with a knife. Toss the asparagus with oil, salt and freshly ground black pepper.

Heat a heavy-based frying pan over medium–high heat. Add the asparagus and a splash of oil and cook for 5–6 minutes, turning regularly.

Arrange the asparagus on a platter, crumble the feta on top, drizzle with vinegar and serve.

Asparagus with hollandaise sauce
Cook the asparagus in boiling water for about 2-3 minutes. Drain and, while still warm, serve with Hollandaise sauce (page 454).

Asparagus with prosciutto
Wrap a slice of prosciutto around each asparagus spear and cook as directed.

Broad beans braised with pancetta

Broad beans generally have to be double-podded to be enjoyed at their best. It's a bit of work, but the flavour of these beans makes it worth every minute of effort. Serves 4

1 kg (2 lb 3 oz) broad beans
1 tablespoon olive oil
1 onion, finely diced
4 slices pancetta, thinly sliced and diced
250 ml (8½ fl oz/1 cup) chicken stock
40 g (1½ oz) butter

Remove the beans from their large pods. Bring a large saucepan of water to the boil. Add the broad beans and cook for 1 minute. Drain and refresh under cold running water.

Remove the pale green skins from the beans. This is easily done by inserting a small knife or your thumbnail into the skin and creating a slit, then pushing the vivid green bean halves from their skins. Discard the skins.

Heat a saucepan over medium heat. Add the oil and onion and cook for 3–4 minutes until soft, stirring often. Add the pancetta and cook until it begins to colour, stirring often. Add the beans and stock and bring to the boil. Reduce to a simmer and cook, uncovered, until the beans are tender.

Raise the heat and cook until the stock has evaporated. Add the butter, season with salt and freshly ground black pepper and serve.

Broad beans with extra-virgin olive oil
Pod the beans and cook them in boiling water for 2-3 minutes. Drizzle with your best extra-virgin olive oil, salt and some shavings of parmesan.

Moroccan broad beans

A simple dish, but one that requires quality ingredients. All the elements can be prepared in advance and then assembled just before you eat. Make sure you serve the broad beans and breadcrumbs either slightly warm, or at room temperature. Serves 4

2 teaspoons cumin seeds

1 teaspoon coriander seeds

250 g (9 oz) sourdough bread

Oil for frying

1 kg (2 lb 3 oz) broad beans

Zest and juice of 1 lemon

250 g (9 fl oz/1 cup) natural yoghurt

2 teaspoons tahini

2 tablespoons chopped coriander (cilantro) or mint, or a mixture of both

½ red onion, finely diced

3 tablespoons fruity extra-virgin olive oil

2 tablespoons shredded mint

Heat a small frying pan over medium heat and toast the cumin seeds until golden brown and fragrant. Remove and set aside to cool. Repeat with the coriander seeds. Once cool, grind roughly in a mortar and pestle. Set aside until needed.

Remove the crusts from the bread and chop the bread into rough breadcrumbs.

Heat a large heavy-based frying pan over medium–high heat. Add a very generous splash of oil and the breadcrumbs and cook for 4–5 minutes, stirring often until the breadcrumbs are golden and crunchy. When they are just about cooked, sprinkle the ground spices over the top and toss well to coat the breadcrumbs with the spices.

Blanch the broad beans in boiling water for about 2–3 minutes, then refresh under cold water.

Remove the pale green skins from the beans. This is easily done by inserting a small knife or your thumbnail into the skin and creating a slit, then pushing the vivid green bean halves from their skins. Discard the skins. Put the beans in a bowl.

Put the lemon zest, yoghurt, tahini and chopped coriander in a bowl and season well with salt and freshly ground black pepper.

Add the lemon juice to the broad beans along with the red onion, extra-virgin olive oil and shredded mint. Leave at room temperature until ready to serve.

To serve, spoon the yoghurt onto a serving platter, add the broad beans and top with the crispy breadcrumbs.

Wok-fried snake beans with cashews

Snake, long or yard-long beans are a common sight at markets nowadays, especially those with Asian stallholders. These beans are really great to cook as they always retain a light crunch. Serves 4

1 tablespoon peanut oil

4 spring onions (scallions), thinly sliced

1 teaspoon grated fresh ginger

1 bunch snake (yard-long) beans, cut into 3 cm (1¼ in) pieces

1–2 tablespoons soy sauce

50 g (1¾ oz/⅓ cup) roasted cashew nuts

200 g (7 oz) firm tofu, cut into cubes

Heat a wok over high heat. Add the oil, swirling to cover the side of the wok, then add the spring onion, ginger and snake beans. Toss to coat with oil and cook for 1 minute, until fragrant. Add a generous splash of water and cover with a lid. Allow to steam for 3–4 minutes.

Add the soy sauce, cashew nuts and tofu. Toss, cover with the lid and cook for 1–2 minutes. Serve immediately.

Wok-fried brussels sprouts

This will make you fall in love with brussels sprouts all over again – or maybe for the first time!
Serves 4 as a side dish

500 g (1 lb 2 oz) brussels sprouts
1 tablespoon peanut oil
2 teaspoons grated fresh ginger
1 tablespoon soy sauce
1 teaspoon sesame oil
1 teaspoon toasted sesame seeds

Trim the brussels sprouts of their darker green outside leaves and cut the sprouts in half. Bring a large saucepan of water to the boil. Add the brussels sprouts and cook them for 4–5 minutes.

Heat a wok over high heat. Add the oil and ginger and cook briefly. Add the drained, hot brussels sprouts and toss quickly to coat them with the ginger and oil. Add the soy sauce and cook for 2–3 minutes, stirring frequently to allow the liquid to evaporate. Add the sesame oil and sesame seeds and serve.

Brussels sprouts with almonds and parsley

You may be getting the idea that I love brussels sprouts. I do, and so does every other member of the family, and we eat lots of them over winter – in fact, we even fight over them.
Serves 4 as a side dish

20–40 g (¾–1½ oz) butter
500 g (1 lb 2 oz) brussels sprouts
Handful of flaked toasted almonds
2 tablespoons chopped flat-leaf (Italian) parsley

Trim the brussels sprouts of their darker green outside leaves and cut the sprouts in half. Bring a large saucepan of water to the boil. Add the brussels sprouts and cook them for 4–5 minutes.

Heat a heavy-based frying pan over medium heat. Add the butter and, when melted, add the drained brussels sprouts and cook for 3–4 minutes, stirring well. Sprinkle with the almonds and parsley and season with salt and freshly ground black pepper. Serve.

Brussels sprouts with chestnuts
Substitute chunks of cooked chestnut for the almonds.

Brussels sprouts with anchovies
Blanch the brussels sprouts as directed. Heat a heavy-based frying pan over medium–high heat, add a splash of oil, four diced anchovies and one diced red chilli and cook for 3-4 minutes or until fragrant. Add the hot brussels sprouts to the pan and toss to combine. Season with salt and freshly ground black pepper, add 1 tablespoon chopped flat-leaf (Italian) parsley and serve.

Brussels sprouts with bacon and tamari almonds
Blanch the brussels sprouts as directed. Heat a heavy-based frying pan over medium–high heat, add a splash of oil and 200 g (7 oz) diced bacon and cook for 4-5 minutes or until crispy and golden brown; if necessary, drain the excess oil away. Add the hot brussels sprouts to the pan along with 100 g (3½ oz) tamari almonds. Toss to combine, season with salt and freshly ground black pepper, add 1 tablespoon chopped flat-leaf (Italian) parsley and serve.

Sicilian brussels sprouts

This is probably my favourite brussels sprout dish. Serve it with Roast beef rib (page 169), Slow-roasted lamb shoulder (page 174) or any slow-cooked winter dish. Serves 4 as a side dish

85 g (3 oz) currants
60 ml (2 fl oz/¼ cup) brandy
500 g (1 lb 2 oz) brussels sprouts
Butter for cooking
2 tablespoons toasted pine nuts
1 tablespoon chopped flat-leaf (Italian) parsley

Soak the currants in the brandy for 20 minutes.

Trim the brussels sprouts of their darker green outside leaves and cut the sprouts in half. Bring a large saucepan of water to the boil. Add the brussels sprouts and cook them for 4–5 minutes.

Heat a heavy-based frying pan over medium heat. Add the butter and, when melted, add the drained brussels sprouts. Cook for 3–4 minutes, stirring well. Add the soaked currants and any remaining liquid, toss together and cook for 1–2 minutes. Add the pine nuts and parsley, season with salt and freshly ground black pepper and serve.

Red cabbage with sweet and sour flavours

This sweet-and-sour cabbage is perfect with roast pork. Serves 4 as a side dish

½ red cabbage
75 g (2¾ oz) butter
80 ml (2½ fl oz/⅓ cup) red-wine vinegar
80 ml (2½ fl oz/⅓ cup) redcurrant juice or
  blackcurrant cordial

Cut the cabbage into quarters and trim away the central stalk. Thinly slice the cabbage.

Heat a large heavy-based saucepan over medium–high heat. Melt the butter, add the cabbage and toss well. Stir in the vinegar and redcurrant juice, cover and cook for 20–30 minutes, stirring often. Serve.

Roast carrots

These carrots can be added to a traditional roast, cooked separately and served as a side dish, or added to salads for their extra-sweet flavour. Look out for different-coloured carrots to mix it up a bit. Serves 4 as a side dish

1 bunch baby (Dutch) carrots or 3 large carrots
Oil for cooking
1 tablespoon balsamic vinegar
1–2 thyme sprigs

Preheat the oven to 180°C (350°F).

If using baby carrots, scrub them lightly. If using normal carrots, peel and then cut them into even-sized pieces.

Place the carrots in a baking tin. Drizzle with oil, vinegar and thyme and season with salt and freshly ground black pepper. Cook in the oven for 20–30 minutes, tossing occasionally, until tender.

Honey-roasted carrots
Add 1 tablespoon honey to the baking dish.

Roast cauliflower

Roasting may not be the first cooking method that springs to mind for cauliflower but it works extremely well. For extra flavour you can also sprinkle the cauliflower with a little spice, such as sweet paprika or ground cumin. Serves 6 as a side dish

1 medium cauliflower
Oil for cooking

Preheat the oven to 180°C (350°F).

Cut the large stalk out of the cauliflower to leave the separated florets. Try to ensure they are a similar size.

Toss the cauliflower in oil and season with some salt and freshly ground black pepper. Place in a baking tin and cook in the oven for 20 minutes, or until golden brown and tender.

Moroccan stir-fried cauliflower

Make this recipe when you want a quick cauliflower dish with plenty of flavour and oomph. If you like, you can toss all the ingredients together and roast them in a preheated 180°C (350°F) oven for 8–10 minutes. Serves 4 as a side dish

½ cauliflower
Oil for cooking
1 teaspoon ground cumin
1 teaspoon ground coriander
1 tablespoon chopped coriander (cilantro)

Cut the large stalk out of the cauliflower to leave the separated florets. Try to ensure they are a similar size.

Heat a heavy-based frying pan over medium heat and add a generous splash of oil. Add the cauliflower and toss to combine. Cook for 4–5 minutes, tossing and stirring often. Add the spices and season with salt and freshly ground black pepper. Continue cooking for another 2–3 minutes or until the cauliflower is just cooked – I like to retain quite a bit of bite.

Add the chopped coriander, transfer to a serving dish and serve immediately.

Cauliflower rice

If you're on a gluten-free diet, want to avoid carbs or just want to eat as many veggies as possible, this cauliflower rice is a great substitute for rice or couscous to serve alongside curries and tagines. I first came across this method when working on Jane Kennedy's book, *Fabulous Food, Minus the Boombah*. It's a winner. Serves 2 as a side dish

½ cauliflower

Cut the cauliflower into small florets and place them in a microwave-safe container with a lid – there's no need to add water. Microwave on High (100%) for 5 minutes.

Remove the lid, taking care as steam will escape.

Using either a hand-held blender or food processor, pulse the cauliflower until it resembles rice. Serve while still hot or microwave to heat it though.

Cauliflower cheese

Cauliflower cheese is a classic British dish. It tastes great and encourages children to eat cauliflower – so why not serve it to the family tonight? Serves 4

1 medium cauliflower
40 g (1½ oz) butter
500 ml (17 fl oz/2 cups) milk
2 tablespoons plain (all-purpose) flour
1 teaspoon dijon mustard
200 g (7 oz) grated cheddar

Preheat the oven to 180°C (350°F).

Cut the large stalk out of the cauliflower to leave the separated florets.

Bring a large saucepan of water to the boil and cook the cauliflower in boiling water for 6–7 minutes, or until just tender. Drain well and transfer the cauliflower to a buttered casserole dish.

Warm the milk to a gentle simmer. Heat a small saucepan over medium heat and melt the butter. Reduce the heat to low and add the flour. Stir to form a roux and allow to 'cook out' the flour for 1–2 minutes. Raise the heat, add the warm milk and whisk until a smooth sauce forms. Simmer for 5 minutes, until the sauce has thickened slightly.

Remove from the heat and add the mustard and cheese. Stir until melted. Season to taste with salt and freshly ground black pepper. Pour the sauce over the cauliflower and place in the oven. Cook for 20 minutes, or until bubbling and beginning to brown on top.

Mustard cauliflower bake

Cauliflower is one of my favourite vegetables, hence all the recipes! This Yotam Ottolenghi-inspired dish has all the yumminess of cauliflower, but none of the fuss. Serves 4 as a side dish

125 g (4½ oz/1 cup) grated cheddar

200 g (7 oz/3⅓ cups) panko crumbs

½ cauliflower, cut into florets

250 ml (8½ fl oz/1 cup) thickened (whipping) cream

2 teaspoons dijon mustard

2 tablespoons chopped flat-leaf (Italian) parsley

Preheat the oven to 180°C (350°F) and grease a baking dish.

In a bowl, mix together the grated cheddar and panko crumbs to combine.

Bring a large saucepan of water to the boil and blanch the cauliflower for 2–3 minutes. Drain and set aside.

Put the cream and mustard in a saucepan over medium–high heat and season well with salt and freshly ground black pepper. Bring to the boil. Add the hot blanched cauliflower and half of the cheddar mixture and toss to combine. Spoon the cauliflower into the baking dish.

Add the chopped parsley to the remaining cheddar mixture and sprinkle this over the top of the cauliflower. Bake in the oven for 15–20 minutes until golden brown.

Stir-fried Chinese greens

You can use any type of Asian greens you like in this dish, such as baby bok choy (pak choy) or Chinese cabbage (wombok), or use a combination. Serves 4

1 bunch Chinese broccoli (gai larn)

Oil for cooking

2 garlic cloves, crushed

2 tablespoons grated fresh ginger

1 bunch broccolini, ends trimmed

60 ml (2 fl oz/¼ cup) chicken stock or water

1–2 tablespoons soy sauce

Wash the Chinese broccoli well, taking care to remove all dirt. Discard any big or old leaves. Thinly slice the stems – on an angle is best.

Heat a wok over high heat. Add a splash of oil, the garlic and ginger and cook for 2–3 minutes, stirring often, making sure the garlic doesn't burn. Add the Chinese broccoli and broccolini and toss for 1–2 minutes. Add the stock and cover with a lid. Cook for 3–4 minutes, tossing occasionally to ensure the greens cook evenly.

Remove the lid, season with soy sauce and serve.

Barbecued corn cobs

This is a must-try recipe, as corn is great when it's cooked on the barbecue. If you can get your hands on some Spanish smoky paprika, it'll be an absolute knockout. Serves 4

4 corn cobs

2 tablespoons olive oil

2 teaspoons smoky Spanish paprika or sweet paprika

To prepare the corn, roll back and remove the green husks, then pull off the silky tassels. Wash the cobs briefly to ensure that all the tassels have been removed. Cut the cobs in half or into smaller pieces as required.

Preheat a barbecue grill to high.

Brush the cobs all over with oil, then sprinkle with the paprika and some salt and freshly ground black pepper. Place the corn cobs on a the barbecue grill and cook for 10 minutes, turning often.

Chargrilled corn with queso and lime

This dish makes a great appetiser or pre-dinner nibble, or you can serve it alongside a Mexican-inspired feast. Serves 4

4 corn cobs

½ teaspoon cumin seeds, toasted

2 teaspoons pepitas (pumpkin seeds), toasted

2 teaspoons chipotle powder

1 teaspoon smoked paprika

½ teaspoon cayenne pepper

Grated zest of 1 lime

Oil for cooking

Chipotle mayonnaise (page 463)

100 g (3½ oz) grated parmesan

Lime wedges

Blanch the corn cobs in boiling water, then refresh under cold water.

Grind the cumin seeds and pepitas together using a mortar and pestle. Add the chipotle, smoked paprika, cayenne pepper, lime zest and 1 teaspoon salt and mix together.

Brush the corn cobs with oil and cook on the barbecue or in a chargrill pan over medium–high heat until lightly charred. Remove the corn, brush with the chipotle mayonnaise, roll in the grated cheese and sprinkle with the spice mix. Serve immediately with the lime wedges.

Sichuan eggplant

Eggplant is a vegetable that seems to go in and out of favour with great regularity. This easy recipe should put it right back up there in the popularity stakes. Serves 4 as a side dish

2 eggplants (aubergines)

Oil for cooking

60 ml (2 fl oz/¼ cup) kecap manis

2 teaspoons sesame oil

1 teaspoon Sichuan salt and pepper spice (page 467) (optional)

Preheat the oven to 180°C (350°F).

Cut the eggplants in half, then cut each half into three wedges. Sprinkle with salt and set aside for 20 minutes until the juices bead. Rinse well and pat dry.

Heat a heavy-based frying pan over medium–high heat. Add a generous splash of oil and cook the eggplant until lightly brown on the flesh side. Place in a baking tray, skin side down.

Mix the kecap manis and sesame oil together. Brush over the eggplant and sprinkle with the salt and pepper spice (if using). Bake in the oven for 10–15 minutes, until the eggplant is cooked through. Serve immediately.

Roast vegetable ratatouille

Give ratatouille a modern-day makeover with this delicious recipe. Chop all the vegetables into small dice, about 5 mm (¼ in). This is delicious with roast lamb or pan-fried fish. Serves 4

1 small eggplant (aubergine)

1 onion, chopped

2 small zucchini (courgettes), chopped

1 red capsicum (bell pepper), chopped

1 tomato, coarsely chopped

1 garlic clove, crushed

1 tablespoon chopped flat-leaf (Italian) parsley

1 tablespoon chopped thyme

Oil for cooking

Preheat the oven to 180°C (350°F).

Cut the eggplant into dice. Sprinkle with salt and set aside for 20 minutes until the juices bead. Rinse well and pat dry.

Combine the eggplant, onion, zucchini, capsicum and tomato in a roasting dish. Scatter with the garlic and herbs, season well with salt and freshly ground black pepper and drizzle with oil.

Place the dish in the oven and cook for 40 minutes, stirring the ratatouille occasionally. Continue cooking until the vegetables are tender.

Caponata

Serve this Sicilian eggplant dish with pan-fried lamb or veal, or with chicken cooked with a hint of spice. Serves 6 as a side dish

2 eggplants (aubergines), cut into 1 cm (½ in) dice

Oil for cooking

1 onion, diced

2 celery stalks, cut into 1 cm (½ in) dice

1 red capsicum (bell pepper), cut into 1 cm (½ in) dice

75 g (2¾ oz/½ cup) pitted green olives

2 teaspoons salted capers, soaked and rinsed

80 ml (2½ fl oz/⅓ cup) white-wine vinegar

2 tablespoons caster (superfine) sugar

Chopped basil and flat-leaf (Italian) parsley

Place the diced eggplant in a colander and sprinkle with salt. Leave for 20–30 minutes until the juices bead. Rinse well and pat dry.

Place a large heavy-based frying pan over medium heat and add enough oil to cover the base of the pan. Cook the eggplant in batches until golden brown, adding more oil if necessary. Remove from the pan and cook the onion, celery and capsicum until soft.

Return the eggplant to the pan and add the olives, capers, vinegar and sugar. Cook a little until the sugar has dissolved, taking care not to overcook the eggplant. Remove from the heat and allow to cool at room temperature. Before serving, add the herbs to taste, and salt and freshly ground black pepper if needed.

Sumac eggplant chips with yoghurt dressing

Sumac is a red Middle Eastern berry. It has a slightly astringent, lemony flavour. There is no need to salt the eggplants in this recipe, unless they are particularly old and bitter.
Serves 4 as a side dish

12 long thin eggplants (aubergines)

Oil for cooking

1–2 teaspoons sumac

Yoghurt dressing (page 461)

Preheat the oven to 180°C (350°F).

Cut the eggplants in half lengthways. Place them, skin side down, in a baking dish and brush oil over the cut surface. Sprinkle with the sumac and some salt and freshly ground black pepper. Bake in the oven for 25–30 minutes or until crispy. Serve the warm eggplant chips drizzled with the yoghurt dressing.

Fennel fritters

Serve these fritters as a side dish in autumn (fall) and winter, when fennel is at its seasonal best. Makes 5–6 fritters

1 fennel bulb
1 egg
125 ml (4 fl oz/½ cup) milk
50 g (1¾ oz/½ cup) dry breadcrumbs
40 g (1½ oz/½ cup) grated parmesan
Oil for cooking

Remove the fennel's tough outer skin and trim off the feathery tops. Cut the fennel into 5 mm (¼ in) slices across the bulb.

Bring a saucepan of water to the boil and cook the fennel briefly in the boiling water. Refresh under cold running water and dry well.

Beat the egg and milk together in one bowl and combine the breadcrumbs and parmesan in another. Dip the fennel first in the egg mixture and then in the breadcrumbs.

Heat a heavy-based frying pan over medium heat. Add a generous splash of oil and cook the fritters until golden and crispy.

Jerusalem artichoke purée

A fine accompaniment to a classic Roast beef rib (page 169). Serves 4

1 kg (2 lb 3 oz) Jerusalem artichokes
80 ml (2½ fl oz/⅓ cup) thickened (whipping) cream
40 g (1½ oz) butter
1 tablespoon chopped flat-leaf (Italian) parsley

Peel the artichokes and place them in a large saucepan. Cover them with water and bring to the boil. Reduce to a simmer and cook for 10 minutes, until tender.

Drain the artichokes well, then return them to the saucepan. Place the saucepan over low heat and warm the artichokes for 1–2 minutes, shaking the pan occasionally to evaporate any excess moisture.

Place the artichokes in a food processor and purée roughly. Add the cream and butter and continue puréeing until smooth. Season with salt and freshly ground black pepper.

Gently reheat the artichoke purée in a saucepan over low heat, stirring well. Stir through the chopped parsley and serve immediately.

Caramelised onions

Serve these caramelised onions with grilled steaks, use them on pizza or toss them through cooked pasta with chopped rocket (arugula) and parmesan. Serves 4

80 ml (2½ fl oz/⅓ cup) olive oil
4 onions, sliced
2 garlic cloves, peeled
1 small red chilli, halved
2 thyme sprigs

Heat the olive oil in a saucepan over medium heat and add the onion, garlic, chilli and thyme. Cook for 20–30 minutes on a low heat, stirring often, until the onions soften and caramelise. Season with salt and freshly ground black pepper if needed.

Pan-fried kale or cavolo nero

You can use either kale or cavolo nero in this recipe, or even a mixture of both. The garlic is an optional extra – your choice. Serves 4 as a side dish

250 g (9 oz) kale or cavolo nero
Oil for cooking
2 garlic cloves (optional)

Remove the thick stalks from the kale and cut the leaves into 4 cm (1½ in) pieces. Wash well and set aside to drain. I like to keep a bit of water on the leaves as it helps them to steam as they cook in the pan.

Heat a heavy-based frying pan over medium–high heat and add a generous splash of oil. If using garlic, add it now and cook for 1 minute, stirring often, making sure it doesn't burn. Add the greens and stir well to ensure they are coated with oil and garlic. Cook for 2–3 minutes, stirring often. If needed, add a splash of water to help the greens soften. Cook until tender, season with salt and freshly ground black pepper, then serve immediately.

Kale with chilli and rosemary

There's only one thing better than pan-fried kale, and that's pan-fried kale with chilli and rosemary – delicious with any roast and so good for you. Serves 2–3 as a side dish

2 tablespoons olive oil
1 onion, diced
2 rosemary sprigs, leaves picked
2 small red chillies, seeded and diced
2 garlic cloves, crushed
250 g (9 oz) kale

Remove the thick stalks from the kale. Cut the leaves into 1 cm (½ in) slices. Wash well and set aside to drain.

Heat a large heavy-based saucepan over medium–high heat. Add the oil and onion and cook for 3–4 minutes, stirring often, until the onion is soft. Add the rosemary leaves, chilli and garlic and cook for a further 2 minutes. Add the sliced kale and season with salt and freshly ground black pepper. Cover with a lid, reduce the heat to low and cook for 4–6 minutes, stirring occasionally.

Kale chips

Ah, the great invention of our time: the one recipe guaranteed to get anyone to start eating kale. Resistance is futile. Serves 2 as a side dish

250 g (9 oz) kale
Oil for cooking

Preheat the oven to 180°C (350°F) and line a baking tray with baking paper.

Tear the kale into 5 cm (2 in) pieces, removing the tough stalks as you go. Place the kale in a bowl, add just enough oil to coat, season well with salt and freshly ground black pepper and toss to combine well.

Spread the kale onto the prepared baking tray and cook in the oven for 10–15 minutes or until the kale is crisp. Enjoy.

Parmesan kale chips
Add 50 g (1¾ oz/½ cup) grated parmesan to the kale before cooking.

Smoky paprika kale chips
Add 2 teaspoons smoky sweet paprika to the kale before cooking.

Pan-fried mushrooms

Mushrooms are one of the simplest things to pan-fry. Try using button, Swiss brown or sliced field mushrooms, or a combination of more exotic varieties, such as shiitake and enoki. In autumn (fall), try this method with wild orange pine mushrooms. Serves 4

500 g (1 lb 2 oz) mushrooms
2 tablespoons olive oil
40 g (1½ oz) butter
1–2 tablespoons chopped herbs

Wipe the mushrooms with a damp cloth, then cut them to a similar size, if necessary, to allow even cooking.

Heat a heavy-based frying pan over medium–high heat, then add the oil and butter. Add the mushrooms and toss to coat. Cook for 8–10 minutes, moving the mushrooms around so that they cook evenly and start to soften. Season with salt and freshly ground black pepper, add the fresh chopped herbs and serve.

Pesto mushrooms
Pan-fry large field mushrooms and serve with a dollop of Basil pesto (page 476) on top.

Garlic mushrooms

Mushrooms cope really well with the heat of a barbecue, and taste especially good when they are drizzled with this lovely garlic oil. Serves 4–6

12 Swiss brown or field mushrooms
60–80 ml (2–2½ fl oz/¼–⅓ cup) olive oil
2 garlic cloves, crushed

Wipe the mushrooms with a damp cloth. Preheat a barbecue plate to medium–high. Alternatively, place a medium frying pan over medium–high heat.

Mix the olive oil with the garlic and some salt and freshly ground black pepper. Place the mushrooms on the barbecue plate or add to the hot pan and brush with oil. If barbecuing, cook for 4 minutes, brushing with oil, rotating once. Turn over and brush with oil again. Cook for a further 4 minutes, rotating once, then serve. If frying, cook for 4–5 minutes, tossing occasionally to ensure that the mushrooms cook evenly.

Soy mushrooms

These mushrooms are delicious with roast beef or Teriyaki beef (page 119). Any leftovers are also good in a simple noodle salad. Serves 4 as a side dish

Oil for cooking
2 spring onions (scallions), thinly sliced
½ tablespoon grated fresh ginger
300 g (10½ oz) mixed mushrooms, such as shiitake, oyster and enoki
60 ml (2 fl oz/¼ cup) Chinese rice wine
60 ml (2 fl oz/¼ cup) soy sauce

Heat a wok until very hot, add a splash of oil and the spring onion and ginger. Cook briefly, then add the mushrooms. Cook for 1–2 minutes, stirring often. Add the wine and soy sauce, cover with a lid and steam for 2–3 minutes.

Crispy stuffed mushrooms

Whoever said life's too short to stuff a mushroom obviously hasn't tasted these!
Serves 4 as an appetiser (makes 24)

150 g (5½ oz) goat's cheese or ricotta

2 garlic cloves, crushed

2 tablespoons chopped fresh herbs (basil, flat-leaf/
  Italian parsley, thyme and oregano)

1 tablespoon thickened (whipping) cream

350 g (12½ oz) medium button mushrooms
  (6 per person)

1 egg

125 ml (4 fl oz/½ cup) milk

Plain (all-purpose) flour for coating

50–100 g (1¾–3½ oz/½–1 cup) dry breadcrumbs

Oil for deep-frying

500 g (1 lb 2 oz) salad leaves

Lemon dressing (page 460)

Mix the goat's cheese, garlic, herbs, cream and some freshly ground black pepper.

Remove the stems from the mushrooms. Use a teaspoon to fill the mushroom cavities with the cheese mixture, rounding the tops to form 'balls'.

Lightly beat the egg with the milk in a bowl. Fill another bowl with the flour and a third with the breadcrumbs. Coat the mushrooms in the flour, then the egg and finally the breadcrumbs, one at a time. Repeat this coating to prevent the mushrooms from leaking during cooking.

In a deep-fryer or saucepan, heat the oil to 180°C (350°F). Deep-fry six to eight mushrooms at a time until golden brown. Drain on paper towel.

Dress the salad leaves and pile them onto four plates. Arrange six mushrooms around each salad and serve.

Roast parsnips

Parsnips herald the arrival of winter, so what better way to enjoy them than cooked alongside the weekly roast. Serves 4 as a side dish

1 kg (2 lb 3 oz) parsnips

60 ml (2 fl oz/¼ cup) olive oil

2 tablespoons sherry vinegar

Preheat the oven to 180°C (350°F).

Peel the parsnips and cut them into even-sized pieces, or just cut them in half lengthways if they are not too big. Place them in a bowl and mix well with the oil and vinegar. Season with salt and freshly ground black pepper.

Spread the parsnips in a shallow baking dish and cook in the oven for 45 minutes, or until golden brown and tender. Turn the parsnips occasionally during cooking to ensure that they brown evenly.

Roast parsnips with worcestershire sauce and honey
Substitute 2 tablespoons honey and 1 tablespoon worcestershire sauce for the oil and vinegar.

Roast parsnips with chestnuts
Omit the sherry vinegar and add 100 g (3½ oz) peeled chestnuts before cooking.

Stir-fried snow peas with cashews and soy

Snow peas are eaten whole, as their pod is thin and very sweet. They excel in a stir-fry, retaining their crunch and vibrant colour. Serves 4

600 g (1 lb 5 oz) snow peas (mangetout)
Oil for cooking
1 garlic clove, crushed
1 teaspoon grated fresh ginger
4 spring onions (scallions), thinly sliced
2–3 tablespoons chicken stock or water
1–2 tablespoons soy sauce
75 g (2¾ oz) roasted cashew nuts

Carefully pull the tip away from each snow pea, then pull the tip along the pod to tear off the string. Repeat from the other end.

Place a wok over high heat. Add a splash of oil and the garlic, ginger and spring onion and cook for 1 minute, stirring frequently. Add the snow peas and stock or water. Cover the wok with a lid and cook for 3–4 minutes, stirring once or twice. Remove the lid, stir well and add the soy sauce and cashew nuts. Toss to combine and serve immediately.

Sugar snap peas with lemon butter

Sweet sugar snap peas appeal to young and old alike. If you have younger members in the family, they may prefer their sugar snaps without the lemon. Serves 4

600 g (1 lb 5 oz) sugar snap peas
40 g (1½ oz) butter
2 tablespoons lemon juice

Carefully pull the tip away from each sugar snap pea, then pull the tip along the pod to tear off the string. Repeat from the other end.

Bring a large saucepan of water to the boil. Add the sugar snap peas and cook for 3–4 minutes, until tender. Drain and add the butter and lemon juice. Season with salt and freshly ground black pepper and serve immediately.

Minted peas

To pod peas, simply snap the ends off the pod and open it by running your finger along the seam. Remove the peas and discard the pod – 1.5 kg (3 lb 5 oz) peas will yield 500 g (1 lb 2 oz) podded peas. Serves 4 as a side dish

500 g (1 lb 2 oz) podded peas
1 mint sprig
40 g (1½ oz) butter

Bring a saucepan of water to the boil. Add the peas and mint and cook for 5–6 minutes, until tender. Drain the peas, add the butter and season with salt and freshly ground black pepper before serving.

Smashed pea mash
Boil the peas as directed. Drain well, remove the mint and season the peas with salt and pepper. Add the butter and mash roughly. Pea mash is great with pan-fried salmon, lamb cutlets or roast chicken.

Mashed potatoes

What could be better to serve for a large family gathering than great mashed potatoes?
Serves 6 as a side dish

1.5 kg (3 lb 5 oz) potatoes, such as bintje, nicola, sebago or spunta, or any other waxy potato

50 g (1¾ oz) butter, diced

2–3 tablespoons hot milk

Chopped flat-leaf (Italian) parsley

Peel the potatoes and chop them into even-sized pieces. Place the potatoes in a large saucepan and cover with water. Bring to the boil, reduce the heat and cook for 12–15 minutes, until tender.

Drain the potatoes well, then return them to the saucepan and place over low heat. Warm the potatoes for 1–2 minutes, shaking the pan occasionally to evaporate any excess moisture.

Mash the potatoes well, then stir in the butter, milk and chopped parsley. Season to taste with salt and freshly ground black pepper before serving.

Mashed potatoes with goat's cheese
To give an extra flavour boost to your mashed potatoes, substitute 50 g (1¾ oz) soft marinated goat's cheese for the hot milk.

Roast potatoes

There's nothing quite like perfectly cooked roast potatoes. They are also delicious when cooked in the same tray as a roast chicken or piece of beef, as the flavour from the meat adds that extra-special something. Serves 6 as a side dish

1.5 kg (3 lb 5 oz) potatoes, such as desiree, nicola, king edward or roseval, or any floury or all-purpose potato

Oil for cooking

Preheat the oven to 200°C (400°F).

Peel the potatoes and cut them into large, even-sized pieces. Place the potatoes in a baking tin, toss with oil and sprinkle with salt and freshly ground black pepper.

Cook the potatoes in the oven for 1 hour, turning them occasionally. They should be crispy and golden.

Goose-fat roast potatoes
Prepare the potatoes as directed, then toss with 3 tablespoons melted goose fat, salt and freshly ground black pepper. Cook the potatoes in a preheated 200°C (400°F) oven, turning them occasionally. They should be crispy and golden when ready.

Rosemary garlic potatoes

This is a true family favourite in our household – try it just once and it may become yours, too. These potatoes go well with roast lamb or any pan-fried meats. Serves 4 as a side dish

1 kg (2 lb 3 oz) potatoes, such as desiree, nicola, king edward or roseval, or any other all-purpose or floury potato

Oil for cooking

2–3 rosemary sprigs, leaves picked

20 garlic cloves, unpeeled

Preheat the oven to 180°C (350°F).

Peel and dice the potatoes into 2–3 cm (1¼ in) chunks. Place them in a deep baking tin with lots of oil, rosemary, garlic, salt and freshly ground black pepper. Mix well. Bake in the oven for 1 hour, stirring occasionally, until the potatoes are golden and cooked through.

Potato varieties

Waxy potatoes are great for boiling, potato grain and rösti as they will not collapse. Floury potatoes are high in starch and very good for baking, mashing and frying, and they also make great chips and roast potatoes. All-purpose potatoes have been developed in recent years, and can be used in a variety of ways.

Variety	Boil	Roast	Mash	Fry	Bake	Chips	Gnocchi
Desiree (waxy)	**	***		**	**		**
Bintje (waxy)	***	**	**	**	**		**
Nicola (waxy)	*	***	**	**	*		
Sebago (all-purpose)	**	*	**	**	*		
King Edward (floury)	**	***			**		
Toolangi Delight (all-purpose)	**	*	**		**	**	***
Spunta (all-purpose)	*	**	**		**	***	
Roseval (waxy)		***		***	**		
Pink eye (waxy)	***				*		
Patrone (waxy)	***			**	**		
Russet Burbank (floury)				***	**		

* Good   ** Very good   *** Excellent

Potato wedges

A simple but fantastic accompaniment to any grilled dish. Serves 4

Oil for cooking

2 tablespoons rosemary leaves

1 tablespoon chopped flat-leaf (Italian) parsley

1 kg (2 lb 3 oz) potatoes, such as desiree, nicola, king edward or roseval, or any other floury or all-purpose potatoes, cut into thick wedges

Preheat the oven to 180°C (350°F).

Place the oil, herbs and some salt and freshly ground black pepper in a large bowl. Add the potato wedges and toss well.

Place the wedges on a large baking tray, skin side down. Cook in the oven for 45–55 minutes. The potato wedges will be golden brown when ready.

Spiced potato wedges
Omit the herbs and instead add 1 teaspoon chilli powder, 1 teaspoon ground cumin and 1 teaspoon ground coriander.

Dukkah potato wedges
Omit the herbs and add 2–3 teaspoons Dukkah (page 469).

Sesame and cumin potato wedges
Omit the herbs and add 1 teaspoon sesame seeds and 1 teaspoon ground cumin.

Potato gratin

A gratin is classic dinner party stuff and minimal work once it's in the oven. You might like to serve the potatoes with steamed vegetables or a simple green salad. Serves 6

1.5 kg (3 lb 5 oz) potatoes, such as desiree or bintje, or any other waxy or all-purpose potato
185 ml (6 fl oz) thickened (whipping) cream
185 ml (6 fl oz) milk
2 garlic cloves, sliced
Freshly grated nutmeg

Preheat the oven to 180°C (350°F).

Peel the potatoes and place them in a large saucepan. Cover with water and bring to the boil. Cook for 5 minutes – you don't want the potatoes to be completely cooked.

Drain the potatoes well, then return them to the saucepan. Place the saucepan over low heat and warm the potatoes for 1–2 minutes, shaking the pan occasionally to evaporate any excess moisture.

Butter an ovenproof dish – one that you can serve at the table. Slice the potatoes into 5 mm (¼ in) thick slices and arrange them in the buttered dish.

Mix the cream and milk together and pour over the potatoes. Scatter the garlic slices over, season with salt and freshly ground black pepper and grate some fresh nutmeg over. Cover with foil and cook in the oven for 40 minutes. Remove the foil and return the dish to the oven for a further 10 minutes so the potatoes can brown a little.

Catalan potatoes

A mix of braising and roasting occurs in this dish. The stock is absorbed into the potatoes as they cook in the oven, yet they end up crisp and full of flavour from the smoky paprika. Serves 6 as a side dish

1.5 kg (3 lb 5 oz) desiree potatoes, or any other floury or all-purpose potato
1 teaspoon smoky paprika
Olive oil
500–750 ml (17–25½ fl oz/2–3 cups) chicken stock

Preheat the oven to 200°C (400°F).

Peel the potatoes and cut them in half lengthways. Place them in a roasting tin and sprinkle with the paprika and some salt and freshly ground black pepper. Add a good splash of oil and toss to coat the potatoes with the seasoning. Carefully pour in enough stock to half-cover the potatoes. Cook for 1½ hours, tossing the potatoes occasionally. Cook until they're golden brown and the liquid has been absorbed.

Roast potatoes with chorizo, chilli and coriander

If you haven't fallen in love with chorizo yet, this dish may well be the one that tips you over the edge. When using chorizo, always pan-fry it first, as this removes all the excess fat and caramelises the meat, adding a sweet flavour. Serves 4

Olive oil
500 g (1 lb 2 oz) baby potatoes
½ spicy or mild chorizo sausage
1–2 sliced red chillies
Handful of coriander (cilantro) leaves

Preheat the oven to 180°C (350°F).

Heat a heavy-based frying pan over medium heat. Add a generous splash of oil and pan-fry the potatoes until golden brown. Place the potatoes in a roasting tin and season with salt and freshly ground black pepper and place the tin in the oven.

Put the chorizo in the frying pan and pan-fry until golden brown. Drain the chorizo on paper towel, and add it to the potatoes in the oven. Cook for 30–40 minutes, or until the potatoes are cooked through.

Place the roast potatoes and chorizo in a serving dish and top with the sliced red chilli and coriander leaves.

Potato rösti

Use waxy potatoes for this recipe, as they'll hold together best. Serves 4

4 potatoes, such as bintje, desiree or spunta, or any other waxy potato
1 tablespoon chopped flat-leaf (Italian) parsley
Oil for cooking

Preheat the oven to 180°C (350°F).

Coarsely grate the potatoes, then squeeze any excess starch out of the potatoes.

Place the grated potato in a bowl, along with the parsley and some salt and freshly ground black pepper. Mix well.

Heat a heavy-based pan over medium–high heat. Pour in a generous amount of oil and add 6 cm (2½ in) wide mounds of the grated potato mix. Allow to cook for 3–4 minutes. The mixture will begin to brown and hold itself together. Flatten the mounds of potato a little using a spatula, then loosen the base, turn them over and cook for a further 5 minutes.

Remove the potato rösti from the pan, place them on a baking tray and cook in the oven for 8–10 minutes.

Pumpkin and parmesan mash

Mashed pumpkin is not the most inspiring of vegetables; that is, until you give it a lift with parmesan, chopped basil and a drizzle of your best olive oil. Serves 4

1 kg (2 lb 3 oz) pumpkin (squash)
40 g (1½ oz) grated parmesan
10 basil leaves, chopped
2 tablespoons olive oil

Peel the pumpkin and remove the seeds. Cut into 2–3 cm (¾–1¼ in) dice. Place the pumpkin in a medium saucepan and cover with water. Bring to the boil, then simmer for 10 minutes, until the pumpkin is just tender.

Drain the pumpkin, then return it to the saucepan. Place the saucepan over low heat and warm the pumpkin for 1–2 minutes, shaking the pan occasionally to evaporate any excess moisture.

Remove from the heat. Mash the pumpkin and stir in the parmesan, basil and oil. Season with salt and freshly ground black pepper and serve.

Pumpkin and nutmeg mash
Substitute a knob of organic butter and plenty of ground nutmeg for the parmesan, basil and olive oil.

Sweet potato mash
Substitute sweet potatoes for the pumpkin, then mash well and season with salt and freshly ground black pepper. The final touch is to stir in a decent splash of good cream.

Spiced pumpkin wedges

A trio of spices adds flavour to these wedges of pumpkin, then a little pomegranate molasses is drizzled over them to add a sweet–sour finish. If needed, balsamic vinegar can be substituted for the pomegranate molasses. Serves 4

1 kg (2 lb 3 oz) pumpkin (squash)
Oil for cooking
1 teaspoon ground cumin
1 teaspoon ground coriander
1 teaspoon ground sweet paprika
2 tablespoons pomegranate molasses

Preheat the oven to 180°C (350°F).

Cut the pumpkin into thick wedges. Remove the seeds but leave the skin on each wedge.

Heat a heavy-based frying pan over medium–high heat and add a splash of oil. Cook the pumpkin wedges on each side until golden brown. Transfer to a baking tray.

Combine the cumin, coriander, sweet paprika and some salt and freshly ground black pepper. Sprinkle the spices over the wedges and cook the pumpkin in the oven for 20 minutes, or until tender. Drizzle with the pomegranate molasses and serve immediately.

Pumpkin mole

You can serve this pumpkin mole as a dip with corn (taco) chips, as part of a Mexican-inspired feast, or you can stuff it into baby pumpkins and bake until tender for a substantial vegetarian dish. Serves 6–8 as a side dish

500 g (1 lb 2 oz) peeled and diced pumpkin (squash)

80 ml (2½ fl oz/⅓ cup) agave syrup or honey

Zest and juice of 2 limes, plus 2 extra tablespoons lime juice

80 ml (2½ fl oz/⅓ cup) olive oil

2 teaspoons ground cumin

2 teaspoons smoky sweet paprika

½ teaspoon cinnamon

½ teaspoon allspice

1 tablespoon tahini

1 red onion, finely diced

1 red chilli, chopped

2 tablespoons chopped coriander (cilantro)

Preheat the oven to 200°C (400°F). Line a roasting tin with baking paper.

Put the pumpkin in a large bowl along with the agave syrup, the zest and juice of 2 limes, the oil and spices and season well with salt and freshly ground black pepper. Toss to combine. Spread out in the prepared roasting tin and cook in the oven for 30–40 minutes, or until the pumpkin is tender.

Allow the pumpkin to cool slightly then put it in a bowl and mash it roughly. Add the tahini, diced onion, chilli, chopped coriander and the extra 2 tablespoons lime juice. Season well with salt and pepper and serve at room temperature.

Roast pumpkin with bacon and feta

I love the contrast of salty bacon and feta with the sweetness of the roast pumpkin. This is delicious with any lamb dish. Serves 4 as a side dish

1 kg (2 lb 3 oz) wedge of pumpkin (squash)

Olive oil

3–4 garlic cloves

1 teaspoon dried chilli flakes

1 red onion, cut into wedges

6 rashers (slices) of bacon, chopped

150 g (5½ oz) feta cheese

1–2 tablespoons pomegranate molasses

15 g (½ oz/½ cup) flat-leaf (Italian) parsley leaves

Preheat the oven to 180°C (350°F).

Remove the seeds from the pumpkin, and the skin if desired. Cut into 2 cm (¾ in) thick wedges and place in a deep baking tin. Add a good slug of olive oil, the garlic, chilli, red onion, bacon and some salt and freshly ground black pepper and toss to combine.

Cook in the oven for 30–40 minutes, turning once. Crumble the feta over the top and return to the oven for a further 10 minutes. Drizzle with the pomegranate molasses and parsley. Toss to combine and serve.

Roasted root vegetable chips

I'm very keen on roasting vegetables in this way, as it gives them such a tasty golden coating. I eat them whether I'm having a roast dinner or not. Serves 6

3 swedes (rutabaga)

3 large carrots

4 parsnips

6 large floury or all-purpose potatoes

Oil for cooking

Preheat the oven to 180°C (350°F).

Peel the swedes, carrots and parsnips and cut them into long, fat wedges. Place in a bowl.

Scrub the potatoes and cut each into eight wedges. Add the potatoes to the bowl with the other vegetables, sprinkle with salt and freshly ground black pepper and toss with enough olive oil to coat.

Arrange in a single layer on baking trays and cook on the top shelf of the oven for 40 minutes or until golden brown and crispy.

Roast sweet potato chilli chips

I love sweet potatoes, but this is probably my favourite way of cooking them – the chilli adds a lovely contrast to the sweetness of the potato. Delicious with everything or just on their own. Serves 4 as a side dish

2 sweet potatoes

2 tablespoons olive oil

1 teaspoon chilli flakes

Preheat the oven to 180°C (350°F). Line a baking tray with paper.

Cut the sweet potatoes in half lengthways, then cut each half into six to eight wedges. Place in a bowl along with the oil and chilli, and season with salt and freshly ground black pepper. Toss to coat the wedges.

Place the sweet potato wedges, skin side down, on the baking tray. Bake in the oven for 20–30 minutes, or until the sweet potato chips are crisp and golden brown.

Sesame sweet potato chips
Substitute sesame seeds for the chilli.

Mashed swede

If you find the flavour of swede a little too strong, try a mix of swede and potato or carrot. Serves 4

4 small swedes (rutabaga)

60 g (2 oz) butter

Peel the swedes and cut them into large chunks. Place the swede in a saucepan of water and bring to the boil. Cook for 15–20 minutes, until tender. Drain the swede and return to the saucepan. Place the saucepan over low heat and cook for 1–2 minutes, shaking the pan occasionally to evaporate any excess moisture.

Remove from the heat and mash the swede until smooth. Stir in the butter and season with salt and freshly ground black pepper.

Mashed turnips
Prepare exactly as for mashed swedes and finish with butter, chopped flat-leaf (Italian) parsley, salt and freshly ground black pepper. This is particularly good with roast duck.

Spinach with lemon and almonds

This dish is easy to make, tasty and nutritious, so ensure that it's on your family menu this week.
Serves 4

2 tablespoons olive oil

110 g (4 oz) blanched almonds

200 g (7 oz) English spinach leaves

2 tablespoons lemon juice

Heat a large heavy-based frying pan over medium-high heat. Add the oil and blanched almonds. Cook the almonds by tossing the pan regularly until they're golden brown. Add the spinach leaves and cook, stirring, until they collapse and soften. Add the lemon juice and some salt and freshly ground black pepper. Stir well to combine and remove from the heat. Serve immediately.

Roasted roma tomatoes

Egg-shaped roma tomatoes are at their peak in autumn (fall). They are excellent to cook with as they have lots of flesh, few seeds and little juice, so they hold their shape well when cooked.
Serves 4

250 g (9 oz) roma (plum) tomatoes

60 ml (2 fl oz/¼ cup) olive oil

2 garlic cloves, crushed

1 tablespoon balsamic vinegar

1 teaspoon sugar

1–2 thyme or oregano sprigs

Preheat the oven to 180°C (350°F).

Cut the tomatoes in half and place them, skin side down, in a baking tin.

Mix the oil, garlic, vinegar and sugar and brush the mixture onto the cut side of the tomatoes. Scatter the fresh herbs over the tomatoes and sprinkle with salt and freshly ground black pepper. Place the tin in the oven and cook for 30 minutes, or until the tomatoes are tender.

Roasted roma tomatoes with feta and basil
When the roasted tomatoes come out of the oven, sprinkle 75 g (2¾ oz) marinated goat's feta and chopped basil leaves over them.

Zucchini spaghetti (zoodles)

I'm not sure these are really my thing, but I do eat them. While I'm not a coeliac, I do tend to bloat after eating pasta. Some days I don't mind, but other days I do and that's when I make this recipe.

1 zucchini (courgette) per person

Oil or butter (optional)

Zucchini noodles are basically julienned zucchini. You can julienne them by using a julienne peeler, a mandoline or food processor. You can eat them raw if you like, but I prefer to heat a heavy-based pan over medium heat and add a splash of olive oil or butter (sometimes a combination of both), add the 'zoodles' and cook them for 2–3 minutes, really just to heat them through. One of the more popular ways to eat them as a meal is to stir through some pesto, but use them where you would pasta or noodles.

Zucchini with raisins and pine nuts

This is a classic southern Italian dish that blends pan-fried zucchini with sweet and sour flavours.
Serves 4

250 g (9 oz) small zucchini (courgettes)

Oil for cooking

1 garlic clove, thinly sliced

50 g (1¾ oz/⅓ cup) pine nuts

55 g (2 oz) raisins

6 mint leaves, thinly sliced

2 tablespoons lemon juice

Trim the ends off the zucchini, then cut them into 5 mm
(¼ in) thick slices.

Heat a large frying pan over medium–high heat and
add a splash of oil. Add the zucchini and garlic and cook
until the zucchini slices are pale gold on each side.

Add the pine nuts and stir well for 1–2 minutes. Add
the raisins, mint leaves and lemon juice and remove
from the heat. Season with salt and freshly ground
black pepper and serve.

Zucchini with red-wine vinegar and basil
Cook the zucchini in the oil as directed, then remove
from the heat and drizzle with red-wine vinegar and
freshly chopped basil. Season with salt and freshly
ground black pepper.

Zucchini flower fritters with feta and basil

These zucchini-flower fritters are filled with a creamy combination of feta and fresh basil,
then fried until crisp. If you have a wok burner on the side of your barbecue, use it to cook the
fritters and keep all the cooking aromas outside. Serve the flowers in a paper serviette with a
sprinkling of salt. Serves 4

150 g (5½ oz/1 cup) plain (all-purpose) flour

1 teaspoon olive oil

1 egg, separated

16 zucchini (courgette) flowers

150 g (5½ oz) soft feta (or Persian feta)

10 basil leaves

Oil for deep-frying

Sift the flour and ½ teaspoon salt together in a bowl.

Whisk 250 ml (8½ fl oz/1 cup) water, the olive oil and
egg yolk together, then whisk this mixture into the flour
until combined. Allow to rest for 30 minutes.

Beat the egg white until soft peaks form, then fold it
through the batter just prior to using.

Gently open each zucchini flower and remove the
stamen. Wash gently if needed and dry well.

Mash the feta slightly with a fork. Chop the basil
leaves and add them to the feta, seasoning with
some freshly ground black pepper. Place a heaped
teaspoonful of the filling into each flower and press the
petals back around it firmly.

Pour a 4–5 cm (1½–2 in) layer of oil into a large
saucepan or wok and heat over medium–high heat.

Dip the zucchini flowers, one at a time, in the batter. Fry
in the hot oil until golden. Drain on paper towel, season
with salt and serve immediately.

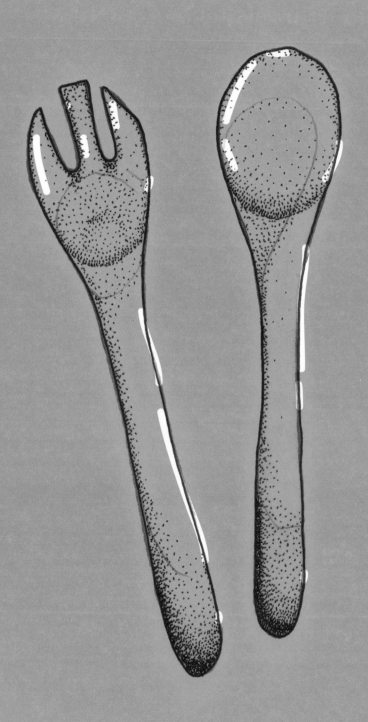

Salads

There's the salad you have every day –
maybe a simple dish of green leaves
tossed with your favourite dressing as
a palate cleanser after dinner – and there's
the salad that's a dish in its own right,
which can be served for lunch, as an
appetiser or a main course for dinner.

All-rounders

Some people think of salads as summer food, when in fact they're an important part of our diet all year round. At the very least we should eat a green salad with a main meal every day. The simplest salads are made up of good, fresh leaves – all you need to do is toss them in a bowl with some vinegar and extra-virgin olive oil, and they're ready to go.

The variety of fresh leaves available these days is phenomenal, from baby cos (romaine) lettuce, frisée, lamb's lettuce (corn salad), oakleaf and mignonette, to wild rocket (arugula) and baby English spinach leaves. Of course, salads can be far more than just leaves. They can contain raw or cooked vegetables, olives, feta and other cheeses, seafood and meats. Others are ideal as appetisers, offering a perfect blend of flavours without being too filling.

Then there's the multitude of grains and seeds you can incorporate into a salad, including quinoa (white, red, black, or a mixture of all three), freekeh, rice (wild, red or brown) and barley. I love the black barley that you can find in speciality shops. Let's not forget noodles either (rice, soba or vermicelli).

Rather than washing lettuce each night, I tend to wash one or two whole lettuces at a time; I spin the leaves to dry them well, then store them in a special salad container in the refrigerator. They keep well for up to a week and I simply need to grab a handful of leaves anytime I want a salad.

Similarly I tend to make up enough dressing for a week. I store mine in a squeezy bottle in the cupboard and simply squeeze dressing over the leaves when I'm ready to eat.

The great thing about salads is you can add your favourite vegetables and ingredients to suit your tastes. If a salad calls for goat's cheese and you prefer feta, simply swap. This, too, can depend on what you have in the refrigerator.

Things you need to know
about salads

- All salad leaves must be washed. Some lettuces, such as English spinach and frisée, usually need two attempts to remove all the grit.

- Lettuce must be dried well. This keeps it crisp and ensures that the dressing will stick to it. A salad spinner is an essential tool to make sure your lettuce leaves are perfectly dry. You'll also need a large bowl for tossing salads and a couple of good platters and bowls for serving.

- Salads need to be dressed, whether it's a squeeze of lemon juice and a splash of extra-virgin olive oil, or more complex variations.

- Most salad dressings are a ratio of 3 parts oil to 1 part vinegar (or other acid, such as lemon juice).

- Add your seasoning to the vinegar or juice to dissolve it. You cannot successfully season dressing once the oil is added.

- Different vinegars will add variety to your salads; I generally alternate between red-wine, sherry and balsamic vinegar.

- Likewise, your oil will make a difference; this is where good-quality extra-virgin olive oil shines. I usually have fruity and a peppery extra-virgin olive oil on hand as well as lemon-infused.

- You can also use mustard, walnut or almond oil, and peanut oil for Asian-influenced salads.

- You can swap red vinegar for herb, white-wine or balsamic vinegar; use lime juice instead of lemon; exchange the extra-virgin olive oil for lemon, peanut or parmesan-infused oil; or go for wholegrain mustard instead of dijon. Place all the ingredients in a jar, put on the lid and shake well, and the dressing is ready to use.

- Only ever add just enough dressing to barely coat the leaves; an over-dressed salad will cause the leaves to wilt, and the dressing will overpower the other flavours.

- To add slivers or shavings of vegetables, use a vegetable peeler. The long, thin strips are much easier to eat in salads than chunky, diced or sliced vegetables.

- Roasted and barbecued vegetables also work, as they introduce flavours and textures that you can't achieve with raw ingredients.

- I like to soak raw onion slices in hot tap water to remove the worst of the onion's powerful taste. Don't leave them to soak too long or they will lose their crispness.

Salad recipes

Rocket, pear, parmesan and pomegranate salad

The combination of peppery rocket leaves and crunchy pomegranate seeds is amazing in this salad. The easiest way to shave parmesan is to use a sharp peeler. Serves 6 as a side dish

1 pomegranate
100 g (3½ oz) rocket (arugula)
1 pear, sliced
60 g (2 oz/¾ cup) shaved parmesan
Pomegranate dressing (page 461)

Remove the seeds from the pomegranate. You need to ensure that all the yellow inside skin has been removed, as it is quite bitter. Toss the seeds with the rocket, pear and parmesan. Drizzle with the pomegranate dressing to serve.

Pear, candied walnut, goat's cheese and rocket salad

You can add radicchio leaves to this salad to vary it a bit if you wish. Serves 4 as a side dish

100 g (3½ oz) rocket (arugula)
80 g (2¾ oz/⅔ cup) Candied walnuts (page 471)
1 pear
60 g (2 oz) goat's cheese, crumbled
Classic salad dressing (page 460)

Place the rocket and walnuts in a bowl. Just before serving, quarter the pear and slice it thinly. Add the pear to the salad, along with the crumbled goat's cheese. Drizzle with the salad dressing and serve.

Rocket, fig, blue cheese and crispy prosciutto salad
Swap the pear for three quartered figs and the goat's cheese for blue cheese. Toast six prosciutto slices until crispy and crumble them over the top of the salad.

Cherry tomato and pomegranate salad

Use a variety of cherry tomatoes in this salad. If you can find heirloom cherry tomatoes, they will add great colour and flavour to this dish. Serves 4–6 as a side dish

1 pomegranate
750 g (1 lb 11 oz) cherry tomatoes
25 g (1 oz/½ cup) chopped coriander (cilantro)
4 spring onions (scallions), thinly sliced (optional)
Pomegranate dressing (page 461)

Remove the seeds from the pomegranate. You need to ensure that all the yellow inside skin has been removed, as it is quite bitter. Rinse and set aside.

Cut the cherry tomatoes in half (or in quarters, if they are on the larger side), aiming to have them all a similar size. Place in a bowl along with the pomegranate seeds, coriander and spring onion (if using) and season well with salt and freshly ground black pepper. Add enough dressing to just coat, then serve.

The broccoli salad

This recipe was passed down from one chef to another and then found its spiritual home at The Food Smith in Melbourne, where it was one of the best-selling salads. If you can't find barberries then fresh pomegranates are a perfect substitute. Serves 4–6 as a side dish

2 heads of broccoli
25 g (1 oz/⅓ cup) barberries, plus extra for garnish
120 g (4½ oz/1 cup) toasted slivered almonds
125 g (4½ oz/½ cup) natural yoghurt
100 g (3½ oz) mayonnaise
1 tablespoon chopped dill
2 tablespoons chopped coriander (cilantro)

Remove the florets from the broccoli and slice them thinly. If you have a mandoline this will save some time. I also like to use the stems and julienne them; you can use a mandoline or julienne peeler, or use a knife to first slice the stems thinly and then cut the slices into long thin slices.

Place the broccoli in a bowl and add the barberries, almonds, yoghurt, mayonnaise and herbs. Season well with salt and freshly ground black pepper, sprinkle with the extra barberries and serve.

Cabbage, pea, mint and chilli salad

The original recipe is Melbourne chef Karen Martini's creation. Again, it's been passed down through kitchens where I have worked and it's always been insanely popular. Karen's original recipe uses parsley, mint and lemon juice; I have never added these. She also uses fresh peas that are podded and cooked; I just use frozen ones. And if I don't have fresh chillies at hand, dried chilli flakes work a treat, too. Serves 4–6 as a side dish

½ green cabbage, shredded
150 g (5½ oz/1 cup) frozen peas, defrosted
1 small red chilli, seeded and diced or ½ teaspoon dried chilli flakes
80 g (2¾ oz/1 cup) grated parmesan
25 g (1 oz/½ cup) shredded mint
1 bunch red radishes, sliced (optional)
125 ml (4 fl oz/½ cup) fruity extra-virgin olive oil

Place all the ingredients in a bowl, season well with salt and freshly ground black pepper and toss to combine.

Blood orange and fennel salad

My lovely friend Sophie Allen has some great ideas. One New Year's Eve she decided we should have an Inspector Montalbano–inspired dinner party to welcome in the New Year. My contribution was this salad to accompany the barbecued snapper. If blood oranges aren't in season (and they're not in December), substitute normal oranges. Serves 4 as a side dish

2 fennel bulbs

4 blood oranges

90 g (3 oz/½ cup) kalamata olives

Generous handful of flat-leaf (Italian) parsley

1 tablespoon sherry vinegar

60 ml (2 fl oz/¼ cup) olive oil

Remove the tough outer layer from the fennel bulbs. Cut the fennel in half, remove the core and slice thinly. Place in a bowl.

Using a sharp knife, remove all the peel and pith from the oranges. Then remove the segments from the membrane, so that each segment is free from any pith or seeds. Squeeze any excess juice from the orange membrane into a bowl and set aside for the dressing. Add the blood orange segments to the fennel, along with the olives, parsley and vinegar.

Add salt and freshly ground black pepper to the blood orange juice and whisk together. Add the oil. Drizzle the dressing over the salad and toss together gently.

Potato salad

Potato salad is an essential summer experience, though I often serve it in the cooler months, too, with pan-fried sausages or Classic beef and mushroom kebabs (page 138). Serves 6 as a side dish

1.5 kg (3 lb 5 oz) waxy potatoes, washed (peeled if preferred)

6 rashers (slices) bacon, diced

10 cornichons, chopped

7 g (¼ oz/¼ cup) chopped flat-leaf (Italian) parsley

3 hard-boiled eggs, diced

Mayonnaise (page 463)

Boil the potatoes until just cooked. Drain and allow to cool. Cut into 1 cm (½ in) slices, or dice if preferred. Place in a bowl.

Heat a small frying pan over medium–high heat. Cook the bacon until crispy, then break it into small pieces.

Mix the potatoes, bacon, cornichons, parsley, egg and mayonnaise together, season well with salt and freshly ground black pepper, then serve.

Potato, kale and tahini salad

When *In The Kitchen* was first released, there were no kale recipes – hard to believe when I think how much I cook with it now. This is just one of the recipes that's better with kale.
Serves 6 as a side dish

1 kg (2 lb 3 oz) kipfler (fingerling) potatoes
2 tablespoons tahini
2 tablespoons lemon juice
125 g (4½ oz/½ cup) natural yoghurt
3 tablespoons chopped flat-leaf (Italian) parsley
250 g (9 oz) kale
Oil for cooking

Cut the potatoes in half, place them in a saucepan, cover with water and bring to the boil. Reduce to a simmer and cook for 12–15 minutes or until the potatoes are tender. Drain and set aside to cool.

Mix the tahini, lemon juice and yoghurt together until smooth. Add to the potatoes, along with the parsley. Season well with salt and freshly ground black pepper and toss to combine.

Cut the kale into 5 cm (2 in) pieces, then wash it well and drain.

Heat a heavy-based frying pan over medium–high heat. Add a splash of oil and the kale and cook, stirring often, for 3–4 minutes or until the kale softens. Season with salt and pepper.

Add the cooked kale to the potatoes and serve.

Slaw

Slaw has become incredibly popular. Feel free to add other ingredients to the mix if you like. You can swap the parsley for coriander (cilantro) or mint, and I often make the dressing with yoghurt or even just a mixture of lemon juice and extra-virgin olive oil. Serves 4

125 g (4½ oz/½ cup) sour cream
2 tablespoons lemon juice
¼ red or green cabbage, shredded
4 spring onions (scallions), thinly sliced
1 green apple, grated
1 carrot, julienned
2 tablespoons chopped flat-leaf (Italian) parsley

Mix the sour cream with the lemon juice and season with salt and freshly ground black pepper.

Mix together the cabbage, spring onion, apple, carrot and parsley. Pour the sour cream over, season well with salt and pepper and toss to combine.

Red cabbage and pomegranate slaw

To make this salad you will need to slice the cabbage, fennel and radish thinly. It's easiest to do this with a mandoline but it can also be achieved with a sharp knife. What makes this salad so good is the cut of the vegetables, so try to be consistent. Serve with any grilled meat or fish. Serves 4 as a side dish

¼ red cabbage, shredded

1 baby fennel bulb, thinly sliced

4–6 radishes, thinly sliced

Seeds of ½ pomegranate

1 tablespoon chopped mint

2 tablespoons chopped flat-leaf (Italian) parsley

1 crisp apple, julienned

2 tablespoons lemon juice

2 tablespoons olive oil

Place the cabbage, fennel and radish in a bowl along with the pomegranate seeds and herbs.

Place the apple in a small bowl, add the lemon juice and toss well. Transfer the apple to the bowl with the other vegetables. Add the olive oil, season with salt and freshly ground black pepper, toss to combine and serve.

Asian coleslaw

This salad is good if you're having a large group over. It's excellent just as it is, or you can top it with roast beef, roast duck or barbecued chicken pieces. Serves 6 as a side dish

½ Chinese cabbage (wombok), sliced

2 carrots, shredded

6 spring onions (scallions), thinly sliced

15 g (½ oz/½ cup) coriander (cilantro) leaves

1 tablespoon shaved palm sugar (jaggery)

2 tablespoons fish sauce

60 ml (2 fl oz/¼ cup) lime juice

60 ml (2 fl oz/¼ cup) peanut oil

Toss the Chinese cabbage, carrot, spring onion and coriander together.

Dissolve the palm sugar in the fish sauce and lime juice. Add some freshly ground black pepper and whisk in the peanut oil.

Toss the vegetables with the dressing and pile the salad onto a platter.

Soba noodle salad with eggplant, soy cashews and coriander

I love noodle salads and this one makes a great lunch dish on a warm day. If you don't have time to make up a batch of soy cashews, use tamari almonds or toasted cashew nuts. Podded edamame are delicious in this recipe, too, if you can get your hands on some. Serves 2–3

Oil for cooking

2 smallish eggplants (aubergines), cut into 1 cm (½ in) dice

3 tablespoons rice vinegar

1 tablespoon caster (superfine) sugar

Grated zest of 1 lime

1 tablespoon lime juice

1 small red chilli, finely diced (seeds removed if you like)

1 teaspoon sesame oil

180 g (6½ oz) soba noodles

100 g (3½ oz/⅔ cup) Soy cashews (page 471)

½ finely diced red onion

Handful each of basil and coriander (cilantro) leaves, roughly chopped

Heat a heavy-based frying pan over medium–high heat and add a generous splash of oil. Cook the eggplant for 5–6 minutes or until cooked through and golden brown. Set aside on paper towel to drain and season with salt and freshly ground black pepper

Slightly warm the rice vinegar, add the caster sugar and stir until dissolved. Add the lime zest and juice, diced chilli and sesame oil.

Cook the soba noodles for 4 minutes until tender, then drain and refresh under cold water. Place the noodles in a bowl and toss with the dressing. Add the eggplant, soy cashews, diced red onion and basil and coriander leaves. Toss to combine.

Pan-fried haloumi with asparagus and roasted cherry tomato salad

A delicious light lunch or candlelit supper dish! Serves 2 as a light meal

250 g (9 oz) cherry tomatoes

Olive oil for cooking

1 bunch asparagus (approximately 200 g/7 oz)

Handful of flat-leaf (Italian) parsley leaves

Handful of torn basil leaves

200 g (7 oz) haloumi

Juice of 1 lemon

Red-wine vinegar

Extra-virgin olive oil

Preheat the oven to 180°C (350°F).

Cut the cherry tomatoes in half and place them on a baking tray. Sprinkle with salt and freshly ground black pepper and drizzle with olive oil. Bake in the oven for 15–20 minutes or until soft. Remove and allow to cool.

Bring a saucepan of water to the boil. Remove and discard the woody asparagus ends. Cut the stems in half if preferred. Blanch the asparagus for 2 minutes, then cool under cold water. Drain and set aside.

Place the cooled tomatoes, asparagus and herbs in a bowl.

Heat a heavy-based frying pan over medium–high heat. Once hot, add a splash of oil. Cut the haloumi into slices and pan-fry them on both sides until golden brown. Once brown, squeeze the lemon juice over and remove from the heat.

Add the haloumi slices to the bowl, add a sprinkling of vinegar and olive oil, season with salt and pepper and toss lightly to combine. Divide between two plates and serve immediately.

Roast pumpkin, chickpea, feta and coriander salad

When using feta in salads such as this, go for the softer-style feta in olive oil rather than the usual firm cheese in brine. It adds a rich and salty hit. This salad is also nice with the addition of pomegranate seeds or slivers of roasted red capsicum (bell pepper). Serves 4–6 as a side dish

300 g (10½ oz) pumpkin (squash)

Oil for cooking

Dukkah (page 469) or Za'atar (page 470) (optional)

100 g (3½ oz) rocket (arugula)

400 g (14 oz) tinned chickpeas, drained

150 g (5½ oz) feta, crumbled

30 g (1 oz/1 cup) coriander (cilantro) leaves

Pomegranate dressing (page 461)

Preheat the oven to 180°C (350°F).

Dice the pumpkin, toss it with the oil and season with salt and freshly ground black pepper. If desired, sprinkle it with either dukkah or za'atar. Roast the pumpkin in the oven for 15–20 minutes or until golden brown and tender. Set aside to cool.

Place the rocket in a bowl and arrange the cooled roasted pumpkin over it. Top with the chickpeas and feta. Garnish with coriander leaves, add the dressing and serve.

Ramen noodle and sesame salad

This salad is somewhat more delicate than the other noodle recipes in this book. It's an ideal accompaniment to Steamed Thai fish (page 151) or Soy ginger salmon with green vegetables and noodles (page 116). Serves 4 as a side dish

180 g (6½ oz) ramen noodles

2 spring onions (scallions), thinly sliced

7 g (¼ oz/¼ cup) coriander (cilantro) leaves

1 small cucumber, sliced

1 teaspoon toasted sesame seeds

6 slices Pickled ginger (page 439)

250 g (9 oz) cooked asparagus (optional)

Chinese dressing (page 461)

Bring a saucepan of water to the boil. Add the noodles and cook for 3–4 minutes, or until al dente. Drain and refresh under cold running water.

Mix the noodles with the spring onion, coriander, cucumber, sesame seeds, pickled ginger and asparagus (if using). Toss with the dressing and serve.

Asian noodle and vegetable salad

You can swap the vegetables to suit your own tastes and depending on what you have in the refrigerator. Baby bok choy (pak choy) is also great in this salad. You could always use green tea noodles for a change, too. Serves 3–4

270 g (9½ oz) vermicelli noodles

1 bunch broccolini

100 g (3½ oz) snow peas (mangetout)

1 carrot

½ red capsicum (bell pepper), thinly sliced

¼ red cabbage, thinly sliced

90 g (3 oz/1 cup) bean sprouts

10 g (¼ oz/⅓ cup) coriander (cilantro) leaves

5 g (¼ oz/¼ cup) mint leaves (regular or Vietnamese)

4 spring onions (scallions), thinly sliced

Asian dressing (page 462)

Bring a saucepan of water to the boil. Add the noodles, cook for 4 minutes or until tender, then drain and refresh under cold running water.

Bring another saucepan of water to the boil, add the broccolini and cook for 2–3 minutes. Remove and refresh under cold running water. Add the snow peas to the boiling water and cook for 1–2 minutes; drain and refresh.

Slice the broccolini and snow peas into long lengths, then add them to the noodles.

Using a vegetable peeler, peel long thin slices from the carrot and add these to the noodles, along with the red capsicum, cabbage, bean sprouts, herbs and spring onion. Toss to combine, add enough dressing to coat and serve.

Asian noodle and tofu salad
Add 300 g (10½ oz) sliced tofu to the salad.

Asian noodle and chicken salad
Add a thinly sliced, grilled boneless skinless chicken breast to the salad.

Pan-fried fish with Asian noodle salad
Pan-fry four firm white fish fillets and serve alongside the salad.

Roasted summer vegetable and quinoa salad

You can add or remove vegetables from this recipe as the mood takes you. Use any colour quinoa you like, or even a mixture of two colours for variety. This is a meal in its own right or a side to slow-cooked pulled meat or pan-fried fish. Serves 6

1 eggplant (aubergine), cut into 2 cm (¾ in) dice

Olive oil for cooking

1 red capsicum (bell pepper)

8 yellow baby (pattypan) squash, cut in half

1 red onion, peeled and cut into 8 wedges

8 baby tomatoes, cut in half

100 g (3½ oz/1 cup) quinoa

400 g (14 oz) tinned chickpeas, drained and rinsed

1 tablespoon chopped mint

2 tablespoons chopped basil or coriander (cilantro)

2 tablespoons chopped flat-leaf (Italian) parsley

2 tablespoons lemon juice

3 tablespoons extra-virgin olive oil

100 g (3½ oz) Spiced nuts (page 470)

Preheat the oven to 180°C (350°F).

Sprinkle the diced eggplant with salt and set aside until the juices bead. Rinse the eggplant and dry well. Toss it with 1–2 tablespoons of oil, season with salt and freshly ground black pepper and roast in the oven until tender, about 20 minutes.

Cut the capsicum into quarters and then into 2 cm (¾ in) triangles. Toss with the baby squash and onion wedges and 1–2 tablespoons oil. Season with salt and pepper and roast in the oven until tender, about 15 minutes.

Place the tomato halves, skin side down, on a baking tray. Drizzle with olive oil and season with salt and pepper and roast for about 10 minutes, until just cooked through.

Allow all the vegetables to cool.

Rinse the quinoa in a small sieve. Place in a small saucepan with 500 ml (17 fl oz/2 cups) water and bring to the boil. Reduce the heat to a simmer, cover and cook for 10–12 minutes until the water is absorbed and the grains appear translucent. Allow to cool.

When the quinoa is cool, add the roasted vegetables, chickpeas, chopped herbs, lemon juice, olive oil and spiced nuts. Season with salt and pepper and serve.

Asparagus and broad bean mograbieh

This mograbieh (Lebanese couscous) salad makes an impressive offering on a large white platter. Serve as a side with Middle Eastern dishes. Serves 6

350 g (12½ oz/1⅔ cup) mograbieh

500 g (1 lb 2 oz) asparagus

750 g (1 lb 11 oz) broad beans

100 g (3½ oz) rocket (arugula), washed

1 red onion, thinly sliced

½ Preserved lemon (page 434), soaked in cold water, then diced

20 g (¾ oz/1 cup) flat-leaf (Italian) parsley leaves

60 ml (2 fl oz/¼ cup) lemon juice

1 teaspoon sumac

Extra-virgin olive oil

Cook the mograbieh in a saucepan of boiling water for 20–30 minutes, until tender. Drain and refresh under cold running water.

Bring a large saucepan of water to the boil. Remove and discard the woody asparagus ends and cook the spears in boiling water for 1–2 minutes. Refresh under cold running water, then cut the asparagus into 3 cm (1¼ in) pieces on an angle.

Pod the broad beans and cook for 2–3 minutes in boiling water. Drain and refresh under cold running water, then remove the pale green skins (see Broad beans braised with pancetta, page 242).

Place the asparagus in a large bowl along with the broad beans, mograbieh, rocket, onion, preserved lemon and parsley.

Make the dressing by placing the lemon juice, sumac, oil, salt and freshly ground black pepper in a small jar. Shake together to mix. Add enough dressing to coat the salad and serve on a platter.

Mexican black barley with corn, tomato and avocado

This salad can be a great as a side to a Mexican-inspired meal or as a meal in its own right, especially if you add cooked chicken breast or pan-fried fish. Serves 4

75 g (2¾ oz/½ cup) black barley

2 corn cobs

Oil for cooking

Smoky paprika (optional)

200 g (7 oz) cooked tinned red kidney beans

200 g (7 oz) cherry tomatoes

1 avocado

100 g (3½ oz) salad greens, such as baby kale, silverbeet (Swiss chard) or English spinach

2 spring onions (scallions), thinly sliced

2 tablespoons chopped mint

2 tablespoons chopped coriander (cilantro)

2 tablespoons lime juice

3 tablespoons olive oil

Bring a small saucepan of water to the boil. Add the barley and bring back to the boil. Reduce to a simmer and cook for 35–45 minutes or until the barley is cooked. Drain, refresh and place in a bowl.

Rub the corn with oil, season with salt and freshly ground black pepper and the paprika (if using), and chargrill until brown, using either a barbecue or chargrill pan. Allow to cool, then remove the kernels from the corn cobs using a sharp knife, and add them to the black barley.

Add the kidney beans to the barley. Cut the cherry tomatoes in half and dice the avocado flesh roughly. Add both to the barley along with the greens, spring onion, herbs, lime juice and olive oil. Season well with salt and pepper, then serve.

Beetroot fattouche

You may well have noticed my obsession with beetroot, but feel free to make this salad with other vegetables, such as tomato, asparagus, green beans or artichokes. Serves 4

1 bunch baby beetroot (beets), or 3 large

1 red onion, sliced

1 teaspoon sumac

Olive oil

125 g (4½ oz) pide bread or focaccia, cut into 1 cm (½ in) chunks

1 baby cos (romaine) lettuce, washed

1 Lebanese (short) cucumber, halved and thickly sliced

Handful of flat-leaf (Italian) parsley leaves

2 tablespoons lemon juice

60 ml (2 fl oz/¼ cup) olive oil

Remove and discard the leaves from the beetroot. Place the beetroot in a saucepan and cover with water. Bring to the boil, reduce to a simmer and cook until tender, about 30 minutes. Drain and allow to cool. When cool remove the skins from the beetroot, then cut the flesh into evenly sized wedges and place in a bowl.

Pour hot water onto the onion and allow to stand for 2 minutes before draining. When cool, toss the onion slices with the sumac.

Heat a heavy-based pan over medium heat, then add a generous splash of olive oil and the bread chunks. Stir until the bread becomes quite toasty, about 6–8 minutes.

Mix the beetroot with the onion, bread chunks, lettuce, cucumber and parsley.

Whisk the lemon juice and some salt and freshly ground black pepper together, then whisk in the olive oil. Dress the salad when ready to serve.

Red salad with berries and spiced nuts

If you don't have spiced nuts to hand, you can add a mixture of toasted seeds and nuts, such as sunflower seeds, almonds, pistachio nuts or cashew nuts. You can also swap the red quinoa or rice for freekeh or farro. Serves 4

100 g (3½ oz/½ cup) red quinoa

100 g (3½ oz/½ cup) red rice

200 g (7 oz)/1 cup) red lentils

35 g (½ cup) barberries

70 g (2½ oz) goji berries or cranberries

75 g (2¾ oz/½ cup) pomegranate seeds (approximately ½ pomegranate)

125 g (4½ oz/½ cup) Spiced nuts (page 470)

Handful of chopped herbs, such as flat-leaf (Italian) parsley, mint or coriander (cilantro)

Lemon dressing (page 460)

Yoghurt tahini sauce (page 455) (optional)

Cook the quinoa, red rice and lentils in separate saucepans. Bring the water to the boil, add the grains and return to the boil. Simmer until cooked – the quinoa will take 15 minutes, the red rice 20 and the lentils 18–20 minutes. Drain once cooked, then refresh under cold running water and drain again. Especially make sure the lentils are well rinsed.

Place all three grains in a large bowl along with berries, pomegranate seeds, nuts and herbs. Season well with salt and freshly ground black pepper and add enough lemon dressing to just coat. Place in a serving bowl and drizzle the tahini sauce over the top (if using).

Black quinoa and baby carrot salad

Try to track down some heirloom varieties of carrots for this recipe – your local farmers' market is the best option. Ideally, choose baby carrots of a similar size. To prepare them, simply scrub to remove the skins. Try to keep them quite rustic looking and retain 1 cm (½ in) of the green tops. This is delicious on its own, or served with Kashmiri quail (page 134) or Pomegranate-glazed beef (page 170). Serves 4

100 g (3½ oz/1 cup) black quinoa

500 g (1 lb 2 oz) baby carrots (about 2 bunches), scrubbed and peeled if necessary

Olive oil for cooking

2 tablespoons fennel seeds, roasted and roughly smashed

150 g (5½ oz) shredded kale

2 oranges

50 g (1¾ oz/⅓ cup) toasted almonds

50 g (1¾ oz/⅓ cup) toasted pistachio nuts

2 tablespoons chopped mint

2 tablespoons chopped flat-leaf (Italian) parsley

2–3 tablespoons extra-virgin olive oil

Cook the quinoa in a saucepan of salted boiling water, stirring often, until tender, about 12 minutes. Drain and allow to cool.

Place the carrots in a single layer on a lined baking tray and drizzle with olive oil. Scatter the fennel seeds over and season well with salt and freshly ground black pepper. Roast in the oven for 15–20 minutes, or until the carrots are just cooked. Remove and set aside to cool slightly.

Heat a heavy-based frying pan over medium–high heat and add a splash of oil. Add the kale and cook for 2–3 minutes or until softened and cooked. Add a splash of water if needed. Allow to cool.

Take the oranges and remove the segments, reserving any juice. Place the segments in a bowl, along with the quinoa, carrots, kale, almonds, pistachio nuts, mint and parsley. Season well with salt and pepper. Add the reserved orange juice and the extra-virgin olive oil and toss to combine. This salad is best served while the carrots are still warm or at room temperature.

Black quinoa and roasted cauliflower salad
Swap the roasted carrots for Roast cauliflower (page 246). You can swap the fennel seeds for cumin seeds, and swap the kale for baby English spinach or silverbeet (chard), too.

Freekeh and chickpea salad

Freekeh is green wheat, or unripe wheat grains, which are partially smoked. You can find freekeh in most good food stores and health shops. Try to buy cracked freekeh, as it takes less time to cook and isn't so chewy. You prepare it in a similar manner to burghul (bulgur wheat). Serves 4

2 tablespoons olive oil

½ onion, finely diced

85 g (3 oz/½ cup) cracked freekeh

60 g (2 oz) almonds (skin on), toasted

60 g (2 oz) pistachio nuts, toasted

7 g (¼ oz/¼ cup) chopped flat-leaf (Italian) parsley

15 g (½ oz/¼ cup) chopped coriander (cilantro)

2 tablespoons chopped mint

½ Preserved lemon (page 434), soaked and pulp removed, finely diced (optional)

400 g (14 oz) tinned chickpeas, drained and rinsed

Seeds of ½ pomegranate (optional)

Pomegranate dressing (page 461)

2 handfuls of rocket (arugula)

Heat a small saucepan over medium heat. Add the olive oil and the onion and cook for 3–4 minutes, stirring often, until the onion softens. Add the freekeh and 180 ml (6 fl oz) water and bring to the boil. Reduce to a simmer and cook for 10 minutes until all the liquid has been absorbed and the freekeh is tender. Remove the freekeh from the saucepan, tip into a bowl and allow to cool slightly.

Add the nuts, herbs, preserved lemon, chickpeas, pomegranate seeds (if using), and the dressing to the freekeh and toss to combine. Place the rocket on a platter and spoon the freekeh salad on top.

Freekeh and chickpea salad with chicken
Add two sliced Pan-fried herb chicken breasts (page 125).

Watercress tabouleh

Tabouleh really gets a lift by using watercress instead of the usual parsley. I often serve this salad with Moroccan roast turkey (page 165) at Christmas lunch and on any other salad-friendly days. Serves 6

150 g (5½ oz) burghul (bulgur wheat)

1 bunch watercress, picked and washed

½ red onion, finely diced

500 g (1 lb 2 oz) firm ripe tomatoes, diced

2 tablespoons lemon juice

60 ml (2 fl oz/¼ cup) extra-virgin olive oil

Rocket tabouleh
Swap the watercress for 100 g (3½ oz) washed and chopped rocket (arugula).

Pomegranate tabouleh
Add the seeds of one fresh pomegranate seeds to the salad

Soak the burghul in cold water for 20 minutes, then drain well.

Chop the watercress roughly and place it in a bowl with the burghul, onion and tomato. Mix well. Add the lemon juice and olive oil, season to taste with salt and freshly ground black pepper and serve.

Roast vegetable, brown rice and goat's cheese salad

I am rather partial to brown rice, but you can also make this salad with cooked quinoa, freekeh, red rice or barley, if you prefer. Serves 6–8

1 eggplant (aubergine)

1 red capsicum (bell pepper), seeded and cut into 2 cm (¾ in) dice

2 carrots, peeled, halved and thickly sliced

2 small zucchini (courgettes), halved and cut into 2 cm (¾ in) slices

1 red onion, cut into wedges

Oil

100 g (3½ oz) brown rice

75 g (2¾ oz/1⅔ cups) baby English spinach leaves

Lemon dressing (page 460)

90 g (3 oz) goat's cheese to serve

Preheat the oven to 180°C (350°F).

Cut the eggplant in half, then slice each half to form 1 cm (½ in) thick semicircles. Sprinkle with salt and set aside for 20 minutes until the juices bead on the surface. Rinse the eggplant and dry well.

Place all the vegetables in a roasting dish. Toss with oil, salt and freshly ground black pepper and roast for 30–40 minutes, or until the vegetables are tender and golden brown. Set aside to cool.

Place the brown rice in a saucepan. Cover with plenty of water and bring to the boil. Reduce to a simmer, cover and cook for 20–30 minutes, or until the rice is tender. Drain and refresh under cold running water.

Mix together the roast vegetables, brown rice and spinach leaves. Just before serving, toss the dressing through. Pile onto a platter and crumble the goat's cheese over the top.

Barbecued chicken, haloumi and green olive salad

You can use whatever type of lettuce leaves you like in this salad. Weather permitting, you can cook the chicken and haloumi on the barbecue; if not, simply pan-fry them. Serves 4

2 tablespoons olive oil, plus extra for brushing

Grated zest of 1 lemon

2 tablespoons chopped herbs, such as flat-leaf (Italian) parsley, basil, thyme and/or oregano

2 boneless skinless chicken breasts

300 g (10½ oz) haloumi, sliced

200 g (7 oz) salad leaves

175 g (6 oz/1 cup) green olives

250 g (9 oz) cherry tomatoes, halved

Pomegranate dressing (page 461)

Preheat the barbecue to hot.

Mix together the olive oil, lemon zest, chopped herbs and season with salt and freshly ground black pepper. Rub over the chicken breasts.

Cook on the barbecue grill for 5–6 minutes on each side until cooked through. When the chicken is almost cooked, brush the haloumi with oil and cook it for 2–3 minutes on each side until golden brown. Thinly slice the chicken and haloumi.

Make the salad by mixing together the salad leaves, olives and tomatoes. Add the warm chicken and haloumi to the salad and add enough pomegranate dressing to just coat the salad.

Thai chicken salad

A classic salad and perfect for lunch or dinner on a hot summer's day – ideal with a nice glass of chilled white wine. Serves 4

2 boneless skinless chicken breasts

250 ml (8½ fl oz/1 cup) coconut milk

1 lemongrass stem, white part only, thinly sliced

2 small red chillies, halved, plus 1 small red chilli, seeded and diced

1 iceberg lettuce, washed and torn into bite-sized pieces

1 cucumber, peeled, halved and sliced

Handful of bean sprouts

6 French shallots, sliced

30 g (1 oz/1 cup) coriander (cilantro) sprigs

150 g (5½ oz) roasted peanuts

1 tablespoon shaved palm sugar (jaggery)

2 tablespoons lime juice

1 tablespoon fish sauce

60 ml (2 fl oz/¼ cup) olive oil

Place the chicken in a saucepan and cover with the coconut milk. Add the lemongrass and halved chillies. Bring to the boil, lower the heat and cook, covered, for 5 minutes. Turn the chicken over and cook for a further 5 minutes. Check that the chicken is cooked through. Allow to cool completely in the coconut milk, then drain and slice thinly. Discard the cooking liquid.

Combine the lettuce, cucumber, bean sprouts, shallots, coriander, peanuts and cooked sliced chicken.

Prepare the salad dressing by dissolving the palm sugar in the lime juice. Stir in the fish sauce, diced chilli and some freshly ground black pepper and whisk in the olive oil. Toss the dressing through the salad and arrange on a large platter.

Coconut chicken and noodle salad
Combine cooked chicken with Asian noodle and vegetable salad (page 278) instead.

Thai prawn salad
Substitute 500 g (1 lb 2 oz) cooked peeled prawns (shrimp) for the chicken.

Thai beef salad
Combine 2 tablespoons fish sauce and ¼ teaspoon chilli paste and spread over two 200 g (7 oz) sirloin steaks. Allow to marinate for at least 20 minutes. Place the steaks on a hot barbecue and cook for 6 minutes, rotating as needed. Turn the steaks over and cook for a further 4-5 minutes, again rotating as needed. Allow the steaks to rest on a cool part of the barbecue for 5 minutes before serving. Thinly slice the steaks and place them on top of the prepared salad in place of the chicken.

Crispy belly pork and watermelon salad

Imagine you live with a teenage boy who likes pizza, burgers and ribs. Imagine your surprise when he asks for salad for dinner. That's exactly what Luke did and, while technically this is a salad, it wasn't the bowl of green leaves I pictured. This has become a family favourite, one that both children ask for if I offer to cook for a special occasion. Serves 4

Master stock (page 451)

1 kg (2 lb 3 oz) pork belly

2 teaspoons sesame seeds

2 tablespoons lime juice

2 tablespoons fish sauce

1 tablespoon honey

¼ watermelon, cut into chunks

2 tablespoons Pickled ginger (page 439)

4 spring onions (scallions), thinly sliced

30 g (1 oz/1 cup) coriander (cilantro) leaves

Bring the stock to the boil, add the pork belly and allow to just simmer for 1½ hours. Allow the pork to cool in the stock for 2–3 hours, then transfer the pork to a plate and leave overnight in the refrigerator, uncovered.

Cut the pork into 1 cm (½ in) dice, removing any bones.

Prepare the dressing by mixing together the sesame seeds, lime juice, fish sauce and honey.

Place the watermelon, ginger, spring onion and coriander leaves in a large bowl.

Heat a heavy-based frying pan over medium–high heat and add the pork – there is no need to add oil as the pork will render out its fat as it cooks. Cook the pork for 8–10 minutes, stirring often until golden brown and crispy all over. Drain any excess fat away. Add the dressing and toss to combine.

Add the pork to the large bowl with the watermelon and other ingredients and toss lightly to combine. Spoon onto a large platter and serve immediately.

Tuna, brown rice and egg salad

This salad is amazing, and you can make it from stock you have in your cupboard. It reminds me of an English kedgeree. It makes a great meal for a hot summer's night. Serves 2–3

200 g (7 oz) brown rice

3 eggs

475 g (1 lb 1 oz) tinned tuna, drained

2 tablespoons soaked capers

75 g (2¾ oz) kalamata olives, halved

Handful of chopped flat-leaf (Italian) parsley

Grated zest and juice of 1 lemon

2–3 tablespoons extra-virgin olive oil

Bring a saucepan of water to the boil, add the rice and allow to return to the boil. Reduce to a low simmer and cook for 15–20 minutes until the rice is cooked. Drain and refresh.

Bring a small saucepan of water to the boil, add the eggs and boil for 6–7 minutes. Drain and refresh under cold running water. Once cool, peel and dice roughly.

Mix the rice, eggs and remaining ingredients together. Season with freshly ground black pepper (you probably don't need to add salt as the capers and tuna are salty). Toss to combine and serve.

Tuna niçoise

Here's a great salad that can be whipped up with ingredients on hand (more or less). I often make it for myself for lunch – just reduce the quantity of ingredients accordingly. Serves 4

1 baby cos (romaine) lettuce, washed and torn into bite-sized pieces

4 potatoes, diced and boiled

500 g (1 lb 2 oz) green beans, blanched

2 tomatoes, cut into wedges

4 boiled eggs, cut into wedges

100 g (3½ oz) kalamata olives

300 g (10½ oz) tinned tuna

Anchovy dressing (page 462)

Chopped flat-leaf (Italian) parsley to serve

Crusty bread to serve

On a large platter, first add a layer of lettuce. Then add a layer of potato, beans, tomato, egg and olives. Drain the tuna and scatter it over the other ingredients. Drizzle the anchovy dressing over, sprinkle with parsley and serve with crusty bread.

Fresh tuna niçoise
Grill four 200 g (7 oz) tuna steaks and serve them on top of the salad in place of the tinned tuna.

Salmon niçoise
Grill four 200 g (7 oz) salmon steaks and serve them on top of the salad in place of the tinned tuna.

Smoked trout, avocado and asparagus salad

This is one of those salads where you can add other ingredients you may have on hand, such as cooked cold potatoes, olives or pickles; and free feel to use other salad leaves, such as baby cos (romaine), oakleaf or butter lettuce. Serves 4

500 g (1 lb 2 oz) asparagus

2 smoked trout fillets

100 g (3½ oz/2¾ cups) rocket (arugula)

150 g (5½ oz) cherry tomatoes, halved

2 avocados, peeled and sliced

2 tablespoons chopped flat-leaf (Italian) parsley

1 cucumber, sliced

Lemon dressing (page 460)

Bring a large saucepan of water to the boil. Remove and discard the woody asparagus ends and cook the spears in boiling water for 1–2 minutes. Refresh under cold running water and then cut the asparagus into 3 cm (1¼ in) pieces, on an angle.

Break the trout fillets into chunks, removing all the bones. Place in a bowl, along with the asparagus, rocket, tomato, avocado, parsley and cucumber. Toss with the dressing to serve.

Smoked chicken, avocado and asparagus salad
Swap the smoked trout for two sliced, smoked, boneless skinless chicken breasts.

Smoked salmon, avocado and asparagus salad
Swap the smoked trout fillets for two hot-smoked salmon fillets (these are thick pieces of smoked salmon, not the thin type).

Hot Thai salmon and lychee salad

This salad combines spicy chillies, pungent fish sauce, slippery sweet lychees and chunks of just-cooked salmon. Serves 4–6

1 tablespoon fish sauce

1 teaspoon grated palm sugar (jaggery)

2 small red chillies, chopped

2 × 200 g (7 oz) salmon fillets

Oil for cooking

1 Lebanese (short) cucumber, peeled

3 spring onions (scallions), thinly sliced

10 mint leaves, shredded

30 g (1 oz/1 cup) coriander (cilantro) sprigs

150 g (5½ oz) roasted peanuts

20 lychees, peeled, halved and seeded

Dressing

1 tablespoon grated palm sugar (jaggery)

2 tablespoons lime juice

1 tablespoon fish sauce

2 small red chillies, seeded and diced

Make the marinade by mixing together the fish sauce, palm sugar and chopped chillies. Pour it over the salmon in a shallow dish and set aside to marinate for at least 40 minutes, but no longer than 4 hours. Drain the salmon.

To cook the salmon, heat a small frying pan or chargrill pan over medium–high heat. Add a splash of oil and cook the salmon for 4 minutes on each side, or until the salmon is medium–rare. Set aside to cool.

Use a vegetable peeler to cut long thin strips from the cucumber, discarding the inner seeds. Place the cucumber in a colander and drain for 10 minutes.

Place the spring onion, mint leaves, coriander, peanuts and lychees in a large bowl.

Prepare the salad dressing by dissolving the palm sugar in the lime juice, then adding the fish sauce and diced chillies.

Remove the skin and any bones from the salmon. Flake the salmon into pieces and add it to the salad, along with the cucumber. Toss the dressing through the salad and season with freshly ground black pepper. Divide between plates or arrange on a large platter to serve.

Eggplant, pine nut and coriander salad

This eggplant salad is seriously good. It's similar to caponata, and has a touch of the Middle East with the coriander, currants and pine nuts. It's great with roast beef, barbecued lamb chops or roast chicken. Serves 4–6 as a side dish

3 eggplants (aubergines)

Oil

35 g (1¼ oz/¼ cup) currants

1 tablespoon red-wine vinegar

3 tomatoes, diced

30 g (1 oz/1 cup) coriander (cilantro) leaves

100 g (3½ oz/⅔ cup) toasted pine nuts

160 g (5½ oz) pitted green olives, halved

2 tablespoons capers, soaked in cold water

60 ml (2 fl oz/¼ cup) extra-virgin olive oil

Preheat the barbecue to hot.

Cut the eggplants in half, then slice each half to form 1 cm (½ in) thick semicircles. Sprinkle with salt and set aside for 20 minutes until juices bead on the surface. Rinse the eggplant and dry well.

Brush the eggplant with oil and barbecue it until tender and golden brown on each side. Set aside to cool.

Soak the currants in the vinegar for 20 minutes. Place them in a large bowl, along with the cooled eggplant, diced tomato, coriander leaves, pine nuts and olives.

Drain the capers, chop them coarsely and add them to the eggplant salad. Add the extra-virgin olive oil, season with salt and freshly ground black pepper and toss all the ingredients together. Place in a bowl to serve.

Vietnamese prawn and mint salad

I often serve this salad as an appetiser when I have friends over for dinner. It goes well with an aromatic white wine and is packed with flavour and texture. It can also be adapted for chicken or beef, if you prefer. Serves 4–6

500 g (1 lb 2 oz) small cooked prawns (shrimp)

1 cucumber, peeled and thinly sliced

2 carrots, peeled and grated

1 small Chinese cabbage (wombok), thinly shredded

3 Asian shallots, thinly sliced

2 kaffir lime leaves, shredded

10 mint leaves, shredded

15 g (½ oz/½ cup) loosely packed coriander (cilantro) leaves

45 g (1½ oz) chopped roasted peanuts

2 small red chillies, seeded and diced

2 cm (¾ in) piece of fresh ginger, grated

1 garlic clove, crushed

80–100 ml (2½–3½ fl oz) lime juice

2 tablespoons oil

2 tablespoons fish sauce

½ teaspoon white sugar

Peel the prawns and cut them in half lengthways. Place them in a large bowl with the cucumber, carrot, Chinese cabbage, shallots, kaffir lime leaves, mint leaves, coriander and peanuts. Mix together well.

Place the remaining ingredients in a separate bowl and whisk well. When ready to serve, toss the dressing through the salad and mix well. Serve on a large platter to share.

Vietnamese chicken and mint salad
Pan-fry two boneless skinless chicken breasts. Allow to cool, then slice thinly and use instead of the prawns.

Vietnamese beef and mint salad
Pan-fry 500 g (1 lb 2 oz) beef fillet. Allow to cool, then slice thinly and use instead of the prawns.

Asparagus and green tea noodle salad with Thai prawns

The zingy dressing used in this recipe doubles as a marinade for the prawns. Serves 6

2 tablespoons grated palm sugar (jaggery)

80 ml (2½ fl oz/⅓ cup) lime juice

60 ml (2 fl oz/¼ cup) fish sauce

2 small red chillies, seeded and diced

60 ml (2 fl oz/¼ cup) peanut or olive oil

200 g (7 oz) green tea noodles

4 bunches asparagus

30 g (1 oz/1 cup) coriander (cilantro) leaves

10 g (¼ oz/½ cup) Vietnamese mint leaves

25 g (1 oz/½ cup) Thai basil leaves

1 kg (2 lb 3 oz) green (raw) prawns (shrimp)

Mix the palm sugar, lime juice and fish sauce together in a bowl. Stir until the sugar dissolves. Add the chilli and oil. Set aside 60 ml (2 fl oz/¼ cup) of the liquid for use as a marinade; the remainder will be used as a dressing.

Bring a large saucepan of water to the boil and cook the green tea noodles for 8 minutes, or until al dente. Drain and cool under running water. Place in a bowl.

Bring another saucepan of water to the boil. Remove and discard the woody asparagus ends. Cook the asparagus in boiling water for 2–3 minutes, depending on the thickness. Refresh under cold running water. Cut the asparagus into 5 cm (2 in) lengths. Place in the bowl with the noodles and add the herbs. Refrigerate until needed.

Peel and devein the prawns, leaving the tails attached, and place in a bowl. Add the 60 ml (2 fl oz/¼ cup) of marinade liquid. Marinate the prawns for about 30 minutes before cooking.

Heat a large frying pan, barbecue or chargrill pan over high heat. Add the prawns and cook for 2–3 minutes on each side. Remove from the heat and add to the noodle salad, along with the dressing. Toss to combine. Divide between six plates and serve immediately.

Lively mushroom salad

Make this salad in advance and toss it with the dressing just before serving. You may also like to cook the mushrooms the day before. If so, allow them to reach room temperature before serving. If you want to bulk this salad out, add some cooked soba noodles or freekeh to make it more substantial. Serves 6

Oil

500 g (1 lb 2 oz) mushrooms (Swiss brown, oyster and shiitake)

2 garlic cloves, crushed

60 ml (2 fl oz/¼ cup) chicken stock or water

2 tablespoons soy sauce

10 g (¼ oz/½ cup) flat-leaf (Italian) parsley leaves

15 g (½ oz/¼ cup) torn basil leaves

2 tablespoons lemon juice

2 tablespoons lime juice

60 ml (2 fl oz/¼ cup) olive oil

Heat a large frying pan over medium heat. Add a generous splash of oil and the mushrooms and garlic and season with freshly ground black pepper. Toss to combine and cook for 5–6 minutes, stirring often. Add the stock or water and the soy sauce, cover with a lid and cook for a further 5 minutes. Remove from the frying pan and set aside to cool.

When cool, add the herbs, the citrus juices to taste and the olive oil. Season to taste with salt and pepper, then pile into a serving bowl.

Sumac beef salad with lentils, grapes and parsley

I love the contrast of tangy beef and sweet juicy grapes in this salad. If grapes aren't in season, try using olives or fresh pomegranate seeds in their place. Serves 4–6

2 tablespoons pomegranate molasses

60 ml (2 fl oz/¼ cup) extra-virgin olive oil

80 ml (2½ fl oz/⅓ cup) lemon juice

2 teaspoons sumac

½ teaspoon ground coriander

½ teaspoon ground cumin

Pinch of ground allspice

3 garlic cloves, crushed

2 × 250 g (9 oz) porterhouse steaks

100 g (3½ oz/½ cup) puy lentils or tiny blue-green lentils

200 g (7 oz) small white grapes, halved

½ red onion, thinly sliced

½ bunch flat-leaf (Italian) parsley, coarsely chopped

60 ml (2 fl oz/¼ cup) olive oil

Mix together the pomegranate molasses, extra-virgin olive oil, half the lemon juice, the spices, one-third of the garlic and some salt and freshly ground black pepper. Rub over the beef and refrigerate for 4 hours.

Place the lentils in a saucepan, cover with water and bring to the boil. Reduce to a simmer and cook for 20–30 minutes until the lentils are tender. Drain and set aside.

Prepare the salad by mixing the grapes, onion, parsley and lentils together. Make the dressing by mixing the remaining lemon juice, garlic and olive oil together. Season the dressing with salt and pepper.

Drain the excess marinade from the beef. Cook the meat for 3–4 minutes on each side on a hot barbecue grill or in a heavy-based frying pan over medium–high heat. Allow to rest for 5–10 minutes. Slice the beef and add it to the salad. Add enough dressing to coat, toss to combine and serve immediately.

Beef salad with hot and sour flavours

This Thai-influenced salad will wake up anyone's tastebuds. It's worth searching out green mango or papaya as it adds a lovely crunch to the salad. Serves 6

Oil

500 g (1 lb 2 oz) beef fillet

60 ml (2 fl oz/¼ cup) lime juice

60 ml (2 fl oz/¼ cup) fish sauce

2 tablespoons Sweet chilli sauce (page 437)

1 green mango or papaya (optional)

2 tomatoes

1 cucumber, peeled

2 spring onions (scallions), thinly sliced

15 g (½ oz/½ cup) coriander (cilantro) leaves

30 g (1 oz/½ cup) Thai basil

4 Asian shallots, thinly sliced

1 small red chilli, seeded and diced

1 tablespoon toasted sesame seeds

Preheat the oven to 180°C (350°F).

Heat a small ovenproof frying pan over medium heat. Rub some oil over the beef and cook for 5 minutes until the beef is brown all over. Transfer to the oven and bake for 15 minutes. Set aside to cool.

Mix the lime juice, fish sauce, sweet chilli sauce and some freshly ground black pepper together. Rub 1 tablespoon over the beef and marinate until ready to serve.

To peel the mango (if using), take a small sharp knife, trim the top and bottom off so the mango will stand upright and, following the curve of the mango, cut down over the flesh to remove the skin. Then cut down between the flesh and stone, removing the cheek of the mango. Slice each cheek thinly. If using the papaya, remove the skin, cut the papaya in half, discard any seeds and slice thinly.

Cut the tomatoes into quarters and slice thinly. Slice the cucumber thinly using a peeler. Toss these ingredients with the spring onion, herbs, shallots and chilli.

Slice the beef thinly and add it to the salad, drizzling over just enough dressing to coat. Toss gently and serve on individual plates, or on one large platter so guests can help themselves. Scatter the sesame seeds over.

Salad of Peking duck with bean sprouts, coriander and mint

If you live near an Asian roast house, you can buy a Peking duck from them, remove all the skin and bones and slice the flesh thinly in place of the duck breast. Serves 4

2 boneless skinless duck breasts

Chinese five-spice (page 468)

Oil for cooking

2 tablespoons hoisin sauce

2 tablespoons light soy sauce

1 tablespoon honey

½ Chinese cabbage (wombok), thinly sliced

Handful of bean sprouts

5 g (¼ oz/¼ cup) Vietnamese mint leaves

10 g (¼ oz/⅓ cup) coriander (cilantro) leaves

4 spring onions (scallions), thinly sliced

½ red capsicum (bell pepper), thinly sliced

2 tablespoons crispy shallots (optional)

Take the duck breasts and score the fat on top of the meat. Season with salt, freshly ground black pepper and a sprinkling of Chinese five-spice.

Heat a large heavy-based frying pan over medium–high heat. Add a splash of oil and cook the duck breasts for 3–4 minutes on each side, until just cooked. Cover and rest for 5 minutes.

Prepare the dressing by mixing together the hoisin sauce, soy sauce and honey.

Toss together the Chinese cabbage, bean sprouts, herb leaves, spring onion, red capsicum and crispy shallots (if using).

Thinly slice the duck breasts, add to the other salad ingredients and add enough dressing to just coat. Toss together to combine and serve.

Pea and asparagus salad with feta and prosciutto

What better way to celebrate the arrival of asparagus than with this beautiful salad? Serves 4

1 small bunch asparagus

155 g (5½ oz/1 cup) peas

150 g (5½ oz) snow peas (mangetout)

8 thin slices of prosciutto

40 g (1½ oz) toasted pine nuts

5 g (¼ oz/¼ cup) mint leaves

10 g (¼ oz/½ cup) flat-leaf (Italian) parsley leaves

100 g (3½ oz) snow pea (mangetout) shoots

50 g (1¾ oz) baby English spinach leaves

50 g (1¾ oz) rocket (arugula)

Honey dressing (page 462)

100 g (3½ oz) feta, crumbled

Bring a saucepan of water to the boil. Remove and discard the woody asparagus ends and cook the spears briefly for 1–2 minutes. Remove and refresh under cold running water.

Add the peas and snow peas to the boiling water and cook for 1–2 minutes. Drain and refresh under cold running water.

Heat a large frying pan over medium–high heat and cook the prosciutto slices for 2–3 minutes on each side until crisp. Drain on paper towel.

Place the asparagus, peas and snow peas in a large bowl along with the pine nuts, herbs, shoots, spinach and rocket. Add the honey dressing when ready to serve and toss to combine. Arrange on a platter, crumble the feta over the top and add the crisp prosciutto slices, crumbling them a little if necessary.

Pastry

There's a knack to making pastry and, for many people, it takes a few attempts to get it right. Pastry is greatly influenced by the weather – too humid, and the pastry becomes sticky; too cold, and it's hard to manipulate. A cool, light touch seems to work best so, if your hands are too hot, rinse them under cold water. Working in a cool, well-ventilated spot will also help.

Savoury and sweet

The most important rule when making pastry is – don't give up. Once you've mastered the art you will be able to whip up quiches, tarts and pies at the drop of a hat. There are no shortcuts when it comes to making good sweet or shortcrust pastry, though – it needs to be rested for at least 20 minutes every time it has been worked, or it will shrink during cooking.

A stash of puff pastry in the freezer can be a great stand-by. I would love to say I make my own, but the reality is I don't have time, unless I make the effort for some special occasion. Instead, I keep some puff pastry in the freezer for a backup. Spend the extra money and buy the frozen all-butter puff pastry from the supermarket. It has far fewer nasties in it.

Some people swear by a food processor to make pastry so if that works well for you, that's great. However, I've always stuck to the tried-and-tested rubbing-in method, which takes the same amount of time as a food processor but results in less washing up.

Tips for cooking
with pastry

- Don't be afraid of pastry. I reckon that pastry, like dogs, can sense fear and will play up to it.

- Making pastry is like riding a bike – make it right once and you'll have the knack forever.

- Climate will affect pastry. If your kitchen is hot and humid you're not going to have much luck. Keep ingredients and your work area as cool as possible.

- Always dust your work surface and rolling pin with a little flour to stop the pastry sticking.

- To check you have rolled out your pastry to the right size, place your tin on top of the pastry and allow an extra 2–3 cm (¾–1¼ in) for the sides.

- Try not to roll pastry out too thin – 3 mm (¼ in) is perfect.

- To line a pastry tin, place your rolling pin on top of the pastry at the edge closest to you. Pick up the edge of the pastry and roll the pastry around the pin. Transfer the rolling pin to the edge of the tin and unroll the pastry onto the tin. Push the pastry down into the tin and push the edges over it. Roll the rolling pin across the top to trim off the excess pastry. Lastly, work your fingers around the sides of the tin, making sure the pastry is pushed down into the corners. Trim off any excess pastry using a small knife.

- Pastry is often cooked in the oven before any filling is added to prevent the bottom becoming soggy. This is known as blind baking. Make a baking paper liner (see page 359) and place it in the rested raw pastry shell. Weigh down with baking beans or raw rice. I keep a container of 'baking' rice in the cupboard just for this purpose.

- All the fillings in this chapter are based on a 23 × 3 cm (9 × 1¼ in) non-stick loose base flan (tart) tin. The pastry recipes will suit most tart tins, allowing for some that are slightly wider, deeper or shallower.

Pastry recipes

Basics

Shortcrust pastry

This is the basic pastry used for all savoury tarts. It can also be used for sweet tarts, especially if the filling is very sweet. Makes 1 × 23 cm (9 in) pastry shell

300 g (10½ oz/2 cups) plain (all-purpose) flour, plus extra for dusting
150 g (5½ oz) butter, diced
60–80 ml (2–2½ fl oz/¼–⅓ cup) cold water

For the dough, sift the flour and a pinch of salt into a bowl. Rub in the butter to produce a breadcrumb-like texture. Add enough cold water to bring the pastry together and knead briefly. Wrap the dough in plastic wrap and chill for 30 minutes.

For the pastry shell, preheat the oven to 180°C (350°F).

Roll out the pastry on a lightly floured work surface to a 3 mm (¼ in) thickness. Line a buttered 23 cm (9 in) flan (tart) tin with the pastry, working your fingers around the sides of the tin to make sure the pastry is pushed down into the corners. Trim off any excess pastry using a small knife.

Prick the base of the pastry shell with a fork and rest for 30 minutes. Line the pastry with baking paper, then add baking beans, pastry weights or rice. Bake blind for 15 minutes in the oven.

Remove the paper and pastry weights and bake for a further 5 minutes to crisp the pastry.

Gluten-free shortcrust pastry
Swap the plain flour for Gluten-free flour (page 484).

Sweet crust pastry

Sweet crust pastry is easier to work with because the sugar breaks down the protein in the flour and makes the pastry more supple. Use it for sweet tarts. Makes 1 × 23 cm (9 in) pastry shell

300 g (10½ oz/2 cups) plain (all-purpose) flour, plus extra for dusting
150 g (5½ oz) soft butter, diced
1 egg
55 g (2 oz/¼ cup) caster (superfine) sugar

For the dough, place the flour, butter and a pinch of salt in a bowl and rub together until the mixture resembles fine breadcrumbs. Break the egg into a separate bowl, add the caster sugar and mix lightly. Add to the flour mixture and mix until the pastry comes together. Wrap in plastic wrap and chill for 30 minutes.

For the pastry shell, preheat the oven to 180°C (350°F).

Roll out the pastry on a lightly floured work surface to a 3 mm (¼ in) thickness. Line a buttered 23 cm (9 in) flan (tart) tin with the pastry, working your fingers around the sides of the tin to make sure the pastry is pushed down into the corners. Trim off any excess pastry using a small knife.

Prick the base of the pastry shell with a fork and rest for 30 minutes. Line the pastry with baking paper, then add baking beans, pastry weights or rice. Bake blind for 15 minutes in the oven.

Remove the paper and pastry weights and bake for a further 5 minutes to crisp the pastry.

Gluten-free sweet crust pastry
Swap the plain flour for Gluten-free flour (page 484).

Chocolate sweet crust pastry
Swap 50 g (1¾ oz/⅓ cup) of the flour for unsweetened (Dutch) cocoa powder.

Almond sweet crust pastry

Here, ground almonds replace some of the flour to introduce a nutty flavour to the pastry.
Makes 1 × 23 cm (9 in) pastry shell

200 g (7 oz/1⅓ cups) plain (all-purpose) flour, plus extra for dusting
100 g (3½ oz/1 cup) ground almonds
150 g (5½ oz) soft butter, diced
2 egg yolks
55 g (2 oz/¼ cup) caster (superfine) sugar

For the dough, rub the flour, almonds, butter and a pinch of salt together until the mixture resembles fine breadcrumbs. Lightly beat the egg yolks and dissolve the caster sugar in them.

Make a well in the centre of the flour mix, pour in the egg and sugar and knead lightly to form a ball. Wrap in plastic wrap and chill for 30 minutes.

For the pastry shell, preheat the oven to 180°C (350°F).

Roll out the pastry on a lightly floured work surface to a 3 mm (¼ in) thickness. Line a buttered 23 cm (9 in) flan (tart) tin with the pastry, working your fingers around the sides of the tin to make sure the pastry is pushed down into the corners. Trim off any excess pastry using a small knife.

Prick the base of the pastry shell with a fork and rest for 30 minutes. Line the pastry with baking paper, then add baking beans, pastry weights or rice. Bake blind for 15 minutes in the oven.

Remove the paper and pastry weights and bake for a further 5 minutes to crisp the pastry.

Rough puff pastry

This is the 'quick' version of puff pastry. It's perfect when time is tight and you need a top for your pie. What you're doing here is three folds in one go, rather than six folds with resting time in between, as for true puff pastry (see opposite). Makes 500 g (1 lb 2 oz)

250 g (9 oz/1⅔ cups) plain (all-purpose) flour, plus extra for dusting
250 g (9 oz) butter, diced
Squeeze of lemon juice
100–120 ml (3½–4 fl oz/⅓–½ cup) iced water

Place the flour and a pinch of salt in a food processor. Add the butter to the flour and pulse three to four times. Don't try to make the butter disappear; it should still be nice and lumpy.

Place the pastry in a large bowl, add the lemon juice and iced water, then knead lightly to bring the pastry together; don't over-knead. Wrap in plastic wrap and rest in the refrigerator for 30 minutes.

Dust the pastry with flour and roll it into a long 50–60 cm (20–24 in) rectangle. Fold the bottom third of the pastry up over the centre and the top third down to cover it, like a letter. Turn it 90 degrees (a quarter turn) and roll again into a long rectangle. Again fold into three and turn it 90 degrees. Roll one last time into a long rectangle (three times in total), fold into three, wrap it in plastic wrap and pop it back in the refrigerator for 30 minutes before using.

Parmesan flaky pastry
Add 50 (1¾ oz) finely grated parmesan along with the lemon juice and water.

Puff pastry

Puff pastry is usually thought best left to the experts but, in fact, it's quite easy. It takes a few hours because of all the resting time, but you can do plenty of other things in between. Makes 500 g (1 lb 2 oz)

250 g (9 oz/1⅔ cups) plain (all-purpose) flour, plus extra for dusting
Squeeze of lemon juice
100–120 ml (3½–4 fl oz/⅓–½ cup) iced water
250 g (9 oz) butter

Sift the flour and a pinch of salt together in a large bowl. Add the lemon juice and enough iced water to bring the pastry together.

Tip onto a floured work surface and roll the pastry into a 20 cm (8 in) square. Wrap in foil and chill for 30 minutes.

Remove the butter from the refrigerator 30 minutes before using and cut it into thick slices. It is essential that the butter and pastry share a similar temperature and softness, so the butter will be thoroughly incorporated.

Place the chilled pastry on a floured work surface and roll it out to a 30 cm (12 in) square, leaving a thick centre that is about twice as thick as the sides. Place slices of butter in the centre of the pastry and press all over with your fingertips to soften the butter a little more. Fold in all the edges, ensuring that the butter is completely encased in the pastry.

Turn the pastry over, dust with flour and roll it into a long 50–60 cm (20–24 in) rectangle. Fold the bottom third of the pastry up over the centre and the top third down to cover it, like a letter. Make a single indentation with your finger on top of the pastry to signify the first fold. Wrap in foil and chill for 30 minutes.

Remove the pastry from the refrigerator. Turn it 90 degrees (a quarter turn) and roll again into a long rectangle. Again fold into three, like a letter, and mark two indentations. Cover and chill for 30 minutes. Repeat until a total of six folds have been completed. Remember to mark them as you go.

After the last fold, roll the pastry as required and allow to rest 30 minutes before baking.

If not using the pastry immediately, divide it into two portions and freeze.

Choux pastry

Choux pastry makes delectable things such as profiteroles and cheesy puffs. Makes enough for 40 profiteroles or 10–15 éclairs.

125 ml (4 fl oz/½ cup) milk
100 g (3½ oz) butter
150 g (5½ oz/1 cup) plain (all-purpose) flour
5 eggs

Place 125 ml (4 fl oz/½ cup) water, the milk, butter and a pinch of salt in a saucepan and bring to the boil. Tip in the flour, stir and return to a low heat. Cook for 2–3 minutes, stirring constantly, until the mixture begins to come away from the side of the saucepan.

Tip the contents into a food processor. Start the processor, allowing the mixture to cool slightly.

Break the eggs into a jug and beat lightly. Slowly add the egg mix to the pastry mixture, ensuring that the eggs are well incorporated after each addition. Continue adding the eggs until the pastry is of a dropping consistency – not too runny. You may not need to add all the eggs; it tends to vary a bit from batch to batch.

Savoury

Traditional quiche or savoury tart

Quiche lorraine is the type most people know, with a filling that includes lots of cooked onion and bacon. No wonder it's so popular. Serves 8

Oil for cooking

1 onion, diced

4 rashers (slices) bacon, cut into strips

4 eggs

125 ml (4 fl oz/½ cup) pouring (single/light) cream

2 tablespoons chopped flat-leaf (Italian) parsley

125 g (4½ oz/1¼ cups) grated parmesan

1 × 23 cm (9 in) Shortcrust pastry shell (page 299)

Preheat the oven to 180°C (350°F).

Heat a heavy-based frying pan over medium heat, add a splash of oil and onion and cook for 4–5 minutes, stirring often until the onion softens but doesn't colour. Add the bacon and cook for a further 3–4 minutes. Remove from the heat and allow to cool.

Beat the eggs with the cream, parsley and cheese and season with salt and freshly ground black pepper. Spoon the onion and bacon mix into the cooked pastry shell. Pour the egg mixture into the pastry shell and bake in the oven for 30 minutes until golden brown and set.

Leek and feta tart
Substitute two thinly sliced leeks for the onion, and feta for 60 g (2 oz) of the parmesan.

Asparagus and goat's cheese tart
Cook the onion until soft and add the bacon if you want to. Place blanched, chopped asparagus spears in the pastry shell along with the onion before the egg mixture.

Caramelised onion tart
Cook four sliced onions in 60 ml (2 fl oz/¼ cup) olive oil with some salt, freshly ground black pepper and a sprig or two of fresh thyme for 30 minutes. Stir often. The onion will turn dark brown and gloriously rich. Drain and allow to cool before placing it in the cooked pastry shell. This is also delicious with goat's cheese rather than parmesan.

Mushroom quiche
Add 125 g (4½ oz) sliced mushrooms to the pan while cooking the onion. Cook for a further 5-6 minutes, or until the mushrooms are softened. Allow to cool, then add to the pastry shell before the egg mixture.

Roast pumpkin and feta tart
Add diced roasted pumpkin (squash) to the pastry shell and crumble feta cheese over the top. Pour the egg mixture over and cook as directed. You can also use blue cheese instead of feta.

Tomato and anchovy tart

This tart is perfect for those of you who love the salty combination of anchovies and olives.
Serves 8

Olive oil for cooking

1 onion, diced

1 garlic clove, crushed

6 tomatoes, diced

2 tablespoons tomato paste (concentrated purée)

2 eggs

1 × 23 cm (9 in) Shortcrust pastry shell (page 299)

12 anchovy fillets

12 black olives

Preheat the oven to 180°C (350°F).

Heat a heavy-based frying pan over medium heat, add a splash of olive oil and cook the onion and garlic until soft. Add the tomatoes and tomato paste and continue to cook until soft, about 10 minutes. Remove from the heat and allow to cool. Add the eggs and season to taste with salt and freshly ground black pepper.

Pour the mixture into the cooked pastry shell.

Cut the anchovy fillets in half lengthways, remove the stones from the olives and cut them in half. Lay the anchovy strips over the tomato in a diamond lattice formation and put one olive half in each diamond. Bake in the oven for 40 minutes, or until the tomato filling is set and lightly brown.

Sausage rolls

The sausage meat typically offered for sausage rolls is not something I'm all that keen to eat. Instead, I buy really good sausages and use them; then I know exactly what's in there. (You can take the skins off or leave them on.) Makes 20

1 quantity Puff pastry (page 301) or 4–6 sheets frozen puff pastry

20 small skinless frankfurter sausages or baby bratwurst

Dijon or wholegrain mustard (optional)

Egg wash (see page 419)

Roll out the pastry to a 3 mm (¼ in) thickness – either a square or a rectangle will do. Use one sausage as a guide to cut out 20 evenly sized rectangles. They should be wide enough to wrap completely around the sausage one and a half times.

Spread a small amount of mustard on the lower half of each pastry rectangle. Place a sausage on top of the mustard and brush the top half of the pastry with the egg wash. Roll the sausage up in the pastry.

Preheat the oven to 200°C (400°F).

Place the sausage rolls on a lined baking tray with the pastry join underneath. Brush with egg wash and slash each top with a knife in a few places to expose the sausage. Rest for 30 minutes. Bake the sausage rolls for 15–20 minutes, or until the pastry is cooked and golden brown.

Roast pumpkin, feta and pine nut puff slice

A glorious combination of sweet roast pumpkin, salty feta and crunchy pine nuts. Serve with a green salad. Serves 4

1 kg (2 lb 3 oz) pumpkin (squash), cut into 2 cm (¾ in) dice

Olive oil for cooking

½ quantity Puff pastry (page 301) or 2 sheets frozen puff pastry

100 g (3½ oz) rocket (arugula)

200 g (7 oz) feta

80 g (2¾ oz/½ cup) pine nuts

Preheat the oven to 180°C (350°F). Line baking trays with baking paper.

Toss the pumpkin with olive oil to coat, season with salt and freshly ground black pepper and roast in the oven for 30 minutes or until the pumpkin is tender and golden brown.

Roll out the puff pastry to a 3 mm (¼ in) thick square and cut into four smaller squares measuring about 12 cm (4¾ in). If using frozen puff pastry, cut the sheets into quarters. Place on the prepared baking trays. Scatter rocket leaves over the base and top with the cooked pumpkin. Crumble the feta over the pumpkin and scatter the pine nuts on top.

Bake in the oven for 15–20 minutes or until the pastry is crisp and golden brown. Cut the slice into four pieces to serve.

Sumac beef and pine nut tarts

Assuming you have puff pastry on hand, this is a quick and easy pie option for dinner. Serves 4

Oil for cooking

1 onion, diced

1 garlic clove, crushed

375 g (13 oz) minced (ground) beef

2 teaspoons sumac

Grated zest of 1 lemon

1 tablespoon pomegranate molasses

2 tablespoons toasted pine nuts

1 quantity Puff pastry (page 301) or 2 sheets frozen puff pastry

Egg wash (see page 419)

250 g (9 oz) cherry tomatoes, quartered

5 g (¼ oz/¼ cup) flat-leaf (Italian) parsley leaves

7 g (¼ oz/¼ cup) coriander (cilantro) leaves

1 tablespoon chopped mint

2 tablespoons extra-virgin olive oil

1 tablespoon lemon juice

Yoghurt tahini sauce (page 455)

Preheat the oven to 200°C (400°F). Line a baking tray with baking paper.

Heat a heavy-based frying pan over medium–high heat. Add a splash of oil and the onion and cook for 3–4 minutes, stirring often. Add the garlic and cook for a further 1–2 minutes until fragrant. Add the beef and cook until browned. Add the sumac, lemon zest and pomegranate molasses and cook for a further 5 minutes. Season with salt and freshly ground black pepper and stir through the pine nuts.

Roll out the puff pastry to a 3 mm (¼ in) thick rectangle and cut it into four smaller rectangles measuring about 12 × 16 cm (4¾ × 6¼ in). If using frozen puff pastry, cut the sheets into halves. Place on the prepared baking tray.

Divide the beef mixture between the four pieces of pastry and fold over 2 cm (¾ in) of the edge on each piece of pastry. Brush with the egg wash and bake in the oven for 25 minutes until golden brown.

Toss together the tomatoes, herbs, extra-virgin olive oil and lemon juice. Season with salt and pepper.

When the tarts are cooked, drizzle the yoghurt tahini sauce over the top of each and divide the tomato salad between them. Serve.

Tomato tarte tatin

A delicious savoury variation on a classic dish. Perfect for a light lunch with a simple salad.
Serves 6

80 ml (2½ fl oz/⅓ cup) olive oil, plus extra for drizzling

4 onions, sliced

2 garlic cloves, peeled

1 small red chilli, halved

2 thyme sprigs

4 roma (plum) tomatoes

1–2 tablespoons balsamic vinegar

2–3 tablespoons chopped basil

½ quantity Parmesan flaky pastry (page 300)

Egg wash (see page 419)

Heat the oil in a saucepan and add the onion, garlic, chilli and thyme. Cook for 20–30 minutes on a low heat, stirring often, until the onion softens and caramelises.

Preheat the oven to 180°C (350°F).

Cut the tomatoes in half lengthways. Place them on a baking tray, drizzle with olive oil and balsamic vinegar and season with salt and freshly ground black pepper. Roast in the oven for 20–30 minutes, or until cooked and golden brown.

Increase the oven temperature to 200°C (400°F).

Grease and line a shallow baking dish or flan (tart) tin with baking paper. Place the tomatoes, cut side down, in the dish, arranging them so they fit snugly. Scatter the caramelised onion and chopped basil over the top.

Roll out the pastry to a 3 mm (¼ in) thickness. Place the pastry over the tomatoes. Tuck the edges down slightly around the edge of the baking dish. Brush with the egg wash and trim the excess pastry away.

Bake in the oven for 15–20 minutes or until the pastry is golden brown and crisp. Allow to cool briefly, then place a board or serving plate over the baking dish and turn upside down, allowing the tart to come out.

Free-form roast summer vegetable tart

A delicious summer tart, perfect for lunch or as an appetiser before dinner. Serves 6

1 eggplant (aubergine)

3 tomatoes

2 zucchini (courgettes)

1 red onion

5–6 garlic cloves, left whole

Olive oil

2 thyme sprigs

Handful of basil leaves

2–3 oregano sprigs

1 quantity Shortcrust pastry dough (page 299)

Egg wash (see page 419)

Cut the eggplant in half, then cut each half into six wedges. Cut the tomatoes into quarters. Cut the zucchini in half lengthways and then into 4 cm (1½ in) chunks. Cut the red onion into thick wedges.

Place the vegetables and garlic in a deep baking tin and toss them with the olive oil, salt and freshly ground black pepper. Roughly chop the herbs and scatter them on top. Roast for 30–40 minutes or until the vegetables are cooked and golden brown. Set aside to cool.

Roll out the pastry on a lightly floured work surface to make a circle about 40 cm (16 in) in diameter and 3 mm (¼ in) thick. Place the pastry on a baking tray lined with baking paper and leave to rest for 30 minutes.

Preheat the oven to 180°C (350°F).

Arrange the roasted vegetables on the pastry, leaving a 5 cm (2 in) border. Fold the pastry over the edge of the vegetables to form a 3 cm (1¼ in) lip. Brush the egg wash over the sides of the tart. Bake the tart in the oven for 30–35 minutes, or until the pastry is cooked and golden brown.

Moroccan chicken rolls

If you like your food spicy, double the quantities of spice recommended in this recipe. Makes 20

Oil

1 onion, finely diced

500 g (1 lb 2 oz) minced (ground) chicken

2 teaspoons ground cumin

2 teaspoons ground coriander

1 teaspoon smoky paprika

2–3 tablespoons chopped coriander (cilantro)

1 egg yolk

1 quantity Puff pastry (page 301) or 4–6 sheets
  frozen puff pastry

Plain (all-purpose) flour for dusting

Egg wash (see page 419)

Sesame seeds for sprinkling

Heat a small frying pan over medium–high heat. Add a splash of oil and the onion. Cook for 4–5 minutes, stirring often, until soft.

Mix the onion, chicken, spices, coriander and egg yolk together and season with salt and freshly ground black pepper.

Roll out the pastry on a lightly floured work surface to a 3 mm (¼ in) thickness – either a square or a rectangle.

Roll the chicken mixture to form a long snake, 2 cm (¾ in) wide. Place the chicken on the puff pastry – you may need two to three 'snakes', depending on the length of your pastry.

Brush one edge of the puff pastry with egg wash and fold the pastry over to totally enclose the meat. Crimp the pastry to ensure that it sticks together, then cut it into 20 small rolls. Place the chicken rolls on a lined baking tray. Brush the rolls with egg wash and slash each top with a knife in a few places to expose the filling. Sprinkle with sesame seeds and rest for 30 minutes.

Preheat the oven to 200°C (400°F).

Bake the chicken rolls for 15–20 minutes, or until the pastry is cooked and golden brown, ensuring the chicken is cooked through.

Spinach and feta rolls
Use the spinach and ricotta filling from Spanakopita (page 309), in place of the minced chicken.

Breakfast tarts

Perfect for social brunches, or even picnics, what better way to eat bacon and eggs than to wrap them up in flaky pastry? Makes 12

12 cherry tomatoes

12 button mushrooms

Oil for cooking

6 bacon rashers (slices), rind removed

½ quantity Puff pastry (page 301) or 2–3 sheets
  frozen puff pastry

40 g (1½ oz) grated parmesan

12 eggs

7 g (¼ oz/¼ cup) chopped flat-leaf (Italian) parsley

Preheat the oven to 180°C (350°F). Grease a 12-hole muffin tin.

Place the tomatoes and mushrooms on a baking tray. Sprinkle with salt and freshly ground black pepper and drizzle with oil. Bake in the oven for 15–20 minutes or until soft and golden brown. Place the bacon on another baking tray and cook in the oven for 5–8 minutes or until crispy.

Roll out the pastry on a lightly floured work surface to a 3 mm (¼ in) thickness. Cut circles of pastry using a 10 cm (4 in) cutter and place each pastry circle into the holes of the muffin tin. Sprinkle 1 tablespoon grated parmesan into each tart shell. Arrange half a bacon rasher in each shell, along with one mushroom. Crack an egg into each shell. Cut the cherry tomatoes in half and add two halves to each tart. Sprinkle with chopped parsley, salt and pepper.

Bake in the oven for 15–18 minutes or until the eggs have set. Serve while still warm.

Egg and bacon pie

A good egg and bacon pie is a beautiful thing. If you like, you could also use pancetta or prosciutto, or make individual pies. Serves 6–8

1 quantity Rough puff pastry (page 300) or
  4–6 sheets frozen puff pastry

Plain (all-purpose) flour for dusting

Butter for greasing

2 tablespoons olive oil

2 onions, finely diced

400 g (14 oz) rashers (slices) bacon, cut into strips

2 tablespoons chopped flat-leaf (Italian) parsley

4 eggs, lightly beaten

Egg wash (see page 419)

Preheat the oven to 190°C (375°F).

Divide the pastry in half and roll out each piece on a lightly floured board to a 3 mm (¼ in) thickness.

Line a 23 cm (9 in) buttered pie dish with one piece of pastry.

Heat a heavy-based frying pan over medium heat. Add the oil and onion and cook for 3–4 minutes, stirring often, until the onion softens. Add the bacon and cook for a further 3–4 minutes, stirring often to stop the bacon catching. Season well with freshly ground black pepper. Add the parsley and eggs and stir well to combine. Spoon the filling into the prepared pie dish.

Brush the edge of the bottom piece of pastry with egg wash and cover with the remaining piece of pastry. Crimp the edges to join the pastry pieces together. Brush the pastry top with egg wash and bake in the oven for 30 minutes, or until the pastry is risen and golden brown.

Chicken and mushroom pie

There's something special about serving a pie at the table. It always looks as if you've gone to a lot of trouble, whereas in fact it's just a casserole with pastry on the top – but don't tell anyone. Serves 4

1 kg (2 lb 3 oz) boneless skinless chicken thighs, diced

Seasoned flour

Olive oil

6 bacon rashers (slices), cut into strips

200 g (7 oz) mushrooms, sliced

125 ml (4 fl oz/½ cup) white wine

125–250 ml (4–8½ fl oz/½–1 cup) chicken stock

1 teaspoon fresh thyme leaves

1 tablespoon chopped flat-leaf (Italian) parsley

½ quantity Puff pastry (page 301) or 1 sheet frozen puff pastry

Egg wash (see page 419)

Toss the chicken in the seasoned flour and shake well to remove any excess. Heat a heavy-based saucepan over medium heat. Add the oil and cook the chicken in batches until golden brown. Set aside.

Using the same pan, cook the bacon and mushrooms until softened and beginning to colour. Add the white wine and allow to come to the boil.

Return the chicken to the saucepan and add enough stock to just cover. Add the herbs and season to taste with salt and freshly ground black pepper, then reduce the heat and allow to cook for 30–45 minutes.

Preheat the oven to 180°C (350°F).

Ensure the pastry is rolled out to a 3 mm (¼ in) thickness. Spoon the hot chicken mixture into the pie dish. Cover the chicken with the puff pastry, trim the edges and brush with the egg wash. Place in the oven and bake for 20–30 minutes, or until the pastry is cooked and golden brown. Remove and serve.

Spiced eggplant parcels

These eggplant parcels are a great vegetarian option for a cocktail party. You can even make them larger for a lunch option if you prefer. Makes 36

Oil
1 onion, diced
1 eggplant (aubergine), cut into 1 cm (½ in) dice
1 garlic clove, crushed
1 teaspoon grated fresh ginger
2 teaspoons Harissa (page 467)
Pinch of saffron threads
1 teaspoon ground coriander
1 teaspoon ground cumin
¼ teaspoon ground cardamom
¼ teaspoon allspice
1 tablespoon tomato paste (concentrated purée)
250 ml (8½ fl oz/1 cup) chicken or vegetable stock
15 g (½ oz/¼ cup) chopped coriander (cilantro)
2 quantities Puff pastry (page 301) or 8–12 sheets
  frozen puff pastry
Plain (all-purpose) flour for dusting
Egg wash (see page 419)
Cumin or sesame seeds for sprinkling

Heat a large frying pan over medium–high heat. Add a generous splash of oil, the onion and eggplant and cook for 3–4 minutes, stirring often. Add the garlic, ginger, harissa and spices. Cook for 1–2 minutes, stirring often, until fragrant.

Add the tomato paste and cook briefly, then add the stock and bring to the boil. Season with salt and freshly ground black pepper, reduce the heat and simmer for 10–15 minutes, or until the eggplant is cooked and the liquid has reduced to form a thick sauce. Remove from the heat and allow to cool. Check the seasoning and add the chopped coriander.

Divide the pastry into four pieces and roll each one out on a lightly floured work surface to form a 30 cm (12 in) square. Cut each square into nine smaller squares. Place 1 heaped teaspoon of the eggplant mixture in each square.

Brush two edges of the pastry with the egg wash and fold over diagonally to form small triangles. Crimp the pastry edges to ensure that the pastry sticks together. Place the parcels on a lined baking tray, brush with the egg wash and sprinkle with the cumin or sesame seeds. Rest for 30 minutes.

Preheat the oven to 200°C (400°F).

Bake the parcels for 10–12 minutes, or until the pastry is cooked and golden brown. Serve while still warm.

Chipotle beef empanadas
Swap the eggplant filling for Braised chipotle beef ribs (page 197). This is a great way to use leftovers.

Cheesy choux puffs

These are ideal as a nibble before dinner. I find their light cheese flavour is perfect with a glass or two of sparkling wine. Makes 30

90 g (3 oz) gruyère or parmesan, grated
1 quantity Choux pastry dough (page 301)

Preheat the oven to 200°C (400°F).

Add the cheese to the choux pastry mixture. Spoon or pipe teaspoonfuls of the choux pastry dough onto lined baking trays. Place the trays in the oven at the same time. (With choux pastry it is important not to open the door in the first 10 minutes of cooking, as cold draughts will make the pastry sink.)

Cook for 10 minutes, then reduce the temperature to 180°C (350°F). Cook for another 10 minutes, then try one. They should be quite brown (more than golden brown) and relatively dry inside. Resist the urge to pull them out too soon, as they will be doughy inside. When ready, set aside to cool.

Chicken and vegetable pasties

On a long car trip, a picnic or bushwalk, a good chicken pastie can be just the thing. The pasties can also be made into small cocktail-sized nibbles and served with a tomato relish. Makes 6

2 × 200 g (7 oz) boneless skinless chicken thighs

2 tablespoons olive oil

1 onion, finely diced

2 medium potatoes, finely diced

1 small carrot, finely diced

1 garlic clove, finely crushed

1 tablespoon tomato paste (concentrated purée)

250 ml (8½ fl oz/1 cup) chicken or vegetable stock

2 tablespoons chopped flat-leaf (Italian) parsley

1 quantity Puff pastry (page 301) or 4–6 sheets frozen puff pastry

Plain (all-purpose) flour for dusting

Egg wash (see page 419)

Cut the chicken thighs into 2 cm (¾ in) dice. Heat the oil in a saucepan over medium–low heat and add the chicken and onion. Stir together and cook for 5 minutes. Add the potato, carrot, garlic and tomato paste and cook for a further 5 minutes, stirring well. Add the stock and bring to a simmer. Cover and cook for 10 minutes. Uncover the saucepan, raise the heat to high and cook for 6–7 minutes, stirring, until the liquid has evaporated. Stir in the chopped parsley, season to taste with salt and freshly ground black pepper and allow to cool.

Preheat the oven to 180°C (350°F).

Divide the puff pastry into six equal pieces. Roll out each piece of pastry on a lightly floured work surface to a rough 18 cm (7 in) circle. Brush generously with egg wash. Place one-sixth of the chicken mixture in the centre of each pastry circle in a heaped oval. Bring the two opposite sides up around the filling and press to seal on top of the chicken mix. Crimp the edges to give them a decorative look. Continue until all six pasties are made. Place on a buttered baking tray and brush with egg wash. Cook for 30 minutes or until golden brown.

Spanakopita

The classic Greek spanakopita (cheese pie) is a winning light meal in my book. It can also be made into small cocktail-sized party food. Serves 4–6

150 g (5½ oz/3 cups) English spinach leaves

125 g (4½ oz/½ cup) ricotta

1 egg, lightly beaten

150 g (5½ oz) mashed feta

Pinch of freshly grated nutmeg

2 tablespoons chopped flat-leaf (Italian) parsley

6 sheets filo pastry

100 g (3½ oz) melted butter

Preheat the oven to 180°C (350°F).

Blanch the spinach leaves in boiling water. Refresh immediately under cold running water, squeeze the excess water out and chop finely. Mix the spinach with the ricotta, egg, feta, nutmeg, some freshly ground black pepper and the chopped parsley until smooth.

Brush one sheet of filo pastry with the melted butter. Lay another sheet of filo pastry on top, brush again with butter and repeat until you have six sheets of filo pastry buttered together.

Lay the filo pastry layers in a 23 cm (9 in) flan (tart) tin. Spoon in the spinach and ricotta mixture. Fold the pastry ends over to enclose the filling completely and brush the top with melted butter. Bake in the oven for 30 minutes, or until golden brown and slightly puffy.

Bistella

I've come to love these Moroccan chicken pastries through the cooking and writing of Melbourne-based chef Greg Malouf. Traditionally, they're made with pigeon, but I find that chicken pies are easier to re-create in the home kitchen. While it may seem unusual to sprinkle the pastry with icing sugar to serve, it is an essential part of the finished dish. Serves 6–8

Oil

1 onion, diced

1 garlic clove, crushed

500 g (1 lb 2 oz) boneless skinless chicken thighs, diced

½ teaspoon ground ginger

½ teaspoon ground cinnamon

½ teaspoon ground allspice

125 ml (4 fl oz/½ cup) chicken stock

1 tablespoon tomato paste (concentrated purée)

2 tablespoons chopped coriander (cilantro)

8 sheets filo pastry

150 g (5½ oz) melted butter

150 g (5½ oz/1⅔ cups) flaked toasted almonds

45 g (1½ oz) icing (confectioners') sugar

1 teaspoon ground cinnamon

Heat a heavy-based frying pan over medium heat. Add a splash of oil and the onion and cook for 3–4 minutes, stirring often. Add the garlic and chicken and cook for 5–6 minutes, or until the chicken is golden brown. Add the spices and cook for 1–2 minutes, until fragrant. Add the stock and tomato paste and season with salt and freshly ground black pepper. Bring to the boil. Reduce to a simmer and cook for 6–8 minutes, stirring often, until the chicken is cooked and most of the stock has been absorbed. Check the seasoning and add the chopped coriander.

Preheat the oven to 180°C (350°F).

Brush each sheet of filo pastry with melted butter. Lay three to four sheets in the base of a buttered 23 cm (9 in) flan (tart) tin, allowing plenty of pastry to hang over the edges. Add the chicken filling and sprinkle on the toasted almonds. Top with another three to four sheets of buttered filo. Fold the edges over to totally encase the filling.

Bake in the oven for 15–20 minutes, or until golden brown and the chicken is heated through.

Sift the icing sugar and cinnamon together. Dust the bistella with this mixture and serve hot.

Potato, rosemary and goat's cheese tarts

The secret to the success of this tart is to use good-quality potatoes and goat's cheese. Opt for kipfler (fingerling) potatoes for maximum flavour. Serve with a simple green salad. Makes 4

4 potatoes, peeled (preferably kipfler/fingerling)

½ quantity Puff pastry (page 301) or 2–3 sheets frozen puff pastry

2 tablespoons chopped rosemary

200 g (7 oz) goat's cheese

Olive oil

Cook the potatoes in boiling water until just tender. Drain, allow to cool and cut into 5 mm (¼ in) slices.

Preheat the oven to 180°C (350°F). Line baking trays with baking paper.

Roll out the puff pastry to a 3 mm (¼ in) thick square and cut into four smaller squares measuring about 12 cm (4¾ in). If using frozen puff pastry, cut the sheets into quarters. Place on the prepared baking trays.

Divide the potato slices between each rectangle, leaving a 1 cm (½ in) border. Scatter with chopped rosemary and add two to three slices of goat's cheese on top. Drizzle with olive oil and season with salt and freshly ground black pepper. Bake in the oven for 20–25 minutes, until puffed and golden brown.

Sweet

Lemon tart

Here are two lemon tarts. This first recipe is smoother and more sophisticated and is quite the dinner party item. Serves 8

6 eggs
125 g (4½ oz) mascarpone
200 g (7 oz) caster (superfine) sugar
250 ml (8½ fl oz/1 cup) lemon juice
Grated zest of 2 lemons
1 × 23 cm (9 in) Sweet crust pastry shell (page 299)

Preheat the oven to 140°C (275°F)

Beat the eggs, mascarpone, sugar and lemon zest and juice together. Allow to stand for 30 minutes before pouring into the still-warm, blind-baked pastry shell.

Cook for 30 minutes. By this stage the filling will be just set on top. This is the time to remove it from the oven for a perfect consistency. Allow to cool, during which time it will finish setting.

Passionfruit tart
Swap the lemon juice for passionfruit pulp. Strain after sitting for 30 minutes to remove the seeds.

Lime tart
Swap the lemon zest and juice for lime zest and juice.

Raspberry and mascarpone tart
Add 200 g (7 oz) raspberries after pouring the filling into the pastry shell.

Lemon curd tart
Fill the pastry shell with Lemon curd (lemon butter) (page 445) or Passionfruit curd (page 445). Better still, line individual flan (tart) tins with sweet crust pastry and bake blind, then fill with lemon curd.

Lemon tart #2

Few people can say no to a classic lemon tart, especially when it's as delectable as this. Serves 8

3 eggs
150 g (5½ oz) caster (superfine) sugar
Grated zest of 2 lemons
60 ml (2 fl oz/¼ cup) lemon juice
175 g (6 oz) melted butter
100 g (3½ oz) ground almonds
1 × 23 cm (9 in) Sweet crust pastry shell (page 299)
Cream to serve

Preheat the oven to 160°C (320°F).

Beat the eggs and sugar until light and doubled in size, about 10 minutes. Add the lemon zest and juice, butter and almonds, then mix to incorporate.

Pour into the blind-baked tart shell. Bake in the oven for 20–30 minutes, or until golden brown and set. Serve at room temperature with the cream.

Ricotta tart

A simple and easy tart to make, and one that can be adapted in many ways. The list of variations below should keep most tart lovers happy for a long time. Serves 8

250 g (9 oz/1 cup) ricotta

110 g (4 oz) caster (superfine) sugar

3 eggs

1 teaspoon natural vanilla extract

125 ml (4 fl oz/½ cup) pouring (single/light) cream

2 tablespoons plain (all-purpose) flour

Grated zest of 1 lemon

1 × 23 cm (9 in) Sweet crust pastry shell (page 299)

2 tablespoons lemon juice

Ground cinnamon

Preheat the oven to 180°C (350°F).

In a bowl, whisk together the ricotta, caster sugar, eggs, vanilla, cream and flour with the grated zest and lemon juice. Spoon the ricotta mixture into the cooked pastry shell. Sprinkle with cinnamon and bake in the oven for 40 minutes, or until firm.

Quince and ricotta tart
Slice two cooked quinces. Add to the cooked pastry shell, then pour the ricotta mix over.

Port-soaked prune and ricotta tart
Soak 300 g (10½ oz) pitted prunes in 2 tablespoons port for 20 minutes. Add to the cooked pastry shell, then pour the ricotta mixture over.

Other ideas
Add any fruit you like, such as raspberries, pear slices or roasted nectarine wedges. You can also swap the ricotta for fresh goat's curd, mascarpone or fromage frais.

Apricot and frangipane tart

Frangipane is a gorgeous almond tart filling that is delicious on its own and even better when you pour it over roasted apricots. Serves 8

8 ripe apricots, halved and stoned

110 g (4 oz) caster (superfine) sugar, plus
  3 tablespoons caster sugar

100 g (3½ oz) soft butter

2 eggs

100 g (3½ oz/1 cup) ground almonds

1 tablespoon plain (all-purpose) flour

1 × 23 cm (9 in) Sweet crust pastry shell (page 299)

Preheat the oven to 180°C (350°F).

Place the apricot halves on a baking tray, skin side down and sprinkle with the 3 tablespoons sugar. Roast the apricots in the oven for 20–30 minutes, until they soften and brown slightly.

Prepare the frangipane by creaming the butter and sugar until pale. Add the eggs and combine. Add the ground almonds and flour and stir until well combined.

Place the roasted apricot halves, skin side down, in the pastry shell. Spoon the frangipane over them and bake in the oven for 30 minutes, until the frangipane is set and golden brown.

Peach and frangipane tart
Swap the apricots for two peaches. Cut the peaches into wedges and discard the stones. Place them on a baking tray, skin side down. Sprinkle with caster sugar and roast in the oven for 20-30 minutes, until the peaches soften and brown slightly.

Pear and frangipane tart
Substitute poached pear slices for the apricots.

Cherry and frangipane tart
Omit the apricots. Spoon the frangipane mix into the tart shell and then scatter 200 g (7 oz) pitted cherries over the top, pushing down on the cherries to submerge them.

Salted peanut chocolate tart

This tart is incredibly rich so you will only need small slices for each portion. There are a couple of steps to create this dish, but it's well worth it. Serves 8–10

65 g (2¼ oz) brown sugar

100 g (3½ oz) butter

2 tablespoons golden syrup

380 ml (13 fl oz) pouring (single/light) cream

200 g (7 oz) roasted salted peanuts, chopped

1 × 23 cm (9 in) Chocolate sweet crust pastry shell (page 299)

300 g (10½ oz) dark chocolate, chopped

2 tablespoons crunchy peanut butter

200 ml (7 fl oz) thickened (whipping) cream

2 tablespoons icing (confectioners') sugar

½ tablespoon cornflour (cornstarch)

Place the brown sugar, 50 g (1¾ oz) of the butter and the golden syrup in a small saucepan over medium heat and cook until melted. Add 80 ml (2½ fl oz/⅓ cup) of the pouring cream and bring to the boil. Remove and set aside to cool. When cool, stir through the chopped peanuts. Spread into the base of the cooked chocolate pastry shell.

Make a ganache by placing the remaining pouring cream in a saucepan and bringing it to the boil. Pour the hot cream over the chopped chocolate and remaining butter in a bowl, and stir until melted and mixed together. Remove and set aside approximately 125 ml (4 fl oz/½ cup) of the ganache.

Add the peanut butter to the remaining ganache and stir until combined. Beat the thickened cream until soft peaks form and add the icing sugar and cornflour. Fold through the peanut chocolate ganache and spread the mousse over the peanut caramel. Chill until set.

When set, soften the reserved ganache and spread it over the top. Set aside until ready to serve.

Bitter chocolate tarts

These tiny chocolate tarts are incredibly decadent, especially if you can source some gold leaf to decorate the tops. Make them in mini tart shell trays or mini muffin tins and serve with coffee at the end of a meal. Makes 18 tarts

1 quantity Sweet crust pastry dough (page 299)

150 ml (5 fl oz) pouring (single/light) cream

150 g (5½ oz) dark chocolate, chopped

1 teaspoon tokay or brandy

2 egg yolks

Gold leaf (optional)

Preheat the oven to 180°C (350°F).

Roll the pastry out on a lightly floured work surface. Cut out eighteen 7.5 cm (3 in) circles. Lightly butter mini tart shells or mini muffin tins and place a pastry circle in each hole. Press the circles down gently with your fingers. Prick the pastry with a fork.

Cook in the oven for 6–8 minutes, or until the pastry is dry and just beginning to colour. Allow the pastry shells to cool.

Place the cream in a saucepan and bring it to the boil. Remove from the heat and add the chocolate. Whisk until the chocolate is completely melted. Set aside to cool, whisking occasionally.

Whisk in the tokay or brandy and egg yolks. Spoon the chocolate mixture into the tart shells. Allow to cool completely. If desired, decorate with a tiny sprinkling of gold leaf to serve.

Raw coconut and chocolate tart

Not only is this recipe gluten-free, it's dairy-free and contains no processed sugar; in fact you can omit the agave syrup altogether if you like. For the disbelievers of 'raw' desserts, this is a game changer. Use this base for other desserts, such as cheesecakes and banoffee pie, if you want a gluten-free option. You need to use a high-quality coconut cream for this recipe, and it has to be cream because it needs the fat content in order to set. Serves 8

60 g (2 oz/¼ cup) coconut oil, melted

200 g (7 oz/2 cups) ground almonds

1–2 tablespoons agave syrup

250 ml (8½ fl oz/1 cup) coconut cream

225 g (8 oz) dark chocolate (70% cocoa solids), chopped

Lightly grease a 23 cm (9 in) flan (tart) tin with some of the melted coconut oil.

Place the ground almonds and coconut oil in the food processor and whiz until combined. Add enough agave syrup to taste. Place the mixture in the prepared flan tin and refrigerate until set.

Place the coconut cream in a small saucepan over medium heat and bring to the boil. Pour the coconut cream over the chocolate and stir until the chocolate melts and the mixture is smooth. Pour the chocolate–coconut mixture onto the almond base and refrigerate until set.

Remove from the refrigerator approximately 20 minutes before serving, to allow it to soften slightly. Beware on super-hot days, as it may soften too much – if so, simply return to the refrigerator to allow it to set before cutting.

Lemon meringue tart

Italian meringue is a bit harder to prepare than traditional meringue, but worth the effort. Serves 8

4 eggs

185 ml (6 fl oz) thickened (whipping) cream

150 g (5½ oz/⅔ cup) caster (superfine) sugar

100 ml (3½ fl oz) lemon juice

Grated zest of 2 lemons

1 × 23 cm (9 in) Sweet crust pastry shell (page 299), blind-baked (see Apple pie recipe, opposite, for instructions)

Italian meringue

220g (1 cup) caster (superfine) sugar

4 egg whites

Pinch of cream of tartar

Preheat the oven to 160°C (320°F). Make the lemon filling by beating the eggs, cream, sugar, lemon juice and lemon zest together. Pour into the blind-baked tart shell and cook in the oven for 30 minutes or until the filling is just set. Set aside to cool.

Make the Italian meringue by placing the sugar and 200 ml (7 fl oz) water in a small saucepan. Bring to the boil, stirring, until the sugar dissolves. Cook until the syrup reaches hard ball stage (see page 388), 121°C (250°F) on a sugar thermometer (approximately 10 minutes).

While the sugar is cooking, beat the egg whites with the cream of tartar until stiff peaks form. Gradually add the hot syrup to the egg whites, until all the syrup is added and the meringue is thick and glossy. Continue to beat until the meringue cools to room temperature.

Place the cool meringue in a piping (icing) bag and pipe it on top of the lemon filling. You can eat this as is or, if you prefer, you can brown the top of the meringue by either using a cook's blow torch or by placing the tart in a preheated 220°C (430°F) oven or under a hot grill (broiler) until golden brown. Take care as the sugar will burn easily.

Apple pie

Custard powder has an interesting effect on pastry. Firstly it makes it nice and yellow, making it more appealing to the eye, but it also adds a flakiness that is lighter than traditional pastry.

Serves 6–8

300 g (10½ oz (2 cups) plain (all-purpose) flour

40 g (1½ oz/⅓ cup) custard powder

100 g (3½ oz) icing (confectioners') sugar

200 g (7 oz) butter, diced

6 granny smith apples

110 g (4 oz) caster (superfine) sugar plus extra for sprinkling

½ teaspoon ground cinnamon

Egg wash (see page 419)

Sift the flour, custard powder and icing sugar together. Rub in the butter to produce a breadcrumb-like texture. Add enough water to bring the pastry together and knead briefly. Wrap in plastic wrap and chill for 30 minutes.

Peel, core and thinly slice the apples. Place in a saucepan with the caster sugar, cinnamon and 125 ml (4 fl oz/½ cup) water. Bring to the boil, reduce the heat and simmer for 5–10 minutes until the apples are tender, but still holding their shape.

Divide the pastry in half. Roll out one half on a lightly floured work surface to a 3 mm (¼ in) thickness. Either line a greased 23 cm (9 in) pie dish or shallow flan (tart) tin with the pastry, working your fingers around the side of the tin to make sure the pastry is pushed down into the corners. Trim off any excess pastry using a small knife. Return to the refrigerator to rest for 30 minutes. Roll the remaining half to the same thickness.

Preheat the oven to 180°C (350°F).

To blind-bake, prick the base of the pastry shell with a fork. Line with baking paper and then add baking beans or rice. Bake for 15 minutes in the oven. Remove the pastry weights and paper and bake for a further 5 minutes to crisp the pastry.

Add the cooked apples. Top with the remaining pastry, press down the border and then trim the edges into a neat circle. Brush the top with the egg wash and sprinkle with caster sugar. Bake in the oven for 30–40 minutes or until the pastry is cooked and golden brown.

Caramel apple pie
Dot 1 teaspoonful amount of Dulce de leche (page 489) over the top of the cooked apple before covering with pastry.

Apple and raspberry pie
Place cooked apple slices on the cooked pastry base. Arrange 250 g (9 oz/2 cups) fresh raspberries on top. Cover with pastry and continue.

Apple and rhubarb crumble tart
Forget the pastry top, cover with the crumble mix from Nutty rhubarb crumble (page 329) and bake for 15–20 minutes, or until golden brown and crunchy.

Free-form berry tart

Make this with your choice of berries or whatever is in season. I love it with raspberries and blackberries, or gooseberries. But most of all I love it with lashings of runny cream. Serves 4–6

200 g (7 oz/1⅓ cups) plain (all-purpose) flour, plus extra for dusting

125 g (4½ oz) soft butter, diced

Cold water

800 g (1 lb 12 oz) fresh or frozen berries

75 g (2¾ oz) caster (superfine) sugar

Egg wash (see page 419)

Cream to serve

Sift the flour with a pinch of salt, then rub in the butter to produce a breadcrumb-like texture. Add enough water to bring the pastry together, then knead briefly. Wrap in plastic wrap and chill for 30 minutes.

Preheat the oven to 200°C (400°F).

Roll out the pastry on a lightly floured work surface to form a rough circle, 5 mm (¼ in) thick. Place the pastry on a flat, buttered baking tray. Arrange the berries in the middle, sprinkle them with caster sugar and pinch the pastry up to overlap and form sides (don't expect them to meet in the middle).

Brush the edges of the pastry with the egg wash. Bake in the oven for 30–35 minutes, or until the pastry is cooked and golden brown. Serve with cream.

Fruit mince pies

What would Christmas celebrations be without a few mince pies to munch on? Makes 18

75 g (2¾ oz/½ cup) currants

90 g (3 oz/¾ cup) sultanas (golden raisins)

½ apple, grated

40 g (1½ oz/¼ cup) blanched almonds

50 g (1¾ oz) brown sugar

½ teaspoon ground cinnamon

Grated zest of 1 lemon

Grated zest of 1 orange

1 tablespoon lemon juice

1 tablespoon orange juice

1 tablespoon brandy or rum (optional)

1 quantity Sweet crust pastry dough (page 299)

Egg wash (see page 419)

2–3 tablespoons caster (superfine) sugar

Combine the fruits, almonds, brown sugar, cinnamon, citrus zests and juice and alcohol (if using). Stir well and set aside to macerate for 2 hours. This step can be done weeks, if not months, in advance. The longer the macerating, the better the final flavour.

Preheat the oven to 180°C (350°F).

Roll two-thirds of the pastry out on a lightly floured work surface. Cut out eighteen 7.5 cm (3 in) circles. Lightly butter mini tart shells or mini muffin tins and place a pastry circle in each hole. Press the circles down gently with your fingers. Prick the pastry with a fork. Cook in the oven for 6–8 minutes, or until the pastry is dry and just beginning to colour. Allow the pastry shells to cool.

Fill the shells with the fruit mince. Roll the remaining pastry out and cut it into 5 cm (2 in) circles or stars and place it on top of the fruit mince. Brush the pastry pie tops with the egg wash and sprinkle with the caster sugar. Bake in the oven for 6–8 minutes, or until the pastry tops are cooked.

Shortbread-topped mince pies
Make some Shortbread dough (page 391), roll it out to a 3 mm (⅛ in) thickness and cut out stars to place on top of each pie.

Tarte tatin

This is without a doubt the most incredible upside-down apple pie experience you're ever likely to have. Ideally, you need a 22 cm (8¾ in) Le Creuset or deep-sided cast-iron pan for this recipe. If you have neither of these, cook the apples in a heavy-based frying pan, then tip them into a similar-sized pie dish and top with pastry. Serves 6

½ quantity Rough puff pastry (page 300)
75 g (2¾ oz) butter
150 g (5½ oz) caster (superfine) sugar
4 apples, peeled, cored and cut into eighths
Egg wash (see page 419)
Thick (double/heavy) cream to serve

Preheat the oven to 190°C (375°F).

Roll out the pastry to a 5 mm (¼ in) thickness and set aside to rest for 30 minutes.

Heat a 22 cm (8¾ in) cast-iron pan (or a heavy-based frying pan) over medium–high heat, add the butter and sugar and cook for 8–10 minutes, stirring constantly. Cook until the sugar and butter have cooked to a golden caramel colour. Carefully add the apple pieces, watching out for splashes, and cook for just 2–3 minutes, stirring or tossing the pan to coat the apples with the caramel. The apples will begin to release their juice and stop the caramel overcooking.

Set the pan aside to cool a little. Either leave the apples in the pan you cooked them in, or transfer to a 22 cm (8¾ in) pie dish. Place the pastry over the apples and tuck down the sides to completely cover the apples. Trim the excess pastry away. Brush the pastry with the egg wash and place in the oven. Cook for 20–25 minutes, or until the pastry is risen, golden brown and cooked. Remove from the oven.

To serve, place a large plate or platter over the pan or pie dish. Then, using oven gloves or tea towels (dish towels), tip the pan over and remove the pie, leaving the apples on top and the pastry on the bottom. Take care, as this is very hot. Serve immediately with thick cream.

Berry and almond tart

This is where frozen puff pastry comes in handy. This is an impressive dessert made from ingredients on hand. Serves 4

1 sheet butter puff pastry
300 g (10½ oz) frozen berries

Frangipane
100 g (3½ oz) soft butter
110 g (4 oz) caster (superfine) sugar
Grated zest of 1 lemon
2 egg yolks
100 g (3½ oz/1 cup) ground almonds

Preheat the oven to 200°C (400°F). Line a baking tray with baking paper.

Place the puff pastry on the prepared tray and prick it with a fork. Place another tray on top of the pastry to weigh it down and bake in the oven for 15–20 minutes, until brown and cooked through.

Prepare the frangipane by beating the butter, sugar and lemon zest until creamy. Add the egg yolks and ground almonds and stir to combine.

Spread the frangipane thinly over the cooked pastry sheet. Scatter the berries over the top. Bake in the oven for 25–30 minutes until lightly browned.

Peach and raspberry puff pastry squares

A summery dessert making the most of the in-season fruits. Peaches and raspberries are a classic combination. Serves 4

1 sheet butter puff pastry

Raspberry sauce (page 487)

2 peaches

Caster (superfine) sugar

Egg wash (see page 419)

Preheat the oven to 180°C (350°F). Line a baking tray with baking paper.

Cut the puff pastry sheet into four squares. Place a spoonful of raspberry sauce in the centre of each square. Cut the peaches in half and thinly slice each half. Place the sliced peach half on top of the raspberry sauce. Brush the exposed puff pastry with the egg wash and fold the outside edge in, to form a border. Sprinkle with the caster sugar.

Place the squares on the prepared baking tray and bake in the oven for 20–25 minutes or until they are crisp and golden brown.

Toffee pear galettes
Substitute pears for the peaches and swap the raspberry sauce for Dulce de leche (page 489).

Chocolate éclairs

I'm a big fan of a well-made chocolate éclair and have been known to travel quite a distance to my favourite cake shop to get a fix. Alternatively, I whip up a batch at home and indulge to my heart's content. Makes 12–15

1 quantity Choux pastry (page 301)

1 quantity Thick custard (pastry cream) (page 490)

1 quantity Chocolate ganache (page 492)

Preheat the oven to 200°C (400°F).

Pipe 8 cm (3¼ in) lengths of choux pastry onto lined baking trays. Place the trays in the oven at the same time. It is important not to open the door during the first 10 minutes of cooking, as cold draughts will make the pastry sink.

Cook the éclairs for 10 minutes, then reduce the oven temperature to 180°C (350°F). Cook for another 10 minutes, then try one. They should be quite brown (more than golden brown) and relatively dry inside. Resist the urge to take them out too soon, as they will end up doughy inside. When ready, set aside to cool.

Spoon the thick custard into a piping (icing) bag, if you have one, then poke the piping nozzle into the choux pastry base and squeeze to fill the éclairs with the thick custard. If not using a piping bag, slit the éclairs with a knife and fill with custard.

Spread ganache over the top of each éclair to finish.

Passionfruit éclairs
Swap the ganache for Passionfruit icing (page 491).

Coffee éclairs
Swap the ganache for Coffee icing (page 491).

Profiteroles with white chocolate and raspberries

In this great variation on the theme of choux pastry profiteroles, the profiteroles are filled with white chocolate custard, drizzled with white chocolate sauce, then scattered with raspberries. This would be a sensational dessert to complete a summer dinner party. Makes 30

1 quantity Choux pastry (page 301)

2 egg yolks

55 g (2 oz/¼ cup) caster (superfine) sugar

1 tablespoon plain (all-purpose) flour

500 ml (17 fl oz/2 cups) milk

½ teaspoon natural vanilla extract

100 g (3½ oz) white chocolate, chopped

1 quantity White chocolate sauce (page 489)

300 g (10½ oz) raspberries

Preheat the oven to 200°C (400°F).

Spoon teaspoonfuls of choux pastry onto lined baking trays. Place the trays in the oven at the same time. It is important not to open the door during the first 10 minutes of cooking, as cold draughts will make the pastry sink.

Cook the profiteroles for 10 minutes, then reduce the oven temperature to 180°C (350°F). Cook for another 10 minutes, then try one. They should be quite brown (more than golden brown) and relatively dry inside. Resist the urge to take them out too soon, because you will not fit enough cream in them if they are doughy inside. When ready, set aside to cool.

Beat the egg yolks and caster sugar together until pale, then stir in the flour until smooth.

In a saucepan, bring the milk and vanilla to the boil. Whisk the hot milk into the egg yolk mixture and return to a clean saucepan over low heat. Stir constantly as the custard comes to the boil and thickens. Remove from the heat. Add the chopped chocolate and stir until it dissolves.

When cold, spoon the custard into a piping (icing) bag, if you have one, then poke the piping nozzle into the choux pastry base and squeeze to fill each one. If not using a piping bag, slit the profiteroles with a knife and fill with custard. Refrigerate until ready to serve.

To serve, either arrange three to four profiteroles on each plate (piled if you wish) or the entire batch on a large platter. Warm the chocolate sauce until it melts, then drizzle it over the profiteroles. Scatter the raspberries over and serve.

Passionfruit profiteroles
Fill the pastry balls with Passionfruit curd (page 445) and drizzle with Lemon icing (page 491).

Egyptian bread and butter pudding

This bread and butter pudding is quite different from the typical version, and unlike any other filo pastry dish in general. Try it once – you'll love it. Serves 6–8

100 g (3½ oz) (8–10 sheets) filo pastry
50 g (1¾ oz) melted butter
60 g (2 oz/⅓ cup) dried apricots, diced
60 g (2 oz/½ cup) sultanas (golden raisins)
30 g (1 oz/⅓ cup) flaked almonds, toasted
30 g (1 oz) shelled pistachio nuts, toasted
30 g (1 oz) pine nuts, toasted
500 ml (17 fl oz/2 cups) milk
150 ml (5 fl oz) thickened (whipping) cream
55 g (2 oz/¼ cup) caster (superfine) sugar
2 tablespoons pomegranate molasses
Freshly grated nutmeg

Preheat the oven to 160°C (320°F). Line two baking trays with baking paper.

Brush each sheet of filo with butter, crumple loosely and arrange on the prepared baking trays. Bake in the oven for 20 minutes, or until crisp and golden.

Increase the oven temperature to 220°C (430°F).

Butter a 20 cm (8 in) pie dish. Crumple the filo sheets, retaining some largish pieces. Mix together the dried fruit and nuts and layer alternately with the filo pastry in the pie dish.

Place the milk, cream and sugar in a saucepan over medium heat and bring to the boil. Pour the boiling milk over the pastry and fruit, drizzle with pomegranate molasses and sprinkle the nutmeg over. Bake in the oven for 15–20 minutes.

Pistachio, almond and orange blossom baklava

This recipe is inspired by Claudia Roden's *A New Book of Middle Eastern Food*. This book is well worth checking out if you're at all interested in food of the Middle East. Serves 12

220 g (8 oz) caster (superfine) sugar
60 ml (2 fl oz/¼ cup) lemon juice
1 tablespoon orange blossom water
325 g (11½ oz/3¼ cups) ground almonds
100 g (3½ oz) ground pistachio nuts
½ teaspoon ground coriander
125 g (4½ oz) melted butter
8 filo pastry sheets, cut in half

Preheat the oven to 170°C (340°F).

Make orange blossom syrup by placing the sugar, 125 ml (4 fl oz/½ cup) water and the lemon juice in a saucepan. Simmer until the sugar has dissolved. Allow to cool completely, then stir in the orange blossom water. Set aside.

Mix together the ground almonds, pistachio nuts and ground coriander.

Brush a 24 × 22 cm (9½ × 8¾ in) baking dish with the melted butter. Lay two sheets of filo in the bottom. Sprinkle a thin layer of nuts on top, folding the hanging edges over. Place two sheets of filo on top and brush with melted butter. Continue adding layers of nuts and filo until all the ingredients are used. Finish with a layer of pastry. Brush the top with plenty of butter.

With a sharp knife, cut the baklava into small diamond shapes and bake in the oven for 45 minutes.

When the baklava comes out of the oven, pour the orange blossom syrup over and allow to cool completely. To serve, run a knife along the lines previously cut and cut into diamond-shaped pieces.

Kataifi nests with sweet labne and rosewater-poached rhubarb

Despite all the small steps, this is an easy dessert to make, and very impressive. You can also increase the recipe to serve more by making extra nests and rhubarb. Serves 6

375 g (13 oz/1⅔ cups) natural yoghurt

1½ teaspoons ground cardamom

1 tablespoon icing (confectioners') sugar

½ teaspoon ground allspice

½ tablespoon caster (superfine) sugar

75 g (2¾ oz) ground almonds

200 g (7 oz) kataifi pastry

150 g (5½ oz) melted butter

Poached rhubarb

110 g (4 oz) caster (superfine) sugar

2 tablespoons rosewater

8 stems of rhubarb, cut into 3 cm (1¼ in) lengths

Make the sweet labne by mixing the yoghurt, 1 teaspoon of the cardamom and the icing sugar together. Set a sieve over a bowl, and line it with muslin (cheesecloth) or a clean tea towel (dish towel). Spoon the yoghurt into the sieve, cover and refrigerate for at least 4 hours, to allow the whey to drip through the cloth.

Preheat oven to 180°C (350°F).

Mix together the remaining cardamom, allspice, caster sugar and ground almonds.

Take the kataifi pastry and divide it into six 20 cm (8 in) lengths, approximately 2 cm (¾ in) wide. Drizzle melted butter over the pastry and sprinkle the almond mixture over. Twirl the pastry up to form circular 'nests'. Transfer to a lined baking tray. Drizzle with a little extra butter. Bake in the oven until crisp, about 10–12 minutes. Remove and set aside.

To poach the rhubarb, put 750 ml (25½ fl oz/3 cups) water, the caster sugar and the rosewater in a large saucepan. Cook over low heat until the sugar dissolves, then bring to the boil. Add the rhubarb pieces and cook gently – you want the rhubarb to retain its shape. Remove the rhubarb when tender and set aside.

Return the syrup to the heat and cook until reduced by half. Return the rhubarb to the syrup when the syrup is cool.

Remove the labne from the cloth in the refrigerator and discard the whey (liquid). Arrange a nest of pastry on each plate and add a spoonful of labne in the centre. Arrange five to six pieces of rhubarb around the nest, drizzle with a spoonful of the poaching syrup and serve.

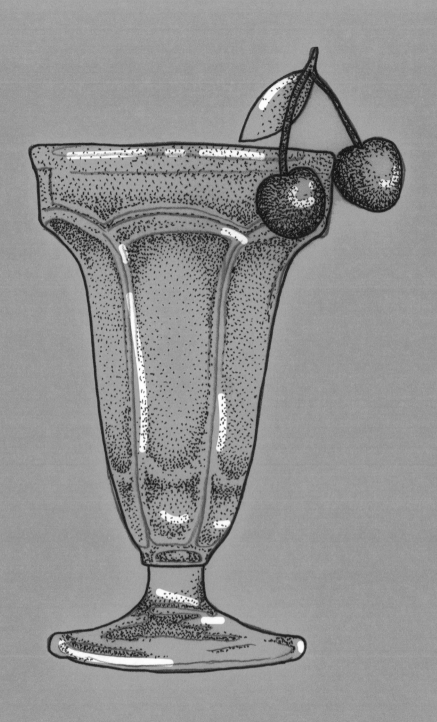

Desserts & puddings

Whether it's a platter of fresh fruit or a simple apple or slice of watermelon, fruit is the ultimate quick and easy dessert. Other quick dessert staples are ice cream or yoghurt. Then there are the more decadent delights, such as mousses, soufflés and trifle.

For the sweet tooth

If you have a sweet tooth, this is the chapter for you. You'll find all manner of delights, from crumbles and luscious puddings, to tarts and fruit desserts.

Chocolate is just about everyone's passion and you can spend as much or as little as you can afford on this ingredient. Always buy dark chocolate for cooking (unless of course the recipe specifically calls for milk or white chocolate) – the packet will have a percentage number, which indicates the level of cocoa solids in the chocolate. The higher the percentage the better the chocolate and the health qualities it possesses, such as the alkaloids that have a physiological effect on the body and the serotonin levels in the brain. Dark chocolate also contains a high level of antioxidants, which reduce the production of free radicals in the body. Typical milk chocolate contains at least 25 per cent milk solids and most dark chocolates start at 60 per cent.

Take care when melting chocolate. You can do it in the microwave on Low, in bursts, or by placing it in a bowl over a simmering pan of water (but don't let the water come in contact with the bottom of the bowl). Either way is fine, but slow and steady wins the race or the chocolate may seize.

The recipes in this chapter can be mixed and matched to make amazing flavour combinations. Poached quinces (page 327) can be served with Vanilla panna cotta (page 332), or Rosewater meringues (page 411) can be served with Chocolate mousse (page 330). Also check out the Pastry (page 295), Cakes (page 357) and Cookies & slices (page 385) chapters for more sweet ideas.

Things to remember
about desserts & puddings

- Never be afraid to try something new. However, it's best to tackle the more complicated desserts only when time permits.

- Leaf gelatine is miles better than powdered, which often doesn't dissolve easily and has an unusual taste. (All of my recipes use titanium-strength leaves that weigh 5 g/¼ oz.)

- A tub of ice cream in the freezer can be your stand-by dessert if you have a complete failure in the kitchen. Melt some good-quality chocolate and cream together to make a ganache to serve over the top of your ice cream for an instant dessert.

Quick dessert ideas

Here are some ideas for simple desserts for those times when you have unexpected guests or just have a craving for something sweet.

- Vanilla ice cream (page 349) with fresh berries and Raspberry sauce (page 487)

- Sliced bananas, Simple chocolate ice cream (page 348) and Butterscotch sauce (page 488)

- Strawberries tossed with 1–2 tablespoons balsamic vinegar

- Affogato – Vanilla ice cream (page 349) with a shot of espresso and liqueur

- Make banana splits with ice cream, Chocolate sauce (page 489) or Dulce de leche (page 489) and flaked toasted almonds

- Cut fresh figs in half, top with a splash of sweet wine and serve with Vanilla ice cream (page 349)

- Sprinkle plums with ground cinnamon, ground ginger and sugar and roast until tender. Serve with cream.

- Make a rhubarb fool by folding whipped cream through rhubarb purée

- Try a shot of limoncello over Vanilla ice cream (page 349) for a great adult dessert

- Segment blood oranges and add 1 tablespoon of shredded mint and 1 tablespoon orange blossom water

- Poach a bunch of rhubarb with a splash of water and 55 g (2 oz/¼ cup) caster (superfine) sugar. Once cooked, remove and add 125 g (4½ oz) halved strawberries and 2 tablespoons rosewater

Dessert & pudding recipes

Vanilla poached fruit

Poaching fruit is extremely easy – it's nothing more than heating water and sugar in a saucepan, adding a few aromatic spices if you feel like it, and then simmering the fruit of your choice until it's tender. This will take anything from 5 minutes for berries, to up to 1½ hours for quinces. Poached fruit retains its shape during cooking; that's why I prefer it to stewed fruit, which disintegrates during cooking. Try berries, cherries, apricots, rhubarb, pineapple, peaches, pears or plums. Serves 4

---

220 g (8 oz) caster (superfine) sugar
Juice of 1 lemon
1 vanilla bean cut in half lengthways
500 g (1 lb 2 oz) fruit, cut into pieces if needed

Place 500 ml (17 fl oz/2 cups) water, the sugar, lemon juice and vanilla bean in a large heavy-based saucepan over medium heat. Stir until the sugar is dissolved. Bring to a gentle boil.

Place the fruit in the poaching syrup and cook until just softened. Remove and either serve warm with some of the poaching liquid or allow to cool and serve in the strained poaching liquid.

Spiced poached fruit
Add cardamom pods, cinnamon sticks, star anise, sliced fresh ginger or even chillies to add a touch of spice.

Dessert wine poached fruit
Substitute half the water with dessert wine and reduce the sugar by half.

Poached pears with chocolate
Peel, quarter and core four pears and poach in liquid for 15-20 minutes. Serve the warm pears with Chocolate sauce (page 489).

Poached quinces

Bright yellow quinces are one of my favourite autumn (fall) fruits – not only because their perfume will scent a room for weeks, but also because of the incredible transformation they undergo during cooking. Virtually rock hard and inedible when ripe, they develop a deep ruby-red colour and an intense, glorious flavour as a result of poaching. Serves 4–6

---

220 g (8 oz) caster (superfine) sugar
1 vanilla bean, split lengthways and seeds scraped
1 lemon, cut in half
2 cloves
4–6 quinces
Cream or Vanilla ice cream (page 349) to serve

Prepare the poaching liquid by placing 1 litre (34 fl oz/4 cups) water, the sugar, vanilla bean and seeds, lemon and cloves in a large heavy-based saucepan. Bring the liquid to a rolling boil.

Peel, quarter and core the fruit, adding the quinces immediately to the poaching liquid to prevent discolouration. Reduce to a simmer, cover and cook for about 1½ hours, or until the quinces are tender and ruby red.

Serve the quinces with a little of the strained warm syrup along with cream or vanilla ice cream.

Sugar-roasted stone fruit with fresh cheese and honey

This is one of my favourite easy-to-prepare desserts. Roasting the stone fruit with a little sugar on top intensifies all the natural flavours. It is best done in summer when stone fruit is at its best; ripe nectarines, plums, peaches or apricots will all work a treat. Serves 4–6

8 nectarines or peaches, or 16 apricots or small plums
55 g (2 oz/¼ cup) caster (superfine) sugar
100 g (3½ oz/½ cup) ricotta or goat's curd
Full-flavoured honey

Preheat the oven to 200°C (400°F).

Cut the fruit in half and remove the stones. Place the fruit halves, flesh side up, on a baking tray. Sprinkle the sugar on top. Place in the oven and cook for 20–30 minutes, or until the fruit is beginning to brown on top.

Place the sugar-roasted fruit on a platter, spoon a dollop of ricotta or curd into the centre of each, then drizzle with honey.

Spiced roasted stone fruit
Sprinkle ground cinnamon, freshly grated nutmeg, allspice, cardamom or ground ginger onto the fruit before cooking.

Sugar-grilled stone fruit
Cook the stone fruit under a hot grill (broiler) for 3-4 minutes.

Baked plums with amaretti biscuits

Plums are best for this simple but stunning dessert, but you can use nectarines or peaches if you prefer. I had the most success with this recipe when I used the giant plums that appear towards the end of the stone-fruit season in early autumn (fall). Serves 4

8 plums, halved and stoned
75 g (2¾ oz) amaretti biscuits
2 tablespoons brown or raw sugar
40 g (1½ oz) butter, diced
Pinch of ground cinnamon
Pinch of grated nutmeg
2 tablespoons sweet sherry
185 ml (6 fl oz/¾ cup) pouring (single/light) cream
150 g (5½ oz) mascarpone
1 tablespoon icing (confectioners') sugar

Preheat the oven to 200°C (400°F).

Place the plum halves, flesh side up, in a deep baking dish so they fit snugly.

Crush the amaretti biscuits with your hands and place them in a bowl along with the brown sugar, butter and spices. Toss to combine.

Spoon the amaretti crumble into the plums. Don't worry if some of the filling spills into the base of the baking dish. Drizzle half the sweet sherry over the top and bake in the oven for 15–20 minutes, or until the crumble mixture is golden brown and the plums have cooked through.

Whip the cream until it forms soft peaks. Fold through the mascarpone, icing sugar and remaining sweet sherry.

Serve two plum halves per person with a dollop of the sherry cream.

Rhubarb crumble

Rhubarb crumble is probably the most popular of all crumbles (along with apple). Crumbles are a great thing for teenagers to try if they show an interest in cooking, as they are virtually foolproof.
Serves 4

1 bunch of rhubarb
55 g (2 oz/¼ cup) caster (superfine) sugar
150 g (5½ oz) soft butter, diced
250 g (9 oz/1⅔ cups) plain (all-purpose) flour
150 g (5½ oz/¾ cup firmly packed) soft brown sugar
Cream or custard to serve

Trim off the leaves and root ends from the rhubarb and cut the stems into 2 cm (¾ in) chunks.

Heat a heavy-based saucepan over medium heat. Add the rhubarb, sugar and 2 tablespoons water. Reduce the heat to low, cover with a lid and cook for 5–10 minutes, stirring often. Remove from the heat and allow to cool.

Preheat the oven to 180°C (350°F).

Using your fingertips, rub together the soft butter, flour and brown sugar until they resemble fine breadcrumbs.

Place the stewed rhubarb in a baking dish, top with the crumble mixture and bake in the oven for 20 minutes, or until golden brown. Serve with cream or custard.

Nutty rhubarb crumble
Add 60 g (2 oz/⅔ cup) flaked almonds or chopped hazelnuts to the crumble mix.

Rhubarb and raspberry crumble
Add 200 g (7 oz) raspberries to the cooked rhubarb.

Rhubarb oat crumble
Substitute 60 g (2 oz/⅓ cup) of the flour with rolled (porridge) oats.

Cinnamon rhubarb crumble
Add 1 teaspoon ground cinnamon to the crumble mix.

Apple and cinnamon crumble
Substitute the rhubarb with six peeled, cored and sliced apples and add ½ teaspoon ground cinnamon.

Quince crumble
Swap the rhubarb for four cooked and sliced quinces. A combination of rhubarb and quince is also lovely.

Pear, chocolate and hazelnut crumble
Substitute rhubarb for four cooked and sliced pears. Add 90 g (3 oz/½ cup) small chocolate chips and 65 g (2¼ oz/½ cup) chopped hazelnuts to the crumble topping.

Lemon mousse

Fruit mousses are seen as fairly old-fashioned – the sort of thing Grandma used to serve up. It's a pity, as mousses are easy to make and last for a couple of days in the refrigerator. They can be made with almost any fruit, are light as air and perfect in warmer weather or after a big meal. Serves 4–6

2 × 5 g (¼ oz) gelatine sheets

Grated zest of 2 lemons

125 ml (4 fl oz/½ cup) lemon juice

3 eggs, separated

110 g (4 oz) caster (superfine) sugar

250 ml (8½ fl oz/1 cup) thickened (whipping) cream

Soak the gelatine in cold water for 2 minutes. Squeeze well to remove the excess water. Place the lemon zest and juice in a small saucepan and bring to the boil over medium heat. Remove from the heat, add the soaked gelatine and stir until dissolved.

Whisk the egg yolks and sugar until pale and creamy. Fold the lemon mixture into the egg yolks. Beat the egg whites until stiff. Whip the cream until soft peaks form.

Add a spoonful of cream and egg whites to the lemon base. Stir until well combined; this will allow you to fold the remaining egg whites and cream in without losing their 'air'. Gently fold in the remaining egg whites and cream. Spoon into serving bowl(s). Refrigerate until set, about 3–4 hours, or overnight.

Passionfruit mousse
Reduce the lemon zest by half and substitute strained passionfruit pulp for the lemon juice.

Chocolate mousse

A good chocolate mousse is a joy to behold – and to eat, of course. This is my favourite chocolate mousse because it tastes brilliant, it's incredibly simple to make and it can easily have lots of other flavours added to it. Serve with fresh raspberries and cream. Serves 4

3 egg yolks

55 g (2 oz/¼ cup) caster (superfine) sugar

200 g (7 oz) dark chocolate, chopped

250 ml (8½ fl oz/1 cup) thickened (whipping) cream

Place the egg yolks and sugar in a bowl set over a saucepan of simmering water. Whisk continuously for 6–8 minutes until the mixture thickens and the eggs cook through. Melt the chocolate by placing it in a bowl over a saucepan of simmering water or in a microwave on Low for 1–2 minutes. Add the egg mixture to the melted chocolate and whisk to combine.

Whip the cream until soft peaks form. Add a spoonful of cream to the chocolate mixture and beat it in; this will allow you to fold in the remaining cream without losing its 'air'. Gently fold in the remaining cream, spoon into a serving dish and allow to set in the refrigerator for 2–3 hours or overnight.

Chocolate coffee mousse
Add 2 tablespoons strong black coffee to the melted chocolate with the egg yolks.

Jaffa mousse
Add the finely grated zest of two oranges to the melted chocolate.

Chocolate brandy mousse
Add 2 tablespoons brandy to the egg yolks.

Frozen chocolate mousse
Line a loaf (bar) tin with plenty of plastic wrap, leaving lots of overhang. Spoon the chocolate mousse into the tin and smooth the top. Completely cover the top of the mousse with plastic wrap and freeze overnight. Cut into thin slices to serve.

Pedro Ximénez chocolate mousse
Add 2 tablespoons Pedro Ximénez to the egg yolks.

Coffee and cardamom mousse

I am keen on blending the flavours of coffee and cardamom, so you'll find it in lots of my dessert recipes, including here in this mousse. Serve with Orange and walnut florentines (page 393). Serves 4–6

2 × 5 g (¼ oz) gelatine sheets

125 ml (4 fl oz/½ cup) hot strong black coffee

3 eggs, separated

80 g (2¾ oz/⅓ cup) caster (superfine) sugar

¼ teaspoon ground cardamom

250 g (9 oz) mascarpone

Soak the gelatine in cold water for 2 minutes. Squeeze well to remove the excess water.

Add the soaked gelatine to the hot coffee, stir well to dissolve, then strain. Set aside until cool and just beginning to set, about 10–15 minutes.

Beat the egg yolks, sugar and cardamom until white and creamy. Add the mascarpone and the cooled coffee mixture. Mix well.

Beat the egg whites until stiff peaks form. Stir 1 tablespoon egg white into the coffee mixture, then fold the rest through gently. Spoon into serving bowl(s) and allow to set in the refrigerator.

Chocolate soufflé

I expect that the name 'chocolate soufflé' might get your attention, but you will put it in the too-hard basket before you move on to the next page. Well, don't! This way of making a soufflé is how I was taught at catering college, and if 17-year-old apprentices can make it, so can you. Go on, give it a go, just this once. Serves 6

2 eggs, separated, plus 2 extra egg whites

55 g (2 oz/¼ cup) caster (superfine) sugar, plus extra for sprinkling

2 tablespoons plain (all-purpose) flour

500 ml (17 fl oz/2 cups) milk

125 g (4½ oz) dark chocolate, chopped

Grease six 175 ml (6 fl oz) ramekins with butter, then sprinkle them with caster sugar.

In a bowl, beat the egg yolks and sugar until pale. Stir in the flour until smooth.

Put the milk and chocolate in a saucepan over medium heat, until the chocolate melts. Whisk the milk into the egg yolk mixture and return to a clean saucepan over low heat. Stir constantly while the custard comes to the boil and thickens. Remove from the heat.

Preheat the oven to 200°C (400°F).

Whip all the egg whites until stiff, then carefully fold them into the warm chocolate mixture.

Place the buttered soufflé dishes on a flat baking tray. Divide the soufflé mixture between the dishes, allowing room for rising. Cook in the oven until the soufflés are well risen and firm to the touch, about 12–15 minutes. Remove the soufflés carefully from the oven and serve immediately.

Coffee soufflé
Omit the chocolate. Instead add 2–3 tablespoons strong black coffee to the milk as it comes to the boil.

Raspberry soufflé
Omit the chocolate. Purée 60 g (2 oz/½ cup) raspberries and strain to remove the seeds. Stir the purée into the cooked custard. Scatter a few extra raspberries on top of each soufflé as they go into the oven.

Tiramisu

This creamy, chocolate and coffee–flavoured Italian trifle is always popular, and there is almost no cooking involved, other than making the coffee. Serves 4–6

6 egg yolks

55 g (2 oz/¼ cup) caster (superfine) sugar

500 g (1 lb 2 oz) mascarpone

125 ml (4 fl oz/½ cup) strong black coffee

60 ml (2 fl oz/¼ cup) sweet marsala or Baileys

250 ml (8½ fl oz/1 cup) thickened (whipping) cream

24 Italian sponge finger biscuits (savoiardi)

Unsweetened (Dutch) cocoa powder or grated chocolate

Beat the egg yolks with the sugar until pale and creamy. Gently whisk in the mascarpone.

Mix the coffee and marsala together.

Whip the cream to firm peaks, then fold this into the mascarpone mixture.

Lay half the sponge fingers in the bottom of a 1.5 litre (51 fl oz/6 cup) serving dish and drizzle with half of the coffee. Pour half the mascarpone mixture over. Top with the remaining biscuits and drizzle with the remaining coffee. Top with the remaining mascarpone mixture.

Refrigerate for 3–4 hours to allow the flavours to develop fully. Sift the cocoa over the top just before serving.

Vanilla panna cotta

This is a simple yet stylish dessert, which you can add just about any flavouring to, such as citrus zest, spices or flavour extracts. Serve with fresh berries, figs or roasted stone fruit. Serves 6

375 ml (12½ fl oz/1½ cups) milk

375 ml (12½ fl oz/1½ cups) thickened (whipping) cream

80 g (2¾ oz/⅓ cup) caster (superfine) sugar

1 teaspoon natural vanilla extract

3 × 5 g (¼ oz) gelatine sheets

Soak the gelatine sheets in cold water for 2–3 minutes or until soft, then squeeze out the excess water and set aside.

Bring the milk, cream, sugar and vanilla to the boil in a saucepan. Remove from the heat. Add the gelatine and stir until dissolved. Strain the liquid, then pour into six 125 ml (4 fl oz/½ cup) moulds. Refrigerate overnight.

To serve, use a small spatula or knife to work the puddings away from the edges of the moulds, then stand the moulds in boiling water for 4–5 seconds. Place a plate on top of each mould, then turn over carefully so the plate is on the bottom. Shake to dislodge the pudding. Remove the mould and serve with fruit of your choice.

Buttermilk panna cotta
Swap the milk for buttermilk.

Rosewater panna cotta
Add 2 tablespoons rosewater to the strained milk mixture.

Lime panna cotta
Add the chopped zest of two limes to the milk mixture, then bring to the boil.

Coffee panna cotta
Swap 125 ml (4 fl oz/½ cup) of the milk for strong black coffee. Add two crushed cardamom pods to the milk mixture.

Jelly-topped panna cotta
Heat 125 ml (4 fl oz/½ cup) fruit juice, such as raspberry, add one 5 g (¼ oz) gelatine sheet and stir to dissolve. Divide between seven 125 ml (4 fl oz/½ cup) moulds and set. Pour the cool panna cotta onto the firm jelly and refrigerate until set.

Coconut panna cotta
Swap the cream for coconut cream. This is particularly yummy served with Poached quinces (page 327).

Yoghurt panna cotta with caramelised peaches

A tangy twist on the classic panna cotta. Be sure to use a good quality-natural yoghurt.
Serves 6

2 × 5 g (¼ oz) sheets gelatine
250 ml (8½ fl oz/1 cup) pouring (light/single) cream
80 g (2¾ oz/⅓ cup) caster (superfine) sugar
1 teaspoon natural vanilla extract
375 (13 oz/1½ cups) natural yoghurt
6 peaches
Icing (confectioners') sugar for sprinkling
Salted praline (page 413), chopped

Soak the gelatine sheets in cold water for 2–3 minutes or until soft, then squeeze out the excess water and set aside.

Bring the cream, caster sugar and vanilla to the boil. Remove from the heat. Add the gelatine and stir until dissolved. Strain the liquid, whisk in the yoghurt and then pour into six 125 ml (4 fl oz/½ cup) dariole moulds. Refrigerate until set, for at least 4 hours, or overnight.

To serve, preheat a grill (broiler) to hot.

Cut the peaches in half and remove the stones. Sprinkle the cut side lightly with icing sugar. Cook under the hot grill for 5–10 minutes, or until the peaches just begin to brown.

Use a small spatula or knife to work the puddings away from the edges of the moulds, then stand the moulds in boiling water for 4–5 seconds. Place a plate on top of each mould, then turn each one over carefully so the plate is on the bottom. Shake to dislodge the panna cotta. Remove the moulds.

Serve two peach halves alongside the panna cotta and sprinkle the chopped praline over the top.

Wobbly berry jelly

I love jellies as they look very impressive and are easy to make. They are best made the day before to ensure they set well. You could set the jelly in a kugelhopf tin or other decoratively shaped mould. Serves 8

5 × 5 g (¼ oz) gelatine sheets
110 g (4 oz) caster (superfine) sugar
375 ml (12½ fi oz/1½ cups) dessert wine
600 g (1 lb 5 oz) mixed berries – raspberries,
  blueberries and strawberries

Soak the gelatine sheets in cold water for 2–3 minutes or until soft, then squeeze out the excess water and set aside.

Put the sugar and 500 ml (17 fl oz/2 cups) water in a saucepan and cook over low heat to dissolve the sugar. Bring to the boil, add the dessert wine and bring back to the boil. If you want to evaporate most of the alcohol in the wine, continue boiling for 5 minutes. If not, remove from the heat, add the gelatine and stir until dissolved. Strain into a jug and allow to cool slightly – you don't want to pour hot liquid over the berries as this will cook and soften them.

Wash the berries and drain well; if necessary, cut the strawberries in half. Divide the berries equally between eight 125 ml (4 fl oz/½ cup) dariole moulds. Pour the just-warm liquid over and cover the moulds. Refrigerate to set, for at least 4–6 hours, or overnight.

Use a small spatula or knife to work the jellies away from the edges of the moulds, and then stand the moulds in boiling water for 4–5 seconds. Place a plate on top of each mould, then turn over carefully so the plate is on the bottom. Shake to dislodge the jelly.

Crème caramel

Crème caramel is a light, refreshing dessert. Do you need more temptation? No? Good, then make it tonight. Serves 6

145 g (5 oz/⅔ cup) caster (superfine) sugar
600 ml (20½ fl oz/2⅓ cups) milk
½ teaspoon natural vanilla extract
Grated zest of 1 orange
3 eggs
3 egg yolks

Place 90 g (3 oz) of the sugar and 60 ml (2 fl oz/¼ cup) water in a saucepan. Cook, stirring, over low heat until the sugar dissolves. Raise the heat and bring the liquid to a boil. Stop stirring once the liquid is clear; otherwise, the mixture will caramelise. Cook for 12–15 minutes, or until the liquid begins to colour; the desired colour is a lovely mix of gold and caramel, not dark brown. If needed, carefully swirl the saucepan to mix the caramel.

Allow to cool for 1 minute, then pour the caramel into six 175 ml (6 fl oz) individual ovenproof moulds. Tilt and turn the dish so that the caramel covers the base and goes up the side a little.

Preheat the oven to 160°C (320°F).

Warm the milk, vanilla and orange zest in a saucepan over medium heat. Remove just as it comes to the boil, then infuse for 10 minutes. Beat the eggs, egg yolks and remaining sugar together until pale and thick. Whisk the warm milk into the egg mixture. Strain the mixture, then pour it on top of the caramel.

Place the moulds in a deep baking tin. Pour hot water in to come halfway up the sides. Cook for 35–45 minutes. The custard should be firm to the touch, with a slight wobble when it's ready. Remove from the oven and refrigerate overnight.

To serve, run a knife around the edge of the custard, then place a plate on top of the dish and quickly turn the dish upside down to remove the crème caramel.

Molten chocolate puddings

No dinner party is complete without a decadent chocolate dessert. You can make the pudding mix in advance and put it to one side until ready to cook after the main course. It's lovely with a glass of tokay, my favourite dessert wine. Serves 6

350 g (12½ oz) dark chocolate, chopped into chunks
50 g (1¾ oz) soft butter
50 g (1¾ oz) caster (superfine) sugar
4 eggs, lightly beaten
2 tablespoons plain (all-purpose) flour
Cream to serve

Grease six 125 ml (4 fl oz/½ cup) ramekins and place them on a baking tray.

Melt the chocolate by placing it in a bowl over a saucepan of simmering water or in a microwave on Low for 1–2 minutes.

Using an electric mixer, beat the butter and caster sugar together until light and fluffy. With the mixer still going, gradually add the beaten eggs. Add the flour and ensure that all the ingredients are well combined. Add the melted chocolate and beat to a smooth paste.

Divide the chocolate mixture evenly between the ramekins. If you want, you can now set the puddings aside until you are ready to cook them.

Preheat the oven to 180°C (350°F).

Place the ramekins in the oven and cook for about 18–20 minutes. Check the puddings by inserting a skewer: you want them to be gooey in the middle, but cooked at least 1 cm (½ in) inside from the edge.

When ready, turn the puddings out onto serving plates and serve immediately with cream.

Chestnut creams with rich chocolate sauce

An unusual dessert, but beautifully decadent and perfect in the cooler months. Chestnut purée is available from most good food shops. Serves 6

1 × 5 g (¼ oz) gelatine sheet
250 ml (8½ fl oz/1 cup) pouring (light/single) cream
125 ml (4 fl oz/½ cup) milk
55 g (2 oz/¼ cup) caster (superfine) sugar
435 g (15½ oz) tinned unsweetened chestnut purée
75 g (2¾ oz) cooked chopped chestnuts (optional)

Chocolate sauce

½ teaspoon natural vanilla extract
90 g (3 oz) dark chocolate, chopped into chunks
20 g (¾ oz) butter
2 tablespoons brandy
80 ml (2½ fl oz/⅓ cup) pouring (light/single) cream

Grease six 125 ml (4 fl oz/½ cup) dariole moulds.

Soak the gelatine sheet in cold water for 2–3 minutes, until soft. Squeeze the excess water out and set aside.

Put the cream, milk and sugar in a small saucepan and bring to the boil. Remove from the heat, add the gelatine and stir until dissolved. Add the chestnut purée. Strain the mixture through a sieve into a bowl. Add the chopped chestnuts (if using) – they add a bit of texture if you like that.

Pour the mixture into the greased dariole moulds. Refrigerate to set, for 3–4 hours or overnight.

Make a chocolate sauce by putting all the remaining ingredients in a heatproof bowl. Set the bowl over a saucepan of simmering water and cook for 5–6 minutes. Stir often until everything has melted together smoothly. Keep warm.

Use a small spatula or knife to work the puddings away from the edges of the moulds, then stand the moulds in boiling water for 4–5 seconds. Place a plate on top of each mould, then turn over carefully so the plate is on the bottom. Shake gently to dislodge the pudding. Remove the mould and serve the puddings with the warm chocolate sauce.

Lemon delicious pudding

With its light-as-a-feather crust floating over tangy lemon sauce, it's no wonder that few people can resist lemon delicious pudding. It's the type of pudding that is perfectly at home as a weeknight family dessert, as well as at a weekend dinner party. I often make it with other citrus fruit, such as lime, orange or tangelo. Serves 4–6

75 g (2¾ oz) soft butter
220 g (8 oz) caster (superfine) sugar, plus extra for sprinkling
Grated zest of 2 lemons
3 eggs, separated
125 ml (4 fl oz/½ cup) lemon juice
250 ml (8½ fl oz/1 cup) milk
100 g (3½ oz/⅔ cup) self-raising flour

Preheat the oven to 180°C (350°F).

Butter a 1 litre (34 fl oz/4 cup) pudding bowl and sprinkle with caster sugar.

Cream the butter with the lemon zest and caster sugar. Add the egg yolks and mix well. Add the lemon juice, milk and flour and mix to incorporate.

Beat the egg whites until stiff and fold them through the batter. Spoon the mixture into the pudding bowl and place the bowl in a deep baking dish. Pour hot water into the dish until it comes halfway up the bowl. Cook in the oven for 45 minutes, or until golden brown and puffed.

Steamed lemon pudding

A good steamed pudding is one of the most popular desserts. Despite the minimal ingredients and the easy cooking method, a huge variety of different puddings can be made by swapping the lemon with other flavours. Serves 4–6

125 g (4½ oz) soft butter
125 g (4½ oz) caster (superfine) sugar
2 medium eggs
200 g (7 oz/1⅓ cups) self-raising flour
Grated zest and juice of 2 lemons
Thin custard (page 490) to serve

Cream the butter and sugar until light and fluffy. Add the eggs, one at a time, allowing each to be incorporated before adding the next. Stir in the flour, then stir in the lemon zest and juice.

Butter a 1 litre (34 fl oz/4 cup) pudding bowl and spoon in the pudding mixture. Cover with buttered baking paper and foil. Tie down tightly with string under the rim of the pudding bowl or, easier still, use a large elastic band.

Place the pudding bowl in a large saucepan and pour in enough water to come three-quarters of the way up the bowl. Bring the water to the boil, reduce to a simmer, place the lid on the saucepan and cook for 1½ hours. Check the water level from time to time and add more if needed.

Remove the pudding bowl from the water and allow to stand for 10 minutes. Remove the foil and baking paper. Run a small spatula around the edge of the pudding and unmould it onto a platter. Serve with the custard.

Steamed orange pudding
Substitute orange, tangelo or blood orange zest and juice for the lemon.

Steamed chocolate pudding
Replace 60 g (2 oz) of the flour with unsweetened (Dutch) cocoa. Sift the two together. Omit the lemon zest and juice. Add 90 g (3 oz/½ cup) small chocolate chips as an optional extra.

Steamed jam or marmalade pudding
Spoon 100 g (3½ oz) of your favourite jam or marmalade into the bottom of the bowl, then spoon the pudding mix over the top. Omit the lemon juice and zest and add ½ teaspoon natural vanilla extract.

Steamed ginger pudding
Add 2 teaspoons ground ginger to the pudding mix and omit the lemon juice and zest. Stir in 60 g (2 oz) chopped glacé ginger.

Steamed golden syrup or maple syrup pudding
Spoon 100 ml (3½ fl oz) golden syrup or maple syrup into the bottom of the bowl, then spoon the pudding mix over the top. Omit the lemon juice and zest and add ½ teaspoon natural vanilla extract.

Steamed rhubarb pudding
Chop the stems from one bunch of rhubarb into 1 cm (½ in) pieces. Toss with 2 tablespoons raw sugar, ½ teaspoon freshly grated nutmeg and ½ teaspoon cinnamon. Omit the lemon juice and zest and stir in the rhubarb, sugar and spices instead.

Self-saucing lemon and coconut pudding

I seem to have developed a thing for self-saucing puddings. Serves 4–6

200 g (7 oz/1⅓ cups) self-raising flour

410 g (14½ oz) caster (superfine) sugar, plus extra for sprinkling

45 g (1½ oz/½ cup) desiccated coconut

Grated zest and juice of 1 lemon

125 ml (4 fl oz/½ cup) milk

1 egg

60 g (2 oz) melted butter

1 tablespoon cornflour (cornstarch)

150 ml (5 fl oz) boiling water

80 ml (2½ fl oz/⅓ cup) lemon juice

Cream to serve

Preheat the oven to 180°C (350°F).

Butter a 1 litre (34 fl oz/4 cup) ovenproof dish and sprinkle with caster sugar.

Mix the flour, 260 g (9 oz) of the caster sugar the and desiccated coconut together in a bowl.

Whisk together the lemon zest and juice, milk, 110 g (4 oz) of the caster sugar, the egg and melted butter until smooth, then pour into the flour mixture. Mix until smooth. Spoon into the greased ovenproof dish.

Mix the remaining caster sugar and the cornflour together and sprinkle over the pudding mix.

Stir the boiling water and lemon juice together and pour over the pudding. Place the pudding in the oven and cook for 45 minutes, or until a skewer comes out clean. Serve with cream.

Chocolate self-saucing pudding

This is an incredibly popular style of dessert – partly because it's so easy and partly because of the apparently magical way the sauce starts on top of the pudding and ends up on the bottom. Serves 4

60 g (2 oz) melted butter

125 ml (4 fl oz/½ cup) milk

130 g (4½ oz) caster (superfine) sugar, plus extra for sprinkling

1 egg

150 g (5½ oz/1 cup) self-raising flour

40 g (1½ oz/⅓ cup) unsweetened (Dutch) cocoa

250 ml (8½ fl oz/1 cup) boiling water

Preheat the oven to 180°C (350°F).

Butter a 1 litre (34 fl oz/4 cup) ovenproof dish and sprinkle with caster sugar.

Whisk the melted butter, milk, 75 g (2¾ oz) of the sugar and the egg together lightly.

Sift the flour and half the cocoa together, then whisk into the milk. Pour this into the ovenproof dish.

Place the remaining cocoa and sugar together in a bowl, whisk in the boiling water until smooth, then pour this over the chocolate pudding. Place in the oven and cook for 30–40 minutes, or until a skewer comes out clean.

Sticky date pudding with toffee sauce

This chapter wouldn't be complete without a sticky date (sticky toffee) pudding recipe. It's classic winter fare. Serves 6

185 g (6½ oz/1 cup) pitted dates, chopped

1 teaspoon bicarbonate of soda (baking soda)

250 ml (8½ fl oz/1 cup) boiling water

80 g (2¾ oz) butter

300 g (10½ oz) soft brown sugar

2 medium eggs

175 g (6 oz) self-raising flour

250 ml (8½ fl oz/1 cup) pouring (light/single) cream

½ teaspoon natural vanilla extract

Preheat the oven to 180°C (350°F).

Mix the dates and bicarbonate of soda in a bowl. Pour the boiling water over and leave to stand.

Cream 60 g (2 oz) of the butter and half the sugar until pale and thick. Add the eggs, one by one, incorporating each one before adding the next. Fold in the flour until well mixed, then fold through the date mixture. Spoon into a greased and lined 20 cm (8 in) cake tin. Bake for 35–40 minutes, or until a skewer comes out clean.

To make the toffee sauce, place the remaining brown sugar, the cream, vanilla and the remaining butter in a saucepan and cook over medium heat, stirring often until the sauce comes to the boil. Reduce to a simmer and allow to cook for 10–15 minutes until the sauce reduces and thickens slightly.

Cut the pudding into wedges to serve and pour the hot toffee sauce over.

Banoffee pie

One of my favourite desserts and super-quick to make, assuming you have dulce de leche on hand. The pretzels add a nice salty kick, but you can substitute them with regular cookies if you like. Use the base from the Raw coconut and chocolate tart (page 314), if you would like to make it gluten-free. Serves 6–8

200 g (7 oz) digestive biscuits (sweet wholemeal cookies) or graham crackers

50 g (1¾ oz) pretzels

60 g (2 oz) melted butter

250 g (9 oz) Dulce de leche (page 489)

2 bananas

250 ml (8½ fl oz/1 cup) thickened (whipping) cream, whipped

Good-quality dark chocolate to garnish

Place the biscuits and pretzels in a food processor and whizz to form small crumbs. Add the melted butter and process briefly.

Press the biscuit mixture into the bottom of a greased 20 cm (8 in) springform cake tin and place in the refrigerator to set for at least 20 minutes.

Spread the dulce de leche over the biscuit base, top with the banana slices and then add whipped cream to cover. Grate the dark chocolate over the cream and serve immediately.

Bread and butter pudding

Bread and butter pudding is best made with day-old bread to absorb the egg mixture better. This is a simple dish that any member of the family could make. Serves 4

10 slices white bread, crusts removed

Butter as required

30 g (1 oz/¼ cup) sultanas (golden raisins)

3 eggs

55 g (2 oz/¼ cup) caster (superfine) sugar

500 ml (17 fl oz/2 cups) milk

1 teaspoon natural vanilla extract

Preheat the oven to 180°C (350°F).

Lightly butter each slice of bread, then cut each into quarters to form triangles.

Butter a pie dish and lay the bread triangles in it so that they overlap each other. Scatter the sultanas over the top.

Beat the eggs, sugar, milk and vanilla extract together in a bowl. Pour the egg mixture over the bread slices.

Allow to stand for 10–15 minutes, then push the bread down to soak up the egg mixture, adding the remaining egg mixture if there is any.

Bake in the oven for 45 minutes. When ready, the pudding will be puffed and golden.

Bread and jam pudding
Spread strawberry or raspberry jam onto the buttered bread triangles.

Pain au chocolat pudding
Substitute two to three pain au chocolat (chocolate-filled croissants) for the white bread and butter. Omit the sultanas.

Chai bread and butter pudding
Place the milk with 2 tablespoons chai tea in a small saucepan and bring to the boil. Remove from the heat and allow to brew for 4-5 minutes. Strain and use the infused milk. Omit the sultanas.

Summer pudding

Summer pudding is an old-fashioned English dessert. It's the sort of thing to serve when you're having a large group over on a hot summer's day. Serves 6–8

10–15 slices day-old white bread, crusts removed

500 g (1 lb 2 oz/3⅓ cups) strawberries

200 g (7 oz) raspberries

200 g (7 oz) blackberries

200 g (7 oz) redcurrants

200 g (7 oz) loganberries

220 g (8 oz) caster (superfine) sugar

Clotted cream to serve

Line a 1 litre (34 fl oz/4 cup) pudding bowl with the slices of bread. Sort through the berries and remove any stalks.

Bring 500 ml (17 fl oz/2 cups) water and the sugar to the boil in a saucepan. Place all the fruit in the hot syrup and allow to heat through for 1 minute. Drain immediately, reserving the liquid.

Return the cooking liquid to the pan and boil until reduced by half. Allow the fruit and syrup to cool completely before gently mixing the two together again.

Spoon the fruit into the bread-lined bowl. Add enough cooking liquid to cover, then top with more bread. Place a small plate on top of the pudding (one that fits inside the rim of the bowl) and put a heavy weight on it. Refrigerate overnight.

To serve, remove the pudding from the bowl by placing a plate over the top of the bowl, turning it upside down and shaking gently. Serve with the clotted cream.

Cherry berry pudding
Replace the strawberries with 500 g (1 lb 2 oz) pitted cherries and cook them for 1 minute before adding the remaining fruit. The cherries add a richness to the pudding.

Panettone and raspberry pudding

This is a marvellous way to use up any left-over panettone from Christmas Day. It's a simple variation on a bread and butter pudding but with a heady aroma from the panettone and little bursts of flavour courtesy of the berries. Serves 4–6

10 slices panettone

150 g (5½ oz) raspberries

3 eggs

55 g (2 oz/¼ cup) caster (superfine) sugar, plus an extra 1–2 tablespoons for sprinkling

500 ml (17 fl oz/2 cups) milk

1 teaspoon natural vanilla extract

Preheat the oven to 180°C (350°F).

Butter a pie dish and arrange the panettone slices so that they overlap each other. Scatter the raspberries over the top.

Beat the eggs, caster sugar, milk and vanilla together in a bowl, then pour this mixture over the panettone slices. Allow to stand for 10–15 minutes, then push the panettone down to soak up the egg mixture. Sprinkle the extra caster sugar over the top.

Bake in the preheated oven for 40–45 minutes. When ready, the pudding will be puffed and golden.

Rice pudding

This is the easiest rice pudding recipe I know. I often serve it with a dollop of raspberry jam. It's also a recipe children enjoy learning how to make. In fact, it was one of the first recipes that my daughter, Mia, mastered. Serves 4

1 litre (34 fl oz/4 cups) milk

110 g (4 oz) caster (superfine) sugar

1 teaspoon natural vanilla extract

220 g (8 oz/1 cup) short-grain rice

Place the milk, sugar, vanilla and rice in a large heavy-based saucepan. Bring to the boil, then reduce to a very low heat and cook for 20 minutes, stirring often.

When the rice is tender, remove from the heat, cover and allow to rest for 15 minutes before serving. This will allow time for any remaining liquid to be absorbed. Spoon the warm rice pudding into serving bowls.

Middle Eastern rice pudding
Prepare as directed, then add 50 g (1¾ oz/⅓ cup) toasted pine nuts and 50 g (1¾ oz/⅓ cup) currants. Drizzle with pomegranate molasses to serve.

Chocolate rice pudding
Add 60 g (2 oz) chopped dark chocolate to the pudding once cooked. Stir until melted.

Adult's rice pudding
Soak 110 g (4 oz) sultanas (golden raisins) in 125 ml (4 fl oz/½ cup) muscat or tokay as the rice is simmering, then add them to the pudding.

Risotto of chocolate and nougat
Make the rice pudding as above. When cooked, stir through 2 tablespoons thickened (whipping) cream and 80 g (2¾ oz) chopped glacé fruit. Spoon the warm rice into serving bowls. Scatter 100 g (3½ oz) chopped dark chocolate and 100 g (3½ oz) chopped almond nougat over the rice and serve immediately.

Christmas pudding

This recipe originated from Allan's mum, Teresa, who came across it in Ireland, hence the Guinness in the recipe. The mix makes three large puddings – one for the day itself, one as a gift and one to put away for mid-year Christmas. Makes 3 large puddings

175 g (6 oz) self-raising flour

½ teaspoon freshly ground nutmeg

1 teaspoon ground cinnamon

1 teaspoon mixed spice

225 g (8 oz) fresh breadcrumbs

500 g (1 lb 2 oz) brown sugar

450 g (1 lb/3 cups) currants

225 g (8 oz) raisins

225 g (8 oz) sultanas (golden raisins)

100 g (3½ oz) mixed peel or candied orange peel

50 g (1¾ oz) slivered almonds

Grated zest of 1 orange

Grated zest of 1 lemon

225 g (8 oz) margarine

3 eggs

65 ml (2¼ fl oz/¼ cup) brandy

275 ml (9½ fl oz) Guinness

Butter three 1 litre (34 fl oz/4 cup) pudding bowls.

Sift together the flour and spices. Stir in the breadcrumbs, brown sugar, currants, raisins, sultanas, mixed peel, almonds and citrus zests.

Melt the margarine and mix it with the eggs, brandy and stout in a separate bowl.

Stir the wet mixture into the dry mixture, combining both thoroughly. It may look quite runny at this stage but it will thicken in the refrigerator. Cover the mixture and refrigerate overnight.

Divide the pudding mixture between the three pudding bowls. Cover with buttered baking paper and foil. Tie down tightly with string under the rim of each pudding bowl or, easier still, use a large elastic band.

Place each pudding bowl in a large saucepan. Pour in enough water to come three-quarters of the way up the bowl. Bring to the boil, reduce to a simmer, cover and cook for 4 hours.

Check the water level from time to time and add more if needed. Test the puddings with a skewer as you would a cake, to make sure they are cooked. Either serve while still hot or wrap carefully and store in a cool dark place for up to 6 months.

Australian Christmas pudding
This is the variation I developed as I grew to love great native Australian ingredients. It is quite different from the original, but also delicious. Add to the pudding mix: 1 teaspoon ground ginger, ¾ teaspoon ground wattle seed, 175 g (6 oz) chopped glacé ginger in place of the mixed peel, and 150 g (5½ oz) macadamias in place of the almonds. Use Australian dark rum instead of brandy and a South Australian stout instead of Guinness.

Ginger parkin with spiced cream

If you thought British food was a write-off, you have never tried this dessert, which is heavenly on a cold winter's night. The parkin improves with age, becoming even gooier and stickier, so make it in advance if you can. To complete the dessert, serve the parkin with poached pears.
Serves 8

100 g (3½ oz/⅔ cup) self-raising flour

2½ teaspoons ground ginger

1½ teaspoon mixed spice

½ teaspoon freshly ground nutmeg

100 g (3½ oz/1 cup) rolled (porridge) oats

175 g (6 oz/½ cup) golden syrup

50 g (1¾ oz) black treacle

100 g (3½ oz) soft butter

100 g (3½ oz) soft brown sugar

1 egg, lightly beaten

1–2 tablespoons milk

300 ml (1¼ cups) thick (double/heavy) cream

Preheat the oven to 140°C (275°F).

Sift the flour, a pinch of salt, 2 teaspoons of the ground ginger, ½ teaspoon of the mixed spice and the nutmeg together in a large bowl. Add the rolled oats and stir them through.

Place the golden syrup, treacle, butter and brown sugar in a small saucepan and melt over gentle heat. Do not boil. Add to the flour, along with the egg and milk, to create a soft cake consistency. If needed, add a little more milk.

Spoon the mixture into a buttered 23 cm (9 in) round cake tin and bake in the oven for 1 hour. Check if it's cooked by inserting a skewer in the centre. If the skewer comes out clean, the cake is cooked. If not, cook for a further 5 minutes and try again. Allow the cake to cool in the tin for 10 minutes before turning it out onto a wire cooling rack. Once cold, wrap the cake in plastic wrap and store in an airtight container for up to 2 weeks.

Mix the cream and the remaining ground ginger and mixed spice together.

Warm the parkin by either heating it in the microwave for 2 minutes or by wrapping it in foil and heating it in a preheated 180°C (350°F) oven for 10 minutes. Cut the parkin into eight wedges and serve with the spiced cream.

Zuccotto

This is a slightly different type of dessert, but still a crowd-pleaser. You can make your own cake, or buy a good-quality cake if time is tight. Serves 4–6

500 g (1 lb 2 oz) Butter cake (page 361)

80 ml (2½ fl oz/⅓ cup) Tia Maria

375 ml (12½ fl oz/1½ cups) thickened (whipping) cream

110 g (4 oz) icing (confectioners') sugar

100 g (3½ oz) toasted slivered almonds

60 g (2 oz) chopped glacé apricots

100 g (3½ oz) dark chocolate chips

100 g (3½ oz) melted dark chocolate

Cut the butter cake into 1 cm (½ in) thick slices. Arrange a layer of cake slices in a 1.5 litre (51 fl oz/ 6 cup) bowl. Moisten with half of the Tia Maria.

Whip the cream with the icing sugar until stiff. Fold through the toasted almonds, apricots, chocolate chips and melted chocolate. Spoon the cream mixture into the cake-lined bowl. Cover with the remaining cake, moistening with the remaining Tia Maria. Cover with plastic wrap and refrigerate overnight.

Remove the zuccotto from the bowl, turning it out onto a serving plate. Cut into wedges to serve.

Christmas trifle

I love trifle, particularly in summer when fresh fruit is so magnificent. I usually have panettone left over after Christmas and so I use it in this dish instead of sponge. Combined with the sparkling wine jelly and real custard, this is a spectacular dish. Serves 6–8

3 × 5 g (¼ oz) gelatine leaves

250 ml (8½ fl oz/1 cup) apple juice

165 g (6 oz) caster (superfine) sugar

500 ml (17 fl oz/2 cups) sparkling wine

4 peaches, sliced

150 g (5½ oz/1¼ cups) raspberries

6–8 slices panettone

2 egg yolks

1 tablespoon plain (all-purpose) flour

500 ml (17 fl oz/2 cups) milk

½ teaspoon natural vanilla extract

300 ml (10 fl oz) thickened (whipping) cream

2 tablespoons sliced pistachio nuts, or 2 tablespoons flaked almonds

Soak the gelatine sheets in cold water for 2–3 minutes, or until soft. Remove from the soaking dish and squeeze away the excess water. Set aside.

Put the apple juice and 110 g (4 oz) of the sugar in a saucepan and bring to the boil. Remove from the heat, add the gelatine and sparkling wine and stir until the gelatine is dissolved. Strain into a large serving bowl and refrigerate for 4–6 hours, until almost set.

Add the peach slices and raspberries at this point; if you add the fruit too early it will sink to the bottom. Arrange the panettone slices on top of the jelly.

To make the custard, beat the egg yolks and the remaining caster sugar together until pale, then stir in the flour until smooth.

Bring the milk and vanilla to the boil. Whisk the hot milk into the egg yolk mixture and return to a clean saucepan over low heat. Stir constantly as the custard comes to the boil and thickens. Remove from the heat and allow to cool. Spread the custard over the panettone and chill until ready to serve.

To serve, whip the cream, spread it over the custard and sprinkle with nuts.

Raspberry and gin trifle

A huge bowl of trifle will have your friends coming back for seconds. If you don't have any gin in the house, use any other white spirit or dessert wine. Serves 8–10

3 × 5 g (¼ oz) gelatine leaves

750 ml (25½ fl oz/3 cups) apple juice

95 g (3¼ oz) caster (superfine) sugar

60 ml (2 fl oz/¼ cup) gin

4 peaches, sliced

150 g (5½ oz) raspberries

6–8 slices panettone

2 egg yolks

1 tablespoon plain (all-purpose) flour

500 ml (17 fl oz/2 cups) milk

½ teaspoon natural vanilla extract

300 ml (10 fl oz) thickened (whipping) cream

2 tablespoons sliced pistachio nuts, or 2 tablespoons flaked almonds

Soak the gelatine sheets in cold water for 2–3 minutes or until soft, then squeeze out the excess water and set aside.

Put the apple juice and 2 tablespoons of the sugar in a saucepan and bring to the boil. Remove from the heat, add the gelatine and gin and stir until the gelatine is dissolved. Strain into a large serving bowl. Refrigerate until almost set, at least 3–4 hours. At this point add the peach slices and raspberries – if you add them too early they will sink to the bottom. Arrange the panettone slices on top of the jelly. Set aside in the refrigerator.

To make the custard, beat the egg yolks and remaining sugar until pale, then stir in the flour until smooth. Bring the milk and vanilla to the boil. Whisk the milk into the egg yolk mixture, then return to a clean saucepan over low heat. Stir constantly as the custard comes to the boil and thickens. Remove from the heat. Allow to cool.

Spread the custard over the panettone and chill until ready to serve. Whip the cream, spread it over the custard and sprinkle with nuts.

Raspberry cranachan trifle

Assembling this traditional Scottish dessert as a trifle, rather than stirring all the ingredients together, as is normal for a cranachan, allows the flavours of each ingredient to be savoured. Use Scottish whisky for authenticity. Serves 6–8

125 g (4½ oz) butter

80 g (2¾ oz) honey

200 g (7 oz/2 cups) rolled (porridge) oats

110 g (4 oz) caster (superfine) sugar

100 g (3½ oz) chopped hazelnuts

55 g (2 oz) plain (all-purpose) flour

250 ml (8½ fl oz/1 cup) thickened (whipping) cream

80 ml (2½ fl oz/⅓ cup) whisky

250 g (9 oz) mascarpone

140 g (5 oz) icing (confectioners') sugar

300 g (10½ oz) raspberries

Preheat the oven to 180°C (350°F).

Melt the butter and honey in a saucepan over low heat. Add the oats, sugar, hazelnuts and flour. Stir well until the oats are coated. Spread the mixture out on a baking tray lined with baking paper and bake for 20 minutes until crisp. Allow to cool and then crumble.

Whisk the cream and whisky together. Add the mascarpone and icing sugar and beat together. To serve, put four to five raspberries in the bottom of each bowl. Add a spoonful of the whisky cream, then a handful of the crunchy oats, and continue layering two or three times, finishing with a layer of oats. Be generous with the oats – you should use nearly all of them. They go gloriously gooey in the cream.

Mango and orange blossom trifle

The combination of mangoes, citrus jelly and almond-flavoured cookies is hard to beat. Once the jelly is made, the rest of the preparation is plain sailing. The pistachio praline is an decadent extra, but it's like air-conditioning in the heat of summer – you've just got to have it. Serves 8

3 × 5 g (¼ oz) gelatine sheets

220 g (8 oz) caster (superfine) sugar

Grated zest of 2 oranges

Grated zest of 2 lemons

250 ml (8½ fl oz/1 cup) orange juice

80 ml (2½ fl oz/⅓ cup) lemon juice

250 ml (8½ fl oz/1 cup) apple juice

80 ml (2½ fl oz/⅓ cup) orange blossom water

2 mangoes, peeled and diced into 1 cm (½ in) pieces

75 g (2¾ oz/½ cup) shelled pistachio nuts

200 g (7 oz) amaretti biscuits, crushed

250 g (9 oz) mascarpone

Icing (confectioners') sugar to taste (optional)

Soak the gelatine sheets in cold water for 2–3 minutes or until soft, then squeeze out the excess water and set aside.

Place half the caster sugar and 250 ml (8½ fl oz/ 1 cup) water in a saucepan and heat gently until the sugar dissolves. Add the citrus zests and fruit juices and bring to the boil.

Remove from the heat, add the gelatine and stir until dissolved. Strain, discarding the zest, and cool slightly.

Add half the orange blossom water and stir to combine. Pour into a large glass bowl or eight individual glasses. Place in the refrigerator until almost set, then add the diced mango. If you add the mango before this stage it will sink to the bottom. Refrigerate the jelly until set.

To make the caramel for the pistachio praline, place the remaining caster sugar and 80 ml (2½ fl oz/⅓ cup) water in a saucepan. Cook over low heat until the sugar dissolves. Raise the heat and boil the liquid. Cook for 12–15 minutes, or until the liquid begins to colour. The desired colour is a mix of gold and caramel, not dark brown. If needed, carefully swirl the saucepan to mix the caramel. Remove from the heat, add the pistachio nuts and tip the mixture onto a tray lined with baking paper. Allow the praline to cool, then chop roughly.

Lightly crush the amaretti biscuits and spoon onto the jelly. Sprinkle with the remaining orange blossom water.

Beat the mascarpone until smooth and add icing sugar to taste, if desired. Spoon the mascarpone on top of the amaretti and refrigerate until ready to serve. Serve the trifle topped with the chopped praline.

Pavlova

The pavlova is a marvellous version of meringue, almost always topped with cream, then finished with berries or other fruit. There's no real secret to making one; if you can whip egg whites you can whip up a pavlova. It's traditionally served at barbecues all through summer in Australia, so who am I to break a great custom? Serves 8–10

6 egg whites

440 g (15½ oz) caster (superfine) sugar

1 teaspoon natural vanilla extract

1 tablespoon cornflour (cornstarch)

1½ teaspoons white vinegar

250 ml (8½ fl oz/1 cup) thickened (whipping) cream

Pulp from 6 passionfruit

200 g (7 oz) raspberries

Preheat the oven to 180°C (350°F).

Beat the egg whites until stiff peaks form. Add the sugar, one-third at a time, allowing each third to be well incorporated before you add the next, so that you end up with a thick glossy meringue. Fold through the vanilla, cornflour and vinegar.

Either spoon the mixture into a greased and lined 23 cm (9 in) springform cake tin, or pile in a high circle on a sheet of baking paper on a baking tray. Place in the oven, lower the temperature to 120°C (250°F) and bake for 45 minutes. Turn the oven off, leaving the pavlova to cool inside the oven, preferably overnight.

Place the cool pavlova on a serving platter and cover it with whipped cream. Scoop the passionfruit pulp on top and scatter the raspberries over.

Baby pavlovas
Spoon pavlova mix into 12 individual rounds and bake for 30 minutes. Allow to cool in the oven.

Baby pavlovas with banana and honeycomb
Make baby pavlovas as described in the variation above. When cool, top with spoonfuls of Dulce de leche (page 489), slices of fresh banana, whipped cream and either crushed Honeycomb (page 410) or chopped dark chocolate.

Chocolate meringue discs
Make the meringue as described, but add 2 tablespoons unsweetened (Dutch) cocoa powder with the cornflour. Line three baking trays with baking paper and divide the meringue between them. Smooth into large circles, about 20 cm (8 in) in diameter – they don't have to be perfect. Cook for 1 hour, then leave to cool in the oven overnight. Fill the layers with cream and top with whipped cream and berries.

Mousse and meringue stacks
Make the chocolate meringues as described. Top each meringue with Coffee and cardamom mousse (page 331) before it sets, then layer the meringues on top of each other. Refrigerate for 2–3 hours until the mousse sets before serving.

Eton mess

A great way to use up left-over meringues, or slight failures. Serves 4–6

375 ml (12½ fl oz/1½ cups) thickened (whipping) cream

Pavlova (see above)

300 g (10½ oz) fresh berries

Raspberry sauce (page 487) to serve

Whip the cream until stiff. Crumble the pavlova into a large serving bowl or individual bowls. Layer the crumbled pavlova with cream and berries. Repeat until you have two layers of each. Refrigerate for at least 30 minutes, but no longer than 4 hours. If you leave the Eton mess too long the cream will break down the meringue, and you'll lose the gorgeous crunchy bit. Serve with the raspberry sauce.

Passionfruit meringue roulade

A simple dish that is perfect to serve on a hot summer's day as dessert after a long lazy lunch.
Serves 6–8

4 egg whites

220 g (8 oz) caster (superfine) sugar

Pinch of cornflour (cornstarch)

200 g (7 oz/1 cup) Passionfruit curd (page 445)

250 ml (8½ fl oz/1 cup) thickened (whipping) cream, whipped to firm peaks

Extra whipped cream, passionfruit pulp and icing (confectioners') sugar to serve

Preheat the oven to 180°C (350°F).

Butter a 25 × 30 cm (10 × 12 cm) Swiss roll tin (jelly roll tin) and line the sides and bottom with baking paper.

Beat the egg whites until stiff peaks form. Add the sugar, one-third at a time, allowing each third to be well incorporated before adding the next, so that you end up with a thick glossy meringue. Fold through the cornflour.

Spoon the mixture into the prepared tin. Transfer to the oven and bake for 10–12 minutes. Allow the cake to cool for 5–10 minutes.

Place a clean tea towel (dish towel) on a work surface, cover with a sheet of baking paper and sprinkle over a little caster sugar. Turn the meringue out onto the paper-lined tea towel.

Spread the passionfruit curd over two-thirds of the meringue (leave the last third free so that as you roll it up it allows room for the curd to spread). Top with the whipped cream.

Using the tea towel as a guide, carefully roll the meringue up widthways, leaving the tea towel outside.

Place the roulade, seam side down, on a platter. If you like, decorate with extra whipped cream and fresh passionfruit pulp. Dust with icing sugar.

Rosewater meringue stack with red summer berries

This dessert is basically an overgrown layered pavlova with lots of extras. You'll definitely need one of these if you're entertaining a large group of people during summer. Serve it in all its glory and allow everyone to help themselves. Serves 8–10

6 egg whites

440 g (15½ oz) caster (superfine) sugar

2 tablespoons rosewater

1 tablespoon cornflour (cornstarch)

1½ teaspoons white vinegar

600 ml (20½ fl oz) thickened (whipping) cream

500 g (1 lb 2 oz) cherries, pitted

250 g (9 oz) redcurrants, stalks removed

300 g (10½ oz) raspberries

Preheat the oven to 180°C (350°F). Line three baking trays with baking paper.

Beat the egg whites until stiff peaks form. Add the caster sugar, one-third at a time, allowing each third to be well incorporated before adding the next, so that you end up with a thick, glossy meringue. Fold through the rosewater, cornflour and vinegar.

Shape one disc of meringue onto the three prepared baking trays, the first 20 cm (8 in) wide, the second 15 cm (6 in) and the last 10 cm (4 in) wide. Place the trays in the oven, lower the temperature to 120°C (250°F) and bake for 45 minutes. Turn the oven off, leaving the meringue to cool inside the oven.

Whip the cream until thick. Combine the fruit in a bowl.

Place the largest meringue disc on a serving platter, spread it with the cream and top with almost half the fruit. Add the medium-sized meringue disc and top with cream and fruit. Repeat with the final meringue, using up the remaining cream and fruit.

Pancakes

Pancakes are a popular dessert or breakfast option. They were one of the first dishes that my son, Luke, mastered – mainly because he wanted them for dessert everyday. Serves 4

1 egg
250 ml (8½ fl oz/1 cup) milk
150 g (5½ oz/1 cup) plain (all-purpose) flour
2 tablespoons melted butter
Caster (superfine) sugar to serve
2 lemons, cut into wedges, to serve

Place the egg, milk and a pinch of salt in a bowl and whisk lightly. Whisk in the flour, a little at a time, until the pancake batter has the consistency of thin custard. Allow to rest for 30 minutes. Strain the batter if there are any lumps.

Heat a heavy-based frying pan over medium heat. When hot, brush the base of the pan with 1½ teaspoons melted butter, then pour in just enough batter to coat the bottom of the pan thinly. Allow to cook until golden, then turn the pancake over and cook the other side. Repeat until the mixture is used up, adding more melted butter as needed.

Luke liked to serve each pancake with a sprinkling of caster sugar and a wedge of lemon as it was ready, but you can keep the cooked pancakes warm in a 180°C (350°F) oven if you want to serve them together

Berry pancakes
Top the pancakes with fresh berries (or stewed apricots or sliced banana) and roll them up. Place the filled pancakes in a buttered ovenproof dish and cook in a preheated 180°C (350°F) oven for 10 minutes. Serve with cream or ice cream.

The simplest ice cream

Okay, I may not have been completely honest. I'm addicted to ice cream. This is the easiest recipe and it requires no churning so you don't need an ice cream machine. You can add whatever flavours you like to this; the ideas are limited only by your imagination.
Makes 750 ml (25½ fl oz/3 cups)

500 ml (17 fl oz/2 cups) thickened (whipping) cream
220 g (8 oz) caster (superfine) sugar
400 g (14 oz) tinned sweetened condensed milk
2 teaspoons natural vanilla extract

Whip the cream and sugar to soft peaks and then pour in the condensed milk and vanilla extract and whisk again to form soft peaks. Pour the mixture into a freezer-proof container. Cover with a lid and freeze for at least 4–6 hours, preferably overnight.

Simple chocolate ice cream
Add 250 g (9 oz) melted dark chocolate (or white, orange-flavoured, ginger-flavoured or any flavoured chocolate) at the end and stir it through. You can also add 100 g (3½ oz) chocolate chips.

Simple raspberry ripple ice cream
Add 125 ml (4 fl oz/½ cup) Raspberry sauce (page 487) at the end and stir it through.

Simple passionfruit ice cream
Add 250 g (9 oz/1 cup) passionfruit pulp (from about 12–15 passionfruit) at the end and stir it through.

Simple Christmas cake ice cream
Add ¼ teaspoon ground cinnamon, ¼ teaspoon ground nutmeg, 100 g (3½ oz) mixed fruit (currants, raisins or sultanas/golden raisins), 3 tablespoons brandy, 50 g (1¾ oz/⅓ cup) roasted almonds and 50 g (1¾ oz) glacé cherries.

Vanilla ice cream

This recipe, which has a high proportion of cream, enabled me to get by for years without an ice cream machine. The cream is folded through at the last minute before the mixture goes into the freezer. You just have to give it a stir each hour until it freezes – around four or five times. Serves 8–10

4 eggs
125 g (4½ oz) caster (superfine) sugar
2 teaspoons natural vanilla extract
500 ml (17 fl oz/2 cups) thickened (whipping) cream

Beat the eggs, caster sugar and vanilla until thick and doubled in size, about 5 minutes.

Whip the cream until it forms stiff peaks. Fold the whipped cream gently into the egg mixture.

If you have an ice cream machine, churn the ice cream according to the manufacturer's instructions. If not, pour the mixture into a bowl. Place in the freezer. Remove after 1 hour and stir well to break up the ice particles. Return to the freezer and repeat every hour for 4–5 hours or until just about frozen.

On the last stir, transfer the ice cream into a sealable container. Allow to set in the freezer for at least 24 hours before serving.

Chocolate ice cream
Add 250 g (9 oz) melted dark chocolate to the mixture just before adding the whipped cream. You can also add 100 g (3½ oz) chocolate chunks.

Hazelnut ice cream
Add 200 g (7 oz) roasted hazelnuts and 60 g (2 oz) ground roasted hazelnuts to the mix just before adding the whipped cream.

Tiramisu ice cream

If you're a fan of tiramisu – and that's probably about 90 per cent of the population – then you're going to love this frozen version. A big thank you to Rosemary Di Benedetto for the recipe. This is delicious with Butterscotch sauce (page 488). Serves 6

125 ml (4 fl oz/½ cup) strong black coffee
2 tablespoons coffee liqueur
400 g (14 oz) tinned sweetened condensed milk
600 ml (20½ fl oz) thickened (whipping) cream
60 ml (2 fl oz/¼ cup) milk
12 sponge fingers (savoiardi)

Line a medium (21 × 9 × 6 cm/8¼ × 3½ × 2½ in) loaf (bar) tin with plastic wrap.

Mix the prepared coffee and the coffee liqueur together and allow to cool.

Place the condensed milk, cream and milk in a large bowl and beat until thick. Add half of the coffee mixture and beat well.

Lay six sponge fingers in the prepared loaf tin, spoon in the milk and cream mixture and drizzle over half of the remaining coffee mixture. Top with six sponge fingers, then drizzle with the remaining coffee mixture. Freeze overnight.

Remove the ice cream from the tin and cut into 1 cm (½ in) slices to serve. Cut each slice in half diagonally.

Rocky road ice cream

This recipe works well without an ice cream machine, and you could also make it with a good-quality store-made vanilla ice cream if you wished. Serves 8–10

4 eggs

110 g (4 oz) caster (superfine) sugar

2 teaspoons natural vanilla extract

500 ml (17 fl oz/2 cups) thickened (whipping) cream

½ quantity Rocky road (page 411)

Beat the eggs, caster sugar and vanilla together for 5 minutes, until thick and doubled in size.

Whip the cream until it forms stiff peaks, then gently fold the cream into the egg mixture.

If you have an ice cream machine, churn the ice cream according to the manufacturer's instructions. If you don't have an ice cream machine, pour the mixture into a bowl and place it in the freezer. Remove it after 1 hour and stir well to break up the ice particles. Return it to the freezer and repeat every hour for 4–5 hours, or until just about frozen.

Chop the rocky road into bite-sized pieces. On the last stir of the ice cream, add the chopped rocky road. Spoon the ice cream into a sealable container. Cover and allow to set in the freezer for at least 24 hours before serving.

To serve, allow the ice cream to stand in its container at room temperature for 10 minutes before scooping.

Frozen nougat

Melbourne chef Arnie Sleeman created a method for what he calls frozen nougat. I persuaded him to allow me to include it here. His recipe uses glucose, which means the ice cream never really freezes, so in many ways it's more like a semifreddo than an ice cream. It doesn't require an ice cream machine and can have virtually any flavour added. How good is that? Serves 6

100 g (3½ oz) honey

65 g (2¼ oz) liquid glucose

8 egg whites

4 egg yolks

130 g (½ oz) caster (superfine) sugar

330 ml (11 fl oz) thickened (whipping) cream

165 g (6 oz) flavouring of your choice (lemon, lime, berries, toasted nuts, lemon curd or whatever takes your fancy)

Place the honey and glucose in a saucepan, cook over medium heat until the mixture boils, then remove and allow to cool slightly.

Beat the egg whites until soft peaks appear, then slowly pour the honey mixture onto the whites and continue beating until incorporated.

In a separate bowl, beat the egg yolks and sugar until white and silky in appearance.

Whip the cream until soft peaks form. Gently whip a large spoonful of beaten egg white and whipped cream into the egg yolks. When this is fully incorporated, gently fold in the remaining egg white and cream. Fold in the flavouring of your choice. Place the mixture in a freezer-proof bowl, cover with foil and freeze overnight.

Liquorice frozen nougat
Melt 165 g (6 oz) liquorice with the honey and glucose; it will take an extra 2–3 minutes to melt.

Chocolate and chestnut frozen nougat
Add 90 g (3 oz) melted chocolate and 90 g (3 oz) chestnut or hazelnut pieces.

Frozen nougat ice cream cake
Because of the no-churn policy, this can be poured into a 22 cm (8¾ in) springform cake tin and frozen. Add Strawberry sauce (page 487) or 165 g (6 oz) melted chocolate. It's perfect for birthday parties.

Banana and peanut butter ice cream

A simple sugar-free, dairy-free ice cream alternative. Makes 500 ml (17 fl oz/2 cups)

4 ripe bananas

2 tablespoons peanut butter

½ teaspoon ground cinnamon

Grated chocolate and toasted almonds to serve (optional)

Peel the bananas, chop them into chunks, place in a sealed container and freeze until frozen.

When the bananas are frozen, place them in the food processor along with the peanut butter and cinnamon and process until a smooth consistency is reached. Transfer to a sealed container and freeze for 1 hour. Best enjoyed within 48 hours. Serve with grated chocolate and toasted almonds, if you like.

Banana, chocolate and hazelnut ice cream
Substitute chocolate and hazelnut spread for the peanut butter.

Strawberry frozen yoghurt

This is the easiest dessert recipe ever, and it's healthy! Use any type of frozen fruit and, depending on your taste, you may not need to add the agave. It will become very solid if left in the freezer for any length of time, so just pop it back in the food processor if needed. Serves 4

500 g (1 lb 2 oz) frozen strawberries

1 tablespoon lemon juice

2 tablespoons agave nectar

375 g (13 oz/1½ cups) natural yoghurt

Place all the ingredients in a food processor and pulse until smooth. Check for sweetness – you may need to add more agave depending on your taste buds and the acidity of the strawberries.

Freeze in a sealable container until frozen. Keep for up to 1 month. Allow to sit at room temperature for 10 minutes before serving.

Raspberry and coconut frozen yoghurt
Swap the strawberries for raspberries and the natural yoghurt for coconut yoghurt. The added bonus is that it's now also dairy-free!

Mango and coconut frozen yoghurt
Swap the strawberries for frozen mango and the natural yoghurt for coconut yoghurt.

Raspberry and pistachio torronata

A simple but effective dessert with the added bonus of being able to make it in advance. Serves 8

375 g (13 oz/1½ cups) ricotta

110 g (4 oz) caster (superfine) sugar

150 g (5½ oz) nougat, finely chopped

Grated zest of 1 lemon

2 tablespoons chopped pistachio nuts, plus extra to serve

250 ml (8½ fl oz/1 cup) whipped cream

125 g (4½ oz) raspberries, plus extra to serve

Mix the ricotta and caster sugar until combined. Add the nougat, lemon zest, pistachio nuts and whipped cream. Add the raspberries and stir through until just combined. Line a loaf (bar) tin with plastic wrap and spoon the ricotta mix in. Cover well and freeze for at least 8 hours.

Once frozen and ready to eat, remove the torronata from the tin and cut it into 1 cm (½ in) slices. Serve with the extra fresh raspberries and pistachio nuts.

Raspberry and Campari sorbet

An ice cream machine makes this dish easy, but if you don't have one you can still give it a go. Best eaten within 2 days of making it. Serves 6–8

200 g (7 oz) caster (superfine) sugar

300 g (10½ oz) raspberries

1½ tablespoons lemon juice

2 tablespoons Campari, plus extra for serving

Prepare a syrup by placing the sugar and 375 ml (12½ fl oz/1½ cups) water in a saucepan. Stir over medium heat until the sugar dissolves. Allow to cool for 5 minutes.

Place the berries, lemon juice and cooled syrup in a food processor and blitz until smooth. Strain the liquid to remove the raspberry seeds. Add the Campari to the strained liquid.

Pour into an ice cream machine and churn according to the manufacturer's instructions. Alternatively, pour the liquid into a shallow freezer-proof tray and freeze for 1 hour. Remove the tray and stir the sorbet well. Freeze for a further hour and repeat the stirring. Pour into a freezer-proof bowl, cover and freeze overnight.

Place the sorbet in the refrigerator for 10 minutes before serving. Serve scoops of the sorbet with additional Campari drizzled over.

Watermelon granita with summer fruit

Granita is a semi-frozen dessert, which is so refreshing in the summer months. Spoon the dessert into chilled glass bowls to prevent the granita from melting too quickly when it's served. Serves 6

1 kg (2 lb 3 oz) watermelon

75 g (2¾ oz) caster (superfine) sugar

60 ml (2 fl oz/¼ cup) white spirit (vodka, gin, tequila or white rum)

3 pink grapefruit or 4 oranges

½ rockmelon

200 g (7 oz/1½ cups) strawberries

Chop the watermelon, discarding the skin and pips.

Place the watermelon in a food processor, along with the caster sugar and white spirit, and blend until smooth. Strain through a sieve and discard any remaining pulp. Tip the watermelon juice into a shallow baking tray and freeze overnight.

Remove the skins and pith of the citrus fruit. Remove the segments from the membrane so that each segment is free from any pith or seeds.

Either dice the rockmelon or scoop it into balls using a melon baller. Remove the leaves from the strawberries, cut them in half if necessary and wash. Combine all the fruit in a bowl and set aside.

Remove the granita from the freezer and flake with a fork. Divide the fruit salad between six chilled glass bowls, add a large spoonful of granita and serve.

Blood plum granita

This granita is delicious served with Vanilla panna cotta (page 332). Serves 4–6

110 g (4 oz) caster (superfine) sugar

500 g (1 lb 2 oz) blood plums, seeded and chopped

2 tablespoons lemon juice

2 tablespoons finely shredded mint

Place the caster sugar and 125 ml (4 fl oz/½ cup) water in a medium saucepan over low heat. Stir until the sugar dissolves. Raise the heat and bring to the boil. Simmer for 2–3 minutes. Allow to cool.

Place the chopped plums and lemon juice in a food processor and purée until smooth. Strain through a fine sieve. Add 100 ml (3½ fl oz) of the sugar syrup and 100 ml (3½ fl oz) water and stir to combine.

Pour the mixture into a deep rectangular tin and place it in the freezer. Every hour, remove the mixture from the freezer and using a fork scrape it into flakes. Continue to do so every hour as it's freezing, until all the mixture is flaked.

The granita can then be stored in the freezer until ready to serve, but no longer than 2–3 days.

Salted caramel parfait

The simplest and most awesome recipe ever – thanks Andrew Wood! Every year my family has a Christmas feast, thanks to Phillippa Grogan, which is the social event of the year. A select group of foodies indulge in way too much food and wine of the highest standard, and this dessert made an appearance several years ago. Despite the excess alcohol consumed, this parfait stood out and lives on. Serves 8

440 g (15½ oz) caster (superfine) sugar

950 ml (32 fl oz) thickened (whipping) cream

10 egg yolks

Place the sugar and 250 ml (8½ fl oz/1 cup) water in a saucepan. Cook over low heat, stirring, until the sugar dissolves. Raise the heat and boil the liquid. Stop stirring once the liquid is clear; otherwise, the mixture will caramelise. Cook for 12–15 minutes, or until the liquid begins to colour – the desired colour is a lovely mix of gold and caramel, not dark brown. If needed, carefully swirl the saucepan to mix the caramel. Add ½ teaspoon salt and 200 ml (7 fl oz) of the cream carefully – the caramel may splutter. Allow the mixture to come back to the boil, then whisk until smooth. Remove from the heat and allow to cool.

Beat the egg yolks until pale and slightly thickened. Slowly add the caramel and beat until cool.

Whip the remaining cream and fold it through the cool caramel mixture. Pour into a sealable container and place in the freezer until frozen, at least overnight.

Strawberry, rosewater and pistachio semifreddo

A beautiful light and delicate dessert to serve in summer, heralding the arrival of the new season's berries. Serves 6–8

500 g (1 lb 2 oz) strawberries, washed and hulled

1 tablespoon rosewater

6 egg yolks

110 g (4 oz) caster (superfine) sugar

350 ml (12 fl oz) thickened (whipping) cream

75 g (2¾ oz/½ cup) shelled unsalted pistachio nuts

1 tablespoon finely chopped mint leaves

Place half the strawberries in a bowl with the rosewater and mash roughly (a potato masher is ideal).

Beat the egg yolks and sugar until pale and creamy.

Whip the cream until it forms stiff peaks.

Add a spoonful of cream to the egg yolk mixture and stir until well combined. Fold through the remaining cream, the mashed strawberries and pistachio nuts. Pour into a sealable plastic container and place in the freezer. For the next 3–4 hours, about every hour, remove the semifreddo from the freezer and stir well to break up the ice crystals.

Line a 1.5 litre (51 fl oz/6 cup) capacity loaf (bar) tin with plastic wrap and spoon in the mixture. Cover the top with plastic wrap and place in the freezer overnight.

Chop the remaining strawberries into quarters and toss them with the mint. Allow to stand at room temperature for 2–3 hours before serving.

Remove the semifreddo from the freezer 10 minutes before serving, to allow it to soften a little. Slice the semifreddo into 1.5 cm (½ in) thick slices. Arrange on serving plates, add the minted strawberries and serve.

Espresso semifreddo with butterscotch sauce

Butterscotch sauce can be used in many ways – drizzle it over Vanilla ice cream (page 349), Baby pavlovas (page 346) or this espresso semifreddo. Serves 8

200 g (7 oz) dark chocolate, chopped into chunks

6 egg yolks

110 g (4 oz) caster (superfine) sugar

165 ml (5½ fl oz) strong black coffee

350 ml (12 fl oz) thickened (whipping cream)

Butterscotch sauce (page 488) to serve

Line a medium (21 × 9 × 6 cm/8¼ × 3½ × 2½ in) loaf (bar) tin with plastic wrap.

Melt the chocolate by placing it in a bowl over a saucepan of simmering water, or in a microwave on Low for 1–2 minutes.

Beat the egg yolks and caster sugar until pale and thick. Add the coffee and chocolate and beat to incorporate.

Whip the cream to form soft peaks. Add a spoonful of whipped cream to the chocolate base and stir it through, then gently fold through the remaining cream. Spoon into the prepared tin, cover and freeze overnight.

To serve, allow the semifreddo to stand in its tin at room temperature for 10 minutes. Turn it out onto a board and cut into slices. Arrange the slices on plates and drizzle with the butterscotch sauce.

Cherry ripe sundaes

It's often hard for me to get cherries home from the shop because everyone tucks into them on the journey. But it's well worth making the effort so you can enjoy this dish. Serves 4

100 g (3½ oz) white chocolate
60 ml (2 fl oz/¼ cup) thickened (whipping) cream
75 g (2¾ oz) caster (superfine) sugar
500 g (1 lb 2 oz) cherries, halved and pitted
25 g (1 oz) shredded coconut
Vanilla ice cream (page 349)

Make a white chocolate ganache by melting the white chocolate with the cream in a bowl set over a saucepan of simmering water. Whisk until smooth and set aside.

Preheat the oven to 180°C (350°F).

Make a syrup by placing the caster sugar and 75 ml (2½ fl oz) water in a small saucepan. Dissolve the sugar in the water over low heat. Raise the heat and cook for 5–6 minutes, or until the mixture reduces to a light syrup. Add the cherries, bring to the boil, then remove from the heat. Drain the cherries and reserve the syrup.

Toast the shredded coconut in the oven for 6–7 minutes until golden brown.

In four tall glasses layer the vanilla ice cream, white chocolate ganache, cherries and toasted coconut. Drizzle with the reserved syrup.

Simple banana split with Mars Bar sauce

An old-fashioned dessert, but still a winner. Good-quality ice cream adds a lot to this recipe. It's also delicious with Dulce de leche (page 489). Serves 4

90 g (3 oz) chopped Mars Bars (Milky Way Bars)
20 g (¾ oz) butter
80 ml (2½ fl oz/⅓ cup) thickened (whipping) cream
4 bananas
Vanilla ice cream (page 349)
Toasted almond flakes

Make a chocolate sauce by placing the Mars Bars, butter and cream in a bowl. Set the bowl over a saucepan of simmering water and cook for 5–6 minutes. Stir often until everything has melted together smoothly.

Peel and split the bananas in half and lay each banana in an individual dish. Add one to two scoops of vanilla ice cream, drizzle the warm chocolate sauce over and sprinkle with the toasted almond flakes.

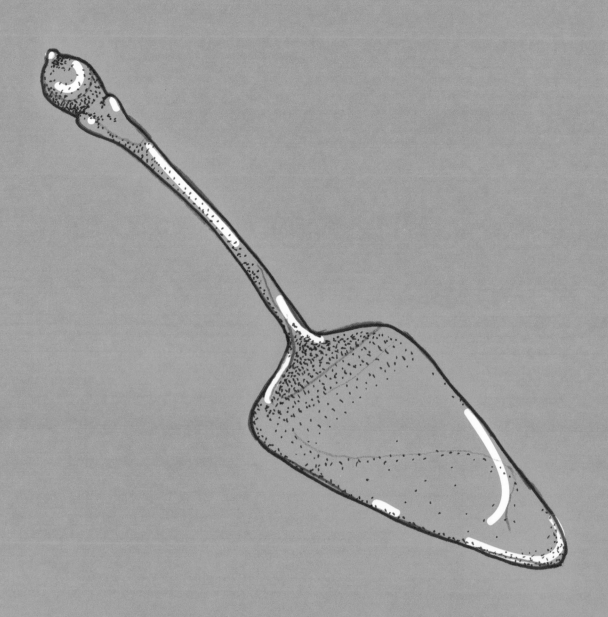

Cakes

There is nothing more welcoming than the aroma of a cake baking in the oven; nothing that rekindles childhood memories more than the scent of a tray of cupcakes cooling on a rack, or a still-warm sponge being spread with raspberry jam.

Home baked

For kids today, freshly home-baked cakes are an increasingly rare occurrence. Many people are too busy to cook dinner, let alone go to the bother of dipping cubes of sponge into chocolate and coconut to make lamingtons, or whipping up a batch of cupcakes. Sadly, the result will be a new generation of adults who have no experience of home baking. To ensure that this is not the future for your household, I've gathered a selection of recipes that may well become your family favourites.

It has to be said that I've managed to bring up two children who are equally passionate about 'procrastabaking' as I am. Deadline looming? Housework to do? Phone calls to make? Ignore them all and make a cake instead! Somehow as the magic of baking takes over, whatever task you have been avoiding or unable to get your head around doesn't seem so bad after all. And if you don't believe me, here's a whole chapter of recipes to try the theory out on.

Things you need to know
about cakes

Basic baking equipment:
20 cm (8 in) cake tin
22 cm (8¾ in) cake tin
23 cm (9 in) cake tin
Loaf (bar) tin (21 × 9 × 6 cm/8¼ × 3½ × 2½ in)
Muffin tins, either 2 × 6 large (two rows of three) or
  3 × 6 small (three rows of six)
Wire cooling rack

- Grease tins with the fat you are cooking with. This means butter with most cakes, oil when used and so on. Grease the tin, line it with baking paper and then grease again.

- Needless to say, a freestanding electric mixer will make light work of any beating, whisking or blending to be done.

- Always line tins with baking paper to make sure cakes come out easily and to keep washing up to a minimum. The easiest way to line a round cake tin is to tear off a square piece of paper that's big enough to sit the tin on without much excess. Fold the paper in half, then in half again sideways, then in half again diagonally to end up with a wedge-shaped piece of paper. Mark a curve on the paper with your scissors, using the cake tin as a guide, then cut along the curve. Unfold the paper and it should fit your tin perfectly.

- It's much easier to make a cake with soft butter than with hard. Zap hard butter in the microwave for 20 seconds, or grate it, to soften it quickly. I normally use unsalted butter for baking.

- The better the quality of your chocolate, the better your chocolate cakes, so when a recipe calls for chocolate use cooking couverture. Dark couverture is best, and melts (buttons) or chips melt more easily.

- Natural vanilla extract has a far superior flavour to vanilla essence. Yep, it's more expensive, but you only have to use half as much.

- Use unsweetened (Dutch) cocoa powder for better flavour – again, the better the quality, the better the cake.

- All eggs used in these recipes are medium (59 g/2 oz).

- For preference, use espresso coffee where coffee is called for, adding extra coffee grounds for a stronger brew. A stove-top espresso machine makes great cooking coffee. Otherwise, the simplest thing to do is to dissolve 1–2 teaspoons instant coffee in the required amount of boiling water.

- To test whether a cake is ready, insert a skewer or cake tester into the centre of the cake. The skewer should come out free of cake mix or crumbs. If it doesn't, cook the cake for a further 5 minutes, then try again.

- When a cake is cooked, place the tin on a wire cooling rack and allow to stand for 10–15 minutes before removing the cake from the tin.

- A simple way to jazz up a cake is to dust it with icing (confectioners') sugar or cocoa powder.

- Head to your nearest health food store, rather than the supermarket, to buy baking powder. The supermarket brands all contain aluminium (they don't have to list it in the ingredients because of the small quantities). The health food store brands are usually gluten-free, too.

- I have made many of the cakes in this chapter with commercially bought gluten-free flour and, for the most part, with good results. However, I find sometimes the cakes are a bit heavier. If you'd like to make your own gluten-free flour, see the recipe on page 484.

- I often substitute coconut sugar for caster (superfine) sugar with good results, particularly with 'heavier' cakes, such as chocolate and dried fruit. The coconut sugar adds a caramelly richness, making the cakes heavier and more pudding-like.

- I have also reduced the amount of sugar in some of the recipes and you can't tell the difference. While baking is a careful chemistry of flour, eggs, fat and sugar, you can reduce the quantity of sugar if you think the amount sounds excessive.

Cake recipes

Allan's easy sponge cake

There's something special about a good sponge cake filled with a little whipped cream and a layer of raspberry jam. This is a really easy recipe, and it cooks in no time. Serves 6–8

4 eggs

110 g (4 oz) caster (superfine) sugar

100 g (3½ oz/⅔ cup) plain (all-purpose) flour

Raspberry jam as required

250 ml (8½ fl oz/1 cup) thickened (whipping) cream, whipped

Icing (confectioners') sugar to dust

Preheat the oven to 180°C (350°F). Butter a 20 cm (8 in) springform cake tin and line the side and bottom with baking paper. Butter the paper and sprinkle it with a little plain flour to ensure the batter won't stick.

Beat the eggs and caster sugar together until very thick and light. Carefully fold in the flour, then spoon the mix into the prepared cake tin and cook in the oven for 15–20 minutes. Test the cake by inserting a skewer. If it comes out clean, the cake is ready; if it doesn't, cook for a further 2–3 minutes and test again.

Allow the cake to cool on a wire rack. When cool, remove the cake from the cake tin and peel away the baking paper. Cut the sponge in half and spread a layer of jam and whipped cream on the bottom half of the cake. Replace the top, then sprinkle with icing sugar.

Passionfruit sponge cake
Fill the sponge with a layer of Passionfruit curd (page 445) instead of jam.

Butter cake

Also known as Madeira cake, this is one of my favourite types of cake: quiet and unassuming, but somehow extremely more-ish. If you can leave it alone for a few days, it gets better with age. You can simply dust this cake with icing sugar, or top it with Butter icing (page 491 – match the flavour to suit the icing), or turn it into a drizzle cake. Serves 6–8

220 g (8 oz) soft butter

180 g (6½ oz) caster (superfine) sugar, plus extra for sprinkling

Grated zest of 2 lemons

3 eggs

200 g (7 oz/1⅓ cups) self-raising flour

90 g (3 oz) plain (all-purpose) flour

60 ml (2 fl oz/¼ cup) lemon juice

Preheat the oven to 170°C (340°F). Grease and line a 23.5 × 13.5 × 7 cm (9¼ × 5¼ × 2¾ in) loaf (bar) tin.

Cream the butter and sugar until light and fluffy. Add the lemon zest. Add the eggs one at a time, allowing each to be incorporated before adding the next. Stir in the flours and lemon juice and keep stirring until incorporated. Spoon into the prepared tin, sprinkle with the extra caster sugar and bake for 1 hour. Test the cake by inserting a skewer. If it comes out clean the

cake is ready, if it doesn't, cook for a further 5 minutes and test again. Allow to cool in the tin before removing.

Lemon and poppy seed tea cake
Add 1 tablespoon poppy seeds to the flour.

Orange tea cake
Substitute orange zest and juice for the lemon.

Passionfruit tea cake
Substitute strained passionfruit juice for the lemon juice.

Chocolate tea cake
You can swap 1 tablespoon of flour for unsweetened (Dutch) cocoa powder.

Lemon drizzle cake
Add 80 g (2¾ oz/⅓ cup) caster (superfine) sugar to 60 ml (2 fl oz/¼ cup) lemon juice. Stir together – the sugar will not dissolve, but that's fine. Pour the icing over the still-warm cake.

One-pot chocolate cake

This has to be the best, simplest chocolate cake in the whole world! There's no need for a mixer or any equipment at all, other than a pan and a wooden spoon. The further in advance you make it, the moister and deeper the flavours become. As I've gotten older I've discovered that good things take time and this cake is a classic example of this. I now cook it at a lower temperature and it makes all the difference – it's fudgier and it cooks better. Serves 6–8

250 g (9 oz) soft butter
150 g (5½ oz) dark chocolate, chopped
165 g (6 oz) caster (superfine) sugar
250 ml (8½ fl oz/1 cup) strong coffee
150 g (5½ oz/1 cup) plain (all-purpose) flour
100 g (3½ oz/⅔ cup) self-raising flour
50 g (1¾ oz) unsweetened (Dutch) cocoa powder
2 eggs

Preheat the oven to 160°C (320°F). Grease a 22 cm (8¾ in) round cake tin and line the side and bottom with baking paper.

Place the butter, chocolate, caster sugar and coffee in a large saucepan. Cook over medium heat, stirring occasionally, until everything melts. Remove from the heat and allow to cool slightly.

Sift the flours and cocoa together and add to the cooled chocolate mixture, along with the eggs. Beat well until all the ingredients are combined.

Spoon the batter into the prepared cake tin and bake in the oven for 45 minutes. Test the cake by inserting a skewer. If it comes out clean, the cake is ready; if it doesn't, cook for a further 5 minutes and test again.

Chocolate fudge cake
Increase the self-raising flour to 150 g (5½ oz/1 cup), omit the plain flour and add 100 g (3½ oz/1 cup) ground almonds to produce a fudgier cake.

Flourless chocolate and almond cake

This is my variation on the classic Elizabeth David cake, which I find every bit as good as everyone says it is. Serves 6–8

250 g (9 oz) dark chocolate, chopped
1 tablespoon brandy
130 g (4½ oz) ground almonds
250 g (9 oz) soft butter
165 g (6 oz) caster (superfine) sugar, plus an extra
  2 tablespoons
6 eggs, separated
Chocolate ganache (page 492) for topping

Preheat the oven to 180°C (350°F). Grease a 22 cm (8¾ in) springform cake tin and line the side and bottom with baking paper.

Melt the chocolate gently, then mix in the brandy and ground almonds. Cream the butter and sugar until light and fluffy. Add the egg yolks, then beat to incorporate.

Add the chocolate and almond mixture and stir lightly to blend.

Beat the egg whites with the extra 2 tablespoons of caster sugar until they form stiff peaks.

Add 1 tablespoon egg white to the chocolate mixture and stir in well. Gently fold through the remaining egg white. Spoon into the prepared cake tin and bake in the oven for 50 minutes.

Test the cake with a skewer. If it comes out clean, the cake is ready; if it doesn't, cook for a further 5 minutes before trying again. Allow the cake to cool in the tin for 15 minutes before turning it out onto a wire rack. When cool, cover with the chocolate ganache.

Rich chocolate and hazelnut cake
You can replace the ground almonds with roasted ground hazelnuts.

Chocolate buttermilk cake

Buttermilk adds a lovely softness to this cake recipe. You have the option to make one larger 'everyday' kinda cake, or divide the mix into two smaller tins, which then get sliced horizontally after cooking to make a four-layered 'celebration' cake. No one will judge you if you're just celebrating surviving the day. You can also make this mix into chocolate cupcakes. Serves 6–8

200 g (7 oz) butter, diced
50 g (1¾ oz) unsweetened (Dutch) cocoa powder
450 g (15½ oz/3 cups) self-raising flour
550 g (1 lb 3 oz) caster (superfine) sugar
3 eggs
180 ml (6 fl oz) buttermilk
Chocolate fudge icing (page 492)

Preheat the oven to 160°C (320°F). Grease a 23 cm (9 in) round cake tin and line the side and bottom with baking paper.

Place 375 ml (12½ fl oz/1½ cups) water, the butter and cocoa in a small saucepan and cook over medium heat until the butter is melted.

Place the flour and sugar in a large mixing bowl, stir to combine and then add the cocoa mixture and mix together. Add the eggs and buttermilk and beat until smooth and combined.

Pour into the prepared cake tin and bake in the oven for 50–60 minutes. Test with a skewer. If it comes out clean, the cake is ready; if it doesn't, cook the cake for a further 5 minutes before trying again. Allow the cake to cool in the tin for 15 minutes before turning it out onto a wire rack. When the cake is completely cool, cover it with the chocolate fudge icing.

Chocolate buttermilk layer cake
For a special occasion, divide the cake mixture between two lined and greased 20 cm (8 in) cake tins. Bake for 40 minutes. Check the cakes are cooked and allow to cool. When cool, trim the tops of the cakes if necessary to flatten them slightly and then slice in half horizontally. Place one cake on a serving platter, cover with icing and repeat with the remaining layers until you have a four-layer cake. Top with frosting.

Green cake

Well, this almost didn't make it. For me, and now my children, this is the ultimate comfort cake. My mum used to make it for my brother and me as a birthday cake and I'm rather fond of it. It's not everyone's cup of tea, hence why it almost didn't make the cut, but I love it. Serves 6–8

200 g (7 oz) soft butter
250 g (9 oz) caster (superfine) sugar
3 eggs
225 g (8 oz/1½ cups) self-raising flour
1½ teaspoons almond essence
1 teaspoon natural green food colouring
Chocolate icing (page 491)

Preheat the oven to 180°C (350°F). Grease and line a 23 cm (9 in) springform cake tin.

Cream the butter and sugar until light and fluffy. Add the eggs one by one, allowing each to be incorporated before adding the next. Add flour, almond essence and colouring and beat until smooth.

Spoon the batter into the prepared tin and bake for 40 minutes. Test the cake by inserting a skewer. If it comes out clean, the cake is ready; if it doesn't, cook for a further 5 minutes and test again.

Allow to cool for 15 minutes, then remove the cake from the tin. When cool, top with the chocolate icing.

Red velvet cake

I just want everyone to know how hard it was to limit this part of the book to five chocolate cake recipes – but I couldn't leave out red velvet cake, everyone's favourite. Serves 6–8

225 g (8 oz) soft butter
275 g (9½ oz) caster (superfine) sugar
1 teaspoon natural vanilla extract
3 eggs
300 g (10½ oz/2 cups) self-raising flour
2 tablespoons unsweetened (Dutch) cocoa powder
180 ml (6 fl oz) buttermilk
2–3 teaspoons natural red food colouring
Cream cheese frosting (page 493)

Preheat the oven to 170°C (340°F). Grease a 20 cm (8 in) round cake tin and line the side and bottom with baking paper.

Cream the butter, sugar and vanilla until light and fluffy. Add the eggs one at a time, allowing each to be fully incorporated before adding the next. Sift in the flour and cocoa, then add the buttermilk and red food colouring and keep stirring until incorporated. Make sure you add enough food colouring to get a vibrant shade of red. Spoon the batter into the prepared tin and bake for 1 hour. Test the cake by inserting a skewer. If it comes out clean, the cake is ready; if it doesn't, cook for a further 5 minutes and test again. Allow to cool in the tin before removing.

When cool, trim the top of the cake if necessary to flatten slightly, then slice the cake in half horizontally. Place one half on a serving platter, cover with the frosting and repeat with the remaining layer. Top with more frosting.

Red velvet cupcakes
Pour the mixture into lined muffin tins to make cupcakes. Reduce the cooking time to 20–25 minutes.

White chocolate and raspberry cake

White chocolate and raspberry is a classic combination, and this produces a dense, fudgy cake. You can also double this recipe and make a large celebration cake as I did for my daughter Mia's eighteenth birthday party. I covered the whole cake with cake pops, fairy floss and edible glitter. Still trying to get most of that glitter out of the carpet! Serves 6–8

200 g (7 oz) soft butter
220 g (8 oz) caster (superfine) sugar
3 eggs
Grated zest of 1 lemon
75 g (2¾ oz) sour cream or natural yoghurt
200 g (7 oz) small white chocolate chips
350 g (12½ oz/2⅓ cups) self-raising flour
200 g (7 oz) raspberries
White chocolate ganache (page 492)

Preheat the oven to 160°C (320°F). Grease a 23 cm (9 in) round cake tin and line the side and bottom with baking paper.

Cream together the butter and sugar until light and fluffy. Add the eggs, one by one, beating well after each addition. Add the lemon zest, sour cream and chocolate and mix well. Finally add the flour.

Spoon the cake mix into the prepared tin. Bake in the oven for 40 minutes. Check the cake with a skewer. If it comes out clean, the cake is cooked; if it doesn't, cook for a further 5–10 minutes and try again.

When cool, cover with the white chocolate ganache and top with fresh raspberries.

Blueberry pound cake
Substitute cream cheese for the white chocolate. Cream the cheese with the butter and sugar and swap the raspberries for blueberries.

Choc chip pound cake
Substitute cream cheese for the white chocolate. Cream the cheese with the butter and sugar and swap the raspberries for small dark chocolate chips.

Sicilian flourless orange cake

Cakes are great for dessert as they can be baked in advance and thus save you the drama of any last-minute assembling. This one is wonderful after any Mediterranean-influenced main course, as it's rich, moist and full of flavour. Serves 8

2 oranges

5 eggs

220 g (8 oz) caster (superfine) sugar

250 g (9 oz) ground almonds

1 teaspoon baking powder

Icing (confectioners') sugar

Marmalade cream (page 488) to serve

Put the oranges in a small saucepan, cover with water and bring to the boil. Reduce the heat to a simmer and cook for 30–40 minutes, or until the fruit is soft. Allow to cool. Cut the oranges into quarters, removing the pips. Purée in a food processor until smooth.

Preheat the oven to 180°C (350°F). Grease a 22 cm (8¾ in) round cake tin and line the side and bottom with baking paper.

Beat the eggs and sugar together until pale and doubled in size, about 5 minutes.

Mix the ground almonds and baking powder together. Add the orange purée and almond mixture to the beaten eggs and beat to incorporate completely. Pour the mixture into the prepared cake tin. Bake in the oven until light brown and firm in the centre, about 1 hour. Allow to cool.

Dust the cake with icing sugar, cut into slices and serve with the marmalade cream.

Baby orange and almond cakes
Line eighteen 125 ml (4 fl oz/½ cup) muffin tin holes with paper cases, then spoon the mixture into the tins and bake in the oven for 20 minutes, or until light brown and firm in the centre. Test the cakes by inserting a skewer into one of them. If it comes out clean, they are ready; if it doesn't, cook for a further 5 minutes and test again. Allow to cool on a wire rack.

Pear, pistachio and chocolate loaf

Vary the type of chocolate you use in this recipe to add a different flavour – maybe an orange- or ginger-flavoured dark chocolate or an intensely bitter chocolate high in cocoa solids. Serves 6–8

225 g (8 oz/1½ cups) self-raising flour

165 g (6 oz) caster (superfine) sugar

200 g (7 oz) soft butter

4 eggs

100 g (3½ oz) mini dark chocolate chips

2 peeled, cored and diced pears

130 g (4½ oz/1 cup) chopped pistachio nuts

Grated zest of 1 orange

Preheat the oven to 180°C (350°F) Grease and line a 22 × 11.5 × 7 cm (8¾ × 4½ × 2¾ in) loaf (bar) tin.

Mix together the flour, sugar, butter, eggs and a pinch of salt until smooth. Add the chocolate, diced pear, pistachio nuts and the orange zest and mix until evenly combined. Pour the mixture into the prepared tin and bake in the oven for 50–60 minutes or until a skewer inserted into the cake comes out clean. Allow to cool in the tin for 5–10 minutes before turning out.

Serve as a luscious afternoon tea cake, or as a dessert, alongside some whipped cream and fresh berries.

Passionfruit ring cake

I love using passionfruit in cakes, tarts and desserts. This recipe follows the classic French method called 'quatre-quart', which combines equal quantities of ingredients. A kugelhopf tin is ideal if you have one; if not, a 22 cm (8¾ in) springform cake tin will work. Serves 6–8

250 g (9 oz) soft butter

250 g (9 oz) caster (superfine) sugar

4 eggs

250 g (9 oz/1⅔ cups) self-raising flour, sifted

Passionfruit icing (page 491)

Preheat the oven to 180°C (350°F). Grease either a kugelhopf tin or a 22 cm (8¾ in) cake tin and line the side and bottom with baking paper.

Cream the butter and caster sugar until light and fluffy. Add the eggs, one by one, fully incorporating each one before adding the next. Carefully fold in the flour.

Spoon the mixture into the prepared cake tin. Bake in the oven for 40 minutes. Check the cake with a skewer. If it comes out clean, the cake is cooked; if it doesn't, cook for a further 5–10 minutes and try again.

When the cake is cool, cover with the passionfruit icing.

Boil-and-bake fruit cake

This is easy to make and great for taking away on a weekend camping trip or just for having on hand in the cupboard. Also yummy with walnuts or pecans. Serves 8–10

150 g (5½ oz) butter

300 g (10½ oz) sultanas (golden raisins)

300 g (10½ oz) currants

200 g (7 oz) brown sugar

1 teaspoon ground allspice

1 teaspoon ground cinnamon

1 teaspoon ground ginger

1 teaspoon bicarbonate of soda (baking soda)

2 eggs, beaten

150 g (5½ oz/1 cup) plain (all-purpose) flour

150 g (5½ oz/1 cup) self-raising flour

Preheat the oven to 180°C (350°F). Grease a 22 cm (8¾ in) round cake tin and line side and bottom with baking paper.

Combine the butter, sultanas, currants, sugar, spices, bicarbonate of soda and 250 ml (8½ fl oz/1 cup) water in a saucepan. Cook over medium heat until the mixture comes to the boil, stirring often. Remove from the heat and allow to cool.

Add the eggs and beat well. Sift the flours together, add to the mixture and beat well.

Spoon the mixture into the prepared cake tin and bake for 1 hour. Check the cake with a skewer. If it comes out clean, the cake is cooked; if it doesn't, cook for a further 5–10 minutes and try again.

Apple fruit cake
Swap half the dried fruit for grated fresh apple.

Fig or date fruit cake
Replace half the currants with figs or dates.

Chadwick family Christmas cake

My friends John and Ann Marie Chadwick have agreed to share their Christmas cake recipe. John first made the cake to remind himself of his English roots and it has now become their family tradition. They recommend making it at the beginning of December to allow the fullest flavour to develop in time for the big day. It takes 5 hours to cook but it's well worth the time and effort. Serves 20

Batter

250 g (9 oz) butter

300 g (10½ oz) brown sugar

4 eggs

250 g (9 oz/1⅔ cups) plain (all-purpose) flour, sifted

½ teaspoon baking powder

½ teaspoon salt

Fruit

320 g (11½ oz) sultanas (golden raisins)

300 g (10½ oz/1⅔ cups) dried apricots, sliced

170 g (6 oz) pitted dried dates, sliced

190 g (6½ oz) dried figs, sliced

125 g (4½ oz/⅔ cup) mixed peel

100 g (3½ oz) glacé cherries

55 g (2 oz) blanched almonds

50 g (1¾ oz/½ cup) walnuts

250 ml (8½ fl oz/1 cup) sweet sherry

2–3 tablespoons brandy

Icing

Apricot jam

250 g (9 oz) marzipan icing (store-bought)

Royal icing (page 491)

Preheat the oven to 200°C (400°F). Butter a 25 cm (10 in) square cake tin, line the sides and bottom with baking paper and butter it lightly. If you have a smaller tin, you can use it instead and reduce the cooking time a little.

Cream the butter and brown sugar until light and fluffy. Add the eggs, one by one, fully incorporating each one before adding the next.

Sift the flour, baking powder and salt together. Stir this into the butter and sugar.

Place all the dried fruit and nuts together in a large bowl. Add the sherry and stir to combine. Add the fruit and nuts to the batter and stir to mix well. The secret here is for every member of the family to have a stir and make a wish!

Spoon the mixture into the prepared cake tin and smooth the top. Cover with foil and bake in the oven for 20 minutes. Reduce the oven temperature to 175°C (345°F) and bake for another 20 minutes. Remove the foil and reduce the oven temperature to 125°C (255°F) and bake the cake for a further 3 hours and 20 minutes. Test the cake by inserting a skewer. If it comes out clean, the cake is ready; if not, cook for a further 20 minutes and test again.

Allow the cake to cool for 10 minutes. Remove the cake from the tin and place it upside down on a wire rack. The bottom of the cake is quite flat and will now become the top. This will make icing the cake much easier. Brush the top and sides of the cake with the brandy while still warm, then allow to cool completely on a wire rack. Wrap the cool cake in foil and store in a cool place. Wait a few days before icing.

To ice the cake, thickly spread the jam over the top and sides. Roll out the marzipan and cover the top and sides with a thin layer. Use a palette knife to spread a layer of royal icing all over the cake. Decorate further if desired.

Spiced Italian fruit cake

This is a glorious blending of candied fruits, chocolate, a multitude of spices and the heady aroma of marsala. Resistance is useless. When the cake mix is in the tin you can add additional sliced glacé fruit in a decorative pattern on top if you wish. Serves 8–10

125 g (4½ oz/1 cup) sultanas (golden raisins)

80 ml (2½ fl oz/⅓ cup) marsala

250 g (9 oz) blanched almonds, chopped

90 g (3 oz) pine nuts

250 g (9 oz) candied fruit, such as orange, apricots, figs, pears or lemon, chopped

125 g (4½ oz) dark chocolate, chopped

125 g (4½ oz) caster (superfine) sugar

125 g (4½ oz) plain (all-purpose) flour

1 teaspoon ground cinnamon

¼ teaspoon ground cloves

½ teaspoon freshly grated nutmeg

½ teaspoon ground cardamom

½ teaspoon baking powder

2 tablespoons honey

60 g (2 oz) butter

3 eggs

Soak the sultanas in the marsala for at least 1 hour, or ideally overnight. (If you are short of time, cooking the sultanas in the marsala for 1–2 minutes in the microwave will hurry the soaking along.)

Preheat the oven to 180°C (350°F). Grease and line a 22 cm (8¾ in) springform cake tin.

Mix the soaked, drained sultanas with the nuts, candied fruit and chocolate. Add the sugar and mix to combine.

In a bowl, sift the flour with the spices and baking powder. Mix through the nut mixture.

In a small saucepan over low heat, melt the honey and butter together.

Beat the eggs until light and fluffy and doubled in size. Add the warm butter and honey mixture to the eggs, then fold this through the fruit and nut mixture until well combined. Spoon into the prepared tin. Bake in the oven for 45–50 minutes, or until a skewer comes out clean.

Sherry-soaked raisin and almond cake

I've been making almond cakes for many years now and they always go down a treat. In this variation, raisins soaked in sherry add richness to the cake, which also makes a great dessert when served with Marmalade cream (page 488). Serves 6–8

170 g (6 oz) raisins

60 ml (2 fl oz/¼ cup) sweet sherry

125 g (4½ oz) soft butter

220 g (8 oz) caster (superfine) sugar

2 eggs

125 g (4½ oz/1¼ cups) ground almonds

225 g (8 oz/1½ cups) self-raising flour

250 g (9 oz/1 cup) natural yoghurt

1 teaspoon almond essence

Icing (confectioners') sugar to serve

Soak the raisins in sherry overnight. If time is tight, microwave on High (100%) for 1 minute or place in a small saucepan and warm through for a few minutes. Cool before using.

Preheat the oven to 180°C (350°F). Grease a 22 cm (8¾ in) cake tin and line the side and bottom with baking paper.

Cream the butter and caster sugar until light and fluffy. Add the eggs, one by one, allowing the first to be incorporated before adding the second. Fold in the ground almonds, flour, yoghurt and almond essence.

Spoon the mixture into the prepared cake tin and bake in the oven for 35 minutes. Test the cake by inserting a skewer. If it comes out clean, the cake is ready; if it doesn't, cook for a further 5 minutes and test again.

When cool, dust the cake with icing sugar and serve.

Upside-down pear and ginger cake

There's something magical about preparing a cake from the top down. I love the fact that the top starts on the bottom and, when it's flipped over, it looks amazing. This pear and ginger version tastes particularly fine. Serves 6–8

5 poached pear halves (see Vanilla poached fruit, page 327), cooking liquid reserved

200 g (7 oz) golden syrup, plus 2 tablespoons

125 g (4½ oz) butter

265 g (9½ oz) brown sugar

2 eggs

225 g (8 oz/1½ cups) self-raising flour

2 teaspoons ground ginger

Icing (confectioners') sugar to dust

Preheat the oven to 180°C (350°F). Grease a 22 cm (8¾ in) cake tin and line the side and bottom with baking paper.

Arrange the pear halves, cut side down, in the base of the prepared cake tin. Reserve any cooking liquid. Drizzle with the 2 tablespoons golden syrup.

Cream the butter and brown sugar until light and fluffy. Beat in the remaining golden syrup. Add the eggs, one by one, fully incorporating the first before adding the second. Sift the flour and ginger together and fold them in carefully. Add enough cooking liquid to form a soft cake mix.

Spoon into the prepared cake tin over the pear slices and bake in the oven for 40 minutes. Test the cake by inserting a skewer. If it comes out clean, the cake is ready; if it doesn't, cook for a further 5 minutes and test again.

Allow the cake to cool for 15 minutes, then remove it from the tin and flip it over to reveal the top. Dust with icing sugar to serve.

Coconut cake

This is a beautiful cake with a dense texture, which can easily be sliced and passed around. Try it as your next birthday cake. Serves 6–8

250 ml (8½ fl oz/1 cup) coconut milk

100 g (3½ oz) desiccated coconut

200 g (7 oz) soft butter

220 g (8 oz) caster (superfine) sugar

4 eggs

250 g (9 oz/1⅔ cups) self-raising flour, sifted

Icing (confectioners') sugar to dust

Preheat the oven to 180°C (350°F). Grease a 22 cm (8¾ in) cake tin and line the side and bottom with baking paper.

Place the coconut milk and desiccated coconut in a small saucepan over medium heat. Allow to simmer for 2–3 minutes, then remove from the heat, set aside and allow to cool.

Cream the butter and sugar until light and fluffy. Add the eggs one by one, fully incorporating each one before adding the next. Alternately fold in the sifted flour and coconut mixture until well combined.

Spoon the mixture into the prepared tin. Bake in the oven for 40 minutes. Test the cake by inserting a skewer. If it comes out clean, the cake is ready; if it doesn't, cook for a further 5 minutes and test again.

Allow to cool, dust with icing sugar and serve.

Rhubarb lemon cake

The best kind of fruit to include in cakes are those with a good amount of acid. That's why plums, apricots, quinces and rhubarb feature so heavily in my baking. I find they balance the sweetness and richness of cakes. Try this rhubarb lemon cake, and you'll see what I mean.
Serves 6–8

250 g (9 oz) rhubarb stalks, cut into 2 cm (¾ in) pieces

65 g (2¼ oz) brown sugar

125 g (4½ oz) soft butter

170 g (6 oz/¾ cup) caster (superfine) sugar

Grated zest of 1 lemon, plus 2 tablespoons lemon juice

3 eggs

150 g (5½ oz/1 cup) plain (all-purpose) flour

50 g (1¾ oz/⅓ cup) self-raising flour

100 g (3½ oz) sour cream

Icing (confectioners') sugar for dusting

Preheat the oven to 180°C (350°F). Grease a 22 cm (8¾ in) round cake tin and line the side and bottom with baking paper.

Toss the rhubarb with the brown sugar and set aside.

Cream the butter and caster sugar until light and fluffy. Add the lemon zest and then the eggs, one by one, fully incorporating each one before adding the next. Stir through the lemon juice.

Sift the flours together and fold them into the cake mix carefully, alternating with sour cream. Finally, fold the rhubarb through. Spoon the mixture into the prepared tin and bake for 40 minutes. Test the cake by inserting a skewer. If it comes out clean, the cake is ready; if it doesn't, cook for a further 5 minutes and test again.

Allow the cake to cool for 15 minutes, then remove from the tin. Dust with icing sugar and serve.

Apple, olive oil and pistachio cake

I love a good apple cake. Make sure you use a mild olive oil so it doesn't overpower the cake.
Serves 8

2 cooking apples, grated (approximately 1½ cups)

200 g (7 oz) brown sugar

125 ml (4 fl oz/½ cup) olive oil

2 eggs

150 g (5½ oz/1 cup) plain (all-purpose) flour

30 g (1 oz/¼ cup) semolina

2 teaspoons baking powder

Grated zest of 2 lemons

65 g (2¼ oz/½ cup) chopped pistachio nuts

Icing (confectioners') sugar for dusting

Preheat the oven to 160°C (320°F). Grease a 22 cm (8¾ in) cake tin and line the side and bottom with baking paper.

Beat the eggs and sugar until light and fluffy. Add the olive oil and beat together.

Sift together the flour, semolina and baking powder and stir this mixture through the batter. Pour into the prepared tin and bake in the oven for 40 minutes. Check the cake with a skewer. If it comes out clean the cake is cooked; if it doesn't, cook for a further 5–10 minutes and try again. Dust with icing sugar.

Orange and yoghurt syrup cake

Who doesn't love a syrup cake? They're always beautifully moist and keep that extra day or two. This recipe also works well as small cakes as a dessert alternative. Serves 6–8

125 g (4½ oz) soft butter

300 g (10½ oz) caster (superfine) sugar

3 eggs, separated

Grated zest of 4 oranges

160 ml (5½ fl oz) orange juice

250 g (9 oz/1 cup) natural yoghurt

300 g (10½ oz/2 cups) self-raising flour

2 tablespoons lemon juice

Preheat the oven to 180°C (350°F). Grease a 22 cm (8¾ in) cake tin and line the side and bottom with baking paper.

Cream the butter and 220 g (8 oz) of the sugar until light and fluffy. Add the egg yolks along with half the orange zest. Add 60 ml (2 fl oz/¼ cup) of the orange juice and the yoghurt. Mix briefly, then add the flour and beat until smooth.

Beat the egg whites until stiff, then fold through the cake mix. Spoon into the prepared cake tin and bake in the oven for 40 minutes. Test the cake by inserting a skewer. If it comes out clean, the cake is ready; if it doesn't, cook for a further 5 minutes and test again.

To make the syrup, place the remaining sugar in a small saucepan with the remaining zest and juice. Stir to dissolve the sugar, then bring to the boil. Allow to simmer for 2–3 minutes. Pour the warm syrup topping over the cake and allow to cool.

Lime and blueberry syrup cake
Swap all things orange for lime and add 200 g (7 oz) blueberries as you fold through the egg whites.

Orange poppy seed cake
Add 150 g (5½ oz) poppy seeds to the batter. Omit the syrup topping.

Guinness gingerbread cake

Who said you can't have your cake and eat it too? With this recipe you can have your cake and Guinness all at the same time. If you don't like the idea of adding alcohol, simply substitute it with water. Serves 8–10

75 g (2¾ oz) butter

150 g (5½ oz) golden syrup

100 g (3½ oz) brown sugar

125 ml (4 fl oz/½ cup) Guinness

1 teaspoon ground ginger

½ teaspoon ground cinnamon

Pinch of ground cloves

150 g (5½ oz/1 cup) plain (all-purpose) flour

1 teaspoon bicarbonate of soda (baking soda)

150 g (5½ oz) sour cream

1 egg

Preheat the oven to 180°C (350°F). Grease a 20 cm (8 in) square cake tin and line the sides and bottom with baking paper.

Combine the butter, golden syrup, sugar, Guinness, spices and ½ teaspoon salt in a saucepan and cook over medium heat until everything melts. Sift together the flour and bicarbonate of soda and add to the butter mix and beat well. Add the sour cream and egg and beat until a smooth batter forms.

Pour into the prepared cake tin and bake in the oven for 35–40 minutes. Test the cake by inserting a skewer. If it comes out clean, the cake is ready; if it doesn't, cook for a further 5 minutes and test again.

Caramel banana cake

At last, I've found a use for those bananas lurking at the bottom of the fruit bowl. The riper the bananas and the blacker the skins, the better this cake will be. Serves 6–8

125 g (4½ oz) soft butter
220 g (8 oz) brown sugar
1 tablespoon golden syrup
1 teaspoon natural vanilla extract
2 eggs
150 g (5½ oz/1 cup) plain (all-purpose) flour
75 g (2¾ oz/½ cups) self-raising flour
1 teaspoon baking powder
1 teaspoon ground cinnamon
2 ripe bananas, mashed
90 g (3 oz) walnuts, chopped (optional)
Caramel icing (page 492)

Preheat the oven to 180°C (350°F). Grease a 22 cm (8¾ in) cake tin and line the side and bottom with baking paper.

Cream the butter, sugar, golden syrup and vanilla until light and fluffy. Add the eggs, one by one, incorporating well after each addition. Sift together the flours, baking powder and cinnamon and stir through with the banana and walnuts (if using).

Spoon into the prepared cake tin and bake in the oven for 35–40 minutes. Check the cake with a skewer. If it comes out clean, the cake is cooked; if not, cook for a further 5–10 minutes and try again. Top with the caramel icing.

Carrot cake

When I first heard about carrot cakes in the 1980s, I was very sceptical of the whole idea. This delicious cake proves just how wrong I was. Serves 8–10

300 g (10½ oz/2 cups) self-raising flour
1 teaspoon cinnamon
1 teaspoon mixed spice
4 eggs
330 g (11½ oz) caster (superfine) sugar
1 teaspoon natural vanilla extract
300 ml (10 fl oz) olive oil
60 g (2 oz) hazelnuts
60 g (2 oz/½ cup) chopped walnuts
150 g (5½ oz) sultanas (golden raisins)
3 large carrots, grated
Cream cheese frosting (page 493)

Preheat the oven to 180°C (350°F). Grease a 23 cm (9 in) cake tin and line the side and bottom with baking paper.

Sift the flour, cinnamon and mixed spice together into a large bowl. Add the eggs, sugar, vanilla, oil and a pinch of salt. Mix lightly, then incorporate the hazelnuts, walnuts, sultanas and grated carrot.

Pour into the prepared cake tin. Bake in the oven for 1 hour. Check the cake with a skewer. If it comes out clean, the cake is cooked; if it doesn't, cook for a further 5–10 minutes and try again.

Allow to cool in the tin for 15 minutes, then remove and cool on a wire rack. Top with the cream cheese frosting.

Carrot, cardamom and cashew cake
Substitute ground cardamom for the cinnamon and omit the mixed spice. Substitute cashew nuts for the hazelnuts and walnuts.

Pecan coffee cake

This is a very simple tea cake – or should that be coffee cake? Serves 6–8

150 g (5½ oz) soft butter

90 g (3 oz) caster (superfine) sugar

2 eggs

150 g (5½ oz/1 cup) self-raising flour

1 teaspoon baking powder

60 ml (2 fl oz/¼ cup) strong coffee

90 g (3 oz/¾ cup) chopped pecans, plus pecan halves to decorate

Coffee icing (page 491)

Pecan halve to decorate

Preheat the oven to 180°C (350°F). Grease a 20 cm (8 in) round cake tin and line the side and bottom with baking paper.

Cream the butter and sugar until light and fluffy. Add the eggs, one by one, incorporating well after each addition. Sift together the flour and baking powder. Add the flour mixture and coffee to the other mixture and mix until well combined. Fold through the chopped nuts.

Spoon into the prepared cake tin and bake in the oven for 30–35 minutes. Check the cake with a skewer. If it comes out clean, the cake is cooked; if it doesn't, cook for a further 5 minutes and try again.

Allow to cool, then top with the coffee icing and decorate with the pecan halves.

Persian love cake

This has been a family favourite ever since I saw the recipe by Gerald Yaxley from Qöm in *Gourmet Traveller* magazine. I tend to call it 'lurve cake', or the 'Barry White special' and, as you would expect, I have fallen in love with it. Serves 6–8

360 g (12½ oz) ground almonds

220 g (8 oz) raw sugar

200 g (7 oz) brown sugar

120 g (4½ oz) soft butter

2 eggs, lightly beaten

250 g (9 oz/1 cup) natural yoghurt

1 teaspoon freshly grated nutmeg

45 g (1½ oz) pistachio nuts, roughly chopped

Rose petals (organic and unsprayed)

Preheat the oven to 180°C (350°F). Grease a 20 cm (8 in) round cake tin and line the side and bottom with baking paper.

Combine the ground almonds, sugars, butter and 1 teaspoon salt in a bowl, then rub with your fingertips until a breadcrumb-like texture forms. Spoon half the mixture into the prepared cake tin, gently pressing to evenly cover the base.

Add the eggs, yoghurt and nutmeg to the remaining crumble mixture in the bowl and beat with a wooden spoon until smooth and creamy. Pour over the prepared base in the tin, smooth the top, scatter the pistachio nuts around the edge and bake for 30–35 minutes or until golden brown and set.

Allow to cool. Scatter with rose petals to serve.

Castagnaccio

Here it is for all you fans out there. This cake has had quite an impact on certain friends of mine. Once tried, never forgotten. You can jazz it up even more by serving it with poached pears for a dessert. You have been warned! Serves 8

155 g (5½ oz/1 cup) chestnut flour

155 g (5½ oz/1 cup) self-raising flour

185 g (6½ oz) butter, diced

300 g (10½ oz) brown sugar

1¼ teaspoons bicarbonate of soda (baking soda)

310 ml (10½ fl oz/1¼ cups) milk

1 egg, plus 1 egg yolk

70 g (2½ oz) raisins, soaked in hot water to soften

2 tablespoons rosemary leaves

40 g (1½ oz/¼ cup) pine nuts

2 tablespoons olive oil

Preheat the oven to 170°C (340°F). Line a 20 × 30 cm (8 × 12 in) shallow baking tin with baking paper.

Process the flours, butter and ¼ teaspoon salt until the mixture forms a breadcrumb-like texture. Add the brown sugar. Divide the mixture in two and press half in to the base of the prepared baking tin.

Mix the bicarbonate of soda with the milk, egg and extra yolk, then add to the remaining flour mixture. Add the drained raisins and mix to combine. Pour over the base in the tin. Scatter over the rosemary leaves, pine nuts and drizzle over the olive oil.

Bake in the oven for 40 minutes. Check the cake with a skewer. If it comes out clean, the cake is cooked; if it doesn't, cook for a further 5–10 minutes and try again. Allow to cool in the tin.

Banana bread

You could serve this for breakfast, slightly toasted with fresh banana slices, honey and yoghurt, but's it's also just as good as an afternoon tea treat, too. Feel free to add chopped walnuts or pistachio nuts, if you like. Makes 1 loaf

80 g (2¾ oz) soft butter

150 g (5½ oz) coconut sugar

1 egg

1 teaspoon natural vanilla extract

150 g (5½ oz/1 cup) self-raising flour

2 ripe bananas, mashed

50 g (1¾ oz) small dark chocolate chips (optional)

Preheat the oven to 170°C (340°F). Grease and line a 23.5 × 13.5 × 7 cm (9¼ × 5¼ × 2¾ in) loaf (bar) tin with baking paper.

Cream the butter and coconut sugar until light and fluffy. Add the egg, vanilla, flour and bananas and mix well. Fold through the chocolate chips (if using).

Spoon the mixture into the prepared tin and bake in the oven for 40 minutes. Check the cake with a skewer. If it comes out clean, the cake is cooked; if it doesn't, cook for a further 5–10 minutes and try again. Allow the cake to cool in the tin.

My kind of cheesecake

This cheesecake is made in the traditional way, but is cooked in a deep baking tray surrounded by hot water. This method means the cheesecake cooks slowly. The result is my kind of cheesecake: one with an extraordinarily soft, silky texture. My mate Macka substitutes 375 g (13 oz) of the cream cheese for quark, for a slightly different texture. He also says blood orange zest and juice is 'bonza' in place of the lemon. I also think he's in love with this recipe.
Serves 6–8

150 g (5½ oz) digestive (sweet wholemeal) biscuits or graham crackers
60 g (2 oz) melted butter
500 g (1 lb 2 oz/2 cups) cream cheese
110 g (4 oz) caster (superfine) sugar
Grated zest of 2 lemons
2 eggs, plus 3 egg yolks
150 ml (5 fl oz) thickened (whipping) cream
100 ml (3½ fl oz) lemon juice

Grease a 20 cm (8 in) round cake tin and line the side and bottom with baking paper.

Place the biscuits in a food processor and whizz to form small crumbs. Add the melted butter and process briefly. Press the biscuit base into the bottom of the prepared cake tin. Place in the refrigerator to set for at least 20 minutes.

Preheat the oven to 170°C (340°F).

Beat the cream cheese until smooth. Add the sugar and lemon zest and then whisk in the eggs and yolks one at a time. Stir in the cream and lemon juice.

Take the cake tin and wrap the outside base with foil, using two pieces to cover the base. (This prevents water seeping into the cake during cooking.) Place the cake tin inside a deep baking tin.

Pour the cheesecake filling over the biscuit base. Pour boiling water into the baking tin to come halfway up the side of the cake tin. Place carefully in the oven. Cook for 1 hour, or until the cheesecake is just set, still with some hint of wobble. Allow to cool on a wire rack before refrigerating, preferably overnight.

Passionfruit cheesecake
Substitute strained passionfruit pulp for the lemon juice and serve the chilled cake with additional pulp on top.

White chocolate cheesecake

If white chocolate isn't your thing, simply use dark chocolate instead. Serves 6–8

150 g (5½ oz) chocolate ripple cookies
60 g (2 oz) melted butter
150 g (5½ oz) white chocolate
500 g (1 lb 2 oz/2 cups) soft cream cheese
150 g (5½ oz) caster (superfine) sugar
250 g (9 oz/1 cup) sour cream

Grease a 23 cm (9 in) round cake tin and line the side and bottom with baking paper.

Place the cookies in a food processor and whizz to form small crumbs. Add the melted butter and process briefly. Press the cookie mixture into the bottom of the prepared cake tin and place in the refrigerator to set for at least 20 minutes.

Melt the chocolate by placing it in a bowl over a saucepan of simmering water, or in a microwave on Low for 1–2 minutes.

Beat the cream cheese and caster sugar until well softened and creamy. Add the sour cream and melted chocolate and stir until well combined. Pour on top of the cookie base and chill until set.

Double-chocolate jaffa cheesecake
Swap the white chocolate for dark chocolate, add the grated zest of two oranges to the butter and sugar, and beat until creamy.

Lemon cheesecake

This is the simplest cheesecake of all, with lots of chopped lemon zest and lemon juice to balance the creamy filling. One to be enjoyed regularly. Serves 6–8

150 g (5½ oz) digestive (sweet wholemeal) biscuits or graham crackers

60 g (2 oz) melted butter

500 g (1 lb 2 oz/2 cups) soft cream cheese

145 g (5 oz/⅔ cup) caster (superfine) sugar

125 ml (4 fl oz/½ cup) lemon juice

2 × 5 g (¼ oz) gelatine sheets

125 ml (4 fl oz/½ cup) thickened (whipping) cream

Grated zest of 2 lemons

Grease a 20 cm (8 in) cake tin and line the side and bottom with baking paper.

Place the biscuits in a food processor and whizz to form small crumbs. Add the melted butter and process briefly. Press the biscuit mix into the bottom of the prepared cake tin and place in the refrigerator to set for at least 20 minutes.

Beat the cream cheese and caster sugar until well softened and creamy.

Soak the gelatine in water for 2 minutes, then squeeze out the excess water.

In a small saucepan, bring the lemon juice to the boil, add the gelatine and stir until dissolved. Add the cream and lemon zest and stir until well combined. Stir the lemon mixture into the cream cheese until combined. Pour on top of the biscuit base and chill until set.

Orange cheesecake
Substitute orange juice and zest for the lemon juice and zest.

Chocolate tofu cheesecake

Not only is this recipe gluten-free, but it's also dairy-free and has the most amazing silky smooth texture. Be sure to use silken tofu to get the right consistency. Serves 8

200 g (7 oz/2 cups) ground almonds

60 g (2 oz) coconut oil, melted

1 tablespoon agave syrup

350 g (12½ oz) dark chocolate

500 g (1 lb 2 oz) soft silken tofu

1–2 tablespoons raspberry jam

Unsweetened (Dutch) cocoa powder for dusting

Grease a 22 cm (8¾ in) tart (flan) tin and line the side and bottom with baking paper.

Place the ground almonds, coconut oil and agave syrup in a food processor and whizz to blend. Press the mixture into the bottom of the prepared cake tin and place in the refrigerator to set for at least 20 minutes.

Melt the chocolate by placing it in a bowl over a saucepan of simmering water, or in a microwave on Low for 1–2 minutes.

Place the tofu and jam in a food processor and blitz until puréed. Add the melted chocolate and whisk together. Pour the mixture over the chilled base and refrigerate for 2–3 hours.

When set, remove the cheesecake from the tin, dust with cocoa powder and serve.

Cupcakes

All cupcakes should be beautifully light and sponge-like, just like these. The real fun of cupcakes is in the decorating. You can go simple, perhaps with Chocolate ganache (page 492) and silver cachous, or try white icing with those pretty iced flowers from cake-decorating shops. You can also use jelly beans, Smarties, M&Ms, crushed Honeycomb (page 410) or just about any form of chocolate. Makes 10

175 g (6 oz) butter
150 g (5½ oz) caster (superfine) sugar
1 teaspoon natural vanilla extract
3 eggs
225 g (8 oz/1½ cups) self-raising flour
Basic icing (page 491)

Preheat the oven to 180°C (350°F). Line ten 125 ml (4 fl oz/½ cup) holes of a muffin tin with paper cases.

Cream the butter and sugar until light and fluffy. Add the vanilla, then the eggs one by one, fully incorporating each one before adding the next. Sift the flour and fold it in carefully.

Spoon the mixture into the prepared tin and bake for around 15 minutes, or until a skewer inserted into the centre of a cake comes out clean.

Allow to cool completely, then spread the icing on the cakes and decorate as you wish.

Killer cupcakes

Children and adults alike will be won over by these chocolate-enriched cupcakes. Makes 10

100 g (3½ oz) soft butter
130 g (4½ oz) brown sugar
1 egg
1 teaspoon natural vanilla extract
95 g (3¼ oz) dark chocolate, melted and cooled
200 g (7 oz/1⅓ cups) self-raising flour
60 ml (2 fl oz/¼ cup) milk
Chocolate fudge icing (page 492)

Preheat the oven to 180°C (350°F). Line ten 125 ml (4 fl oz/½ cup) holes of a muffin tin with paper cases.

Cream the butter and brown sugar until light and fluffy. Add the egg and vanilla and beat until well incorporated. Stir in the cooled melted chocolate. Fold through the flour and milk, and mix until just combined.

Spoon the mixture into the prepared tin and bake in the oven for 15 minutes, or until a skewer inserted into the centre of a cake comes out clean.

Allow to cool completely, then top with the chocolate fudge icing to serve.

Lamingtons

Lamingtons are one of the classics of Australian baking. The simple squares of sponge dipped in light chocolate icing and then rolled in coconut are worth making for the tradition alone. Luckily, they taste amazing, too. Makes 18

100 g (3½ oz/⅔ cup) plain (all-purpose) flour

4 eggs

110 g (4 oz) caster (superfine) sugar

390 g (14 oz) icing (confectioners') sugar

50 g (1¾ oz) unsweetened (Dutch) cocoa powder

280 g (10 oz) desiccated coconut

Preheat the oven to 180°C (350°F).

Line a 20 × 30 cm (8 × 12 in) shallow baking tin with baking paper, ensuring there is plenty of overhang. This will allow the sponge to rise without going over the edge. Butter the paper and sprinkle with a little plain flour to ensure that the batter won't stick.

Beat the eggs and caster sugar together until very thick and light. Carefully fold in the flour. Spoon the sponge mixture into the tin, ensuring it is relatively flat on top. Bake in the oven for around 10 minutes, or until risen and golden.

Allow to cool for 5 minutes on a wire rack, then carefully lift the sponge onto a chopping board and peel away the paper. Allow to cool completely.

Place the icing sugar, cocoa powder and 185 ml (6 fl oz) water in a saucepan and bring to the boil, whisking well. Reduce the heat and simmer for 1–2 minutes. Remove from the heat and allow to cool slightly.

Place the coconut in a shallow dish. Using a serrated knife, carefully cut the sponge into 18 even-sized cubes. Dip the pieces of sponge in the chocolate icing until well covered, then place on a wire rack, set over some baking paper, to drain. When most of the excess icing has dripped off, but the sponge cubes are still moist, dunk them into the coconut, ensuring that each side is coated. Leave to dry on a wire rack.

Jelly lamingtons
Make up some raspberry jelly (gelatin dessert) according to the instructions on the packet. Dip the lamingtons in the jelly mixture instead of the chocolate mix.

Jam-filled lamingtons
Cut the sponge pieces in half. Spread with jam and sandwich them back together. Dip the lamingtons in the chocolate icing and roll in the coconut as normal.

Basic muffins

My basic muffin mixture is exceptionally easy to make and you can vary it by adding berries, chocolate chips or anything else that takes your fancy. Makes 6 large muffins

150 g (5½ oz/1 cup) self-raising flour

110 g (4 oz) caster (superfine) sugar

1 teaspoon natural vanilla extract

1 egg

125 ml (4 fl oz/½ cup) milk

50 g (1¾ oz) melted butter

Preheat the oven to 180°C (350°F). Line six 125 ml (4 fl oz/½ cup) holes in a muffin tin with paper cases.

Mix the flour, caster sugar and a pinch of salt together. Add the vanilla, egg, milk and melted butter and beat until smooth.

Spoon the mixture into the prepared tin and bake in the oven for 15–20 minutes, or until risen and golden brown. Allow to cool.

Chocolate muffins
Substitute 30 g (1 oz) unsweetened (Dutch) cocoa powder for 30 g (1 oz) of the flour.

Brown sugar muffins

This recipe makes the best muffins. You can add anything to the mix – however, take care not to add too much or it all sinks to the bottom. Go crazy! Makes 8

150 g (5½ oz/1 cup) self-raising flour
150 g (5½ oz) brown sugar
60 g (2 oz) melted butter
1 egg
1 teaspoon natural vanilla extract
Fruit of your choice
80 ml (2½ fl oz/⅓ cup) thickened (whipping) cream (approximately)
Frosting of your choice (see page 493)

Preheat the oven to 180°C (350°F). Line eight 125 ml (4 fl oz/½ cup) holes of a muffin tin with paper cases.

Sift the flour into a bowl, add the brown sugar and stir it through.

Whisk the melted butter, egg and vanilla together and add them to the dry mix. Whisk together until it forms a smooth batter. Fold through the fruit of your choice. Add enough of the cream to bring the mixture to a good cake consistency. This will vary depending on how wet the fruits are that you choose to add.

Spoon the mix into the prepared muffin tin and bake in the oven for 20 minutes, or until risen and golden brown. Allow to cool, then top with frosting.

Raspberry and white chocolate muffins
Add the grated zest of one lemon to the flour and sugar mix. Fold 100 g (3½ oz) raspberries and 95 g (3¼ oz) white chocolate chips through the muffin batter.

Rhubarb, cinnamon and yoghurt muffins
Add 1 teaspoon ground cinnamon to the flour and sugar mix. Thinly slice three rhubarb stalks and fold them through, along with 125 g (4½ oz/½ cup) natural yoghurt.

Blueberry and coconut muffins
Add 35 g (1¼ oz) desiccated coconut and 155 g (5½ oz/1 cup) blueberries.

Spiced apple and sour cream muffins
Dice one granny smith apple finely and toss with 1 teaspoon ground cinnamon and 2 tablespoons brown sugar. Add this to the muffin mixture. Substitute the thickened cream with sour cream.

Banana and maple syrup muffins
Add two mashed bananas and 2 tablespoons maple syrup to the mix. You could also add a handful of chopped pecans or walnuts.

Triple chocolate muffins

Triple chocolate muffins are created by studding dark and white chocolate chips through a chocolate muffin base, then topping the finished product with chocolate icing. Not the sort of thing you'd want to eat every day, but fantastic every now and then. Makes 8

150 g (5½ oz/1 cup) self-raising flour
50 g (1¾ oz) unsweetened (Dutch) cocoa powder
100 g (3½ oz) soft brown sugar
165 ml (5½ fl oz) milk
60 g (2 oz) butter, melted and cooled
1 egg
45 g (1½ oz/¼ cup) dark chocolate chips
45 g (1½ oz/¼ cup) white chocolate chips
Chocolate fudge icing (page 492)

Preheat the oven to 180°C (350°F). Line eight 125 ml (4 fl oz/½ cup) holes of a muffin tin with paper cases.

Sift the flour and cocoa together, then add the brown sugar and stir it through. Whisk the milk, melted butter and egg together. Add the wet mix to the dry mix and whisk together until it forms a smooth batter. Fold through the chocolate chips.

Spoon the mix into the prepared muffin tin and bake in the oven for 20 minutes, or until risen and golden brown. Allow to cool, then top with the chocolate fudge icing.

Chocolate cheesecake muffins

These are a bit trickier to make than some of my other muffin recipes, but they are well worth the extra hassle. Makes 8 large or 16 small muffins

90 g (3 oz/⅓ cup) cream cheese

110 g (4 oz) caster (superfine) sugar, plus 2 extra tablespoons

150 g (5½ oz/1 cup) self-raising flour

30 g (1 oz/¼ cup) unsweetened (Dutch) cocoa powder

1 egg, beaten

175 ml (6 fl oz) milk

80 ml (2½ fl oz/⅓ cup) oil

Preheat the oven to 180°C (350°F). Line eight 125 ml (4 fl oz/½ cup) holes of a muffin tin with paper cases.

Beat the cream cheese and the 2 tablespoons sugar until soft and smooth. Set aside.

Sift the flour, cocoa and a pinch of salt together in a large bowl. Add the remaining sugar and mix together.

Beat the egg, milk and oil together, then add to the flour mix and beat until well combined.

Half-fill the paper cases with the chocolate batter. Add about 1 teaspoon of the cream cheese mix, then cover with the remaining chocolate batter. Bake in the oven for 15–20 minutes, or until risen and golden brown.

'Doughnut' muffins

No tricky names here, just muffins that taste like doughnuts, with only a fraction of the work. Makes 10–12 large muffins

250 g (9 oz/1⅔ cup) self-raising flour

2 teaspoons ground cinnamon

80 ml (2½ fl oz/⅓ cup) oil

260 g (9 oz) caster (superfine) sugar

1 egg

175 ml (6 fl oz) milk

75 g (2¾ oz) butter

Preheat the oven to 180°C (350°F). Line 10–12 holes of a muffin tin with paper cases.

Sift the flour, 1 teaspoon of the cinnamon and a pinch of salt into a large bowl.

In a separate bowl, mix together the oil, 150 g (5½ oz) of the sugar, the egg and milk. Add to the flour mixture and stir well until combined. Spoon into the prepared muffin tin and bake in the oven for 20 minutes, or until risen and golden brown.

While cooking, melt the butter. Mix the remaining sugar and cinnamon together.

When the muffins are cooked, remove them from the tins and dip the tops into the melted butter, then into the cinnamon–sugar mixture. Place on a wire rack to cool.

Jam doughnut muffins
Half-fill the muffin holes with batter, then add
½ teaspoon strawberry jam to each muffin. Cover
with the remaining batter and cook in the same way.

Flourless chocolate muffins

As with most flourless cakes, these muffins use ground almonds to keep them moist.
Makes 20 small or 10 large muffins

150 g (5½ oz) dark chocolate, chopped

125 g (4½ oz) soft butter

3 eggs, separated

90 g (3 oz) caster (superfine) sugar, plus 2 extra
tablespoons

90 g (3 oz) ground almonds

Preheat the oven to 170°C (340°F). Line twelve 125 ml
(4 fl oz/½ cup) holes of a muffin tin with paper cases.

Place the chocolate and butter in a bowl over a
saucepan of simmering water to melt. Remove the

pan from the heat and add the egg yolks, sugar and
ground almonds.

Whisk the egg whites until stiff peaks form, then fold in
the 2 tablespoons sugar.

Fold the egg white mixture into the chocolate mixture
and spoon into the muffin tin. Bake in the oven for
30–35 minutes, or until a skewer comes out clean.

Flourless white chocolate and raspberry muffins
Add 50 g (1¾ oz) white chocolate chips and 125 g
(4½ oz/1 cup) raspberries to the chocolate mixture
before folding in the egg whites.

Spicy cheddar muffins

It's worth searching out the best farmhouse cheddar you can for these muffins. This recipe
was supplied by food writer and friend Siu Ling Hui. Makes 6 large or 12 small muffins

250 ml (8½ fl oz/1 cup) milk

2 tablespoons melted butter

1 egg, lightly beaten

Generous pinch of cayenne pepper

200 g (7 oz/1⅓ cups) plain (all-purpose) flour

1 tablespoon baking powder

1 tablespoon caster (superfine) sugar

150 g (5½ oz) grated farmhouse cheddar

100 g (3½ oz/1 cup) walnuts, lightly roasted and
chopped, or 1 grated apple

Preheat the oven to 180°C (350°F). Line twelve 25 ml
(4 fl oz/½ cup) holes of a muffin tin with paper cases.

Combine the milk, butter, egg and cayenne pepper in
a large bowl.

In another bowl, sift together the flour, baking powder,
sugar and a pinch of salt. Toss the grated cheddar with
the flour to mix well. Add the cheese and flour mixture
to the wet mixture and stir well. Add the walnuts or
grated apple.

Spoon the mixture into the muffin tin and cook in the
oven for 15–20 minutes, or until risen and golden brown.

Zucchini, corn and bacon muffins

You can make these muffins with gluten-free flour, but you will need to allow an extra 10 minutes of cooking time. The recipe works just as well without the bacon if you're catering for vegetarians. Makes 12

150 g (5½ oz/1 cup) self-raising flour
125 ml (4 fl oz/½ cup) olive oil
5 eggs, beaten
500 g (1 lb 2 oz) grated zucchini (courgettes)
1 onion, diced
100 g (3½ oz) bacon, chopped
400 g (14 oz/2 cups) corn kernels
100 g (3½ oz) grated cheddar

Preheat the oven to 180°C (350°F). Line twelve 125 ml (4 fl oz/½ cup) holes in a muffin tin with paper cases.

Mix together the flour, oil and eggs to form a smooth batter. Add the remaining ingredients and season well with salt and freshly ground black pepper. Pour into the muffin tin and bake in the oven for 20–25 minutes until golden brown and risen.

Pumpkin and feta savoury muffins
Swap the corn for 200 g (7 oz) diced roasted pumpkin and add 100 g (3½ oz) crumbled feta – you can remove the bacon if you want.

Friands

You can add whatever flavours you like to this recipe. Swap the lemon zest for orange or lime, add berries, or nuts or even glacé fruits – let your imagination go wild. Makes 9

200 g (7 oz) icing (confectioners') sugar, plus extra
　for dusting
150 g (5½ oz/1 cup) Gluten-free flour (page 484)
125 g (4½ oz/1¼ cups) ground almonds
5 egg whites
180 g (6½ oz) melted butter
Grated zest of 1 lemon

Preheat the oven to 200°C (400°F). Butter nine friand moulds, or line nine 125 ml (4 fl oz/½ cup) holes of a muffin tin with paper cases.

Sift the icing sugar and flour into a bowl and mix in the ground almonds.

Lightly beat the egg whites with a fork for 30 seconds, then stir into the dry ingredients. Add the melted butter and lemon zest and stir well.

Divide the mix between the buttered friand moulds and bake in the oven for 15 minutes. Test the friands by inserting a skewer into one of them. If it comes out clean, they are ready; if it doesn't, cook for a further 5 minutes and test again.

When ready, cool for 10 minutes, then unmould onto a wire rack. Dust the friands with icing sugar to serve.

Hazelnut friands
Replace the ground almonds with ground roasted hazelnuts.

Orange and poppy seed friands
Replace the lemon zest with the grated zest of one orange. Add 2 tablespoons ground poppy seeds.

Blueberry friands
Dot three to four blueberries on top of each friand just before they go in the oven.

Raspberry friands
Dot three to four raspberries on top of each friand just before they go in the oven.

Scones

Many people claim that they, and only they, know how to make the perfect scone. Try the recipe below and you'll realise that now you have the knack! Makes 6–8

300 g (10½ oz/2 cups) self-raising flour

2 teaspoons caster (superfine) sugar

125 ml (4 fl oz/½ cup) thickened (whipping) cream, plus extra for brushing

125 ml (4 fl oz/½ cup) milk

Jam and whipped cream to serve

Preheat the oven to 200°C (400°F). Line a baking tray with baking paper.

Sift the flour, caster sugar and a pinch of salt into a bowl.

Mix the cream and milk together, then stir the wet mix into the dry mix. Stir gently until the mixture is just combined. Tip the mixture onto a lightly floured work surface.

Pat the scone dough out with lightly floured hands until it is 2 cm (¾ in) thick. Cut out scones using a 5.5 cm (2¼ in) cutter. Mix together the left-over bits, re-roll and cut out more scones.

Place the scones, touching each other, on the lined baking tray, then brush the tops with the additional cream. Cook in the oven for 12–15 minutes until risen and golden brown.

Remove the baking trays from the oven and cover the scones with a clean tea towel (dish towel) until cool. Split the scones and spread them with jam and whipped cream to serve.

Cinnamon scones
Sift 1 teaspoon cinnamon with the flour.

Date scones
Add six to eight finely chopped dates to the dough.

Strawberry shortcakes

These shortcakes make a great Sunday afternoon treat. Makes 8

325 g (11½ oz) plain (all-purpose) flour

1 tablespoon baking powder

55 g (2 oz/¼ cup) caster (superfine) sugar, plus 2 extra tablespoons

125 g (4½ oz) soft butter, chopped

1 egg, beaten, plus 1 egg white, lightly beaten

125 ml (4 fl oz/½ cup) thickened (whipping) cream

300 g (10½ oz) strawberries, sliced

250 ml (8½ fl oz/1 cup) whipped cream to serve

Preheat the oven to 220°C (430°F). Line a baking tray with baking paper.

Sift the flour, baking powder and a pinch of salt into a bowl. Add the sugar and butter and rub in with your fingertips to produce a fine breadcrumb-like texture.

Whisk the egg into the cream, then pour this mixture into the flour mixture, little by little, stirring it with a fork until the mixture holds together.

Turn the dough out onto a lightly floured work surface and roll out to a thickness of 2 cm (¾ in). Cut out circles using a 6 cm (2½ in) cutter. Continue re-rolling dough and cutting out circles – you should get eight in total.

Place the shortcakes on the prepared baking tray, brush with the egg white and sprinkle with the extra 2 tablespoons caster sugar. Bake for 10–15 minutes, until golden brown.

Split the shortcakes, as you would a scone, while they are still warm. Fill them with the sliced strawberries and whipped cream, and serve immediately.

Cookies & slices

You'll find many of my favourite sweet things in this chapter. There's a recipe here for every occasion, from afternoon tea to children's birthday parties, or for a rainy Saturday afternoon when you're in need of a little something sweet.

Sweet snacks

Cookies are great because one batch seems to go quite a long way – unlike a cake, which can disappear almost as soon as it's made. It's also possible to jazz up simple cookies such as macarons by sandwiching them together with Chocolate ganache (page 492).

The simplest slice (bar) mixture generally takes only a few minutes to stir together and requires simply spooning into a baking tray and popping in the oven or setting in the refrigerator. There is very little chance that it will fail.

Raw slices or health bars have sneaked into my cooking vocabulary and, while they still contain sugar (but in a more natural or unprocessed form), and coconut oil in place of animal fats such as butter, they certainly have a part to play in the kitchen. What I like most about raw slices is that because they are made of natural ingredients they tend to be more filling. And because many of them require refrigeration they tend to keep longer, allowing a late-night trip to the refrigerator for something that's a little bit naughty, but not all bad. Get to know a whole range of new ingredients with rice malt syrup, agave syrup, cacao nibs, bunikins and nut butters. Keep a stash of Protein balls (page 407) on hand for a healthier snack option and surprise people with recipes such as Bounty balls (page 407) and Raw salted caramel slice (page 406).

I've also provided a collection of other sweet treats. I make such things as Rocky road (page 411) and Almond nougat (page 409) at Christmas time to give as gifts to friends. Many of these are simple enough to make with children, though some do require a sugar thermometer to ensure accuracy. Always take care when boiling sugar, otherwise it can lead to nasty burns.

Things you should know
when making cookies and slices

Basic baking equipment
Baking tray (27.5 × 13 × 3.5 cm/11 × 5 × 1½ in)
Brownie tin (27.5 × 17.5 × 3.5 cm/11 × 7 × 1½ in)
Two to three flat baking trays
Wire cooling rack

- Grease baking trays with butter and line them with baking paper to give yourself a better chance of removing slices in one piece and keep washing up to a minimum.

- I often cut slices into smallish squares and offer a selection of different slices.

- On average, each slice recipe can be cut into 10 or 12 regular portions, or a number of thin fingers. It's difficult to accurately estimate how many people each recipe will feed, because it depends how much they can eat!

- It's much easier to make a slice or cookies with soft butter than with hard. Zap hard butter in the microwave for 20 seconds, or grate it, to soften it quickly. I normally use unsalted butter for baking.

- Natural vanilla extract has a far superior flavour to vanilla essence. It's more expensive, but you only have to use half as much.

- The better the quality of your chocolate, the better your baking, so when a recipe calls for chocolate use cooking couverture. Dark couverture is best, and buttons (or chips) melt more easily.

- Use unsweetened (Dutch) cocoa powder for better chocolate flavour. Again, the better the quality, the better the result.

- All eggs used in these recipes are medium (59 g/2 oz).

- Test to see whether a slice is cooked in the same way as for cakes: insert a skewer or cake tester into the centre of the slice. The skewer should come out free of mix or crumbs. If it doesn't, cook for a further 5 minutes, then try again.

- Needless to say, a freestanding electric mixer will make light work of any beating, whisking or blending to be done.

Cooking with sugar

Sugar is used for many different purposes when baking sweet treats, and is cooked to different stages. A sugar, or confectionery, thermometer will make life much easier when testing these different stages, but you can get by without one if you use the following practical method.

TO COOK SUGAR

1 Place the sugar in the saucepan with water and cook over low heat until the sugar melts. Raise the heat and allow the liquid to boil.

2 Don't stir, but do keep the side of the pan clear of any splatters as they will crystallise and may cause the sugar to also crystallise. A pastry brush dipped in cold water is best for this purpose.

3 To test the different cooking stages without a sugar thermometer, drop small quantities of the sugar into iced water.

SOFT BALL (116°C/241°F): If the sugar is ready, you will be able to roll it into a soft ball with your fingers.

HARD BALL (121°C/250°F): As above, but the sugar will roll into a firmer ball.

SMALL CRACK (140°C/284°F): The sugar should peel off your fingers in a pliable film, which sticks to your teeth when chewed.

HARD CRACK (153°C/307°F): The sugar will break like glass.

CARAMEL (176°C/349°F): Continue cooking until golden brown.

Cookies & slices recipes

Anzac biscuits

The Australian Anzac biscuit is one of the easiest and most delicious cookies to make. Makes 24

100 g (3½ oz/1 cup) rolled (porridge) oats
70 g (2½ oz) desiccated coconut
185 g (6½ oz/1¼ cups) plain (all-purpose) flour
130 g (4½ oz) brown sugar
125 g (4½ oz) butter
2 tablespoons golden syrup
1 teaspoon bicarbonate of soda (baking soda)

Preheat the oven to 180°C (350°F). Line a baking tray with baking paper.

Mix the oats, coconut, flour and brown sugar together in a large bowl.

Place the butter, golden syrup and 80 ml (2½ fl oz/ ⅓ cup) water in a small saucepan and bring to the boil.

Remove from the heat, add the bicarbonate of soda and stir until the mixture becomes frothy. Pour the frothy mixture into the dry ingredients and mix quickly.

Roll the mixture into golfball-sized balls and place on the prepared trays, allowing some room for spreading. Press down gently. Bake in the oven for 15–20 minutes, or until golden brown but still slightly soft.

Allow to cool for 5 minutes. Remove the biscuits from the trays and leave to cool on a wire rack. Store in an airtight container for up to 1 week.

Macadamia Anzacs
Substitute 150 g (5½ oz) macadamia nuts for the desiccated coconut.

Raspberry jam drops

The quality of the jam you use will make a big difference, and you can use jams other than raspberry if preferred. It's best to dust your hands with flour when making these cookies, in order to roll the mixture successfully into balls for baking. Makes 30

150 g (5½ oz) soft butter
150 g (5½ oz) caster (superfine) sugar
65 g (2¼ oz) icing (confectioners') sugar
2 eggs
A few drops of natural vanilla extract
185 g (6½ oz/1¼ cups) self-raising flour
75 g (2¾ oz/½ cup) plain (all-purpose) flour, plus extra for dusting
150 g (5½ oz) (½ cup) raspberry jam

Preheat the oven to 180°C (350°F). Line a baking tray with baking paper.

Cream the butter and sugars until pale and fluffy. Beat in the eggs and vanilla. Sift the flours and a pinch of salt together, then gently stir into the butter mixture. Place in the refrigerator for 15 minutes to make it easier to handle.

Dust your hands with flour and roll heaped spoonfuls of the mixture into balls and place them on the baking trays. Flatten each cookie slightly, then use a teaspoon to make an indent in the middle. Spoon jam into the indent.

Bake in the oven for 12–15 minutes, or until golden. Remove the cookies from the trays and leave to cool on a wire rack. Store in an airtight container for up to 1 week.

Lemon gems
Substitute lemon curd for the jam.

Chocolate drops
Replace the jam with one large chocolate chip on each cookie (or use Smarties if the cookies are for a child's party).

Chocolate-hazelnut drops
Substitute chocolate-hazelnut spread for the jam.

Chocolate vanilla drops
Melt 100 g (3½ oz) dark chocolate by placing it in a bowl over a saucepan of simmering water or in a microwave on Low. Using a spoon, drizzle melted chocolate over the cookies. Allow the chocolate to set before storing the cookies in an airtight container.

Shortbread

There's something essentially wholesome about shortbread; it's always so crisp and satisfying. It can also be adapted to produce new versions with flavours such as orange, chocolate and spice. Makes 30

260 g (9 oz/1¾ cups) plain (all-purpose) flour

115 g (4 oz/⅔ cup) rice flour

250 g (9 oz) soft butter, diced

125 g (4½ oz) caster (superfine) sugar

Water, if required

Preheat the oven to 170°C (340°F). Line a baking tray with baking paper.

Rub together the flours, butter, sugar and a pinch of salt. Knead well until combined. Add a little water if the mixture is very dry.

Roll out the dough to a 5 mm (¼ in) thickness and cut into large fingers or 5 cm (2 in) circles. Bake in the oven until crisp, about 10–12 minutes. Store in an airtight container for up to 1 week.

Orange shortbread
Add the zest of two oranges to the basic mixture.

Chocolate shortbread
Substitute unsweetened (Dutch) cocoa powder for 30 g (1 oz) of the plain flour.

Spiced shortbread
Add 1 teaspoon mixed spice to the basic mixture.

Lemon-glazed shortbread
Dissolve 2 tablespoons caster (superfine) sugar in 2 tablespoons lemon juice and brush over the cool shortbread.

Kourabiedes

A classic Greek cookie, often made at Christmas time, but easily enjoyed year round. Makes 30

250 g (9 oz) soft butter

1 teaspoon natural vanilla extract

Grated zest of 1 lemon

2 egg yolks

200 g (7 oz/2 cups) ground almonds

90 g (3 oz/¾ cup) icing (confectioners') sugar, plus extra for dusting

300 g (10½ oz/2 cups) plain (all-purpose) flour

120 g (4½ oz/1⅓ cups) flaked almonds

Preheat the oven to 170°C (340°F). Line a baking tray with baking paper.

Beat the butter, vanilla and lemon zest until light and fluffy. Add the egg yolks, one at a time, beating well after each addition. Stir through the ground almonds, icing sugar and flour and mix to combine.

Take a tablespoon of dough, roll it into a 3 cm (1¼ in) log and then shape it into a crescent. Roll the crescent in the flaked almonds. Repeat with the remaining mixture and place the Kourabiedes on the prepared baking trays. Ensure you leave enough space on the trays for the cookies to spread slightly.

Bake in the oven for 15–18 minutes or until pale golden. Allow to cool and then dust heavily with the additional icing sugar. Store in an airtight container for up to 1 week.

Passionfruit yoyo cookies

Also known as melting moments, yoyo cookies are a classic combination where two cookies are joined with a vanilla filling. I like to think I have improved on this classic by using a passionfruit filling – I'll leave it to you to decide. Makes 18

300 g (10½ oz/2 cups) plain (all-purpose) flour

300 g (10½ oz) soft butter, plus 60 g (2 oz) melted butter

350 g (12½ oz) icing (confectioners') sugar

100 g (3½ oz) (¾ cup) custard powder

½ teaspoon natural vanilla extract

2 passionfruit

Preheat the oven to 180°C (350°F). Line a baking tray with baking paper.

Beat together the flour, the 300 g (10½ oz) butter, 100 g (3½ oz) of the icing sugar, the custard powder, vanilla and a pinch of salt. Roll the mixture into 36 small balls and place them on the prepared baking tray. Press down with the prongs of a fork to form round cookies. Bake in the oven for 10–15 minutes, until cooked but not coloured. Allow to cool completely.

Strain the pulp from the passionfruit to remove the seeds. Mix with the melted butter and remaining icing sugar until smooth. Spoon a small amount of passionfruit butter onto one cookie half and top with another cookie. Continue until all the cookies are ready. Store in an airtight container for up to 1 week.

Ginger kisses

A nod to Ian, aka Mr Ginger Kiss (or Mr GK for short), who likes to indulge in a daily ginger kiss. Makes 10

165 g (6 oz) soft butter

220 g (8 oz) caster (superfine) sugar, plus extra for rolling

1 eggs

60 g (2 oz) treacle

1 tablespoon water

300 g (10½ oz/2 cups) plain (all-purpose) flour

20 g (¾ oz) ground ginger

½ teaspoon ground cinnamon

1 teaspoon baking powder

Butter icing (page 491)

Preheat the oven to 165°C (330°F). Line a baking tray with baking paper.

Cream the butter and sugar until light and fluffy. Add the eggs, treacle and water and mix to combine. Sift the flour, spices, baking powder and ½ teaspoon salt into the mixture and mix to combine.

Divide the mixture into 20 and shape into balls. Roll in the additional caster sugar.

Place the balls on the prepared baking trays, allowing room for spreading. Press each cookie gently. Bake for 12–15 minutes and allow to cool completely. When cool, sandwich two cookies together with the vanilla butter icing. Store in an airtight container for up to 1 week.

Gingerbread

Ginger is a flavour that people either love or can't stand; this one is for all the ginger lovers I know. Makes 30 cookies

125 g (4½ oz) soft butter

70 g (2½ oz) brown sugar

Finely chopped zest of 1 orange

1 egg, plus 1 egg lightly beaten

125 ml (4 fl oz/½ cup) warm honey

450 g (1 lb/3 cups) self-raising flour

4 teaspoons ground ginger

½ teaspoon ground cinnamon

30 blanched almonds

Raw sugar for sprinkling

Cream the butter and sugar until light and fluffy. Add the orange zest and whole egg and beat until smooth.

Stir in the honey. Sift together the flour, ginger and cinnamon and stir into the wet mixture. Wrap the mixture in plastic wrap and chill for 30 minutes.

Preheat the oven to 170°C (340°F). Line a baking tray with baking paper.

Roll the gingerbread mixture out on a floured work surface and cut out heart shapes, or other shapes to suit your fancy. Lay the cookies on the prepared baking tray. Push an almond into the centre of each, brush each cookie with the beaten egg and sprinkle the raw sugar over. Bake in the oven for 8–10 minutes. Allow the gingerbread to cool before eating. Store in an airtight container for up to 1 week.

Orange and walnut florentines

This twist on the classic florentine recipe brings a great orange taste to the existing toffee and chocolate flavours. Makes 24

45 g (1½ oz) butter

125 ml (4 fl oz/½ cup) thickened (whipping) cream

125 g (4½ oz) caster (superfine) sugar

100 g (3½ oz/1 cup) walnuts, roughly chopped

Finely chopped zest of 1 orange

50 g (1¾ oz/⅓ cup) plain (all-purpose) flour

100 g (3½ oz) dark chocolate, chopped

Preheat the oven to 160°C (320°F). Line a baking tray with baking paper.

Place the butter, cream and sugar in a small saucepan and bring to the boil over medium heat, then remove immediately. Stir in the nuts, orange zest and flour. Leave to cool for 5 minutes.

Drop heaped teaspoonfuls of the mixture onto the prepared baking trays, leaving 4 cm (1½ in) between each one. Bake in the oven for 15–20 minutes. The florentines should be golden at the edges and firm to the touch. Allow to cool on the trays.

Melt the chocolate and spread it onto the back of each florentine. Allow the chocolate to set completely before serving. Store in an airtight container for up to 1 week.

Salted chocolate cookies

Jumping on the salted bandwagon, these cookies are very yummy – even more so when sandwiched together with a generous dollop of dulce de leche. Makes 15

230 g (8 oz) soft butter
185 g (6½ oz) brown sugar
75 g (2¾ oz) caster (superfine) sugar
270 g (9½ oz) plain (all-purpose) flour
45 g (1½ oz) unsweetened (Dutch) cocoa powder
1 teaspoon bicarbonate of soda (baking soda)
200 g (7 oz) small dark chocolate chips
1 teaspoon salt flakes
Dulce de leche (page 489)

Cream the butter and sugars until light and fluffy. Sift the flour, cocoa and bicarbonate of soda into the mixture and mix to combine. Add the chocolate chips and salt flakes and mix to combine.

Roll into two logs, roll in plastic wrap and refrigerate for 30 minutes.

Preheat the oven to 170°C (340°F). Line a baking tray with baking paper.

Divide the mixture into 30 and shape into even-sized balls. Place the cookies on the prepared baking trays, allowing room for spreading. Press each cookie gently.

Bake for 12–15 minutes and allow to cool completely. When cool, sandwich the cookies together with the dulce de leche. Store in an airtight container for up to 1 week.

Triple chocolate chip cookies

These rich triple chocolate cookies have cocoa powder in the mix and chocolate chips studded through them. Makes 35

150 g (5½ oz) soft butter
150 g (5½ oz) caster (superfine) sugar
100 g (3½ oz) brown sugar
1 teaspoon natural vanilla extract
1 egg
150 g (5½ oz/1 cup) self-raising flour
100 g (3½ oz/⅔ cup) plain (all-purpose) flour
50 g (1¾ oz) unsweetened (Dutch) cocoa powder
190 g (6½ oz) small chocolate chips (a mix of dark and white)

Preheat the oven to 180°C (350°F). Line a baking tray with baking paper.

Cream the butter, sugars and vanilla until light and fluffy. Add the egg, then beat well until combined.

Sift the flours and cocoa together, then stir into the butter mix. Finally, stir through the chocolate chips.

Roll level teaspoonfuls of the mixture into balls and place them 3 cm (1¼ in) apart on the prepared baking tray. Flatten slightly using a fork.

Bake in the oven for 12–15 minutes. The cookies should be dry on top and still slightly soft in the centre. Remove the cookies from the trays and leave to cool on a wire rack. Store in an airtight container for up to 1 week.

Salted peanut chocolate cookies

Peanut butter and chocolate chips might sound like an unusual combination, but it really works. Trust me! Makes 30

125 g (4½ oz) soft butter

125 g (4½ oz/½ cup) crunchy peanut butter

100 g (3½ oz) brown sugar

110 g (4 oz) caster (superfine) sugar

1 teaspoon natural vanilla extract

1 egg

225 g (8 oz/1½ cups) self-raising flour

90 g (3 oz/½ cup) chocolate chips

90 g (3 oz) chopped peanuts (optional)

Preheat the oven to 180°C (350°F). Line a baking tray with baking paper.

Cream the butter, peanut butter, sugars and vanilla until pale and fluffy. Add the egg and beat until combined. Sift in the flour and ½ teaspoon salt and mix to combine. Stir in the chocolate chips and peanuts (if using).

Roll level teaspoonfuls of the mixture into balls and place them 3 cm (1¼ in) apart on the prepared baking tray. Flatten slightly using a fork.

Bake in the oven for 10–12 minutes, or until golden brown. Remove the cookies from the trays and leave to cool on a wire rack. Store in an airtight container for up to 1 week.

Cranberry and white chocolate cookies

A lighter alternative to the traditional chocolate chip cookie – deliciously rich because of the condensed milk, and nicely contrasted by the tartness of the cranberries. Makes 20

170 g (6 oz) soft butter

80 g (2¾ oz/⅓ cup) caster (superfine) sugar

1 teaspoon vanilla extract

150 g (5½ oz) sweetened condensed milk

300 g (10½ oz/2 cups) plain (all-purpose) flour

3 teaspoons baking powder

50 g (1¾ oz) craisins (dried cranberries)

75 g (2¾ oz) small white chocolate chips

Preheat the oven to 160°C (320°F). Line a baking tray with baking paper.

Cream the butter, sugar and vanilla until light and fluffy. Add the condensed milk and mix to combine. Sift in the flour and baking powder and mix to combine. Add the dried cranberries and chocolate chips and again mix to combine.

Divide the mixture into 20 and shape into even-sized balls. Place the cookies on the prepared baking tray, allowing room for spreading. Press each cookie gently.

Bake in the oven for 12–15 minutes. The cookies should be dry on top but still slightly soft in the centre. Remove the cookies from the tray and leave to cool on a wire rack. Store in an airtight container for up to 1 week.

Earthquake cookies

These earthquake cookies – so named because as they cook they erupt and look like an earthquake, all cracked and oozy – are delicious. Makes 35

125 g (4½ oz) dark chocolate

125 ml (4 fl oz/½ cup) oil

330 g (11½ oz) caster (superfine) sugar

4 eggs

350 g (12½ oz/2⅓ cups) plain (all-purpose) flour

2 teaspoons baking powder

125 g (4½ oz) small dark chocolate chips

Icing (confectioners') sugar as needed

Preheat the oven to 180°C (350°F). Line a baking tray with baking paper.

Place the chocolate in a heatproof bowl and set it over a saucepan of simmering water until it has melted, or melt it in the microwave on Low.

Whisk the melted chocolate and oil together, then stir through the sugar. Add the eggs one at a time, stirring well after each addition. Sift the flour and baking powder into the mix and stir through. Add the chocolate chips and stir to combine. Refrigerate the mix until it's completely cool (this will stop them from spreading too much during baking).

Remove from the refrigerator and roll the dough into even-sized balls and flatten them slightly. Roll the cookies in the icing sugar, then place them on the prepared baking tray, allowing room for spreading.

Bake in the oven for 12–15 minutes. The cookies should be dry on top but still slightly soft in the centre. Remove the cookies from the tray and leave to cool on a wire rack. Store in an airtight container for up to 1 week.

Crunchy muesli cookies

Natural muesli (granola) adds flavour and texture to these cookies, but be warned – it's hard to stop at just one! Makes 30

100 g (3½ oz/1 cup) rolled (porridge) oats

150 g (5½ oz/1 cup) plain (all-purpose) flour

220 g (8 oz) caster (superfine) sugar

2 teaspoons cinnamon

35 g (1¼ oz) cranberries

45 g (1½ oz) chopped dried apricots

60 g (2 oz/½ cup) slivered almonds

125 g (4½ oz) butter

2 tablespoons golden syrup

½ teaspoon bicarbonate of soda (baking soda)

1 tablespoon boiling water

Preheat the oven to 170°C (340°F). Line a baking tray with baking paper.

Place the oats, flour, sugar, cinnamon, dried fruits and almonds in a large bowl.

Place the butter and golden syrup in a small saucepan and melt over low hear. Add the bicarbonate of soda and boiling water and stir to combine. Add to the dry ingredients and mix to combine.

Roll level teaspoonfuls of the mixture into balls and place them 5 cm (2 in) apart on the prepared baking tray. Flatten slightly using a fork.

Bake in the oven for 18–20 minutes. Remove the cookies from the tray and leave to cool on a wire rack. Store in an airtight container for up to 1 week.

Biscotti

Biscotti are an Italian-style dry cookie, usually served after a meal with coffee and grappa. I prefer them at 11 am with a cup of tea. Makes 24–30

250 g (9 oz/1⅔ cups) plain (all-purpose) flour

1 teaspoon baking powder

250 g (9 oz) caster (superfine) sugar

1 teaspoon natural vanilla extract

2 eggs, plus 1 egg yolk

100 g (3½ oz/⅔ cup) blanched toasted almonds

Preheat the oven to 180°C (350°F). Line a baking tray with baking paper.

Sift the flour, baking powder and sugar into a large bowl. Add the vanilla, eggs and egg yolk and mix until the ingredients form a ball. Add the almonds and knead until they are combined.

Divide the dough into two and form into two log-shaped pieces, about 25 cm (10 in) in length. Place both pieces on the lined baking tray, allowing room for spreading. Bake in the oven for 30 minutes, or until firm to the touch and golden brown. Remove and allow to cool.

Reduce the oven temperature to 140°C (275°F). Slice the logs diagonally to a 1 cm (½ in) thickness. Place the slices on the lined baking tray and return to the oven for 20 minutes, or until quite dry. Store in an airtight container for up to 1 week.

Pistachio biscotti
Substitute pistachio nuts for the almonds.

Chocolate and hazelnut biscotti
Substitute hazelnuts for the almonds and unsweetened (Dutch) cocoa powder for 30 g (1 oz) of the flour.

Raspberry macarons

You can vary this recipe by changing the filling ingredients. Sandwich with Dulce de leche (page 489) and swap the white chocolate for dark for chocolate macarons. There's a lot of talk about triple-sifting the icing sugar, using day-old egg whites and letting the macarons stand for a couple of hours after piping to get perfect results. These things do add an extra finesse to the finished product, but I have also made them without these steps and only an expert pastry chef would be able to taste the difference. Makes 20

130 g (4½ oz) pure icing (confectioners') sugar

110 g (4 oz) ground almonds

105 g (3½ oz) egg whites

65 g (2¼ oz) caster (superfine) sugar

Natural food colouring of your desired colour

White chocolate ganache (page 492)

50 g (1¾ oz) raspberries

Line a baking tray with baking paper.

Triple-sift the icing sugar into a bowl, add the ground almonds and mix to combine.

Whisk 90 g (3 oz) of the egg whites until soft peaks form. Gradually add the caster sugar until a thick meringue forms, then add enough food colouring to reach your desired shade. Fold this mixture through the almond mix and add enough of the remaining egg whites to just loosen the mix.

Preheat the oven to 140°C (275°F).

Spoon the mixture into a piping (icing) bag and pipe forty 3 cm (1¼ in) rounds onto the prepared tray. Ideally, allow to stand for 3–4 hours.

Bake the macarons until firm but not coloured, around 10–12 minutes. Set aside to cool.

Fold the raspberries through the ganache and use this mixture to sandwich the macarons together. Store in an airtight container for up to 1 week.

Amaretti

You can add any type of candied fruit to this recipe. Try quinces in season, glacé oranges, cherries or citron. Makes 20

330 g (11½ oz) caster (superfine) sugar
540 g (1 lb 3 oz) ground almonds
6 egg whites
130 g (4½ oz/1 cup) chopped pistachio nuts

Preheat the oven to 160°C (320°F). Line a baking tray with baking paper.

Mix together the sugar and ground almonds.

Whisk the egg whites until soft peaks form. Fold the egg whites through the sugar and almond mixture.

Roll the mixture into tablespoon-sized balls and roll each ball in the chopped pistachio nuts.

Place the cookies on the prepared baking trays, allowing room for spreading. Press each cookie gently.

Bake in the oven for 12–15 minutes. The cookies should be dry on top and still slightly soft in the centre. Remove the cookies from the tray and leave to cool on a wire rack. Store in an airtight container for up to 1 week.

Sour cherry amaretti
Substitute chopped sour (morello) cherries for the pistachio nuts and fold them through the cookie mix.

Coconut macaroons

The variations on these cookies are enormous and limited only by the different types of nuts available. Makes 48

3 egg whites
300 g (10½ oz) caster (superfine) sugar
300 g (10½ oz/3⅓ cups) desiccated coconut
2 tablespoons plain (all-purpose) flour, plus extra flour as required

Preheat the oven to 180°C (350°F). Line a baking tray with baking paper.

Beat the egg whites to stiff peaks. Slowly beat in the sugar until thick and glossy.

Mix together the coconut and flour. Fold the dry mix into the beaten egg whites.

Dust your hands with a little flour and roll heaped teaspoonfuls of the cookie mixture into balls. Place the macaroons on the prepared baking tray. Bake in the oven for 10–15 minutes, or until golden brown and firm to the touch. Store in an airtight container for up to 1 week.

Chocolate macaroons
Substitute unsweetened (Dutch) cocoa powder for 30 g (1 oz) of the coconut. Then be really decadent and sandwich the cooked macaroons together with Chocolate ganache (page 492).

Almond macaroons
Substitute ground almonds for the coconut.

Brandy snaps

Brandy snaps are considered the epitome of dinner party chic by many people. Although I don't hold them quite that high, these traditional cookies, often filled with brandy cream and berries, are well worth knowing how to make. Makes 20–24

90 g (3 oz) butter
90 g (3 oz/¼ cup) golden syrup
200 g (7 oz) icing (confectioners') sugar
90 g (3 oz) plain (all-purpose) flour
1 teaspoon ground ginger

Preheat the oven to 160°C (320°F) Line a baking tray with baking paper.

Place the butter, golden syrup and icing sugar in a saucepan over medium heat. Stir until melted, then remove from the heat. Sift the flour, ginger and a pinch of salt together and add to the melted mixture. Beat until well combined.

Drop teaspoonfuls of the mix onto the prepared baking trays. Use a spatula to spread the mixture into 8 cm (3¼ in) circles. Bake in the oven for 5 minutes. The cookies should be just golden at the edges and pale in the centre. Allow to cool, then transfer the brandy snaps to an airtight container. Store for up to 1 week.

Brandy snap baskets
Brandy snaps, when still warm, can be draped over moulds to form basket shapes, or rolled around the handle of a large wooden spoon to form tubes. Fill with whipped cream.

Oatcakes

These are wonderful with cheese – cheddar in particular – and make a change from packets of water crackers, which are pretty unexciting. Makes 20

110 g (4 oz/¾ cup) wholemeal (whole-wheat) flour
75 g (2¾ oz/½ cup) plain (all-purpose) flour
110 g (4 oz) oatmeal
110 g (4 oz) soft butter, diced
50 g (1¾ oz) brown sugar
1 egg

Preheat the oven to 190°C (375°F). Line a baking tray with baking paper.

Mix the flours and oatmeal together and rub in the butter, using your fingertips, to produce a breadcrumb-like texture. Add the sugar and egg and mix together until a smooth dough forms.

Roll out the dough to a 3 mm (¼ in) thickness and cut it into 5 cm (2 in) circles. Place the circles on the prepared baking tray and cook for 20–25 minutes, or until the cookies are crisp. Store in an airtight container for up to 1 week.

Goat's cheese cookies

These cookies are great spread with a little tapenade, or topped with fresh goat's curd and a slice of roasted tomato. A formal thank you to Grace. Makes 40

350 g (12½ oz) soft butter

250 g (9 oz) fresh goat's cheese

60 g (2 oz) grated parmesan

½ teaspoon cayenne pepper

425 g (15 oz) plain (all-purpose) flour

Preheat the oven to 160°C (320°F). Line a baking tray with baking paper.

Using a food processor, beat the butter, goat's cheese, parmesan, cayenne pepper and a pinch of salt to a smooth paste. Put the paste in a bowl and mix in the flour.

Roll the dough into 5 cm (2 in) logs and wrap in plastic wrap. Freeze for 30 minutes to allow easy slicing. Slice the logs into 1 cm (½ in) thick discs. Place the cookies on the prepared tray and bake in the oven for 20–25 minutes, until pale gold in colour. Allow to cool, then store in an airtight container for up to 1 week.

Cheese bickies

These cookies are easy to make, easy to cook and easy to eat. What more could you want in life? Makes 20–25

150 g (5½ oz) soft butter

225 g (8 oz/1½ cups) plain (all-purpose) flour

125 g (4½ oz/1 cup) grated cheddar

½ teaspoon cayenne pepper

Place all the ingredients plus a pinch of salt in a mixing bowl. Beat until the mixture forms a ball.

Roll the dough into two long sausage shapes, about 3 cm (1¼ in) thick. Wrap in plastic wrap and refrigerate for 30 minutes.

Preheat the oven to 180°C (350°F). Line a baking tray with baking paper.

Slice the logs into 1 cm (½ in) thick discs. Place on the prepared tray and bake in the oven for 10–12 minutes or until slightly browned.

Seed crackers

A great gluten-free option for serving with cheese, or just for snacking on. Makes 250 g (9 oz)

250 ml (8½ fl oz/1 cup) water

80 g (2¾ oz) linseeds (flax seeds)

2 tablespoons chia seeds

60 g (2 oz/½ cup) sunflower seeds

70 g (2½ oz/½ cup) pepitas (pumpkin seeds)

40 g (1½ oz/¼ cup) sesame seeds

1 tablespoon coconut oil

Preheat the oven to 180°C (350°F). Line a baking tray with baking paper.

Combine all the ingredients with 1 teaspoon salt and stir until well combined. Allow to stand for 30 minutes or until all the water has been absorbed.

Spread the mixture out on the prepared tray. Bake for 20 minutes, then remove from the oven and turn the crackers over and cook for a further 20 minutes. Remove from the oven and allow to cool. Break into pieces and store in an airtight container for up to 1 week.

Chocolate brownies

A good chocolate brownie is a wondrous thing, and that's exactly what you'll get with this recipe. I've been making and enjoying these for years, and I hope to do so for many more to come. Swap the walnuts for pecans or hazelnuts if you like, or omit them altogether. Makes 12

180 g (6½ oz) butter

180 g (6½ oz) dark chocolate, chopped

3 eggs

1 teaspoon natural vanilla extract

250 g (9 oz) caster (superfine) sugar

110 g (4 oz/¾ cup) plain (all-purpose) flour

185 g (6½ oz/1½ cups) chopped walnuts

Preheat the oven to 180°C (350°F). Butter and line a 27.5 × 17.5 × 3.5 cm (11 × 7 × 1½ in) brownie tin with baking paper.

Melt the butter and chocolate together by placing them in a bowl over a saucepan of simmering water or in a microwave on Low for 1–2 minutes.

Beat the eggs, vanilla and sugar together until light and doubled in size.

Sift the flour and ½ teaspoon salt together. Add the flour, melted chocolate and walnuts to the beaten eggs and sugar and mix to combine. Pour the mixture into the prepared tin and bake in the oven for 25 minutes. Take care not to overcook the brownies or they will lose their deliciously gooey texture. Allow to cool before cutting into 12 pieces.

Dulce de leche brownies
Substitute half the sugar for Dulce de leche (page 489). Continue as directed. When the brownie mix is in the tin, dot the top of the raw brownie with teaspoons of dulce de leche. If you like, scatter with salt flakes and then bake as directed.

Raspberry brownies
Add 125 g (4½ oz/1 cup) raspberries in place of the walnuts.

Pistachio, white chocolate and raspberry blondies

I have a love affair with blondies, and this particular combination of pistachio nuts, white chocolate and raspberries is a match made in heaven. Makes 12

200 g (7 oz) soft butter

400 g (14 oz) white chocolate melts (buttons)

220 g (8 oz) caster (superfine) sugar

4 eggs

2 teaspoons natural vanilla extract

300 g (10½ oz/2 cups) plain (all-purpose) flour

100 g (3½ oz/⅔ cup) self-raising flour

180 g (6½ oz) pistachio nuts

200 g (7 oz) raspberries (frozen are fine)

Preheat the oven to 150°C (300°F). Butter and line a 27.5 × 13 × 3.5 cm (11 × 5 × 1½ in) baking tray with baking paper.

Melt the butter and chocolate together, either by placing them in a bowl over a saucepan of simmering water, or in the microwave on Low.

Transfer to a mixing bowl and whisk in the sugar, eggs and vanilla. Fold through the sifted flours. Finally stir through the chocolate melts and pistachio nuts.

Pour the mixture into the prepared tray and scatter the raspberries over the top. Bake for 35 minutes or until just cooked. Allow to cool before cutting into 12 pieces.

Gluten-free raspberry and almond brownies

These brownies are incredibly rich. If you like, you can swap the almonds for other nuts, such as macadamia nuts or pecans, and swap the raspberries for Turkish delight or Dulce de leche (page 489). Makes 24 small squares

265 g (9½ oz) caster (superfine) sugar

200 g (7 oz) brown sugar

80 g (2¾ oz) unsweetened (Dutch) cocoa powder

250 g (9 oz) butter

200 g (7 oz) dark chocolate

1 teaspoon natural vanilla extract

4 eggs

50 g (1¾ oz) slivered almonds

200 g (7 oz) raspberries

Preheat the oven to 160°C (320°F). Butter and line a 27.5 × 17.5 × 3.5 cm (11 × 7 × 1½ in) brownie tin with baking paper.

Mix together the sugars and cocoa powder in a bowl.

Melt the butter and chocolate over a simmering saucepan of water, then add to the sugar and cocoa mixture, along with the vanilla and eggs, and stir to combine. Stir through the almonds and raspberries.

Pour into the prepared brownie tin and bake for 40 minutes. Remove from the oven and allow to cool. Place in the refrigerator for a while to make it easier to cut into 24 small squares.

Cheesecake brownies

Here it is: what lovers of cheesecake and brownies have been looking for. A recipe that combines both! Makes 12

100 g (3½ oz) chocolate

100 g (3½ oz) butter

4 eggs

50 g (1¾ oz/⅓ cup) plain (all-purpose) flour

225 g (8 oz) caster (superfine) sugar

250 g (9 oz/1 cup) soft cream cheese

Grated zest of 1 lemon

Preheat the oven to 180°C (350°F). Butter and line a 27.5 × 17.5 × 3.5 cm (11 × 7 × 1½ in) brownie tin with baking paper.

Melt the chocolate and butter by heating them in a bowl over a saucepan of simmering water, or in a microwave on Low for 1–2 minutes.

Beat three of the eggs with the flour and 150 g (5½ oz) of the caster sugar until white and doubled in size. Add the melted chocolate and pour into the prepared tin.

Beat the cream cheese, lemon zest, remaining egg and remaining sugar until combined. Pour over the chocolate mix. Swirl to incorporate, aiming for a marbled effect.

Bake in the oven for 40 minutes, or until cooked through and bouncy to the touch. Allow to cool before cutting into 12 pieces.

Millionaire's shortbread (caramel slice)

I always knew this recipe as caramel slice, but have recently found out that it's also called 'millionaire's shortbread' – a much more fitting name. Makes 12

90 g (3 oz) brown sugar

150 g (5½ oz/1 cup) plain (all-purpose) flour

80 g (2¾ oz) soft butter, plus 120 g (4½ oz) melted butter

600 ml (20½ fl oz) condensed milk

65 g (2¼ oz) golden syrup

150 g (5½ oz) dark chocolate, chopped

Preheat the oven to 160°C (320°F). Butter and line a 27.5 × 17.5 × 3.5 cm (11 × 7 × 1½ in) brownie tin with baking paper.

Mix together the brown sugar and flour. Add the melted butter and stir to combine.

Press the mixture into the prepared tin. Bake in the oven for 15–20 minutes, or until just cooked. (It's going to go back into the oven for another 15 minutes, so it doesn't have to be brown.)

Place the condensed milk, golden syrup, remaining butter and a pinch of salt in a small saucepan over low heat and cook until everything melts together, stirring often to prevent the condensed milk catching and burning. Pour the caramel over the cooked pastry base.

Return to the oven and cook for a further 20 minutes, or until the caramel has turned golden brown. Set aside to cool.

When the caramel is set, melt the chocolate and coat the top of the caramel. Top evenly, leave to set, then cut into squares.

Hedgehog

This is one of those 'stir together and pour into a tin' recipes that is incredibly quick and easy to make. Hedgehog is best kept chilled as it softens at room temperature. Makes 24

250 g (9 oz) digestive biscuits (sweet wholemeal biscuits) or graham crackers

75 g (2¾ oz/¾ cup) walnuts, chopped

250 g (9 oz) butter

150 g (5½ oz) caster (superfine) sugar

50 g (1¾ oz) unsweetened (Dutch) cocoa powder

2 eggs

100 g (3½ oz) dark chocolate, chopped

Preheat the oven to 180°C (350°F). Butter and line a 27.5 × 17.5 × 3.5 cm (11 × 7 × 1½ in) brownie tin with baking paper.

Break the cookies into roughly 1 cm (½ in) pieces. Mix with the walnuts and set aside.

Melt the butter in a saucepan over medium heat. Remove from the heat, then add the sugar and cocoa to the pan. Return to the heat and stir until the sugar dissolves. Remove from the heat and allow to cool.

Beat in the eggs, then add the broken cookies and nuts. Spoon the mixture into the prepared tin and press down well until the cookies are covered with the chocolate mixture. Refrigerate until set.

Melt the chocolate and coat the top evenly. Allow to set, then cut into small squares.

Raspberry coconut slice

I've tasted a few versions of this slice, and then taken the best aspects of each one and blended them to make my own variation. The combination of a simple pastry base with berries and coconut is hard to beat. Makes 12

225 g (8 oz) soft butter

165 g (6 oz) caster (superfine) sugar

½ teaspoon natural vanilla extract

3 eggs

225 g (8 oz/1½ cups) self-raising flour

60 ml (2 fl oz/¼ cup) milk

160 g (5½ oz/½ cup) raspberry jam

155 g (5½ oz/1¼ cups) raspberries

225 g (8 oz) shredded coconut

50 g (1¾ oz/⅓ cup) plain (all-purpose) flour

Icing (confectioners') sugar to serve

Preheat the oven to 180°C (350°F). Line a 27.5 × 17.5 × 3.5 cm (11 × 7 × 1½ in) brownie tin with baking paper.

Cream 125 g (4½ oz) of the butter, 55 g (2 oz/¼ cup) of the caster sugar and the vanilla until white and fluffy. Add 1 egg, mix to combine, then fold in the flour and milk. Mix until it forms a sticky dough.

Press the dough into the prepared tin. Spread the jam over the uncooked base, then sprinkle evenly with the whole raspberries.

Cream the remaining butter and sugar together until pale and fluffy. Add the remaining eggs one at a time, beating well after each addition. Stir in the shredded coconut and flour, then gently spoon the mix over the raspberry base.

Bake in the oven for 35–40 minutes. Check that the topping is cooked in the centre. If not, cook for another 5–10 minutes and check again. Allow to cool before cutting into slices. Dust with icing sugar to serve.

Free muesli slice

I call this 'free muesli slice' because it's free from gluten, dairy and nuts. However, luckily it's far from taste-free. Makes 12

100 g (3½ oz/½ cup) cooked quinoa

75 g (2¾ oz) craisins (dried cranberries)

75 g (2¾ oz) sliced dates

125 g (4½ oz/1 cup) sultanas (golden raisins)

70 g (2½ oz) sunflower seeds

75 g (2¾ oz/½ cup) pepitas (pumpkin seeds)

40 g (1½ oz/⅔ cup) shredded coconut

50 g (1¾ oz) chia seeds

35 g (1¼ oz) sesame seeds

3 eggs

2 tablespoons agave syrup

½ teaspoon ground cinnamon

1 teaspoon natural vanilla extract

Preheat the oven to 160°C (320°F). Line a 27.5 × 17.5 × 3.5 cm (11 × 7 × 1½ in) brownie tin with baking paper.

Put all the ingredients in a bowl and mix well until combined. Spoon the mixture into the prepared tin, pressing it down to smooth the top. Bake in the oven for 25–30 minutes, or until set and golden brown. Allow to cool before cutting into slices.

Lemon slice

A classic recipe, and it's easy to make either lime or passionfruit variations too. Makes 12

125 g (4½ oz) condensed milk
100 g (3½ oz) butter
200 g (7 oz) digestive biscuits (sweet wholemeal biscuits) or graham crackers
90 g (3 oz/1 cup) desiccated coconut
Grated zest of 2 lemons
250 g (9 oz/2 cups) icing (confectioners') sugar
2–3 tablespoons lemon juice

Grease and line a 20 × 30 cm (8 × 12 in) baking tin with baking paper.

Melt the condensed milk and butter together either by heating them in a small saucepan over medium heat or by microwaving on Low.

Process the cookies in a food processor until they form fine crumbs. Add the coconut, half the zest and the melted butter mixture and mix to combine. Press the mixture into the prepared tin. Refrigerate until set, approximately 2 hours.

Sift the icing sugar into a bowl. Add the remaining zest and enough lemon juice to just bring the icing sugar together – you want it to stay quite thick.

Spread the icing over the chilled base and return to the refrigerator until set. Cut into 12 pieces and enjoy.

Lime slice
Substitute lime zest and juice for the lemon.

Passionfruit slice
Substitute strained passionfruit juice for the lemon juice and zest. I like to add a few passionfruit seeds for appearance – but not too many, as they can be unpleasant to eat.

Dream slice

I love this slice. The combination of pistachio nuts, dried apricots and chocolate, combined with caramelised condensed milk, is a winner. Not one to try if you're on a diet though! Makes 24

400 g (14 oz) digestive biscuits (sweet wholemeal biscuits) or graham crackers
250 g (9 oz) melted butter
130 g (4½ oz) chopped dried apricots
130 g (4½ oz/1 cup) slivered or chopped pistachio nuts
150 g (5½ oz) small dark chocolate chips
800 g (1 lb 12 oz) condensed milk
Additional white and dark chocolate for melting (optional)

Preheat the oven to 160°C (320°F). Grease and line a 20 × 30 cm (8 × 12 in) baking tin with baking paper.

Place the cookies in a food processor and blitz until they form fine crumbs. Add the melted butter and mix to combine. Press the mixture into the prepared tin.

Scatter the apricots, pistachio nuts and chocolate chips over the top. Pour the condensed milk over, covering everything. Bake in the oven for 20–25 minutes until golden. Remove and allow to cool.

Remove from the tin. If desired, melt the additional chocolates (separately) and drizzle them over the top to decorate. Allow to set and then cut the slice into 24 pieces.

Sticky date slice

This is the perfect midwinter slice; a bit like a sticky date (toffee) pudding but with a cookie base. You can omit the macadamia nuts if you prefer. Makes 12

240 g (8½ oz) unsalted butter, chopped, plus 40 g (1½ oz) melted butter

110 g (4 oz) caster (superfine) sugar

300 g (10½ oz/2 cups) plain (all-purpose) flour

300 g (10½ oz) brown sugar

160 ml (5½ fl oz) golden syrup

2 teaspoons natural vanilla extract

2 eggs, lightly beaten

240 g (8½ oz) pitted dates, thinly sliced

125 g (4½ oz) chopped macadamia nuts

Preheat the oven to 180°C (350°F). Line a 27.5 × 17.5 × 3.5 cm (11 × 7 × 1½ in) brownie tin with baking paper, leaving 4 cm (1½ in) overhang on all sides.

Whiz the chopped butter and caster sugar in a food processor for 30 seconds until light and fluffy. Add the flour and pulse to form medium crumbs (don't let them form a ball).

Spread the mixture in the prepared tin, pressing it firmly into the base. Chill for 10 minutes. Bake in the oven for 20–25 minutes until light brown. Cool for 5 minutes.

Meanwhile, whisk the melted butter, brown sugar, golden syrup, vanilla and eggs to combine, then pour over the base. Scatter over the dates and macadamia nuts. Bake for 25 minutes or until set. Leave to cool completely in the tin.

Use the overhanging paper to lift the slice out of the tin. Cut the slice into 12 squares and serve. Store in an airtight container between layers of baking paper in the refrigerator for up to 1 week.

Raw salted caramel slice

If you didn't know this was a 'raw' slice it would be hard to pick; it's deliciously rich and more-ish. It will keep in the refrigerator for a couple of weeks – if you don't eat it before that! Makes 12

225 g (8 oz) cashew nuts

40 g (1½ oz) desiccated coconut

150 g (5½ oz) pitted dates, plus an extra 8–10 dates

125 ml (4 fl oz/½ cup) rice malt syrup, plus 2 tablespoons for the base

60 ml (2 fl oz/¼ cup) melted coconut oil

125 g (4½ oz) almond butter

1 teaspoon natural vanilla extract

Raw chocolate coating (see Bounty balls, opposite)

Line a 27.5 × 17.5 × 3.5 cm (11 × 7 × 1½ in) brownie tin with baking paper.

Place the cashew nuts in a food processor and blitz until fine. Add the coconut, the extra 8–10 dates and the 2 tablespoons rice malt syrup and process until combined.

Spread the mixture into the prepared tray, pressing it down firmly into the base. Refrigerate until set, about 30 minutes.

Make the caramel layer by placing the remaining dates, coconut oil, almond butter, the remaining rice malt syrup, the vanilla and 1 teaspoon salt in a food processor and blitzing until smooth. Spread the mixture over the base and return to the refrigerator.

When the slice is set, pour the chocolate coating over the slice and spread evenly. Return to the refrigerator to set, about 1 hour or ideally overnight. Cut into 12 portions and store in the refrigerator for up to 3 weeks.

Protein balls

You can use any type of seeds or nuts in these protein balls. Use your favourite, or whatever you have to hand. Makes 12–15

200 g (7 oz) dried dates, soaked in hot water for 30 minutes

1 tablespoon coconut oil, melted

1 tablespoon desiccated coconut

250 g (9 oz) mixed nuts and seeds – raw almonds, sunflower seeds and pepitas (pumpkin seeds)

Drain the dates and place them in a food processor along with the oil, coconut and a pinch of salt and process until smooth. Add the nuts and seeds and process until combined. Roll into small balls and refrigerate until set.

Bounty balls

These little balls really pack a punch of flavour. I find them incredibly rich, so I can't imagine you'll be able to manage more than one or two in a row. The chocolate coating will soften at room temperature so keep them in the refrigerator for late-night snacks. Makes 18–20

75 g (2¾ oz) cashew nuts, soaked in water

60 ml (2 fl oz/¼ cup) coconut cream

120 g (4½ oz/1⅓ cups) desiccated coconut

60 ml (2 fl oz/¼ cup) melted coconut oil

50 ml (1¾ fl oz) rice malt syrup

Raw chocolate coating

125 ml (4 fl oz/½ cup) melted coconut oil

55 g (2 oz) cacao powder

80 ml (2½ fl oz/⅓ cup) maple syrup

Drain the soaked cashew nuts and place them in a food processor along with the coconut cream, desiccated coconut, coconut oil and rice malt syrup. Process until smooth and combined.

Roll the mixture into balls and place in the freezer to set.

Prepare the raw chocolate coating by whisking together the coconut oil, cacao powder and maple syrup. If it hardens, simply pop it in the microwave for 20 seconds.

Coat the balls in the chocolate and place on a wire rack to allow the excess chocolate to drain off (place baking paper or a plate under the rack). Store the balls in the refrigerator.

White Christmas

What better treat to serve at Christmas? If preferred, you can spoon the mix into paper cases rather than serving it as a slice. Makes 12–16

180 g (6½ oz) white chocolate
70 g (2½ oz) desiccated coconut
70 g (2½ oz) puffed rice cereal
130 g (4½ oz) icing (confectioners') sugar
160 g (5½ oz) sultanas (golden raisins)
150 g (5½ oz) dried apricots, diced
140 g (5 oz) craisins (dried cranberries)
250 ml (8½ fl oz/1 cup) coconut cream

Line a 20 × 30 cm (8 × 12 in) baking tin with baking paper.

Melt the chocolate, either in a bowl over a saucepan of simmering water or in a microwave on Low.

In a large bowl, mix the coconut, puffed rice cereal, icing sugar, sultanas, apricots and craisins and toss until well combined. Add the coconut cream and melted chocolate and stir together.

Pour into the prepared tin and press down firmly to form a flattish surface, taking care not to squash the puffed rice too much. Leave to set. Cut into wedges to serve.

Chocolate and hazelnut panforte

This is my own version of panforte, a firm toffee-like cake of Italian origin. Use new season's hazelnuts and the best chocolate you can afford. Look for citron in speciality food stores. Serves 18–20

Hazelnut or olive oil for greasing
150 g (5½ oz) dark chocolate, chopped
150 g (5½ oz) caster (superfine) sugar
350 g (12½ oz/1 cup) honey
500 g (3⅓ cups) hazelnuts, skins removed
200 g (7 oz) citron, diced
50 g (1¾ oz/⅓ cup) plain (all-purpose) flour
50 g (1¾ oz) Dutch unsweetened cocoa powder
2 teaspoons ground cinnamon
1 teaspoon ground nutmeg
¼ teaspoon freshly ground black pepper
¼ teaspoon ground cloves
¼ teaspoon mixed spice

Preheat the oven to 150°C (300°F). Line the base and side of a 23 cm (9 in) springform cake tin with baking paper (this step is essential). Lightly grease with hazelnut or olive oil.

Place the chocolate, sugar and honey in a large saucepan and dissolve over low heat, stirring regularly.

Place the hazelnuts and citron in a large bowl. Sift the flour, cocoa and spices into the nut mix and combine well.

Pour the hot chocolate mixture over the dry ingredients and stir together quickly. Press firmly into the prepared tin. Bake in the oven for 60 minutes. During cooking the mixture will start to bubble at the edges of the tin. When the bubbles have almost reached the middle, the cake is ready. Remove and, if necessary, smooth the top using a butter knife. Cool for 15 minutes, then remove from the tin. Allow to cool completely before cutting.

To serve, cut into quarters, then into thin slices with a sharp knife and serve with coffee. Panforte can be wrapped in silicone paper and stored in a cool dark place for up to 6 months.

Almond nougat

This nougat has endless variations – you can swap the almonds for hazelnuts, pistachio nuts or macadamia nuts, or add chocolate or glacé fruit, such as oranges or figs. Makes 18

Rice paper (optional)
550 g (1 lb 3 oz) caster (superfine) sugar
250 ml (8½ fl oz/1 cup) liquid glucose
60 ml (2 fl oz/¼ cup) honey
2 egg whites
200 g (7 oz) blanched almonds
100 g (3½ oz) glacé fruit (optional)

Line a 20 × 30 cm (8 × 12 in) baking tin with rice paper, if desired, with enough set aside to put on top at a later stage. Rice paper is traditionally used to set nougat in, but you could line the tin with baking paper instead.

Combine the caster sugar, glucose and honey in a saucepan and stir over medium heat until the sugar has dissolved. Increase the heat to high and boil until the mixture reaches the small crack stage (see page 388), 140°C (284°F) on a sugar thermometer.

When the sugar reaches temperature, beat the egg whites until stiff. Carefully pour the boiling sugar into the egg whites while still beating – a freestanding electric mixer is ideal for this. Beat until well combined. Fold through the almonds and glacé fruit (if using).

Pour into the prepared tin, cover with rice paper (if using) and put aside until set. Cut into long bars and wrap in cellophane.

Chocolate hazelnut nougat
Add 100 g (3½ oz) melted chocolate and substitute 200 g (7 oz) hazelnuts for the almonds.

Christmas nougat
Use pistachio nuts instead of almonds and add 95 g (3¼ oz) craisins (dried cranberries).

Coconut ice

Coconut ice is an old favourite and extremely sweet. Best eaten in small quantities! Makes 18

1 egg white
650 g (1 lb 7 oz) icing (confectioners') sugar
350 g (12½ oz) desiccated coconut
270 ml (9 fl oz) coconut cream
Natural pink food colouring

Line a 20 × 30 cm (8 × 12 in) baking tin with baking paper.

Beat the egg white slightly to soft peaks.

Sift the icing sugar into a large bowl, add the coconut, coconut cream and egg white. Mix until well combined.

Place half the mixture in the prepared tin. Press down firmly to ensure that it's even (I use an empty jar as a rolling pin).

Add a few drops of pink food colouring to the remaining coconut mixture and stir well so the colour is evenly distributed. Spread on top of the white coconut ice and press down firmly until evenly spread. Refrigerate until set. Cut into long rectangles or small squares as desired. Keep refrigerated.

Chocolate truffles

This recipe is extremely versatile. You can use milk chocolate instead of dark, and add different types of alcohol or flavoured essences to create myriad flavours. Makes 25–30

90 g (3 oz) butter
125 ml (4 fl oz/½ cup) thick (double/heavy) cream
300 g (10½ oz) dark chocolate
2 tablespoons brandy
Unsweetened (Dutch) cocoa powder for rolling

Place the butter and cream in a medium saucepan over medium–low heat, and cook just until the butter melts. Add the chocolate and heat until it melts. (You can melt this in the microwave on Low, if you prefer.)

Remove the pan from the heat and let it stand for 2–3 minutes. Add the brandy and set aside to cool, stirring occasionally to keep the butter incorporated. When cool, place in the refrigerator to firm up.

Take teaspoonfuls of the mixture and roll them into balls. You'll have to work quickly as the mixture will quickly melt when it comes in contact with your warm hands. Roll the truffles in the cocoa until well covered. Refrigerate until set.

Kahlua truffles
Swap the brandy for Kahlua.

Grand Marnier truffles
Swap the brandy for Grand Marnier.

White chocolate and rosewater truffles
Swap the dark chocolate for white chocolate and the brandy for rosewater.

Honeycomb

Honeycomb is simply amazing to make. Once you add the bicarbonate of soda, it explodes upwards and outwards, so take care as it is essentially boiling sugar. Use good-quality baking paper for this rather than greaseproof (wax) paper, as greaseproof paper often tears when the honeycomb hardens. Makes 18

220 g (8 oz) caster (superfine) sugar
100 ml (3½ fl oz) honey
1 tablespoon bicarbonate of soda (baking soda), sifted

Line a large baking tray with good-quality baking paper.

Place the caster sugar, honey and 2 tablespoons water in a large heavy-based saucepan. Cook over low heat until the sugar dissolves, stirring once or twice. Once the sugar has dissolved, raise the heat and bring to the boil. Cook for 3–4 minutes, until the liquid starts to change colour. Remove from the heat.

Fold through the bicarbonate of soda – be careful, as the honeycomb will expand quickly! Spoon the mixture into the prepared baking tray and allow to cool.

Simply break into chunks to use. It can be stored in an airtight container for 1–2 days, but it does get affected by moisture and may dissolve away.

Chocolate-coated honeycomb
Simply cover the cooled honeycomb with melted chocolate. I once saw chef Raymond Capaldi set honeycomb in a cake tin, then coat it with melted chocolate - amazing!

Rocky road

Rocky road is all about personal taste. Some people like it with coconut; others prefer Turkish delight or chocolate-coated marshmallows. Personally, I make it a different way each time, but my all-time favourite addition has to be Clinkers, inspired by chef and friend Megan Lilburn. If you can't find Clinkers, Maltesers are a good substitute. Makes 12

125 g (4½ oz) dark chocolate

125 g (4½ oz) milk chocolate

75 g (2¾ oz) mini marshmallows

100 g (3½ oz) Clinkers (optional)

75 g (2¾ oz) nuts (almonds, brazil nuts, macadamia nuts – whatever)

300 g (10½ oz) rosewater-flavoured Turkish delight

35 g (1¼ oz) shredded coconut

Line a deep log tin with baking paper.

Melt the chocolates, either in a bowl set over a saucepan of simmering water, or in a microwave on Low.

Chop the marshmallows, Clinkers, nuts and Turkish delight, so they are all a similar size. Place them in a large bowl and toss well to evenly mix. Stir through the shredded coconut.

Pour the melted chocolate over the ingredients and mix well to combine – use your hands, it's more fun. Tip into the prepared tin and refrigerate until set. Cut into slices.

Rosewater meringues

A delicate white meringue is one of the wonders of baking. How is it that two basic ingredients, namely egg whites and sugar, can be transformed into such a delicious food by mere beating and cooking? The technique becomes irrelevant with the first mouthful of these crispy delights with their marshmallow centres. Makes about 20

6 egg whites

300 g (10½ oz) caster (superfine) sugar

1 tablespoon rosewater

Preheat the oven to 160°C (320°F). Line a baking tray with baking paper.

Beat the egg whites until stiff peaks form. Add the sugar, one-third at a time, and continue beating until the meringue is glossy and firm. Fold through the rosewater.

Spoon large dollops of the meringue onto the prepared tray. Bake in the oven for 30 minutes. Turn the oven off, and leave the meringues to cool in the oven for 30 minutes more. Enjoy them just as they are!

Passionfruit marshmallow

Who doesn't love marshmallow – especially when it's passionfruit flavoured? Makes 12

Icing (confectioners') sugar for dusting
180 ml (6 fl oz) strained passionfruit juice
20 g (¾ oz) powdered gelatine
440 g (15½ oz) caster (superfine) sugar
80 ml (2½ fl oz/⅓ cup) boiling water
2 egg whites
Natural colouring (optional)

Lightly grease a 20 cm (8 in) square cake tin and dust it liberally with icing sugar. Set aside.

Combine the gelatine and passionfruit juice and set aside to absorb.

Place the sugar and boiling water in a small saucepan and heat gently to dissolve the sugar, then bring to the boil. Swirl the liquid over the heat (do not stir) to prevent sugar crystals forming, and cook to 125°C (257°F) – you will need a sugar thermometer to check this. Remove and allow to cool to 100°C (212°F). Add the passionfruit mixture and stir until the gelatine dissolves.

Meanwhile, in a freestanding electric mixer, whisk the egg whites until stiff peaks form. Gradually add the passionfruit mixture and whisk continuously on full speed until doubled in size and the mixture cools. Pour the mixture into the sugar-lined tin and allow to set at room temperature.

When ready to cut, dust the surface with icing sugar and, as you cut the marshmallow into squares, dust all the cut sides with icing sugar.

Chocolate bark

You can add as few or as many toppings as you like to this chocolate bark, and in any combination (see the variations for some ideas). Makes 300 g (10½ oz)

200 g (7 oz) dark chocolate
100 g (3½ oz) white chocolate

Line a baking tray with baking paper.

Place the dark chocolate in one bowl and the white chocolate in another. Melt the chocolate by placing the bowls over simmering saucepans of water, stirring often until the chocolate melts.

Pour the melted dark chocolate onto the prepared tray and spread it out evenly using a spatula, making it as thin or thick as you like. Splodge dollops of white chocolate across the top and, using a skewer or toothpick, draw swirls in the chocolate. Scatter the topping of your choice over the chocolate and set aside to cool. You may need to pop it in the refrigerator if it's a hot day. When set, break the bark into pieces by chopping roughly with a sharp knife, and enjoy.

Pistachio and sea salt bark
Sprinkle sea salt flakes and 60 g (2 oz) slivered pistachio nuts over the top of the melted chocolate.

Honeycomb bark
Crumble 50 g (1¾ oz) Honeycomb (page 410) over the top of the melted chocolate

Cranberry and macadamia bark
Scatter 30 g (1 oz) cranberries and 30 g (1 oz) chopped macadamia nuts over the top of the melted chocolate.

Salted praline

Praline is great for adding a little something special to dessert or the top of cakes.
Makes 160 g (5½ oz)

80 g (2¾ oz/⅓ cup) caster sugar
½ teaspoon salt
80 g (2¾ oz/½ cup) blanched almonds, toasted

Line a baking tray with baking paper.

Place the sugar and 2 tablespoons water in a small saucepan over low heat. Heat to dissolve the sugar, then bring to the boil. Swirl the liquid over the heat (do not stir) to prevent sugar crystals from forming, and cook to a light brown colour.

Remove from the heat and stir in the salt and toasted almonds. Pour onto the lined baking tray. Try to make it as flat as possible. Don't touch it as it's very hot, but simply tilt the tray to get the praline to spread out, or use the back of an oiled wooden spoon. Leave until set hard.

When completely cold, remove the praline from the tray and chop it into bite-sized pieces with a sharp knife.

Peanut brittle
Substitute toasted peanuts for the almonds.

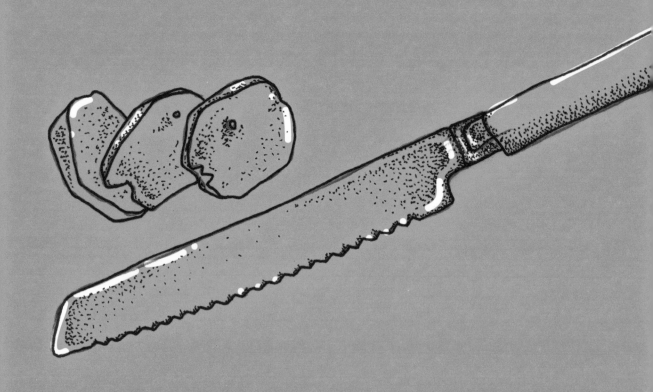

Bread

The world of bread offers a range of wonderful things to eat. It's also an area of cooking that's quick and easy to learn if you consider the following two points:

1 The base of virtually every recipe uses the same ingredients: flour, salt, water and yeast.
2 Once you've mastered making the simplest bread dough, you're set: with all other breads, the method changes only slightly.

Freshly baked

Most of the recipes here are for fairly rustic breads – the type that I make at home – and are quite easy to execute. What you won't find here are recipes for sourdough bread (which can take a day or two to make), tricky French baguettes and intricate croissants. My recipes don't necessarily follow traditional methods; rather, they are recipes that are perfect for the home kitchen.

Many people swear by bread-making machines. However, I'm not convinced that they are that easy, or that the bread is all that good. If I could teach everyone how easy it is to make a simple loaf of bread, they would soon find their bread machine was unnecessary. However, if you love your bread maker and it stops you buying fluffy white square loaves from the supermarket, then don't let me stop you.

One you have mastered a simple loaf of bread you can turn your mind to other yeasty delights, such as Focaccia (420), Naan bread (page 424) and Tortillas (page 424), and then the good stuff – Sticky cinnamon buns (page 427), Doughnuts (page 428) and an incredible Rhubarb Danish pastry slice (page 429). For the more healthy minded, I've included a recipe for Protein bread (page 428), a great gluten-free option for breakfast – make a loaf, slice it and freeze it, and you can be assured of a good start to the day.

Things you need to know
about bread

- Yeast is available in two main forms: fresh and dried. Fresh is fine if you do baking on a daily basis; sachets of dried yeast are better if you use it no more than once a week, as these keep for many months in the cupboard.

- Yeast is often mixed with a little warm water and a pinch of sugar in order to bring it to life.

- 7 g (¼ oz) dried yeast is equal to 1 sachet.

- Use plain (all-purpose) unbleached flour, unless otherwise stated. If you have a supply of baker's or strong flour, use that instead.

- Kneading dough is an essential part of making any yeast product. To knead, sprinkle a little plain (all-purpose) flour on a smooth work surface. Place the dough in front of you, grab the far edge of the dough with your fingertips and bring it into the centre. Then press it down with the heel of your hand. Repeat this until the dough takes on a smooth, almost silky feel. This can be anywhere from 5–10 minutes. This is wonderful therapy for getting any grievances out of the way. It's also much better for everyone in the house if you take your bad thoughts out on the dough rather than them.

- Kneading can be done in a freestanding electric mixer by using a dough hook attachment, if you have one, and running it on the lowest speed.

- All doughs need a warm place to rise, which is not that easy on a cool day. Here are a few tricks to try:
  - Place the covered bowl of dough on top of a warm heater.
  - Cover the dough and float the bowl in a sink of warm water.
  - Keep the covered dough on top of the stove with the oven on below.
  - Warm the oven for 5 minutes, then turn it off and use this as a warm place for your dough to rise.
  - On hot days you can set your dough in a sunny spot in the garden.

- Flat baking trays are best for baking bread and pizza. If you're really enthusiastic you can also buy a ceramic or terracotta tray. These hold the heat well and will create nice crusty bottoms on your baked goods.

- A light brushing of butter or olive oil is enough to stop bread and pizza sticking to trays. I often add a light sprinkling of fine polenta or semolina, too, a little of which sticks to the finished bread, adding a nice texture and crunch. Baking paper can also be used; this will also leave your baking tray much cleaner.

- Scrolls, scones and loaves of bread can also be made in cake tins, loaf (bar) tins and even large muffin tins. Never feel you need to spend a lot of money on special baking trays or other accessories.

- The breads and sweet doughs you make at home don't keep as well as store-bought products, which is all the more reason for eating them as soon as they come out of the oven.

Bread recipes

Bread rolls

This bread roll recipe is so easy that absolutely everybody should try it. Makes 12 rolls

1 sachet (7 g/¼ oz) dried yeast

1 teaspoon sugar

100 ml (3½ fl oz) warm water

60 g (2 oz) soft butter

450 g (1 lb/3 cups) unbleached plain (all-purpose)
  flour

175 ml (6 fl oz) water mixed with Egg wash (see below)

Mix the dried yeast with the sugar and warm water. Leave in a warm place until the mixture bubbles.

In a large bowl, rub the butter into the flour and 1 teaspoon salt. Add the yeasty water. Mix together well, then place on a floured work surface.

Knead the dough until smooth and no longer sticky, around 6–8 minutes. Place the dough in a large bowl and cover with plastic wrap. Leave to prove in a warm place until the dough doubles in size, 1–2 hours.

Preheat the oven to 200°C (400°F).

Knead the proven dough for 1–2 minutes. Divide the dough into 12 even-sized pieces. Shape into balls and place on a greased baking tray. Cover with a clean cloth and leave to prove in a warm place for 20 minutes.

Brush the rolls with the water and egg wash mixture and bake in the oven for 10–12 minutes until golden brown.

Sesame seed rolls
When the rolls are proven, brush with egg wash and sprinkle with sesame seeds, then bake as described.

Poppy seed rolls
When the rolls are proven, brush with egg wash and sprinkle with poppy seeds, then bake as described.

Square white loaf
Turn this recipe into a simple white loaf by placing the risen dough in a tin lined with baking paper. Allow to prove for 30 minutes in a warm place, then bake for 30 minutes. A perfectly cooked loaf will sound hollow when tapped on the bottom.

Knot rolls
Take the divided dough and roll each piece into a long snake-like shape about 15 cm (6 in) in length. Tie each piece of dough into a knot, then prove and bake as directed.

Egg wash

TIP

Lightly beat 1 egg yolk with a splash of milk. Use this to brush on top of proven dough to add a shiny finish to cooked breads and pastries.

A great crusty loaf

I find that this loaf is best on the day it's made, after which I use it for toast. Makes 1 loaf

500 g (1 lb 2 oz/3⅓ cups) unbleached flour
60 g (2 oz) soft butter
1 sachet (7 g/¼ oz) dried yeast
250–300 ml (9–10½ fl oz/1–1¼ cups) warm water
Egg wash (page 419)

Sift the flour and 2 teaspoons salt into a large bowl. Rub in the butter. Add the yeast and mix briefly. Add water – 250 ml (8½ fl oz/1 cup) should do it, but you may need more. Mix with a wooden spoon until the mixture comes together.

Tip the dough onto a floured work surface. Knead until smooth and no longer sticky, around 6–8 minutes.

Place the dough in a large bowl and cover with plastic wrap. Leave to prove in a warm place until the dough doubles in size, 1–2 hours.

Preheat the oven to 200°C (400°F).

Knead the proven dough for 1–2 minutes. Make it into a loaf shape and either place it on a greased and lined baking tray, or in a greased and lined 23.5 × 13.5 × 7 cm (9¼ × 5¼ × 2¾ in) loaf (bar) tin. Cover loosely with a tea towel (dish towel) and set aside to prove in a warm place for 30 minutes.

Brush the top of the dough with egg wash and slash the top three to four times with a small knife. Bake in the oven for 25–30 minutes, or until well risen and golden brown and the base sounds hollow when tapped.

Focaccia

Focaccia is one of the easiest styles of bread to make. It's the usual blend of yeast, water, salt and flour with a little olive oil added. It can be made into virtually any shape you like: a huge oval loaf, a couple of thin round ones or even small individual ones. Makes 2 focaccias

1 sachet (7 g/¼ oz) dried yeast
Pinch of sugar
60 ml (2 fl oz/¼ cup) olive oil, plus extra for brushing
500 g (1 lb 2 oz/3⅓ cups) unbleached plain
  (all-purpose) flour
Salt flakes

Mix the dried yeast with the sugar and 80 ml (2½ fl oz/⅓ cup) tepid water. Leave in a warm place until the mixture bubbles. Stir in 250 ml (8½ fl oz/1 cup) tepid water, the olive oil and 1 teaspoon salt. Stir in the flour until combined.

Place the dough on a lightly floured work surface. Knead until smooth and no longer sticky, 6–8 minutes. Place the dough in a large bowl and cover with plastic wrap. Leave to prove in a warm place until the dough doubles in size, 1–2 hours.

Preheat the oven to 200°C (400°F).

Knead the proven dough for 1–2 minutes. Shape into two 25 cm (10 in) rounds about 2 cm (¾ in) thick, or another size if you prefer. Place on greased baking trays and allow to prove for 15 minutes.

Brush the dough with olive oil and sprinkle with the salt flakes. Bake in the oven for 10–12 minutes, or until golden brown.

Olive focaccia
Press 125 g (4½ oz) pitted kalamata olives into the proved loaves, then brush with oil and sprinkle the salt flakes over.

Garlic focaccia
Slice four to five large peeled and sliced garlic cloves and press them into the dough after the olive oil and salt.

Za'atar focaccia
Add 1 tablespoon Za'atar (page 470) with the flour. Sprinkle additional za'atar over the top after brushing with olive oil.

Polenta bread

Adding polenta to bread dough introduces a delightful yellow colour, as well as a robust flavour and texture, to the finished loaf. It is good for making sandwiches with fillings of roasted vegetables, goat's cheese and pesto. Makes 2 loaves

2 × 7 g (¼ oz) sachets dried yeast

1 teaspoon caster (superfine) sugar

250 ml (8½ fl oz/1 cup) warm water

500 g (1 lb 2 oz/3⅓ cups) unbleached plain (all-purpose) flour

250 g (9 oz/1⅔ cups) polenta

2 eggs, lightly beaten

Egg wash (page 419)

Mix the yeast with the sugar and warm water. Leave in a warm place until the mixture bubbles.

In a large bowl sift together the flour, polenta and 1 teaspoon salt. Add the yeast mixture and the eggs. Mix together well, then place on a floured work surface.

Knead the dough until smooth and no longer sticky, around 6–8 minutes. Place the dough in a large bowl and cover with plastic wrap. Leave to prove in a warm place until the dough doubles in size, 1–2 hours.

Preheat the oven to 200°C (400°F).

Knead the proven dough for 1–2 minutes. Divide the dough into two equal-sized pieces. Shape into loaves and place on a greased baking tray. Cover with a clean cloth and leave to prove in a warm place for 20 minutes.

Brush the dough with egg wash and bake in the oven for 15–20 minutes, or until golden brown and the bottom sounds hollow when tapped.

Rosemary polenta bread
Add 1 teaspoon chopped fresh rosemary to the flour and polenta mix.

Soda bread

Soda bread is perfect for those who want a quick and easy loaf. This old-fashioned Irish recipe uses bicarbonate of soda and baking powder for rising and the dough is simply stirred together, then shaped and baked until golden. Makes 1 loaf

375 g (13 oz/2½ cups) wholemeal (whole-wheat) self-raising flour

375 g (13 oz/2½ cups) self-raising flour

2 teaspoons baking powder

1 teaspoon bicarbonate of soda (baking soda)

500 ml (17 fl oz/2 cups) buttermilk, or milk soured with a little lemon juice, plus additional buttermilk for brushing

Preheat the oven to 210°C (410°F).

Sift together the flours, baking powder, bicarbonate of soda and 1 teaspoon salt. Stir in the buttermilk and mix until combined to a firm dough.

Shape the dough into a round about 4 cm (1½ in) high on a lined baking tray. Slash a deep cross into the top of the bread, then brush it with additional buttermilk.

Bake in the oven for 20 minutes. Remove the bread from the oven and brush it with additional buttermilk. Reduce the oven temperature to 180°C (350°F) and cook the bread for a further 40 minutes. A perfectly cooked loaf will sound hollow when tapped on the bottom. Wrap the bread in a dry tea towel (dish towel) as it cools; this will help to keep the moisture in.

Fruity soda bread
Add 250 g (9 oz) dried fruit to the dough – try a mix of raisins, apricots, currants and sultanas (golden raisins). Adding ½ teaspoon cinnamon, mixed spice or nutmeg goes well with the fruit.

Pizza

Pizza, it seems, is universally popular. No matter what your favourite topping might be, your enjoyment of pizza can only be improved by making your own base. This recipe makes a thick and chewy pizza base and is the sort of thing I prepare on weekends. Makes 2 pizza bases

1 sachet (7 g/¼ oz) dried yeast
Pinch of caster (superfine) sugar
80 ml (2½ fl oz/⅓ cup) olive oil
500 g (1 lb 2 oz/3⅓ cups) unbleached plain
   (all-purpose) flour

Mix the dried yeast with the caster sugar and 80 ml (2½ fl oz/⅓ cup) tepid water. Leave in a warm place until the mixture bubbles.

Stir in the oil and 250 ml (8½ fl oz/1 cup) tepid water. Add the flour and 1 teaspoon salt and mix briefly. Tip the dough onto a lightly floured work surface.

Knead the dough for 6–8 minutes, until smooth and no longer sticky. Place the dough in a large bowl and cover

with plastic wrap. Leave to prove in a warm place until the dough doubles in size, 1–2 hours.

Preheat the oven to 190°C (375°F).

Knead the proven dough for 1–2 minutes. Divide into two equal pieces and roll each into a ball. Place on oiled baking trays and use your fingers to press and flatten the dough out until it's 20 cm (8 in) across and 2 cm (¾ in) thick. Cover and let it prove for 20 minutes.

Add the toppings of your choice (see the ideas below) and bake in the oven for 10–15 minutes, or until the pizza bases are dry and golden underneath.

Pizza toppings

TIP

While I usually make my own pizza bases, good-quality store-bought bases are a must in the freezer as an after-school snack or for those times when unexpected guests drop in for dinner.

The only rule for pizza is to limit yourself to two to three toppings on each one, so you can really enjoy the flavours. Here are some topping suggestions:

- Ham, olives and tomato
- Ham, tomato and grilled eggplant (aubergine)
- Salami, tomato and olives
- Salami, artichokes and goat's cheese
- Roasted capsicum (bell pepper), basil and goat's cheese
- Artichokes, eggplant (aubergine) and bocconcini
- Tapenade (page 477), tomato and goat's cheese
- Caramelised onions (page 252) and anchovies

Pizzas are also often topped with tomato, baked and then finished with raw ingredients such as:

- Smoked salmon and Horseradish cream (page 456)
- Prosciutto, mozzarella and figs
- Prosciutto, blue cheese and rocket (arugula)

Pizza bianco, or white pizza, has no tomato base and is usually simply brushed with olive oil and topped with ingredients such as the following:

- Thinly sliced potato, rosemary and onion
- Roast pumpkin (squash), English spinach and goat's cheese (with pine nuts if you like)
- Three cheeses: mozzarella, blue cheese and parmesan

Pissaladière

Pissaladière is a pizza topped with caramelised onions, anchovies and olives. As you can imagine, it is for those people, like me, who enjoy robust, concentrated flavours on their pizza. Cut into fingers and serve as a nibble. Serves 4

½ quantity Pizza dough (see opposite)

1 quantity Caramelised onions (page 252)

Anchovies as required, halved lengthways

Pitted kalamata olives as required

Roll the dough out to a rough rectangular shape of around 30 × 15 cm (12 × 6 in). Spread the caramelised onions on top. Arrange the anchovy halves in a diamond lattice formation and stud each diamond centre with an olive.

Preheat the oven to 190°C (375°F).

Set the pizza aside to prove in a warm place for 15 minutes. Bake in the oven for 15–20 minutes, or until risen and golden brown.

Roasted vegetable calzone

Calzone is basically an enclosed pizza parcel, so anything you can put on pizza you can put into a calzone. Calzone can be cooked with a sweet filling as well. Makes 6 calzone

1 eggplant (aubergine), cut into 1 cm (½ in) dice, salted and rinsed

1 zucchini (courgette), halved and cut into 1 cm (½ in) slices

1 onion, diced

¼ pumpkin (squash), peeled and diced

1 red capsicum (bell pepper), diced

Oil

3–4 oregano sprigs

1 quantity Pizza dough (see opposite)

125 ml (4 fl oz/½ cup) tomato passata (puréed tomatoes)

125 g (4½ oz) mozzarella, grated

Egg wash (page 419)

Polenta for sprinkling

Preheat the oven to 200°C (400°F).

Toss together the eggplant, zucchini, onion, pumpkin, capsicum, oil and oregano and season with salt and freshly ground black pepper. Place in a baking tin and cook in the oven for 40 minutes, until soft and cooked. Set aside to cool.

Divide the pizza dough into six 150 g (5½ oz) pieces. Roll each piece of dough into an oval shape about 20 cm (8 in) long.

Toss the roasted vegetables with the passata and cheese. Divide the vegetables between each dough oval, placing them on the lower half of the dough oval. Brush around the vegetables with egg wash. Fold the dough over and press the edges together firmly.

Transfer to greased baking trays sprinkled with polenta. Brush the top of each calzone with egg wash. Set aside to prove in a warm place for 15 minutes. Bake in the oven for 20 minutes, or until golden brown.

Naan bread

Naan bread is loved by one and all at my place, so I was determined to master it. This recipe follows a similar principle to other doughs, with the addition of a few other simple ingredients. When it's ready it can be cooked in a hot pan or, even better, outside on the barbecue hot plate. Makes 16 naan

2 × 7 g (¼ oz) sachets dried yeast
1 tablespoon caster (superfine) sugar
50 ml (1¾ fl oz) warm water
1 egg
125 g (4½ oz/½ cup) natural yoghurt
125 ml (4 fl oz/½ cup) milk
50 g (1¾ oz) melted butter
700 g (1 lb 9 oz/4⅔ cups) unbleached plain (all-purpose) flour
Olive oil

Mix the yeast with 1 teaspoon of the sugar and the warm water. Leave in a warm place until the mixture bubbles.

Stir in the remaining sugar, the egg, yoghurt, milk, 125 ml (4 fl oz/½ cup) water, the melted butter and 1 teaspoon salt. Add the flour, mix briefly, then tip the dough onto a lightly floured work surface.

Knead until smooth and no longer sticky, around 6–8 minutes. Place the dough in a large bowl and cover with plastic wrap. Leave to prove in a warm place until the dough doubles in size, 1–2 hours.

Knead the proved dough for 1–2 minutes. Divide into 16 equal-sized portions (about 80 g/2¾ oz each), and roll into balls.

Using a rolling pin or your fingers, shape and flatten out each bread until it's 20 cm (8 in) across. Place a tight layer of plastic wrap on a dinner plate and lay one of the naan breads on it. Cover with more plastic and repeat until all the portions are flattened.

Heat a flat barbecue plate to medium–hot, or a heavy-based frying pan over medium–high heat. Brush the breads with a thin layer of olive oil, then cook the naan until golden, about 2 minutes each side.

Garlic naan
Brush both sides of each naan with melted garlic butter as it finishes cooking.

Spice naan
Add 3 teaspoons spice, such as ground cardamom, cumin and coriander, to the dough.

Tortillas

Of all the processed foods in the supermarket I am most shocked by how many artificial things there are in pre-made tortillas. Do yourself a favour and make your own, which are delicious with any Mexican-inspired feast. Makes 8 tortillas

300 g (10½ oz/2 cups) plain (all-purpose) flour
1 teaspoon baking powder
60 ml (2 fl oz/¼ cup) oil
180 ml (6 fl oz) warm water
Oil for cooking

Sift together the flour, baking powder and 1 teaspoon salt. Add the oil and warm water and turn out onto a floured work surface. Knead for 2–3 minutes until you get a smooth dough. Add more water or flour as necessary if the dough is dry or sticky.

Divide the dough into eight pieces, roll into rough ball shapes and set aside to rest for 15 minutes. Roll the balls into 15 cm (6 in) circles.

Heat a heavy-based frying pan over medium–high heat, add a splash of oil and cook each tortilla for 1 minute on each side until lightly brown.

Simple brioche

Brioche is a yeast loaf often served for breakfast in France. This recipe is for one large brioche, but you could make several smaller ones instead. Brioche is scrumptious toasted and served with butter and jam and it makes the most amazing bread-and-butter pudding. Makes 1 brioche

2 × 7 g (¼ oz) sachets dried yeast
1 teaspoon sugar
2 tablespoons warm water
200 g (7 oz/1⅓ cups) plain (all-purpose) flour
2 medium eggs, beaten
60 g (2 oz) melted butter

Mix the yeast with the sugar and warm water and set aside until the yeast bubbles.

Sift the flour and 1 teaspoon salt together. Add the yeast, eggs and melted butter to the flour. Mix briefly, then tip the dough onto a lightly floured work surface.

Knead the dough until smooth and no longer sticky, around 6–8 minutes. Place the dough in a large bowl and cover with plastic wrap. Leave to prove in a warm place until the dough rises, about 1 hour.

Preheat the oven to 190°C (375°F).

Knead the proven dough for 1–2 minutes. Shape the dough into a loaf and place in a greased 23.5 × 13.5 × 7 cm (9¼ × 5¼ × 2¾ in) loaf (bar) tin. Cover with a cloth and leave to prove in a warm place for 20 minutes.

Bake in the oven for 15–20 minutes, or until golden brown and the bottom sounds hollow when tapped.

Orange brioche
Add the chopped zest of one orange to the flour.

Sticky currant buns

I love a sticky currant bun! You can swap the currants for sultanas (golden raisins), or use a combination of both, if you prefer. Makes 12 buns

400 g (14 oz/2⅔ cups) plain (all-purpose) flour
1 teaspoon mixed spice
2 × 7 g (¼ oz) sachets dried yeast
60 g (2 oz) caster (superfine) sugar
100 g (3½ oz) melted butter
2 medium eggs, lightly beaten
125 ml (4 fl oz/½ cup) milk
90 g (3 oz) currants
Sugar syrup (page 486)

Sift the flour and mixed spice together in a large bowl. Add the yeast, sugar and a pinch of salt and mix briefly.

Mix the melted butter with the beaten eggs and milk. Pour into the flour mixture and mix briefly with a wooden spoon. Tip the dough out onto a floured work surface. Knead for 4–5 minutes or until you have a smooth and silky dough.

Place the dough in a bowl, cover with plastic wrap and leave it to prove in a warm place until doubled in size, about 1 hour. When proven, tip the dough onto a floured work surface, add the currants and knead well to incorporate the fruit. Divide the dough into 12 equal-sized pieces. Roll each one into a small bun shape and place the buns on a greased and lined baking tray. Cover the tray with a tea towel (dish towel) and leave to prove in a warm place for 20 minutes.

Preheat the oven to 200°C (400°F).

Place the buns in the oven and bake for 15–20 minutes, or until risen and golden brown. When the buns are cooked, brush them liberally with the sugar syrup and allow to cool slightly before eating them warm.

Orange and currant buns
Add 60 g (2 oz) diced candied orange peel along with the currants.

Chelsea buns

Chelsea buns are a touch more complicated to make than currant buns, but the end result is well worth the effort. Makes 12 buns

400 g (14 oz/2⅔ cups) plain (all-purpose) flour

2 × 7 g (¼ oz) sachets dried yeast

115 g (4 oz/½ cup) caster (superfine) sugar

100 g (3½ oz) melted butter, plus an extra 3 tablespoons

2 eggs, lightly beaten

125 ml (4 fl oz/½ cup) milk

30 g (1 oz) currants

60 g (2 oz/½ cup) sultanas (golden raisins)

Sugar syrup (page 486)

Sift the flour into a large bowl. Add the yeast, 60 g (2 oz) of the sugar and a pinch of salt and mix briefly.

Mix the melted butter with the beaten eggs and milk. Pour into the flour, mix briefly with a wooden spoon and then tip the dough out onto a floured work surface. Knead for 4–5 minutes or until the dough is smooth and silky.

Place the dough in a bowl, cover with plastic wrap and set aside in a warm place to prove until doubled in size, about 1 hour.

Tip the dough onto a floured work surface and knead well. Roll out to a large square, about 30 cm (12 in).

Brush with the additional melted butter, then sprinkle liberally with the remaining caster sugar. Sprinkle with the dried fruits.

Roll up from one end to form a large Swiss roll (jelly roll) shape. Cut into 2 cm (¾ in) slices. Place the slices, cut side up, on a lined baking tray. Cover the tray with a tea towel (dish towel) and leave to prove in a warm place for 20 minutes.

Preheat the oven to 200°C (400°F).

Place the proven buns in the oven and bake for about 15–20 minutes, or until risen and golden brown. When the buns are cooked, brush liberally with sugar syrup and allow to cool slightly before eating them warm.

Swiss buns
Drizzle the cooked buns with Basic icing (page 491).

Jam swirls
Omit the butter, sugar and fruit and spread the dough with jam instead.

Hot cross buns
Add 60 g (2 oz) chopped candied orange peel or mixed peel to the bun dough. Slash the tops with a knife to form cross shapes.

Sticky cinnamon buns

These cinnamon buns are rich, sticky and very more-ish. They're guaranteed to make your morning tea better than ever. Makes 12 buns

400 g (14 oz/2⅔ cups) unbleached plain (all-purpose) flour
130 g (4½ oz) caster (superfine) sugar
2 × 7 g (¼ oz) sachets dried yeast
50 g (1¾ oz) butter, plus 75 g (2¾ oz) soft butter
1 medium egg
200 ml (7 fl oz) milk
1 teaspoon ground cinnamon
Egg wash (page 419)

Sift the flour, 55 g (2 oz/¼ cup) of the sugar, the yeast and ½ teaspoon salt together in a large bowl.

Melt the 50 g (1¾ oz) butter and mix with the egg and milk. Pour into the flour mixture, mix briefly with a wooden spoon and then tip out onto a floured work surface. Knead for 4–5 minutes or until the dough is smooth and silky. Place the dough in a bowl, cover with plastic wrap and set aside in a warm place to prove until doubled in size, about 1 hour.

Tip the dough onto a floured work surface and knead well. Roll the dough out to a large square about 30 cm (12 in). Mix the 75 g (2¾ oz) soft butter, the remaining sugar and the cinnamon together and spread liberally over the dough.

Roll up from one end to form a large Swiss roll (jelly roll) shape. Cut into 2 cm (¾ in) slices. Place the slices, cut side up, in a lined baking tin. Cover the tray with a tea towel (dish towel) and leave to prove in a warm place for 20 minutes.

Preheat the oven to 200°C (400°F).

Brush the buns with egg wash. Place the proven buns in the oven and bake for 15–20 minutes, or until risen and golden brown. Best eaten warm.

Fruit bread

Everyone seems to love fruit bread, my family included. This loaf is excellent served warm from the oven with a decent smear of butter on top. Makes 2 loaves

125 g (4½ oz) dried apricots
60 g (2 oz) currants
125 g (4½ oz/1 cup) sultanas (golden raisins)
2 × 7 g (¼ oz) sachets dried yeast
1 teaspoon caster (superfine) sugar
60 ml (2 fl oz/¼ cup) warm water
500 g (1 lb 2 oz/3⅓ cups) unbleached plain (all-purpose) flour
1 teaspoon mixed spice
175 ml (6 fl oz) milk
1 medium egg
Egg wash (page 419)

Place the dried fruit in a bowl and pour boiling water over to cover. Allow to stand for 15–20 minutes, then drain, discarding the water. Set aside.

Mix the yeast with the sugar and warm water. Leave in a warm place until the mixture bubbles.

Sift the flour and mixed spice together. Add the yeast mixture, soaked fruit, the milk and egg. Mix briefly, then tip the dough out onto a lightly floured work surface. Knead until smooth and no longer sticky, around 6–8 minutes. Place the dough in a large bowl and cover with plastic wrap. Leave to prove in a warm place until the dough doubles in size, 1–2 hours.

Preheat the oven to 210°C (410°F).

Knead the proven dough for 1–2 minutes. Divide the dough into two equal-sized pieces, then shape into loaves and place on a greased baking tray. Cover with a cloth and leave to prove in a warm place for 20 minutes.

Brush the loaves with egg wash, slash the tops three to four times, then bake for 15–20 minutes, or until golden brown and the bottom sounds hollow when tapped.

Doughnuts

Believe it or not, I don't make these every day. But I'm always glad when I do. You can pipe a dollop of jam or custard into the centre when the doughnuts have cooled – if they last that long! Makes 10 doughnuts

55 g (2 oz/¼ cup) caster (superfine) sugar, plus extra for rolling

1 sachet (7 g/¼ oz) dry yeast

2 tablespoons tepid water

300 g (10½ oz/2 cups) unbleached plain (all-purpose) flour

150 g (5½ oz) soft butter, diced

3 medium eggs

Oil for deep-frying

A little ground cinnamon

Mix the sugar, yeast, water and a pinch of salt together. Leave in a warm place until the mixture bubbles.

Place the flour in a large bowl, add the butter and rub it in with your fingertips until a breadcrumb-like texture is achieved. Make a small well in the centre, add the yeast mixture and stir lightly. Add the eggs, one by one, mixing well after each addition.

Turn the dough onto a floured work surface. Knead until smooth and no longer sticky, around 6–8 minutes. Place the dough in a bowl, cover with plastic wrap and set aside in a warm place to prove until doubled in size, about 1 hour.

Tip the dough onto a floured work surface and knead well for 1–2 minutes. Divide the dough into 10 evenly sized pieces. Shape into balls and place on a greased baking tray. Cover with a clean cloth and leave to prove in a warm place for 20 minutes.

Heat the oil in a deep-fryer or large saucepan to a temperature of 175°C (345°F).

Mix the extra caster sugar and a little cinnamon together on a plate or piece of baking paper.

Cook the doughnuts in batches until golden brown, turning once during cooking. Drain briefly on paper towel, then roll them in the caster sugar and cinnamon mixture while still warm.

Protein bread – gluten-free

You will be surprised by how much you like this bread. If you want to go gluten-free, this is nice and easy to make at home. To make it really wholesome you can double the amount of seeds. Makes 1 loaf

1 sachet (7 g/¼ oz) dry yeast

80 ml (2½ fl oz/⅓ cup) extra-virgin olive oil

375 ml (12½ fl oz/1½ cups) warm water

120 g (4½ oz) besan (chickpea flour)

110 g (4 oz) rice flour

100 g (3½ oz/1 cup) ground almonds

50 g (1¾ oz/⅓ cup) pepitas (pumpkin seeds)

50 g (1¾ oz) linseeds (flax seeds)

50 g (1¾ oz) chia seeds

50 g (1¾ oz) sunflower seeds

4 eggs, lightly beaten

Preheat the oven to 190°C (375°F). Grease and line a 21 × 9 × 6 cm (8¼ × 3½ × 2½ in) loaf (bar) tin.

Add the yeast and oil to the warm water, mix to combine and set aside to prove.

Place the besan, ground almonds, all the seeds and 1 teaspoon salt in a large bowl and mix to combine. Add the eggs and mix to combine and then add the yeast mixture, stirring as you go to bring the mixture to a thick batter. It will look quite wet at this stage, but that's normal.

Pour into the prepared tin and bake in the oven for 30–40 minutes or until golden brown and cooked through. Allow to cool before slicing.

Rhubarb Danish pastry slice

This Danish pastry slice is an absolute beauty and comes from my Danish mother. It makes a huge pastry so it's great to enjoy with a large group of people. I have made it for a traditional Easter Sunday brunch/free-for-all at the local park. It's extremely easy; don't be put off by the vast quantities of butter. Feeds 5000!

310 g (11 oz/1⅓ cups) caster (superfine) sugar, plus extra for sprinkling

8 stalks of rhubarb, cut into 3 cm (1¼ in) lengths

2 × 7 g (¼ oz) sachets dried yeast

2 tablespoons warm water

3 eggs

500 g (1 lb 2 oz/3⅓ cups) plain (all-purpose) flour

475 g (1 lb 1 oz) butter, softened

100 g (3½ oz) marzipan, grated

Egg wash (page 419)

Handful of flaked almonds

Prepare the rhubarb by placing 750 ml (25½ fl oz/ 3 cups) water and 110 g (4 oz) of the sugar in a large saucepan. Cook over low heat until the sugar dissolves. Bring to the boil. Add the rhubarb pieces. Cook gently for 3–4 minutes – you want the rhubarb to retain its shape. Remove the rhubarb and set aside.

Preheat the oven to 220°C (430°F).

Make the dough by dissolving the yeast in the warm water. Set aside to prove.

Lightly beat the eggs and add the yeast mixture.

Place the flour, 350 g (12½ oz) of the butter, 75 g (2¾ oz) of the sugar and the egg and yeast mixture in a freestanding electric mixer fitted with a dough hook. Knead the dough until smooth. If you don't have a dough hook you can mix the dough by hand.

Divide the dough into thirds. Take two-thirds and roll this out to approximately 25 × 35 cm (10 × 12 in), or a similar size, to fit a baking tray. Place the dough on the greased and lined baking tray, stretching and kneading the dough if necessary to fit into the corners.

Mix together the remaining butter, the remaining sugar and the grated marzipan. Sprinkle the mixture over the dough. Arrange the poached rhubarb slices on top.

Roll the remaining third of the dough out flat and cut it into long strips. Arrange the strips diagonally over the top of the pastry, twisting to add a decorative edge. Brush with the egg wash, sprinkle with the flaked almonds and sprinkle with caster sugar. Bake in the oven for 15–20 minutes, or until the pastry is golden brown and risen. Serve warm.

Preserves

Whether you're a keen gardener or simply love picking up a bargain at your local market, preserving is the best way to secure a taste of the season for later in the year. Some recipes are kitchen must-haves, such as preserved lemons; others are a daily indulgence, such as berry jam and tomato relish; and some are just for the fun of it, or great to give as a gift.

Savour the seasons

Making preserves gives you the opportunity to preserve a taste of one season to carry through to the next. Hoard all your empty jars for that day when you have a glut of a fruit or vegetable and get busy making jam, chutney or relishes. There's something in this chapter for both sweet and savoury tastes, from classic berry jams and citrus marmalades, to good old faithful tomato kasoundi and the more exotic chilli jam and pickles to complement many foods.

Key things to know
when making preserves

- You need the best-quality produce to make the best preserves. The ingredients have to be just right – neither underripe nor overripe.

- Some fruit can be roasted before being made into jam to intensify the flavour. Always remove the stones before cooking.

- Jars must be sterilised before use. The easiest way to do this is in the dishwasher on a hot cycle. Failing this, wash them well and place them in a hot oven for a couple of minutes.

- Soak the jar lids in boiling water for 10 minutes.

- When the jars have been filled, check that the lids are airtight. If not, air can get in and ruin all your hard work.

- Always label the preserves with the name of the product and the date on which it was made.

- Pass on a few jars to food-loving friends. Hopefully, you'll get a few in return!

Preserves recipes

Preserved lemons

Preserved lemons are stored in salty brine for later use. I use them in Middle Eastern salads, rolled up inside a leg of lamb and to add a burst of lemon flavour to tagines and couscous.
Makes 8 preserved lemons

2–3 cloves

1 cinnamon stick

8 lemons, cut into quarters

Place 4 tablespoons salt, the cloves and cinnamon in a large saucepan of water and bring to the boil. When boiling, add half the lemon wedges and allow the water to return to the boil. Cook the lemon, skin side down, for 7–8 minutes. Remove the lemon, drain and cook the next batch. Reserve the cooking liquid.

Squash the lemons into sterilised jars and push down firmly. When each jar is full, cover the lemons with the reserved cooking liquid. Store in a cool dark place for 3–4 weeks before using.

To use the preserved lemon, soak a wedge in cold water for 10 minutes, cut out and discard the pulpy centre, then use the preserved lemon rind in your recipe. Keep in a cool dark place for up to 6 months.

Marinated olives

I've tried numerous recipes over the years in my search for a simple way to prepare fresh olives. This recipe from my friend Daniele gives great results. Daniele prefers to remove the stones completely, while I tend to leave them in – the choice is yours. Makes 1 kg (2 lb 3 oz)

1 kg (2 lb 3 oz) olives

1 lemon, sliced

White vinegar

1 tablespoon fennel seeds

2 garlic cloves, sliced

4 bay leaves

4 oregano sprigs

2 small chillies

Olive oil as required

Cut a slit in the base of each olive with a sharp knife. You might like to follow Daniele's example and bash them with a beer bottle so the seed can be completely removed! Place the olives in a large container and cover with water and the sliced lemon. Leave for 24 hours.

Strain and rinse the olives a few times. Dry well. Sprinkle the olives with salt and leave for 24 hours.

Rinse well in fresh water. Cover with the vinegar and leave for 24 hours. Drain well.

Mix the olives with the fennel seeds, garlic, bay leaves, oregano and chillies. Place in sterilised glass jars and cover with olive oil.

The olives will take at least 6 weeks to mature. Test regularly until you are happy with the flavour. Keep in a cool dark place for up to 6 months.

Tomato kasoundi

This fantastic tomato chilli pickle is based on a recipe by Christine Manfield, who was inspired by Charmaine Solomon. It's an excellent addition to curries, noodles or barbecued meats.
Makes 500 ml (17 fl oz/2 cups)

1 tablespoon black mustard seeds

125 ml (4 fl oz/½ cup) cider vinegar

2 kg (4 lb 6 oz) tomatoes

2 tablespoons cumin seeds

125 ml (4 fl oz/½ cup) oil, plus extra as needed

Pinch of cloves

2 teaspoons ground turmeric

2 tablespoons grated fresh ginger

10 garlic cloves, peeled

10 small chillies

85 g (3 oz) grated palm sugar (jaggery)

60 ml (2 fl oz/¼ cup) fish sauce

Place the mustard seeds and vinegar in a saucepan and cook over medium heat for 10 minutes. Remove from the heat and set aside for 2 hours.

Cut a cross in the base of each tomato and cut out the core. Bring a large saucepan of water to the boil. Add the tomatoes, a few at a time, and cook for 30 seconds, then place them in cold water. The tomatoes can then be peeled and cut into quarters.

Dry-roast the cumin seeds in a dry frying pan over medium heat, stirring well, until fragrant. Cool, then grind to a fine powder.

Heat the oil in a heavy-based saucepan. Fry the cumin, cloves and turmeric gently, until fragrant. Remove from the heat.

Place the soaked mustard seeds, ginger, garlic and chillies in a food processor and whizz until smooth. Add the mixture to the saucepan with the oil and spices, along with the prepared tomatoes. Bring to a simmer and cook for 1 hour, stirring frequently. Add the palm sugar and fish sauce and cook for a further 30 minutes. Season to taste with salt and freshly ground black pepper, if needed.

Spoon into sterilised jars and cover with a thin layer of oil. Keep in a cool dark place for up to 6 months.

Mango chutney

Mangoes have a relatively short season, and they are a sign of the warmer weather about to arrive. Make this chutney and you can keep the wonderful flavour of mango going for a few more months.
Makes 1.25 litres (42 fl oz/5 cups)

165 ml (5½ fl oz) white-wine vinegar

100 g (3½ oz) brown sugar

1 onion, finely diced

4 garlic cloves, peeled

1 teaspoon ground ginger

4 mangoes, peeled and sliced

Bring the vinegar, sugar, onion, garlic and ginger to the boil in a saucepan. Cook until reduced by half. Add the mango and cook for a further 5 minutes. Remove from the heat and pour into sterilised jars. Keep in a cool dark place for up to 6 months.

Capsicum relish

This relish reminds me of summer. Use it in sandwiches or as an accompaniment to barbecued beef or pork. Makes 625 g (1 lb 6 oz/2½ cups)

5 red capsicums (bell peppers)

Olive oil

2 onions, diced

2 garlic cloves, crushed

220 g (8 oz/1 cup) raw sugar

125 ml (4 fl oz/½ cup) white-wine vinegar

1 teaspoon cinnamon

Preheat the oven to 200°C (400°F).

Rub the red capsicums with oil and roast them in the oven for 20–25 minutes, until their skins blister.

Place the capsicums in a plastic bag and seal to allow the steam to lift their skins.

When cool, remove the skins and seeds and dice the flesh roughly.

Add a splash of oil to a large saucepan and cook the onion and garlic for 3–4 minutes, until soft. Add the capsicum, sugar, vinegar, cinnamon, 1 teaspoon freshly ground black pepper and 125 ml (4 fl oz/½ cup) water. Allow the sauce to come to the boil, then reduce the heat and simmer for 30 minutes, until the sauce thickens slightly. Season and spoon into sterilised jars. Keep in a cool dark place for up to 6 months.

Beetroot relish

Vibrant beetroot relish is stunning with cold meats and is ideal for picnics or in the cold of winter with the weekly roast. It's fantastic in burgers, too. Makes 500 ml (17 fl oz/2 cups)

3 beetroot (beets)

250 ml (8½ fl oz/1 cup) white-wine vinegar

60 g (2 oz/¼ cup firmly packed) brown sugar

2 whole cloves

2 teaspoons grated fresh ginger

2 garlic cloves, sliced

1 small red chilli, seeded and chopped

12 peppercorns

Trim the beetroot, wash them well and place them in a saucepan. Cover with water and bring to the boil. Cook for 30–40 minutes, depending on the size of the beetroot, until tender. Drain, and allow to cool before peeling and grating.

Place 250 ml (8½ fl oz/1 cup) water, the vinegar, sugar, cloves, ginger, garlic, chilli and peppercorns in a small saucepan. Bring to the boil and cook until reduced to about 125 ml (4 fl oz/½ cup).

Strain the liquid over the grated beetroot, return to a clean saucepan and simmer for 10 minutes. Store in an airtight container for up to 6 months.

Chilli jam

This classic Thai sauce is a cupboard staple at my house. I use it to add flavour to Asian meatballs and noodles and it's great as a barbecue marinade. Makes 500 g (1 lb 2 oz/2 cups)

500 ml (17 fl oz/2 cups) oil

500 g (1 lb 2 oz) Asian shallots, peeled and thinly sliced

2 garlic cloves, thinly sliced

10 long red chillies, seeded and sliced

2 tablespoons tamarind pulp

250 ml (8½ fl oz/1 cup) boiling water

260 g (9 oz) grated palm sugar (jaggery)

25 g (1 oz) dried shrimp paste

60 ml (2 fl oz/¼ cup) fish sauce

1 teaspoon salt

Heat a wok over high heat. Add the oil, then deep-fry the shallots, garlic and chillies in separate batches. Drain on paper towel. Allow the oil to cool and then strain and reserve.

Place the fried ingredients in a food processor and add one-third of the cooled, strained cooking oil (around 100 ml/3½ fl oz). Process until smooth, adding more oil if needed to obtain a smooth paste.

Soak the tamarind in the boiling water for about 5–10 minutes. Use your fingers to work the pulp free from the tamarind seeds. Strain the tamarind, reserving the liquid.

Place the shrimp paste in a heavy-based pan and add the tamarind liquid and remaining ingredients. Heat over low heat until the palm sugar dissolves, then bring to the boil. Reduce the heat and cook for 5 minutes, stirring frequently, until the jam thickens slightly. Pour into sterilised jars and store in a cool dark place for up to 3 months.

Sweet chilli sauce

Why make sweet chilli sauce when you can buy a bottle? Because it tastes about 100 times better, that's why. I find that it's best made with milder, long red chillies, such as the cayenne, poblano or serrano varieties. You can, of course, use hotter chillies if you prefer.
Makes 300 ml (10 fl oz)

250 g (9 oz) chillies (cayenne, poblano or serrano)

4 garlic cloves, crushed

220 g (8 oz) caster (superfine) sugar

1 tablespoon white vinegar

Remove the seeds and membrane from the chillies and slice the flesh thinly.

Place the chillies in a saucepan with the garlic, 375 ml (12½ fl oz/1½ cups) water, the caster sugar, vinegar and 1 tablespoon salt. Bring to the boil, then reduce the heat and simmer for 30 minutes, until most of the liquid has evaporated.

Whizz the sauce in a blender to produce a thick consistency with speckles of chilli. Pour into sterilised jars and store in a cool dark place for up to 3 months.

Onion marmalade

This gorgeous condiment is great with roast meats and in sandwiches of all types, but particularly those with a good cheddar cheese. Makes 750 g (1 lb 11 oz/3 cups)

80 ml (2½ fl oz/⅓ cup) olive oil

4 onions, sliced

2 garlic cloves, peeled

1 small red chilli, halved (optional)

2 thyme sprigs

1 teaspoon yellow mustard seeds

1 teaspoon mixed spice

125 ml (4 fl oz/½ cup) white-wine vinegar

100 g (3½ oz/½ cup firmly packed) soft brown sugar

Put the oil in a saucepan over low heat and add the onion, garlic, chilli (if using) and thyme. Season well with salt and freshly ground black pepper. Cook for 20 minutes, stirring often, until the onion softens and turns a pale gold colour. Add the remaining ingredients and bring to the boil. Stir well to ensure the brown sugar dissolves. Reduce to a simmer again and continue cooking until the mix has a shiny, jam-like consistency.

Allow to cool, then spoon into sterilised jars. Store in the refrigerator for 3–4 weeks.

Asian pickles

Make these pickles in advance and serve them as you need them. They are good as a side dish to Asian food. Serves 6–8

500 ml (17 fl oz/2 cups) rice vinegar

110 g (4 oz) caster (superfine) sugar

2 tablespoons light soy sauce

2 garlic cloves, sliced

2 black peppercorns

6 slices fresh ginger

2 small red chillies, halved

¼ cauliflower, broken into bite-sized florets

2 carrots, cut into sticks

2 Lebanese (short) cucumbers, cut into sticks

1 daikon (white radish), halved and cut into 1 cm (½ in) slices

¼ Chinese cabbage (wombok), cut into 4 cm (1½ in) chunks

Place the rice vinegar, 250 ml (8½ fl oz/1 cup) water, the caster sugar, soy sauce, garlic, peppercorns, ginger and chillies in a large saucepan. Bring to the boil, stirring to dissolve the sugar. Remove the pan from the heat.

Bring a large saucepan of water to the boil and blanch the cauliflower and carrot for 1–2 minutes. Refresh under cold running water.

Place all the vegetables in a large sterilised jar. Pour the pickling liquid over, ensuring that all the vegetables are covered. Set aside to mature for 48 hours before using. Keep refrigerated for up to 3 weeks.

Pickled ginger

Pickled ginger is available at most Asian supermarkets but, when there is plenty of ginger around, you may like to make your own. Makes 500 g (1 lb 2 oz/2 cups)

500 g (1 lb 2 oz) fresh ginger

350 ml (12 fl oz) rice vinegar

2 small red chillies, halved

2 garlic cloves, sliced

12 peppercorns

220 g (8 oz) caster (superfine) sugar

Using a very sharp knife, peel and thinly slice the ginger. Blanch it briefly in boiling water.

To prepare the pickling liquid, place 150 ml (5 fl oz) water, the rice vinegar, chillies, garlic, peppercorns and caster sugar in a saucepan. Bring to the boil, then simmer for 20 minutes. Strain, discarding the solids.

Place the ginger in sterilised jars, cover with the pickling liquid and seal well. The ginger will turn pinkish over time. Will keep for up to 3 months.

Pickled cabbage

'Pickled cabbage' is a general term, I know, but this isn't quite sauerkraut and it isn't quite kimchi – it's somewhere is the middle. You can use any type of cabbage or it could be a mix of green cabbage, Chinese cabbage (wombok) and/or mustard greens, or even some vegetables such as carrot or daikon (white radish). Makes 500 g (1 lb 2 oz/2 cups)

300 g (10½ oz) shredded cabbage

2 carrots, or 1 carrot and 1 daikon (white radish) or red radishes, grated or julienned

2 garlic cloves, crushed

1 tablespoon grated fresh ginger

1 tablespoon chilli paste or Harissa (page 467)

1 tablespoon caster (superfine) sugar

3 tablespoons rice vinegar

Toss the vegetables and 2 teaspoons salt together and set aside to stand for 1 hour.

Mix the remaining ingredients together and mix through the salted vegetables – I wear disposable gloves for this and try to make sure all the vegetables get completely covered with the mixture.

Leave to stand at room temperature for 4 hours, then drain the excess liquid away and refrigerate for up to 2 weeks.

Seed mustard

Mustard is a great condiment to make for friends at Christmas – or at any time of the year. It's not difficult to do and the recipe can be easily adapted to incorporate flavours, such as walnuts, herbs or brandy, once you get the hang of it. Makes 750 g (1 lb 11 oz/3 cups)

100 g (3½ oz) yellow mustard seeds

100 g (3½ oz) brown mustard seeds

250 ml (8½ fl oz/1 cup) vegetable oil

250 ml (8½ fl oz/1 cup) dry white wine or white vinegar

250 ml (8½ fl oz/1 cup) vermouth

Place the yellow and brown mustard seeds, 1 tablespoon freshly ground black pepper, 1 tablespoon salt, the oil, wine and vermouth in a food processor. Process for 5 minutes.

At this stage the mustard will look like a thin dressing with mustard seeds floating around in it. Don't be alarmed; this is normal. Cover and set aside overnight.

The next day, process again for 5 minutes. The mustard will begin to thicken, though it may need a further 5 minutes on the following day to be just right. If it's still too thin, cover and set aside overnight again.

When you are happy with the consistency, spoon the mustard into sterilised jars. Store in a cool dark place for up to 12 months.

Walnut and sage mustard
Add 100 g (3½ oz/1 cup) walnuts and 12 sage leaves at the final stage in the food processor.

Barbecue sauce

When Allan and I wrote the first edition of this book, Allan thought he had the ultimate recipe for barbecue sauce, until he came across this easy version in one of Keith Floyd's books. Makes 375 ml (12½ fl oz/1½ cups)

2 garlic cloves, peeled

½ teaspoon salt

½ teaspoon smoky paprika

80 ml (2½ fl oz/⅓ cup) honey

60 ml (2 fl oz/¼ cup) tomato passata (puréed tomatoes) or tomato sauce (ketchup)

80 ml (2½ fl oz/⅓ cup) orange juice

80 ml (2½ fl oz/⅓ cup) red-wine vinegar

125 ml (4 fl oz/½ cup) soy sauce

Put all the ingredients in a food processor and purée until smooth. Pour into a saucepan and bring to the boil. Reduce to a simmer and cook for 10 minutes. Season if required. Store in the refrigerator for up to 6 weeks.

Berry jam

You can make this simple jam with a mixture of berries – blackberries, raspberries and strawberries – or just use one kind of berry, such as raspberries. Makes 1 litre (34 fl oz/4 cups)

1 kg (2 lb 3 oz) berries
2 tablespoons lemon juice
1 kg (2 lb 3 oz/4⅓ cups) caster (superfine) sugar

If using strawberries and a mixture of other berries, cut the strawberries in half. Wash the berries. Place the fruit, lemon juice and sugar in a large heavy-based saucepan. Cook over low heat until the sugar dissolves, stirring often. Raise the heat and cook at a boil for 15–20 minutes.

After 15 minutes, check to see if the jam has reached setting point by placing a teaspoon of the mixture onto a chilled plate. Tip the plate; if the jam runs, cook for a further 5 minutes, then try again. Pour into sterilised jars while still hot. Keep in a cool dark place for up to 6 months.

Peach and almond jam

This is the perfect way to capture the flavour of summer peaches and then be able to enjoy them in the cooler months. Makes 500 g (1 lb 2 oz/2 cups)

1 kg (2 lb 3 oz) peaches
500 g (1 lb 2 oz) caster (superfine) sugar
2 tablespoons amaretto (optional)
70 g (2½ oz) slivered toasted almonds

Cut the peaches in half, remove the stones and cut each half into wedges. Place in a large heavy-based saucepan, add the caster sugar and amaretto (or 2 tablespoons water if not using amaretto) and bring to the boil. Cook at a gentle boil for 20–30 minutes.

After 20 minutes, check to see if the jam has reached setting point by placing a teaspoon of the mixture onto a chilled plate. Tip the plate; if the jam runs, cook for a further 5 minutes, then try again. Add the toasted almonds and pour into sterilised jars while still hot. Keep in a cool dark place for up to 6 months.

Apricot jam
Substitute apricots for the peaches. Omit the almonds and use 2 tablespoons water instead of the amaretto.

Backyard plum jam

The plum tree in the backyard is a great Australian tradition, providing plums for summer cooking and the opportunity to make a stunning jam like this one. Makes 1litre (34 fl oz/4 cups)

2 kg (4 lb 6 oz) plums, quartered and stoned
2 tablespoons lemon juice
1.5 kg (3 lb 5 oz) caster (superfine) sugar

Place the plums, lemon juice and 250 ml (8½ fl oz/ 1 cup) water in a large heavy-based saucepan. Bring to the boil over medium heat and cook for 20 minutes, or until the fruit is soft.

Meanwhile, warm the caster sugar, either by placing it in a heatproof bowl in the oven, or in the microwave.

Add the sugar to the stewed fruit and stir well until the sugar dissolves. Raise the heat to medium–high and cook for 15–20 minutes, stirring often.

After 15 minutes, check to see if the jam has reached setting point by placing a teaspoon of mixture onto a chilled plate. Tip the plate; if the jam runs, cook for a further 5 minutes, then try again. Pour into sterilised jars while still hot. Keep in a cool dark place for up to 6 months.

Fig jam

My friends around the corner have the most magnificent fig tree, and boxes of figs appear on my doorstep each summer as if by magic. This recipe is a bit trickier than most jams, but it works beautifully.

Figs
Caster (superfine) sugar

Take your figs – as many as you want, but at least 1 kg (2 lb 3 oz). Remove the stems. Weigh the figs and then place them in a large bowl. Add half their weight in caster sugar (for example, if you have 1 kg/2 lb 3 oz of fig, add 500 g/1 lb 2 oz sugar). Leave to stand overnight.

Place the figs and sugar in a large heavy-based saucepan and bring to the boil. Using a slotted spoon, remove the fruit and set aside. Continue to boil the

syrup until it reaches pearl stage (see page 388), 106°C (223°F) on a sugar thermometer. Carefully return the figs to the syrup and cook gently for 15 minutes, stirring often to prevent the jam from catching. Pour into sterilised jars while still hot. Keep in a cool dark place for up to 6 months.

Fig and ginger jam
For every 1 kg (2 lb 3 oz) of fruit, add 50 g (1¾ oz) chopped crystallised ginger.

Orange marmalade

You can make this marmalade with any citrus fruit. Try blood oranges, tangelos, mandarins – or cumquats, which makes for my all-time favourite version. Makes 750 g (1 lb 11 oz/3 cups)

1 kg (2 lb 3 oz) oranges
600 g (1 lb 5 oz) caster (superfine) sugar
60 ml (2 fl oz/¼ cup) Cointreau (optional)

Place the oranges in a large saucepan and cover with water. Bring to the boil and cook for 1 hour, until soft. Remove the oranges and reduce the cooking liquid to about 80 ml (2½ fl oz/⅓ cup). Reserve the cooking liquid in the pan.

When the oranges have cooled, peel them, reserving the peel but discarding the pips, then purée the flesh in a food processor. Strain the purée and add it to the cooking liquid.

Finely shred the orange peel – you're aiming to get about 100 g (3½ oz) – and add it to the cooking liquid, along with the caster sugar. Bring to the boil, add Cointreau (if using) and reduce the heat. Cook until it achieves a syrupy consistency, stirring frequently.

Test for setting point by putting a teaspoon of the marmalade on a chilled plate. Tip the plate – if the marmalade runs, cook for a further 5 minutes, then try again. Pour into sterilised jars while still hot and enjoy as soon as it's cool. Keep in a cool dark place for up to 6 months.

Cranberry and pear conserve

The mix of tangy cranberries, pear and orange creates an unusual yet sensational conserve. Makes 1.5 kg (3 lb 5 oz/4 cups)

500 g (1 lb 2 oz) craisins (dried cranberries) or
   frozen cranberries
4 pears, peeled, cored and chopped
1 orange, peeled and flesh roughly chopped
700 g (1 lb 9 oz) soft brown sugar
1 teaspoon ground cinnamon
¼ teaspoon ground cardamom
170 g (6 oz) raisins

Place all the ingredients in a large bowl and leave to stand overnight.

Transfer the fruit to a large saucepan and bring to the boil. Reduce the heat and simmer for 30–45 minutes, or until thick. Ladle into sterilised jars while still hot. Keep in a cool dark place for up to 6 months.

Pumpkin conserve

A true autumn (fall) treat, this conserve is great on toast in the morning.
Makes 500 ml (17 fl oz/2 cups)

500 g (1 lb 2 oz) caster (superfine) sugar

500 g (1 lb 2 oz) pumpkin (squash), peeled, seeded and flesh grated

Grated zest of 2 limes

60 ml (2 fl oz/¼ cup) lime juice

125 ml (4 fl oz/½ cup) water

50 g (1¾ oz) butter

Place all the ingredients in a heavy-based saucepan over medium heat. Bring to the boil and cook at a gentle boil for 20–30 minutes, or until the conserve reaches setting point.

Check to see if the conserve has reached setting point by placing a teaspoon of the mixture onto a chilled plate. Tip the plate; if it runs, cook for a further 5 minutes, then try again. Pour into sterilised jars while still hot. Keep in a cool dark place for up to 6 months.

Cumquat jelly

Cumquat jelly is incredibly easy to make because you don't have to chop the peel or try to remove hundreds of tiny pips. The end result will be an intensely flavoured citrus jelly that's amazing on hot buttered toast. Makes 750 ml–1 litre (25½–34 fl oz/3–4 cups)

1 kg (2 lb 3 oz) cumquats

Caster (superfine) sugar as needed

Cut the cumquats in half and place them in a saucepan. Add enough cold water to cover and bring to a gentle boil. Reduce the heat to a simmer and cook the fruit for 2 hours. Regularly skim off the froth as it comes to the surface.

Allow the liquid and fruit to cool slightly, then ladle it into a colander or sieve lined with cloth – a large clean tea towel (dish towel) is fine, or muslin (cheesecloth) is good if you have it. Allow the liquid to drip through into a large bowl.

When the dripping begins to slow, gather the edges of the cloth together and tie it with string. Hang the cloth in an elevated position and allow the remaining liquid to drip through for a few hours, or overnight if time permits.

Measure the cumquat liquid into a saucepan and add an equal amount of caster sugar to the liquid. For example, you would add 500 g (1 lb 2 oz) sugar if you had 500 ml (17 fl oz/2 cups) liquid.

Return the liquid and sugar to the heat and bring to the boil. Reduce to a simmer and regularly skim off the froth as it comes to the surface. Cook until it achieves a syrupy consistency, stirring frequently.

To see if the jelly has reached setting point, place a teaspoon of the mixture onto a chilled plate. Tip the plate; if the jelly runs, cook for a further 5 minutes, then try again. Pour into sterilised jars while still hot. Keep in a cool dark place for up to 6 months.

Lemon curd (lemon butter)

This is arm-breaking work but well worth the effort for this rich and yummy treat.

Makes 500 ml (17 fl oz/2 cups)

4 egg yolks

200 g (7 oz) caster (superfine) sugar

200 g (7 oz) soft butter

Grated zest of 2 lemons

80 ml (2½ fl oz/⅓ cup) lemon juice

Beat the egg yolks and sugar in a large heatproof bowl until pale and creamy. Add the butter, lemon zest and juice.

Place the bowl over a simmering saucepan of water and whisk continuously until thickened, 20–30 minutes.

Store the lemon curd in sterilised jars in the refrigerator for up to 3 weeks.

Passionfruit curd
Substitute 60 ml (2 fl oz/¼ cup) passionfruit pulp for the lemon juice.

The pantry

This is the backbone of the book, where you will find all those recipes that make a dish complete – though, it has to be said, for every recipe in here, you can pretty much find a pre-packaged alternative. If time is an issue, you may prefer to buy pre-made stock, spice mixes and sauces. If quality and trying to omit processed foods are a high priority, you will need to make everything from scratch.

The pantry recipes

Stocks

Chicken stock

Keep chicken stock on hand for many uses besides soup – risotto, gravy, casseroles and curries also benefit from the addition of good-quality stock. Bone broth is essentially stock, often cooked for more than 6 hours to extract all the nutrients.
Makes 2–3 litres (68–101 fl oz/8–12 cups)

1 kg (2 lb 3 oz) chicken bones
1 onion, roughly chopped
1 leek, roughly chopped
2 carrots, roughly chopped
2 celery stalks, roughly chopped
2–3 whole black peppercorns
2 bay leaves
Flat-leaf (Italian) parsley stalks

Place the chicken bones in a large stockpot. Add the vegetables, peppercorns, herbs and 2–3 litres (68–101 fl oz/8–12 cups) water and bring to the boil. Remove any scum from the surface, reduce to a simmer and cook for 2–3 hours. Strain and press down hard on the ingredients to extract all the flavour.

When the stock has cooled slightly, refrigerate to allow the fat to set on the surface. Skim the fat off the surface and the stock is ready to use.

Store in the refrigerator for up to 3 days.

Asian chicken stock
Add a 3 cm (1¼ in) piece of fresh ginger (sliced), 2 tablespoons soy sauce, 1 sliced lemongrass stem and a sliced chilli or two, if desired.

Rich chicken stock
Place the bones on a baking tray and roast in a preheated 180°C (350°F) oven for 30-40 minutes until golden brown, turning once or twice and occasionally draining any excess oil off. The bones can then be added to the vegetables and herbs and cooked in the usual way.

Duck stock
Use the same quantity of duck bones instead of chicken bones, and roast them as described for the chicken stock. This stock can also be reduced to 250 ml (8½ fl oz/1 cup) for an amazingly rich, sticky duck sauce.

Turkey stock
Use the same quantity of turkey bones instead of chicken bones, and roast them as described for the chicken stock. This stock can also be reduced to 250 ml (8½ fl oz/1 cup) for a rich turkey sauce.

Master stock

Master stock can be used as a base for Asian soups, but more commonly it is used for the Chinese practice of cooking poultry and pork in stock to retain moisture and add flavour. The stock can be reused for poaching many times over, becoming more flavoursome each time it is used. I use this recipe for Crispy belly pork and watermelon salad (page 286), Crispy duck with spiced plum sauce (page 168) and Crispy-skin quail with sichuan pepper and salt (page 134). Makes 1.75 litres (60 fl oz/7 cups)

1.5 litres (51 fl oz/6 cups) water
250 ml (8½ fl oz/1 cup) soy sauce
125 ml (4 fl oz/½ cup) Chinese rice wine
3–4 slices fresh ginger
1 lemongrass stem, sliced
2–3 pieces tangerine peel (optional)
2 star anise
80 g (2¾ oz/⅓ cup) caster (superfine) sugar

Place all the ingredients in a large stockpot and bring to the boil. Reduce to a simmer, then use the stock to poach the meat as directed in your recipe. After cooking, the stock can be refrigerated and used many times. Will keep for up to 1 week.

Fish stock

Fish bones need only 20 minutes of cooking to produce a well-flavoured stock – any longer and the stock may turn bitter. It's best to use bones from white fish rather than oily varieties. I also recommend ladling the fish stock into a sieve before using it. Makes 2–3 litres (68–101 fl oz/8–12 cups)

1 kg (2 lb 3 oz) fish bones
250 ml (8½ fl oz/1 cup) white wine
1 onion, roughly chopped
1 leek, roughly chopped
2 carrots, roughly chopped
2 celery stalks, roughly chopped
Top of 1 fennel bulb, if available
2–3 whole black peppercorns
2 bay leaves
Flat-leaf (Italian) parsley stalks

Heat a stockpot over medium heat. Add the bones and white wine, then cook for 2–3 minutes. Add the vegetables, peppercorns, herbs and 2–3 litres (68–101 fl oz/8–12 cups) water and heat until almost boiling. Remove any scum from the surface, reduce to a simmer and cook for 20 minutes.

Strain by ladling the stock through a sieve, then set aside. When the stock has cooled slightly, refrigerate it for up to 3 days.

Home-made stock vs packaged stock cubes

TIP

In an ideal world we all have plenty of time and the stockpot is forever bubbling away on ohe back of the stove ready for us to dip into whenever we need it. The reality is that you probably rush in the door after 6 pm, grab some chicken, veggies and a stock cube and go for a one-pot wonder.

Generally speaking, supermarket packaged liquid stocks are high in salt. Check the nutritional panel as they can range from 600 mg per 250 ml (8½ fl oz/1 cup) to more than 1300 mg per 250 ml (8½ fl oz/1 cup), even the low-salt varieties! Stock cubes and stock powders are generally high in salt, too, so check the nutritional panels carefully.

The best liquid stocks are from high-end producers, but these are expensive. The liquids are the most expensive, with powders the cheapest, closely followed by stock cubes. Making your own stock at home works out to very little per serve, and you can make a large batch and freeze it in portions.

Vegetable stock

Vegetable stock is perfect when you want a lightly flavoured base for your finished dish or are cooking a strictly vegetarian meal. It's quick to prepare and is easily made as required.
Makes 2–3 litres (68–101 fl oz/8–12 cups)

2 tablespoons oil
3 onions, roughly chopped
2 leeks, roughly chopped
3 carrots, roughly chopped
2 celery stalks, roughly chopped
2 tomatoes, chopped
2–3 whole black peppercorns
2 bay leaves
Flat-leaf (Italian) parsley stalks

Heat the oil in a stockpot, add the vegetables and stir for a few minutes. Add the pepper, herbs and 2–3 litres (68–101 fl oz/8–12 cups) water and bring to the boil. Remove any scum from the surface, reduce to a simmer and cook for 20 minutes.

Strain and press down hard on the vegetables to extract all the flavour. Set aside. Store in the refrigerator for up to 5 days.

Sauces

Ponzu sauce

This sauce is served with the Beef tataki (page 136) and adds a lovely zing. Makes 100 ml (3½ fl oz)

2 tablespoons shoyu or tamari

1 tablespoon lemon juice

1 tablespoon lime juice

1 tablespoon rice vinegar

½ teaspoon grated fresh ginger

Combine all the ingredients. Store in the refrigerator for up to 1 week.

Romesco sauce

Romesco is a little like a Spanish-flavoured pesto, and is absolutely amazing served with barbecued chicken, seafood and lamb. Try it just once, and it's sure to become a favourite. Makes 500 g (1 lb 2 oz/2 cups)

1 red capsicum (bell pepper), seeded

1 small red chilli, seeded

1 tomato, halved

4 garlic cloves, peeled

Olive oil

80 g (2¾ oz/½ cup) blanched almonds

75 g (2¾ oz) hazelnuts

2 tablespoons smoky paprika

Large pinch of saffron threads, soaked in 2 tablespoons boiling water

1 thick slice of bread, toasted and diced

1 tablespoon chopped flat-leaf (Italian) parsley

2 tablespoons red-wine vinegar

½ teaspoon salt

½ teaspoon freshly ground black pepper

Preheat the oven to 180°C (350°F).

Place the capsicum, chilli, tomato and garlic on a baking tray and drizzle with oil. Place in the oven and cook for 30 minutes, or until all the ingredients are tender.

Place the almonds and hazelnuts on a separate baking tray and cook in the oven for 15 minutes until golden. Place the hazelnuts in a clean tea towel (dish towel) and rub to remove the skins.

Peel the capsicum and tomato. Add to a food processor, along with all the other ingredients (including the saffron's soaking liquid) and whizz to a coarse paste. Spoon the mixture into a bowl, stir well and add more oil to form a thick paste-like consistency. Season with extra vinegar, salt and pepper as needed. The sauce should have a smoky, full-flavoured taste. It will keep, refrigerated, for up to 6 weeks.

Hollandaise sauce

It may take a few attempts to master this classic sauce of the French kitchen. Once you do, you can serve it over poached eggs and bacon to create Eggs benedict (page 25), or serve it with asparagus. Makes 250 ml (8½ fl oz/1 cup)

3 egg yolks
2–3 tablespoons lemon juice
180 g (6½ oz) melted butter
Boiling water as required

Place the egg yolks, lemon juice and a pinch of salt in a food processor or mixer. Blend for 3–5 minutes until pale and thickened. Slowly add the melted butter in a steady stream. The butter should be just warm rather than hot. When thick, add the boiling water to adjust the consistency. Add salt and freshly ground black pepper to taste.

Pour the sauce into a bowl and keep warm. Either stand the bowl in another bowl of warm water or wrap it in a tea towel (dish towel) and stand it near something warm. Take care, as too much heat will curdle the sauce.

Bearnaise sauce
Add 2 tablespoons chopped tarragon to the egg yolks.

Maltaise sauce
Substitute blood orange juice for the lemon juice.

Saffron sauce
Add a pinch of saffron threads to the egg yolks.

Lemon butter sauce

This sauce can be served with all manner of fish dishes, but my favourite way of serving it is with Tuna patties (page 148). Makes 125 ml (4 fl oz/½ cup)

60 ml (2 fl oz/¼ cup) white wine
100 g (3½ oz) soft butter
2 tablespoons lemon juice

Place the white wine in a small saucepan over medium heat and allow to reduce by half. Lower the heat and whisk in the butter, piece by piece. Add the lemon juice and season with salt and freshly ground black pepper. Keep the sauce warm on the side of the stove until ready to serve.

Blood orange butter sauce
Substitute blood orange juice for the lemon juice and serve with steamed new-season asparagus.

Lime butter sauce
Substitute lime juice for the lemon juice and serve with pan-fried fish fillets.

White sauce (béchamel)

This is the base sauce from which cheese sauce, parsley sauce and a multitude of similar sauces are made. Makes 500 ml (17 fl oz/2 cups)

500 ml (17 fl oz/2 cups) hot milk
40 g (1½ oz) butter
45 g (1½ oz) flour

Warm the milk to a gentle simmer. Place a saucepan over medium heat and melt the butter, without browning. Add the flour and stir well to incorporate. Reduce the heat and cook the 'roux' for 2–3 minutes, stirring often. Raise the heat under the roux and add 1 ladleful of hot milk. Whisk in well, then continue to add milk, 1 ladleful at a time, until it's all incorporated. Reduce the heat and cook for 3–4 minutes, stirring often. Season with salt and freshly ground black pepper.

Cheese sauce
When the sauce is cooked, remove from the heat and add 1 teaspoon dijon mustard and 200 g (7 oz) grated cheddar. Stir until melted. Do not return to a strong heat or the cheese may curdle.

Parsley sauce
Add 2 tablespoons chopped flat-leaf (Italian) parsley.

Mustard sauce
Add 1 tablespoon wholegrain mustard.

Onion sauce
Cook two sliced onions in 2 tablespoons olive oil until soft. Omit the butter, add the flour and cook as directed.

Apple sauce

This is the perfect accompaniment to a roast leg of pork or pan-fried pork chops.
Makes 500 ml (17 fl oz/2 cups)

3 granny smith apples, peeled, cored and thinly sliced
1 tablespoon caster (superfine) sugar
2 tablespoons lemon juice

Place the apple slices in a saucepan over low heat. Add a few tablespoons of water, along with the caster sugar and lemon juice. Cover and cook for 15 minutes, keeping the heat low.

Mash the apples with a fork or a potato masher into a nice, smooth purée. Season to taste with salt and freshly ground black pepper. Store in the refrigerator for up to 1 week.

Yoghurt tahini sauce

This has a lot more body than regular yoghurt sauces, due to the addition of tahini. Serve with kebabs, barbecued chicken and spicy Middle Eastern stews. Makes 250 ml (8½ fl oz/1 cup)

1 tablespoon tahini
2 tablespoons lemon juice
2 garlic cloves, crushed
185 g (6½ oz/¾ cup) natural yoghurt

Mix the tahini and lemon juice together to form a smooth paste. Add the garlic and yoghurt and whisk until smooth. Season to taste with salt and freshly ground black pepper. Keep refrigerated.

Green tahini sauce
Place all the ingredients in a food processor along with 2 tablespoons chopped coriander (cilantro) or flat-leaf (Italian) parsley. Process until smooth.

Horseradish cream

Fresh horseradish is amazing in this cream. If not, a good horseradish sauce will do.
Makes 150 g (5½ oz/½ cup)

125 g (4½ oz/½ cup) sour cream
2 tablespoons grated fresh horseradish or
  2 tablespoons horseradish sauce
1 tablespoon chopped flat-leaf (Italian) parsley

Mix the sour cream, horseradish and parsley together. Add lots of freshly ground black pepper. Keep refrigerated for up to 5 days.

Classic gravy

I had to include this recipe for those not already converted to making their own gravy. It takes only 5 minutes to put together, then 15 minutes to simmer gently. There's nothing hard about that, so give it a try! Makes 500 ml (17 fl oz/2 cups)

40 g (1½ oz) butter
2 tablespoons plain (all-purpose) flour
2 tablespoons red or white wine
1 tablespoon tomato paste (concentrated purée)
375 ml (12½ fl oz/1½ cups) chicken stock

If using a roasting dish, pour away any excess fat and place the dish over medium–low heat on the stove top.

If not using a roasting dish, use a small saucepan. Add the butter and melt. Stir in the flour and cook for 1–2 minutes, stirring often. Add the wine, tomato paste and stock and bring to the boil, whisking often. Reduce the heat and allow to simmer for 10–15 minutes, stirring often.

Season with salt and freshly ground black pepper, add the juices from the resting meat and serve the gravy in a warmed jug.

Red wine onion gravy

A terrific accompaniment to roast meat, beef burgers, sausages or barbecued steak, this recipe uses red wine and beef stock to create a hearty, full-flavoured gravy. I don't like my gravies to be thick but, if you do, simply add 2 tablespoons flour instead of the recommended 1 tablespoon. Makes 500 ml (17 fl oz/2 cups)

Oil for cooking
2 onions, thinly sliced
1 tablespoon plain (all-purpose) flour
125 ml (4 fl oz/½ cup) red wine
250 ml (8½ fl oz/1 cup) beef stock

Heat a heavy-based saucepan over medium–high heat. Add a splash of oil and the onion. Cook for 3–4 minutes, stirring often, until the onions are well

softened and turning a golden colour. Sprinkle in the flour and stir well. Add the wine and stock and bring to the boil, whisking occasionally. Reduce the heat and allow to simmer for 10–15 minutes, stirring occasionally.

Season with salt and freshly ground black pepper, add the juices from the resting meat and serve the gravy in a warmed jug.

Glazes & marinades

Teriyaki glaze

Make your own teriyaki glaze rather than buying a processed one that's full of artificial additives. Use it in stir-fries, as a marinade for meats, or serve it as a dipping sauce.
Makes 200 ml (7 fl oz)

125 ml (4 fl oz/½ cup) soy sauce

80 ml (2½ fl oz/⅓ cup) mirin

1 tablespoon grated fresh ginger

2 teaspoons caster (superfine) sugar or honey (optional)

Place all the ingredients in a small saucepan and bring to the boil. Reduce the heat and simmer for 5 minutes. Remove and allow to cool before storing in the refrigerator until needed. Keeps for up to 2 months.

Barbecue baste

This baste gives a real kick to barbecued meat. I love to use it on chicken wings, chicken drumsticks and beef ribs. Makes 375 ml (12½ fl oz/1½ cups)

1 onion, diced

125 ml (4 fl oz/½ cup) tomato passata (puréed tomatoes)

2 tablespoons worcestershire sauce

2 tablespoons red-wine vinegar

100 g (3½ oz) brown sugar

1 tablespoon dijon mustard

1 garlic clove, crushed

1 teaspoon sweet paprika

1 teaspoon ground coriander

1 teaspoon ground cumin

1 teaspoon freshly ground black pepper

½ teaspoon salt

250 ml (8½ fl oz/1 cup) water

Place all the ingredients in a saucepan and bring to the boil. Reduce to a simmer and cook for 30 minutes.

Place the baste in a food processor and purée until smooth. Adjust the seasoning and allow to cool. Brush onto meat as it is barbecuing.

Chilli and garlic marinade

The perfect marinade for beef or lamb. Makes 80 ml (2½ fl oz/⅓ cup)

2 small red chillies, seeded and diced

2 garlic cloves, crushed

80 ml (2½ fl o/⅓ cup) olive oil

Mix all the ingredients together and season with salt and freshly ground black pepper. Pour over the meat and allow to marinate for at least 30 minutes, or up to 4 hours, before barbecuing.

Ultimate barbecue marinade

This ultimate barbecue marinade is perfect for pork, beef or chicken. Makes 125 ml (4 fl oz/½ cup)

60 ml (2 fl oz/¼ cup) tomato sauce (ketchup)

1 tablespoon worcestershire sauce

1 tablespoon white vinegar

1 tablespoon brown sugar

2 teaspoons dijon mustard

1 teaspoon chilli powder

Dash of Tabasco

Whisk all the ingredients together and brush onto meat as it is barbecuing.

Spicy Mexican marinade

This one really packs a punch. It is great on chicken wings and beef ribs. Makes enough marinade for Mexican pulled pork (page 177)

1 garlic clove, crushed

½ teaspoon salt

½ teaspoon chilli powder

1 teaspoon sweet paprika

½ teaspoon ground coriander

½ teaspoon ground cumin

1 teaspoon mustard seeds, crushed

½ teaspoon freshly ground black pepper

2 tablespoons olive oil

Mix all the ingredients together and brush onto meat as it is barbecuing.

Soy and garlic marinade

This is a simple marinade that works wonders with chicken, fish and pork. Makes 60 ml (2 fl oz/¼ cup)

1½ tablespoons rice vinegar

2 tablespoons soy sauce

1 garlic clove, crushed

Pinch of Chinese five-spice (page 468)

1 teaspoon caster (superfine) sugar

A few drops of Tabasco

Mix all the ingredients together and brush onto meat as it is barbecuing.

Sweet sticky marinade

This marinade goes particularly well with pork neck, which can be bought from any butcher's shop in an Asian shopping area. Serve with Asian noodle and vegetable salad (page 278).
Makes 375 ml (12½ fl oz/1½ cups)

250 ml (8½ fl oz/1 cup) dark soy sauce

125 ml (4 fl oz/½ cup) rice vinegar

2 tablespoons honey

1 teaspoon sesame oil

2 garlic cloves, crushed

2 teaspoons grated fresh ginger

2 tablespoons hot bean paste

½ teaspoon Chinese five-spice (page 468)

Mix all the ingredients together, then marinate the meat for approximately 1–2 hours. Drain the excess marinade before cooking.

Pinchito marinade

A great marinade for beef. Spanish in heritage, this dish is traditionally cooked over charcoal.
Makes 125 ml (4 fl oz/½ cup)

60 ml (2 fl oz/¼ cup) lemon juice

2 tablespoons ground cumin

60 ml (2 fl oz/¼ cup) olive oil

2 garlic cloves, crushed

1 teaspoon smoky paprika

½ teaspoon salt

½ teaspoon freshly ground black pepper

Mix all the ingredients together and brush onto meat as it is barbecuing.

Chimichurri

Perfect with grilled or barbecued steak. Makes 500 g (1 lb 2 oz/1 cup)

½ onion, finely chopped

1 garlic clove, crushed

2 tablespoons finely chopped thyme or oregano

2 tablespoons white-wine vinegar

½ teaspoon sweet paprika

3 tablespoons flat-leaf (Italian) parsley leaves, finely chopped

125 ml (4 fl oz/½ cup) olive oil

Mix all ingredients together and season well with salt and freshly ground black pepper.

Simple Moroccan blend

This blend can be added to just about any meat successfully, particularly lamb and quail.
Makes 3 tablespoons

1 teaspoon ground coriander

1 teaspoon ground cumin

1 teaspoon sweet paprika

½ teaspoon salt

1½ tablespoons lemon juice

2 tablespoons olive oil

Mix the ingredients together to form a smooth paste. Brush it onto lamb or quail just before barbecuing.

Dressings

Classic salad dressing

I usually make double or triple this recipe and keep it in a squeezy bottle in the pantry. Then, whenever I'm making a salad (usually every night), all I have to do is squeeze the dressing over the top. Makes 80 ml (2½ fl oz/⅓ cup)

1 tablespoon red-wine vinegar

½ teaspoon dijon mustard

60 ml (2 fl oz/¼ cup) extra-virgin olive oil

Mix together the vinegar and mustard and season with salt and freshly ground black pepper. Add the extra-virgin olive oil and whisk well.

Lemon dressing

This dressing can be used on just about every salad, but I particularly like it on salads served with fish or chicken. Makes 80 ml (2½ fl oz/⅓ cup)

1 tablespoon lemon juice

½ teaspoon dijon mustard

60 ml (2 fl oz/¼ cup) extra-virgin olive oil
  (lemon-infused, if you like)

Mix together the lemon juice and mustard and season with salt and freshly ground black pepper. Add the extra-virgin olive oil and whisk well.

Pomegranate dressing

Use this pomegranate dressing on any Middle Eastern-inspired salad. Makes 125 ml (4 fl oz/½ cup)

1 tablespoon lemon juice

1 tablespoon pomegranate molasses

1 teaspoon sumac (optional)

80 ml (2½ fl oz/⅓ cup) extra-virgin olive oil

Mix together the lemon juice, pomegranate molasses, and sumac (if using) and season with salt and freshly ground black pepper. Add the extra-virgin olive oil and whisk well.

Yoghurt dressing

Try this dressing in salads served with spiced grilled meats. Makes 250 ml (9 oz/1 cup)

180 g (6½ oz/¾ cup) natural yoghurt

2 tablespoons lemon juice

2 garlic cloves, crushed

1 tablespoon tahini

Mix all the ingredients together and season with salt and freshly ground black pepper. Keep refrigerated.

Chinese dressing

A sweet dressing for Asian-inspired salads. Makes 60 ml (2 fl oz/¼ cup)

2 teaspoons caster (superfine) sugar

1 tablespoon light soy sauce

1 tablespoon Chinese cooking wine

2 teaspoons sesame oil

Mix all the ingredients together, ensuring that the caster sugar dissolves.

Asian dressing

This is the best dressing for any Asian-inspired salad and also makes a good dipping sauce.
Makes 500 ml (17 fl oz/2 cups)

115 g (4 oz/½ cup) caster (superfine) sugar

Grated zest of 2 limes

125 ml (4 fl oz/½ cup) lime juice

125 ml (4 fl oz/½ cup) rice wine vinegar

125 ml (4 fl oz/½ cup) fish sauce

125 ml (4 fl oz/½ cup) Sweet chilli sauce (page 437)

Mix the sugar, lime zest, juice, vinegar and fish sauce until the sugar dissolves.

Add the sweet chilli sauce and stir to combine. Store in the refrigerator for up to 2 weeks.

Honey dressing

This recipe is delicious on the Pea and asparagus salad with feta and prosciutto (page 293).
Makes 80 ml (2½ fl oz/⅓ cup)

1 tablespoon red-wine vinegar

½ teaspoon dijon mustard

1 teaspoon honey

3 tablespoons extra-virgin olive oil

Mix the vinegar and mustard together. Season with salt and freshly ground black pepper. Add the honey and oil and whisk to combine.

Anchovy dressing

Anchovies add a lovely salty burst to many dishes. In a traditional niçoise whole anchovies are used, which many people don't like – but you can sneak them in this way.
Makes 80 ml (2½ fl oz/⅓ cup)

6 anchovy fillets, finely chopped

1 garlic clove, crushed

1 tablespoon lemon juice

60 ml (2 fl oz/¼ cup) olive oil

Freshly ground black pepper

Prepare the dressing by whisking all the ingredients together. (You don't need salt as the anchovies are already salty.)

Mayonnaise

If you're going to make your own salads, you might as well make your own mayonnaise as well. This can easily be done in a mixer or food processor, or by hand if you prefer. In fact, making mayonnaise by hand with a simple bowl and whisk doesn't take as long as you might imagine.
Makes 250 ml (8½ fl oz/1 cup)

2 egg yolks
½ teaspoon dijon mustard
125 ml (4 fl oz/½ cup) extra-virgin olive oil
1 tablespoon white-wine vinegar
White pepper to taste
1–2 tablespoons boiling water, if required

Place the egg yolks and mustard in a food processor or bowl and add a little salt and freshly ground black pepper. Blend or whisk for 2–3 minutes, or until white and creamy. Slowly drizzle in the extra-virgin olive oil until a thick, creamy consistency is reached. If the oil is added too fast, the mayonnaise may separate. Add the vinegar, white pepper to taste and more salt if needed. If the mayonnaise is too thick, add a little boiling water to thin it. The mayonnaise will keep refrigerated for 2 weeks.

Aïoli
Add four (or more if you wish) crushed garlic cloves to the food processor or bowl at the same time as the egg yolks.

Herb aïoli
Add four crushed garlic cloves and 30 g (1 oz/⅔ cup) roughly chopped basil to the food processor or bowl at the same time as the egg yolks.

Chipotle mayonnaise
Add two chipotles en adobo after the oil.

Rocket mayonnaise
Purée a handful of rocket (arugula) leaves in a food processor, adding the mayonnaise until smooth.

Lemon mayonnaise
Substitute lemon juice for the white-wine vinegar. Serve with freshly cooked prawns (shrimp).

Lime and chilli mayonnaise
Substitute lime juice for the white-wine vinegar. Add one crushed garlic clove, 1 teaspoon tomato paste (concentrated purée) and two seeded and finely diced small red chillies to the food processor or bowl at the same time as the egg yolks.

Harissa mayonnaise
Add 1 teaspoon Harissa (page 467) to the finished mayonnaise.

Tartare sauce
Add 2 teaspoons soaked, chopped capers, 30 g (1 oz) chopped cornichons and 1 tablespoon chopped flat-leaf (Italian) parsley to the finished mayonnaise. Great with beer-battered fish.

Smoked paprika mayonnaise
Add 2 teaspoons smoky sweet paprika.

Pastes

Indian Korma paste

Before there was the plethora of good-quality curry pastes on the market, I had to make my own. I have included the recipes here for those curry purists who like to make everything from scratch, but I'll happily admit to using pre-bought curry pastes 90 per cent of the time. This is your basic everyday 'Indian' curry paste. Use it for Indian chicken curry (page 188) or Indian beef curry (page 196). Makes 250 g (9 oz/1 cup)

2 teaspoons cumin seeds

1 teaspoon coriander seeds

½ teaspoon cayenne pepper

1 teaspoon garam masala

½ teaspoon salt

30 g (1 oz/1 cup) coriander (cilantro), leaves, stems and roots

2 garlic cloves

2 green chillies

5 cm (2 in) piece fresh ginger, peeled

2–3 tablespoons oil

Heat a small frying pan over medium heat and dry-toast the cumin and coriander seeds until fragrant, about 4–5 minutes, stirring or tossing often.

Place the toasted spices, along with all the remaining ingredients, in a food processor and process until smooth. Store refrigerated for up to 3 weeks.

Tandoori paste

If you only do it once in your life, make your own tandoori paste just to see how tasty it is. No artificial anything and super tasty. Makes 80 g (2¾ oz)

1 teaspoon paprika

1 teaspoon ground cinnamon

1 teaspoon chilli paste or powder

1 tablespoon garam masala

2 teaspoons ground cumin

2 teaspoons ground coriander

2 tablespoons lemon juice

1 tablespoon grated fresh ginger

2 garlic cloves, crushed

2 teaspoons salt

Place all the ingredients in a bowl and mix together. Keep refrigerated until needed.

Red Thai curry paste

I make my own Thai curry pastes more than other curry pastes. This recipe will make enough for at least two curries, so I often freeze the leftover paste to use later.
Makes 250 g (9 oz/1 cup)

4 long red chillies, seeded and roughly chopped

1 onion, diced

⅓ bunch coriander (cilantro), roots, stems and leaves, roughly chopped

2 cm (¾ in) piece of fresh galangal, thinly sliced and finely diced

1 lemongrass stem, white part only, thinly sliced and finely diced

2 garlic cloves, chopped

1 tablespoon ground coriander

1 tablespoon ground cumin

1 teaspoon ground turmeric

1 teaspoon paprika

2 tablespoons peanut oil

Place the chillies and onion in a food processor and blend to a fine paste. It's best to blend the onion at this stage as onions release their own liquid, making it easier to blend the other ingredients without the need to add water, which can dilute the overall flavour.

Add the coriander, galangal, lemongrass and garlic, and purée until smooth, stopping occasionally to push down the ingredients with a spatula. Add the remaining spices and 1 teaspoon salt and blend until combined.

Store in a clean, dry glass jar and cover the surface with oil. This will keep in the refrigerator for up to 3–4 weeks, or it can be frozen.

Green Thai curry paste

This is the green version of the Red Thai curry paste (above). It packs quite a punch, so approach with caution. Makes 250 g (9 oz/1 cup)

4 large green chillies, seeded and roughly chopped

1 onion, diced

⅓ bunch coriander (cilantro), roots, stems and leaves, roughly chopped

2 cm (¾ in) piece of fresh galangal, thinly sliced and finely diced

2 garlic cloves, chopped

1 lemongrass stem, white part only, thinly sliced and finely diced

2 teaspoons ground coriander

1 teaspoon ground cumin

1 teaspoon ground turmeric

2 tablespoons peanut oil

Place the chillies and onion in a food processor and blend to a fine paste. It's best to blend the onion at this stage as onions release their own liquid, making it easier to blend the other ingredients without the need to add water, which can dilute the overall flavour.

Add the coriander, galangal, garlic and lemongrass, and purée until smooth, stopping occasionally to push down the ingredients with a spatula. Add the remaining spices and 1 teaspoon salt and blend until combined.

Store in a clean, dry glass jar and cover the surface with oil. This will keep in the refrigerator for up to 3–4 weeks, or it can be frozen.

Rendang curry paste

Rendang is a famous Malaysian curry paste that is slowly cooked to tender, aromatic perfection –
see Beef rendang (page 195). Makes 250 g (9 oz/1 cup)

1 onion, diced

1 lemongrass stem, white part only, thinly sliced

2 garlic cloves, peeled

5 cm (2 in) piece of fresh ginger, peeled and chopped

1 teaspoon salt

2 teaspoons ground coriander

2 teaspoons ground cumin

2 dried red chillies, soaked in water

60 ml (2 fl oz/¼ cup) water

30 g (1 oz/⅓ cup) desiccated coconut

Place all the ingredients, except the coconut, in a food processor and blend until smooth. Add more water if too thick.

Transfer to a bowl and stir through the coconut. Store in a clean, dry glass jar and cover the surface with oil. This will keep in the refrigerator for up to 3–4 weeks or it can be frozen.

Tikka paste

Use this paste on Tikka roasted lamb (page 198), Slow-roasted lamb shoulder (page 174) or as
the base for a traditional Indian curry. Makes 125 g (4½ oz)

1 teaspoon ground cumin

1 teaspoon ground coriander

2 garlic cloves

5 cm (2 in) piece of fresh ginger, peeled

1 teaspoon cayenne pepper

1 tablespoon smoked paprika

2 teaspoons garam masala

60 ml (2 fl oz/¼ cup) oil

2 tablespoons tomato paste (concentrated purée)

2 red chillies

Small bunch coriander (cilantro)

2 tablespoons desiccated coconut

Place all the ingredients in a food processor and blend until smooth. Store in the refrigerator for up to 1 month.

Harissa

There are some great brands of pre-made harissa out there. However, making your own brings its own rewards – you can make it spicier if you like, or swap the variety of chillies to add different flavours. If you can find them, dried chillies add an extra dimension.
Makes 125 g (4½ oz)

2 dried chillies, such as chipotle or ancho (optional)

4–5 long red chillies

2–3 garlic cloves

Oil

½ teaspoon caraway seeds

1 teaspoon coriander seeds

1 teaspoon cumin seeds

2–3 tablespoons extra-virgin olive oil

Preheat the oven to 200°C (400°F).

If using dried chillies, place them in a heatproof bowl and cover with boiling water. Leave to stand and soften for at least 30 minutes.

Rub the fresh chillies and garlic with the oil, place on a baking tray and cook in the oven until the skins blister. Remove from the oven and place in a small bag, seal well and leave the chillies to steam for 20 minutes to ensure the skins will slip off easily.

Heat a small frying pan over medium heat and toast the spices until aromatic, about 3–4 minutes, stirring or tossing often. Remove and crush the spices using a mortar and pestle.

If you are using soaked dried chillies, remove the stalks and seeds and place the chillies in a food processor, reserving the soaking liquid.

Remove the stalks and seeds from the roasted fresh chillies and place them in the food processor. Squeeze the garlic from its skin and add it to the chillies along with the toasted spices, ½ teaspoon salt and the olive oil. Process until smooth, adding a splash of the reserved soaking liquid if needed. Scrape the bowl of the food processor down often.

Transfer to a clean jar (if you store harissa in a plastic container it will taint the plastic) and store in the refrigerator for 2–3 weeks.

Spice mixes

Sichuan salt and pepper spice

A classic spice mix that's good with oily fish, quail, chicken and prawns (shrimp).
Makes enough to serve with Crispy-skin quail with sichuan pepper and salt (page 134)

3 teaspoons sichuan pepper

½ teaspoon Chinese five-spice (page 468)

Place the sichuan pepper and ½ teaspoon salt in a dry frying pan and cook over medium heat. Stir until the salt turns golden, about 3 minutes. Crush in a mortar and pestle until very fine. Pass through a sieve to remove the husks, then stir the five-spice powder through. Sprinkle the mixture onto meat or seafood just before barbecuing. Store in an airtight container for up to 6 weeks.

Ras el hanout

A basic Moroccan spice blend that has a lovely aromatic flavour without being overly hot. Double or triple this recipe to keep some on hand, as it's super versatile. Makes 100 g (3½ oz/½ cup)

2 teaspoons sweet paprika

1 teaspoon ground ginger

1 teaspoon chilli powder

1 teaspoon ground cumin

1 teaspoon ground coriander

1 teaspoon ground white pepper

½ teaspoon ground cardamom

½ teaspoon ground cinnamon

½ teaspoon allspice

1 teaspoon salt

Mix the spices and salt together. Store in an airtight container for up to 6 weeks.

Chermoula
Add 2 tablespoons lemon juice and 2 tablespoons olive oil to the spice mix.

Indian spice mix

If you need a quick curry or spice mix, this is the go. Makes 60 g (2 oz)

1 tablespoon ground cumin

1 tablespoon ground coriander

2 teaspoons ground turmeric

1 teaspoon chilli powder or flakes

1 teaspoon ground ginger

½ teaspoon ground cinnamon

¼ teaspoon ground cardamom

Pinch of ground cloves

Mix all the the spices together. Store in an airtight container for up to 6 weeks.

Chinese five-spice

You can buy Chinese five-spice in the supermarket but it's good to make your own to ensure freshness. Makes 2 tablespoons

2 star anise

2 teaspoons sichuan peppercorns

1 teaspoon cloves

1 teaspoon fennel

1 teaspoon coriander seeds

1 cinnamon stick

Heat a small frying pan over medium heat and toast the star anise, peppercorns, cloves, fennel and coriander until fragrant. Toss or swirl often to prevent burning. Allow to cool slightly and then place the toasted spices in a spice grinder along with the cinnamon and grind to a fine powder. Store in an airtight container for up to 6 weeks.

Togarashi

You can sprinkle this classic Japanese seasoning over any Japanese-inspired dish or add it to nori rolls. Makes 125 g (4½ oz)

½ sheet nori

1 tablespoon dried tangerine peel

2 tablespoons sansho or black peppercorns

1 tablespoon chilli powder

2 teaspoons black sesame seeds

2 tablespoons white poppy seeds

2 teaspoons garlic powder

Place the nori and tangerine peel in a spice grinder or food processor and blitz until powdery. Stir through the remaining ingredients. Store in an airtight container for up to 6 weeks.

Italian herb and salt rub

This is a great all-in-one seasoning to have on hand. Try rubbing a few tablespoons onto a leg of lamb or a chicken before roasting. It is also good with barbecued and grilled meats. Makes 500 g (1 lb 2 oz)

500 g (1 lb 2 oz) salt flakes

2 bay leaves

2 small rosemary sprigs

6 sage leaves

2 thyme sprigs

Grated zest of 1 lemon

3 garlic cloves, crushed

Place the salt flakes and 1 teaspoon freshly ground black pepper in a large bowl.

Finely chop the bay leaves, rosemary, sage and thyme. Add the herbs to the salt, along with the lemon zest and garlic. The salt rub should be aromatic and full of herby, lemon and garlic flavour. The salt will dry out any liquid in the herbs, lemon zest and garlic over time. Store in an airtight container for up to 6 weeks.

Spanish herb and spice rub
Add 1 teaspoon Spanish smoky paprika and two chopped small red chillies to the mix.

Dukkah

Dukkah is an Egyptian spice blend that can be used in myriad ways. The simplest is to offer it with a bowl of olive oil and fresh bread. Dunk the bread into the oil, then into the dukkah. Delicious! Makes 250 g (9 oz/1⅓ cups)

80 g (2¾ oz/½ cup) sesame seeds

30 g (1 oz/⅓ cup) coriander seeds

30 g (1 oz/⅓ cup) cumin seeds

45 g (1½ oz/⅓ cup) hazelnuts

50 g (1¾ oz/⅓ cup) almonds

Salt flakes to taste

Toast all the seeds and nuts separately until fragrant, either in a dry frying pan or on a baking tray in a preheated 180°C (350°F) oven.

Allow to cool, then crush roughly in a mortar and pestle or pulse in a food processor – they should not be too finely ground. Add salt flakes to taste. Store in an airtight container for up to 6 weeks.

Za'atar

Some people like to make their own spice blends to ensure freshness, or sometimes it's just because they can't find them for sale anywhere close by. Makes 100 g (3½ oz/½ cup)

2 tablespoons dried thyme

2 tablespoons dried oregano

2 tablespoons sumac

2 tablespoons toasted sesame seeds

Mix all the ingredients together. Store in an airtight container for up to 6 weeks.

Nuts & seeds

Spiced nuts

You can use almost any type of nut you like in this recipe. I like to use larger nuts, such as cashew nuts and pecans, or you can use pepitas (pumpkin seeds) or sunflower seeds, too. Makes 450 g (1 lb/3 cups)

155 g (5½ oz/1 cup) almonds

155 g (5½ oz/1 cup) cashew nuts

150 g (5½ oz/1 cup) pistachio nuts or pecans

1 teaspoon ground coriander

1 teaspoon ground cumin

1 teaspoon smoky sweet paprika

1 tablespoon chopped rosemary

1 egg white

2 tablespoons caster (superfine) sugar

Preheat the oven to 180°C (350°F). Line two baking tins with baking paper.

Sift the spices together and season with salt and freshly ground black pepper.

Beat the egg white until stiff peaks form. Add the sugar and beat until dissolved. Add the spices and rosemary to the egg whites, then fold the nuts through.

Spread the nuts in a single layer in the baking trays. Bake for 10–15 minutes. Stir well to ensure the nuts separate and cook evenly. Cook for a further 10–15 minutes, or until the nuts are golden brown and crisp. Store in an airtight container in the pantry for up to 4 weeks.

Soy cashews

These nuts are irresistible. Eat them as they are or add them to an Asian-inspired salad for extra crunch. Makes 150 g (5½ oz/1 cup)

125 ml (4 fl oz/½ cup) light soy sauce
80 g (2¾ oz/⅓ cup) caster (superfine) sugar
150 g (5½ oz/1 cup) cashew nuts

Preheat the oven to 180°C (350°F). Line a baking tray with baking paper.

Bring the soy sauce, 250 ml (8½ fl oz/1 cup) water and the caster sugar to the boil in a small saucepan. Add the cashew nuts and allow to cook for 4–5 minutes.

Drain and place the cashew nuts on the baking tray and cook in the oven for 5–8 minutes, turning often until golden brown and crunchy. Allow to cool. Store in an airtight container in the pantry for up to 4 weeks.

Candied walnuts

While these are extremely more-ish by themselves, the idea is to use them in salads like Pear, candied walnut, goat's cheese and rocket salad (page 271) or to garnish Carrot cake (page 372). Makes 150 g (5½ oz/1 cup)

230 g (8 oz/1 cup) caster (superfine) sugar
150 g (5½ oz/1 cup) walnuts

Preheat the oven to 180°C (350°F). Line a baking tray with baking paper.

Bring 500 ml (17 fl oz/2 cups) water and the caster sugar to the boil. Add the walnuts and allow to cook for 4–5 minutes. Drain and place the walnuts on the baking tray and cook in the oven for 5–8 minutes. Turn often until golden brown and crunchy. Allow to cool. Store in an airtight container in the pantry for up to 4 weeks.

Tamari seed mix

Quick and easy and a great last-minute nibble idea. This is very more-ish, so make extra and keep it for a quick snack or add to salads for an extra flavour burst. Also good with smashed avocado for breakfast. Makes 260 g (9 oz/2 cups)

260 g (260 g/2 cups) seeds: pepitas (pumpkin seeds), sunflower or sesame, or any combo
2 tablespoons tamari

Preheat the oven to 180°C (350°F). Line a baking tray with baking paper.

Mix the seeds and tamari together. If time permits, leave to stand for a while to increase the flavour.

Spread the mixture out in a single layer on the lined baking tray. Bake in the oven for 10–12 minutes, stirring every 3–4 minutes to ensure they cook evenly. Allow to cool and store in an airtight container for up to 4 weeks.

Spiced chickpeas

You can vary the spice mix in this recipe to suit your taste buds. Try the Spicy Mexican marinade (page 458) or Indian spice mix (page 468). Makes 200 g (7 oz)

200 g (7 oz) cooked chickpeas, or tinned chickpeas (drained and well rinsed)
2 teaspoons Ras el hanout (page 468)
2 tablespoons olive oil

Preheat the oven to 180°C (350°F). Line a baking tray with baking paper.

Mix the chickpeas, spice and oil together. Season well with salt and freshly ground black pepper. Toss together to ensure the chickpeas are well coated.

Spread the mixture out in a single layer on the baking tray. Bake in the oven for 10–15 minutes. Stir well to ensure the nuts separate and cook evenly. Cook for a further 10–15 minutes, or until the nuts are golden brown and crisp.

Dips & spreads

Baba ghanoush

Baba ghanoush is a classic Middle Eastern dip made with eggplants that have been cooked over a flame – this is best done over a gas stove or on a barbecue. It's this that gives the dip its distinctive smoky flavour and aroma. Serve as part of a Middle Eastern antipasto platter. Serves 6–8

2 eggplants (aubergines)
½ teaspoon crushed garlic
1–2 tablespoons lemon juice
3 tablespoons tahini
80 g (2¾ oz) natural yoghurt
Pinch of ground allspice
White pepper to taste
Turkish pide bread to serve

Cook each eggplant over a gas flame until the skin is charred and the flesh is completely softened inside. If the eggplants are not completely softened they can be finished in a preheated 180°C (350°F) oven. Allow to cool completely.

Peel away the charred skin carefully and spoon the flesh into a bowl. Mash with a fork until smooth. Stir in the garlic, lemon juice, tahini and yoghurt along with the allspice and white pepper to taste. Mix well and season to taste with salt. Serve with slices of pide bread.

Pomegranate baba ghanoush
Omit the allspice and add 1 extra tablespoon tahini and 1–2 tablespoons pomegranate molasses to taste. Be extra fancy and serve with fresh pomegranate seeds on top.

Hummus

Hummus is probably the most famous of all the Middle Eastern dips. It's easy to make and the chickpeas give it a delicious nutty taste. Serves 8–10

150 g (5½ oz) chickpeas, soaked overnight in water

2 garlic cloves, chopped

90 g (3 oz) tahini

2 teaspoons ground cumin

2 teaspoons ground coriander

2 tablespoons lemon juice

60 ml (2 fl oz/¼ cup) olive oil

Smoky sweet paprika to garnish

Pitta bread to serve

Drain the chickpeas and place them in a saucepan. Cover with plenty of water and bring to the boil over medium heat. Reduce the heat to low and cook for 30–40 minutes, or until the chickpeas are soft. Drain and reserve the cooking liquid.

Place the cooked chickpeas in a food processor and pulse until they are smooth. Add the garlic, tahini, spices, lemon juice and oil and season with salt and freshly ground black pepper.

Blend until all the ingredients are smooth and well combined. If the hummus is still thick, add some of the cooking liquid. Adjust the seasoning by adding extra spices, lemon juice or salt and pepper. Place the dip in a serving bowl. Drizzle a little olive oil on top and sprinkle with the paprika. Serve with pitta bread.

Roasted carrot and chickpea dip
Peel and dice three carrots. Toss with olive oil and a sprinkling of smoky paprika. Cook in a preheated 180°C (350°F) oven for 20 minutes, or until tender. Allow to cool, then process along with the chickpeas.

Cheat's hummus
Instead of soaking dried chickpeas, take tinned chickpeas, drain them and rinse well. Place them in a bowl with all the other ingredients. Now, you can blend this too if you like, but I like it more rustic. Simply take a potato masher and mash away until everything comes together, but there's still some texture left in the chickpeas. This is also delicious on toast for lunch or for breakfast with sautéed greens and poached eggs.

Broad bean hummus

Perfect as an appetiser or light lunch. Toast some sourdough bread, spread with soft goat's cheese, top with the hummus and snow pea (mangetout) shoots. If you make this for a pre-dinner nibble, keep some aside to have for breakfast the next day – spread it over toast and add a poached egg or two. Makes 500 g (1 lb 2 oz/2 cups)

300 g (10½ oz) peas

300 g (10½ oz) fresh podded broad beans

Grated zest of 2 lemons

2 tablespoons lemon juice

1 garlic clove

1½ teaspoons tahini

125 ml (4 fl oz/½ cup) garlic-flavoured olive oil

Toasted pitta bread or sourdough bread to serve

Bring a saucepan of water to the boil and blanch the peas and broad beans for 1–2 minutes. Drain and refresh under cold running water.

When cool, tip them into a food processor along with the lemon zest, juice, garlic and tahini and process until chunky. With the motor running, slowly add the olive oil. Season with salt and freshly ground black pepper. Try to leave the hummus quite chunky. Drizzle over the garlic-flavoured olive oil and serve with the toasted bread.

Beetroot dip

I was first introduced to beetroot dip many years ago in Turkey, where it is often called beetroot salad. Basically, I love it, and think you will, too. Serve with Pitta crisps (page 35) or slices of baguette. Serves 6–8

3 beetroot (beets)

1–2 tablespoons red-wine vinegar

60 ml (2 fl oz/¼ cup) olive oil

2 garlic cloves, crushed

1–2 teaspoons Horseradish cream (page 456)

Place the beetroot in a saucepan, cover with plenty of water and bring to the boil over medium heat. Once boiling, reduce the heat to low, cover and cook for 30–40 minutes, until the beetroot are tender.

Allow the beetroot to cool, then remove the skins and chop the flesh roughly.

Place the beetroot in a food processor, add the vinegar and oil and process until smooth. Add the garlic and horseradish and season with salt and freshly ground black pepper to taste.

Creamy beetroot dip
For a milder, creamier dip, add 125 g (4½ oz/½ cup) sour cream or natural yoghurt with the garlic and horseradish cream.

Guacamole

This dip is famous all over the world, and when you taste a good 'un you'll realise why – it's tasty, fresh and completely more-ish. As David 'Avocado' Wolfe says, 'It's the best snack food in the world'. You can add and subtract things to suit your tastes. I often make it with just avocado, citrus juice, oil and herbs, and it's still delicious. Serve with toasted pitta triangles or warmed corn (taco) chips. It's delicious with tacos, on top of toast for breakfast or lunch, and makes the ideal healthy snack when teamed up with Seed crackers (page 400). Serves 6–8

2 ripe avocados

2 tablespoons lemon or lime juice

1–2 green chillies, seeded and diced

2 tablespoons chopped coriander (cilantro)

1 spring onion (scallion), sliced, or 1 finely diced red onion (optional)

1 tomato, finely diced

Tabasco (optional)

Peel the avocados and place the flesh in a bowl. Mash to a coarse consistency with a fork. Add the lemon juice, chilli, coriander, spring onion (if using) and tomato. Season with salt and freshly ground black pepper, adding a few drops of Tabasco, if desired. Stir gently and taste, adding more citrus juice or chilli to balance the flavour to your liking.

Almond skordalia

Skordalia is a Greek-style dip, which is great served with crumbed calamari rings, barbecued lamb or pan-fried salmon. Makes 250 ml (8½ fl oz/1 cup)

100 g (3½ oz) day-old bread
115 g (4 oz/¾ cup) toasted blanched almonds
100 g (3½ oz) cooked potatoes, roughly chopped
2 garlic cloves, crushed
60–80 ml (2–2½ fl oz/¼–⅓ cup) lemon juice
60–80 ml (2–2½ fl oz/¼–⅓ cup) olive oil

Place the bread and almonds in a food processor and blend until they form a breadcrumb texture. Add the potato, garlic and enough lemon juice and oil to form a thick paste. Season with salt and freshly ground black pepper, and adjust the consistency with hot water if needed. Store in the refrigerator for up to 5 days.

Tzatziki

Tzatziki appears regularly in our kitchen, as it goes with everything from barbecued lamb kebabs to spicy tagines, or can simply be served as a dip with Turkish bread.
Makes 250 g (9 oz/1 cup)

250 g (9 oz/1 cup) natural yoghurt
1 garlic clove, crushed
1 Lebanese (short) cucumber, grated
Pinch of dried mint
3 tablespoons coarsely chopped coriander
   (cilantro) leaves

Mix all the ingredients together and season to taste with salt and freshly ground black pepper. Store in the refrigerator for up to 4–5 days.

Quince aïoli

Classic aïoli is a garlic-infused mayonnaise. This quince aïoli is a different type of recipe, and goes with virtually all pan-fried or barbecued meats. It's an absolute winner with roast pork.
Makes 250 g (9 oz/1 cup)

3–4 garlic cloves, peeled
250 g (9 oz) quince paste
165 ml (5½ fl oz/⅔ cup) olive oil
60–80 ml (2–2½ fl oz/¼–⅓ cup) lemon juice

Crush the garlic and place it in a large bowl with the quince paste. Mash well with a fork. Whisk the oil in well. Don't worry if it looks a bit lumpy as it all comes together at the end.

Add the lemon juice and season with salt and freshly ground black pepper and whisk until smooth. The aïoli will keep refrigerated for up to 6 weeks. It's best served at room temperature.

Basil butter

You can add just about any flavour you like to butter – see the list of variations for a few ideas.
Makes 100 g (3½ oz)

100 g (3½ oz) soft butter
2 tablespoons chopped basil leaves

Mix the butter, basil and a little freshly ground black pepper until well combined. Place the basil butter onto a square of baking paper and roll the paper around the butter to form a sausage shape. Refrigerate until firm. Store in the refrigerator for up to 1 week, or freeze for up to 4 weeks.

Lemon butter
Omit the basil and add the grated zest of one lemon.

Lime butter
Omit the basil and add the grated zest of one lime.

Miso butter
Omit the basil and add ½ tablespoon miso paste.

Wasabi butter
Omit the basil and add 2 teaspoons wasabi paste.

Pestos & relishes

Basil pesto

This is my version of the classic Italian condiment. Stir it through spaghetti, add it to a bowl of minestrone or serve a dollop with barbecued meats. Makes 375 g (13 oz/1½ cups)

80 g (2¾ oz/½ cup) pine nuts
1 garlic clove, peeled
1 bunch basil, leaves picked
200 ml (7 fl oz) extra-virgin olive oil
100 g (3½ oz/1 cup) grated parmesan

Place the pine nuts and garlic in a food processor and pulse. Add the basil and purée until smooth. Gradually add the extra-virgin olive oil in a thin stream, until everything combines into a creamy consistency. Add the parmesan and blend. Will keep refrigerated for up to 6 weeks.

Almond pesto
Substitute almonds for the pine nuts.

Rocket pesto
Substitute rocket (arugula) for the basil.

Kale pesto
Substitute 100 g (3½ oz) kale leaves for the basil.

Coriander pesto

This pesto adds zing to barbecued foods, tagines or marinades. Makes 375 g (13 oz/1½ cups)

1 bunch coriander (cilantro) leaves and stems
50 g (1¾ oz) baby English spinach leaves
2 large green chillies, seeded
2 garlic cloves, peeled
½ teaspoon grated fresh ginger
2 tablespoons lime juice
½ teaspoon ground coriander
½ teaspoon ground cumin
½ teaspoon sweet paprika
165 ml (5½ fl oz) olive oil

Place the coriander, spinach leaves, chillies, garlic, ginger and lime juice in a food processor. Blend until smooth. Add the spices, ¼ teaspoon salt and ¼ teaspoon freshly ground black pepper and blend again. Gradually add the oil in a thin stream until everything is combined to a creamy consistency.

Tapenade

Try this olive paste on warm toast for a taste sensation. I recommend chopping the ingredients by hand to ensure a coarse texture. Makes 750 g (1lb 11 oz)

100 g (3½ oz) salted capers
700 g (1 lb 9 oz/4⅔ cups) pitted kalamata olives
60 g (2 oz) anchovy fillets in oil, including the oil
6 garlic cloves, crushed
2 tablespoons chopped flat-leaf (Italian) parsley
250–375 ml (9½–12½ fl oz/1–1½ cups) olive oil

Soak the capers in cold water for 10 minutes, then rinse several times to remove any excess salt. Drain well and chop finely.

Coarsely chop the pitted olives and the anchovies. Stir the capers, olives, anchovies (and their oil), the garlic and parsley together in a large bowl. Season with freshly ground black pepper. Add enough oil to make a paste-like consistency.

Place in an airtight container, cover with a layer of olive oil and refrigerate. It will keep for a few weeks.

Coriander relish

This fresh-tasting relish is excellent served with pan-fried meat or fish. Makes 250 g (9 oz)

½ cucumber
30 g (1 oz/1 cup) coriander (cilantro) leaves
1 red onion, diced
2 tablespoons lemon juice
2 tablespoons olive oil
2 tablespoons pomegranate molasses

Cut the cucumber into quarters lengthways, then slice thinly. Place the cucumber in a bowl, along with the coriander and onion.

To serve, season with salt and freshly ground black pepper, add the lemon juice, oil and pomegranate molasses, then toss to combine.

Fennel relish

Simple, but a stunner. Try it with pan-fried fish, veal cutlets or sausages. Makes 250 g (9 oz)

1 fennel bulb, cored and diced finely

2 tablespoons lemon juice

2 tablespoons olive oil

Toss the fennel with the lemon juice and olive oil and season with salt and freshly ground black pepper to taste. Serve immediately.

Salsas

Green olive salsa

This salsa is easy to prepare but it tastes as if you've gone to lots of trouble – that's got to be good. Chop the ingredients by hand to ensure a coarse texture. Makes 375 g (13 oz)

200 g (7 oz) pitted green olives

2 teaspoons capers, soaked and rinsed

2 anchovies

15 g (½ oz/½ cup) chopped flat-leaf (Italian) parsley leaves

80 ml (2½ fl oz/⅓ cup) extra-virgin olive oil

Finely chop the olives, capers and anchovies. Mix together in a bowl and add the parsley and extra-virgin olive oil. Stir well and add lots of freshly ground black pepper to season.

Pineapple salsa

This salsa is delicious with pan-fried fish, chicken kebabs and Thai-marinated chicken (page 125). Serves 4 as a side dish

½ pineapple

Oil for cooking

2 teaspoons coconut sugar

1 tablespoon lime juice

1 tablespoon fish sauce

1 small red chilli, finely diced

2 tablespoons chopped coriander (cilantro)

Cut off the top and bottom of the pineapple, then stand it upright. Slice off the skin by cutting downwards, then cut the pineapple into quarters from the top down and

remove the tough core from each wedge. Cut each quarter into 5 mm (¼ in) slices.

Heat a heavy-based chargrill pan or barbecue to medium–high. Add a splash of oil and the pineapple. Take care to not overcrowd the pan – you may need to cook the pineapple in batches. Cook for 2–3 minutes on each side until golden brown. Set aside until cool.

Make the dressing by dissolving the coconut sugar in the lime juice and fish sauce. Add the chilli and coriander. Season well with freshly ground black pepper and pour the mixture over the pineapple. Toss to combine and serve immediately.

Fresh mango salsa

A stunning recipe that makes the most of fresh mangoes in season. It's best with fish or chicken and especially good with Asian-flavoured dishes. Makes 250 g (9 oz)

1 ripe mango

1 teaspoon caster (superfine) sugar

1 tablespoon lime juice

2 teaspoons fish sauce

2 small red chillies, finely diced

1 tablespoon chopped Thai basil or coriander (cilantro) leaves

Peel the mango, remove the flesh from the stone and dice it finely.

Dissolve the caster sugar in the lime juice and fish sauce. Add the remaining ingredients, season with freshly ground black pepper and mix to combine.

Thai cucumber salsa

Serve this fresh-tasting salsa with spiced foods, such as Chinese crispy-skin chicken (page 161) or Pan-fried fish fillets (page 146). Makes 500 g (1 lb 2 oz)

1 cucumber

½ small onion, finely diced

2 tablespoons palm sugar (jaggery)

½ teaspoon salt

½ teaspoon freshly ground black pepper

2 tablespoons white vinegar

2 teaspoons fish sauce

15 g (½ oz/¼ cup) chopped coriander (cilantro)

50 g (1¾ oz/⅓ cup) chopped peanuts

Peel the cucumber, cut it in half lengthways and scoop out the seeds with a teaspoon. Cut the cucumber flesh into small dice.

Place the cucumber in a bowl with all the remaining ingredients, except the peanuts. Stir well and allow to marinate for at least 30 minutes. Check the seasoning and place the salsa in a serving bowl. Sprinkle with the chopped peanuts.

Tomato and basil salsa

I use this salsa in a multitude of ways, including on top of Crostini (page 36) and Blini (page 35), and as a fresh-tasting dip or spooned over barbecued chicken breasts. Makes 250 g (9 oz)

4 ripe tomatoes

1 small cucumber

6 basil leaves, thinly sliced

Sherry or balsamic vinegar

Olive oil

Dice the tomatoes and cucumber finely. Mix the tomato, cucumber and basil together and season to taste with sherry or balsamic vinegar, oil and salt and freshly ground black pepper.

Tomato and coriander salsa
Substitute coriander (cilantro) leaves for the basil.

Chilli salsa
Add two small seeded and diced red chillies.

Grains

Steamed rice

A rice cooker should take away the fear of cooking rice but, if that doesn't work for you, practise this absorption method until you have it down pat. It's one of the best things you can learn. Once cooked, rice will keep warm for up to 20 minutes. Salt is optional; I rarely add it to steamed rice. Serves 4–6

400 g (14 oz/2 cups) long-grain rice

Place the rice, 625 ml (21 fl oz/2½ cups) water and salt, if desired, in a saucepan. Cover with a lid, bring to the boil and then reduce to a low simmer. It is important to keep the saucepan covered, so the steam doesn't escape. It will take 15–20 minutes for all the water to be absorbed. It is also beneficial to allow the rice to stand for 5–10 minutes, covered, at room temperature before using.

Coconut rice
Substitute half the water with coconut milk.

Saffron rice
Add a large pinch of saffron threads to the cooking water.

Spiced nut rice
Cook 30 g (1 oz) each of almonds, pine nuts and pistachio nuts in 1 tablespoon oil until golden brown. Add a pinch each of ground turmeric, cinnamon and chilli. Add the uncooked rice and cook everything briefly together. Add the water and continue as described.

Kimchi fried rice

This is just a simple twist on steamed rice, when you want something a little bit special. Perfect with Korean or Japanese-inspired dishes. Serves 3–4

150 g (5½ oz/1 cup) kimchi
Oil for cooking
1 tablespoon Korean chilli paste
4 spring onions (scallions), thinly sliced
370 g (13 oz/2 cups) cooked long-grain rice
1 tablespoon toasted sesame seeds
1 tablespoon sesame oil (optional)

Squeeze the excess liquid from the kimchi, then chop it roughly and set aside.

Heat a wok over high heat, add a splash of oil and then the kimchi. Cook for 2–3 minutes, tossing or stirring often. Add the chilli paste and spring onions, cook briefly and then add the rice. Cook, stirring often to ensure the rice breaks up and is coated by the kimchi/chilli paste mix and heated through. Add the sesame seeds and the sesame oil (if using). Serve while still hot.

Persian rice

With its flecks of ruby red, green and brown, this dish is so pretty you could it 'jewelled rice'. Don't worry if you need to omit the pomegranate because it isn't in season, you could use dried barberries in its place. Serves 4–6

2 tablespoons oil

1 onion, diced

80 g (2¾ oz/½ cup) blanched almonds

100 g (3½ oz) pistachio nuts or pine nuts

Pinch of saffron threads

3 cardamom pods

400 g (14 oz/2 cups) basmati rice

750 ml (25½ fl oz/3 cups) vegetable or chicken stock

110 g (3½ oz) sultanas (golden raisins)

1 pomegranate, skin and pith discarded

30 g (1 oz/1 cup) coriander (cilantro) leaves

Heat a heavy-based saucepan over medium heat. Add the oil, onion, almonds, pistachio nuts, saffron and cardamom pods. Cook for 7–8 minutes, stirring often, until the nuts turn golden and the saffron and onion are fragrant. Add the rice and cook for 2 minutes, stirring to coat with the oil. Add the stock, sultanas and a pinch of salt. Cover with a lid and bring to the boil.

Reduce the heat and cook for 15–20 minutes, until the stock is absorbed and the rice is tender; add a splash more water if necessary. Allow to stand for 5 minutes before serving.

Stir through the pomegranate seeds and coriander leaves. Spoon the rice onto a large platter to serve.

Basic pilaf

I cook this when I have had just too much steamed rice and want something a little bit more exciting. I like to serve this with chicken or beef kebabs, roast lamb or a vegetable tagine. You can finish cooking this on the stove top over very low heat, but I find it easier to just pop it in the oven. Serves 4–6

Oil for cooking

1 onion, diced

Pinch of saffron threads

400 g (14 oz/2 cups) long-grain rice

750 ml (25½ fl oz/3 cups) vegetable or chicken stock

2 tablespoons chopped flat-leaf (Italian) parsley

Preheat the oven to 180°C (350°F).

Heat a large heavy-based ovenproof saucepan or casserole dish over medium heat. Add the oil, onions

and saffron and cook for 4–5 minutes, until fragrant and soft. Add the rice and stir for 1–2 minutes. Add the stock and bring to the boil, stirring often.

Reduce the heat, cover and cook in the oven for 30 minutes, or until the rice is tender and the stock has been absorbed.

Allow to stand for 5 minutes before serving. Season with salt and freshly ground black pepper, add the parsley and serve.

Preserved lemon, almond and parsley pilaf

This Middle Eastern–flavoured pilaf is easy to prepare and goes well with dishes like Chermoula chicken (page 160) and Braised lamb shanks with mint and harissa (page 200). Stick to vegetable stock if you want a vegetarian dish, or use chicken stock for a more full-flavoured result. Serves 4–6

½ Preserved lemon (page 434)

2 tablespoons oil

1 onion, diced

1 garlic clove, crushed

Pinch of saffron threads

50 g (1¾ oz/⅓ cup) blanched almonds

400 g (14 oz/2 cups) long-grain rice

750 ml (25½ fl oz/3 cups) chicken or vegetable stock

15 g (½ oz/½ cup) chopped flat-leaf (Italian) parsley

Soak the preserved lemon in cold water for 30 minutes. Drain the lemon, discard the pulpy centre, then dice the rind.

Preheat the oven to 180°C (350°F).

Heat a large heavy-based ovenproof saucepan or casserole dish over medium–high heat. Add the oil, onion, garlic and saffron and cook for 4–5 minutes, until fragrant and soft. Add the almonds and cook until golden brown. Add the rice and stir for 1–2 minutes. Add the stock and preserved lemon rind and bring to the boil, stirring often. Reduce the heat, cover and cook in the oven for 30 minutes, or until the rice is tender and the stock has been absorbed. Allow to stand for 5 minutes before serving. Season with salt and freshly ground black pepper, add the parsley and serve.

Pine nut, sultana and onion pilaf
Swap the almonds for pine nuts and add 110 g (4 oz) sultanas (golden raisins) along with the stock and cook as directed.

Pumpkin, chickpea and saffron pilaf
Roast 500 g (1 lb 2 oz) diced pumpkin (squash), tossed with olive oil, salt and freshly ground black pepper, until golden brown and tender. Omit the almonds, add the roasted pumpkin and 100 g (3½ oz) cooked chickpeas along with the rice, then cook as directed.

Tomato pilaf

This style of dish is typically served with Mexican-influenced dishes, such as Rodriguez pork (page 231) or Braised chipotle beef ribs (page 197). Serves 4–6

2 tablespoons oil

1 onion, diced

Pinch of saffron threads

3 cardamom pods

400 g (14 oz/2 cups) basmati rice

400 g (14 oz) tinned chopped tomatoes

500 ml (17 fl oz/2 cups) vegetable or chicken stock

2 tablespoons chopped coriander (cilantro)

Heat a heavy-based saucepan over medium heat. Add the oil, onion, saffron and cardamom pods. Cook for 7–8 minutes, stirring often, until the saffron and onion are fragrant. Add the rice and cook for 2 minutes, stirring to coat with oil. Add the tinned tomatoes and stock and season with salt. Cover with a lid and bring to the boil.

Reduce the heat and cook for 15–20 minutes, until the stock is absorbed and the rice is tender; add a splash more water if necessary. Allow to stand for 5 minutes before serving. Check the seasoning, adding lots of freshly ground black pepper and chopped coriander.

Quick couscous

I didn't create this method – it's straight from the packet directions! If kept covered, couscous will stay warm for 10 minutes. Serves 4

250 ml (8½ fl oz/1 cup) water or stock
1 tablespoon olive oil
245 g (8½ oz/1¼ cups) instant couscous
Small knob of butter

Place the water or stock, oil and a pinch of salt in a saucepan and bring to the boil. Remove from the heat, stir in the couscous, cover and allow to rest for 2 minutes.

Add the butter to the soaked couscous and place over low heat. Stir with a fork to break up the grains and mix the butter through.

Saffron couscous
Add a pinch of saffron threads to the boiling liquid.

Herb couscous
Add 2 tablespoons chopped fresh herbs, such as flat-leaf (Italian) parsley or coriander (cilantro), as you stir in the butter.

Spiced couscous
Add a pinch each of allspice, cinnamon and nutmeg, and ¼ teaspoon each of ground cumin and ground coriander to the stock.

Pine nut and coriander couscous
Heat a heavy-based saucepan over medium heat. Add a splash of oil, a diced onion and 2 tablespoons pine nuts and cook for 5 minutes, or until the pine nuts are golden brown. Add 2 tablespoons currants, then add the stock and continue as above. Stir in a handful of coriander (cilantro) leaves to serve.

Soft polenta

Using half water and half stock adds richness to the finished polenta. If you don't have stock available, it's fine to just use water. Sometimes I double the recipe and set half aside to make Polenta wedges (page 484) for later in the week. Serves 4

500 ml (17 fl oz/2 cups) chicken or vegetable stock
185 g (6½ oz/1¼ cups) polenta
65 g (2¼ oz/⅔ cup) grated or shaved parmesan

Bring 500 ml (17 fl oz/2 cups) water and the stock to the boil in a heavy-based saucepan. Sprinkle in the polenta and stir constantly to prevent any lumps forming. Reduce to a low simmer and cook for 10–15 minutes, stirring often, until the mixture thickens – take care as the polenta can splutter and burn. A long-handled spoon is ideal.

Remove from the heat and stir in the cheese. Season to taste with salt and then serve immediately.

Herb polenta
Add 1-2 tablespoons chopped herbs, such as flat-leaf (Italian) parsley, thyme, basil or rosemary, along with the cheese.

Truffle polenta
Add 1 teaspoon truffle oil to the polenta just before serving. You may also like to add 250 g (9 oz) Pan-fried mushrooms (page 254).

Goat's cheese polenta
Add 100 g (3½ oz) fresh goat's cheese to the polenta just before serving.

Polenta wedges

These amazing wedges are perfect with just about everything. They're a fantastic alternative to potatoes. Serves 4–6

500 ml (17 fl oz/2 cups) chicken or vegetable stock

185 g (6½ oz/1¼ cups) polenta

65 g (2¼ oz/⅔ cup) grated or shaved parmesan

Bring 500 ml (17 fl oz/2 cups) water and the stock to the boil in a heavy-based saucepan. Sprinkle in the polenta, whisking well to prevent any lumps forming. Reduce to a low simmer and cook for 10 minutes, stirring often, until the mixture thickens – take care as the polenta can splutter and burn. A long-handled spoon is ideal. Add more stock or water if it becomes too thick to stir.

Remove from the heat and stir in the cheese. Season to taste with salt, then pour the cooked polenta into a deep baking dish and allow to set for at least 4 hours.

Cut the set polenta into wedges or triangles.

Preheat the oven to 180°C (350°F).

Arrange the wedges on an oiled baking tray and bake for 20 minutes, until crispy and golden. Alternatively, you can cook the wedges on a hot barbecue plate.

Gluten-free flour

Rather than buying gluten-free flour, which often has additives and all sorts in it, you can make your own using this formula. Makes 400 g (14 oz/2⅔ cups)

200 g (7 oz) rice flour

100 g (3½ oz) soy flour

100 g (3½ oz) potato, corn or tapioca flour

1 teaspoon xanthan gum

Sift all the ingredients three times and mix well before using. Store in an airtight container for up to 3 months.

Gluten-free self-raising flour
Add 2 teaspoons gluten-free baking powder per 150 g (5½ oz/ 1 cup) of the flour.

Stuffings

Sage and onion stuffing

Sage and onion is a classic combination for stuffing a chicken. This one uses sourdough bread, which adds an extra gutsy flavour. Makes enough to stuff 1 chicken

200 g (7 oz) day-old sourdough bread

40 g (1½ oz) butter

3 onions, sliced

2 tablespoons chopped sage

1 tablespoon chopped flat-leaf (Italian) parsley

1 egg

Tear the bread into large chunks and soak in cold water. Squeeze the bread well to remove all the liquid, then place the bread in a bowl.

Heat a small saucepan over medium heat. Add the butter and onion and cook for 7–8 minutes, stirring often, until the onion softens but doesn't burn.

Add the cooked onion, sage, parsley, egg and lots of salt and freshly ground black pepper to the bread in the bowl. Mix well to combine.

Spoon the stuffing into a chicken and roast as directed. Alternatively, line a loaf (bar) tin with buttered foil and spoon the stuffing into the tin. Cook alongside the roast for 30 minutes, or until crunchy on top.

Lemon, herb and almond stuffing

This is a fresh and zesty stuffing with fruit for sweetness, nuts for texture and herbs for a savoury flavour. I use a mix of whatever herbs are best at the time – perhaps thyme, rosemary, oregano, chives, flat-leaf (Italian) parsley and a few mint leaves. Makes enough to stuff 2 chickens

2 tablespoons olive oil

Knob of butter

1 onion, finely diced

2 garlic cloves, crushed

75 g (2¾ oz) dried dates, pitted and chopped

3 tablespoons chopped fresh herbs

40 g (1½ oz/¼ cup) roasted blanched almonds

Grated zest and juice of 1 lemon

150 g (5½ oz) fresh breadcrumbs

1 egg

Heat a small saucepan over medium heat. Add the oil and butter. Allow the butter to melt, then add the onion and garlic and cook for 7–8 minutes, until soft.

Place in a large bowl and allow to cool. Add the dates, herbs, almonds, lemon zest and juice, breadcrumbs and egg. Season with salt and freshly ground black pepper and mix well.

Spoon the stuffing into a chicken and roast as directed. Alternatively, line a loaf (bar) tin with buttered foil and spoon the stuffing into the tin. Cook alongside the roast for 30 minutes, or until crunchy on top.

Chestnut stuffing

Chestnuts can be tiresome to prepare, but this recipe is your hard-earned reward. It's wonderful with chicken, pheasant or turkey. You can add 90 g (3 oz/¾ cup) raisins or cranberries at Christmas time. Makes enough to stuff 2 chickens

250 g (9 oz) chestnuts
2 tablespoons olive oil
1 onion, finely diced
2 garlic cloves, crushed
4 bacon rashers (slices), chopped
2 tablespoons chopped flat-leaf (Italian) parsley
75 g (2¾ oz/¾ cup) dry breadcrumbs
1 egg

Using a sharp knife, make two slits in the chestnuts from top to bottom. Place them in a saucepan, cover with water and bring to the boil. Reduce to a simmer and cook for 10 minutes. Allow the chestnuts to cool, then peel, removing both the outside shell and inside skin. Chop roughly and place in a bowl.

Heat a small saucepan over medium heat. Add the olive oil, onion and garlic and cook until soft. Add the bacon and cook it lightly. Add this mixture to the chestnuts. Add the parsley, breadcrumbs and egg and season with salt and freshly ground black pepper. Mix well.

Either stuff into a chicken and cook as directed or spoon into a small greased baking dish and cook alongside the roast for 30 minutes, or until crunchy on top. This recipe makes enough for two chickens, so I usually freeze half for another roast.

Sweet sauces

Sugar syrup

Sugar syrup can be used for poaching fruit and as a base for making berry sauces, or it can be reduced to make caramel sauce. If desired, ingredients such as lemon zest or a cinnamon stick can be added to give flavour to the basic sugar syrup. Makes 200 ml (7 fl oz)

115 g (4 oz/½ cup) caster (superfine) sugar

Place the caster sugar and 125 ml (4 fl oz/½ cup) water in a medium saucepan over low heat. Stir until the sugar dissolves.

Increase the heat and bring to the boil. Simmer for 2–3 minutes. Allow to cool and use as directed.

Lemon syrup
Add 2 tablespoons lemon juice and the finely grated zest of one lemon to the cooled syrup.

Lime syrup
Add 2 tablespoons lime juice and the finely grated zest of one lime to the cooled syrup.

Orange blossom syrup
Add 2 tablespoons orange juice, 1 tablespoon orange blossom water and the finely grated zest of one orange to the cooled syrup.

Rosewater syrup
Add 1 tablespoon rosewater to the cooled syrup.

Raspberry sauce

Try raspberry sauce (also known as raspberry coulis) with almond friands, alongside chocolate cake or over Vanilla ice cream (page 349). Makes 250 ml (8½ fl oz/1 cup)

110 g (4 oz/½ cup) caster (superfine) sugar
250 g (9 oz) raspberries, stalks removed

Heat a medium saucepan over low heat. Add 125 ml (4 fl oz/½ cup) water and the caster sugar and stir until the sugar dissolves. Increase the heat and bring to the boil. Add the raspberries and cook for 1 minute, then remove from the heat.

Purée the raspberries in a food processor, then pass through a sieve to remove the seeds.

Rhubarb sauce
Add 100 g (3½ oz) chopped rhubarb to the simmering syrup, along with 1 tablespoon rosewater. Cook for 2-3 minutes. Remove from the heat and allow to cool. Purée if desired.

Strawberry sauce
Replace the raspberries with an equal quantity of strawberries. Or you could try blackberries, blueberries or loganberries.

Brandy orange butter

This is the classic accompaniment to a hot plum pudding. Makes 1 × 500 g (1 lb 2 oz) log

225 g (8 oz) butter, diced
230 g (8 oz) icing (confectioners') sugar
60 ml (2 fl oz/¼ cup) brandy
Grated zest of 1 orange

Cream the butter and icing sugar together until light and fluffy. Beat in the brandy and orange zest.

Place the butter on a square of baking paper and fold the paper over the top. Using your hands, roll it into a log shape. Twist the ends of the paper to seal well. Refrigerate until completely cold. Unwrap and slice as needed.

Honeycomb butter

Use this sweet butter for the Gingerbread waffle cakes with honeycomb butter and banana (page 20). It's also delicious on French toast (page 22) – just putting it out there. Makes 1 × 185 g (6½ oz) log

125 g (4½ oz) soft butter
60 g (2 oz) Honeycomb (page 410), crushed

Mash the butter with a fork and fold in the honeycomb. Place the butter on a piece of baking paper. Roll up tightly to form a large sausage. Chill until required.

Marmalade cream

Super-simple and super-delicious, this cream goes perfectly with a freshly baked Baby orange and almond cakes (page 365). Makes 250 g (9 oz)

3 tablespoons orange marmalade
125 g (4½ o) mascarpone
1 teaspoon orange blossom water
90 g (3 oz/⅓ cup) Greek yoghurt
Icing (confectioners') sugar to taste

Mix the marmalade, mascarpone and orange blossom water together. Add the yoghurt, then icing sugar to taste.

Caramel sauce

This light caramel has a multitude of uses. Try it with a slice of cake or tart.
Makes 250 ml (8½ fl oz/1 cup)

115 g (4 oz/½ cup) caster (superfine) sugar
185 ml (6½ fl oz) water

Place the caster sugar and 60 ml (2 fl oz/¼ cup) water in a saucepan over low heat and cook until the sugar dissolves. Increase the heat to medium and bring the liquid to a boil. Stir until the liquid is clear, then stop stirring or the mixture will caramelise.

Cook for 12–15 minutes, until the liquid begins to colour; the desired colour is a mix of gold and caramel, not dark brown. If needed, carefully swirl the saucepan to mix the caramel.

Remove from the heat and carefully add 125 ml (4 fl oz/½ cup) more water – the caramel will probably spit and spurt quite a bit at this stage, so take care. Stir well to make sure all the caramel comes off the bottom of the saucepan.

Butterscotch sauce

The addition of butter, brown sugar and cream transforms caramel sauce into an amazing butterscotch creation. This is brilliant over ice cream, served warm with a slice of cake or as the final touch to a steamed pudding. Makes 375 ml (12½ fl oz/1½ cups)

115 g (4 oz/½ cup) caster (superfine) sugar
60 g (2 oz) butter
95 g (3¼ oz/½ cup firmly packed) brown sugar
125 ml (4 fl oz/½ cup) thickened (whipping) cream

Place the caster sugar and 60 ml (2 fl oz/¼ cup) water in a saucepan. Cook over low heat until the sugar dissolves. Increase the heat and bring the liquid to the boil. Stir until the liquid is clear, then stop stirring or the mixture will caramelise.

Cook for 12–15 minutes, until the liquid begins to colour; the desired colour is a mix of gold and caramel, not dark brown. If needed, carefully swirl the saucepan to mix the caramel.

Remove from the heat and carefully add the butter and brown sugar. Return to the heat and simmer until smooth. Stir in the cream and whisk until combined. Set aside to cool. The sauce can be allowed to cool completely, if required; simply melt it over low heat until it's runny once again.

Dulce de leche

I usually 'cook' three tins of condensed milk at a time to make this quick version of dulce de leche. This keeps forever and is great to have on hand to whip up a quick dessert, such as a banana split or Banoffee pie (page 338).

3 tins sweetened condensed milk

Place three, or however many you want, tins of condensed milk in a saucepan where they will fit snugly. Add enough water to cover the tins entirely, and allow an extra couple of centimetres (about an inch) as the water will evaporate while cooking. Place over medium heat and bring to the boil. Reduce to a simmer and allow to cook for 2¼ hours. Make sure the tins are covered by water at all times.

Allow the tins to cool in the water, then remove. Store at room temperature until needed. Once the tin is open, store it in the refrigerator.

Chocolate sauce

Sometimes I make this sauce with Mars Bars (Milky Way Bars), which adds extra caramel flavour to the sauce. Makes 125 ml (4 fl oz/½ cup)

90 g (3 oz) dark chocolate, chopped
20 g (¾ oz) butter
2 tablespoons brandy
80 ml (2½ fl oz/⅓ cup) thickened (whipping) cream

Place all the ingredients in a heatproof bowl. Set the bowl over a saucepan of simmering water and cook for 5–6 minutes. Stir often until everything has melted together smoothly. Serve while hot or warm.

Chocolate brandy sauce
Add 1 tablespoon brandy.

White chocolate sauce
Substitute white chocolate for the dark.

Custards

Thin custard

All lovers of dessert need to know how to make custard. Once you master the classic version, you can play around with it and try brandy or muscat custard. Makes 500 ml (17 fl oz/2 cups)

5 egg yolks
115 g (4 oz/½ cup) caster (superfine) sugar
500 ml (17 fl oz/2 cups) milk
½ teaspoon natural vanilla extract

Beat the egg yolks and caster sugar together until pale and thick.

Place the milk and vanilla in a saucepan over medium heat and bring to simmering point.

Whisk the hot milk into the egg yolk mixture, then pour into a clean saucepan. Place the custard over medium–low heat. Using a wooden spoon, stir constantly in a figure of eight to prevent the custard catching on the bottom of the saucepan. As it approaches (but isn't allowed to reach) the boil, the mixture will begin to thicken. Immediately remove the pan from the heat and strain into a cold bowl. This will slow the cooking and remove any eggy bits from the custard.

Brandy custard
Add 60 ml (2 fl oz/¼ cup) brandy to the custard just before serving.

Muscat custard
Add 60 ml (2 fl oz/¼ cup) liqueur muscat or tokay to the custard just before serving.

Thick custard (pastry cream)

This is for those who like their custard thick. It's also the custard that will set quite firmly and can be used in many desserts, tarts and slices. Makes 500 ml (17 fl oz/2 cups)

2 egg yolks
55 g (2 oz/¼ cup) caster (superfine) sugar
1 tablespoon plain (all-purpose) flour
500 ml (17 fl oz/2 cups) milk
½ teaspoon natural vanilla extract

Beat the egg yolks and caster sugar together until pale, then stir in the flour until smooth.

Place the milk and vanilla in a saucepan and bring to the boil. Whisk the hot milk into the egg yolk mixture, then pour into a clean saucepan. Place the custard over low heat and stir constantly as the custard comes to the boil and thickens. Remove from the heat.

This custard can be made in advance and reheated gently over low heat when needed. If not using within 1 hour, store it in the refrigerator covered with plastic wrap to stop a skin forming.

Icings & frostings

Basic icing

This basic icing is what you'll need for everyday cakes. Makes enough to top a 23 cm (9 in) cake

2 tablespoons melted butter
125 g (4½ oz/1 cup) icing (confectioners') sugar

Whisk 1½ tablespoons water and the butter together. Add it to the icing sugar, bit by bit, until you reach the desired consistency.

Coffee icing
Substitute strong coffee for the water.

Chocolate icing
Substitute unsweetened (Dutch) cocoa powder for 30 g (1 oz/¼ cup) of the icing sugar.

Passionfruit icing
Strain the pulp of two passionfruit and use in place of the water.

Lemon icing
Substitute lemon juice for the water and add the finely grated zest of one lemon.

Orange icing
Substitute orange juice for the water and add the finely grated zest of one orange.

Butter icing

Another basic icing, but with a butter base. Makes enough to top a 23 cm (9 in) cake

250 g (9 oz) soft butter
125 g (4½ oz/1 cup) icing (confectioners') sugar
1 teaspoon natural vanilla extract

Place all the ingredients in a freestanding electric mixer and beat for 5–6 minutes on high speed, until white and fluffy.

Royal icing

Royal icing can be used for formal cakes, such as Christmas and wedding cakes. I've included it here to adorn the the Chadwick Family Christmas cake (page 367). Makes 200 g (7 oz/1 cup)

2 egg whites
195 g (7 oz) icing (confectioners') sugar
2 teaspoons lemon juice

Place the egg whites in a bowl and beat slightly with a wooden spoon. Add the icing sugar very gradually, beating with a spoon. When thick and smooth, add the lemon juice and beat again. Using a palette knife, spread the icing onto your cake.

Caramel icing

Delicious on Caramel banana cake (page 372) or a chocolate cake. Makes enough to top a 22 cm (8¾ in) cake

230 g (8 oz/1 cup firmly packed) brown sugar
60 g (2 oz) butter
80 ml (2½ fl oz/⅓ cup) milk
125 g (4½ oz/1 cup) icing (confectioners') sugar

Place the brown sugar, butter and half the milk in a small saucepan over low heat. Cook, stirring often, until all the ingredients are melted. Remove from the heat.

Sift in the icing sugar and mix to form a smooth icing, adding as much of the remaining milk until you get the correct consistency.

Chocolate fudge icing

A rich chocolate icing that's great for cupcakes, especially Killer cupcakes (page 377), or Red velvet cupcakes (page 364). Makes enough to top and fill a 20 cm (8 in) cake

230 g (8 oz/1 cup) caster (superfine) sugar
50 g (1¾ oz) unsweetened (Dutch) cocoa powder
125 g (4½ oz) butter
60 ml (2 fl oz/¼ cup) milk
350 g (12½ oz/3 cups) icing (confectioners') sugar

Place the caster sugar and cocoa in a saucepan over low heat, then whisk in the butter and milk. Bring to the boil and cook for 3 minutes, stirring well.

Remove from the heat and allow to cool until the saucepan is cool enough to touch. Whisk in the icing sugar and stir until thick. Allow to cool completely before using.

Chocolate ganache

This is the shiny icing used on the delicacies sold in European cake shops. Be sure to place your cake on a cooling rack over a plate before pouring the warm ganache over. Makes 80 g (2¾ oz) or enough to cover a 23 cm (9 in) cake

2 tablespoons thickened (whipping) cream
90 g (3 oz) dark chocolate, chopped

Warm the cream in a small saucepan over medium heat, to just below boiling, then remove the pan from the heat. Add the chocolate and whisk to incorporate.

White chocolate ganache
Substitute white chocolate for the dark.

Cream cheese frosting

This is the classic icing for Carrot cake (page 372), but I love its fresh, creamy flavour and use it on lots of other cakes, too. Makes enough to top a 23 cm (9 in) cake

200 g (7 oz) soft cream cheese
115 g (4 oz/½ cup) caster (superfine) sugar
2 tablespoons lemon juice

Place all the ingredients in a food processor and blend until smooth.

White chocolate frosting

A simple frosting to use on cakes, muffins or brownies. Makes 250 g (9 oz/1 cup)

250 g (9 oz) white chocolate buttons
310 g (11 oz/1¼ cups) sour cream

Melt the chocolate by placing it in a bowl over a saucepan of simmering water, or melt it in a microwave on Low for 1–2 minutes. Beat the melted chocolate into the sour cream.

Coconut frosting

A rich frosting that's good on fruit and nut-based cakes. Makes 250 g (9 oz/1 cup)

60 ml (2 fl oz/¼ cup) coconut milk
125 g (4½ oz/1 cup) icing (confectioners') sugar
30 g (1 oz/⅓ cup) desiccated coconut

Place all the ingredients in a bowl and beat until smooth.

Maple syrup frosting

This frosting is delicious on muffins with a sprinkling of toasted shredded coconut.
Makes 100 g (3½ oz/½ cup)

100 g (3½ oz) soft cream cheese
2 tablespoons maple syrup

Place all the ingredients in a bowl and beat until smooth.

Glossary

Acidulated water

Water with lemon juice added to it, in which ingredients such as artichokes and quinces are soaked in order to avoid discolouring during preparation – 1 litre (34 fl oz/4 cups) water requires 60 ml (2 fl oz/¼ cup) lemon juice.

Agave syrup

A sweetener popular in raw slices, as it doesn't crystallise and dissolves easily. Made from agave plants and native to Mexico. It is highly processed and is higher in fructose than regular sugar, but has a low GI. You can use maple syrup, brown rice syrup or honey as a substitute.

Annatto seeds

These peppery seeds are primarily used to bring a natural red colour to South American marinades and chilli pastes.

Arborio rice

A short-grain rice from northern Italy used for making risotto.

Asian greens

Bok choy (pak choy): A Chinese variety of cabbage with crunchy white stalks and dark green leaves. One of the most readily available Asian greens.

Chinese cabbage (wombok): A large, cylindrical, pale green cabbage with crinkly leaves and thick stems. Perfect for stir-fries, adding to soups and making kimchi. Also very popular as the main ingredient in Thai salads.

Choy sum (Chinese flowering cabbage): One of the most versatile Asian greens with stems that are of uniform thickness, so it cooks evenly. Recognisable by its yellow flowers.

Gai Laan (Chinese broccoli): This vegetable has long stems and leaves that cook quickly and have a slightly bitter aftertaste. Typically stir-fried with garlic and ginger.

Barberries

These small, tart berries are widely used in Persian cooking. Available dried, the berries are delicious when incorporated into rice dishes, couscous, salads and stuffings.

Besan

Besan, or gram, is flour made from chickpeas. It is a staple ingredient in India, Pakistan and Nepal and is gluten-free.

Betel leaves

Lush, shiny, heart-shaped green leaves used in Asian cooking for wrapping around food, such as pork, before grilling and adding to some Thai curries.

Blanch

Briefly cook ingredients in boiling water.

Bouquet garni

A bundle of fresh herbs, which includes bay leaves, thyme, flat-leaf (Italian) parsley and celery leaves, tied with string, or wrapped in muslin (cheesecloth). It is added to stocks and soups for flavour and removed during straining. To make your own, see page 61.

Brown rice syrup

Unlike other sweeteners, which are predominately fructose based, brown rice syrup is made up of glucose, which can be metabolised by all cells in the body. This is unlike fructose, which is metabolised by the liver and can lead to fatty liver and increasing triglycerides in the blood.

Cacao (raw)

Raw cacao is less processed than Dutch cocoa, which is said to result in a product with higher nutritional properties. Terrific in smoothies, cookies, raw bars and drinks.

Calasparra (paella) rice

A brand of rice used to make the perfect Spanish paella. It has been cultivated as a short-grain rice with low starch and an ability to absorb liquid and the flavours of paella.

Caramelised buckwheat (Buckinis)

Raw activated buckwheat, often used in pancakes and waffles, smoothies, salads and cakes.

Cavolo nero

Also know as Tuscan kale or black cabbage, the delicious dark green leaves of this vegetable can be sautéed with garlic, used in salads or added to soups, such as minestrone.

Chia seeds

These seeds are often described as a superfood, due to their high levels of omega 3, protein and fibre. Chia can be added to smoothies, breads and muffins, used as the base of salads and added to soups.

Chillies

There are virtually hundreds of types of chillies from across the world and they are used in a myriad of ways in different cuisines, from Southeast Asian to Mexican. Heat levels vary from very mild to super hot, depending on the season and growing conditions. Start with a little and (carefully) taste as you go!

Chilli paste (sambal oelek): A widely available chilli paste that is readily available and packs a punch. Adjust amounts to suit your taste.

Chipotles en adobo: These are chipotle chillies in adobo sauce. Chipotles are dried smoked jalapeño peppers in a tomato-based sauce. Essential in Mexican cooking.

Chinese barbecued pork (char siu)

A boneless piece of pork marinated in soy sauce, hoisin sauce, salt, sugar and colouring, then roasted by hanging in a special oval-shaped oven.

Chinese rice wine (shaoxing rice wine)

Chinese rice wine with a delicate fragrance and amber colour. Dry sherry can be substituted at a pinch. Made from fermented, glutinous rice.

Chocolate (couverture)

Couverture is the very best form of chocolate to use in cooking. It has a high cocoa butter content and contains less sugar than other chocolate. Dark chocolate is a pretty good substitute, and I recommend 60 per cent or higher cocoa solids as a good starting point.

Chorizo

Spanish air-cured sausage made with paprika.

Citron

Citron is a large variety of citrus with a thick rind. This rind is typically cooked in sugar syrup to preserve it. A small amount of diced citron can be added to cakes and desserts.

Cocoa nibs

Cocoa nibs are actually small pieces of crushed and roasted cocoa bean. They offer an excellent way to get a dark, unsweetened chocolate flavour into your food.

Cocoa (unsweetened/Dutch)

Cocoa brings a delicious, rich chocolate flavour to cakes and desserts. The best-quality cocoa is usually labelled Dutch cocoa, which refers to the process of making it.

Coconut milk and cream

Made from grated coconut soaked in hot water. Coconut milk is lighter and thinner than coconut cream. Both have a myriad of uses, from curries and sauces to desserts and smoothies.

Coconut oil

High in saturated fat, this oil will solidify at ambient temperature and can be used in both sweet and savoury dishes. It's easy to digest (it contains medium-chain triglycerides) and can increase blood levels of ketones. Like olive oil, it can be cold-pressed and extra-virgin, with superior taste and benefits.

Coconut sugar

Made from the sap from the flower of the coconut palm, this has a slightly different taste from traditional palm sugar. Generally speaking, it's less processed than regular white sugar and retains more minerals, especially potassium. It tastes like brown sugar but has a low burning point.

Couscous

This staple of North African cooking comes in different grades. 'Instant' couscous only needs to be soaked in boiling water and then it's ready.

Crispy shallots

Crispy or deep-fried shallots are most commonly used in Asian cooking. They are traditionally sprinkled over curries, noodle dishes, salads and soups where they add a unique, fried onion flavour. You can buy them in packets from Chinese food stores.

Daikon (white radish)

Daikon is a very mild radish used extensively in Asian cooking. The grated flesh is commonly added to ponzu dipping sauce and also served as an accompaniment to sashimi.

Dashi

A Japanese ingredient made from bonito (fish) that's used as a base flavouring for soups.

Dukkah

An Egyptian mixture consisting of roasted and crushed spices, nuts and sesame seeds. To make your own, see page 469.

Dulce de leche

This delectable sauce is made by reducing milk, sugar and vanilla (or condensed milk) until it reaches a thick, rich and sweet sauce consistency. It's amazing on cakes, drizzled onto desserts or ice cream or simply spread on toast. To make your own see page 489.

Fish sauce

A tangy, thin sauce made from salted fish. It's essential in many Asian cuisines and wonderful for adding a salty burst of flavour.

Freekeh

Freekeh is wheat that is harvested while still young, then roasted. It is highly nutritious and can be used in all manner of ways, from salads and stuffings through to breads and in burgers.

Gelatine

Is there a more confusing ingredient to deal with? Not only is it available in sheet or powdered form, but these then come in different strengths!

I prefer to use leaf gelatine, as it's easier to work with and dissolves better. If you choose to use powdered gelatine, you can buy it at the supermarket – simply check the instructions to ensure you're using the correct amount to set the liquid, as there's nothing worse than a rock-hard panna cotta.

With leaf gelatine you may need to visit a speciality food store. Look for titanium or silver gelatine leaves — one leaf will set 250 ml (8½ fl oz/1 cup) liquid to the desired consistency.

Ghee (clarified butter)
Butter that has been melted and had the milk solids removed. It has very good keeping qualities and will not burn during cooking.

Ginger
Fresh ginger: Fresh root ginger is essential in curries, stir-fries and soups. A 5 cm (2 in) piece of ginger will produce 1 tablespoon grated ginger. Use a microplane grater or the fine side of a regular grater.

Ground ginger: Only a little ground ginger is usually required in recipes, as it is quite intense. Excellent in cakes and slices, curry pastes and marinades.

Pickled ginger: This is made by pouring a mixture of hot vinegar, sugar, salt and water over thin slices of fresh ginger. A week or so later you will have pickled ginger to serve with sushi and sashimi. To make your own, see page 439.

Goji berries
Goji berries are packed with nutrients and a significant amount of protein. They are usually bought dried and look like raisins. Use in salads, and add to muesli, yoghurt and breakfast smoothies.

Golden syrup
Golden syrup has quite a distinctive taste and it can be hard to find an exact substitute. Technically, golden syrup is molasses, but a lighter version, and it would be best not to swap it for dark corn syrup or molasses, or you will end up with a darker, more intense dish. Maple syrup or honey would be a better substitute.

Haloumi
Cheese made from sheep's milk. Usually salty and squeaky in texture. Great for pan-frying, or grating and adding to fritters.

Harissa
A Tunisian chilli paste with a smoky flavour. To make your own, see page 467.

Hoisin sauce
Hoisin is a thick, dark, sweet and salty sauce used extensively in Chinese cuisine. Brush it onto meats before roasting or barbecuing. Also popular in dipping sauces for dumplings and Peking duck.

Kaffir lime leaves
These leaves, with a pungent citrus flavour, are used whole in broths or finely shredded for salads and marinades. Each leaf has two oval sections. Search out fresh leaves from Asian grocery stores.

Kataifi pastry
A Middle Eastern–style shredded pastry used in both sweet and savoury dishes. Particularly good wrapped around prawns (shrimp) and baked, or used in Greek-style sweet baklava desserts.

Kecap manis
A thick, sweet Indonesian soy sauce that's widely available at Asian grocery stores and larger supermarkets. If you can't find it, you could substitute with a combination of soy sauce and sugar.

Kimchi
Kimchi is most commonly available as a fermented, pickled cabbage with plenty of added chilli. It is served with Korean dumplings, grilled meats and soups.

Jamon
A Spanish salted air-dried ham that adds a salty bacon flavour to dishes. Similar to prosciutto.

Lentils

Puy lentils are small blue-green lentils that cook quickly and hold their shape very well. Cook them in boiling water until just tender, then drain and rinse until the water flows clear before using. Use in soups, salads and all manner of side dishes.

Liquid glucose

Used when cooking sugar. Available from chemists or cake decorating shops.

LSA

A mixture of ground linseeds (flax seeds), sunflower seeds and almonds.

Mirin

Sweetened Japanese sake used for cooking.

Miso paste

A Japanese paste made from soy beans. Yellow, red or brown miso pastes are most commonly used to form the base of soups and appetisers.

Mograbieh

Large couscous available from speciality food stores and Middle Eastern food stores. Mograbieh requires up to 30 minutes' cooking time.

Mushrooms

Button, field and Swiss brown mushrooms: These mushrooms are readily available and are a great addition to risotto, sauces, casseroles and salads.

Orange pine (saffron milk cap) and slippery jack: These wild picked mushrooms only appear in autumn (fall) and are usually gathered the day before using, or early that morning, from secret spots dotted around the countryside. Only buy these from an experienced mushroom expert.

Shiitake, enoki and oyster mushrooms: These are all excellent in Asian dishes as they have a delicate texture and flavour. Use in omelettes, soups, salads and breakfast dishes.

Noodles

Cellophane noodles (mung bean vermicelli): Most commonly bought in their dried form, cellophane noodles require cooking in boiling water to soften them before they are used in salads and soups.

Chow mein egg noodles: These are used extensively in Chinese cooking for stir-fried dishes. Chow mein egg noodles come in a variety of widths – thin and round or flat and ribbon-shaped. They are available fresh and dried and can be white or yellow.

Hokkien noodles: Also known as Shanghai noodles, these are made in much the same way as chow mein noodles, but are soft and thicker. You will find them in white and yellow, but generally only fresh.

Rice ribbon noodle: These noodles can be bought either dried or fresh, the fresh noodles being more superior in texture and easier to handle. Rice ribbon noodles are most frequently used in broths, such as the traditional Vietnamese pho.

Rice vermicelli noodles: These fine, creamy noodles are made from ground rice and water. To prepare, cover them completely with boiling water for 5 minutes to soften. Drain well, then use as a salad base for grilled meats or in curry laksa.

Soba noodles: These Japanese noodles get their distinctive colour from a combination of wheat and buckwheat flours. Typically bought dried; boil them, then use in soups and as a base for a cold salad.

Nori sheets

Sheets of dried seaweed that are essential in Japanese cooking, particularly in California rolls. You can buy plain or toasted nori (the most commonly used type). You can toast your own by simply holding the nori sheet over a flame.

Orange blossom water

This distinctive, orange-infused liquid is distilled from orange tree blossoms. It is amazing sprinkled over sweet pastries that are still hot from the oven, and is also used in poaching syrups as well as savoury dishes.

Palm sugar

Palm sugar, also known as jaggery, is made from the sap of palm trees, then set into thick, dense cakes. It's best grated using the fine side of a grater, or a microplane grater. It is usually dissolved in an acidic liquid, such as lemon juice or fish sauce. I use coconut sugar (from the coconut palm) in place of palm sugar, as it is already granulated.

Pancetta

An Italian ham made from pork belly and typically made in a round shape. Eat this thinly sliced, or dice it finely and add to pasta sauces and casseroles for a delicious pork flavour.

Pandan leaves

This long, spear-shaped leaf has a distinctive, aromatic, sweet scent like jasmine rice. It is used to perfume rice as it cooks, as noodles for Vietnamese desserts and to wrap around meats to be cooked on a barbecue.

Panko crumbs

Panko crumbs, or Japanese breadcrumbs, are large, flaky breadcrumbs made from white bread. They have a much superior finish to regular breadcrumbs, due to their crunchy texture.

Paprika

A powdered seasoning made from sweet red pepper. Smoky paprika is dried naturally over a wood fire and comes in both sweet and spicy varieties.

Pedro Ximénez

Pedro Ximénez is a super-rich, intensely sweet sherry that is made in Spain. It is amazing drizzled over ice cream or served alongside a great dessert.

Pipis

Small, edible, saltwater clams, popular with Italian cooks. Cook them as you would mussels, with a little white wine and garlic.

Piquilllo pepper

A delightful pepper grown in Spain, which is roasted over a fire, peeled, then packed into jars. Often stuffed and baked or chopped to add a roasted capsicum (bell pepper) flavour to sauces, soups and salads.

Polenta

Ground cornmeal, much used in Italy to produce either a soft mixture to accompany stews or firm blocks to be grilled or pan-fried.

Pomegranate molasses or syrup

A thick, bittersweet fruit syrup available from Middle Eastern grocery stores and good delicatessens.

Preserved lemons

Widely used in Middle Eastern cooking, lemons are salted and left to preserve, increasing their umami and saltiness. Always rinse them well and remove the pulp before cutting them finely and using. To make your own, see page 434.

Prosciutto

An Italian salted, air-dried ham that adds a salty bacon flavour to dishes. Also known as Parma ham.

Quinoa

Quinoa is a grain (actually the seed of the amaranth plant) that contains essential amino acids and is high in protein, making it the most nutrient-rich grain around, while being gluten-free. Its rise in popularity has been incredible, and most people even know how to pronounce it correctly now (keen-wah). Cooked in a similar way to rice, it can be used in soups, breads, salads and braised dishes. The flakes can be used in place of breadcrumbs.

Ras el hanout
This famous spice blend originated in Morocco and traditionally contains a dozen different spices. It's great used in casseroles, in barbecue rubs or rubbed over chicken or whole fish before they are baked. To make your own, see page 468.

Rice flour
Finely ground rice that is used to make shortbread and other cookies.

Rice syrup
A thick, sweet syrup made from brown rice.

Rice vinegar
A Japanese vinegar. Make sure you buy pure rice vinegar, not flavoured 'sushi vinegar'.

Rosewater
Rose-scented liquid from the Middle East. Available at good delicatessens and Middle Eastern grocery stores.

Saffron
Saffron is one of the world's most expensive spices, with each thread coming from the centre of a crocus flower. Luckily, only a few threads are needed to enjoy saffron's aroma and flavour.

Sansho
Traditionally used in Japanese cooking, this pepper has a distinctive lemony citrus flavour and quite a spicy kick.

Seasoned flour
A little salt and pepper is added to flour to coat meats before cooking or crumbing.

Sesame oil
A rich aromatic oil made from roasted sesame seeds. Only a small amount is needed to add flavour to dishes.

Shallots
Small brown or red onion-shaped vegetables. The brown shallots are also known as French shallots. Red Asian shallots are used extensively in Asian cuisines and have a flavour between garlic and onion.

Shiso
Also known as perilla, this fragrant leaf is often served fresh with sashimi.

Sichuan peppercorns
These small red berries, also known as szechwan peppercorns, aren't actually a member of the pepper family, but they have a peppery taste. They are best toasted before use.

Sumac
Ground red berries with a sweet flavour. Available from Middle Eastern grocery stores.

Sushi rice
A traditional short-grain rice for making sushi, available in both white and brown varieties.

Tahini
A paste made from sesame seeds. Available from Middle Eastern grocery stores or the health-food section of the supermarket.

Tamari
Tamari is a gluten-free soy sauce, most commonly used in Japanese food.

Tamari almonds
Also known as the most delicious snack in the world. They are whole almonds soaked in tamari and then roasted. You can buy these at the supermarket or any good food store.

Tamarind
The pulp of the tamarind fruit, sold in clear plastic packets. Soak 60 g (2 oz) of the sour tamarind pulp in 250 ml (8½ fl oz/1 cup) boiling water. Strain and cool, then use the soaking liquid.

Thai basil

A very fragrant plant used extensively in Asian cooking. It has vivid green leaves and an abundance of aniseed flavour with a hint of heat. Great used in salads, soups and curries.

Togarashi

This is a delicious Japanese seasoning with plenty of chilli, black sesame, lemon myrtle and mustard seeds (among other things). Used as a table seasoning on fish, meats and rice. To make your own, see page 469.

Tom yum paste

A Thai paste that's usually used to make spicy soup and broths.

Truffle oil

Oil infused with truffles, available from specialist Italian importers or delicatessens.

Verjuice

Championed by Maggie Beer, who was the first person to produce it commercially, verjuice is made from unfermented grape juice. You can use it in place of wine, especially when you don't want to add alcohol, or in place of lemon juice or vinegar for a gentler acidulant.

Vietnamese mint

This plant has elongated green leaves with a hint of red colouring. It's also known as hot mint, due to its spicy flavour, and is traditionally served as part of a table salad in Vietnamese restaurants.

Vine leaves

Usually bought in brine. Soak in cold water for at least 30 minutes before using.

Wasabi

A fiery lime-green paste extracted from the wasabi root, used extensively in Japanese cuisine.

Wattle seed

A native Australian plant, which is ground and used to add a chocolatey, hazelnut flavour to desserts, ice cream and sauces.

Za'atar

Traditionally made with wild thyme, sesame seeds and sumac, za'atar is used as a seasoning in many Middle Eastern dishes. To make your own, see page 470.

Index

Index | 506

Acknowledgements

This book has existed in many forms since the original gold-cover Campion and Curtis *In The Kitchen* was published back in 2002. Without editor Tracey O'Shaunessy's drive to produce a book that people will actually cook from, this ever-lasting project would never have happened.

Thanks to the lovely folk at Hardie Grant who all made it happen: new publishing director Jane Willson and editor Loran McDougall, and especially Sandy Grant, Fiona Hardie, Julie Pinkham and Fran Berry, who recently called me their oldest author! That may be true, but hopefully she means longest existing! It's been like an old friends reunion, with much love.

Big shout out to Dina Salter, who helped me with the recipe testing; sorry about the extra kilos you may have gained with all that baking.

And to my original partner-in-crime Allan Campion, who is always there.

Thanks also to family and friends, many of who sampled these recipes in the development stage and gave honest feedback. All of the recipes are better for it. Thanks also to those who donated their favourite recipes and allowed me to include them.

References & inspirations

Back when this book was first written, the reference list gave a nod to food authors such as Stephanie Alexander, Martin Boetz, Marcella Hazan, Nigella Lawson, Christine Manfield, Neil Perry, Claudia Roden, Charmaine Solomon and David Thompson. In writing this edition I would also like to acknowledge chefs such as Jamie Oliver, Adam Liaw, Nigel Slater, Karen Martini, Yotam Ottolenghi, Paul Wilson, Kylie Kwong and Thomasina Miers for their inspiration.

Inspiration comes from everywhere: eating out, recipe books, magazines, friends and the internet. Online, you can see how chefs create new techniques, which you can incorporate into your own repertoire.

Some say there's no such thing as an original recipe, and many times I have created something at home, only to open a book or magazine several days later to see a similar dish. Does an original idea exist? Maybe, maybe not – but sometimes it's about taking a classic and giving it a twist. In other words, cooking it to suit your palate so that it becomes your recipe. The lines are very blurred.

As they say in movies (more or less at least), this is a work of fiction (creation). Names (chicken, beef, pork, fish and vegetables), characters (rice, quinoa, noodles and polenta), businesses (frying, steaming, grilling, slow cooking and baking), places (pantry, stove, sink, mixer and oven), events (mixing, chopping, blending and cooking) and incidents (yummy, delicious, mouth-watering and happy places) are products of the authors' imaginations or used in a creative manner. Any resemblance to actual recipes, living or dead, is purely coincidental.

About the authors

Michele Curtis and Allan Campion live and breathe food. Professional chefs and award-winning food authors, they have been writing about the Australian food scene since the mid-1990s. Cooking and eating seasonally has always been at the heart of what they do.

Michele has contributed articles to many food magazines and newspapers. Her latest cookbook is *What's for Dinner?*. Find Michele at Frankie's Top Shop, her cafe and food store, which specialises in delicious take-home meals – and cakes – in Melbourne's St Kilda West.

www.frankiestopshop.com.au

Allan is the founder of Melbourne Food Experiences, a specialist in food tours, corporate team-building events, cooking classes, functions and private parties. All are run in partnership with top Melbourne chefs, chocolatiers, bakers, wine experts, restaurants, bars and cooking schools to offer outstanding food and wine experiences.

www.melbournefoodexperiences.com.au

Published in 2018 by Hardie Grant Books,
an imprint of Hardie Grant Publishing

Hardie Grant Books (Melbourne)
Building 1, 658 Church Street
Richmond, Victoria 3121

Hardie Grant Books (London)
5th & 6th Floors
52–54 Southwark Street
London SE1 1UN

hardiegrantbooks.com

A Cataloguing-in-Publication entry is available from the catalogue
of the National Library of Australia at www.nla.gov.au

In the Kitchen
ISBN 978 1 74379 306 0

Publishing Director: Jane Willson
Managing Editor: Marg Bowman
Project Editor: Loran McDougall
Editor: Ariana Klepac
Design Manager: Mark Campbell
Designer: Vaughan Mossop
Typesetter: Patrick Cannon
Production Manager: Todd Rechner
Production Coordinator: Rebecca Bryson

Colour reproduction by Splitting Image Colour Studio
Printed in China by 1010 Printing International Limited